The Old Testament between Theology and History

Also by Niels Peter Lemche

The Israelites in History and Tradition (Library of Ancient Israel)

The Old Testament between Theology and History

A Critical Survey

Niels Peter Lemche

Westminster John Knox Press
LOUISVILLE • LONDON

Book design by Sharon Adams
Cover design by Mark Abrams
Cover art: Noah's Ark, *engraving after Gustave Doré, The Granger Collection, New York*

First edition
Published by Westminster John Knox Press
Louisville, Kentucky

This book is printed on acid-free paper that meets the American National Standards Institute Z39.48 standard. ∞

PRINTED IN THE UNITED STATES OF AMERICA

08 09 10 11 12 13 14 15 16 17 — 10 9 8 7 6 5 4 3 2 1

Library of Congress Cataloging-in-Publication Data

Lemche, Niels Peter.
    The Old Testament between theology and history : a critical survey / Niels Peter Lemche.—1st ed.
        p. cm.
    Includes indexes.
    ISBN-13: 978-0-664-23245-0 (alk. paper)
    1. Bible. O.T.—Criticism, interpretation, etc.   I. Title.
BS1171.3L46 2008
221.6—dc22

                                                                2008002717

My two comrades in arms

Philip R. Davies
Thomas L. Thompson

Contents

Illustrations   xiii

Preface   xv

Abbreviations   xx

Prolegomena: The Old Testament   1
Facts about the Old Testament   1
The Old Testament: An Overview   8
    The Law   9
    The Prophets: The Former Prophets (Joshua–2 Kings)   13
    The Prophets: The Prophetic Books   18
    The Writings   22

PART I. FROM THEOLOGY TO HISTORY   29

1. The Historical-Critical Paradigm in Its Historical Context   31
A New Context for Scholarship   32
The Origins and Development of Historical-Critical Scholarship   36

2. Reading Texts in the Context of Historical-Critical Scholarship   44
The Purpose of Old Testament Studies—as Seen
    by Historical-Critical Scholarship   44
Literary Criticism   45
Form Criticism/Form History   52
Tradition History   58
Redaction History   64

3. Historical-Critical Scholarship and Ancient Israel   70
The History of Israel   70
    "The Histories of Israel"   70
    The History of Ancient Israel   73
The History of the Religion of Ancient Israel   80
    "The Histories of Israelite Religion"   80
    The History of Religion in Ancient Israel   81

The History of Israel's Literature   87
   Introductions to the Old Testament   87
   The History of Ancient Israel's Literature   88
     The Pentateuch   91
     The Deuteronomistic History   92
     The Chronicler's History   94
     The Prophetic Literature   95
     The Book of Psalms   97
     The Remaining Books of the Old Testament   97
   Summary   98

PART II. THE CRISIS FOR HISTORY   99

4. The Old Testament and the Changing Sciences   101
New and Old in Science   101
The Study of the Old Testament in the Twentieth Century   106

5. The Crisis of Historical-Critical Scholarship   110
The Hermeneutical Circle   110
External Evidence   112
   Inscriptions   112
   Archaeological "External Evidence"   119
Historical Criticism   124
   The Time of the Patriarchs   124
   Exodus and the Wilderness   128
   The Conquest   132
   The Period of the Judges   139
   The Empire of David and Solomon   143
   The Divided Kingdom   146
   The Exile   154
   The Persian Period   156
The Logical Problem: The Three (Four) Different "Israels"   161

PART III. FROM HISTORY AND BACK TO THEOLOGY   165

Introduction: The Text and Its Author *or* the Text and Its Reader   167

**6. Written or Oral Transmission of Literature:
A Renewed Critical Study of the Old Testament I   173**
Canonical, Religious Texts in Ancient Times—
   Outside of the Old Testament   173
Written and Oral Tradition   175
The Alphabet and Missing Inscriptions from Palestine
   in the Iron Age   177
Who Wrote the Old Testament?   180

The Art of Writing in Palestine in the Iron Age   180
The Iron Age as the Background for the Writing
   of History in the Old Testament   183

7. **The Constructed History:**
   A Renewed Critical Study of the Old Testament II   **186**
   The Historical Literature, Its Aim and Purpose   186
   The Meaning of History   187
      The Obligations Placed on Humanity   187
      The Promise to the Patriarchs   188
      From Egypt to Canaan   191
      The Lost Possibilities: From Conquest to Exile 196
   Summary   206
   Who Wrote the Great Historical Novel about Biblical Israel?   209

8. **The Prophets as the Spokespersons of Yahweh:**
   A Renewed Critical Study of the Old Testament III   **212**
   The Prophetic Books   212
   The Concept of Prophetism—in a Near Eastern Context   213
   New Vistas on the Prophetic Literature and the Prophets
      in the Old Testament   217
   Why Was the Prophetic Literature Written Down,
      and for Whom?   219
   Summary   233

9. **The Writings in the Intellectual Context of the Old Testament:**
   A Renewed Critical Study of the Old Testament IV   **235**
   The Psalms of David   235
   Wisdom Literature and the Authorship of the Old Testament   240
   The "Ethnogenesis" of Ancient Israel   246
   Summary   251

PART IV. OLD TESTAMENT AND BIBLICAL THEOLOGY   **255**

10. **What Are We Talking About?**   **257**
    Johann Philipp Gabler   257
    An Overview of the Fourth Part   264

11. **Our Text: Canonical History and Theology**   **270**
    The Hebrew Bible or the Greek Bible?   270
    The Canon   273
    The Compilation of Our Canon   276
    How Important Is Canon?   280

12. **Old Testament Theologies of the Twentieth Century**   **284**
    The Old Testament as Part of the Bible   284

Ludwig Köhler   288
Theodor C. Vriezen   289
Walter Eichrodt   291
Gerhard von Rad   294
Otto Kaiser   296
Theology Depends on History: Summary   297

13. **History, Theology, and/or the History of Religion:**
    The Collapse of History; The Theological Consequences I   299
    The Collapse of History   299
    Salvation History and History   304
    Theology or History of Religion   305
    Rainer Albertz and the History of Israelite Religion   309
    Erhard Gerstenberger and the Theologies   310
    Hans Jørgen Lundager Jensen and the Religion
        of the Old Testament   310

14. **Alternative Theologies:**
    The Collapse of History; The Theological Consequences II 313
    History and Its Collapse   313
    The Bible as a Textbook for Colonialism   314
    The Bible and Liberation Theology   316
    Feminist Theology   317
    Liberation Theology—*stricte sensu*—and Postcolonial Exegesis 320

15. **Canonical Theology**   327
    James A. Sanders   328
    Brevard S. Childs   331
    Rolf Rendtorff   334
    Canonical Theology: An Evaluation   336

16. **Salvation Theology and Gerhard von Rad:**
    Theologies of the Old Testament I   339
    Text and Event   339
    Gerhard von Rad, History, and Time   341
    Gerhard von Rad and Salvation Theology   345
    The Tragic History of Israel   347
    Theology or the History of Thought?   348

17. **From the Biblical Theology Movement to Postmodernism:**
    The North American Scene;
    Theologies of the Old Testament II   351
    The Biblical Theology Movement   352
    The Collapse of History and the Biblical
        Theology Movement   355
    Walter Brueggemann and God's Trial   359

18. **The Old and New Testaments: Elements from the Discussion in the Twentieth Century**   365
    The Old and the New Testaments in Christian
        and Jewish Theology   365
    Rudolf Bultmann and the Hermeneutics of Faith   368
    Manfred Oeming and His All Biblical Theology   372
    The Old Testament in the New Testament   373
    The Old Testament in the New Testament:
        According to the Scriptures   376

19. **The Contribution of the Copenhagen School**   379
    The Study of the Bible—Biblical Theology   379
    The Copenhagen School and History   381
    The History of Palestine and the History of Ancient Israel   382
    Who Wrote the Old Testament, and When?   385
    Law and Gospel—Promise and Fulfilment   388

Appendix: The History of Israel or the History of Palestine?   393
    Orientalism   393
    The Correct Perspective: Israel's or Palestine's History
        in Ancient Times?   395
    Principles for History Writing   398
    The History of Palestine   403
        The Long Perspective: The Geography and Climate of Palestine   403
            The Borders   404
            The Physical Landscape   404
            Climate and Fertility   405
        The Middle Perspective: Forms of Occupation   406
            The Natural Fauna and Flora and Human Interference   406
            The Use of the Natural Resources   407
            The Pattern of Occupation   407
            Agriculture and Husbandry; Nomadism   407
            The Differentiated Society   409
            Trade   410
        The Short Perspective: The History of Palestine   412
            The Neolithic Period: The Preceramic Period   412
            Neolithic: The Ceramic Period   415
            The Chalcolithic Period   416
            The Early Bronze Age   418
            The Transition from the Early to the Middle Bronze Age   422
            The Middle Bronze Age   425
            The Late Bronze Age   429
            The Transition from the Late Bronze Age
                to the Iron Age   433

The Iron Age   438
   The Neo-Babylonian Period   441
   The Persian Period   441
   The Hellenistic Period   442
   The Roman Period until 135 CE   445
   An Overview of the History of Palestine
      after the Jewish Rebellions   447
The Long, Middle, and Short Perspective:
   The History of Palestine   448
   . . . and Israel   452

Indexes   455

Illustrations

1. The Tel Dan inscription 113
2. The Assyrians attack Lachish 119
3. Israelite settlements in Bronze- and Iron-Age Palestine 134
4. Ugaritic alphabet 178
5. Deported inhabitants of Lachish—the Assyrian version 227
6. Kuntillet ʿAjrud ostracon 250
7. A reconstruction of the Chalcolithic temple at En-gedí 417
8. The Egyptian Empire in western Asia at the end
    of the Amarna period 431
9. Beersheba Stratum VII (11th–10th century BCE) 436
10. Beersheba Stratum II (10th–9th century BCE) 437
11. The administrative system in Palestine ca. 500 CE 449

Preface

According to a Latin maxim, "libelli habent sua fata," books have their destiny. In the summer of 1983, I wrote the first Danish edition of my introduction to the study of the Old Testament, *Ancient Israel: A New History of Israelite Society* (Danish original title: *Det Gamle Israel: Det israelitiske samfund fra sammenbruddet af bronzealderkulturen til hellenistisk tid*, 1984). When it appeared, this version of a history of ancient Israel represented something new, a kind of synthetic description of Israelite history and religion, paying due regard to social anthropological reflections of the history of this ancient society. Sociology and social anthropology were chosen as presenting the paradigm for history writing. On the back of the first Danish edition, the main theses of the book read as follows:

- Israel emerged as the result of a social development within Canaanite society in Palestine in the last half of the second millennium BCE. It was not a consequence of an "Israelite" migration from the desert.
- Israelite religion was "originally" a Canaanite religion. Only toward the middle of the first millennium did it assume the particular characteristics normally considered "Jewish" monotheism.
- The Old Testament includes practically no historical sources older than, say, the seventh-sixth centuries BCE. It is accordingly not possible on the basis of the narratives in the Old Testament to reconstruct any Israelite history dating back before 1000 BCE. If such a history can be constructed, it demands the inclusion of written and archaeological sources not found in the Old Testament.
- The idea of history in the Old Testament arose as a consequence of political catastrophes that hit the historical Israel toward the middle of the first millennium BCE.

Ancient Israel was originally aimed at introductory courses in religion at the University of Aarhus, but was soon adopted also by theological students and afterwards translated into English by the late Frederick H. Cryer and published by JSOT Press in 1988.

The 1980s did not witness a stiffening of the fronts in Old Testament studies. On the contrary, when *Ancient Israel* appeared, some scholars already considered it partly obsolete.

The development of the field of Old Testament studies after the publication of *Ancient Israel* may be illustrated by a reference to the preface to the fourth Danish edition from 1991. In this preface, three of the four theses from the first edition have been reformulated in this way:

- The concept of "Israel" appeared as the result of an ideological reorientation among the people who were deported from Palestine to Mesopotamia in connection with the Babylonian conquest of Jerusalem and the destruction of the state of Judah.
- Jewish monotheism came into being in the postexilic period, in competition with other contemporary religious currents that confronted Jewish Yahwism both in Palestine and in the exile. The "old" polytheistic religion did not disappear with the exile but continued to exist down into the postexilic period.
- The historiography of the Old Testament is hardly to be dated to the seventh or sixth century BCE. It is most likely a product of the postexilic period.

The fourth thesis survived, but not for long. As early as a lecture from 1997 (never published), I was able to reformulate the theses in this way:

- "Ancient Israel" is an ideological concept created by modern historians and students of the Bible. It has only a peripheral relationship to the historical states of Israel and Judah in Palestine in the Iron Age.
- Israelite religion as found in the Old Testament is already interpreted in the light of Judaism. Judaism appeared as a monotheistic movement among several other similar movements in the first millennium BCE. When it appeared, Judaism was able to construct a history of Israel as its national foundation myth.
- Old Testament writings are mostly to be dated to the Hellenistic period. As a concept and as a canonical collection, the Old Testament hardly predates the appearance of Christianity.

Many colleagues and students have been asking me for a new edition of *Ancient Israel*. My answer is usually that such a new edition will have no purpose, as I would have to rewrite about 90 percent of the book. However, seen in this light, what is the purpose of the present study?

First and foremost, it not only represents a 90 percent rewriting of my earlier textbook, but is a totally new book and follows a totally different context. Second, it must be deemed necessary in the light of the present discussion about the future of historical-critical biblical studies.

Adopting the Indo-European favorite number of three, we may divide historically oriented scholarship into three groups:

1. The conservative—not to say evangelical—studies, having recently received a real boost by the publication of a major history of Israel by Iain Provan, V. Philips Long, and Tremper Longman III, *A Biblical History of Israel* (2003), and by methodological studies, for example, by Jens Bruun Kofoed (*Text and History: Historiography and the Study of the Biblical Text*, 2005).
2. The middle of the road, exemplified by *The History of Ancient Israel and Judah* by J. Maxwell Miller and John H. Hayes, now in its second revised edition (2006).
3. The frontrunners, the so-called minimalist approach, exemplified by Thomas L. Thompson, *The Bible in History* (North American title, somewhat misleading: *The Mythical Past* [1999]).

The first group pay special attention to the idea that the biblical narrative is a historically reliable source presenting a correct image of the past. From a theological point of view, the project is questionable, as it diverts the interest of the reader from the biblical text to events of the past, making these events decisive for the interpretation of present-day positions, political as well as religious.

The second group—undoubtedly the majority position—is also the easy one, both conservative and progressive, and reluctantly accepting revisions whenever the academic discussion has made such revisions necessary. This middle position is thus never stable (it is one of this author's basic maxims that nothing is stable; everything is on the move, although the direction of this movement may not always be evident), but is always being moved, not by itself but by considerations deriving from the first or the third group. I have sometimes called this position the graveyard of young scholars, as the position is characterized by its inability to produce new knowledge. It only absorbs knowledge won from other directions. It may expand an existing scholarly paradigm, but it never creates anything new. Furthermore, representing a kind of compromise, it has the same problems as any good compromise: It satisfies nobody, and can and will be attacked from both the conservative and the progressive sides.

The third group is a child with many names, "minimalist" being only the kindest among them. "Revisionist historians" is another less-than-kind nickname (with an open allusion to so-called revisionist historians who have, for example, in modern times denied the Holocaust). I will not describe the standpoint of this group in detail in this place, as this book is the product of the minimalist school, sometimes dubbed the Copenhagen School of biblical studies (because two of its main proponents teach at the University of Copenhagen). It is, however, certain that the school has never been static but always on the move. It has created a new paradigm for historical studies, although several studies have shown that it is also in its present form safely embedded within the ideologies of modernity, as opposed to postmodernism, because it has never given up the idea of history in itself. Here another trend might be mentioned, a direction within biblical studies that shows express disinterest in historical studies in general and even speaks about "the collapse of history" (Leo G. Perdue).

This study has four parts, introduced by a prolegomena and followed by an appendix on the history of Palestine. This arrangement partly but only partly owes it existence to pedagogical reasons. The prolegomena has in the original Danish version been used for an introductory course in biblical literature. It only tells what everybody interested in biblical studies should know, and produces nothing special. It has, however, been evaluated as an easy and practical entry point to a very complicated collection of writings not too well known in its entirety even among many young students of theology.

The first and second parts have been used for some years as background literature for the basic training in the Old Testament on the BA level. The first part, "From Theology to History," presents an outline of the emergence of historical-critical studies and describes some of its major characteristics. The point of departure for the second part, "The Crisis for History," is the basic logical problem of classic historical-critical study, that is, the kind of circular argumentation used within biblical studies, sometimes called the hermeneutical circle. Basically it will have to be accepted that circular argumentation—even if called hermeneutical—is illegitimate from a logical point of view and therefore has to be disregarded. This observation, evident to everybody outside of biblical studies, spells the end of traditional historical-critical research.

However, in the third part, "From History and Back to Theology"—probably best suited for continuous study of the Bible at the master's level—I try to present a kind of consolation to readers by proposing a new way for critical studies. Even in a postmodern world, it should be possible to do historical analysis based on biblical texts without being caught by the logical problems by which traditional scholarship has been so mightily infested. The main point is that the Old Testament is a book deriving from the past. On the other hand, it is not about the past but about the present time, that is, the time of the authors who wrote the biblical books, and about the future of the "Israel of the new covenant" as exposed by Jeremiah 31.

The fourth part, "Old Testament and Biblical Theology," is devoted to theological discussion about the Old Testament in the twentieth century, although this discussion began in earnest with Johann Philipp Gabler's introductory lecture at the University of Altdorf in 1787. Although Gabler's position was probably misunderstood by posterity and ended in a futile discussion about the relationship between the history as narrated by the Bible and the real, that is, the profane history, it formed a point of departure for all theological discussion until the end of the twentieth century. This theologically oriented discussion replaces a more traditional description of the religion of ancient Israel. Such a history of religion will be mostly redundant in the light of the general attitude toward the history of ancient Israel, simply because the author is very much in doubt about the existence of this ancient Israel, following the definition of ancient Israel proposed by Philip R. Davies. According to Davies, ancient Israel owes its existence to the imagination of modern scholars, combining biblical Israel, the Israel of the narratives of the Old Testament, and historical Israel, the Israel "found in the ground," that is, in archaeological excavations of Iron Age strata in the soil of the Holy Land. Furthermore, the marginalization of Old Testament studies in academics at the present time has to do with theological indifference, at least in my part of the world. A layout and discussion of Old Testament theology addresses this crisis and tries to explain why Christianity will not survive without the first part of its Bible. For Jewish readers this is evident, but it is not so anymore among Christian readers.

As a consequence of the late dating of Old Testament literature common among the members of the Copenhagen School, the Old Testament is not viewed as a collection of ancient Israelite literature. It is a Jewish collection of writings considered to be authoritative. The early Christian community, considering itself to be Jewish, accepted the proposal of Jeremiah to be the Israel of the new covenant, without doubt competing with other similar groups within Judaism, claiming this position for themselves.

The appendix, "The History of Israel or the History of Palestine?" presents a new history of the landscape of Israel/Palestine without the Old Testament. It was originally written in 2001, well before the appearance of Mario Liverani's *Oltre la Bibbia* (2003; ET: *Israel's History and the History of Israel*, 2005). Although Liverani's history is new in layout and intention, it is still, when it comes to the historical part, "biblical" in essence. I hope that this impression of being biblically based will not be evident in the appendix here.

The text aims primarily at students of theology and religion—and the general reader. Footnotes will be restricted and the discussion of technical problems limited. It is therefore my hope that everyone with an interest in the Old Testament and biblical studies will find it rewarding to read this book, even if they disagree with some of its conclusions.

Biblical quotations follow the New Revised Standard Version (NRSV). Most quotations from ancient texts, except the Egyptian ones, are translated by me.

A final note: Throughout the book I use the term Old Testament and not the increasingly common Hebrew Bible. Old Testament is much more than the Hebrew Bible, as it also includes the writings found in other editions of the Bible, e.g., the Septuagint, the Old Testament of the Orthodox Bible, and the Ethiopian or Coptic Bibles.

This book is dedicated to my two comrades in arms, Thomas L. Thompson and Philip R. Davies. Together we have for many years formed a kind of band of brothers. People will know why.

Special thanks to James (Jim) West of Petros, Tenessee, and the staff of WJK for their excellent way of changing my Danish English into proper English.

Lönngården, Scania, December 1, 2007

Abbreviations

ANET	*Ancient Near Eastern Texts Relating to the Old Testament*, ed. J. B. Pritchard, 3rd ed., Princeton, 1969
BZAW	Beihefte zur Zeitschrift für die alttestamentliche Wissenschaft
CANE	*Civilizations of the Ancient Near East*, ed. J. Sasson, 4 vols., New York, 1995
COS	*The Context of Scripture*, ed. W. W. Hallo, 3 vols., Leiden, 1997–2000
ET	English translation
JSOT	*Journal for the Study of the Old Testament*
JSOTSup	Journal for the Study of the Old Testament Supplement Series
KTU	*The Cuneiform Alphabetic Texts from Ugarit, Ras Ibn Hani, and Other Places*, ed. M. Dietrich, O. Loretz, and J. Sanmartin, Münster, 1995
OTL	Old Testament Library
SBL	Society of Biblical Literature
SBLWAW	Society of Biblical Literature Writings from the Ancient World
SBT	Studies in Biblical Theology
SJOT	*Scandinavian Journal of the Old Testament*
VTS	Vetus Testamentum Supplements

Prolegomena

The Old Testament

FACTS ABOUT THE OLD TESTAMENT

The days are surely coming, says the LORD, when I will make a new covenant with the house of Israel and the house of Judah. ³² It will not be like the covenant that I made with their ancestors when I took them by the hand to bring them out of the land of Egypt—a covenant that they broke, though I was their husband, says the LORD. ³³ But this is the covenant that I will make with the house of Israel after those days, says the LORD: I will put my law within them, and I will write it on their hearts; and I will be their God, and they shall be my people. ³⁴ No longer shall they teach one another, or say to each other, "Know the LORD," for they shall all know me, from the least of them to the greatest, says the LORD; for I will forgive their iniquity, and remember their sin no more.

(Jer. 31:31–34)

The term "Old Testament" really means "the old covenant" (the modern word *testament* comes from Latin *testamentum* meaning "covenant," "contract"). The

Old Testament is the name, in a Christian context, for the first part of the Christian Bible, in contrast with the New Testament, the book of the "new covenant." These names have to do with the way early Christianity understood itself, not as a new religion contrasted to an old one, Judaism, but as a new direction within an old religion. The Christian church was the "new Israel" in opposition to the "old Israel," the part of Hellenistic-Roman Jewish society that did not follow the new interpretation of old Scripture proposed by the Christian church. In this way the early church drew lines back to ideas already pronounced by Old Testament Scripture and exemplified in the quotation from Jeremiah 31, which speaks of the new covenant in substitution for the old one, which Israel broke.[1]

In Jewish tradition there is no place for the term "the Old Testament." Often we find the acronym TaNaK used concerning the collection of Jewish literature in our Bible. TaNaK in itself is meaningless but is composed by selecting the first letter in the names of the three groups of writings included in the Bible according to Jewish tradition, respectively the *Torah* ("the Law"), *Nevi'im* ("Prophets"), and *Ketuvim* ("the Writings"). Hellenistic-Roman Judaism already has references to its traditional literature as the Law, the Prophets, and the other books of the fathers (thus in the Prologue to Ecclesiasticus), or—in a Dead Sea scroll—to "the book of Moses, the books of the Prophets and in David" (the last category may be a reference to the book of Psalms, also found among the Dead Sea Scrolls).[2] The Jewish historiographer Josephus, writing toward the end of the first century BCE, consequently characterizes the literature of the Old Testament as "the Law, the Prophets, and the Writings," although the more or less contemporary New Testament usage varies. The normal reference to the sacred writings of Judaism is simply "the Law and the Prophets."

In contrast to the term "the Old Testament" (the Old Testament as opposed to the New Testament), TaNaK has no qualitative meaning. It is rather neutral but subdivides the books of the Old Testament according to the different genres, although within Jewish tradition this arrangement is at the same time highly hierarchical. Priority is always given to the the Law, second place is accorded to the prophetic literature, and finally the Writings are placed at the end of this hierarchical ladder.

---

1. To be honest, the Old Testament never uses the term "the new Israel." The correct terminology is the cumbersome "the Israel of the old covenant," as opposed to "the Israel of the new covenant." In this way, the Old Testament expresses the connection between old and new Israels, a theme that runs through its literature as a red thread and is a governing theme in the historiography of the Old Testament: Israel in exile will one day return to its homeland, where it would be the receiver of the new covenant. When the term "the new Israel" is used in this book, the reference is always to the Israel of the new covenant. It is not an ethnic or national term for a new society differentiated from the old one. The term "ancient Israel" has nothing to do with the differentiation between the Israel of the old covenant and the Israel of the new covenant. It is really only the Israel constructed by modern historians. See p. 162.

2. In 4QMMT, the so-called Halakhic Letter (4Q394–9), translated, e.g., in Florentino García Martínez, *The Dead Sea Scrolls in English* (Leiden: Brill, 1994), 77–85, and in Michael Wise, Martin Abegg Jr., and Edward Cook, *The Dead Sea Scrolls: A New Translation* (San Francisco: Harper, 1996), 358–64.

Often we see another term used about the Old Testament, not least in theological scholarly literature originating in North America: *Biblia Hebraica*, the "Hebrew Bible." This name given to the Old Testament indicates that the Old Testament is primarily a Jewish and not a Christian book. In this connection the traditional name of the Old Testament is regarded as an expression of Christian condescension, placing the Old Testament—the Bible of Judaism—below the New Testament, the Bible of Christianity. From a Christian theological point of view, this understanding is highly problematic. From a more traditionally dogmatic Christian point of view, the Old Testament is not relegated to second place in comparison to the New Testament. It is an integral part of the Christian Bible, which can never be limited to only include the New Testament. So the use of the term *Biblia Hebraica* as the exclusive name of the Jewish part of the Bible is based on two false assumptions. First and foremost, it represents a false interpretation of the relationship between the Old and the New Testaments. Second, it represents a false understanding of the content of the Old Testament. These problems are not part of these prolegomena, but will be discussed in the theological last part of this monograph.[3]

The correct use of the name *Biblia Hebraica* refers to the modern printed editions such as the *Biblia Hebraica Stuttgartensia*, the present standard edition of the Hebrew text, or the *Biblia Hebraica Quinta*, the new edition of Hebrew Scripture supposed to, within a few years, replace *Biblia Hebraica Stuttgartensia*.[4]

The Law is subdivided into the five books of Moses, in scholarly literature usually referred to as the Pentateuch (Greek, meaning "the five books"). This is the most important part of Jewish sacred writings. The five books of Moses have individual names: the first book is named Genesis, the second Exodus, the third Leviticus, the fourth Numeri (Eng. Numbers), and the fifth Deuteronomium (Eng. Deuteronomy). These Latinized Greek names refer to the main subject of each book. Genesis ("the Beginning") says that the book is about the origin of humankind; Exodus ("the Emigration") informs its readers about the deliverance of the Israelites from Egypt; Leviticus ("the Priestly [law]") includes the main part of the priestly legislation in the Old Testament; Numeri (Numbers) owes its name to the censuses that introduce the book; and Deuteronomium (Deuteronomy, "the second law") has its name because the law of Moses is repeated here, although in an edited version.

Jewish tradition has other names for these books. Here the name of the book is simply the first, or one of the first, Hebrew words found in these books. Thus Genesis is called *berešit* ("in the beginning"); Exodus *w'elle šemôt* ("and these are the names"); Leviticus *wayyiqra* ("and [Yahweh] called"); Numbers *bemidbar* ("in

---

3. See chapter 11, pp. 270–73.

4. *Biblia Hebraica Stuttgartensia* was published by the German Bible Society in Stuttgart (therefore the name) between 1967 and 1977. *Biblia Hebraica Quinta*—in many respects a superior edition—began to appear in 2004. There are other publication projects running, such as *The Hebrew University Bible*, founded by Prof. M. H. Goshen-Gottstein, but so far, only a few volumes (Isaiah, Jeremiah, and Ezekiel) have appeared in print.

the desert"); and finally Deuteronomy *'elle devarîm* ("these are the words"). In Jewish exegetical literature the use of these Hebrew names for the books of Moses are quite common.

In the Jewish Bible, the second part, Prophets, includes not only the books of the prophets—the books of the three great prophets, Isaiah, Jeremiah, and Ezekiel, and the books of the Twelve Prophets (Hosea, Joel, Amos, Obadiah, Jonah, Micah, Nahum, Habakkuk, Zephaniah, Haggai, Zechariah, and Malachi)—but also much of the historical literature: the books of Joshua and Judges, the two books of Samuel, and the two books of Kings.

The Writings is a cover name for a collection of literature belonging to many different genres. Here we find books with mainly a historical content, namely the two books of Chronicles and the books of Ezra and Nehemiah. Further, the Writings include the collection of *Megilloth*, "the festival scrolls," that is, Ruth, the Song of Songs, Esther, Ecclesiastes, and Lamentations. Writings also contains three major poetical works: the Psalms of David, a collection of 150 poems, subdivided into five smaller collections; Job, an epic text about the suffering servant of the Lord; and Proverbs, a comprehensive selection of short maxims and more extended wisdom poems. Finally, we also find Daniel among the Writings.

The main part of the Jewish collection of TaNaK is in Hebrew, a language belonging to the Semitic family. Some minor parts are in Aramaic, another Semitic language related to Hebrew.

The order of these books in Christian Bibles is different, and several books are placed in different contexts from the one found in Jewish tradition. Christian Old Testaments, like their Jewish counterparts, are subdivided into three sections. The first consists of the books from Genesis to 2 Kings, the second of several of the books that in the Jewish Bible are placed among the Writings, and the third and final part of the prophetical literature in the narrow sense of the word.

The reason for this change of arrangement of the books of the Old Testament within the Christian tradition is obviously inspired by theological and christological motives. The Law must definitely be considered the most important part in Jewish tradition. In the Christian adaptation, history is much more important. The collection of the laws of Moses is only a subset of the long narrative about biblical Israel running from the creation of the world and the subsequent election of the descendants of Abraham and Sarah as God's chosen people to the destruction of Israel and its temple in Jerusalem. The second part embraces several of the books that according to Jewish tradition have their home among the Writings. In Christian Bibles, Prophets are always found at the end of the collection of Old Testament books, without doubt because the Hebrew prophets in the eyes of the early church were holy men who prophesied about the coming of Christ.

There are, however, more differences between a Jewish Bible and a Christian Old Testament as found in the Protestant, Western tradition. Several of the biblical books have been moved from one group to another. The books of Chronicles and Ezra and Nehemiah in Christian tradition belong among the historical books and have their place after 2 Kings. Ruth is situated between Judges and the books of Samuel, and Esther after Nehemiah. The Jewish collection of Prophets has in the Christian tradition been greatly reduced; the first six books of Prophets according to the Jewish tradition, Joshua through 2 Kings, are in the Christian tradition reckoned as historical books. The collection of prophetic literature in the Christian Old Testament has, on the other hand, been augmented by the transfer of Daniel from the Writings to Prophets. Here it is placed as the fourth of the major prophets, just after Ezekiel. Also Lamentations has been moved from the Writings to Prophets, and placed after Jeremiah. The reason is that the traditional view of Lamentations is that it was composed by Jeremiah. In this way the collection of Writings has been reduced to only five books: Job, Psalms, Proverbs, Ecclesiastes, and Song of Songs. Again the reason may be historical considerations: Job is placed in a distant past; the Psalms are, according to tradition, composed by David; and the three last books are traditionally reckoned to be written by Solomon, David's son and successor.

Protestant Old Testaments are based on the collection of biblical books included in the TaNaK, but they appear in their present order according to Christian tradition since antiquity. The arrangement found in modern Christian Bibles is already in evidence in the oldest known Christian Bible. This Bible was in Greek and included the Old as well as the New Testament. The Greek Old Testament that forms part of this Christian Bible is called Septuaginta (in Eng. Septuagint, or in its short form LXX, "the seventy"—a name that relates to the tradition about the way it was translated from Hebrew into Greek, a tradition we find, among other places, in Josephus [first century CE]). Most of the books included in the Septuagint consist of translations of Jewish Scripture from the TaNaK.

In the Greek Bible, the Septuagint, books appear that are not found among the Hebrew Scriptures of the TaNaK. Thus the first book of Ezra has been added to the collection of historical literature (in the Septuagint, 2 Ezra includes the Hebrew books of Ezra and Nehemiah), but also Judith, Tobit, and the four books of the Maccabees. New parts of the Writings are the Odes of Solomon, the Psalms of Solomon, Ecclesiasticus (the Wisdom of Jesus ben Sira), and the Wisdom of Solomon. Prophetic literature has also grown by the inclusion of the Letter of Jeremiah, Baruch (according to Jeremiah, Baruch was the prophet Jeremiah's scribe), Susanna, and Bel and the Dragon.

There are several ways of explaining the differences between the Hebrew Bible and the Septuagint; one reason has to do with the rationale behind the collection of books in the Hebrew Bible; that is, none of these can be younger than Ezra the Scribe and books definitely younger never became part of the Jewish canon.[5] Because of this, second-century BCE books like Ecclesiasticus and Tobit could not be accepted. Daniel, which, on the other hand, dates from roughly the same period as these two books, the second century BCE, was accepted because it was supposed to narrate events of the time of Nebuchadnezzar, Belshazzar, and Darius, the Persian king.

---

5. Insofar as it is correct to speak about a Jewish canon. See pp. 276.

A second reason might be the language of the book. If there was no Hebrew version of a book in existence, it would of course never make it to the *Hebrew* Bible—translations of biblical books from Greek to Hebrew are unknown. For that reason, but also because of their subject (the Maccabean wars dating from the second century BCE), the four books of the Maccabees would never be accepted into the Hebrew Bible.

The majority of the books of the Septuagint not found in the Hebrew Bible are in Protestant Bibles traditionally reckoned among the Apocryphal books (meaning "hidden" or "secret" books). It is thus quite common in printed versions of Protestant Bibles to see these books forming a separate collection placed between the Old and the New Testament.

However, here the uniformity of the Protestant tradition falls apart, as there is no agreement concerning the exact numbering of the Apocryphal books. In the Lutheran tradition some of these are not even reckoned as Apocryphal in the strict sense of the word, but are relegated to the third category, the Old Testament Pseudepigrapha (meaning "false writings"). Among these we find 3 Maccabees, 4 Maccabees, and the Odes and Psalms of Solomon. The Pseudepigrapha includes several books that are not part of the Hebrew Bible or of the Septuagint, such as the *Testaments of the Twelve Patriarchs, Jubilees, 1 Enoch,* and *4 Ezra.*[6] In his translation Luther thus accepted only Judith, Wisdom, Tobit, Sirach, Baruch, 1 and 2 Maccabees, and the additions to Daniel in the Septuagint as Apocryphal writings.

The Reformed tradition was less restricted in its choice of Apocryphal books, as it also accepted 3 Maccabees, 3 Ezra, and 4 Ezra.

In this way, the Protestant tradition is diversified by its choice of Apocryphal books but is dependent on choices already made in the Catholic tradition as reflected in the Vulgate (meaning "the popular [version]"), the translation into Latin dating from the fourth century CE. The Vulgate is divided into four sections: "historical books," "pedagogical literature" (*libri didactici*—maybe we should call them "wisdom literature"), prophetic literature, and "new historical books." The historical books include all the historical literature present in most Protestant Bibles. To these are added Tobit and Judith. The pedagogical literature also accepts Solomon's Wisdom and Ecclesiasticus. In the fourth group 1 and 2 Maccabees have their place, but 3 and 4 Maccabees are excluded.

This is not the end of divergence among the different Bible traditions. The Coptic and the Ethiopic churches have other canonical collections than these. Although both of them in general are in accordance with early Christian tradition, they also include Enoch among their sacred literature. It would thus be true to say that every Christian community has its own Bible, its own selection of holy writ. They, however, have one thing in common: all the books of the Jewish TaNaK will invariably have their place in all Christian Bibles.

---

6. English translation of the Pseudepigrapha: James H. Charlesworth, *The Old Testament Pseudepigrapha*, I–II (New York: Doubleday, 1983).

Synopsis of four different collections of Old Testament books

Luther	TaNaK	LXX	Vulgate
Genesis	Genesis	Genesis	Genesis
Exodus	Exodus	Exodus	Exodus
Leviticus	Leviticus	Leviticus	Leviticus
Numbers	Numbers	Numbers	Numbers
Deuteronomy	Deuteronomy	Deuteronomy	Deuteronomy
Joshua	Joshua	Joshua	Joshua
Judges	Judges	Judges	Judges
Ruth	1 Samuel	Ruth	Ruth
1 Samuel	2 Samuel	1 Samuel[7]	1 Samuel
2 Samuel	1 Kings	2 Samuel	2 Samuel
1 Kings	2 Kings	1 Kings	1 Kings
2 Kings	Isaiah	2 Kings	2 Kings
1 Chronicles	Jeremiah	1 Chronicles	1 Chronicles
2 Chronicles	Ezekiel	2 Chronicles	2 Chronicles
Ezra	Hosea	1 Ezra	Ezra
Nehemiah	Joel	2 Ezra	Nehemiah
Esther	Amos	Esther	Tobit
Job	Obadiah	Judith	Judith
Psalms	Jonah	Tobit	Esther
Proverbs	Micah	1 Maccabees	Job
Ecclesiastes	Nahum	2 Maccabees	Psalms
Song of Songs	Habakkuk	3 Maccabees	Proverbs
Isaiah	Zephaniah	4 Maccabees	Ecclesiastes
Jeremiah	Haggai	Psalms	Song of Songs
Lamentations	Zechariah	Odes (appendix to Psalms)	Wisdom
Ezekiel	Malachi	Proverbs	Ecclesiasticus
Daniel	Psalms	Ecclesiastes	Isaiah
Hosea	Job	Song of Songs	Jeremiah
Joel	Proverbs	Job	Lamentations
			(continued)

7. Septuagint names 1 and 2 Samuel the 1 and 2 Book of Kings; 1 and 2 Kings therefore are counted as the 3 and 4 Kings.

Synopsis of four different collections of Old Testament books
(continued)

Luther	TaNaK	LXX	Vulgate
Amos	Ruth	Wisdom	Baruch
Obadiah	Song of Songs	Ecclesiasticus	Ezekiel
Jonah	Qohelet	Psalms of Solomon	Daniel
Micah	Lamentations	Hosea	Hosea
Nahum	Esther	Amos	Joel
Habakkuk	Daniel	Micah	Amos
Zephaniah	Ezra	Joel	Obadiah
Haggai	Nehemiah	Obadiah	Jonah
Zechariah	1 Chronicles	Jonah	Micah
Malachi	2 Chronicles	Nahum	Nahum
		Habakkuk	Habakkuk
		Zephaniah	Zephaniah
		Haggai	Haggai
		Zechariah	Malachi
		Malachi	1 Maccabees
		Isaiah	2 Maccabees
		Jeremiah	
		Baruch	
		Lamentations	
		Letter of Jeremiah	
		Ezekiel	
		Susanna	
		Daniel (additions)	
		Bel and the Dragon	

THE OLD TESTAMENT: AN OVERVIEW

This short survey of the literature of the Old Testament follows the sequence of the TaNaK, the Law or the Pentateuch (*torah*) coming first, followed by the Prophets (*nevi'im*)—the former prophets (Joshua through 2 Kings) and the prophetic books—and the Writings (*ketuvim*). The choice to follow the order in the Hebrew Bible, disregarding the Christian way of arranging the books of the

Old Testament, is conventional but also practical, especially in contexts where the Bible's Hebrew text forms the basis of the study of the Old Testament.

The survey of the five books of Moses and the books from Joshua to 2 Kings will present a résumé of the narrative units. When we turn to the Prophetic books and to the Writings, the survey will be cursory and limited to a presentation of the major themes of the individual books.

The Law

Genesis can be subdivided into three sections: the Primeval History (Gen. 1–11), the Patriarchal Narratives (Gen. 12–36), and the Story of Joseph (Gen. 37–50).

The *Primeval History* presents the story of the origin of this world as God's creation (Gen. 1–2). It presents the sad story of the first humans and their rebellion against Yahweh/God, who exiled them from paradise to this harsh world (Gen. 3). After the expulsion of Adam and Eve from paradise, the first murder (Gen. 4: brother killing brother) is followed by the story of the flood (Gen. 6–8) and the story of the tower of Babel (Gen. 11). The Primeval History also presents a series of genealogies, bringing the human race from Adam and Eve to Abraham, the ancestor of Israel (Gen. 4:1,17–26; 5; 9:18–19; 10; 11:10–32). Finally we also hear about the first covenant between God and humankind, concluded after the end of the great flood, in which God promises never again to destroy the earth by flood (Gen. 9).

The *Patriarchal Narratives* are subdivided into two main sections. The first section has the patriarch (derived from Gk. *patriarches*, etymologically "the chieftain of a family") Abraham as its subject (Gen. 12–25:11). The second tells the story of the patriarch Jacob (Gen. 25:19–36:43). Between these two major figures, the third patriarch, Isaac is sandwiched. Isaac is the main figure in only one chapter (Gen. 26).

The story of Abraham and Sarah—at the beginning Abram and Sarai—begins with God's election of Abraham as the founder of his chosen people. Abraham and Sarah travel on the order of God from their homeland in Haran in Mesopotamia to the land of Canaan, their future home. Although Abraham commits a series of blunders, such as his departure for Egypt where he almost loses his wife (Gen. 12), and his affair with the Egyptian woman Hagar (Gen. 16), Yahweh never withdraws his support. Abraham dies in old age, full of days, and his succession is in safe hands (Gen. 25:7–10). Isaac, Abraham's and Sarah's only child, who marries Rebekah, the granddaughter of his father's brother (Gen. 24), begets the twins Esau and Jacob (Gen. 25:20–26).

The beginning of the story about Jacob, the third patriarch, takes as its departure the competition between twin brothers. Jacob, being the second-born of the two, nevertheless obtains the blessing of his father by fraud. Because of his fear of his brother, whom he has cheated so badly, Jacob is forced to leave his home and his parents and run away to Haran to his mother's brother, the crafty Laban (Gen. 27). In Haran Jacob marries the two daughters of Laban, Leah and Rachel, and fathers twelve sons (Gen. 29:15–30:24; 35:16–20), the ancestors of Israel's twelve tribes. From Haran Jacob returns to Canaan (Gen. 33–35), where he buries his father (Gen. 35:29).

This is only the main line of the patriarchal narratives. Dispersed among them are other narratives, anecdotes, genealogies, and more. Here we hear about the origin of Israel's neighbors Ammon, Moab, and Edom (Gen. 19:29–38; 36); about the visits of the patriarchs to foreign peoples: the Egyptians (Gen. 12) and the Philistines (Gen. 20 and 26); and about the acquisition of the family grave cave in Hebron (Gen. 23).

The story of Joseph opens at the moment the story of Jacob has seemingly come to an end and Jacob is living peacefully in his homeland. At this point, Joseph, Jacob's favorite son, is sold by his brothers as a slave and carried away to Egypt (Gen. 37). After many problems Joseph in Egypt obtains the office of a supervisor, second only to Pharaoh himself. After he has reached his high position, his brothers arrive in Egypt, forced to leave Canaan because of hunger (Gen. 42–45), and after them his father (Gen. 46). Jacob dies in Egypt, but he is brought back to Canaan and buried in his family grave. Joseph dies in Egypt and is buried there according to Egyptian custom. The story of Joseph also includes interludes in the form of smaller narrative units like the anecdotal story about Judah and Tamar, the widow of Judah's son who becomes pregnant by her father-in-law and gives birth to the ancestor of the Davidic dynasty (Gen. 38; cf. also Ruth 4:18–22). The Blessing of Jacob (Gen. 49), a poetical compilation that gives characters to the twelve tribes of Israel, not always in the kindest way, is also included.

Exodus-Numbers may, from a literary point of view, be divided into three major sections: the stories about the exodus from Egypt (Exod. 1–15), the introduction to the narratives about Israel's sojourn in the desert (Exod. 16–18), and the concluding part of this story in Numbers (Num. 10–33). The story of Israel's march back to Canaan is interrupted by the Sinai tradition, the story about how Yahweh made his covenant with Israel and gave his law to his chosen people (Exod. 19–Num. 9).

The *exodus narrative* opens with the story of young Moses, who is miraculously saved from the Nile and grows up at the court of Pharaoh. However, forced to flee from Egypt, he encounters Yahweh in the burning bush and is installed by Yahweh himself as the leader of his people who is to bring them out of Egypt (Exod. 3). Now Israel, after having lived in Egypt for 430 years, has become a great nation, but Pharaoh will not allow it to leave. Only the ten plagues of Egypt can convince Pharaoh of the necessity of letting Israel go. In connection with the departure of the Israelites, the festival of the *Passover* is celebrated in memory of the mighty acts of God, who delivered his people from oppression in Egypt (Exod. 12–13). After the departure of Israel, Pharaoh regrets his mildness and starts pursuing the Israelites but meets his fate in the waters of the Sea of Reeds, which divided itself to allow Israel to pass through (Exod. 14–15). From the sea Israel moves into the desert to Mount Sinai (Exod. 18–19). This narrative is interspersed with some minor units. Most remarkable is the Song of the Sea (Exod.

From the Blessing of Jacob (Gen. 49)
and the Blessing of Moses (Deut. 33)

Genesis 49:3–4, 8, 27	Deuteronomy 33:6–7, 12
3 "Reuben, you are my firstborn, my might and the first fruits of my vigor, excelling in rank and excelling in power.	6 May Reuben live, and not die out, even though his numbers are few.
4 Unstable as water, you shall no longer excel, because you went up onto your father's bed; then you defiled it—you went up onto my couch!	
8 Judah, your brothers shall praise you; your hand shall be on the neck of your enemies; your father's sons shall bow down before you.	7 And this he said of Judah: O LORD, give heed to Judah, and bring him to his people; strengthen his hands for him, and be a help against his adversaries.
27 Benjamin is a ravenous wolf, in the morning devouring the prey, and at evening dividing the spoil."	12 Of Benjamin he said, The beloved of the LORD rests in safety— the High God surrounds him all day long— the beloved rests between his shoulders.

15:1–18), a poetical rendering of the prose narrative about the miracle at the sea in Exodus 14.

The narratives about *Israel's sojourn in the desert* bring Israel from the Sea of Reeds to the eastern bank of the Jordan River. It is introduced at the end of the exodus narrative, the passage of the Sea of Reeds (Exod. 14–15), and is followed by the passage of the Jordan in Joshua (Josh. 3). During their wanderings in the desert, bringing Israel from the borders of Egypt to the borders of Canaan, the Israelites stop at several stations, each of them the place of a remarkable act and a place where important decisions for the future have to be made. Characteristic of the attitude of the Israelites toward Moses and their God and benefactor are the many times when the Israelites regret their evil fate in the desert and look back on the stay in Egypt as a lost paradise: "If only we had died by the hand of the LORD in the land of Egypt, when we sat by the fleshpots and ate our fill of bread" (Exod. 16:3). The Israelites are always complaining in spite of being continuously guided by Yahweh, who travels in front of Israel during the day in the form of a pillar of cloud, and in the night as a pillar of fire (Exod. 13:21). As Israel reaches the southern border of Canaan, Moses sends scouts into the country to bring information about conditions there. They report back to Moses in such a way that, stricken by terror, the people decide not to start an invasion. Because of their disobedience Yahweh condemns them to forty years of wandering in the desert, so that nobody except Joshua and Caleb will be allowed to enter the future homeland of Israel (Num. 13–14). The story about the scouts is followed by more episodes until Israel finally arrives at the border of Canaan, putting their tents up on the eastern bank of the Jordan opposite Jericho (Num. 33:41–49).

As already indicated, the narrative about Israel's migration in the desert breaks off with the introduction of the complex of tradition concerning Sinai, the covenant between Yahweh and Israel, and the law of God. This complex is placed in the center of the Pentateuch and occupies more than half of Exodus, all of Leviticus, and the first nine and a half chapter of Numbers. It opens with the story of the theophany at Sinai (Exod. 19), followed by a series of laws: first the Ten Commandments (Exod. 20:1–17), the law of the altar (Exod. 20:24–26), and the book of the covenant (Exod. 21–23). After the laws come the conclusion of the covenant (Exod. 24) and a series of instructions about the arrangement of the sanctuary and its priesthood (Exod. 25–40). Inserted into the middle of this assemblage of instructions is the story of the golden calf and the new tables of the law (Exod. 32–34).

Leviticus is introduced by a series of laws concerning sacrifice: the burnt sacrifice, the sacrifice of flour, and so forth (Lev. 1–7). Then follow the story of the installation of Aaron, the brother of Moses, and his sons as priests (Lev. 8–10) and another series of laws about cleanness and uncleanness (Lev. 11–15). There are extensive instructions for the celebration of the Day of Atonement (Lev. 16). The following laws and instructions about religious and social problems are often summarized as the Law of Holiness (Lev. 17–26). Among these we find sexual laws, laws concerning the Sabbath, and the law of the year of jubilee.

Numbers opens with a series of censuses counting the Israelites tribe by tribe and family by family, and special censuses covering the priests (Num. 1–4). Following these, a series of instructions dealing with the tasks of the Levites and about the sanctuary conclude the Sinai complex (Num. 4–9), and the narrative about the wanderings in the desert continues.

Deuteronomy is formally organized as a long lecture delivered by Moses east of the Jordan before Israel can pass through the river and invade the land of Canaan (Deut. 1–30). At the end we find the story of Moses's death (Deut. 34). Several subjects are joined together to make up Moses's lecture. It opens with a review of the time in the desert (Deut. 1–3), after which follows a series of admonitions that Israel should keep the covenant and obey the law (Deut. 4:1–10), whereupon the law itself follows, introduced as was the case in Exodus with the Ten Commandments (Deut. 5:6–21). In contrast to the laws in Exodus–Numbers, the laws of Deuteronomy are constantly interrupted by new and repeated admonitions to Israel, asking it in the future to stay faithful to Yahweh and obey his law and commandments. This arrangement changes in the central part of Deuteronomy, where the sections with laws on the cost of the admonitions take over (Deut. 12–26). After Deuteronomy 26, a new direction follows: instructions for the building of an altar on Mount Ebal at Shechem (Deut. 27:1–10); a list of blessings and curses following the person who keeps or breaks, respectively, the covenant comes next (Deut. 27:12–28:68). More instructions follow until the lecture is concluded by the installation of Joshua as Moses's successor (Deut. 31), and Deuteronomy ends with the Song of Moses (Deut. 32), the Blessing of Moses (Deut. 33), and the story of Moses's death (Deut. 34). The Blessing of Moses consists of a series of sentences dealing with the tribes of Israel, in many ways similar to the Blessing of Jacob (Gen. 49).

The Prophets: The Former Prophets (Joshua–2 Kings)

Joshua may be subdivided into three sections. The first section tells us about the passage of the Israelites through Jordan and the conquest of Canaan (Josh. 1–12). The second section overviews the distribution of the country among the tribes of Israel (Josh. 13–19). In this section also belongs the chapter on cities of refuge (Josh. 20), the chapter on the Levitical cities (Josh. 21), and the story of the building of an altar to the east of the Jordan (Josh. 22). The final section consists of the story of two meetings. At the first, in Shiloh, Joshua delivers his farewell address to the leaders of Israel (Josh. 23). After this follows his renewal of the covenant in Shechem (Josh. 24). Joshua concludes with a note about the death and burial of Joshua (Josh. 24:29–33).

The narrative about the *conquest of Canaan* is introduced by the story of the Israelite scouts who enter Jericho and are here protected by the whore Rahab (Josh. 2). Thereupon follows the passage through the Jordan, presented as a parallel to the earlier passage through the Sea of Reeds, and the erection of twelve stones in Gilgal (meaning "circle") in commemoration of the passage through the Jordan. This part ends with the celebration of the Passover (Josh. 3–5), whereupon the conquest can start in earnest. First, the Canaanite cities of Jericho and Ai are utterly destroyed and their inhabitants executed (Josh. 6 and 8). In between is inserted the story about the punishment of Achan for having broken the ban on the spoils from Jericho, put aside for God (Josh. 7). A third Canaanite city, Gibeon, is next on the list, but before the Israelites can proceed to destroy this city, its inhabitants by treachery persuade the Israelites to establish a covenant with them (Josh. 9). After these particular incidents, the conquest of the remaining parts of the country are summarized: the southern part of Canaan in Joshua 10 and the northern part in Joshua 11. The last chapter belonging to this section surveys all of Joshua's conquests (Josh. 12).

The central part of Joshua is occupied with the *division of the country among the various tribes.* Here we encounter a meticulous account of the division of Canaan into different tribal territories, including a precise rendering of the borderlines between them. The distribution is subdivided into several passages. First comes an account of the tribal territories to the east of the Jordan, given to the tribes of Reuben, Gad, and half of Manasseh, even before the passage through the Jordan (Josh. 13; cf. Num. 32). After this comes the description of the territories of the tribes of the central part of the country: Judah, Ephraim, and the second half of Manasseh

(Josh. 14–17). In contrast to the remaining tribes, these three tribes receive their territories by divine order. The other tribes receive their territories by lot (Josh. 18–19). For Israelites who unintentionally have committed murders and because of their crime are forced to leave their home and society, a special institution is established, the cities of refuge (Josh. 20). A series of cities is likewise reserved for the Levites, who after having been instituted as a tribe of priests (cf. Exod. 32:25–29) have no longer any territorial claims in the land of Israel (Josh. 21).

The last part of Joshua includes the *farewell address of Joshua in Shiloh* (Josh. 23) and his conclusion of the covenant in Shechem (Josh. 24). In some ways the two narratives duplicate one another. Joshua summons the leaders of the Israelites to Shiloh, where he advises them to remain faithful to Yahweh and to keep the covenant, if Israel does not want to "perish quickly from the good land that he has given to you" (Josh. 23:16). After this meeting, all of Israel is invited to Shechem, where Joshua delivers a speech to the Israelites. A historical review of the past intro-duces the speech, and is followed by an admonition to worship Yahweh and remove idols. The chapter ends with a formal and binding establishment of the covenant. Here Joshua acts as the mediator between Yahweh and the people of Israel. The covenant is marked by the erection of a memorial stone in the sanctuary of Shechem. After having concluded this covenant, Joshua has finished his task and dies.

Judges is subdivided into three sections: the narratives about Israel's judges (Judg. 1–12), the Samson stories (Judg. 13–16), and stories from the time when there was no king in Israel (Judg. 17–21).

The first section, the *narratives about Israel's judges*, opens with a review of the conquests of the tribes of Judah and Joseph (the combination of Ephraim and Manasseh). It is, however, remarkable that emphasis has been put on the parts of Canaan not conquered by the Israelites (Judg. 1). Next comes a chapter describ-ing all of Israel's sins against its God after the death of Joshua, leading to Yahweh delivering his people into the hand of its enemies (Judg. 2).

> Now the angel of the LORD went up from Gilgal to Bochim, and said, "I brought you up from Egypt, and brought you into the land that I had promised to your ancestors. I said, 'I will never break my covenant with you. [2] For your part, do not make a covenant with the inhabitants of this land; tear down their altars.' But you have not obeyed my command. See what you have done! [3] So now I say, I will not drive them out before you; but they shall become adversaries to you, and their gods shall be a snare to you." (Judg. 2:1–3)

This introduces the rather sad story of Israel and its land. In Judges, the stereo-typed stories have this structure: Israel sins against Yahweh, who delivers them into the hands of their enemies. Because of this foreign oppression, Israel cries for help to Yahweh, who sends a judge who vanquishes the enemies and saves the people. As long as this judge lives and rules Israel, there is peace because Israel stays faith-ful to its God. However, when the judge dies, the cycle repeats itself. This happens over and over again, until Israel is torn by internal strife and civil war, and its judge—in this case Jephthah—is forced to fight against his own people (Judg. 12).

The *story of Samson* (Judg. 13–16), which follows the narratives about Israel's judges, has as its main characters the mighty Israelite champion Samson and the ever-scheming Philistine woman Delilah. It explains how Samson delivered Israel from the Philistines but was himself the victim of Delilah's wiles that deliver him into the hands of his opponents, who blind him. It also describes the hero's glorious end, when blind Samson by his last and suicidal act kills 3,000 Philistines.

The *stories of when there was no king*, which conclude Judges, do not contribute to the theme of Israel deserting Yahweh. Here the subject is rather the willfulness of humankind when it has no king to rule over it: "In those days there was no king in Israel; all the people did what was right in their own eyes" (Judg. 21:25). The first narrative (Judg. 17–18) is the story of Micah's sanctuary in the mountains of Ephraim. Migrating Danites plunder it and carry away both priest and idol and bring it to Laish, the future capital of the tribe of Dan. The second narrative (Judg. 19–21) is devoted to the almost complete annihilation of the tribe of Benjamin. This gruesome fate of the Benjaminites is caused by the gang rape of a Levite's concubine in a Benjaminite city. As a consequence of this crime, all the tribes of Israel make war on Benjamin. Only a tiny fraction of the tribe is spared.

First Samuel, like Joshua and Judges, may also be divided into three parts, each having its main character. The first part has the prophet Samuel as its champion, the second Israel's first king, Saul, and the third part young David, Saul's successor as king of Israel. These narratives have, however, been interwoven in such a way that it is rather difficult to separate the three stories as individual literary units. A preliminary division will have the first part to include 1 Samuel 1–8, the second 1 Samuel 9–15, and the third part 1 Samuel 16–31. However, Samuel does not die until 1 Samuel 25, nor Saul until 1 Samuel 31.

In the introduction to 1 Samuel, we hear about the birth of *Samuel*, his upbringing in the temple of Shiloh, and his vocation as the prophet of Yahweh (1 Sam. 1–3). Here the flow of the story is interrupted by the narrative about the fate of the ark of God, which had its place in the sanctuary of Shiloh but is lost in the war between the Israelites and the Philistines. The Philistines place the ark in their own temple, but it destroys their idol and they have to send it away to its provisional home in Kiriath-jearim (1 Sam. 4–6). After this story about the ark, the Samuel narrative goes on and it is recorded that Samuel was the victor in a battle against the Philistines (1 Sam. 7). In spite of Samuel's protests, the people of Israel now want a king to rule over them: "appoint for us, then, a king to govern us, like other nations" (1 Sam. 8:5).

Now follows the story of *Saul*, who travels around in search of his father's donkeys, but finds a kingdom, being anointed king by Samuel (1 Sam. 9–10). Two more times Saul is elected as king, first by lot, then as a consequence of his victory over the Ammonites (1 Sam. 10:17–25 and 1 Sam. 11). Now Samuel delivers his farewell address and warns Israel of the new direction its history has taken, as subject to a king's will (1 Sam. 12). Saul goes on to win a remarkable victory over the Philistines (1 Sam. 13–14) but is soon rejected by Samuel, who instead anoints the boy *David* from Bethlehem as the new king of Israel (1 Sam. 15–16).

The remaining part of 1 Samuel describes the envy between Saul and David, which grows to new heights as David becomes increasingly successful. In the end, Saul is killed in a battle against the Philistines (1 Sam. 31).

Second Samuel continues the narrative of 1 Samuel. Now the antagonists are no more David and Saul but David and the family of Saul, and the civil war goes on until only David is left as the king of Israel. David is chosen as the king of Israel, and conquers his future capital Jerusalem and brings the ark of God to his city (2 Sam. 1–6). In this place, one of the central passages in the historical books of the Old Testament is found, the promise of Nathan to David when Nathan on behalf of Yahweh guarantees an eternal dynasty of the family of David (2 Sam. 7). A new story line opens with 2 Samuel 8, describing the tragedy of the family of David (2 Sam. 8–20, supplemented by 1 Kgs. 1–2). Although victorious in all his wars, David brings upon his family internal fighting, fratricide, incest, and rape because of his infatuation with Bathsheba, the wife of Uriah the Hittite, with whom he fathers his successor, the future king of Israel, Solomon. Especially tragic is the strife between David and his favorite son, Absalom, who ends his days most dishonorably hanging from a tree and pierced by Joab (2 Sam. 14–19). The story of King David is approaching its end when the northern tribes of Israel fight against their king, a rebellion that inaugurated the harsh times that were to follow after Solomon's death (2 Sam. 20). The last four chapters of 2 Samuel bring sundry information from the time of King David, among them the Last Words of David (2 Sam. 23:1–7), a list of David's heroes (2 Sam. 23:8–39), and the story of the plague that killed 70,000 Israelites as a punishment for David's census (2 Sam. 24).

Three version of God's promise to David that his dynasty shall rule forever and ever

2 Samuel 7	Psalm 89	Psalm 132
[11] Moreover the LORD declares to you that the LORD will make you a house. [12] When your days are fulfilled and you lie down with your ancestors, I will raise up your offspring after you, who shall come forth from your body, and I will establish his kingdom. . . . [16] Your house and your kingdom shall be made sure forever before me; your throne shall be established forever.	[3] You said, "I have made a covenant with my chosen one, I have sworn to my servant David: [4] 'I will establish your descendants forever, and build your throne for all generations.' "(thus NRSV; Heb. vv. 4–5)	[11]The LORD swore to David a sure oath from which he will not turn back: "One of the sons of your body I will set on your throne. [12] If your sons keep my covenant and my decrees that I shall teach them, their sons also, forevermore, shall sit on your throne."

The two **books of Kings** tell about the history of the kingdoms of Israel and Judah from David's death to the fall of Jerusalem, the destruction of the temple, the deportation of Israel from its land, and the loss of the ark of the covenant.

First Kings opens with the end of the story about David. He dies and is succeeded by Solomon (1 Kgs. 1–2:11). Solomon's greatness then is the subject of the next chapters of the book (1 Kgs. 2–11). In the center of the story about Solomon stands the description of the building of the temple of Jerusalem and the complex of palace buildings erected next to the temple (1 Kgs. 5–8). Among the extraordinary events of Solomon's reign, the visit of the queen of Sheba must take pride of place (1 Kgs. 10:1–13), but famous also is his acting as a wise judge in the case of the two women who claim one and the same child for both of them (1 Kgs. 3:16–27). The tragedy of "the history of Israel" begins in earnest in 1 Kings 11, and it comes to a bitter end only in 2 Kings 25. The remaining parts of 1 Kings (chaps. 11–22) deal with history from the death of Solomon and the dissolution of his great kingdom into two small states, Israel and Judah (1 Kgs. 12), to the reign of Ahaziah, the son of Ahab. A special part of this narrative deals with the two northern prophets, Elijah and Elisha, and their struggles against King Ahab and his evil Queen Jezebel (1 Kgs. 17–2 Kgs. 9). In this way these prophetic legends bind 1 and 2 Kings together and provide the link to the final part of the history of the kingdom of Israel until the fall of Samaria (2 Kgs. 9–17). Interwoven into this history of Israel is the history of the kingdom of Judah, which develops more or less in parallel with the history of the northern kingdom. The historiographer includes a devastating commentary explaining the reasons for the fall of Israel (2 Kgs. 17:7–23). After this comes the reign of the good King Hezekiah, when Yahweh himself changes the course of history and saves Jerusalem from the hands of King Sennacherib of Assyria (2 Kgs. 18–20), but he is followed by the evil King Manasseh, whose acts bring disaster upon the kingdom of Judah (2 Kgs. 21), and the good acts of Josiah, the best king of Judah since the days of David, can only postpone the inevitable destruction and exile. Thus Josiah introduces a reform of religion in his kingdom that centralizes all forms of cult in the temple of Jerusalem (2 Kgs. 23). The end is bitter, but it is now decided and cannot be changed. Two times King Nebuchadnezzar of Babylonia conquers Jerusalem; the second time he also totally destroys the city and the temple and carries its population away into exile (2 Kgs. 25).

According to the Jewish tradition of the TaNaK, the historical books from Joshua to 2 Kings belong among the prophetic literature. In this light, the history of Israel told by these books cannot be regarded as an independent part of the TaNaK, but should be studied in connection with the fifteen prophetic books, which in the Hebrew Bible follow 2 Kings: the three great prophetic books of Isaiah, Jeremiah, and Ezekiel, followed by the book of the Twelve Minor Prophets. The biblical books from Joshua to Malachi in Jewish tradition are looked upon as two sides of the same coin. Both parts of the Prophets have the same story to tell, the greatness and fall of ancient Israel. It is in accordance with this reading of the prophetic books that several among them are fixed in time. The prophets to whom these books are ascribed are often in the introduction to the books placed within a historical framework created by the historiographers who composed the books of Kings. Apart from that, the prophetic books are all very uneven as far as structure and staging goes. Some of them seem to be anthologies of preprophetic commentaries intersected by a commentary by the compiler of the book; other books are almost prophetic biographies; still other books look more like psalms disguised as prophetic utterances; and one of the books, the book of Jonah, is a short burlesque.

The Prophets: The Prophetic Books

The separation in the Christian tradition of the two parts of the Hebrew prophetic literature has also severed the relation between—in the Christian Bible—the historical literature and the prophetic books. According to the arrangement found in Christian Bibles, the books from Joshua through 2 Kings are about the past, the prophetic books from Isaiah through Malachi about the future.

We will return to the historical and theological connections between these two groups later in this book.[8] It is obvious that the Christian tradition made a mistake by separating these two blocks of biblical literature. However, this separation was necessary, from the specific point of view of Christianity.

Isaiah: the name of the book reflects a development within English of the Hebrew name of the prophet, yeshayahu. Isaiah is particular to the English language tradition. Other Bible traditions often follow the rendering of the name in the Greek Bible, Esaias. The book carrying this prophet's name is a complicated piece of literature that is conveniently subdivided into three sections, respectively Proto-Isaiah, Deutero-Isaiah, and Trito-Isaiah.

Proto-Isaiah, or First Isaiah, covers the first thirty-nine chapters of Isaiah. It is, according to its self-testimony, related to events in the days of the four kings mentioned in the introduction to the book (Isa. 1:1). The main subject of Proto-Isaiah refers to Israel's desertion of Yahweh. Therefore, Israel's land is going to be destroyed by foreign invaders. Only a few among treacherous Israel will survive the ordeal, those lucky few who have not rejected the torah of God. The code word is "a remnant will return/repent" (symbolized by the name of the prophet's son Shear-jashub [Isa. 7:3]). After the punishment and the purification of the people, the country, and Jerusalem, the holy remnant in the future will all live in God's place on Zion governed by the Messiah, God's chosen king, and protected by the very presence of God.

Especially in the first part of Proto-Isaiah (Isa. 1–12), this message is followed by poetry of the highest order. Among these poems we may mention the song of the vineyard (Isa. 5:1–7), a story about God's care and humankind's disbelief. The poetic parts are often parts of prose narratives like the stories about the call of the prophet (Isa. 6) and the meeting between the prophet and King Ahaz "at the end

8. See chapters 7 and 8.

The dates of the prophets according to the superscription to the Prophetic Books

Dates relating to the historical framework in the books of Kings	
Isaiah	Uzziah, Jotham, Ahaz, Hezekiah
Jeremiah	Josiah, Jehoiachim, Zedekiah
Ezekiel	30th year, 5th day, 4th month / five years after the exile of Jehoiachin
Hosea	Uzziah, Jotham, Ahaz, Hezekiah, Jeroboam
Amos	Uzziah, Jeroboam
Micah	Jotham, Ahaz, Hezekiah
Zephaniah	Josiah
Dates relating to the Second Temple	
Haggai	2nd year of King Darius
Zechariah	2nd year of King Darius
Prophetic books carrying no date	
Joel	
Obadiah	
Jonah (but cf. 2 Kgs. 14:25)	
Nahum	
Habakkuk	
Malachi	

of the conduit of the upper pool on the highway to the Fuller's Field" (Isa. 7:3), leading to the prophecy about the birth of Immanuel (a symbolic name meaning "God is with us") (Isa. 7).

The following chapters include a series of prophetic threats against foreign nations: Babylonia, Assyria, the land of the Philistines, Moab, and more (Isa. 13–23). These prophecies introduce a section relating the destruction of the earth, that is, the world known in the culture of and at the time of the prophet, and the salvation of Israel (Isa. 24–27), after which follows another series of admonitions, warnings, and predictions (Isaiah 18–35). The conclusion of the first part of Isaiah (Isa. 36–39) is more or less identical to the story about Sennacherib's attack on Jerusalem in 2 Kings 18–20.

Deutero-Isaiah includes Isaiah 40–55 and has as its main subject the liberation of Israel from captivity in Babylon. This part of Isaiah stages the liberation as another exodus arranged by the God of Israel using Cyrus, the king of Persia, as his agent.

A series of passages in Deutero-Isaiah have for more than a hundred years received special attention, the so-called Servant of the Lord Songs (Isa. 42:1–9; 49:1–13; 50:4–11; 52:13–53:17). These songs have often been regarded as constituting a coherent and maybe originally independent complex of literature within the confines of the book of Isaiah. The first song (Isa. 42:1–9) praises the Servant because of his noble constitution and describes him as the one who is going to liberate Israel from its prison. In the second song (Isa. 49:1–13) the servant praises God for having elected him as the one who is going to bring Israel home. The third song (50:4–11) praises the Servant as endowed with power from God and as the one "who walks in darkness and has no light" and punishes evil. In the fourth song (Isa. 52:13–53:12) the Servant is described as destroyed and rejected by God, harassed by death, and delivered as an atonement sacrifice for the world.

Trito-Isaiah includes Isaiah 56–66. It mainly concerns the temple, the Sabbath, Jerusalem, and Israel's salvation.

The arrangement of **Jeremiah** is quite different from the one found in Isaiah. In this book, there is a definite emphasis on the biographical parts. Thus Jeremiah includes large sections of prose narrative describing both the prophet's encounters with the king and his retainers and the prophet's reactions to the many disasters that struck his country until the fall of Jerusalem—and beyond that event, until the murder of Gedaliah, the Babylonian governor, and Jeremiah's exile in Egypt. The prosaic parts of Jeremiah display a certain similarity to ideas and sentiments found in the former prophets, the historical literature, and Deuteronomy. Another part of the book, the so-called confessions, plays an important role. These confessions are often believed to express the personal sentiments of the prophet himself but are now often reckoned as psalm literature, akin to the songs of lamentations in the book of Psalms.

The essential message of Jeremiah is more or less the same as found in Isaiah. Yahweh will punish Israel because of its idolatry, and Israel will be deported into exile at the same time the enemy will plunder its land. The people have declined to follow the instructions in Yahweh's torah and have pursued their own evil path. In an important chapter (Jer. 31) a new hope comes forth, however, involving not the people of the old covenant but the people of the new covenant. In this way Jeremiah shares the hopes of Isaiah that when Israel has been punished and the godless part removed from its midst, it will see a new era of greatness bound to God by a covenant that cannot be broken. At the end of Jeremiah we find a series of curses against foreign nations (Jer. 46–51), similar to the prophecies against foreigners in Isaiah, and also the narrative about the fall of Judah and destruction of Jerusalem, identical to 2 Kings 24–25 (Jer. 52).

Ezekiel tells the story of the prophet Ezekiel, who before the fall of Jerusalem is carried away into exile in Mesopotamia. Here, in a series of visions he sees the destruction of Jerusalem. The explanation for this disaster in Ezekiel is very similar to that found in Isaiah and Jeremiah. The idolatry of the Israelites and Judeans, which in Ezekiel is expressed in images that some scholars have dubbed "religious pornography" (e.g., Ezek. 16), led to the downfall of the two nations. Ezekiel also allows for prophecies directed against foreign nations (Ezek. 25–32; 35) and predicts that Israel in the future will regain its possession of "the mountains of Israel" (Ezek. 36). The final part of Ezekiel is a vision of the new temple of Jerusalem. In this vision Ezekiel is brought by an angel from Mesopotamia to Jerusalem, where he witnesses the reconstruction of the temple and all its institutions (Ezek. 40–48).

The book of the **Twelve Prophets** is a collection of sundry prophetic books, among them six dated by their headings: Hosea, Amos, Micah, and Zephaniah all belong to the time before the fall of Jerusalem, and Haggai and Zechariah evidently belong to the time of King Darius of Persia. The remaining six undated books are Joel, Obadiah, Jonah, Nahum, Habakkuk, and Malachi.

In *Hosea* we meet prophecies concerning the fall of Israel, that is, Samaria. Hosea is described as a prophet living in Israel before the Assyrian conquest. Hosea follows the three major prophets in his explanation of the reason for Israel's downfall: lack of knowledge of God paired with idolatry, because they had forgotten the torah of Yahweh (Hos. 4:6). The desert has a special role to play in the prophecies about future exile and stay in Egypt: The desert is the place where true relations may be reestablished between Israel and its God.

Also in *Amos*, the expectations that the state of Israel will be destroyed are in the center, and again the punishment comes because Israel has forgotten Yahweh's torah (Amos 2:4–5). The punishment is unavoidable but will one day be a thing of the past when a new Israel shall appear, living in its country forever and ever (Amos 9:11–15).

Micah opens with a series of prophecies about the impending punishment and destruction, but ends with a vision of the coming salvation, when the nations are traveling to Zion and Jerusalem, the mountain where Yahweh's temple is built, from whence his torah will shine forth. Here the new David, the prince of everlasting peace, shall rule (Mic. 5).

Zephaniah follows the preceding books in its pronouncement of impending punishment and extinction, because unfaithful Israel has rejected the torah of Yahweh (Zeph. 3:4). Zephaniah, however, also envisions a return for the rest of Israel.

Haggai and *Zechariah* are connected to the reconstruction of the temple of Jerusalem a few years after the end of the exile. The context in this case is not a period found in the former prophets, that is, in Joshua through 2 Kings. The context of these two prophetic books is presented by their placement in the collection of the minor prophets and their relation to the books of Chronicles and of Ezra and Nehemiah. This is of especial importance for Haggai and Zechariah 1–6, whereas Zechariah 6–12 (also sometimes named Deutero-Zechariah) consists of a series of prophecies about the coming kingdom of David and the restoration of Israel.

The remaining six undated prophetic books are very different in style and content. Some of them are rather short. *Obadiah* consists of only one chapter.

The subject of *Joel* is a plague of locusts to be countered by repentance and prayer to Yahweh, who will replace what has been lost and restore the wealth of the country (Joel 1–2). In its choice of subject, the final part of the book is quite similar to other prophetic books: Words of condemnation are directed against foreign nations, and the restored Israel will live on Zion, the holy mountain of God (Joel 3–4).

As already mentioned, *Obadiah* consists of only one chapter. The subject is the condemnation of Edom and the salvation of Israel.

Jonah is absolutely different in scope and layout from the prophetic literature so far mentioned. It is a minor novel, having as its hero the prophet Jonah, the son of Amittai, who is sent by Yahweh to Nineveh to preach coming judgment and repentance. Jonah tries to escape this burden, expecting the citizens of Nineveh to kill him. He enters a ship in Joppa but is swallowed by a big fish that after three days spits him up on the coast. Now Jonah travels to Nineveh and to his great surprise—and outspoken dissatisfaction—the people of Nineveh do not kill him, but repent and turn to Yahweh.

The single subject of *Nahum* is Yahweh's impending destruction of Nineveh and the Assyrian Empire.

Habakkuk opens with a complaint about the success of the enemy, the Chaldeans, and a prediction of their and their king's downfall (Hab. 1–2). The third and last chapter is a psalm about the coming of Yahweh, the punishment of the enemy, and the salvation of Israel.

Malachi consists of three parts: speeches about the punishment of the wicked and the salvation of the pious ones, an admonition to Israel that it shall keep Moses's torah, and the prediction of the coming of the prophet Elijah.

The Writings

The third part of the Hebrew Bible or the TaNaK consists of the Writings, *ketuvim*. It is a collection of very different forms of literature and not connected by any kind of red thread. The sequence and number of books differs among the various Bible traditions, for example, between the Hebrew tradition and the Christian one. In keeping with the principles behind the Christian collection, anything that has even a remote allusion to history is placed at the beginning of the collection. For that reason, the two books of Chronicles follow in the Christian tradition immediately after 2 Kings, and are followed by Ezra and Nehemiah.[9] In Christian Bibles, Esther comes directly after Nehemiah—another consequence of the historically oriented principle for the Christian Bible. Job comes before Psalms, probably also a result of historical considerations. Although Job does not belong to any historical period, and lives in Uz, an otherwise unknown place, he is considered a person who really lived "once upon a time," east of the sun and west of the moon.

Psalms introduces the third part of the TaNaK. There may be several reasons for this place of honor. When New Testament writers refer to the Old Testament,

---

9. It is, however, remarkable that the Leningrad and the Aleppo codices have Chronicles following Malachi, i.e., they place Chronicles at the beginning of the Writings and not at the end.

The beginning and the end of the Psalms of David

Psalms 1–2	Psalms 149–150

Happy are those
who do not follow the advice of the wicked,
or take the path that sinners tread,
or sit in the seat of scoffers;
[2]but their delight is in the law of the LORD,
and on his law they meditate day and night.
[3]They are like trees
planted by streams of water,
which yield their fruit in its season,
and their leaves do not wither.
In all that they do, they prosper.

[4]The wicked are not so,
but are like chaff that the wind drives away.
[5]Therefore the wicked will not stand in the judgment,
nor sinners in the congregation of the righteous;
[6]for the LORD watches over the way of the righteous,
but the way of the wicked will perish.

2 Why do the nations conspire,
and the peoples plot in vain?
[2]The kings of the earth set themselves,
and the rulers take counsel together,
against the LORD and his anointed, saying,
[3]"Let us burst their bonds asunder,
and cast their cords from us."

[4]He who sits in the heavens laughs;
the LORD has them in derision.
[5]Then he will speak to them in his wrath,
and terrify them in his fury, saying,
[6]"I have set my king on Zion, my holy hill."

[7]I will tell of the decree of the LORD:
He said to me, "You are my son;
today I have begotten you.
[8]Ask of me, and I will make the nations your heritage,
and the ends of the earth your possession.
[9]You shall break them with a rod of iron,
and dash them in pieces like a potter's vessel."

Praise the LORD!
Sing to the LORD a new song,
his praise in the assembly of the faithful.
[2]Let Israel be glad in its Maker;
let the children of Zion rejoice in their King.
[3]Let them praise his name with dancing,
making melody to him with tambourine and lyre.
[4]For the LORD takes pleasure in his people;
[5]he adorns the humble with victory.
Let the faithful exult in glory;
let them sing for joy on their couches.
[6]Let the high praises of God be in their throats
and two-edged swords in their hands,
[7]to execute vengeance on the nations
and punishment on the peoples,
[8]to bind their kings with fetters
and their nobles with chains of iron,
[9]to execute on them the judgment decreed.
This is glory for all his faithful ones.
Praise the LORD!

150 Praise the LORD!
Praise God in his sanctuary;
praise him in his mighty firmament!
Praise him for his mighty deeds;
[2]praise him according to his surpassing greatness!

[3]Praise him with trumpet sound;
praise him with lute and harp!
[4]Praise him with tambourine and dance;
praise him with strings and pipe!
Praise him with clanging cymbals;
[5]praise him with loud clashing cymbals!
[6]Let everything that breathes praise the LORD!
Praise the LORD!

(continued)

The beginning and the end of the Psalms of David
(continued)

Psalms 1–2

[10]Now therefore, O kings, be wise;
be warned, O rulers of the earth.
[11]Serve the LORD with fear,
with trembling [12] kiss his feet,
or he will be angry, and you will perish in
the way;
for his wrath is quickly kindled.

Happy are all who take refuge in him.

---

they stress that it happened according to what is written in "the law and the prophets" (e.g., Matt. 5:17; 7:12; 11:13). But in one place the reference is to "the law of Moses, the prophets, and the psalms" (Luke 24:44). Maybe the third part of the Hebrew Bible was a kind of terra incognita to the writers of the New Testament. The reason might be that there was at the time of writing no official canon of Jewish Scripture. The New Testament writers knew the collection of psalms and also knew the correct numbering, at least when Psalm 2 is quoted as Psalm 2 in the Acts of the Apostles (Acts 13:33). Because of this, but certainly also for more substantial reasons, we know that a collection of psalms definitely existed at least in the first century BCE recognizable to people of the time.[10]

The collection of psalms consists of 150 poems of different sorts. They are subdivided into five minor collections: Psalms 1–41, Psalms 42–73, Psalms 73–89, Psalms 90–106, and Psalms 107–50. Most of the poems have the heading in Hebrew *lĕdavid,* "for David" (this is found also in the Greek translation: *to David*), but it is in most translations rendered as "of David," following the tradition which sees David as the author of most of the psalms. Some of the headings refer to events in David's life, such as Psalm 54 with the heading "To the leader: with stringed instruments. A Maskil of David, when the Ziphites went and told Saul, 'David is in hiding among us'"—a reference to the story told in 1 Samuel 23:19 and 26:1.

The Psalms are quite varied and may be subdivided into genres, such as king psalms, psalms of lamentation, hymns, and more. However, the collection has as its frame Psalms 1 and 2 on one side and Psalms 149 and 150 on the other. The frame not only indicates who created the collection but also says how they wanted their collection to be read. In Psalm 1, the collectors present themselves as law-

---

10. Most notably the existence of manuscripts of the collection of Psalms among the Dead Sea Scrolls, especially the Psalm manuscript from Qumran cave 11. Altogether about forty Psalm manuscripts or fragments of manuscripts have been found, representing the text of 126 of the collection's 150 psalms.

obeying Jews, studying the Torah day and night, and the Psalms are supposed to be read as messianic hymns, as indicated by the introduction of the king as *messiah* (Heb. *mašiaḥ*, "the anointed one") at the beginning of Psalm 2 (Ps. 2:2). This king and messiah is undoubtedly David. It is therefore the intention of the collectors to present their collection as a messianic collection, and they ask their readers to study it as such, disregarding at the same time any other meaning a psalm may have had before it was incorporated into the collection of Psalms. In this way, the Psalms may be read as messianic poems announcing the coming of the messiah and the creation of the new Israel. In this way, the interest behind the collection of Psalms seems similar to the one behind the creation of the prophetic corpus.

Job follows Psalms in the Hebrew Bible. The story is set in a remote past in a place far away. The frame of the book consists of chapters 1 and 42. The first chapter is a prologue that takes place "in heaven," as God allows Satan,[11] "the enemy," to destroy righteous Job in order to test his belief in God. The book has a "happy ending" (Job 42) when Job receives back seven times all things lost. In between, readers are told how everything is taken away from Job. He will not accept that his misfortune is caused by any personal fault or sin, but his three friends try to convince him of his guilt in a series of long speeches. Job declines, however, to repent (Job 4–26). After the friends have run out of arguments, a fourth person, Elihu, delivers a long speech in which he attacks Job for being self-righteous (Job 32–37). Following this series of accusations and admonitions, Job is allowed in God's presence to present his case, but receives an answer from God "out of the whirlwind," telling him that he doesn't understand anything, as he had no part in the creation of the world (Job 38–41). Job's story ends with his confession that he really doesn't understand anything. Job is normally considered the first example of a discussion that has been going on for now more than 2,000 years, about the righteousness of God. There is no satisfying answer to be found in the book of Job, and it is most likely impossible to present such an answer. It might therefore be reasonable to say that Job does not concern the righteousness of God as much as humankind's inability to understand the ways of God.

Proverbs follows Job, often categorized as *Wisdom literature*, in the Hebrew Bible and belongs to the same category. According to its heading, the book of Proverbs—in the scholarly tradition often simply rendered as *proverbia*—is written by the wise King Solomon, who had a reputation as a composer of proverbs (1 Kgs. 5:12). Proverbs is made up of a series of minor collections. In some sections we find short proverbs; in others, sermons in which the wise author addresses his "son." These sermons are mostly found at the beginning of the book (Prov. 1–9). In other sections, the short sentence dominates, especially in Proverbs 10–22. The philosophy expressed here is quite simplistic: the hard-working will succeed, and misery will follow the lazy. The collection in Proverbs

---

11. In the Hebrew text we have *hassatan*, literally "the satan." The book of Job belongs to a time when the personalized Satan did not yet exist. In Hebrew *satan* means "the enemy."

22:17–24:22 is special. It is obviously an edited translation from an Egyptian wisdom book, the Wisdom of Amenope.[12] It shows that biblical wisdom is rooted in a general Near Eastern wisdom tradition.

The **Megillot**, in the TaNaK, follow Proverbs. Megillot, meaning "scrolls," are in Jewish tradition the texts attached to five Jewish festivals: The *Song of Songs* belongs to Passover, *Ruth* to Pentecost, *Lamentations* to the lamentations because of the destruction of the temple, *Ecclesiastes* to the feast of Tabernacles, and *Esther* to the Purim festival. The two most important Hebrew Bible manuscripts from the Middle Ages, Leningradensis from the eleventh century CE and the Aleppo manuscript from the tenth century CE, have a slightly different arrangement: Ruth, Song of Songs, Ecclesiastes, Lamentations, and Esther.

Ruth is a short novella or even pastoral narrative about a Moabite woman, Ruth, who marries into an Israelite family. When her husband dies childless, she by cunning forces a relative to marry her. Although her acts do not accord with the expectations of an Israelite girl, she saves the future of her family and becomes the great-grandmother of David. At the end of the book, a minor genealogy is included, relating Ruth via Perez to Tamar, who in a similarly cunning way and by transgressing normal societal rules became pregnant with her father-in-law and became the great-great-grandmother of David (Ruth 4:18–22).

The *Song of Songs* is a minor collection of love poems composed by Solomon, according to tradition. Through history the relationship between the woman and her lover has been understood in different ways, for example, as symbolizing the connections between Yahweh and Israel or between Christ and the church.

Ecclesiastes is also traditionally seen as the product of Solomon, in this case as disillusioned old king whose meaningless life passes in review before his eyes.

Lamentations is said to have been composed by Jeremiah. It is made up of five poems about the sad fate of Jerusalem.

Esther is a story about Esther, the Jewish wife of Ahasuerus, the king of Persia, who saves her people from the machinations of evil Haman and institutes the Purim festival commemorating the salvation of the Jews.

Daniel, like Esther, has as its subject the life of the pious Jew in a foreign land.[13] The first part of the book (Dan. 1–6) consists of a series of anecdotes about the pious Daniel as he explains the meaning of his dreams to King Nebuchadnezzar of Babylon, among these the vision of the statue with clay feet (Dan. 2). We also find the story of Daniel's three friends who are placed in a burning oven but survive the ordeal unharmed (Dan. 3), and the incident of the inscription on the wall—MENE, MENE, TEKEL, and PARSIN—that Daniel is the only one who can understand (Dan. 5). The second part of Daniel (Dan. 7–12) includes

---

12. Translations can be found in James B. Pritchard, ed., *Ancient Near Eastern Texts relating to the Old Testament* (Princeton: Princeton University Press, 1955), 421–25, and in William W. Hallo, ed., *COS I* (Leiden: Brill, 1997), 115–22.

13. There is in recent time an ongoing discussion about the place of Daniel among the Writings. It has been proposed that the book is originally a prophetic book and has its rightful place among the prophets, even in the old Jewish tradition.

visions of Daniel, some of them about mighty and haughty monsters symbolizing the empires of this world. The visions also tell about the elevation of Israel after the downfall of the empires. The language is special, for Daniel at its central part (Dan. 2:4–7:28) is not in Hebrew, but in Aramaic.

Ezra. Irrespective of scholarly discussion about the book of Daniel, which generally places the composition of the book in the second century BCE, according to its own testimony, it tells about things that happened in the reigns of Nebuchadnezzar and Belshazzar, both kings of Babylon, and King Darius of Media. It is, accordingly, natural for the Jewish tradition to place the book of Ezra immediately after Daniel, and the activities of Ezra the scribe belong to the reign of King Artaxerxes of Persia (Ezra 7:1). The first six chapters of Ezra have, however, nothing to do with Ezra's mission. The subject here is the return of the Jews from Babylon and the beginning of the rebuilding of the temple in the days of King Cyrus and King Darius of Persia. The final part of the book (Ezra 7–10) tells about the mission of Ezra, who is instructed by the king of Persia to travel to Jerusalem to clear up problems recorded from there. Ezra travels to Jerusalem and introduces a series of new rules, among these the demand that Jewish men divorce their foreign wives (Ezra 10), creating in this way an antecedent for the unhappy praxis of ethnic cleansing.

The book of **Nehemiah** continues the narrative from the book of Ezra and tells the story of Nehemiah, a high-ranking Persian official of Jewish descent. Nehemiah is sent to Jerusalem, where he inspects the conditions of the destroyed city wall (Neh. 2:11–15). In spite of local resistance, he manages to get the wall reconstructed and conditions in and outside of the city returned to more normal forms (Neh. 2–6). Now the focus of the book changes, and Ezra is again the main character (Neh. 7–13). There is some overlap between Ezra and Nehemiah (Neh. 7; cf. Ezra 2). The final part of Nehemiah consists of census lists covering the inhabitants of Jerusalem and the priests (Neh. 11–12). A central place is accorded in the story to the person of Ezra, who in the presence of the people recites the Law of Moses (Neh. 8) and binds the inhabitants of Jerusalem to obeying it (Neh. 10).

First and Second Chronicles form the last part of the Writings and are therefore the final books of the Hebrew Bible. They are in many respects very similar to the books of Samuel and Kings, and many narratives in Chronicles are almost verbatim the same stories as told by the authors of Samuel and Kings. Thus 2 Samuel and the two books of Kings may for good reason be considered a source for the books of Chronicles. The authors of Chronicles include extensive passages from Samuel and Kings, but they generally present a different interpretation and include a comprehensive amount of narrative material not found in Samuel and Kings. Sometimes they directly oppose the version of Israel's history found in Samuel and Kings. Thus David is far more involved in the building of the temple in the books of Chronicles. Solomon's only feat is to construct the temple exactly as he was instructed by his father (1 Chr. 22; 28–29). Toward the end of the history of Judah, Hezekiah and not Josiah is in their version the great reformer of the cult in the temple of Jerusalem (2 Chr. 29–31).

Here ends the review of the canonical parts of the Old Testament, at least as far as it concords with the selection of holy literature in the Hebrew Bible. We shall later return to the question of the canonization of this literature. It was on this textual basis that the procedures of the historical-critical study of the Old Testament were formed. At a time when scholars knew of very few ancient records, their investigations were more or less limited to the study of the Bible.

PART I
FROM THEOLOGY
TO HISTORY

Chapter 1

The Historical-Critical Paradigm in Its Historical Context

There has been a lot of talk recently about a paradigm shift in the study of the Old Testament.[1] "Paradigm shift" is a very loaded expression and presupposes quite a lot. We should therefore question the idea of such a shift. It may, in fact, only be a correction within the same paradigm. It must be said, however, that in the last generation the field of Old Testament studies has experienced many important changes, and some of them will be important also in the years to come.

Such changes do not occur without a general mental shift that may have little to do with Old Testament studies in particular. They may be caused by a general redirection of the way humans think that affects all aspects of human life. This chapter will attempt to place the historical-critical paradigm that dominated biblical studies for most of the twentieth century in its philosophical context. This context may explain why it appeared and how it was embedded in the European

1. Discussions about shifts of paradigm have been popular among scholars for the last forty years, ever since Thomas Kuhn published his famous *The Structure of Scientific Revolution* (Chicago: University of Chicago Press, 1962). This book may probably best be characterized as a sociology of science, as the subject of the book is the way such shifts of paradigm occur, and not what really happened. Kuhn's book is is still completely comprehensible, although not always edifying in the way it describes nonscholarly—often very personal—reasons for changes in the scholarly world.

scholarly tradition that was formed during the Enlightenment and dominated the nineteenth and twentieth centuries. This context may also be described as the era of the *modern* world. We will return at a later point to the ideological situation found in scholarship at the end of the twentieth century and the beginning of the twenty-first century, a development that will certainly have the most important consequences for the study of the Old Testament.

A NEW CONTEXT FOR SCHOLARSHIP

Historical-critical scholarship is a child of the Enlightenment and the positivism of nineteenth-century scholarship. Positivism originated in natural science following Isaac Newton. Newton's great discovery was his demonstration of natural laws, unchangeable rules for the organization of the world. It is impossible to exaggerate the importance of the discovery of such rules or laws, because they prove that the world is predictable from a mechanical point of view. The apple that falls from a tree will always hit the ground. No magical or mythical explanations are needed; the world follows its own rules.

Traditional scholarship possessed its own rules, first and foremost the logical teaching of Aristotle and rules for the development of a scholarly argument. Many philosophers had contributed to the development of these rules, but a major breakthrough occurred in the period of the Enlightenment when Immanuel Kant introduced his theory of categories, thereby creating a framework for human knowledge, placing it in a universe consisting of time and space. The attribution of cause in ancient times, but particularly in the Middle Ages, to an external, divine agent or divinely inspired factor—we might call it a "third" space, a mythical space—became unnecessary. Humanity is placed in a mechanical universe and functions within this universe following its laws.

This reorientation of science meant that humanistic scholarship—and theology belongs here as far as methodology and general scholarly outlook are concerned—never again was able to decide the scholarly agenda. This had since the Middle Ages been the prerogative especially of theology. However, the modern breakthrough changed the power structure within scholarship. Humanistic scholarship lived on, but only on conditions decided upon by natural science.

The scientist proceeded with his or her research with the conviction that if a stringent method was followed and all natural laws observed, the reward would consist of new discoveries, that is, the demonstration of new natural laws. The validity of such laws was indisputable, and they were also a benefit for humanity in general.

There are many examples of the importance of this reorientation within natural science. Consider the discovery of steam power and of electricity. It caused no problems to make practical use of these and other discoveries, as long as the aim was to improve the living conditions of humankind. However, the assurance of the value of natural science for humankind in general was, and is, problematic, because this claim involved ethics, formerly the exclusive responsibility of humanistic, not to say theological, scholarship. Again, this may be taken as a proof that humanistic scholarship and theology would nevermore dominate the world. They would never again be of primary value to humankind. They were reduced in importance to a kind of pastime for scholars who wanted to relax from more important tasks, that is, natural science and its benefits.[2]

In order not just to give up when confronted by emerging natural science, the humanities had to produce results of the same kind found in natural science. Accordingly, humanistic scholars began to develop methodologies aimed at producing *positive*, meaning *correct*, results. Like scientists seeking to discover natural laws, humanistic scholars saw as their goal, by applying such methods, to produce results *acceptable as the consequence of objective scholarship*.

It was the prerogative of natural science to consider itself objective and positivistic. The basis for this claim is of course the character of the procedures it follows: any test within natural science may be repeated indefinitely, and it will always produce the same result, if the test has been correctly executed. It was accordingly the goal of humanistic studies, borrowing its ideology from natural science, to be able to produce similar positive or objective results. If there was no reason to doubt it, the conclusion must be correct. The criteria for good scholarship were bound to the result. If no one questioned it, it was deemed valuable in an absolute sense.

Most scholars working within the field of the humanities soon saw that it was endowed with many obstacles in achieving objective results of the kind their colleagues in natural science took for granted. Although the problem was correctly diagnosed, it took more than a hundred years to present the consequences of this situation. The scientist studied his or her subject meticulously and in isolation and disregarded information that would have disturbed the outcome of the investigation. He or she assumed it possible to discover laws that are independent of the eyes of the scholar who demonstrated their presence. In this way there is a direct connection between the governing natural law and the object scrutinized by the scientist.

Within humanities the situation was felt to be totally different. Here the investigations of scholars continued to produce results that were no more secure and indisputable than was the case before the revolution within natural science. This problem must solved by introducing new methods. Most scholars of that time agreed on one thing, that the connection between a subject and the circumstances that produced the subject was a primary one. It was accepted that it was far more difficult to trace these circumstances than was the case within natural science. It was no longer possible, as was the case in the Middle Ages, to appeal to God as

2. One problematic consequence of this development is the victory of the use of the results of natural science for practical purposes over science as such. Science must pay for itself, and only science is able to do that—it will never happen with humanistic scholarship. For that reason alone, humanistic scholarship is unable to attract more than a fraction of the funding available for natural science, including medicine.

a kind of Aristotelian *prima causa*. The scholar was forced to find the *natural cause*, an explanation kept within the Kantian categories of time and space. It was assumed that any phenomenon has a natural cause, meaning that it should be traceable for human investigators. When disagreement arose, it was not because of a basically wrong approach to humanistic scholarship; it was simply because of a faulty methodology.

Under the influence of natural science, humanistic scholarship aimed at the formulation of definitions and the development of methods allowing the scholar to obtain the correct sort of knowledge. It was almost never acknowledged that the difficulties of humanistic scholarship that prevented it from achieving results that would be uniformly accepted had their root in the inability of the scholars to understand the correct nature of humanistic scholarship. The connection between a scholar and his or her subject continued to be considered of secondary importance in comparison to the primary connection between the subject and its basis in the real world.

When a new branch of humanistic studies, history, began to develop during the Enlightenment and especially in the early Romantic period, the lack of understanding of the special conditions for humanistic research became decisive. In antiquity, history was considered a part of rhetoric, which in Hellenistic-Roman academic circles covered all subjects considered relevant for the education of the sons (and generally only the sons) of the elite: philosophy, philology, and history. History was the *magistra vitae*, the teacher of life, but had far less in common with modern history than is generally assumed. History in ancient times was didactic and moralistic and was taught to educate future generations rather than to reconstruct the past. The past was important only insofar as it had something to say that was deemed useful for the upbringing of the young generation.

History writing in the Middle Ages mostly continued in the path of ancient historiographers. The Middle Ages was interested in the past as a help to understand the present. Like historiography in antiquity, it possessed little of the critical awareness of modern history writing, and we may doubt if the historiographers were really interested in the past as it was. Historiography was also annalistic. Thus, when sources were available—and we here speak about contemporary sources—the historiographers were incapable of distinguishing between important and unimportant information. The selection of information to be preserved in their histories was casual and not governed by what in modern terms would be considered a historical-critical orientation.

As already mentioned, modern critical history writing began to appear during the Enlightenment, and the first scientific definitions of history as an academic discipline were published. From the beginning, modern historical studies kept and developed its didactic purpose providing identity and coherence in the new national states that came into being after the French revolution of 1789. Formerly, the inhabitants of most states were the subjects of their king, a kind of client to their patron. However, after the decapitation of the symbol of the state, the king, a new symbol was needed to create a new national unity among the inhabitants of the formerly royal state. Now the great "national" heroes and heroines of the past were called upon to act as guides to national unity in the new nation-states.[3]

The new historiographers were of the opinion that their studies were in the interest of historical truth, although in the course of the nineteenth century this "truth" changed, from being a truth embedded in the narrative about the past to becoming a truth firmly connected to what really happened in the past. The change implied that the historical *narrative*, which formerly constituted the center of interest of the historians, was now relegated to a second place, replaced by the *events* of the past. Modern historians considered the historical narrative to be of little value except as a *source* of the past. Historians were therefore always looking for better methods to penetrate their sources in order to get back to the real events of the past, events which they considered reflected by their sources.

The early nineteenth century saw a series of improvements in the historian's craft, not least the development of modern source criticism, whose "father" was the German historian Johann Gustav Droysen (1808–84). The aim of source criticism is to enable the historian to distinguish between primary and secondary sources, and in a given source to sift essential information from indifferent "noise." In this way, a historian analyzing a source from ancient times should be able to deduct from his or her source all information deemed unimportant. What is left is a kind of relic (*Überreste*). Here the historian will find the kind of information that enables him or her to reconstruct the past.

Droysen's source criticism was soon acknowledged as the single most important part of the historian's craft in most of the world, although it did not happen without criticism. As an example of Droysen's critics, we may mention the Danish historian Kristian Erslev (1852–1930), who argued against Droysen that any narrative going back to antiquity is at the same time a relic. The important point is therefore not to sort out parts of a certain ancient text that are primary, but to recognize that every part of the text is a relic. The question is now, a relic of what? This criticism has never played any important role, for example, in the study of the history of ancient Israel—after all, this study was until recent times dominated by German scholars following the lead of the great German historians of the past. It is, however, important because it says that every part of an ancient text is important and a source of information. We have only to ask about the type of information we find in an ancient source. Does the source present information of the past or information of the present, seen from the perspective of the historiographer who wrote the text?[4]

Historical research became a most important aspect of humanistic studies in the modern world because it pretended to be able to deliver objective results. This had been expressed programmatically by Droysen's contemporary Leopold von

---

3. It is ironic that in the state where it all began, France, the hero who united the country into a nation-state did not belong to the past but to the present, i.e., Napoleon, whose *gloire*—especially after his death—developed into an overpowering national symbol.

4. More on this in chapter 8 (pp. 151–52).

Ranke (1795–1886), who deemed it the historian's duty to reconstruct what really happened (*wie es eigentlich gewesen*).[5] The historian was obliged to present the past exactly as it really was, and the quality of the historian was determined by whether he or she was able to deliver what was expected. History became a *positivistic* enterprise, and its results were always respected as valid and timeless.

A second factor that endowed historical studies with respect was the link between history and the modern nation-state. The interest in the national past came into focus as never before, and it was the duty of historians to produce material that might kindle this interest. The production of many national histories was the ultimate aim of the historians.[6] One of the more dire consequences of this new trend was the concept of the spirit of the nation (*das Völkergeist*), which dominated much nineteenth-century history writing after the days of von Ranke, who coined the expression. According to this concept, any nation is mentally different from its neighbors. The concept led to xenophobia and political persecution, and it contaminated historical research understood as an objective enterprise, because it introduced criteria in no respect "objective."

THE ORIGINS AND DEVELOPMENT OF HISTORICAL-CRITICAL SCHOLARSHIP

Exegetical scholarship, the study of the Old and New Testaments, has through its long history experienced a series of paradigm shifts. In the ancient church two such "paradigms" competed for predominance: the school of Alexandria, dominated by allegorical interpretation, and the Antiochene school, whose reading of the Bible was "plain." The methods of the first school were victorious and dominated exegesis through the Middle Ages. The Reformers, especially Luther and his successors, argued in favor of a plain reading to replace the allegorical interpretation dominant in the Catholic Church. In this way Luther, himself a professor of biblical studies in the University of Wittenberg, referred to an old tradition of exegesis and did not invent a new way of reading and understanding the Bible. We should, however, not be mistaken; Luther's reading was not "modern" in the sense that it was historical-critical. Rather, it was rooted in theology,

---

5. Droysen never shared the opinion of Ludwig von Ranke (1795–1886) that it was possible to reconstruct the past as it really was. The following quote from Droysen shows him as amazingly modern in his idea of history: "The subject of historical study is not the past, because the past is the past. The subject is what has not yet happened, whether or not we are talking about the memory of what happened, or relics going back to what was and what happened" (*Grundriß der Historik*, ed. Peter Leyh [Stuttgart-Bad Cannstatt: Frommann Holzboog, 1977], 422). [Das Gegebene für die historische Forschung sind nicht die Vergangenheiten, denn diese sind vergangen, sondern das von ihnen in dem Jetzt und Hier noch Unvergangene, mögen es Erinnerungen von dem, was war und geschah, oder Überreste des Gewesenen und Geschehenen sein.]

6. This interest also boosted the interest in archaeology, transforming it from the pastime of a few intellectuals to a national obsession.

and the fundamental principle behind his interpretation of the Old Testament was christological.

When the Reformers insisted on the principle of *sola scriptura,* arguing that the Bible is the only authority whose meaning is not decided by the tradition of the church, this invariably led to the liberation of the interpretation of the Old Testament from the control of the church and the rejection of the christological interpretation advocated by Luther and used by Lutheran orthodoxy to strangle all endeavors for a critical study of the Bible. Although censured by church officials, biblical scholarship could not escape being influenced by the general intellectual development in western Europe. Sooner or later, plain-reading students of the Bible would start asking critical questions. The sharpening of the historical awareness during the Enlightenment, which made ancient documents sources for studying the past, also decided that the texts of the Old Testament must be such sources about the past. It had nothing to do with contemporary circumstances.

After 1750 the rules of critical biblical scholarship were formed. Critical scholars first addressed the question of the Pentateuch, where it was easy to demonstrate—for example, a series of problems in the story of the flood—that the Pentateuch did not constitute a single composition by one hand but instead was a collection of literature with a long prehistory, although it could no longer be considered the work of Moses. The critical study of the Pentateuch culminated toward the end of the nineteenth century, when the so-called Graff-Kuenen-Wellhausen documentary hypothesis appeared, dividing the Pentateuch into four originally independent sources.[7]

Old Testament scholars, who grew up within the German tradition of scholarship, were soon to study possible source divisions within the biblical texts. Already in the sevententh and eighteenth centuries—long before the introduction of the modern concept of history—scholars like the philosopher Baruch Spinoza and the French physician Jean Astruc formulated critical questions, for example, about who wrote the books of Moses. When Deuteronomy concludes with the story about Moses's death, it might be reasonable to assume that Moses at least did not write that chapter (Deuteronomy 34). In the period of the Enlightenment and in the early Romantic period, this emerging critical scholarship developed further into a truly critical form of scholarship, which even today surprises because of its radicalism, especially when seen in the light of the development of biblical studies in the second half of the nineteenth century. The critical study of the sources of the Pentateuch (often labeled "higher criticism") developed into a highly technical enterprise making it possible—this was at least the opinion of its proponents—to study any text in the Old Testament in order to divide it into original and secondary elements.

In the eyes of critical scholars, source criticism and its ever-more-refined analysis of biblical texts enabled the scholar to reconstruct not only the history of the

7. See also pp. 45–47.

An example of changes in the understanding of a text from the Old Testament from the Reformation to the end of the Enlightenment

> Again he uttered his oracle, saying:
> "Alas, who shall live when God does this?
> ²⁴But ships shall come from Kittim
> and shall afflict Asshur and Eber;
> and he also shall perish forever."
> (Num. 24:23–24)
>
> Luther understood the passage as referring to the Romans: Thus a marginal note in his translation of the Bible (*Die Gantze Heilige Schrifft Deudsch*, Wittenberg 1545):
>
> "[Chittim] are from Europe / the great Alexander and the Romans / who also perished. And shows the truth of the prophecy / that every kingdom on earth will perish, one after the other / except the people of Israel / which will exist for ever and ever / because of Christ."⁸
>
> Luther considered the passage a prophecy about the future and understood Israel to be the Christian church.
>
> Two hundred fifty years after Luther, the German biblical scholar Karl David Ilgen (1763–1834) presented this interpretation of Numbers 24:23–24:
>
> "It is reasonable to assume that the Pentateuch as we know it hardly predates the time of the Maccabees, because we find traces dating from such a late period in it. The most conspicuous places are Deut 28:68, which informs about a resettlement in Egypt, and Num 24:24, where we find a reference to the Macedonians, who are going to destroy Assyria. It will, however also perish."⁹
>
> According to Ilgen, Numbers 24:23–24 talks about Alexander's conquest of the east. Unlike Luther, he did not consider it a prophecy but as a *vaticinium ex eventu* (a prophecy that comes after the event), which places Numbers 24:23–24 in the period after Alexander.

biblical text, but also the history of ancient Israel and ancient Israelite society and religion. By the middle of the twentieth century, this scholarship had increasingly led to the assumption that it had solved all problems. All that remained was to scrutinize the last few details.

Old Testament scholarship also applied this methodology to the issue of ancient Israelite religion. Scholars reconstructed the religion of ancient Israel by

---

8. "[Chittim] Sind die aus Europa / Als der grosse Alexander und Römer / welche auch zu letzt untergehen. Vnd zeigt hie die Weissagung / das alle Königsreich auff Erden eins nach dem andern vntergehen müssen / neben dem volck Jsrael / welchs ewig bleibet / vmb Christus willen."

9. "Man könnte mit einiger Wahrscheinlichkeit annehmen, daß der Pentateuch seine gegenwärtige Gestalt nicht vor der Zeit der Makkabäer erhalten habe, denn es sind Spuren eines solch späten Zeitalters darinnen. Die auffallendsten Stellen sind Deut. 28,68, wo von der Verpflanzung nach Egypten geredet wird; und Numer. 24,24, wo von den Macedoniern geredet wird, daß sie das

applying source criticism, making it possible to distinguish between the original religion and later additions to it. It became especially important to be able to differentiate between ancient Israelite religion and its later Jewish transformation.[10]

The contemporary broadening of the horizon of the European intellectuals to include the cultures of the ancient Near East was a contributing factor behind the success of critical Old Testament scholarship. The exploration of the Middle East and its ancient environment began in earnest during the Enlightenment, when a series of European travelers visited and described the area. Among the best planned and most important expeditions, we may count the Danish Arabia expedition (1761–67), although only one of its members, the surveyor Carsten Niebuhr (1733–1815), lived to see Europe again.[11]

Interest in Egypt—never absent in European tradition[12]—was enormously boosted by the scientific results from Napoleon's expedition there between 1798 and 1801, which provided the material for the subsequent decipherment of the Egyptian hieroglyphs.[13]

When Mesopotamian cuneiform writing was deciphered, the scholarly world had access to only a rather limited selection of handwritten copies of inscriptions meticulously produced by Carsten Niebuhr. Because of his exactness, these copies enabled German and British scholars to break the code and make the documents available to the scholarly world of Europe.[14] The French scholar Jean-François Champollion (1790–1832) managed at the same time to decipher the hieroglyphs of Egypt—*hieroglyph* being a Greek word meaning "holy letters"—known since antiquity and incised on the walls of the many spectacular monuments from ancient Egypt still in existence. An almost miraculous object discovered by French scholars during the French expedition to Egypt was the Rosetta stone, a trilingual inscription with the same text in a Greek and two Egyptian versions.[15]

Assyrische Reich zerstören würden, sie aber würden auch selbst umkommen." Ilgen's text is found in Bodo Seidel, *Karl David Ilgen und die Pentateuchforschung im Umkreis der sogenannten Älteren Urkundenhypothese: Studien zu Geschichte der exegetischen Hermeneutik in der späten Aufklärung*, BZAW 213 (Berlin: Walter de Gruyter, 1993), 173.

10. We will return to this subject below and especially to the part played by the German scholar Julius Wellhausen. See pp. 268–87.

11. Niebuhr soon published his preliminary report, *Beschreibung von Arabien* (Copenhagen, 1792). The first two volumes of his major report *Reisebeschreibung nach Arabien und andern umliegenden Ländern*, 1–2, appeared in Copenhagen, 1774–78. ET: *Travels through Arabia and Other Countries in the East* (Edinburgh: Printed for R. Morison, 1792), but the final part was published in Hamburg only after his death in 1837.

12. Probably still the best book on the subject: Erik Iversen, *The Myth of Egypt and Its Hieroglyphs in European Tradition* (Copenhagen: G. E. C. Gad, 1961).

13. Published in twenty volumes as *Description de l'Égypte ou Recueil des observations et recherches qui ont été faites en Égypte pendant l'expédition française* (Paris, 1809 and 1828). French-speaking readers may access the whole collection at http://gallica.bnf.fr/Catalogue/noticesInd/FRBNF33341149.htm.

14. On the history of the discovery of ancient Mesopotamia, see Mogens Trolle Larsen, *The Conquest of Assyria: Excavations in an Antique Land* (London: Routledge, 1996).

15. On the subject of the decipherment of these writing systems, see Peter T. Daniels, "The Decipherment of Ancient Near Eastern Scripts," in Jack M. Sasson, ed., *Civilizations of the Ancient Near East*, vol. I (New York: Charles Scribner's Sons, 1995), 81–94.

The nineteenth century also saw the emergence of Near Eastern archaeology, concentrating on Mesopotamia and Egypt. Of special importance for Old Testament studies were the thousands of inscriptions from Mesopotamia and elsewhere uncovered by excavators and now at least partially readable and available to scholars. Toward the end of the nineteenth century, the reading and understanding of cuneiform and hieroglyphs and the languages in which they were written were now so secure that scholars saw a new (old) world opened for them. Before the decipherment of these ancient writing systems, the only sources available to students of the ancient Near East had mostly been Greek and Roman authors and their often rather fanciful descriptions of the civilizations of the ancient Near East. Now it was possible to read the literature produced by these cultures, thereby gaining direct access to the background of the Old Testament, or so it was believed.

By opening the gate to this new world, students of the Bible soon realized that the Old Testament had its roots in the ancient Near Eastern world. Several persons known from the Old Testament—among these a series of Assyrian and Babylonian kings—had commissioned inscriptions to be set up and produced documents that scholars were now able to decipher and read. The narrative about the history of Israel in the Old Testament was not just legend and fable but included much information that was confirmed by discoveries in the Middle East.

However, as is often the case when important new discoveries are made, scholars were prone to exaggerate the importance of their new knowledge. Around 1900, Old Testament scholarship was affected by the so-called Pan-Babylonism movement, which traced almost everything written in the Old Testament back to ancient Mesopotamia. This tendency resulted in the *Babel-Bibel-Streit* (Babel Bible Controversy), which ended in a compromise: It is undoubtedly possible to trace Mesopotamian influence in the narratives of the Old Testament. It is on the other hand just as clear that the stories of the Old Testament are about a society living in Palestine along the shores of the Mediterranean, not in Mesopotamia proper.[16] Thus, instead of looking for the origins of religious ideas and sentiments expressed by Old Testament authors in Mesopotamia, it seemed preferable to assume that the Old Testament was influenced by the society in which it came into being, that is, ancient Israel, which stands at the center of the narratives of the Old Testament.

Around 1900, scholarly interest in Palestine and its neighboring countries, Syria, Lebanon, and Jordan, was rather limited, mostly because there was so little in the way of spectacular discoveries, such as important inscriptions and magnificent monuments, comparable to the discoveries in Egypt and Mesopotamia. The nineteenth century had already seen archaeological excavations in Palestine on a limited scale, mostly in and around Jerusalem. However, only around 1900 did more extensive excavations also begin to be conducted in Palestine. There fol-

---

16. On the Babel Bible Controversy, see Mogens Trolle Larsen, "The 'Babel/Bible' Controversy and Its Aftermath," in Sasson, ed., *Civilizations of the Ancient Near East*, 1:95–106.

lowed soon important discoveries that might be combined with information in the Old Testament—not least at Jericho in the Jordan Valley and Megiddo in the northwestern part of the country. The archaeologists found few inscriptions, but these were written in a language very similar to the Hebrew of the Old Testament. In this way the basic assumption that the Old Testament was rooted in the soil of Palestine was confirmed.

Such discoveries had an immediate impact on biblical studies and changed the outlook of the scholars who intended to reconstruct the ancient history of Israel. It now seemed possible to place the historical information in the Old Testament in its real context within the history of Palestine in the so-called Old Testament Period, which means the time that the literature of the Old Testament has as its subject. Biblical historians generally accepted the story line of the Old Testament, although supplemented by information supplied by archaeological excavations in Palestine and its neighboring countries, as the basis of their historical reconstructions. Most scholars agreed that not all information in the Old Testament contributed to the historical reconstruction. Thus they did not accept stories about miracles caused by God changing the course of history. No scholarly analysis is likely to make any progress based on such "supernatural" events. It was accepted that stories about angels, miracles, and the like were parts of the worldview of ancient human beings also found in Greek and Roman literature. They are to be considered "paraphernalia" to the stories in which they appear and therefore expendable. It was the conviction of many Old Testament historians that they had only to remove such elements, and they would be in possession of documents directly of use for their reconstruction of the past.

The result has been that most textbooks in the history of Israel of the nineteenth and twentieth centuries use the Old Testament historical literature as a framework for their historical reconstructions. Their histories are different only in the way they handle the biblical stories. Some scholars are more faithful to the testimony of the biblical narratives; other scholars are more critically minded and more ready to remove what they consider to be secondary elements in the narratives. Basically they agree on most.[17]

The study of the religion of ancient Israel was generally conducted in parallel with the study of its history. Before World War I, scholars were in possession of very few sources from the Levant in the form of inscriptions that might provide information, not only about myth and legend, but also about ritual life among ordinary people. Classical authors provided quite a number of materials relevant, or so it seemed, to the religion of Phoenicia, that is, Lebanon, and Syria. Such information was, at the beginning of the twentieth century, still used as the primary

---

17. The best way to illustrate this basic uniformity of the histories of ancient Israel may be by confronting the respected histories of Israel from the middle of the twentieth century. Martin Noth, *Geschichte Israels* (Göttingen: Vandenhoeck & Ruprecht, 1950), ET, *The History of Israel* (New York: Harper, 1960), and John Bright, *A History of Israel* (Philadelphia: Westminster, 1959), are considered two poles with the historical reconstructions of ancient Israel, but in light of later developments amazingly similar in outlook.

source for the reconstruction of the religion of the Phoenicians and their neighbors, although some scholars began to question the value of classical authors' testimonies, as more and more documentation from the ancient Near East became known, at first embedded in Mesopotamian documents, but also in the years separating the two world wars, from Syria.

Mesopotamian sources dominated the study of the religion at the beginning of the twentieth century, but were in the eyes of the students of the history of religion replaced by documents from ancient Ugarit. In 1929 a series of excavations started on an ancient mount in northwestern Syria, Tell Ras Shamra, close to the modern Syrian city of Latakia. These excavations, which are still going on, have unearthed an amazing variety of documents, mostly in Akkadian and in Ugaritic, the ancient language of the people inhabiting the place. The scholarly world was at first confused by the writing of these documents, in a kind of cuneiform not previously known. However, a breakthrough in the decipherment of the documents followed after a few years of investigation. Behind the cuneiform of the Ugaritic tablets, scholars discovered a language closely related to Hebrew, mostly going back to the Late Bronze Age (ca. 1550–1300 BCE), and especially the fourteenth century BCE (see table, The historical periods of Palestine, p. 394). In this way, the Ugaritic documents predate even the oldest parts of the Old Testament. Some of these newly excavated texts turned out to be religious epic literature, in many respects similar to the Homeric poems from ancient Greece. Now scholars were for the first time in possession of primary sources of the religious ideas of the Levantine coast, including, or so it was believed, not only the religion of Palestine but also the religion described by the Old Testament as an expression of pre-Israelite "Canaanite" religion.[18]

Over a period of almost two hundred years, the historical-critical form of biblical studies developed until around the middle of the twentieth century it had become the dominant paradigm for biblical studies. Scholars were still discussing and evaluating minor details, but in general they believed themselves to have solved all possible historical problems. Around 1970 a kind of standstill had taken root: there was no more to discuss. It turned out to be the silence before the storm.

In a Christian context, the Old Testament is part of the study of theology, the Old Testament being the first part of the Christian Bible. Within this context, the raison d'être of Old Testament studies is to find such a place for the Old Testament on the Christian firmament that it is not only used in defense of its traditional position but also may contribute to the development of modern

18. On the excavations of Ugarit, its history, and documents, see Marguerite Yon, *The City of Ugarit at Tell Ras Shamra* (Winona Lake, IN: Eisenbrauns, 2006). The standard edition of the cuneiform texts in Ugaritic is Manfried Dietrich, Oswald Loretz, and Joaquín Sanmartín, *The Cuneiform Alphabetic Texts from Ugarit, Ras Ibn Hani and Other Places* (*KTU*, 2nd, enlarged edition) (Münster: Ugarit-Verlag, 1995). There exists a great variety of translations into English: Among the more comprehensive and recent, we may mention N. Wyatt, *Religious Texts from Ugarit: The Words of Ilimilku and His Colleagues*, The Biblical Seminar 53 (Sheffield: Sheffield Academic Press, 1998). Ritual texts are available in an English translation in Dennis Pardee, *Ritual and Cult at Ugarit*, SBLWAW 10 (Atlanta: SBL, 2002).

theology. The ever-increasing concentration among Old Testament scholars on historical issues was likely to create problems for this traditional position of the Old Testament within Christian theology. If the Old Testament had as its main subject ancient Israel—a society that in New Testament times already belonged to the past—would it still at the beginning of the twenty-first century be a relevant part of theology? When asked such questions, many historical-critical scholars had no answer to present. They simply had little understanding of the use to which Old Testament studies were put within theology, and often replied to the question by referring to the Old Testament as a *prolegomenon* to the New Testament or simply placing the Old Testament as a subsidiary subject within biblical studies in general.[19]

The final outcome of historical-critical studies would transform the Old Testament into a collection of sources for religious studies in general relevant for the study of ancient Near Eastern religion. The Old Testament would end up as part of the study of the ancient Near East, and would have trouble defending its position as part of the Christian canon.

For decades, historical-critical study was absolutely dominant. However, recent developments have put pressure on the dominating role of the historical-critical approach to Old Testament studies. Modern scholars, not only from the evangelical part of the Christian community but also from more liberal sources, are increasingly questioning the basic assumptions behind the development of the historical-critical paradigm. In many ways this has already had consequences, not only for the way Old Testament texts are read in the present scholarly community, but also for the understanding of the Old Testament as a historical document.

The next two chapters will describe the essentials of the historical-critical paradigm and the image it painted of ancient Israel and its religion. Later follows an explanation of how all of this has changed. The conclusion of this book includes a discussion of the future of Old Testament studies within theology.

---

19. Further on the theological rejection of the Old Testament already before World War I, see pp. 285–86.

Chapter 2

Reading Texts in the Context of Historical-Critical Scholarship

THE PURPOSE OF OLD TESTAMENT STUDIES—
AS SEEN BY HISTORICAL-CRITICAL SCHOLARSHIP

In an introduction to the theological study for new students at the University of'
Copenhagen, Eduard Nielsen, professor of Old Testament from 1956 to 1991,
saw this as the primary the task of Old Testament studies:

> It is the first task of exegetical studies to define the meaning of an Old Tes-
> tament text for its "author" and for his original readership.[1]

This definition of Old Testament studies would still be seen as relevant more than
fifty years later. However, Nielsen in the following paragraph broadens his view
of the purpose of the exegesis of Old Testament literature:

---

1. Eduard Nielsen, "Det gamle Testamente," in Bent Noack, ed., *Teologien og dens fag* (Copenhagen, 1960), 13–42, 17. On Eduard Nielsen as a representative of the Scandinavian tradition of Old
Testament studies (the so-called Uppsala School), see Douglas A. Knight, *Rediscovering the Traditions
of Israel*, 3rd ed., Studies in Biblical Literature 16 (Atlanta: SBL, 2006), 264–75.

In the moment the exegete turns to the interpretation of the passage in Isa 7,10–17 about the young woman who will give birth to a son, whom she will call Immanuel, it is his first obligation with all possible means to explain the historical situation of this prophecy of Isaiah. When he has placed the text in its correct context, he will go on to explain, how Isaiah looked upon his prophecy, and how it was looked upon by King Ahaz, to whom this prophecy was directed in a very critical situation in 734 BCE.

According to Eduard Nielsen the historical-critical analysis paves the way for all other approaches to an Old Testament text, and for the use of a biblical text as part of the theological agenda and basically also in the church.

It is hardly wrong to claim that these quotations from a long-forgotten Danish introduction might just as well have been written by any other historical-critical exegete of that time. Most scholars would have seen it as an absolutely adequate description of their task. In order to get to this basic historical-critical understanding of the text, scholars have at their disposal a series of methods developed over many generations, such as literary criticism, form history (or form criticism), tradition history, and redaction history.

LITERARY CRITICISM

Biblical scholars in the eighteenth century had already demonstrated several inconsistencies in the Pentateuch. In the nineteenth century they sharpened their analysis of the literature of the Pentateuch and were able to point out many more cases of difference between its various parts. These meticulous studies led to *literary criticism*, and the formulation of the theory of four sources as the basis of the composition of the Pentateuch, also called the Graf-Kuenen-Wellhausen four-source hypothesis, named after three of its major proponents, Karl Heinrich Graf (1815–69), Abraham Kuenen (1828–91), and Julius Wellhausen (1844–1918).

According to the four-source hypothesis, the five books of Moses represent a collage of four written documents, normally called, respectively, the Yahwist (J), the Elohist (E), the Priestly document (P), and the Deuteronomist (D). These scholars believed that redactors, using a kind of cut-and-paste method, had in antiquity pieced these four documents together in a rather mechanical way.[2]

Some may entertain the notion that the hypothesis of the four documents blended together in this way resulted from madness. How could it be that such a haphazard procedure had been able to put together a piece of literature as rich in

2. The basis of this hypothesis, the assumption of redactors at work, has recently been severely criticized by John Van Seters, *The Edited Bible: The Curious History of the "Editor" in Biblical Criticism* (Winona Lake, IN: Eisenbrauns, 2006). According to Van Seters, the redactor made his introduction into Old Testament studies around 1800 under the influence of the study of Homer's poems. When classical philologists a few years later gave up the idea of finding originally independent sources in these poems, the basic elements of their theory survived for generations in biblical studies. The concept of the redactor is, however, an anachronism; such redactors did not exist in antiquity.

content as the Pentateuch? But the hypothesis is dependent on a series of observations that, when combined, show that it definitely is not without any foundation. Some observations have to do with minor differences and "breaks" in the narratives of the Pentateuch; other observations note redundancy in these texts, the classical example being the duplication of the story of creation in Genesis 1–2.

To illustrate the kind of divergences pointed out by critical scholarship, we may mention as an example the minor issue of the different identities of Moses's father-in-law. In the story of Moses's marriage to Zipporah (Exod. 2:16–22), Moses's father-in-law is named Reuel and is the priest of Midian. In the narrative about the visit of this man to Moses's camp in the desert (Exod. 18), he is called Jethro.[3] Such minor divergences may be more serious and have more enduring consequences. Literary criticism therefore created a fine system for the distribution of such divergences between the different documents.

The basic and most discussed divergence concerns the name of God in the Pentateuch. Sometimes God is referred to by his name, *Yahweh*,[4] sometimes by his title, *Elohim*, and in a few cases by Yahweh Elohim. In the story of the creation of the world in Genesis 1, Elohim is the active God. *Elohim* is Hebrew and simply means "God." In the narrative about the creation of the world and humankind in Genesis 2 and in the story of the first sin (Genesis 3), the creator is named Yahweh Elohim. In Genesis 4, the story of Cain and Abel, Yahweh interrogates Cain, but in Genesis 9 it is God who concludes his covenant with Noah and humankind—and so it continues. The different ways of referring to God made it possible to name two of the documents, respectively the Yahwist, which uses Yahweh as the name of God, and the Elohist, where God appears as Elohim.[5]

The third document, the Priestly source, also uses Elohim as its preferred way of referring to God. Scholars of the nineteenth century therefore divided the Elohim-parts of the two Pentateuchal sources into two originally independent documents, giving one of these documents the name the Priestly document, because of its predilection for calendars, a systematic approach, genealogies, and religious legislation.

The Deuteronomistic document appears primarily in the book of Deuteronomy, deriving its name from that book. Because of its language, style, and theological outlook, it was obviously an originally independent source. Literary critics discussed for many years whether or not the Deuteronomist also appears in other parts of the Pentateuch. They never agreed, although it is not uncommon to see references to a Deuteronomistic stratum, for example, in the stories of the covenant between God and Abram in Genesis 15 and in the call of Moses in Exodus 3.

---

3. It does not make the life of the exegete easier when the same person appears in Judges 4:11 as Hobab of a Kenite family, although this has no bearing on the hypothesis of the documentary hypothesis.

4. In most translations of the Bible rendered as the "LORD," respecting the Jewish tradition which does not accept that God's name is pronounced. A Jewish reading of the four Hebrew letters YHWH pronounces it *adonai*, "lord." A misreading of the Hebrew resulted in the word *Jehovah*, a common form of the name of God in English-language literature. The vowels in *Jehovah* come from *adonai*.

5. The documentary hypothesis originated in Germany, which explains the form the "Jahwist."

Over a period of more than a hundred years, literary criticism has produced many important results from its study of the Pentateuch. Some of these results are of the highest order and indisputable. Sometimes, however, modern scholars consider the outcome of a literary critical analysis almost ridiculous and absurd. Two examples of literary criticism will illustrate these tendencies. The first example is the story of the flood in Genesis 6–8, divided by literary criticism into two main sources, the Yahwist and the Priestly document. The second example comes from the introduction to the book of Exodus, Exodus 1, and in its present form goes back to the German scholar Otto Eissfeldt (1887–1973) and his synoptical presentation of the five books of Moses and Joshua.

This analysis of the flood narrative really seems to reveal the presence of two different strata in Genesis 6–8, each presenting their original version of the flood, put together in such a way that neither of them is included in its entirety. The collector of the two stories has chosen not to remove inconsistencies and, although his voice may be heard in passages that presuppose the presence of both narratives, Genesis 7:7–10 and 7:22–23 may be isolated as the collector's work. Here they are placed in the column of the Yahwist, but they could just as well belong to the column of the Priestly document.

Both narratives come from the same source, the Babylonian story of the flood, most likely in the version preserved in the so-called classical version of the epic of Gilgamesh.[6] It is, accordingly, likely that two different stories emerged out of one original source, the Babylonian text, and that a third person melded them together into one narrative, the biblical story of the flood.

In the light of narratives like creation in Genesis 1–2 and the flood in Genesis 6–8, the documentary hypothesis seems well founded. In other places, it seems absolutely meaningless, and the result of the meticulous analysis of the literary critics totally absurd. Here Otto Eissfeldt's division of Exodus 1 will be introduced as an example of a literary critical analysis that does not solve, but rather magnifies, the problems of this chapter.

Having been analyzed in such a way, divided into three or four source documents, not much of the story about Israel's serfdom in Egypt remains intact. It seems more reasonable to think of one and only one story, and not about four different stories put together by an editor. The example presented here, not atypical, shows very well some of the problems of literary critical methodology. In a minute way, scholars analyze the text in order to demonstrate the presence of dissonances that may indicate the presence of two or more documents or a redactor at work. Nothing has been insignificant to the literary critic, and we sometimes end up in a textual situation where Moses is, so to speak, shouting to himself across four columns representing different documents. The strict application of

6. Translated by Ephraim A. Speiser in *ANET*, 72–99, the flood story 93–97, and by Benjamin R. Foster in *COS* 1:458–61. The story of the flood has a long pedigree within Mesopotamian tradition but seems to have found its classical form around 1000 BCE. Another version of the story is known from the Babylonian epic of *Atra-Ḥasis* (ET: Benjamin R. Foster, *COS* 1:450–53).

The story of the flood, Genesis 6:5–8:21

The Yahwist	Priestly Document
6:5 The LORD [Yahweh] saw that the wickedness of humankind was great in the earth, and that every inclination of the thoughts of their hearts was only evil continually. 6 And the LORD was sorry that he had made humankind on the earth, and it grieved him to his heart. 7 So the LORD said, "I will blot out from the earth the human beings I have created—people together with animals and creeping things and birds of the air, for I am sorry that I have made them."	
8 But Noah found favor in the sight of the LORD.	6:9 These are the descendants of Noah. Noah was a righteous man, blameless in his generation; Noah walked with God [Elohim]. 10 And Noah had three sons, Shem, Ham, and Japheth.
	11 Now the earth was corrupt in God's sight, and the earth was filled with violence. 12 And God saw that the earth was corrupt; for all flesh had corrupted its ways upon the earth. 13 And God said to Noah, "I have determined to make an end of all flesh, for the earth is filled with violence because of them; now I am going to destroy them along with the earth. 14 Make yourself an ark of cypress wood; make rooms in the ark, and cover it inside and out with pitch. 15 This is how you are to make it: the length of the ark three hundred cubits, its width fifty cubits, and its height thirty cubits. 16 Make a roof for the ark, and finish it to a cubit above; and put the door of the ark in its side; make it with lower, second, and third decks. 17 For my part, I am going to bring a flood of waters on the earth, to destroy from under heaven all flesh in which is the breath of life; everything that is on the earth shall die. 18 But I will establish my covenant with you; and you shall come into the ark, you, your sons, your wife, and your sons' wives with you. 19 And of every living thing, of all flesh, you shall bring two of every kind into the ark, to keep them alive

(continued)

The story of the flood, Genesis 6:5–8:21 (continued)

The Yahwist	*Priestly Document*
	with you; they shall be male and female. [20] Of the birds according to their kinds, and of the animals according to their kinds, of every creeping thing of the ground according to its kind, two of every kind shall come in to you, to keep them alive. [21] Also take with you every kind of food that is eaten, and store it up; and it shall serve as food for you and for them." [22] Noah did this; he did all that God commanded him.
7 Then the LORD said to Noah, "Go into the ark, you and all your household, for I have seen that you alone are righteous before me in this generation. [2] Take with you seven pairs of all clean animals, the male and its mate; and a pair of the animals that are not clean, the male and its mate; [3] and seven pairs of the birds of the air also, male and female, to keep their kind alive on the face of all the earth. [4] For in seven days I will send rain on the earth for forty days and forty nights; and every living thing that I have made I will blot out from the face of the ground." [5] And Noah did all that the LORD had commanded him.	
	[7:6] Noah was six hundred years old when the flood of waters came on the earth. [7] And Noah with his sons and his wife and his sons' wives went into the ark to escape the waters of the flood. [8] Of clean animals, and of animals that are not clean, and of birds, and of everything that creeps on the ground, [9] two and two, male and female, went into the ark with Noah, as God had commanded Noah.
[10] And after seven days the waters of the flood came on the earth.	
	[11] In the six hundredth year of Noah's life, in the second month, on the seventeenth day of the month, on that day all the fountains of the great deep burst forth, and the windows of the heavens were opened.
[12] The rain fell on the earth forty days and forty nights.	

(continued)

The story of the flood, Genesis 6:5–8:21 (continued)

The Yahwist	*Priestly Document*
	[13] On the very same day Noah with his sons, Shem and Ham and Japheth, and Noah's wife and the three wives of his sons entered the ark, [14] they and every wild animal of every kind, and all domestic animals of every kind, and every creeping thing that creeps on the earth, and every bird of every kind—every bird, every winged creature. [15] They went into the ark with Noah, two and two of all flesh in which there was the breath of life. [16] And those that entered, male and female of all flesh, went
and the LORD shut him in.	in as God had commanded him;
[17] The flood continued forty days on the earth; and the waters increased, and bore up the ark, and it rose high above the earth.	
	[18] The waters swelled and increased greatly on the earth; and the ark floated on the face of the waters. [19] The waters swelled so mightily on the earth that all the high mountains under the whole heaven were covered; [20] the waters swelled above the mountains, covering them fifteen cubits deep. [21] And all flesh died that moved on the earth, birds, domestic animals, wild animals, all swarming creatures that swarm on the earth, and all human
[22] everything on dry land in whose nostrils was the breath of life died. [23] He blotted out every living thing that was on the face of the ground, human beings and animals and creeping things and birds of the air; they were blotted out from the earth. Only Noah was left, and those that were with him in the ark.	beings;
	[24] And the waters swelled on the earth for one hundred fifty days.
	8 But God remembered Noah and all the wild animals and all the domestic animals that were with him in the ark. And God made a wind blow over the earth, and the waters subsided; [2] the fountains of the deep and the windows of the heavens were
the rain from the heavens was restrained,	closed,

(continued)

The story of the flood, Genesis 6:5–8:21 (continued)

The Yahwist	Priestly Document
[3] and the waters gradually receded from the earth.	
	At the end of one hundred fifty days the waters had abated; [4] and in the seventh month, on the seventeenth day of the month, the ark came to rest on the mountains of Ararat. [5] The waters continued to abate until the tenth month; in the tenth month, on the first day of the month, the tops of the mountains appeared.
[6] At the end of forty days Noah opened the window of the ark that he had made [7] and sent out the raven; and it went to and fro until the waters were dried up from the earth. [8] Then he sent out the dove from him, to see if the waters had subsided from the face of the ground; [9] but the dove found no place to set its foot, and it returned to him to the ark, for the waters were still on the face of the whole earth. So he put out his hand and took it and brought it into the ark with him. [10] He waited another seven days, and again he sent out the dove from the ark; [11] and the dove came back to him in the evening, and there in its beak was a freshly plucked olive leaf; so Noah knew that the waters had subsided from the earth. [12] Then he waited another seven days, and sent out the dove; and it did not return to him any more.	
and Noah removed the covering of the ark, and looked, and saw that the face of the ground was drying.	[13] In the six hundred first year, in the first month, on the first day of the month, the waters were dried up from the earth;
	[14] In the second month, on the twenty-seventh day of the month, the earth was dry. [15] Then God said to Noah, [16] "Go out of the ark, you and your wife, and your sons and your sons' wives with you. [17] Bring out with you every living thing that is with you of all flesh—birds and animals and every creeping thing that creeps on the earth—so that they may abound on the earth, and be fruitful and multiply on the earth." [18] So Noah went out with his sons and his wife and his sons' wives. [19] And every animal, every creeping thing,

(continued)

The story of the flood, Genesis 6:5–8:21 (continued)

The Yahwist	Priestly Document
[20] Then Noah built an altar to the LORD, and took of every clean animal and of every clean bird, and offered burnt offerings on the altar. [21] And when the LORD smelled the pleasing odor, the LORD said in his heart, "I will never again curse the ground because of humankind, for the inclination of the human heart is evil from youth; nor will I ever again destroy every living creature as I have done."	and every bird, everything that moves on the earth, went out of the ark by families.

literary critical method may seem a rather unpromising approach, pretending to produce more critical results than is really possible.

Literary criticism has become a method that is no longer au courant with present developments within literary studies. To its credit, it contributed to the development of other methods used by historical-critical scholars to penetrate the textual form of the account of the past in order to get back to the world hiding behind these texts. We know the methods that arose from the cradle of literary criticism as *form criticism* or *form history*, *tradition history*, and *redaction history*.[7]

FORM CRITICISM/FORM HISTORY

One serious objection to literary criticism suggests that the followers of this method do not try to *read* a text; they dissolve the text into its many components (as many as possible). Literary criticism has in this way become a mechanical procedure trying to reconstruct the history of the editorial work behind the text as we have it. The basis of the analysis consists of the four aforementioned documents, J, E, P, and D.

However, a study of the Yahwist's document in its entirety, using one of the traditional literary critical keys to the definition of the extent of the Yahwist, will tell the scholar—even if he or she is in favor of the documentary hypothesis—that this source is in no way homogenous. On the contrary, the Yahwist is made up of a quite heterogeneous series of short stories and novels. Very little speaks in favor of these stories as having belonged to a Yahwistic document from their inception. Also the Yahwist makes use of stories and legends that must have been in existence in some way before they were incorporated into his work. We may say the same about the stories normally attributed to the Elohist.

7. Jean-Louis Ska has recently published a convenient and up-to-date report on the study of the Pentateuch: *Introduction to Reading the Pentateuch* (Winona Lake, IN: Eisenbrauns, 2006).

The introduction to Exodus, Exodus 1:1–14[8]

L[9]	J	E	P
			The oppression of the Israelites in Egypt [1] These are the names of the sons of Israel who came to Egypt with Jacob, each with his household: [2] Reuben, Simeon, Levi, and Judah, [3] Issachar, Zebulun, and Benjamin, [4] Dan and Naphtali, Gad and Asher. [5] The total number of people born to Jacob was seventy. Joseph was already in Egypt.
	The death of Joseph. The oppression of the Israelites in Egypt [6] Then Joseph died, and all his brothers, and that whole generation.		
			[7] But the Israelites were fruitful and prolific;
The oppression of the Israelites in Egypt they multiplied and grew exceedingly strong,			
	[8] Now a new king arose over Egypt, who did not know Joseph.		so that the land was filled with them. *(continued)*

8. Excerpt from Otto Eissfeldt, *Hexateuch-Synopse* (Leipzig: J. C. Heinrichs Verlag, 1922), 107. Here the NRSV is used.

9. According to Eissfeldt, L represents a special source, *Laienquelle* (popular source), a kind of proto-Yahwist.

The introduction to Exodus, Exodus 1:1–14 (continued)

L	J	E	P
[9] He said to his people, "Look, the Israelite people are more numerous and more powerful than we. [10] Come, let us deal shrewdly with them,			
	or they will increase and, in the event of war, join our enemies and fight against us and escape from the land."		
[11] Therefore they set taskmasters over them to oppress them with forced labor. They built supply cities, Pithom and Rameses, for Pharaoh.			
	[12] But the more they were oppressed, the more they multiplied and spread,		
		The oppression of the Israelites in Egypt	
		so that the Egyptians came to dread the Israelites.	
			[13] The Egyptians became ruthless in imposing tasks on the Israelites, [14] and made their lives bitter with hard service
	in mortar and brick and in every kind of field labor.		
			They were ruthless in all the tasks that they imposed on them.

The story of the flood in Genesis 6–8 illustrates the point in an excellent way. From a literary critical point of view, this story can be divided into two originally independent novels which have been joined together. Both stories are dependent on the ancient Mesopotamian tradition of the flood. The Yahwist and the composer of the Priestly document have the same source for their respective versions of the flood story. Probably neither the Yahwist nor the Priestly writer ever saw the product of his colleague, but their common source decided for each the structure of his own version of the story. Both stories belong to the same tradition and perhaps also originated within a common cultural environment.

There is nothing new here. At the end of the nineteenth century, on the basis of the rapidly increasing knowledge of the ancient Near East, a number of scholars, the most influential undoubtedly the German Old Testament scholar Hermann Gunkel (1862–1932), traced many parallels between the narratives of the Old Testament and Mesopotamian documents. They showed that the authors of narratives of the Old Testament firmly belonged within this ancient Near Eastern world and used its traditions as sources for their own stories. They also argued that the biblical authors likewise included information about the world behind their stories. Gunkel and his colleagues also introduced folklore studies as a new discipline within biblical studies. The study of popular literature emerged in the late eighteenth century and developed immensely during the nineteenth century, when scholars began in earnest to collect and systematize popular stories, fairy tales, and anecdotes still preserved in their own societies. What we had in those days was still basically agrarian societies with a history going back many centuries—if not millennia. In Germany the best known exponents of this new interest were the two Grimm brothers, Jakob Grimm (1785–1863) and Wilhelm Grimm (1786–1859). In 1812–13 they published their *Kinder und Hausmärchen* and in 1816 *Deutsche Sagen*.[10] Scholars in other countries produced similar collections.

On the basis of such editions of popular literature, scholars soon had at their disposal a rich collection of popular traditional narratives, mostly transmitted to their own time in the form of oral tradition or literature. It was now accepted that even ordinary persons might produce literature and that this was not a prerogative of the intellectual elite. Most of such traditional stories were short—fairy tales, anecdotes, and legends—but not all. Traditional societies considered such stories important and meaningful and found in them information about their own society. Sometimes these narratives were etiological in nature, meaning that they explained something in the society that kept them in memory: for example, a special social organization, a political allegiance, a natural phenomenon.

Gunkel and his colleagues in contemporary biblical scholarship[11] were able to isolate many elements in the biblical narratives that they considered remnants of

---

10. There are many English translation of these stories known to every child, too many to list here.
11. See Hermann Gunkel, *Folktale in the Old Testament*, published with an introduction by John W. Rogerson, Historic Texts and Interpreters in Biblical Scholarship (Sheffield: Almond, 1987).

Etiological narrative

In Joshua 7, we hear about Achan's theft of goods taken as the booty of war from Jericho. The story begins with the Israelites moving on to conquer the Canaanite city of Ai. They fail miserably and turn to Yahweh for a reason for their defeat. Yahweh informs Joshua of the theft and its consequences. The following day, Joshua proceeds with the investigation of the theft. The guilty party would be found by drawing lots. First, the tribe of the thief must be found. It turns out to be the tribe of Judah. Next come the families of Judah, and the lot points at the clan of Zerah. Within this clan the family of Zabdi is said to be the home of the thief, and Achan's lot comes out. Joshua and the Israelites find the stolen property in Achan's tent and the story has this brutal ending:

Then Joshua and all Israel with him took Achan son of Zerah, with the silver, the mantle, and the bar of gold, with his sons and daughters, with his oxen, donkeys, and sheep, and his tent and all that he had; and they brought them up to the Valley of Achor. [25] Joshua said, "Why did you bring trouble on us? The LORD is bringing trouble on you today." And all Israel stoned him to death; they burned them with fire, cast stones on them, [26] and raised over him a great heap of stones that remains to this day. Then the LORD turned from his burning anger. Therefore that place to this day is called the Valley of Achor.

the old popular literature, mostly of oral origin and transmitted in an oral form. A short story forming part of the Abraham narratives in Genesis was thus not an "invention" by the biblical author but could be traced back to an oral and popular tradition. The author knew it before he or she incorporated it into a narrative, but used it for his or her own purpose. The author kept its original intention—that it was supposed to explain something known to the author and his or her readership. The form critic would conclude on this basis that if it was possible to trace a story back to its oral form and show it to be a folktale of some kind, we would also have information about its original place, its *Sitz im Leben*, "place in life," an expression that became the trademark of form criticism.

Form criticism is not only engaged in the analysis of minor textual units. In the twentieth century, it developed into a complicated system aiming at analyzing Old Testament literature according to its various genres—in German, *Gattungen*—and to find a "place in life" for every genre according to its societal context, which was ancient Israel.[12] Gunkel produced some of the most important contributions to form criticism, especially in his famous commentary on Genesis[13] and in his study of the Psalms, which led to the division of the psalms into several subtypes that are still part of the scholarly agenda: royal hymns, lamentations, and more.[14] His study on Psalms was revitalized and carried on by

12. The classic introduction to form criticism is Klaus Koch, *The Growth of the Biblical Tradition: The Form-Critical Method* (New York: Macmillan, 1968).

13. Gunkel, *Genesis* (Göttingen: Vandenhoeck & Ruprecht, 1902; ET, Macon, GA: Mercer University, 1997).

14. Gunkel, *Die Psalmen* (Göttingen: Vandenhoeck & Ruprecht, 1929; ET, *The Psalms*, Philadelphia: Fortress, 1967).

his student Sigmund Mowinckel (1884–1965), whose studies on Psalms belong to the classics in Old Testament scholarship.[15]

Mowinckel's famous contribution to the study of the Psalms is his hypothesis about the enthronement festival of Yahweh, reflected in the so-called enthronement psalms (e.g., Pss. 47; 93; 97; 99). Mowinckel traced the motives present in these psalms back to religious ideas and concepts in existence in the ancient Near East and used these concepts to formulate a theory about the place in life of these psalms in connection with the celebration of Yahweh's yearly fight against the monsters of chaos and enthronement in his temple at Jerusalem. The chief objection to the hypothesis is that this festival is not mentioned in any part of the Old Testament. But this did not discourage Mowinckel and the many scholars following him. On the contrary, he and his followers agreed that the Ugaritic epic literature[16]—not known when he formulated the theory of the enthronement festival in 1922—more or less confirmed the theory. One of these epics, a series of episodes from the life of the god Baal, tells about Baal's combat with the forces of chaos in the person of Yam, the god of the sea. After having subdued Yam, Baal is installed on his throne as the king of the gods.

Old Testament scholarship soon turned to other subjects for its form-critical interest. The classic studies of Gunkel and Mowinckel concerned the religious life of ancient Israel. Now scholarship also focused on the laws of the Old Testament, resulting in a series of meticulous analyses of both content and form. Among the best known of these studies is the form-critical analysis of the German scholar Albrecht Alt (1883–1956), who divided the biblical laws into two main categories, casuistic laws and apodictic laws.[17]

The first kind of law is the most common. It may have this form: "When individuals quarrel and one strikes the other with a stone or fist so that the injured party, though not dead, is confined to bed, but recovers and walks around outside with the help of a staff, then the assailant shall be free of liability, except to pay for the loss of time, and to arrange for full recovery" (Exod. 21:18–19). This type of law is called *casuistic* because it begins with a description of the matter, the *case*—in Latin *casus*—before it announces the consequence, the punishment. Such laws are common and well known from all around the world.

The second form may have two forms, a positive and a negative one. The Old Testament contains both forms in the Decalogue (Exod 20:1–17): "Honor your father and your mother" and "You shall not murder." Here the case is not presented, and it is not supposed that such cases should appear in court. According

---

15. Mowinckel's main work on Psalms was published as *Psalmenstudien*, I–VI (Kristiania/Oslo: Dybwad, 1921–24; reprinted Amsterdam: P. Schippers N.V, 1961) and was never translated into English. English readers, however, have available his more synthetic work *The Psalms in Israel's Worship* (Oxford: Basil Blackwell, 1962; reprint, Grand Rapids: Eerdmans, 2004).

16. See p. 85.

17. Albrecht Alt, *Die Ursprünge des israelitischen Rechts* (Leipzig: S. Hirzel, 1934), ET, "The Origins of Israelite Law," in Albrecht Alt, *Essays on Old Testament History and Religion*, trans. R. A. Wilson (Oxford: Blackwell, 1966), 79–132.

to Alt, these *apodictic* laws were something special for the Old Testament and accordingly something that characterized Israelite society. Alt believed it was possible to trace the form of these apodictic laws back to the early family-organized Israelite society where there was no need for courts and judges.

These examples may suffice to create an impression of the scope and variety of form-critical studies. When it appeared at the beginning of the twentieth century, form criticism was seen as a fresh new angle of biblical studies aiming at establishing a direct link between Old Testament literature and the society where this literature originated. Form criticism was employed on one hand to find the place in life of Old Testament literature and on the other hand—when this link was established—to use its supposed place in life to paint an image of the society in which it appeared. In this way, form criticism became one of the most important tools used by Old Testament scholarship to reconstruct the history, culture, and religion of ancient Israel.[18]

TRADITION HISTORY

Form criticism succeeded in isolating many parts of the Old Testament in their various forms. It also succeeded in establishing a societal background of these literary forms and genres, tracing their origins back to ancient Israel. Form criticism in its classic version seems not very interested in studying the authorial process leading, for example, from the popular tale to its later incorporation in a major narrative unit like the Pentateuch or the Deuteronomistic History. Two new methods arose in order to allow scholars to reconstruct such literary developments, tradition history and redaction history. These methods may be seen as two sides of the same coin and as overlapping methods, because their subject is one and the same: the established biblical text.

In principle, tradition history is aimed at the analysis of the tradition history of a biblical text. It traces this textual history in its various stages and elements in order to reconstruct the various stages through which the text in question passed before reaching its present form in the Old Testament.

The point of departure for such a reconstruction must be, or should always be, the present text, as it is preserved in *Biblia Hebraica*. Almost every narrative in this collection will reveal a number of problems in the form of textual breaks, fragments, doublets, and so forth. Such problems are the basis of the tradition-historical critic building on the results of form criticism that may already have shown a number of different genres in one and the same text.

Thus a fairy tale might have been supplemented by a motivation of promises or confessions. We find examples of this not least in the patriarchal narratives and

---

18. It should not be forgotten that the impact of Gunkel's form history had just as important consequences for New Testament studies, represented among other scholars in the name of Rudolf Bultmann (1884–1976) (*Die Geschichte der synoptischen Tradition* [Göttingen: Vandenhoeck & Ruprecht, 1921; ET, *History of the Synoptic Tradition* [Harper: San Francisco, 1976]).

the legendary description of Israel traveling in the desert. A narrative may also have been "embellished" by poetic passages such as the story of the sorcerer Balaam, who was invited to curse Israel but ended up blessing it (Num. 22–24), and the story of the crossing of the sea, with the prose version in Exodus 14 supplemented by a poetic version in Exodus 15.

Legal texts may also have experienced such additions and enlargements, often in the form of commentaries. This is the case with the Decalogue. Here a series of commentaries are attached to the older series of probably very short apodictic statements. The secondary nature of the commentaries is apparent when the versions of the Decalogue in Exodus 20 and Deuteronomy 5 are compared. Since the Decalogue is perhaps the most important part of the Old Testament, it is appropriate to devote more space to how a tradition-historical analysis of the Decalogue might proceed.

The student of tradition history will pay special attention to the commandment about the Sabbath and the two different reasons for keeping the Sabbath in Exodus and Deuteronomy. The version in Exodus 20 refers to the creation as the reason for keeping the Sabbath, whereas Deuteronomy 5 invokes the slavery of Israel in Egypt. A tradition-historical analysis of this commandment will begin with the removal of this part of the commandment as secondary in nature and explain the different versions in Exodus 20 and Deuteronomy 5 as the result of two different redactors at work. However, even after the removal of this part of the commentary, the commandment about keeping the Sabbath is still too long and does not have the form of a simple or formal admonition. Therefore, it should be possible to reconstruct a shorter form of the commandment that consisted of only the command itself, "Remember/observe the Sabbath day, and keep it holy."

This result will allow the analyst to proceed and create a series of ten commandments purged of secondary elements:

1. You shall have no other gods before me.
2. You shall not make for yourself an idol.
3. You shall not make wrongful use of the name of the LORD your God
4. Remember (observe) the sabbath day, and keep it holy.
5. Honor your father and your mother.
6. You shall not murder.
7. You shall not commit adultery.
8. You shall not steal.
9. You shall not bear false witness against your neighbor.
10. You shall not covet your neighbor's house (wife). You shall not covet (desire) your neighbor's wife (house), or male or female slave, or ox, or donkey, or anything that belongs to your neighbor.

The analysis of the Decalogue may hereafter change focus. Now the individual commandments will be scrutinized, and the analysis will concentrate on the minor,

The two versions of the Decalogue

Exodus 20:2–17	Deuteronomy 5:6–21
I am the LORD your God, who brought you out of the land of Egypt, out of the house of slavery;	I am the LORD your God, who brought you out of the land of Egypt, out of the house of slavery;
[3] **you shall have no other gods before me.**	[7] **you shall have no other gods before me**.
[4] **You shall not make for yourself an idol**, whether in the form of anything that is in heaven above, or that is on the earth beneath, or that is in the water under the earth. [5] You shall not bow down to them or worship them; for I the LORD your God am a jealous God, punishing children for the iniquity of parents, to the third and the fourth generation of those who reject me, [6] but showing steadfast love to the thousandth generation of those who love me and keep my commandments.	[8] **You shall not make for yourself an idol**, whether in the form of anything that is in heaven above, or that is on the earth beneath, or that is in the water under the earth. [9] You shall not bow down to them or worship them; for I the LORD your God am a jealous God, punishing children for the iniquity of parents, to the third and fourth generation of those who reject me, [10] but showing steadfast love to the thousandth generation of those who love me and keep my commandments.
[7] **You shall not make wrongful use of the name of the LORD** your God, for the LORD will not acquit anyone who misuses his name.	[11] **You shall not make wrongful use of the name of the LORD** your God, for the LORD will not acquit anyone who misuses his name.
[8] **Remember the sabbath day, and keep it holy**. [9] Six days you shall labor and do all your work. [10] But the seventh day is a sabbath to the LORD your God; you shall not do any work—you, your son or your daughter, your male or female slave, your livestock, or the alien resident in your towns. [11] For in six days the LORD made heaven and earth, the sea, and all that is in them, but rested the seventh day; therefore the LORD blessed the sabbath day and consecrated it.	[12] **Observe the sabbath day and keep it holy**, as the LORD your God commanded you. [13] Six days you shall labor and do all your work. [14] But the seventh day is a sabbath to the LORD your God; you shall not do any work—you, or your son or your daughter, or your male or female slave, or your ox or your donkey, or any of your livestock, or the resident alien in your towns, so that your male and female slave may rest as well as you. [15] Remember that you were a slave in the land of Egypt, and the LORD your God brought you out from there with a mighty hand and an outstretched arm; therefore the LORD your God commanded you to keep the sabbath day.
[12] **Honor your father and your mother**, so that your days may be long in the land that the LORD your God is giving you.	[16] **Honor your father and your mother**, as the LORD your God commanded you, so that your days may be long and that it may go well with you in the land that the LORD your God is giving you.
[13] **You shall not murder.**	[17] **You shall not murder.**

(continued)

The two versions of the Decalogue (continued)

Exodus 20	Deuteronomy 5
[14] You shall not commit adultery.	[18] You shall not commit adultery.[19]
[15] You shall not steal.	[19] You shall not steal.
[16] You shall not bear false witness against your neighbor.	[20] You shall not bear false witness against your neighbor.
[17] You shall not covet your neighbor's house; you shall not covet your neighbor's wife, or male or female slave, or ox, or donkey, or anything that belongs to your neighbor.	[21] sYou shall not covet your neighbor's wife; you shall not desire your neighbor's house, or field, or male or female slave, or ox, or donkey, or anything that belongs to your neighbor.

although real, differences between the versions of the fourth and tenth commandments in Exodus 20 and Deuteronomy 5. Here tradition history will have to ask form criticism for further assistance. The scholar may use form criticism in order to divide the commandments into two different genres, on one hand a series of religious commandments (1–4), and on the other a series of commandments establishing basic juridical conditions (5–10). This difference may indicate two different origins of the Decalogue, partly in a religious, partly in a secular environment. In such a case, the Decalogue itself represents a secondary collection of two minor collections with the aim of reaching a round number of ten.

The elementary content of the secular series might indicate a place in life in an environment without any major differentiation among people. Scholars have therefore been looking for a home for these basic juridical rules or laws in a non-sophisticated village culture. Later, four religious commandments were added to the secular laws, resulting in a collection of ten commandments. The next stage in the development of the Decalogue saw this list supplemented with the commentaries shared between the two versions in Exodus 20 and Deuteronomy 5. The collectors behind both Exodus and Deuteronomy included this version in their work but added new and different commentaries. They were probably also responsible for the tiny differences in the wording of the fourth and tenth commandments, especially in the tenth, where the collectors had different priorities, one of them preferring houses to wives.

The student of tradition history might still not be satisfied. Now the question will be, is it possible to reconstruct the Decalogue in such a way that it only has one type of commandment? Two commandments are positive (four and five), the remaining eight are negative. For mnemotechnical reasons (a series of this kind should be as easy as possible to memorize), we should think of an original list of

---

19. The NRSV has "Neither shall you commit adultery" and starts the following commandments with this "neither." It is a misleading translation. The Hebrew text is here exactly the same as in the parallel commandments in Exod. 20.

either ten negative or ten positive commandments. Such a reconstruction might look like this:[20]

1. You shall have no other gods before me.
2. You shall not make for yourself an idol.
3. You shall not make wrongful use of the name of the LORD your God
4. You shall not work on the Sabbath day.
5. You must not show contempt for your father and mother.
6. You shall not murder.
7. You shall not commit adultery.
8. You shall not steal.
9. You shall not bear false witness against your neighbor.
10. You shall not covet your neighbor's house.

In this way it is possible to present a rather complex tradition history of a short text like the Decalogue consisting of perhaps seven or eight stages:

I   Two originally independent minor collections, a religious series (1–4) and a secular one (5–10), each have their own place in life.

II These two collections are placed together to form one series of ten commandments.

III Supplements are added to the collection in the form of additions to some of the commandments.

IIIa Some of the commandments are reformulated (4–5) from a negative to a positive form.

IIIb Commentaries are added to some of the commandments.

IV Two collectors use independently the series of ten commandments for their own purpose and include it in their own work, respectively, in Exodus 20 and Deuteronomy 5.

IVa Some smaller corrections are added, such as the reformulation of a couple of the commandments (house-wife/remember-observe/covet-desire).

IVb The commentary is extended in the version of the Decalogue found in Deuteronomy 5.

The scholar interested in tradition history will be of the opinion that it is possible to trace a biblical text through its many stages of development, from the original tradition to the final version present in the Old Testament. In principle, it does not matter whether we are talking about a short but important text like the Decalogue, an episode taken from the patriarchal narratives, longish novels like the story of Joseph (Gen. 37–50) and David's rise (1 Sam. 16–2 Sam. 7), or

20. Adapted after the reconstruction presented by Eduard Nielsen, *The Ten Commandments in New Perspective: A Traditio-historical Approach* (London: SCM, 1968).

the so-called documents or sources of the Pentateuch, the Yahwist, the Elohist, the Priestly document, and the Deuteronomist.

Among practitioners of tradition history it is common to make a distinction between the continental European methodological approach of tradition history—in German *Überlieferungsgeschichte*—formerly dominating in German scholarship, and the Scandinavian method of tradition history. The main difference is that Scandinavian scholars have put more stress on the importance of *oral tradition* for the development of a text, while German scholars have generally concentrated on the transmission of written sources. The two traditions have more or less melted together, so that it has become increasingly difficult to trace such differences. German scholars became more interested in the oral tradition at the same time their Scandinavian colleagues showed hesitation in their application of the idea of oral transmission.[21]

One of the major problems for Old Testament scholarship when it formulated its ideas about oral tradition was of a practical nature. The theories about *oral* tradition were formed on the basis of *written* documents at the beginning of the twentieth century. Among the dominant folklorists of that time was the Danish scholar Axel Olrik, whose "epic laws," published in German in 1909, obtained a central position.[22] However, Olrik's laws, a collection of rules for folkloristic studies, were based on Norse sagas and legends all of which are available only in written form. Olrik never had access to an oral transmitted saga. It will always be a logical problem to accept theories about oral tradition based on stories transmitted in a written form. The question will always be, how has the process of writing affected these traditions?

Only more recent anthropological and folkloristic studies have been able to study oral literature in illiterate populations. As a consequence, scholars have contributed a series of amendments to the older theories, especially concerning the character of oral transmission in such illiterate cultures. It was a common assumption that traditional people possessed a special ability to retell stories exactly as they were transmitted to them—from one generation to the next. This theory rested on romantic ideas, however misleading, about the role of literature in traditional societies. In reality, oral tradition in such societies is personal, depending on the ability of the storyteller, his time, and the situation, including the audience, in which the story is told.[23]

This modern understanding of the role and technique of the oral transmission of narratives and poems changes the character of such traditions from

21. For an extensive review of tradition history in its German and Scandinavian forms, see Douglas A. Knight, *Rediscovering the Traditions of Israel* (see note 1 in this chapter).

22. "Epische Gesetze der Volksdichtung," *Zeitschrift für deutsche Altertum* 51 (1909): 1–12. ET, "Epic Laws of Folk Narrative," in Alan Dundes, ed., *The Study of Folklore* (Englewood Cliffs, NJ: Prentice-Hall, 1965), 129–41.

23. Especially important for the development of the study of oral tradition was the field research done by two American scholars, Milman Parry and A. B. Lord, in the period between the world wars. The subject was epic poetry in Bosnia-Herzegovina. A popular presentation of the works is A. B. Lord, *The Singer of Tales* (Cambridge, MA: Harvard University, 1960).

unalterable accounts going far back in time into constantly developing traditions, always adapting to time and circumstances. The plea for oral tradition in order to maintain a certain tradition's relevance for studying, for example, the history of ancient Israel, leads nowhere. Tradition history will have to be less ambitious when it deals with the reconstruction of the original form of literature. It would today be wise to say that tradition history can only with many elements of uncertainty reach behind the oldest *written* form of a story, which may or may not originally have been based on oral tradition.

REDACTION HISTORY

Finally, we find redaction history as the last of the four classic ways of studying the text of the Old Testament used by historical-critical scholars. Redaction history is based on the three methods already described and makes extensive use of them. The starting point for redaction history is—as was also the case for the earlier methods—the present text, but redaction history aims at explaining why a certain text appears in its present shape. It may also be described in this way: Literary criticism, form criticism, and tradition history explain the prehistory of the present text. Redaction history concentrates on the composition of the text in question. Thus, proponents of redaction history argue in favor of the individuality of the redactors of the biblical texts. They were certainly not automatons working in a mechanical way; rather, they were governed by ideas and ideologies of their own. In this manner, focus has shifted from the form to the content of a biblical text. Redaction history changed the field of Old Testament studies and paved the way for the development of many modern strategies for reading texts, all agreeing on placing the text, not the history of how it came into being, at the center of scholarly interest.

Like its predecessors, redaction history did not have to develop its methodology from scratch. It was able to draw extensively from the other historical-critical methods, especially literary criticism and form criticism. This dependence on the earlier methods is especially pronounced in the early works of one of the fathers of redaction history, the German scholar Gerhard von Rad (1901–71), in his study of the form-historical problem of the Hexateuch from 1938.[24] In this seminal study, von Rad demonstrates how the Sinai tradition should be considered an intruder in the narratives of the Pentateuch. Von Rad considered his study to be a form-critical one, but in its aim and methods it is very similar to a tradition-historical analysis, and the questions asked definitely belong to redaction history. The basic question must be, what has the Sinai tradition to do in the context where it is placed by an editor? Without doubt it breaks into the narrative of Israel's sojourn in the desert and disrupts the flow of the story in an intolerable manner.

24. Gerhard von Rad, *Das formgeschichtliche Problem des Hexateuch* (Stuttgart: Kohlhammer, 1938); ET, *The Problem of the Hexateuch* (New York: McGraw-Hill, 1966).

No other classical method is aimed at answering the following question: Why did an ancient writer/editor write/edit his story in this way? Redaction history is tuned to produce sensible answers to such questions. The general idea of redaction history is that the ancient writers or redactors of texts had an idea about what they wrote or edited. Although hardly working like modern authors/editors, they were literary people with considerable knowledge, each having his or her ideas, and they were able to express such ideas in writing.

In some way, literary criticism also included themes relevant to redaction criticism. An expression of this interest is the division of the Pentateuch into the four sources or documents already mentioned. Literary critics, however, did not confine themselves to the study of the editorial work behind the combination of these four documents. They also intended to present a history of the composition, dating the four documents in different moments in the history of ancient Israel. They, without doubt, considered the Yahwist stratum to be the oldest one, followed some time later by the Elohist one. The Deuteronomistic stratum came into being at a still later date, and the Priestly source was the youngest. The dating of the documents had nothing to do with the factual information presented by the texts, for example, the appearance of camels in the Abraham narrative or the reference to conditions in Egypt in Exodus.

Literary critics had more serious reasons for dating the four documents to different periods. These reasons had to do with the intellectual content of the individual documents. It was common knowledge that the stories of J were generally more interesting and entertaining, not to say easy reading, than, say, his colleague who produced the Elohistic document. Scholars were also of the opinion that the Elohist represented a more developed stage of the Israelite religion than the Yahwist.[25] The image of God in the Yahwist's document was more "primitive" than the expressions found in the Elohist's, although the Elohist had not yet reached the level of religious reflection found in the Deuteronomist and in the author behind the Priestly document. Therefore the reconstruction of the textual history current among literary critics was dependent on the acceptance of each of the four documents as expressing individual ideas and sentiments. All of them were, for a time, literary units of their own. As a matter of fact, without such an understanding of the individuality of the four documents behind the present Pentateuch, it is doubtful if literary criticism would have succeeded at all in presenting the hypothesis of the four sources in such a persuasive way.

We will return later to these issues in combination with an evaluation of the reconstruction of the literary history of the Old Testament within historical-critical scholarship. Here it will suffice to stress the importance of redaction history as the beginning of a paradigm shift in the study of Old Testament literature. Without redaction history, it is difficult to see how modern literary studies would

---

25. Although they didn't see this as a problem to the Yahwist. Like most scholars of their own generations, they entertained the romantic idea that the original—the literature in its original form—was more valuable than its successors.

have developed. Redaction history combines all the methods of previous approaches in its analyses of biblical texts, with the result that these previous approaches become more or less obsolete.

This effect of a redaction historical approach to a biblical narrative may best be illustrated by the following example: the tale of the matriarch in danger, of which we possess three versions, Genesis 12 (Sarai), Genesis 20 (Sarah), and Genesis 26 (Rebekah). The choice of this example is inspired by the analysis of John Van Seters.[26]

There is no reason to doubt that we have here three different versions of the same story. The story line is the same in all three. The "hero" is frightened while living in a foreign land because of the beauty of his wife. So he lies and explains that she is his sister. In the second part the plot sharpens until the moment when the foreign ruler finds out that he is being tricked. The third and final part includes the direct confrontation between the hero and the foreign ruler, who blames the hero for not having told him the truth.

Classic literary criticism solved the problem of the three versions of one and the same story by assigning them to different sources. They normally reckoned the story in Genesis 12 to belong to the Yahwist, Genesis 20 to the Elohist, and Genesis 26 also to the Yahwist. Otto Eissfeldt in his aforementioned synopsis reckoned Genesis 26 as belonging to his *Laienquelle*, his original Yahwist.

The reader of the three narratives will, however, soon realize that these three versions do not represent independent stories. The relationship between them is more intricate and more sophisticated.

The first version, in Genesis 12, includes a number of unanswered questions. In order to save his life, the patriarch really lies to Pharaoh and receives money for his wife, who now enters Pharaoh's harem. Yahweh is obliged to act in favor of Abram and punish Pharaoh because of his adultery. The angry Pharaoh returns Sarai to Abram and banishes both from his country, although with exorbitant compensation. Two problems remain: How can Abram lie in this way and call Sarai his sister? What happened to Sarai in Pharaoh's harem? Did Pharaoh sleep with her? The version of the story in Genesis provides no answers to these questions.

In the second version, in Genesis 20, the story has been staged not in Egypt but in Gerar, a town in southern Palestine. The change of place is of no consequence to the plot. The story is more or less the same as in Genesis 12, but with some subtle changes. The author had to make these changes to answer the questions left unanswered by the previous narrative. The first question: Did Abram, now Abraham, lie? The answer is yes, but only partly. He tells lies to the foreign ruler—in itself not a noble act—but he does not lie about the status of his wife as his sister, or better, half sister. The answer to the second question, whether the foreign ruler had intercourse with Abraham's wife, is clear: no, he did not,

---

26. John Van Seters, *Abraham in History and Tradition* (New Haven, CT: Yale University, 1975), 167–91.

Example of a redaction historical approach

Genesis 12:10–20	*Genesis 20:1–18*	*Genesis 26:1–11*
Now there was a famine in the land. So Abram went down to Egypt to reside there as an alien, for the famine was severe in the land. [11] When he was about to enter Egypt, he said to his wife Sarai, "I know well that you are a woman beautiful in appearance; [12] and when the Egyptians see you, they will say, 'This is his wife'; then they will kill me, but they will let you live. [13] Say you are my sister, so that it may go well with me because of you, and that my life may be spared on your account." [14] When Abram entered Egypt the Egyptians saw that the woman was very beautiful. [15] When the officials of Pharaoh saw her, they praised her to Pharaoh. And the woman was taken into Pharaoh's house. [16] And for her sake he dealt well with Abram; and he had sheep, oxen, male donkeys, male and female slaves, female donkeys, and camels. [17] But the LORD afflicted Pharaoh and his house with great plagues because of Sarai, Abram's wife. [18] So Pharaoh called Abram, and said, "What is this you have done to me? Why did you not tell me that she was your wife? [19] Why did you say, 'She is my sister,' so that I took her for my wife? Now then, here is your wife, take her, and be gone." [20] And Pharaoh gave his men orders concerning him; and they set him on the way, with his wife and all that he had.	From there Abraham journeyed toward the region of the Negeb, and settled between Kadesh and Shur. While residing in Gerar as an alien, [2] Abraham said of his wife Sarah, "She is my sister." And King Abimelech of Gerar sent and took Sarah. [3] But God came to Abimelech in a dream by night, and said to him, "You are about to die because of the woman whom you have taken; for she is a married woman." [4] Now Abimelech had not approached her; so he said, "Lord, will you destroy an innocent people? [5] Did he not himself say to me, 'She is my sister'? And she herself said, 'He is my brother.' I did this in the integrity of my heart and the innocence of my hands." [6] Then God said to him in the dream, "Yes, I know that you did this in the integrity of your heart; furthermore it was I who kept you from sinning against me. Therefore I did not let you touch her. [7] Now then, return the man's wife; for he is a prophet, and he will pray for you and you shall live. But if you do not restore her, know that you shall surely die, you and all that are yours." [8] So Abimelech rose early in the morning, and called all his servants and told them all these things; and the men were very much afraid. [9] Then Abimelech called Abraham, and said to him, "What have you done to us? How have I sinned against you, that you have brought such great guilt on me and my kingdom? You have done	Now there was a famine in the land, besides the former famine that had occurred in the days of Abraham. And Isaac went to Gerar, to King Abimelech of the Philistines. [2] The LORD appeared to Isaac and said, "Do not go down to Egypt; settle in the land that I shall show you. [3] Reside in this land as an alien, and I will be with you, and will bless you; for to you and to your descendants I will give all these lands, and I will fulfill the oath that I swore to your father Abraham. [4] I will make your offspring as numerous as the stars of heaven, and will give to your offspring all these lands; and all the nations of the earth shall gain blessing for themselves through your offspring, [5] because Abraham obeyed my voice and kept my charge, my commandments, my statutes, and my laws." [6] So Isaac settled in Gerar. [7] When the men of the place asked him about his wife, he said, "She is my sister"; for he was afraid to say, "My wife," thinking, "or else the men of the place might kill me for the sake of Rebekah, because she is attractive in appearance." [8] When Isaac had been there a long time, King Abimelech of the Philistines looked out of a window and saw him fondling his wife Rebekah. [9] So Abimelech called for Isaac, and said, "So she is your wife! Why then did you say, 'She is my sister'?" Isaac said to him, "Because I thought I might die because of her." [10] Abimelech said, "What is this you have done

(continued)

Example of a redaction historical approach

Genesis 12:10–20	Genesis 20:1–18	Genesis 26:1–11
	things to me that ought not to be done." [10] And Abimelech said to Abraham, "What were you thinking of, that you did this thing?" [11] Abraham said, "I did it because I thought, There is no fear of God at all in this place, and they will kill me because of my wife. [12] Besides, she is indeed my sister, the daughter of my father but not the daughter of my mother; and she became my wife. [13] And when God caused me to wander from my father's house, I said to her, 'This is the kindness you must do me: at every place to which we come, say of me, He is my brother.'" [14] Then Abimelech took sheep and oxen, and male and female slaves, and gave them to Abraham, and restored his wife Sarah to him. [15] Abimelech said, "My land is before you; settle where it pleases you." [16] To Sarah he said, "Look, I have given your brother a thousand pieces of silver; it is your exoneration before all who are with you; you are completely vindicated." [17] Then Abraham prayed to God; and God healed Abimelech, and also healed his wife and female slaves so that they bore children. [18] For the LORD had closed fast all the wombs of the house of Abimelech because of Sarah, Abraham's wife.	to us? One of the people might easily have lain with your wife, and you would have brought guilt upon us." [11] So Abimelech warned all the people, saying, "Whoever touches this man or his wife shall be put to death."

because Yahweh prevented such adultery. The patriarch's wife was in danger, but nothing improper really happened.

It is a well-known fact that one lie leads to another. The person who tells lies will end up in a web of lies and will have difficulties extracting himself or herself from this situation. This also happens when Genesis 20 tries to answer the questions put forward in relation to Genesis 12. Now the problem is, did Abraham marry his sister? Is that allowed, even to a patriarch? The Old Testament definitely says no in Leviticus 18:9: "You shall not uncover the nakedness of your sister, your father's daughter or your mother's daughter, whether born at home or born abroad." The punishment is severe: "For whoever commits any of these abominations shall be cut off from their people" (Lev. 18:29). When Abraham answers Abimelech, the king of Gerar, in the way he does, the author creates more problems for Abraham than he solves. He has not only lied, but he has committed a deadly sin. So it is of little help that Abraham prays for Abimelech.

When we move on to the third version, we find that the second question, what happened to Abraham's wife in Pharaoh's/Abimelech's house, found an answer: nothing happened, because the matter never proceeded so far that anything could happen. Rebekah never entered the house of Abimelech. As far as the second part is concerned, the lie is also told in Genesis 26, but there is no reference to the status of Rebekah. This is a natural consequence of Rebekah being not a sister but a cousin of Isaac.

The questions provoked by the narrative in Genesis 12 have been answered in the second version of this story, although hardly in any satisfying way. In Genesis 26, the author has succeeded in solving all problems—but at a cost: not much is left of the original story. The tension has disappeared, and the story seems in this version rather tame.

It is a precondition of the manipulation of one and the same narrative into three versions that the author of the second version has known the first one and the author of the third version probably both the first and the second version. The individuality of these authors shows when they "edit" the original story in this way. From the viewpoint of redaction history, certain problems of the first version of the story have been solved. The lesson to be learned from this example must be that these authors did not work in a mechanical way. They wrote and rewrote the stories at their disposal. A literary-critical distribution of the three variants of the same story among two or three documents does not explain the relationship between these three versions.

Form criticism may explain how the plot of the story has been borrowed from a fairy tale with interchangeable characters—one of the epic laws of Olrik.[27] The cast of the plot may change from one version of the story to the next. This does not make any difference. The plot is stable; the persons participating in the plot are not. A specific fairy tale may appear in many different places and many different disguises. Form criticism cannot, however, present an answer to the problem of the relations between the three versions.

Tradition history has, in this case, nothing to contribute, because the only development between the three versions is a literary one. The changes have nothing to do with tradition history. They are dependent on ethical considerations of three different authors. The three traditional methods for analyzing biblical texts have little to contribute, mainly because they are not interested in the present text but concentrate instead on the history behind it.

27. See pp. 63.

Chapter 3

Historical-Critical Scholarship and Ancient Israel

Historical-critical scholarship is, as the name says, primarily oriented toward historical studies. Therefore historical-critical scholars are interested principally in historical subjects, with the intention of writing histories of ancient Israel and its literature and religion. The secular and religious history of ancient Israel describes the development of ancient Israel and its religion from its beginnings until ancient Israel was displaced by post-exilic Judaism. In the same manner, the history of Israel's literature is aimed at describing the development of the Old Testament from its inception to the canonization of the Hebrew Bible.

THE HISTORY OF ISRAEL

"The Histories of Israel"

The discipline called "the history of ancient Israel" was, from the early nineteenth century, dominated by German scholarship. In the first part of the history of the discipline, scholars had few sources other than the biblical documents, but as the nineteenth century went on, more and more source material from the ancient Near East became available, and the historians soon recognized its importance and incorporated information from the study of the ancient Near East in their own reconstruction of ancient Israel. Egypt and Mesopotamia especially produced a wealth of information, but toward the end of the century excavations in Palestine, Transjordan (the present kingdom of Jordan), and Syria (in those days including Lebanon) also provided important information. German archaeologists were, until the First World War, very active and dug in some of the most important places, like Megiddo and Jericho. After the First World War and especially after the Second World War, their contributions were more modest.

The German tradition has in no way been monolithic. Basically we may divide it into two main directions—disregarding the fact that also very conservative, if not fundamentalist, contributions have appeared in Germany. One direction may be called conservative, the second moderately progressive. The conservative party was in the early part of the twentieth century dominated by scholars like Rudolf Kittel (1853–1929) and Ernst Sellin (1867–1946) and in the second part by Siegfried Herrmann (1926–99).[1] The moderately progressive party was in the first half of the twentieth century represented by Albrecht Alt and his student Martin Noth (1902–68) and in the latter part by, for example, Herbert Donner (b. 1930).[2]

The reason for dividing German scholarship of the last century into conservative and moderately progressive parties is that these directions are rather close, both of them having Julius Wellhausen as their patriarch. All the members of this tradition consider Wellhausen's work as the very basis of their own reconstructions of the history of Israel. Both Siegfried Herrmann and Herbert Donner, representing the two sides of German scholarship, are students of Martin Noth. The real difference has to do with their respective view of the time of the patriarchs. Noth, following a tradition with roots back to de Wette and Wellhausen, regarded this period as legendary and the sources pertaining to it as nonhistorical. More conservative colleagues would argue that even if Abraham, Isaac, and Jacob cannot be traced in history, we may still be able to speak about their time as an introduction to the later history of Israel. Both parties accept Wellhausen's classic thesis that the prophets predate the Law. The Law (the Torah) represents Judaism and belongs to

1. Rudolf Kittel, *Geschichte des Volkes Israel*, vols. 1–2, 6th ed. (Gotha: Leopold Klotz, 1923–1925), vol. 3, bks. 1–2 (Stuttgart: W. Kohlhammer, 1927–29) (orig. *Geschichte der Hebräer*, 2 vols., 1888–92); Ernst Sellin, *Geschichte des israelitisch-jüdischen Volkes*, 2 vols. (Leipzig: Quelle & Meyer, 1924–32); Siegfried Herrmann, *Geschichte Israels in alttestamentlicher Zeit* (Munich, 1973); ET, *A History of Israel in the Old Testament* (Philadelphia: Fortress, 1975).

2. Martin Noth, *Geschichte Israels* (Göttingen: Vandenhoeck & Ruprecht, 1950); ET, *A History of Israel* (1958; rev. ed., London: Adam & Charles Black, 1960); Herbert Donner, *Geschichte des Volkes Israel und seiner Nachbarn in Grundzügen*, 2 vols. (Göttingen: Vandenhoeck & Ruprecht, 1984–86). Alt never wrote a history of Israel, but his three volumes of collected essays belong among the most influential contribution from the German historical tradition: Albrecht Alt, *Kleine Schriften zur Geschichte Israel*, 3 vols. (Munich: Beck, 1953–59). A selection of his articles was published as *Essays on Old Testament History and Religion*, trans. R. A. Wilson (Oxford: Blackwell, 1966).

the postexilic period. The prophets, on the other hand, belong to the preexilic Israelite society which was not yet bound by the obligations expressed by the Law.

Contributions in languages other than German were sporadic and generally late in appearance in comparison with the German histories. Here there is reason to mention from the first part of the twentieth century the complete history of Israel by W. O. E. Oesterley (1866–1950) and Theodore H. Robinson (1881–1964), published in 1932.[3] The American scholarly world saw itself as the counterpart to the German tradition, especially as represented by Martin Noth. Noth's American colleagues regarded him as too critical in his evaluation of the Old Testament as a historical source. The American students of the history of Israel, the most important being William Foxwell Albright (1891–1971), answered the challenge from Germany by referring to "external evidence" as support for the correctness of the biblical version. A reconstruction of the ancient history of Israel cannot rely on the biblical sources exclusively; it also has to incorporate the evidence from archaeological excavations in Palestine and other parts of the Middle East, and here Albright and his students were very active.

We may, however, ask if the American scholars of Albright's generation really wanted to compare biblical narrative with "external evidence." Instead, they used such evidence to bolster the supposed historical content of their biblical sources. This tendency is obvious when we turn to the well-known history of Israel by Albright's disciple John Bright (1908–1995), published in 1959.[4] Still a popular textbook in many American colleges and universities, it definitely has more traditional ideas about the history of Israel than its German counterparts, such as Noth's contemporary history of Israel that had been translated into English in 1958.[5]

Toward the end of the twentieth century the study of the history of Israel in the Anglo-Saxon world reached the level of previous German scholarship. In many ways, American scholars of today not only match their German colleagues, but have in certain aspects surpassed them. Their methodological basis is evident in their handling of external evidence and in their application of other disciplines, such as sociology and social anthropology. The American way of reading texts must also be mentioned, not only because of its adoption of German methods, but also because it has been able to develop independent analytical methods.

A survey of recent developments in American historical scholarship will show that younger American scholars in many ways have accepted the main thrust of Alt, Noth, and their students. They are in many aspects very close to, for instance, Noth's position. In the light of Albright's rejection of the school of Alt and Noth, this situation is quite ironic. Albright's students, and especially their students, ended up as members of the German school. When this is said, however, it should

---

3. Robinson wrote the first volume on preexilic history, and Oesterley the second about the exilic and postexilic periods.

4. John Bright, *A History of Israel* (Philadelphia: Westminster, 1959); 4th ed. (Louisville: Westminster John Knox, 2000).

5. See above, n. 2.

not be forgotten that conservative scholarship still has a much stronger position in North America than in Europe. This is exemplified by the new endeavor to write a major evangelical history of ancient Israel.[6]

Of course the study of the history of ancient Israel was never limited to the German and Anglo-Saxon world. Italian and French scholars have produced a couple of textbooks, and Scandinavia, including Denmark, has produced several versions, most of them never translated into a major language. Non-German European contributions tend to follow the German tradition of historical-critical studies. This also characterizes this writer's contribution from 1988,[7] and certainly also Gösta W. Ahlström's massive *The History of Ancient Palestine* from 1993.[8]

The History of Ancient Israel

In the Old Testament the history of Israel is subdivided into many parts. The story of Israel is preceded by universal history, the history of the world and humanity from creation until it was dispersed after the frustrated attempt to build the tower of Babel. After this introduction follow the patriarchal age, the sojourn in Egypt and the exodus, the wanderings in the desert, the conquest, the period of the judges, the kingdom of Saul, the empire of David and Solomon, the divided kingdom, the exile, and Israel under Persian rule. Ezra and Nehemiah bring this history to an end.

It is also possible to present a different way of organizing this history. First, we have the period before the formation of the Israelite state(s), from Abraham to King Saul, or perhaps from the conquest to Saul. Thereafter follow the period of "the first temple" (of Jerusalem), the exile, and the "second temple" period. The last arrangement is representative of the scholarly way of rewriting the biblical history of Israel. The purpose of this section is to present a traditional historical-critical overview of the history of Israel. It is only a short version of a long story of critical (re)construction. There are scores of more comprehensive histories of Israel to consult for further details.

Traditionally historical-critical scholarship considered the period before the introduction of the kingdom as the seminal era in Israel's history. Thus in the middle of the twentieth century, historical-critical scholarship was of the opinion that it possessed a firm and stable model for understanding the origins of Israel, in the form of the tribal league, or amphictyony, presented by Martin Noth in 1930 as a model of the organization of early Israelite society.[9] The league

---

6. See Iain Provan, V. Philips Long, and Tremper Longman III, *A Biblical History of Israel* (Louisville, KY: Westminster John Knox, 2003).

7. Niels Peter Lemche, *Ancient Israel: A New History of Israelite Society*, Biblical Seminar 5 (Sheffield: JSOT, 1988).

8. Gösta W. Ahlström, *The History of Ancient Palestine from the Neolithic Period to Alexander's Conquest*, ed. Diana Edelman, JSOTSup 146 (Sheffield: JSOT, 1993).

9. Martin Noth, *Das System der zwölf Stämme Israels* (Stuttgart: Kohlhammer, 1930).

Israel's history according to historical-critical scholarship

The Conquest	before 1200 BCE
The Period of the Judges	ca. 1200–1000 BCE
The Empire of David and Solomon	ca. 1000–930 BCE
The Kingdom of Israel	ca. 930–722 BCE
The Kingdom of Judah	ca. 930–587 BCE
The Babylonian Exile	587–538 BCE
The Persian Period	538–331 BCE

consisted of Israel's twelve tribes and was organized in accordance with a Greek pattern with a sanctuary as its center. The tradition about Israel's past had its home within this institution, and the idea of Yahweh as the God of Israel also originated here.

According to Noth and the school of historians following his lead, the history of Israel begins with the period of the judges and the twelve-tribe league. The biblical tradition about the judges is mainly historical and can be used by modern critical scholars in their reconstructions of the life and history of early Israel. But the traditions about the fate of Israel before the migrations leading to the conquest of Palestine must generally be considered legendary and without a historical basis.

Alt and Noth and most of their disciples did not consider the period of the patriarchs to be historical. Israel's history does not begin with Abraham, Isaac, and Jacob. Noth followed Wellhausen's verdict: "You cannot write a history of a people before there is a people." The narratives about the patriarchs are family stories, not a national history, and are therefore not material for a reconstruction of the earliest history of Israel.

Historical-critical scholars belonging to the tradition of Alt and Noth had a similar view on the traditions about the sojourn of the family of Jacob in Egypt and the exodus, as well as the story about the revelation at Sinai and the wanderings in the desert. These stories are not to be considered historical but should be regarded as national foundation myths, handed down by the members of the tribal league. Basically the sacral league of the twelve Israelite tribes created the stories that combined the previous independent histories of the individual Israelite tribes. In this way the tribal league became the cradle of the Israelite nation.

The legends about Joshua's conquest of Canaan were not historical as such. However, some historical truth lay behind them. Although the tribes of Israel had existed before the immigration into Palestine, they acted on their own. There was no coordinated conquest but a process of—at the beginning—peaceful infiltration that led to nomads, looking for grazing for their sheep and goats, assuming control over large parts of Palestine. Although it is not possible on the basis of the biblical tradition about the conquest to reconstruct this process in detail, some historical information may be embedded within the narratives of Joshua. Although there was no ethnic cleansing of the Canaanites as prescribed by the book of Joshua, the settlement of the Israelites led to a competition for the possession of the land between these newcomers and the Canaanites who had lived in the country for hundreds of years.[10]

The period of the judges was, according to the book of Judges, hardly an era of peace and harmony. The twelve tribes were still very individualistic and pursued their own egotistic aims, even if harmful to other Israelite tribes. Only the sacral league kept them together. There are examples of cooperation, for example, when the northern Israelite tribes were attacked by the Canaanites from Hazor. This event is described in two versions, a prose narrative (Judg. 4) and a famous poem, the Song of Deborah (Judg. 5). Just as often, tribes were fighting tribes, as happened in the days of the judge Jephthah (Judg. 12). A real crisis for the tribal league arose when one of the tribes, Benjamin, was attacked by the members of the other eleven tribes because of a hideous crime committed by a Benjaminite. During this civil war, the tribe of Benjamin was almost wiped out.

The Israelite tribes evidently had little in common apart from their sacral league. If Israel was to survive as a coherent nation, another method of government, kingship, was needed. However, only the deadly threat from the Philistines, shortly before 1000 BCE, forced the Israelites to choose a king "like other nations" (1 Sam. 8:5).

The Philistines, who are mentioned several times in the Old Testament and whose name is preserved in the traditional name of the country, Palestine ("[the land of] the Philistines"), were not Canaanites but foreign immigrants into the area, linked to the extensive wave of migration into the Levant and Egypt from around 1200 BCE. Their ethnic roots might be found in the Balkans and in the Aegean archipelago. Shortly after 1200 BCE, they settled—either voluntarily or forced by the Egyptians. By the end of the eleventh century they had developed into a major threat to the survival of the Israelite tribes, mostly settled in the mountains of Palestine.

According to the historical-critical reconstruction of the introduction of the so-called Hebrew kingdom, the problems with the better organized and better equipped Philistines forced kingship upon the Israelites, who were looking for a more permanent type of leadership than the occasional chieftains who at times arose "to save Israel." The establishment of Saul's kingdom was the result of this

---

10. The seminal work about these migrations is Albrecht Alt, "Die Landnahme der Israeliten in Palästina," 1925, in *Kleine Schriften*, 1:89–125, trans. as "The Settlement of the Israelites in Palestine," in Alt, *Essays on Old Testament History*, 133–71. English reading students may, however, get a simplified idea of Alt's reconstruction because his second important contribution to the Israelite immigration, "Erwägungen über die Landnahme der Israeliten," 1939 (*Kleine Schriften*, 1:126–175), has never been translated.

process, although Noth was of the opinion that it lasted for only two years (see 1 Sam. 13:1, where the Hebrew text may have been corrupted). The beginning of Saul's reign was characterized by great victories, but soon disaster followed when in the battle at Gilboa the Philistines killed Saul and Jonathan, his heir, and exposed their bodies on the walls of nearby Beth-shan (1 Sam. 31).

The defeat by the Philistines did not spell the end of Israelite kingship. On the contrary, Saul's death paved the way for a much more able successor, David. Although at the beginning David's success was not a given fact—civil war soon broke out between the northern and southern Israelite tribes, personified in the two figures of Ishbaal[11] and David, a Judean champion from Bethlehem within the tribal area of Judah—David managed to unify all of the Israelite tribes under his rule. Around 1000 BCE, he conquered Jerusalem, a Canaanite (Jebusite) mountain town situated a few miles north of his hometown, and chose it as his capital. Hereafter followed the conquest of the territories of Ammon, Moab, and Edom east of the Jordan River, but this was not the limit of Israelite expansion. Soon also the southern part of Syria became part of his empire. Although conflicts between north and south were not uncommon in David's time, his reign was one of greatness and prosperity. The tradition of this great Israelite kingdom survived for centuries and led in early Judaism to the rise of expectations of a new David, the Messiah, who was supposed to reestablish David's kingdom.

David's success as a king also dominated the first part of the reign of Solomon, David's son and successor. Solomon, like many Near Eastern kings, embellished his capital with great works of construction, among them his palace and the temple of Yahweh. But, as is often the case, his activities drained the resources of the state. Finally several parts of his kingdom rebelled against the oppression and taxation necessary to pay for his building projects. Thus the provinces of Ammon, Moab, and Edom regained their independence, but also internal discontent within Israel itself was in evidence. After Solomon's death, a break occurred between the northern tribes and the Davidic south. The official reason for the dissolution of the kingdom of David and Solomon was the forced labor, already heavy in the days of Solomon, but eventually to be extended by Rehoboam, his son and successor (1 Kgs. 12).

Following the division of Solomon's kingdom shortly before 900 BCE, we have a history of the divided kingdom, or of the two states of Israel and Judah. Most of the time, the two Israelite states competed for control over central Palestine—Israel mostly having the upper hand. Although Jerusalem, the former capital of the empire, was by now the capital of the kingdom of Judah, this state was too small to play any significant role in politics. The true heirs of David and Solomon were the members of the dynasty of Omri, who in the first half of the ninth century at least for a time created a major state in northern Palestine

11. Or Ishbosheth (the man of shame), the form of the name found in the books of Samuel. The real name was Ishbaal as seen in the books of Chronicles, changed for dogmatic reasons: Ishbaal means "the man of Baal."

The kings of Israel and Judah according to historical-critical scholarship [12]

Saul	before 1000		
David	ca. 1000–960		
Solomon	ca. 960–932		
Israel		*Judah*	
Jeroboam	932–911	Rehoboam	932–916
Nadab	911–910	Abijam	916–914
Baasha	910-887	Asa	914–874
Elah	887–886	Jehosaphat	874–850
Zimri	886	Joram	850–843
Omri	886–875	Ahaziah	843–842
Ahab	875–854	Athaliah	842–837
Ahaziah	854–853	Joash	836–797
Joram	853–842	Amaziah	797–769
Jehu	842–815	Azariah/Uzziah	769–741
Jehoahaz	815–799	Jotham	741–734
Joash	799–784	Ahaz	734–715
Jeroboam	784–753	Hezekiah	715–697
Zechariah	753–752	Manasseh	697–642
Shallum	752–751	Amon	642–640
Menahem	751–742	Josiah	640–609
Pekahiah	742–741	Jehoahaz	609
Pekah	741–730	Jehoiakim	609–598
Hoshea	730–722	Jehoiachin	598
		Zedekiah	598–587

with Samaria as its capital. Israel also played a political role in the Syrian power struggle. Perhaps Judah was, in those days, simply a vassal state under the house of Omri.

Israel's many resources also allowed it to take part in international power play, a gamble that at the end proved to be fatal to the survival of this kingdom. In the

12. This list builds on the research done by K. T. Andersen, "Die Chronologie der Könige von Israel und Juda," *Studia Theologica 29* (1969): 69–114, revised as "Noch einmal: Die Chronologie der Könige von Israel and Juda," *SJOT* 3/1 (1989): 1–45.

ninth century, the Omride dynasty ruled Israel (although of foreign extraction).[13] Especially its second king, Ahab, was very active in international politics, and in his time Israel became one of the major military powers in the southern Levant. Sometimes allied to, sometimes opposed to the Omride state of Israel, the Aramaic states of Syria were partners in this game. Especially Hama and Damascus were the centers of important states. When they were threatened by the Assyrian expansion toward the west, the Arameans created a coalition that also included Israel and managed, for the time being, to keep the Assyrians at bay.

Toward the end of the ninth century everything changed. The dynasty of Omri was removed from power and physically extinguished by the usurper Jehu, while at the same time a new dynasty and a new king, Hazael, took over in Damascus. These changes led not only to the dissolution of the former alliance between Aram Damascus and Israel, but also to bitter war between the former allies. Hazael was particularly successful and managed to occupy most of Israel's territories east of the Jordan River.

Ironically it was the former enemy, Assyria, that saved Israel from the Arameans. It conquered and burned Damascus. However, this blessing had another side. Soon Assyria turned against Israel as well. In spite of a new coalition between Israel and Damascus against Assyria, the Assyrians could no longer be stopped. In connection with the so-called Syro-Ephraimite war the king of Assyria, Tiglath-pileser III, conquered Damascus in 735 BCE, whereupon he turned against Israel, which was soon overrun. Only a small state around its capital, Samaria, remained. The rest of the country was divided into a series of Assyrian provinces. In 724 or 723 BCE the Assyrians attacked Samaria, then conquered and sacked it in 722/21 BCE, marking the political end of Israel. A large section of its population was deported to Mesopotamia.

Until the end of Israel, the small kingdom of Judah had played no role internationally. Now in a kind of local power vacuum, the kings of Jerusalem began to dabble in international politics, but definitely without any comprehension of their own weakness. Only twenty years after the fall of Samaria, the king of Judah was witnessing an Assyrian army under the command of King Sennacherib devastating his country and laying siege to his capital. King Hezekiah was forced to surrender and to pay a heavy tribute to the king of Assyria but remained in office, now as an Assyrian vassal without any power extending over his much reduced kingdom.

In the century following this debacle, Judah remained a faithful ally of Assyria. When Assyria succumbed to a foreign coalition including the Babylonians, the Medes (the forerunners of the Persians), and the Lydians from Asia Minor, Josiah, the king of Judah, developed a kind of foreign politics and began to enlarge his territory, now including parts of the former state of Israel, but reduced into Assyrian provinces. Judah soon had to give up its dreams of greatness when in 609 BCE Josiah was killed at Megiddo by the Egyptians.

13. Omri's name is probably Arabic (Omar). See Martin Noth, *Die israelitischen Personennamen im Rahmen der gemeinsemitischen Namengebung* (1928; reprinted, Hildesheim: Georg Olms, 1966), 63.

The remaining twenty years of Judean history were a tragedy. Soon Judah became a Babylonian puppet state, and its king a vassal of King Nebuchadnezzar of Babylon, who in 597 BCE conquered Jerusalem and led its king into exile in Babylonia. The new king, Zedekiah, installed on the throne of Judah by the Babylonians, revolted a few years later. The consequences were disastrous. Jerusalem was sacked, the temple burnt down, and a part of its population dragged away to Mesopotamia.

In the historical literature of the Old Testament, little is said about the Babylonian exile. Most of the information relates to the beginning and the end of the exile. After his conquest of Babylon, King Cyrus of Persia allowed the exiled people from Jerusalem to return to their homeland. A new temple was erected on the remnants of the old one, and the cult of Yahweh was reinstalled in 516 BCE. However, after that, little may have happened until the arrivals of Nehemiah and Ezra. They probably did not arrive at the same time, but within say a decade, about 400 BCE. After their settlement of the affairs of Jerusalem and its inhabitants, nothing is heard about the fate of the city until Hellenistic times. Now the Old Testament has nothing to add. Information about this period we find in the apocryphical books, especially the books of the Maccabees, and in the writing of the Jewish historian Josephus.

This historical-critical reconstruction of the history of ancient Israel may look like a kind of rationalistic paraphrase of the historical books of the Old Testament. The paraphrase has cleansed biblical narrative of supernatural elements and removed some evidently secondary information. Otherwise, the structure of the narrative, including its historical framework, has been retained, at least from the period of the judges until the end of the history of Israel. The relevant question is, why have biblical scholars not done the same to the periods preceding the period of the judges? The answer is that they behaved methodologically correctly by excluding these as nonhistorical. Apparently, information about Israel's earliest times goes back to the period when the judges ruled Israel, when their formation belonged to the intellectual life of the tribes in connection with their sacral league. Such tradition is not information about ancient Israel; rather, it is reflection based on such memories as may have been in circulation at that time. A document from ancient times that is not contemporary with the events it describes, or borrows directly from contemporary sources, will not be of much use in a historical reconstruction of the past.

The best example of this way of handling the past has to do with the tradition of the conquest, which historical-critical scholars generally reject as history. The only part of the tradition reckoned to be old and to include genuine information is the idea of an ethnic difference between the Israelites and the Canaanites. The process of the Israelite settlement was analyzed by Albrecht Alt without much recourse to the biblical story. Instead of biblical paraphrase he employed his so-called territorial-historical method (*Territorialgeschichte*), analyzing the pattern of settlement before and after the Israelite settlement. The changes that had occurred between the first and the second moment represented the effects of the immigration of the Israelites.

When the historical-critical scholars arrived at the period of the judges, their basic assumption was that behind the somewhat later stories in the Old Testament we find a historical nucleus, which can be extracted and analyzed. When scholars moved further into the period of the Hebrew kings, this impression gained in force. Historians were of the conviction that when there was an Israelite state, we also have information having its origins in state archives, for example, king lists and annalistic literature. Now it was possible to write a true history of Israel.

THE HISTORY OF THE RELIGION OF ANCIENT ISRAEL

"The Histories of Israelite Religion"

The traditional historical-critical reconstructions of the history of Israelite religion follow the historical layout closely. Just as there are liberal and more conservative historical constructions, there are also more traditional as well as more advanced histories of religion. In the North American environment, however, the discipline "the religion of ancient Israel" hardly exists. For reasons connected to a special branch of Protestant theology, the religion of the Old Testament is not religion but theology, part of the Christian faith, which according to such opinions is not religion. Thus the comprehensive dictionary of the Bible, the *Anchor Bible Dictionary*,[14] has no entry titled "the religion of ancient Israel." Most of the discussion has therefore been European, and especially German. Books on Israelite religion published in North America are more likely to be translations than local products.

The organization of these histories of religion follows the course of history in the historical textbooks. Thus the Swedish scholar Helmar Ringgren's *Israelite Religion*,[15] opens with "the Pre-Davidic Period," subdivided into "The Religion of the Patriarchs," "The Beginning of Israel's Religion: Moses," and "The Occupation of Canaan and the Period of the Judges." The following chapters are "The Religion in the Period of the Monarchy" and "The Exile and Postexilic Period (Judaism)." The early periods get the lion's share of discussion and description, although Ringgren differs from most German scholars by his special emphasis on the period of the monarchy. All together almost 250 pages are reserved for the time before the exile, while the exilic and postexilic periods are awarded only 50 pages.

The situation is the same if we turn to another influential German contribution, Werner H. Schmidt's textbook on Israelite religion,[16] although a bit more conservative than Ringgren's *Israelite Religion*. Schmidt introduces his book with

---

14. Published in six volumes, edited by David Noel Freedman (New York: Doubleday, 1992).

15. Translated from the German original *Israelitische Religion* (Stuttgart: Kohlhammer, 1963) by David E. Green (Philadelphia: Fortress, 1966).

16. Werner H. Schmidt, *Alttestamentlicher Glaube und seine Umwelt. Zur Geschichte des alttestamentlichen Gottesverständnisses* (Neukirchen: Neukirchener Verlag, 1968); ET, *The Faith of the Old Testament: A History* (Oxford: Blackwell, 1983).

a longish chapter on "nomadic religion," followed by a shorter chapter on the history of religion from the settlement to the end of the period of the judges. The monarchy gets its share as well, but the exilic and postexilic periods are written off in about thirty pages. It is obvious that these European scholars are not really interested in Judaism, and have little understanding of the development of early Judaism.

The History of Religion in Ancient Israel

Syncretism used to be the code word in much previous discussion about the religion of ancient Israel. *Syncretism* comes from Greek and means "mixture." In connection with historical-critical studies of Israelite religion, it indicates both that ancient Israel's origins must be sought outside of Palestine and that after the settlement Israel was influenced by Canaanite ideas and beliefs. In many places, the Old Testament warns the Israelites emphatically that they should not interfere with the Canaanites and worship their gods. If they do so, the Israelites will perish because they have sinned against their God. The war between Yahweh of Israel and Baal of Canaan was, from the beginning of the history of Israel in its land, of fundamental importance for the development of Israelite society. The many attacks on Canaanite religion in the Old Testament were regularly "translated" in this way in historical-critical literature: There was a fundamental dichotomy between Canaanite and Israelite civilization, which could be traced back to the separate origin of the two nations. The Canaanites belonged to an old agricultural society, and their religion mostly related to the fertility of the soil, the productivity of animals and humans. Canaanite religion was a fertility religion. All its myths, cult, and sacred rites concentrated on the fertility of the society, aiming at guaranteeing the survival of the society in the future. Other aspects of religion, like ethics, were less important. The Israelites came from the desert. They were nomads, and their religion could be reconstructed, at least in part, on the basis of the patriarchal narratives, reflecting a special kind of nomadic religion. A study on patriarchal religion by Albrecht Alt played a seminal role in the discussion of "the religion of the fathers" and was widely cited in the relevant literature.[17]

On the nomadic stage, fertility religion was of no concern. The personal relation between the lonely nomad, traveling around in the desert with his animals, and his protecting god and the promise made by this god to assist him when in danger, to guarantee his offspring and a place for his sheep, were of immense importance. The promise to the patriarchs, made several times in Genesis, might be a later version of these promises made by the protecting god to his nomadic worshiper.[18] Fertility religion with its public manifestations was unimportant. The personal relations and ethical questions occupied the nomad's mind. Thus

17. Albrecht Alt, *Der Gott der Väter*, 1929 (*Kleine Schriften*, 1:1–78); ET, "The God of the Fathers," in Alt, *Essays on Old Testament History and Religion*, 1–77.
18. Further on these promises, see pp. 188–91.

there existed a fundamental difference between the nomad's ethically oriented religion and the peasant's fertility cult.

Although the development from nomadic religion to later Israelite religion may have been complicated, the introduction of the Yahwistic religion was made easy because the Israelites were mentally prepared for the personal relationship between Yahweh and his people Israel by the demands of the patriarchal religion of loyalty between human beings and the dominating but personal gods. The religion of the ancestors created special relations between God and human beings. Yahwism established a covenant between God and God's people by setting up a covenant regulating the worship of Yahweh. This covenant, concluded at Mount Sinai in the desert, made Yahweh into the national God of Israel. Like the religion of the ancestors, Yahwism concentrated on ethical issues, formulated in Yahweh's Torah, and was summarized in the so-called "covenant formula" in Exodus 19:5:

> "If you obey my voice and keep my covenant, you shall be my treasured possession out of all the peoples. Indeed, the whole earth is mine."

The biblical idea that all Israel entered this covenant at Sinai could hardly be considered historical, as most historical-critical scholars understood Israel to be a society that was first molded into one nation after its settlement in Palestine. Historical-critical scholarship in the middle of the twentieth century considered the center of the amphictyony—most likely Shechem—to be the place where the Israelites united into the worship of Yahweh, as related in Joshua (Josh. 24).

It was unthinkable that the Israelite Yahweh religion, sharing almost nothing with Canaanite religious practices, could originate within the Canaanite society. The worship of Yahweh should be traced to regions outside of Palestine. According to the Old Testament, Israel became a nation in Egypt, but left Egypt in order to travel to Palestine. In the desert of Sinai, Israel met its God. This story long ago fell into discredit among biblical scholars. The exodus never happened, at least not on the scale described by the biblical book of Exodus. In spite of this, the biblical tradition about the exodus and the wanderings in the desert, placing these events south of Palestine and relating them to the Sinai Peninsula, might be correct. Yahweh had his original home outside of Palestine, most likely on Sinai, where Egyptian sources may include references to a connection between this deity and local nomads, the *š3sw yhw*.[19]

Now two sets of evidence were in conflict. We have, on one hand, the biblical tradition of the exodus and the covenant at Sinai and, on the other hand, the acceptance that the biblical story may not refer to any major migration from Egypt. The historical-critical answer to this problem was to reduce the exodus event considerably. Not all of Israel, but a few clans belonging to the later Israelite tribal system, experienced slavery in Egypt and escaped to Sinai, where they in

---

19. For references, see Rainer Albertz, *A History of Israelite Religion in the Old Testament Period*, 2 vols. (Louisville: Westminster John Knox, 1994), 1:51 with n. 51.

some way met Yahweh at his holy mountain and a covenant was concluded. This minor group carried the tradition of these events with them to Palestine. Here their traditions became part of the common Israelite tradition formed within the confines of the amphictyony. Now the exodus and the revelation at Sinai became the foundation myths of the Israelite nation. In this way the worship of the desert and mountain god Yahweh became the religion of the tribal league in opposition to Canaanite religion, in its essence totally foreign to Israelite ideas and sentiments.

Many scholars also believed that it would be possible to retain Moses as a sort of catalyst. Moses was the mediator who was responsible for the transfer of Yahweh from Sinai to Palestine, although, if the biblical tradition is to be believed, he died before the entry of the Israelites into Palestine. The name of Moses may be derived from Egyptian, meaning "son," and is often a part of royal names from the late second millennium BCE, like Ramesses ("the son of [the sun god] Ra"), Thutmosis ("the son of [the scribal god] Tuth"), and Amenophis ("the son of [the god of Thebes] Amun"). It could therefore be possible that Moses was real, which also indicates that at the center of the legendary tradition about Sinai we have a historical nucleus.

The historical content of the early form of Yahwism may, according to the historical-critical reconstruction, be summarized in this way: Yahweh was the God of Israel, and by entering a covenant with this deity, Israel was obliged to only worship him and no other god. Israel had only one God, but this did not mean that there were no other gods. Biblical authors often stress the fact that other nations had their own gods, for example, Milkom in Ammon, Qaus in Edom, and Kemosh in Moab. It is never said that Baal was not a god or that other Canaanite gods were nonexistent. Israel was, however, forbidden to worship any of them because of its personal contract with Yahweh. Thus Israel's religion was not monotheistic. A lot of gods were in existence, meaning that the religion of Israel could be called monolatry or henotheism.[20] *Monolatry* is a Greek word indicating that only one god is accepted as the God, in this case of Israel. *Henotheism* is also Greek and carries the same meaning. Only one God is accepted, without denying the existence of other gods. Only later did Judaism change the worship of Yahweh into a monotheistic faith, although by that time it was not permissible to use the divine name, for which was substituted *Adonai*, "the Lord."

It is the argument of the Old Testament that Israel broke the covenant with Yahweh and introduced Canaanite worship. Most historical-critical scholars paraphrased this view. It was not that the Israelites deliberately deserted Yahweh. The problem was that the majority of the Canaanites survived and lived on in their cities and hometowns as Canaanites. Thus the Canaanite religion with all its manifestations continued to exist. The Canaanites never assimilated with the Israelite nomads. They continued to work as peasants, tilling their land. The Israelites assimilated with the Canaanites, and that meant—according to modern scholars—that their religion became heavily influenced by Canaanite ideas.

20. See p. 348–49.

From the prologue to the Codex Hammurabi
(first half of the second millennium BCE).
Translated by Theophile J. Meek[21]

> When lofty Anum, king of the Anunaki; (and) Enlil, lord of heaven and earth . . . called Babylon by its exalted name, made it supreme in the world, established for him in its midst an enduring kingship, whose foundations are as firm as heaven and earth—at that time Anum and Enlil named me to promote the welfare of the people, me, Hammurabi, the devout, god-fearing prince, to cause justice to prevail in the land, to destroy the wicked and the evil, that the strong may not oppress the weak, to rise like the sun over the black-headed (people), and to light up the land. Hammurabi, the shepherd, called by Enlil, am I; the one who makes affluence and plenty abound.

It was, perhaps, inevitable that the Israelites began to worship Canaanite gods like El, Baal, Asherah, 'Anat, and many more.

Thus came into being the syncretistic Israelite religion combining genuine Israelite and Canaanite elements. This type of religion was the dominating one in the period of the monarchy. Furthermore, the monarchy represented an institution previously unknown to the Israelites: kingship. The Israelite monarchy was another proof of the ongoing process of assimilation, and it opened the gate for many aspects of religion related to monarchy not formerly shared by the Israelites.

In the ancient Near East the king had a central position in religious life. The king was not a secular leader of the state; his office was preeminently religious, and he acted as a mediator between his subjects and their gods. The precise definition of kingship might be different from one place to another, but basically there were two main types of kingship. One was the divine kingship as found in Egypt; the other was a sacral kingship, generally in force in western Asia. The Egyptian system insisted that the Pharaoh was a god, the incarnation of the sun god on earth. The sacral kingship did not envisage such a divine role for the king: He was the god's personal servant and executor of the divine plan for the earth. His was the obligation to care for the well-being of his subjects.[22]

When we speak about divine kingship in Egypt and sacral kingship in Mesopotamia, this is only true as far as the person of the king is concerned. The institution of kingship was a divine establishment also in Mesopotamia. Kingship was part of creation, as solid as heaven and earth. The king himself was the elected "shepherd" of the god. The Sumerian king list thus opens in this way: "When kingship was lowered from heaven."[23]

21. James B. Pritchard, *ANET* (Princeton: Princeton University, 1950), 164.

22. This basic distinction was established by Henri Frankfort, *Kingship and the Gods: A Study of Ancient Near Eastern Religion as Integration of Society and Nature* (Chicago: University of Chicago, 1948). Although many revisions to Frankfort's basic thesis have since been published, it still stands.

23. Trans. A. Leo Oppenheim, *ANET*, 265.

The discoveries of the Ugaritic epic literature brought new life to the idea of the king's special role in religion. Among these texts, the epic of Kirta[24] has played a preeminent role, because it was understood to provide evidence that the king in Syria and perhaps also pre-Israelite Palestine was, if not a god as in Egypt, at least divine. The theories about sacral kingship developed especially among Scandinavian and Anglo-Saxon scholars.[25] German scholars have generally been much more reluctant, although they were most often in no doubt regarding the importance of kingship for the introduction of Canaanite religion in ancient Israel.

Old Testament scholars also agreed on accepting the Old Testament idea that genuine and pure ethical Israelite religion was compromised by abominable Canaanite religious practice. When the Israelites gained other religious interests, the laws of Yahweh were suppressed, although they were never totally forgotten. The reaction was sometimes violent. Thus the basic narrative in the Elijah and Elisha legends in the books of Kings was found to be a historical reflection of the fight between Yahweh and Baal in the time of the Omride dynasty in the ninth century. Thus, scholars often referred to the role of Jonadab the son of Rechab in the putsch of Jehu that removed the Omrides from power and vanquished their dynasty (2 Kgs. 10:15–16). Jonadab is described in Jeremiah as the epical ancestor of the Rechabites, an ascetical movement in Jeremiah's time that scorned the drinking of wine, declined to live in houses, and did not accept private possessions. The Rechabites were said to follow a nomadic style of life and live in tents (Jer. 35).

Jehu's revolution was seen as an example of a genuine Israelite reaction against Canaanite influence. It was a murderous coup d'état that did not spare a single member of the royal family and was remembered by posterity more because of its cruelty than because of its religious zeal (see Hos. 1:4). However, no major religious change followed Jehu's revolution. In the state of Israel, syncretism was still on the agenda and slowly destroyed whatever was leftover of genuine Israelite religion, including the respect for the individual and general human rights. The politics followed by the kings of the dynasty of Jehu was capitalistic and led to the impoverishment of ordinary people, contrary to the demands of Yahwism that such people must be protected.

It was to be expected that a reaction would follow against the oppressive politics of the kings of Israel. When it manifested itself, it was in the form of the classical prophets. The authors of the books of Samuel and Kings pay great attention

24. Formerly known as Keret. English translations abound. Among the recent ones are Dennis Pardee, in William W. Hallo, ed., *COS* (Leiden: Brill, 1997), 1:333–43; Edward L. Greenstein, in Simon B. Parker, ed., *Ugaritic Narrative Poetry*, SBLWAW 9 (Atlanta: Scholars, 1997), 9–48; and N. Wyatt, *Religious Texts from Ugarit: The Words of Ilimilku and His Colleagues*, The Biblical Seminar 53 (Sheffield: Sheffield Academic Press, 1998), 176–243.

25. Among Scandinavian studies we may mention Ivan Engnell, *Studies in Divine Kingship in the Ancient Near East* (Uppsala: Almqvist & Wiksell, 1943), and among British studies, Aubrey R. Johnson, *Sacral Kingship in Ancient Israel* (Cardiff: University of Wales, 1955). The Scandinavian scholars were often mentioned as members of a school, the so-called Uppsala school. The British direction was called "myth and ritual."

to the role of the prophets as royal advisers, especially when the prophets act in opposition to kings who are not living up to the standards of a just ruler. Now this is literature, and it is not known if reality was the same. However, the many prophets who from the eighth and seventh centuries came forward to criticize the social and religious conditions in the country may be seen as a reaction to the social injustice that was growing in the time of the kings of Israel and Judah. The evidence of this reaction has been handed down in the form of the prophetic literature of the Old Testament. Of course those texts demand careful analysis, in order to dig out such information and clean it of secondary expansions and commentaries. Such an analysis indicates that the prophetic literature represents a message against extortion and social disorder. Israel has deserted its God and has turned to foreign gods. Israel has forgotten its obligation to care for the poor and destitute. Everything depends on rituals and cult. Israel has forgotten the demands of its God.

These prophets are often called prophets of doom, announcing the coming punishment of infidel Israel. In recent times a new definition has been given to the prophets. They are reformers and represent a special religious and sometimes militant group within their society, the "Yahweh-alone Movement." The message of this movement involved the old address to Israel that it could only have one God, Yahweh, who will be its only savior when Israel is punished for its transgressions.[26]

After the fall of Samaria and the kingdom of Israel, Deuteronomism came into being. Scholars formulated the theory of a Deuteronomistic movement as a response to the catastrophe that befell Israel. It arose among refugees from the territory of the former state of Israel, now resettled in Jerusalem. Deuteronomism is a derivation from the Greek name of the fifth book of Moses, Deuteronomy, which has been considered in its central part (Deut. 12–26) a kind of manifesto going back to this circle. The Deuteronomistic "gospel" has Yahweh at its center. To this is added the proclamation that Yahweh has chosen Jerusalem to be his home and the only place on earth where he might be worshiped.

It was not that religious conditions were better in Judah than in Israel. On the contrary, the situation was much the same, and syncretism ruled. However, toward the end of the seventh century BCE, Deuteronomism was becoming a dominating factor in Judean religious and political life and was now in a position to impose reforms on the religious life of Judah. Impressed by Deuteronomism, the young King Josiah directed a religious reform that led to the centralization of all official cults in the temple of Jerusalem. All local sanctuaries were destroyed and their priesthood moved to Jerusalem. The reform also included banishment from the temple and Jerusalem of all gods other than Yahweh. This reform is sup-

---

26. The existence of such a movement was proposed by Morton Smith, in his *Palestinian Parties and Politics that Shaped the Old Testament* (New York: Columbia University, 1971). This proposal was expanded by the German scholar Bernhard Lang in *Monotheism and the Prophetic Minority: An Essay in Biblical History and Sociology*, Social World of Biblical Antiquity Series 1 (Sheffield: Almond, 1983).

posed to have taken place in 623 or 622 BCE. It did not last long. Josiah's successors returned to the old bad ways of the kings of Judah and reintroduced all kinds of pagan worship, a situation the Babylonian conquest brought to an end.

During the Babylonian exile the message of the prophets and the Deuteronomists was never forgotten. After all, they were right. They preached destruction, and it happened. The memory of prophetism bound the exiled together in the hope of a new beginning after they returned to their old country. After all, although in ruins, Jerusalem was still the only place to worship the God of Israel. Directed by such memories, exilic and postexilic Judaism arose. In the postexilic period it was no longer the prophets who dominated religious thinking. They had foreseen the exile but also the restoration. Now it had happened. They had done their duty. Now prophetism was replaced by the Law of Moses—the Torah—which was the dominating factor in early Jewish society. This society had under Persian rule achieved a kind of semi-independence; it was allowed largely to manage its own internal affairs, including religious matters. Many scholars have, in this connection, argued for the existence of a kind of theocratic rule: the high priest and his college of priests at the temple of Jerusalem had assumed practical leadership of society. In this way it was assumed that God was the true and active king. A new religious force, early Judaism, thus came into being and would, during the centuries under first Persian and then later Greek and Roman rule, spread to most of the known world and develop into the Jewish Diaspora. However, this is no longer a part of Old Testament studies, or so it was believed.

This overview of Israelite religion and its history as presented by traditional historical-critical scholarship is of course simplified and pays little respect to the many divergent themes and ideas proposed by the students of religion. The résumé presented here, however, includes a review of the religious developments in ancient Israel that are accepted by most historical-critical scholars. The relationship between this reconstructed history of Israelite religion and the story of Israel's faith presented by the biblical books is evident. Again we may speak of a kind of rationalistic paraphrase presenting answers that the biblical authors were in no position to produce. Just as the historical reconstruction was strongly influenced by its sources, the reconstruction of the religious history was not able to free itself from this influence to become an independent reshaping of religious affairs in Palestine in the Iron Age. Old Testament scholars had an answer for this: the literary history of ancient Israel.

THE HISTORY OF ISRAEL'S LITERATURE

Introductions to the Old Testament

The study of the literature of the Old Testament is mostly considered a discipline of its own, introduction to the Old Testament. Innumerable studies have been published within this special branch of biblical studies, more often than not including meticulous analyses of how every single unit of the biblical literature came into being and arrived at its present form. It was, so to speak, possible to obtain the theological doctoral degree by moving a half verse from one of the documents of the Pentateuch to another. However, this does not mean that scholarship in these matters was unimportant or lacked seriousness. On the contrary, during the last two centuries, biblical scholarship produced a coherent picture of the emergence of Old Testament literature, including every single part of it.

The many detailed studies of the individual parts of the Old Testament have created a basis for the introductions to the Old Testament, of which a great many have been published. Most of these introductions originated within the German academic tradition. Several of the German introductions have been translated into English, although also the Anglo-Saxon world has produced a number of introductions.[27] Most such introductions are not independent works breaking new ground. They simply present what may be called *status quaestionis*.

The History of Ancient Israel's Literature

Without sources there would no history of Israel and its religion. Sources are in this context primarily written sources, more or less from the same time as the events described in these documents. There are other forms of documentation, especially iconography, and tools discovered in archaeological excavations may supplement but not substitute for written sources.[28] The discovery of just one written and contemporary source may change everything. No hypothesis formulated by historians and archaeologists about ancient Israelite society and culture is immune to change. It can always be overturned by new discoveries. We will return to this subject later. In this chapter we will present an overview of the historical-critical reconstruction of the history of Israelite and Old Testament lit-

27. Among the comprehensive German commentaries, Otto Eissfeldt's stands out: *Einleitung in das Alte Testament* (Tübingen: Mohr, 1934). Its third edition (1964) was translated into English by Peter R. Ackroyd as *The Old Testament: An Introduction* (Oxford: Basil Blackwell, 1966). Among the more handy introductions, we may mention Otto Kaiser, *Einleitung in das Alte Testament: Eine Einführung in ihre Ergebnisse und Probleme* (Gütersloh: Gerd Mohn, 1970); ET, *Introduction to the Old Testament: A Presentation of Its Results and Problems* (Oxford: Blackwell, 1976). Two major Anglo-Saxon introductions are worth including in this short list: Samuel Rolles Driver, *An Introduction to the Literature of the Old Testament* (1891; 2nd ed., New York: Charles Scribner's Sons, 1914), and Robert H. Pfeiffer, *Introduction to the Old Testament* (New York: Harper & Bros., 1941). A necessary and updated modern introduction belonging to this tradition is T. C. Vriezen and A. S. van der Woude, *Ancient Israelite and Early Jewish Literature* (Leiden: Brill, 2005).

28. Iconography has traditionally played a minor rule in the reconstruction of ancient Israelite culture. This is a pity, because much is to be gained from the study of such material. A circle of Swiss scholars, with Othmar Keel as their leader, have now presented much of the material in an accessible form. So far, little has been translated into English, apart from single studies, for example, Othmar Keel, *Symbolism of the Biblical World: Ancient Near Eastern Iconography and the Book of Psalms* (Winona Lake, IN: Eisenbrauns, 1997). A systematic edition of the material is in preparation: Silvia Schroer and Othmar Keel, *Die Ikonographie Palästina/Israels und der Alte Orient: Eine Religionsgeschichte in Bildern*, 4 vols. (Fribourg: Academic Press, 2006–).

erature from its inception in the Early Iron Age (ca. 1200–1000 BCE) until parts of it were finally brought together in the composite literary work known as the Old Testament, creating in this way a basis for the reconstruction of the history of ancient Israel and its religion.

The usual ways of reading biblical texts have already been presented. They may all be summarized as "text archaeological methods." They all aim at reconstructing the many stages that the Old Testament literature experienced before it received its final form in the shape of the Hebrew Bible.

Both German and Scandinavian biblical scholarship believe that the earliest stage of transmission of the biblical texts must have been oral, because this literature came into being in a society where reading and writing were almost unknown. Before the settlement the Israelite nomads did not exchange written messages. They communicated only orally and possessed a series of means of expression, from short proverbs and anecdotes to long epic compositions. They told fairy tales and short novels and sang songs about the great heroes of the past. Although oral, this kind of literature may include much that is historical, or so

The fall of Heshbon (Numbers 21:21–31)

Then Israel sent messengers to King Sihon of the Amorites, saying, [22] "Let me pass through your land; we will not turn aside into field or vineyard; we will not drink the water of any well; we will go by the King's Highway until we have passed through your territory." [23] But Sihon would not allow Israel to pass through his territory. Sihon gathered all his people together, and went out against Israel to the wilderness; he came to Jahaz, and fought against Israel. [24] Israel put him to the sword, and took possession of his land from the Arnon to the Jabbok, as far as to the Ammonites; for the boundary of the Ammonites was strong. [25] Israel took all these towns, and Israel settled in all the towns of the Amorites, in Heshbon, and in all its villages. [26] For Heshbon was the city of King Sihon of the Amorites, who had fought against the former king of Moab and captured all his land as far as the Arnon. [27] Therefore the ballad singers say,

"Come to Heshbon, let it be built;
  let the city of Sihon be established.
[28] For fire came out from Heshbon,
  flame from the city of Sihon.
It devoured Ar of Moab,
  and swallowed up the heights of the Arnon.
[29] Woe to you, O Moab!
  You are undone, O people of Chemosh!
He has made his sons fugitives,
  and his daughters captives,
  to an Amorite king, Sihon.
[30] So their posterity perished
  from Heshbon to Dibon,
  and we laid waste until fire spread to Medeba."
[31] Thus Israel settled in the land of the Amorites.

scholars believed. Literature obviously originally oral is sometimes preserved in a written form in biblical prose narrative. Among such fragments of a formerly extensive oral literature belong the Song of the Sea (Exod. 15), the poems of Balaam (Num. 22–24), the Song of Deborah (Judg. 5), and the list of sayings about the tribes by Jacob and Moses (Gen. 49 and Deut. 32).

Conditions for communication changed after the settlement in Palestine. Although orally transmitted literature was still of primary importance among ordinary people, the settlement established contacts with a culture that had for centuries known and used writing. From Palestine's previous inhabitants, the Israelites inherited not only the traditions of the Canaanites but also their system of writing. Therefore it cannot be excluded that at least some of the old traditions going back to the time before the settlement were transmitted into writing by an early stage of Israel's presence in Palestine.

When Martin Noth presented his hypothesis of the Israelite amphictyony, most scholars of his generation accepted this as the place where traditions about the past were collected and handed down in written form from one generation to the next. The stories about early Israel always speak of the people of Israel—the "sons" of Israel—as a combined totality, and are not interested in its individual parts. This is also true even when the narrative obviously relates to only a single element, like the tradition of the settlement of Caleb at Hebron and the reasons for Caleb's favored position (Num. 13:30; 14:6; Josh. 15:13–19; Judg. 1:12–15). According to the stories, the patriarchs are considered the ancestors of all of Israel, and all of Israel lived in Egypt, escaped from the persecution of Pharaoh, and conquered the land, although most scholars agreed on regarding the unity of the Israelite tribes as established only after the settlement.

In this way a common "Israelite" complex of tradition concerning Israel's earliest times existed already in the period of the judges, made available in written form for later authors and redactors of biblical books. Martin Noth talked about the existence of a *Grundschrift*—a basic or foundational document—in which a series of common Israelite "themes" were combined:[29] the exodus, the conquest, the promise to the patriarchs, the wanderings in the desert, and the revelation at Sinai. This thematic group was, at a later date, supplemented by other themes like the plagues of Egypt, the stories of Jacob in Shechem and Caleb in Hebron, and the apostasy at Sinai (the story of the golden calf, Exod. 32). American scholars generally followed Noth but created their own version of his hypothesis. Thus the students of William F. Albright, following a trajectory implied by their teacher, claim that the Pentateuch derives from an Israelite national epic.[30] European scholars have generally dismissed this hypothesis as unfounded and unnecessary.

29. Martin Noth, *Überlieferungsgeschichte des Pentateuch* (Stuttgart: Kohlhammer, 1948); ET, *A History of Pentateuchal Traditions* (Atlanta: Scholars Press, 1981).

30. Frank M. Cross, *Canaanite Myth and Hebrew Epic* (Cambridge, MA: Harvard University Press, 1973).

The Pentateuch

The acceptance of a basic tradition of the kind proposed by Noth became mandatory for the study of the Pentateuch. As already explained, Old Testament scholarship had more or less agreed on the presence of four documents in the Pentateuch, J, E, P, and D.[31] Scholars were also in agreement about the synoptic character of J, E, and P, three documents telling the same basic story with the same episodes and the same main characters. Thus it was possible to place them next to another much in the same way as in Synoptic presentations of the Gospels of the New Testament. But it was also commonplace to argue that these three sources represented three independent versions of the ancient traditions that were formulated within the tribal league. The proponents of the documentary hypothesis were simply obliged to accept this independence, or their reconstruction would be meaningless. If no independence among different source documents existed, there would be no reason to accept more than one document, and here the Yahwistic one was a safe candidate. The remnants of E and P would in this case be considered extras, that is, commentaries and rewritings of the basic document (Ger. *Ergänzungen*). Such ideas were definitely not unknown after the beginning of higher criticism, but most scholars accepted the documentary hypothesis as more reasonable.

The four documents were not contemporary. It has already been mentioned that the Yahwist was considered the oldest testimony of Israel's ancient tradition. Scholars found some of the religious ideas and sentiments present in the Yahwist document old-fashioned if not primitive, although they all accepted the Yahwist as a sophisticated author displaying an amazing openness. The problem was to point to a period in the history of Israel when such an open attitude to the world at large existed. Generally the Davidic and especially the Solomonic period was chosen as the best candidate; the Yahwist belonged to the tenth century BCE. The enlightenment found at the court of Solomon would have been an ideal setting for the production of a piece of literature like that of the Yahwist.[32]

It was commonly accepted that the Elohist must be younger, but, not by much. The Elohist was accordingly placed in the ninth century BCE. The third document, the P document, was, on the other hand, very different in attitude; it definitely displayed a religious interest centered in the Law of Moses. Wellhausen had formulated the verdict that the Law is much later than the Prophets.[33] P therefore had to be much later than J and E, where this interest in the Law was not in evidence. It was a production of postexilic Judaism. P was, for such reasons, often dated to about 400 BCE. Text archaeology, like "dirt" archaeology, always uses the latest stratum as the *terminus a quo,* the moment where something starts. The process of redacting the three documents into one and the same

---

31. See pp. 45–47.
32. Cf. Gerhard von Rad, "Der Anfang der Geschichtsschreibung im Alten Israel" (1944), in his *Gesammelte Studien zum Alten Testament* (Munich: Beck, 1958), 148–88.
33. See pp. 71–72.

narrative, the first four books of Moses, therefore began after 400 BCE and was probably completed by the end of this century, followed by the translation into Greek that belongs to the third century BCE.

The fourth document, D or the Deuteronomistic source, was very different from the other three documents. It never included a narrative that ran in parallel to the story told by J, E, and P. Evidence of this document is found in Deuteronomy, for which it is named. D, accordingly, belongs to the Deuteronomistic tradition, the literary reflections of the Deuteronomistic movement that arose after the fall of Samaria in 722 BCE. This date marks the beginning of the Deuteronomistic tradition and therefore also the beginning of the composition of Deuteronomy.

The Deuteronomistic History

In the same period we should look for the beginning of the historical tradition now collected in the so-called Deuteronomistic History. This has at least been a commonly accepted view of the composition of the historical literature from Joshua to 2 Kings. In this part of the Old Testament there is a plethora of themes normally associated with Deuteronomistic theology. It has therefore been assumed that the author (or authors) who put the historical narrative together was also a member of the Deuteronomistic movement, closely associated with the group that collected Deuteronomy.

Old Testament scholars had for a long time been accustomed to speak about Deuteronomistic influence in the historical literature, but the idea of a coherent historical work covering the history of Israel from Moses's death to the beginning of the Babylonian exile and attributed to an author of the Deuteronomistic school was first published by Martin Noth in 1943.[34] According to Noth, this piece of historiography goes back to the end of the state of Judah but was not fin-

The history of Omri (1 Kings 16:23–28)

In the thirty-first year of King Asa of Judah, Omri began to reign over Israel; he reigned for twelve years, six of them in Tirzah. [24] He bought the hill of Samaria from Shemer for two talents of silver; he fortified the hill, and called the city that he built, Samaria, after the name of Shemer, the owner of the hill. [25] Omri did what was evil in the sight of the LORD; he did more evil than all who were before him. [26] For he walked in all the way of Jeroboam son of Nebat, and in the sins that he caused Israel to commit, provoking the LORD, the God of Israel, to anger by their idols. [27] Now the rest of the acts of Omri that he did, and the power that he showed, are they not written in the Book of the Annals of the Kings of Israel? [28] Omri slept with his ancestors, and was buried in Samaria; his son Ahab succeeded him.

---

34. *Überlieferungsgeschichtliche Studien*, vol. 1, *Die sammelnden und bearbeitenden Geschichtswerke im Alten Testament* (Königsberg, 1943; reprint, Tübingen: Max Niemeyer, 1957), chap. 1, "Das deuteronomistische Werk," 3–110 (ET of the first chapter: *Deuteronomistic History* (Sheffield: JSOT, 1981).

The transgressions and merits of the kings of Judah

Abijam (1 Kings 15:3)

He committed all the sins that his father did before him; his heart was not true to the LORD his God, like the heart of his father David.

Asa (1 Kings 15:11)

Asa did what was right in the sight of the LORD, as his father David had done.

Manasseh (2 Kings 21:2)

He did what was evil in the sight of the LORD, following the abominable practices of the nations that the LORD drove out before the people of Israel.

Josiah (2 Kings 22:2)

He did what was right in the sight of the LORD, and walked in all the way of his father David; he did not turn aside to the right or to the left.

The Transgressions and Merits of the Kings of Israel

Nadab (1 Kings 15:26)

He did what was evil in the sight of the LORD, walking in the way of his ancestor and in the sin that he caused Israel to commit.

Ahab (1 Kings 16:30)

Ahab son of Omri did evil in the sight of the LORD more than all who were before him.

---

ished before the time of the Babylonian exile, the last information having to do with events that happened after the death of Nebuchadnezzar in 562 BCE (see 2 Kgs. 25:27–30).

This hypothesis about a Deuteronomistic History has shown to be firmly rooted in Old Testament scholarship and is still of fundamental importance to most students of history of the period of the kings. Starting with the assumption that such a comprehensive work really exists, scholars have tried to isolate older sections not from the Deuteronomistic school of thought but adapted by a Deuteronomistic author and incorporated into his work. Such old sections include the story of David's rise to power (1 Sam. 16–2 Sam. 7) and the succession history (2 Sam. 8–1 Kgs. 2) about the bitter strife between the sons of David. Also the already-mentioned complex of Elijah and Elisha traditions belongs here (1 Kgs. 17–2 Kgs. 9). Other material used by the Deuteronomistic author might be royal annals from the state archives of Israel and Judah. Such annalistic information might have contained synchronistic notes about the reigns of the kings of Israel and the kings of Judah respectively. It is also possible to refer to notes where the Deuteronomistic author mentions sources for further reading—no longer in existence—such as the Book of the Annals of the Kings of Israel (1 Kgs. 16:27). We have such a case in the short note about the reign of Omri, probably the most important of Israel's kings, but his story covers only six short verses in the Hebrew Bible, and most of this note concerns his transgressions against Yahweh (1 Kgs. 16:25–26).

The Deuteronomistic historiographer has integrated every story acceptable to him into his theological framework, judging every single king of Israel and Judah following the scheme used for Omri: good kings follow the will of Yahweh; bad kings do not. Most kings belong in the second category. Very few kings pass the test. This frame has an etiological purpose. It has to make clear why Yahweh at the end rejected his people and drove it into exile in a foreign country. Thus the frame is in accordance with the general idea of history in the Old Testament, that the relations between Israel and Yahweh regulate the history of Israel. When good relations exist and Israel obeys the obligations of the covenant, everything is well; but when Israel deserts Yahweh, the result is misery.[35]

More recent developments within the study of the Deuteronomistic History tend to split it up into a series of redactions of an original Deuteronomistic document, rewritten several times by Deuteronomistic redactors. We may think here of two distinct schools of thought. The first is German and reckons with three redactions: the basic Deuteronomistic document, a prophetic redaction, and a nomistic (law-oriented) redaction.[36] The second is North American and argues that there are two stages in the formation of the Deuteronomistic History: a late preexilic Deuteronomistic History, and a major exilic revision.[37] In more recent times, scholars are asking questions about the very existence of this Deuteronomistic History.[38]

The Chronicler's History

The Deuteronomists were not the only people in ancient Israel who wrote history. At the same time Martin Noth presented his theory about the Deuteronomistic History, he also argued in favor of a Chronicler's History, which was seen as an alternative to the Deuteronomistic one.[39] The two books of Chronicles make up the main body of the Chronicler's History, but Ezra and Nehemiah also belong here. It is the general opinion that the Chronicler's History is heavily

35. More about this theme in chapter 6 below.
36. This school of thought is sometimes named the Göttingen school, and most authors have relations with the University of Göttingen. The program was formulated by Rudolf Smend, "Das Gesetz und die Völker: Ein Beitrag zur deuteronomistischen Redaktionsgeschichte," in Hans Walter Wolff, ed., *Probleme biblischer Theologie. Gerhard von Rad zum 70. Geburtstag* (Munich: Chr. Kaiser, 1971), 494–509. Among the more substantial contributions we may mention Walter Dietrich, *Prophetie und Geschichte: Eine redaktionsgeschichtliche Untersuchung zum deuteronomistischen Geschichtswerk*, Forschungen zur religion und literatur des Alten und Neuen Testaments 108 (Göttingen: Vandenhoeck & Ruprecht, 1972).
37. See Richard D. Nelson, *The Double Redaction of the Deuteronomistic History*, JSOTSup 18 (Sheffield: JSOT, 1981).
38. See the discussion in T. Römer, ed., *The Future of the Deuteronomistic History* (Louvain: Peeters, 2000), and Thomas Römer, *The So-Called Deuteronomistic History: A Sociological, Historical and Literary Introduction* (London: T. & T. Clark, 2005).
39. *Überlieferungsgeschichtliche Studien*, vol. 1, chap. 2: "Das chronistische Werk," 110–80; ET, *The Chronicler's History*, JSOTSup 50 (Sheffield: JSOT, 1987).

dependent on the Deuteronomistic History, as far as the preexilic period is concerned. The content of the Chronicler's History is not limited to borrowings from the Deuteronomistic literature; it also includes several traditions of its own, and the historiographers behind this work definitely often display an independent position when it comes to the evaluation of the kings of preexilic times. Most important is perhaps their evaluation of King Hezekiah and King Josiah. They see Hezekiah as the great reformer and are not favorable toward Josiah.[40] Another important difference is the attribution of the temple to David: David had arranged everything—Solomon only had to follow his father's instructions.[41] Finally, the chroniclers—the authors of the books of Chronicles—display no interest in the former kingdom of Israel. On the contrary, after the division of Solomon's kingdom, they hardly mention Israel.

In accordance with their general view of history, the authors of the books of Chronicles, Ezra, and Nehemiah do not focus on the preexilic period. They are looking forward to the time to come when Israel—from their perspective—has returned to its country. Thus Chronicles introduces the idea that all of Israel went into exile in Babylonia, and that the country belonging to Israel was empty during the exile.

The date of the books of Chronicles, Ezra, and Nehemiah is more or less provided by the information in these books. They can hardly predate 400 BCE. Most scholars have for a very long time been in agreement and argue that it is unthinkable that the Chronistic literature would have existed before the Jewish era. Thus this literature at the earliest belongs to the fifth or fourth centuries BCE.

The Prophetic Literature

According to classic historical-critical scholarship, other parts of the Old Testament owe their existence to a very complicated history of redaction. We may first of all think about the prophetic literature. Here historical-critical scholars of the old school mostly agreed that the nucleus of these books went back to the prophets who have given their names to the books.

Each prophetic book has its own history of redaction, as do the twelve books now included in the book of the Twelve Prophets. It is not our intention to present the history of redaction in detail. A few examples should be enough.

Scholarship aimed at isolating those parts of a prophetic book that might go back to the prophet in question. This was a text archaeological process where the scholar dug through several strata of redaction in order to get down to bedrock, the ipsissima verba of the prophet. When the scholar had reached this "fundament," he was now in the position of being able to reconstruct the history and religion of the time of the prophet.

If we use Isaiah as our example, prophetic sayings that with certainty may be considered genuine words of the prophet Isaiah—this is what traditional

---

40. Cf. 2 Kgs. 18–20 to 2 Chr. 29–32 (Hezekiah), and 2 Kgs. 22–23 to 2 Chr. 34–35 (Josiah).
41. See 1 Chr. 28–29.

historical-critical scholarship really says—concern historical events covering a period from around 735 BCE to shortly after 701 BCE. This time was, according to the books of Kings, a turbulent period. The kingdom of Israel vanished from history, and the kingdom of Judah was almost overrun by the Assyrians.

Scholars have for more than a hundred years been of the conviction that Isaiah should be divided into three parts, Proto-Isaiah (chaps. 1–39), Deutero-Isaiah (chaps. 40–55), and Trito-Isaiah (chaps. 56–66). The nucleus of the first part is supposed to be the work of the historical prophet Isaiah. The second part belongs to an anonymous exilic prophet whose prophetic remains were at a later date attached to the sayings of Isaiah. The third part belongs to the post-exilic period. Only in the first part we are likely to encounter the true words of Isaiah. Scholars therefore concentrated on the first part to isolate genuine parts from the eighth century BCE, providing information about the society and its problems in the second half of this century. In this way, Proto-Isaiah is a most important historical source for the study of the late eighth century BCE.

The impression gained from the so-called genuine parts of Proto-Isaiah may hereafter be supplemented by similar material from Amos, Hosea, and Micah, all of which include sayings by these prophets, more or less contemporary with Isaiah. When all of these books have been analyzed and the genuine parts separated from the secondary additions, we have ample documentary material allowing us to write the history of ancient Israel in the days of these prophets. The prophetic ipsissima verba must simply be considered a firsthand source for the time of these prophets. Historians are always looking for such primary sources and correctly consider them the most important evidence available.

When we proceed to Jeremiah, we are in the same position. Jeremiah is supposed to have acted as a prophet from the time of King Josiah until shortly after the fall of Jerusalem in 587 BCE. The last information provided by the book relates to events that happened in 582 BCE. A major part of Jeremiah is written in prose and may, for stylistic as well as theological reasons, be considered part of the Deuteronomistic literature. These sections may not go back to the prophet himself, but the poetic passages are definitely a testimony to things that happened in Jerusalem toward the end of the kingdom of Judah, or so scholars have believed.

Deutero-Isaiah, belonging to the exilic period, changes the perspective on the final part of this period. While we are still paying respect to the separation between genuine and secondary parts, we here have a firsthand witness to the exilic situation at the middle of the sixth century BCE. Deutero-Isaiah represents the sentiments and hopes of return of the exilic community.[42]

The books of Haggai and Zechariah present an update of the situation in Jerusalem at the time the new temple was built, about 520 BCE (it was, according to biblical information, inaugurated in 516 BCE). Other books such as Trito-

---

42. A Norwegian "special tradition" should be mentioned, going back to Sigmund Mowinckel: that Deutero-Isaiah did not himself belong to the exiled community but functioned and wrote in Judah. The theory is now in its third generation. See Hans M. Barstad, *The Babylonian Captivity of the Book of Isaiah: "Exilic" Judah and the Provenance of Isaiah 40–55* (Oslo: Novus, 1997).

Isaiah and Malachi allow us some understanding of early postexilic Judaism in the fifth and fourth century BCE.

The collection of the prophetic books is late. For instance, the redaction history of Isaiah shows that it must be so. Although certain parts of the book may go back to the eighth century BCE, its present shape includes prophecies of Trito-Isaiah not older than the fourth century BCE and even later additions to this from perhaps the second century BCE (Isa. 24–27). Jeremiah is not the product of the prophet himself or of his scribe Baruch. It was finalized by Deuteronomistic authors in the sixth century BCE. The same case can be made for other prophetic books. The youngest among them may date to the fourth century BCE (the book of Daniel from the 2nd century BCE is not included in the Hebrew collection of prophetic literature). For reasons such as these, the prophetic collection as such cannot be older than the end of the Persian Period, that is, the end of the fourth century BCE.

The Book of Psalms

The redaction history of the Psalms seems to be different from that of the prophetic collection. The content of the book of Psalms is highly heterogeneous. Historical-critical scholars are in general in agreement that a certain part of the psalms goes back to preexilic times (although they do not agree about how many and which psalms are that old). Psalms, however, does also include clearly postexilic texts like Psalm 137, in which the exile of the Jews in Babylon is remembered as something that now belongs to the past. The redaction of this collection, or rather collections, as the book of Psalms consists of five minor collections of psalms, belongs to the postexilic period. A more precise date is hardly possible. The collection does not include information that allows for a narrowing of its time of production.

The Remaining Books of the Old Testament

The remaining books of the Old Testament are—apart from Daniel—more difficult to date. Daniel is, according to its author, set in a time when Nebuchadnezzar ruled the east, and it continues to the time of King Darius of Persia, that is, the sixth century BCE. Daniel is a wise man living at Nebuchadnezzar's court. Historical-critical scholars are in no doubt that the setting is fictitious. The book reflects political and religious events that belong to the middle of the second century BCE, the Maccabean period. Here the references to acts that took place in 165 BCE, the Seleucid King Antiochus IV's desecration of the temple of Jerusalem, are decisive for the date of Daniel. This piece of "prophetic" literature must accordingly be considered by far the youngest book of the Old Testament; it includes religious ideas belonging to Hellenistic Judaism.

In principle it is not possible to date books like Job, Proverbs, or Ecclesiastes. None of these includes anything in the way of historical information. All of them belong to the corpus of Wisdom literature and are regarded as the outcome of academic discussions, or as belonging to the kind of literature read in ancient schools (often called "scribal schools" by modern scholars, but they were far more than that). As such, they were part of the academic tradition, the prerogative of teachers and students who had time and opportunity to entertain themselves studying wisdom. Ordinary people had no share in Wisdom literature like the specimens found in the Old Testament. It is also exclusive to the degree that entities like Israel are never mentioned, and God is nearly always Elohim, and not Yahweh. Only Ecclesiastes may be datable, if this book really displays, as many scholars think, Greek ideas and is a philosophy book that has a Greek (Cynic) origin.

SUMMARY

In spite of the criticism that will be levelled against classic historic-critical scholarship in this book, nobody can deny that this scholarship, which dominated biblical scholarship for most of the twentieth century, has managed to paint a coherent picture of ancient Israel, which embraces every aspect of ancient Israelite society. The overview presented is not intended to provide a complete review of this discussion. Furthermore, we do not suggest that this scholarship has been uniform or monolithic. On the contrary, the differences between scholars and schools of thought have been prominent as long as historical-critical scholarship has been in charge. Scholars have expended much energy on academic wars.

We should at the same time emphasize that historical-critical scholarship has moved within closed circles, excluding all disagreeing voices from being heard. This scholarship is based on the source criticism borrowed from general history. Biblical scholars saw this source criticism as relevant to their own field and accepted its theoretical background: that it should be possible for scholars belonging to humanities to achieve results that are at least comparable to the results from natural science. The aim of humanistic scholarship was—or so it was believed—to formulate positive and objective conclusions.

Historical-critical scholarship is a child of the nineteenth century and its positivistic idea of scholarship. The next part of this book aims at confronting such scholarship with the consequences of a new view of scholarship prevalent at the beginning of the twenty-first century.

PART II
THE CRISIS FOR HISTORY

Chapter 4

The Old Testament
and the Changing Sciences

NEW AND OLD IN SCIENCE

In the twentieth century, two developments changed the scientific view of the world. In natural science the breakthrough of nuclear physics—theoretical physics—created a new reality, and the humanities have had a similar experience because of the advance of the social sciences, that is, psychology, sociology, and linguistics. This is, of course, not the place to discuss these matters in any detail. The consequences have manifested themselves both within natural science and the humanities as a diminishing self-assuredness of the absolute value of the results obtainable. Einstein's theory of relativity referring to the central position of the observer has created a situation in theoretical physics that may lead to a certain lack of assuredness of the value of classical physics. Natural science in these days may sometimes look more like theology than classical natural science in the mold of Newton. It proposes theories about phenomena that it may not understand or be able to observe. A relevant example of this is the theory of the big bang, about the creation of the universe, and theories about the unending universe.

Because of nuclear physics's ability to create devices that may lead to the destruction of humankind, the positive attitude toward natural science that has dominated the scene for a couple of hundred years may be vanishing. The nuclear device and its use during the Second World War mean that scientists also themselves ask critical questions about the ethics related to its results. The ethics of science—the discussion about why scientists are doing something and why it is legitimate to do so—is part of the academic agenda in modern times. In this way natural scientists must now defend their research. Their position is more or less the same as that of their colleagues in the humanities.

During the twentieth century, the humanities have largely been forced to change their attitude. At the beginning of the last century, the scholarly scene was dominated by optimism and positivism. One hundred years later, the situation shows a fragmented and individualized idea of the subject of humanistic studies. Almost in the same way as natural science, the humanities discovered the importance of the observer. No scholarly hypothesis is independent of the person who formulates it. The hypothesis and the scholar are two sides of the same coin, and the hypothesis exists only because someone has formulated it, and it is of no consequence that other scholars may accept the hypothesis as valid.

The reason for this change has to be psychology and sociology, two sciences that came into being in the years preceding the First World War and gained in importance as the twentieth century grew old. Social anthropology, in the form of ethnology and ethnography, has provided an immense pool of information now available for the historian in his reconstruction of the past.

The difference between the new sciences and classical humanistic scholarship may be that psychology and sociology "individualize" the study of human behavior and create a framework for human acts. Humanistic scholarship—at least in theory—moves on a suprapersonal level, which is not part of the scholar. Whenever a philosopher has created his logical system, it survives independently of the philosopher. This is true about logic. A logical syllogism is valid or invalid according to its own rules, not because somebody uses it. The same may be said about other humanistic disciplines such as philology and history.

We have already referred to the quest of the historian for results that cannot be questioned. However, the philologist also seeks results that can stand up to scrutiny. It is the philologian's task to describe an element of language in a correct way, according to the level of language where this element appears. Thus, when a philologist analyzes an ancient "dead" language like Greek or Latin—or from the ancient Near East Hebrew, Akkadian, Ugaritic, and so on—his or her ultimate duty is to provide a *correct translation* of an ancient text. The methods used are primarily morphology and etymology. Morphology provides precise information to philologists about the element of language that confronts them. If the meaning of this element is unknown, which is certainly not uncommon when the subject is an ancient language, a historical explanation may work, when the meaning of a certain word is traced back to the prehistory of the language in question; that is, the philologist will ask questions about its *etymology*, its original meaning. In this way it is reasonable to classify the part of philology that centers on ancient languages as historical-critical, and the method has generally also been accepted by biblical scholars.

Sigmund Freud and contemporary psychologists initiated a scientific revolution because of their interest in the person who airs an opinion, rather than in the opinion itself. Traditional humanistic scholarship is looking for the relation between scholarly opinion and the subject it seeks to describe. Psychology creates a Copernican revolution by insisting on investigating the reasons a certain person has formulated a certain hypothesis. Just as focus changed in natural science in its more speculative forms from the subject to the scientist, psychology concentrated on the *informer*, the person who provides the information. The relation between a hypothesis and the person who proposes it is of primary concern. The relation between a hypothesis and the subject it seeks to describe is of secondary importance. Or to put it differently, a text from ancient times such as the Bible may provide information about something. The primary object is not the subject of information itself, but its reception among modern readers.

When we talk about a historical analysis of the past, this analysis must first concentrate on the source itself, and leave its testimony about the past to the next stage of the analysis. The task is to identify the author and to describe this author as precisely as possible. Such an analysis puts new demands on the modern scholar, whose historical-critical source analysis must be sharpened. The author has become interesting because he or she is a kind of filter through which information from the past may have been sifted to posterity. In this way, the author may himself or herself be a *source of error*, who has handed down a testimony about the past heavily influenced by his own preferences.

In Old Testament scholarship, this lay behind the shift from classical literary criticism and its source criticism, presuming that the Pentateuch is a collage organized by redactors without a face and identity, to redaction history. Redaction history may, however, be seen as no more than a gate to other, more modern reading strategies, not least the so-called reader-response exegesis.

From its inception, psychology has aimed at practical purposes. The psychologist collects information through interviews. The psychologist seeks individuals, or they come to the psychologist, who will provide him or her with the needed information. Now psychology has no methodological monopoly. Other branches of scholarly pursuit follow the same strategy. Thus the study of folklore would not have existed without interviews in which tales from the past survive. The study of folklore is, on the other hand, aimed at establishing a historical record and formulating general theories about the transmission of traditional literature. Psychology is aimed at the individual to the degree that interviews with a series of individuals may lead to explanations of certain psychological phenomena that are representative and also valid when the task is to explain behavior among people not yet analyzed by the psychologist. Psychology is also experimental because the psychologist may repeat his or her observations, which are never identical, but when combined may lead to a better theory about a certain psychological phenomenon.

In its fieldwork psychology has to work with social phenomena. The psychologist has to interview people from many social strata. With an emphasis on the social differentiation between human beings and different social groups' ability to express themselves in symbols—symbolize themselves—sociology as an academic discipline comes into being, understood to include the study of humanity in all its many forms. Shortly before the First World War, scholars began in earnest to describe societies in a systematic way, and became interested in how societies are influencing their membership. Societies are shown to be absolutely different, each of them including an innumerable variety. The idea that societies are monolithic is a romantic stereotype exemplified by the myth of the *Völkergeist*, the spirit of the nation or simply "the people." Societies are complicated organisms in which people compete and quarrel.

Every modern Western society includes a variety of internal differences. Every Western society is socially and mentally different from other societies. If we move to societies outside our restricted world, our horizon is widened when we encounter social organizations and mental systems that may be from our own time, but are nonetheless very different. In this way sociology develops into social anthropology.

Social anthropology is sociology because it shares the methods of the sociologist. Like the sociologist, the social anthropologist has to do fieldwork among other peoples in order to find and interview informers. The difference between the social anthropologist and the sociologist has to do with the status of the informer, as most of the informers interviewed by social anthropologists belong to groups of which the social anthropologist is not a member. A lot of anthropological fieldwork has been carried out among special groups within modern society, such as gangs in Western cities or sectarian movements. However, the anthropologist is mostly connected to cultures different from ours, which do not share our level of development.

Therefore, anthropologists between the two world wars visited societies far from us on the developmental scale, such as sub-Saharan African societies, the inhabitants of exotic islands in the Pacific, and Indian tribes along the Amazon River. After the Second World War the interest of the social anthropologists moved to include the Middle East and North Africa, where the exotic bedouins especially came to be the focus of attention—this had already happened before the Second World War—and also the agrarian societies and the cities of this corner of the world.[1]

Like all other sciences, social anthropology developed a variety of methods or schools. Among the more influential we may mention the British branch named structural-functionalism. It studies anthropological phenomena as parts of a

1. A dominant figure, and probably the creator of scientific anthropological study of the Middle East, is the Norwegian social anthropologist Fredrik Barth (b. 1928). Among his early studies we may mention *Principles of Social Organization in Southern Kurdistan*, Universitetets etnografiske Museum Bulletin 7 (Oslo: Oslo University, 1953), and *Nomads of South Persia: The Basseri Tribe of the Khamseh Confederacy* (Oslo: Universitetsforlaget, 1964).

structural whole that decides the function of the phenomena in question.[2] Another branch is French structuralism, whose aim is to describe structural connections in society and to present rules that explain these connections. Structuralism is, however, not limited to this quest but also intends to describe mental structures present in other societies and to formulate laws for such processes that can be applied also by scholars from other disciplines. Thus French anthropology, exemplified by Claude Levi-Strauss (b. 1908), has directly contributed to the formulation of an important literary theory, structuralism.[3]

These and similar schools within social anthropology have created an amazing arsenal of knowledge about human societies and the differences among them. Social anthropology provides general sociology with a depth perspective that it would probably not have been able to create without this assistance. This depth perspective is often used in a diachronic, that is, historical sense, exemplified by the anthropologist's reference to traditional societies,[4] our "contemporary ancestors." It is accordingly not a surprise that certain types of social anthropology developed into a kind of social history, studying the origins of different forms of human organization and, in this connection perhaps most interestingly, the development from tribal society to state.

Among such schools the most important part has been played by the mainly North American school of cultural evolution. It is common in cultural evolutionism to present a series of ideal types describing different stages in the development of the organization of humankind, beginning with the hunter and gatherer society, the tribal society, the chiefdoms, and the primitive state. Each ideal type includes a series of variables, which might not always appear in ancient sources but may be added by the anthropologist-historian to the picture gained from these ancient sources, if only some of the necessary variables are present.[5]

Cultural evolutionism became especially important in a North American setting because it seemingly presents a way to understand the history of pre-Columbian America, which has left no written sources.

2. Among the important anthropologists of the British school we may mention Alfred Radcliffe Brown (1881–1955) and Bronislaw Kasper Malinowski (1884–1942), but also from the following generation E. Evans Pritchard (1902–73). All their field work represents the categories mentioned here, sub-Saharan Africa, Pacific islands, and South America.

3. Representative of Levi-Strauss's anthropology are his *Structural Anthropology* (Harmonsworth: Penguin Books, 1972), and *The Savage Mind*, Nature of Human Society Series (London: Weidenfeld & Nicolson, 1966).

4. Traditional societies used to be called primitive societies in anthropological literature. This terminology has been banished, because while third-world societies may be primitive in a technical sense, they are certainly not when it comes to social organization, kinship relations, and the like. "Traditional" means that these societies are basically bound by tradition and seek to preserve it, in contrast to Western societies. In the West, *tradition* is a negative word, as these traditional societies are not oriented toward change.

5. Examples of studies within this school include Elman R. Service, *Primitive Social Organization* (1962; 2nd ed., New York: Random House, 1971) and *Origins of the State and Civilization* (New York: Norton, 1975), and Morton H. Fried, *The Evolution of Political Society* (New York: Random House, 1967).

This anthropological school also became important in the development of archaeological theory, especially among archaeologists specializing in prehistory and historians working in fields where little in the way of written documents has been found. Thus it has helped to organize the earliest history of the ancient Near East, including the early history of Palestine before 2000 BCE. However, cultural evolutionism is, from the perspective of modern science, a step backward; really a child of the nineteenth, not the twentieth century. In many ways it is untouched by scientific developments belonging to the twentieth century.[6]

THE STUDY OF THE OLD TESTAMENT IN THE TWENTIETH CENTURY

If we ask how Old Testament scholarship has reacted to developments within science in general in the last century, the answer must be that it did not react at all until fairly late. As late as 1979, the North American scholar Norman K. Gottwald, in a major study oriented toward the integration of sociology in biblical studies, argued that the attitude of Old Testament scholars toward sociology must be called a scandal. These scholars had deliberately decided not to accept modern scientific knowledge in their own research, which was dominated by history and philology.[7] The first serious application of sociology in Old Testament study—and it was in the form of cultural evolutionism—appeared only after more than two-thirds of the twentieth century had passed.[8]

Old Testament scholarship shared this indifference toward the new human sciences with other disciplines like Assyriology and Egyptology. The reason for this lack of interest in the behavioral sciences must be the self-assuredness displayed by Old Testament scholarship. Scholars were convinced that they had developed a sufficient methodology and saw no need to change it. According to the Italian Assyriologist Mario Liverani, the curriculum of students of the ancient Near East caused this situation. Students—including students of the Old Testament—spent so much time on the ancient languages to be mastered that they hardly managed to upgrade their understanding of what may have been happening in other disciplines.[9] There was simply not time enough left for such undertakings.

The basic assumption is clearly that in order to read and understand ancient documents, it is necessary to master the languages in which these documents are written. Thus a student of the Old Testament must have a fair knowledge not

6. For more on the different schools of anthropology, see Fredrik Barth, Andre Gingrich, Robert Parkin, and Sydel Silverman, *One Discipline, Four Ways: British, German, French, and American Anthropology* (Chicago: University of Chicago, 2005).

7. Norman K. Gottwald, *The Tribes of Yahweh: A Sociology of the Religion of Liberated Israel, 1250–1050 B.C.E.* (New York: Orbis, 1979), chap. 1.2: "The Scandal of Sociological Method," 5–7.

8. George E. Mendenhall, *The Tenth Generation: The Origins of the Biblical Tradition* (Baltimore: Johns Hopkins, 1973).

9. Mario Liverani, "Problemi e indirizzi degli studi storici sul Vicino Oriente antica," *Cultura e Scuola* 20 (1966): 72–79.

only of biblical Hebrew, Aramaic, and Greek but also of other ancient languages like Ugaritic, Akkadian, perhaps Egyptian, and more. In this way the biblical scholar has developed into a kind of mini-Orientalist more or less in command of several disciplines accepted as relevant for his or her studies.

From this perspective, there is no reason to wonder why methodological reflection in Old Testament scholarship was an exception or why a seemingly endless number of histories of ancient Israel appeared, more or less copying other histories without any reflection on method or new ideas on how to approach the subject. This discussion took place within a closed circle, and very few scholars were interested in breaking out of the circle.

In the previously mentioned work, *The Structure of Scientific Revolutions*, Thomas Kuhn says that one of the conditions that lead to a breakdown of a scientific paradigm is the fact that it may become too heavy because it tries to explain everything and does not allow for answers that may pave the way for another paradigm. We may express it in this way: the paradigm becomes so heavy that it collapses in on itself. One day young, enterprising scholars will begin, like termites, to attack the foundation, and sooner or later the paradigm will crumble.

An overview of Old Testament scholarship between, say, 1950 and 1970 will show that this collapse of the traditional paradigm was immanent. The classical historical-critical paradigm had at that time lost most of its energy and had ended up becoming self-affirmative. Young scholars from many countries and scholarly environments had begun to ask critical questions of central parts of the paradigm, among these the basic idea of the tribal league. We will in the following chapter return to the details of this development. These scholars came from Germany, Holland, England, America, and Scandinavia. The only thing they had in common was the basic feeling that the historical-critical paradigm, like an old car, needed service. Still, they did not realize that the problem was the paradigm itself, which was already outdated.

The early revisionist investigations from the 1960s have been preserved only in part. Many studies were never published, or they appeared too late to be of anything but historical interest. The reason was the reaction of more traditional historical-critical scholars of that time, who did not understand what happened and were not prepared to accept the emerging criticism of their own paradigm. A classical example of this was the study of a Danish scholar, Heike Friis, whose thesis from 1968 was titled *The Background in and outside of Israel for the Emergence of David's Empire*. This thesis introduced the idea that biblical historical narrative presupposes the Babylonian exile and has nothing to do with an Israelite tribal league. It took another seven years before this idea began to impress biblical scholarship in earnest. The thesis was not published until 1986—in German.[10]

---

10. Heike Friis, *Die Bedingungen für die Errichtung des Davidischen Reichs in Israel und seiner Umwelt*, trans. Bernd Jörg Diebner, Dielheimer Blätter zu Alten Testament und seiner Rezeption in der Alten Kirche 6 (Heidelberg: Dielheimer Blätter, 1986).

The 1970s witnessed the early stages of the coming reorientation of Old Testament scholarship. Two developments made this change easier: first of all, almost a generation of important scholars in Europe as well as North America died at the same time: the German scholars Martin Noth (1968) and Gerhard von Rad (1971), the American William Foxwell Albright (1971), and the French Roland de Vaux (1971). In Scandinavia Sigmund Mowinckel had already died in 1965. Now the authority of these scholars had vanished. Their shadow had effectively barred the way for different ideas and prevented other scholars from developing into independent minds. The second development was the beginning liberation of North American scholarship from the dominance of German scholars. German scholars had, over a period of more than a hundred years, created the historical-critical paradigm, and it survived in a healthy state in Germany long after it was crumbling in other parts of the world.

In the Anglo-Saxon and North American scholarly world, this opened for a much needed orientation toward other scholarly disciplines. In this connection, historical studies lost their predominant position of the early twentieth century. Scholars more and more concentrated on the reading of texts. The Bible was understood to be literature and was read as such, rather than as a document referring to the past. Numerous strategies for reading texts were introduced into biblical scholarship. They all had in common that they concentrated on the biblical text as a text. They were not interested in the events which may or may not be reflected by the biblical text. Only a few scholars remained faithful to the old paradigm and studied history. The majority of biblical scholars slipped away from history—often without realizing it. It is quite ironic that so many students of literature working with biblical narratives, whenever they returned to historical matters, did it in the form of the old historical-critical paradigm, without knowing that they had already left it behind.

German scholarship was late in recognizing the merits of these new directions. The psychological reason for this slowness may be the extremely strong position of traditional historical-critical research in German universities. They had created the paradigm, and they did not want to part with it, but defended it against all attacks. In the 1970s a circle of young German scholars arose, centered in the University of Heidelberg and led by the German scholar Bernd Jörg Diebner, but they were soon isolated as esoteric. Although this circle of scholars has published their own journal for more than thirty years, the *Dielheimer Blätter zum Alten Testament*, where many ideas have been aired that are only now at the beginning of the twenty-first century generally accepted, they then hardly influenced contemporary German scholarship. The consequence has been that the scholarly focus of attention has changed from central Europe to North America. Few young scholars of this time master German.

At the beginning of the twenty-first century, it is clear that the transformation from the previously dominant historical-critical paradigm is a fact, although it may be too early to predict what will replace it. Many former advocates of historical-critical scholarship will now admit that in many ways it represents a cul-de-sac.

Ideas borrowed from other scholarly disciplines are common, and many changes occur in the curriculum of Old Testament studies. The situation is fluid at the present. When David Noel Freedman, the editor of the acclaimed *Anchor Bible Dictionary*,[11] was asked why it is so heterogeneous, he simply answered that it reflects the present situation in biblical studies in an excellent way.[12] In order to be able to appreciate how different Old Testament scholarship may really be in recent times, we urge the reader to study the comprehensive history of Israelite religion authored by Rainer Albertz and published in 1992 and Thomas L. Thompson's *The Bible in History*, from 1999.[13]

Albertz's history of Israelite religion represents the best of classical historical-critical study and has as its foundation a combination of historical-critical methods and ideas gained from modern social anthropology. This has resulted in a comprehensive but very readable account of Israelite religion from the earliest times to the Persian period. Whether it stands or falls has to do with the survival of the basic paradigm.

Thomas L. Thompson's monograph belongs to a different paradigm. Here the biblical text is no longer regarded as a primary source for ancient Israelite society and its religion. The biblical narrative informs us about ideologies and presumptions shared by its authors and their audience. The depiction of ancient Israel in the biblical narrative is not dependent on how it really was—*wie es eigentlich gewesen*—but reflects ideas about Israel held by people who wrote the stories of the Old Testament.[14]

In the next chapter, the subject is the demonstration of how, in successive steps, the historical-critical edifice of ancient Israel crumbled. This will also indicate some of the consequences of this change.

---

11. David Noel Freedman, ed., *Anchor Bible Dictionary*, 6 vols. (New York: Doubleday, 1992).

12. Oral tradition going back to the Society of Biblical Literature annual meeting of 1992. This author was present.

13. Rainer Albertz, *Religionsgeschichte Israels in alttestamentlicher Zeit*, 2 vols., Grundrisse zum Alten Testament 8, 1–2 (Göttingen: Vandenhoeck & Ruprecht, 1992); ET, *A History of Israelite Religion*, 2 vols. (Louisville, Westminster John Knox, 1994). Thomas L. Thompson, *The Bible in History: How Writers Create a Past* (London: Jonathan Cape, 1999); North American edition, *The Mythic Past: Biblical Archaeology and the Myth of Israel* (New York: Basic Books, 1999).

14. This does not automatically imply that critical scholarship is no longer possible. The focus may, however, have changed, as will be underscored by the third part of this book.

Chapter 5

The Crisis of Historical-Critical Scholarship

THE HERMENEUTICAL CIRCLE

It has already been mentioned a couple of times that traditional historical-critical scholarship existed within a closed room and more or less remained a closed dialogue among the inhabitants of this closed room. At the end of the day, a text in the Old Testament will often be the only source to an event that may have happened in ancient Israel. Other kinds of evidence may not exist at all or are few. Only occasionally do written sources not in the Old Testament relate to information found in the Old Testament. In these few cases, the importance of such external documentation is of course not to be dismissed.

The condition that says a text from the Old Testament used for historical reconstruction will, so to speak, confirm itself has often been referred to as the *hermeneutical circle*, which is in and of itself indispensable. The term hermeneutical circle implies a logically circular argumentation—*circellus logicus vitiosus*: X confirms Y, and Y confirms X. Circular argumentation is, from a logical point of view, false and should never be allowed to be part of a scholarly discourse. This has not deterred biblical scholars, who often make use of this type of argument when they reconstruct the history of ancient Israel and its religion, not to say literature. The German scholar Bernd Jörg Diebner once put it in this way: "You cannot prove anything; however, it is *still* a fact!"[1] Biblical scholars ignore the fact that the method used is wrong and keep arguing that it really happened in the way they imagined.

It is possible to offer many examples of this kind of argumentation in Old Testament scholarship. One example is the thesis of classical literary criticism that the Yahwistic document in the Pentateuch belongs to the time of Solomon because the Yahwist reflects the open-minded and international environment found in the court of King Solomon. This argument is circular because we know about Solomon and his court only from the narrative in 1 Kings. This narrative tells us that the entire world visited Solomon in Jerusalem—paradigmatically illustrated by the visit of the queen of Sheba to Jerusalem (1 Kgs. 10). The discussion among scholars that leads to such a date of the Yahwist can be supported only by the Old Testament, the very source that also includes the Yahwist as reconstructed by the same scholars who use their construct as a basis for arguing that the court of Solomon was international and open-minded.

It is possible to include other examples from the prophetical books. Here scholars have, for generations, been of the conviction that Isaiah would include, apart from secondary additions and revision, the genuine prophecies of a prophet from the eighth century BCE by the name of Isaiah. However, we know about the existence of this prophet only from Old Testament literature and later Jewish tradition based on the information about Isaiah found in the Old Testament. When scholars argue in favor of the existence of a prophet of this name attributable to the eighth century BCE, it is no more than the scholar's assertion, which has no support in other ancient documents. This does not mean that there never was a prophet of the name of Isaiah; it only tells us that we have no information that proves his existence. We *assume* that Isaiah is a historical prophet and proceed on this basis to argue that certain parts of the book carrying his name must go back to the prophet himself.

When the procedure of historical-critical scholarship is dissected in this logical manner, it crumbles like a house of cards. Circular argumentation is false and will always remain false. Nothing can change that. A scholarly assumption may look like a legitimate argument, but contrary to genuine argument it cannot be falsified—to use this concept as coined by the philosopher Karl Popper (1902–94).[2] It is characteristic of such cases that there is no *tertium comparationis,* no external evidence that may prove the argument to be correct and not a baseless assumption.

---

1. "Es lässt sich nicht beweisen, Tatsache aber ist!" with the addition "Sprachfigur statt Methode in der alttestamentlichen Forschung."

2. See Karl Popper, *The Logic of Scientific Discovery* (ET of German original: *Logik der Forschung* [Wien, 1935]; reprint, London: Routledge, 2006). Popper's falsification process is of course not unchallenged by other philosophers of knowledge, among them Paul Feyerabend, *Against Method* (1975; 3rd ed., New York: Verso, 1993). Popper proposed his ideas about falsification in opposition to earlier ideas about variability.

This does not mean that it is impossible to present hypotheses concerning the Old Testament and Israelite society that is at the center of the biblical narrative. It is legitimate to propose a hypothesis, if the premises are correctly formulated. Such hypotheses may be limited to isolated phenomena or episodes, or they may be more comprehensive theories in the shape of "heuristic" (eventually "holistic") models, which play a major role in natural science. However, if it is impossible to provide any evidence supporting a certain hypothesis, it is impossible to decide whether it is correct or false, and so it is a false argument.

For these reasons it is Alpha and Omega for traditional historical-critical analysis of the Old Testament that whatever thesis it proposes can be the subject of a falsification process. If this is not the case, the thesis is false and of no consequence for subsequent scholarship, which should concentrate on proposing new falsifiables, that is, valid hypotheses, to be the subjects of new falsification processes.

If we return to the aforementioned example of Solomon's greatness, only the Old Testament supports the idea. On this basis we present a hypothesis that there once lived a great and mighty King Solomon in Palestine, most likely in the tenth century BCE. The hypothesis is confirmed by information in the Old Testament and in its relation to the Old Testament it can be falsified (or rather verified). As far as the written source is concerned, the hypothesis is correct. But does this lead to the deduction that outside the biblical text there also was a King Solomon?

It has to be firmly stated: a text is not a historical event in the real world. A text may refer to the world outside the text, but it is primarily testimony about itself. Any information found in a text relating to the world outside the text will be valid only if it is in one way or another confirmed by other sources. Historical-critical scholarship has often made deductions from the biblical text to the world that is supposed to be reflected by this text. This is a break against another part of logic, the idea of different logical categories discussed by philosophers since the days of Aristotle. A deduction is made from one category to the next, but is it valid?

EXTERNAL EVIDENCE

In order to get closer to an answer to the question, was Solomon really this mighty king of the southern Levant in the tenth century BCE, it will be necessary to include evidence not found in the Old Testament, but contemporary with the alleged period of Solomon's kingdom or at least not too far removed from it.

Inscriptions

The most important information to look for will be *written sources*. If there appears an inscription that goes back to the tenth century BCE, the period when Solomon is supposed to have ruled, and it even mentions his name, this is information of the highest importance. In itself it does not prove that Solomon was

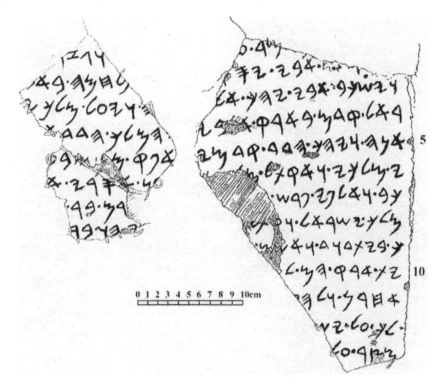

1. The Tel Dan inscription
(After A. Biran and J. Naveh, *Israel Exploration Journal,* 1995. Drawing by Ada Yardeni. Courtesy of the Nelson Glueck School of Biblical Archaeology, Hebrew Union College, Jerusalem.)

the mighty king of biblical narrative, but it makes it likely that the person of Solomon is not totally fictitious.

The fragments of one or more inscriptions found at Tel Dan in northern Palestine some fifteen years ago is a classic example of the importance of such inscriptions. This inscription, written in Aramaic, may mention the house of David, *byt dwd.* Since it was first published, scholars have been debating the date of the inscription—proposals running from about 850 BCE to about 700 BCE. They have also questioned the translation of *byt dwd.* Many scholars agree that it is really a reference to the house of David, most likely meaning the state of Judah, while other scholars question this interpretation. Finally some scholars have questioned the provenance of this inscription, which they consider to be a forgery. This is not the place to present the details of these discussions.[3] Here it is enough

3. A comprehensive review of the studies of this inscription (though not of the question of its status as a genuine artifact from the past) has been published: Halvard Hagelia, *The Tel Dan Inscription: A Critical Investigation of Recent Research on Its Palaeography and Philology,* Acta Universitatis Upsaliensis, Studia semitica Upsaliensia 22 (Uppsala University, 2006).

The Tel Dan inscription in translation[4]

Fragment A

1: [ ] . . . [   ]

2: [ ] . . . my father . . . [   ]

3: and my father died. He went to [*Is-*]

4: rael was be fore in the country of my father [   ]

5: I, and Hadad went before me [   ]

6: . . . my king and I killed . . . [*cha-*]

7: riots and thousands of horse[men   ]

8: king of Israel, and killed [   ]

9: David's house, and I put [   ]

10: their country was [   ]

11: other and . . . [   ]

12 . . . over . . . [   ]

13: siege upon [   ]

Fragments B¹ and B²

1: [ ] and cut . . . [   ]

2: [w]ar in [   ]

3: [ ] . . . and my king entered [   ]

4: [ ] Hadad made king [   ]

5: and I went fro[m] . . . [   ]

6: [ ] . . . prisoners . . . [   ]

7: [ ]rm son [   ]

8: [ ]yhw son [   ]

to stress why the inscription is important and what kind of information may be deduced from this inscription as far as a historical David is concerned. If the inscription really contains a reference to the house of David, it says that there really was a house of this name. The Hebrew word for house, *bayit*, means several things. It may of course refer to a house in the physical sense of a building, big or small, including a royal palace or a temple. It may also refer to the resi-

4. The fragments were published in Avram Biran and Joseph Naveh, "An Aramaic Stele Fragment from Tel Dan," *Israel Exploration Quarterly* 43 (1993): 81–98, and "The Tel Dan Inscription: A New Fragment," *Israel Exploration Quarterly* 45 (1995): 1–18. Most scholars want to combine the fragments in a different way by arguing that fragments B¹ and B². represent the left side of fragments A's broken lines 1–8.

dents of the house in question, for example, a family, and in a royal connection, a dynasty. In the ninth to eighth century, the date of the Tel Dan inscription, almost every single state was ruled by kings, and it was not uncommon to see such states named after the dynasties that ruled them.

The appearance of "the house of David" in the Tel Dan inscription may refer to the kingdom of Judah, but does it prove the historicity of King David? These fragments do not prove it, but if the interpretation of the text presented here is correct, it says that there once was a house—whatever the meaning of *house* in this connection—and the name of this house was "the house of David." However, if we for a moment return to proper categories, a house is not a person. Even if the house is a historical fact, this does not automatically mean that a person of the name of David is also historical. The Tel Dan inscription does not prove that David ever lived and ruled southern Palestine from Jerusalem; it is so-called circumstantial evidence for his existence. Even if this artifact is no proof of his existence, it at least makes it a little more likely that there really was a David.

In Palestine few similar inscriptions have been found, especially compared to Mesopotamia and Egypt. Even Syria and Lebanon are better provided with inscriptions. Until this day, no major royal inscription in which a king of Israel or Judah boasts of his great victories has been discovered.

In this light, scholars are grateful that there is at least a handful of inscriptions from the neighboring states that mention persons, places, and events known from the Old Testament. Assyrian and Babylonian royal inscriptions include, occasionally, important information of value for the reconstruction of Palestinian history in the Iron Age. Some of these inscriptions can be dated very precisely, because of an eclipse that occurred in 853 BCE, the year in which Ahab of Israel, according to Assyrian documents, participated in an anti-Assyrian coalition. In this way, scholars may be able to reconstruct an outline of the history of Palestine in this period, from the middle of the ninth century to the beginning of the sixth century BCE, but hardly more than that; the information does not allow for any detailed historical reconstruction. The question, then, is how to incorporate information from the Old Testament in historical analysis. Most students of the history of Israel have done that for more than a hundred years. Such incorporations of the biblical information, however, demand a careful analysis of the type of material found in the Old Testament and the kind of information this source may include.

The Babylonian record of the capture of Jerusalem provides an example of the dilemma created by external evidence in combination with biblical information. According to the Old Testament, Nebuchadnezzar the king of Babylon conquered Jerusalem two times. The Babylonian Chronicle proves the first conquest, in the seventh year of Nebuchadnezzar, 597 BCE, to be a historical fact. The sad fact is, however, that this chronicle stops only three years later in 594 BCE and therefore makes no reference to the second conquest, which is supposed, because of biblical information, to have taken place in 587 BCE. We are informed by the Old Testament that Nebuchadnezzar took the city two times, but the second conquest cannot be verified from any external source. Although it is more than likely

Two accounts of the capure of Jerusalem

The Babylonian Chronicle[5]	2 Kings 24:10–17
In the seventh year in the month of Kislev, the King of Akkad mustered his army and went to Hattiland. He laid siege on the city of Jerusalem. In the month of Addar, on the second day he captured the city and caught the king. He placed a king after his own heart on the throne and received a heavy tribute from it and brought it to Babylon.	At that time the servants of King Nebuchadnezzar of Babylon came up to Jerusalem, and the city was besieged. [11] King Nebuchadnezzar of Babylon came to the city, while his servants were besieging it; [12] King Jehoiachin of Judah gave himself up to the king of Babylon, himself, his mother, his servants, his officers, and his palace officials. The king of Babylon took him prisoner in the eighth year of his reign.

[13] He carried off all the treasures of the house of the LORD, and the treasures of the king's house; he cut in pieces all the vessels of gold in the temple of the LORD, which King Solomon of Israel had made, all this as the LORD had foretold. [14] He carried away all Jerusalem, all the officials, all the warriors, ten thousand captives, all the artisans and the smiths; no one remained, except the poorest people of the land. [15] He carried away Jehoiachin to Babylon; the king's mother, the king's wives, his officials, and the elite of the land, he took into captivity from Jerusalem to Babylon. [16] The king of Babylon brought captive to Babylon all the men of valor, seven thousand, the artisans and the smiths, one thousand, all of them strong and fit for war. [17] The king of Babylon made Mattaniah, Jehoiachin's uncle, king in his place, and changed his name to Zedekiah. |

that the second capture of Jerusalem really took place and resulted in the destruction of the city and its temple, only the Old Testament includes references to this second capture. Essentially the second conquest is no more than an assertion made by the authors of the biblical narrative.

Also when we turn to the information about the events of 597 BCE, there is not complete harmony between the two main sources. This may indicate that not all information in the biblical version is absolutely reliable, or that the author of

---

5. Translated after the text in D. J. Wiseman, *Chronicles of Chaldaean Kings (626–556 B.C.) in the British Museum* (London: British Museum, 1956). The passage about Jerusalem can be found on pp. 72–73.

Two accounts of the siege of Jerusalem

The Annals of Sennacherib	2 Kings 18:13–16
Hezekiah of Judah did not submit to my yoke, and I laid siege on 46 of his strong cities surrounded by walls, and the many villages surrounding them. I captured all of them by stamped rams on which pile drives were brought close to the walls, while at the same time the infantry attacking by using mining and sapper's work. 200,150 people were forced out of them, young and old, men and women, as well as an innumerable amount of horses, mules, donkeys, camels, and cattle and I made of it my booty. I made Hezekiah a prisoner in Jerusalem, his royal residence, like a bird in a cage. I surrounded him with earthwork in order to catch any person who came out of the gate of the city . . . Hezekiah was overwhelmed by the awe-inspiring might of my rulership, and his soldiers, both ordinary soldiers and his elite force, abandoned him, and later he sent to me in Nineveh, my city of residence, 30 talents of gold, 800 talents of silver, precious stones, antimony, big red stones, beds and arm chairs inlaid with ivory, elephant hides, ebony, and all kinds of precious items, but also his daughters, concubines, and women musicians. He also sent his personal herald to bring this tribute and to throw himself into the dust before me like a slave.	In the fourteenth year of King Hezekiah, King Sennacherib of Assyria came up against all the fortified cities of Judah and captured them. [14] King Hezekiah of Judah sent to the king of Assyria at Lachish, saying, "I have done wrong; withdraw from me; whatever you impose on me I will bear." The king of Assyria demanded of King Hezekiah of Judah three hundred talents of silver and thirty talents of gold. [15] Hezekiah gave him all the silver that was found in the house of the LORD and in the treasuries of the king's house. [16] At that time Hezekiah stripped the gold from the doors of the temple of the LORD, and from the doorposts that King Hezekiah of Judah had overlaid and gave it to the king of Assyria.

the Babylonian Chronicle did not include information that in his eyes was unimportant. Even when there are external written sources, the scholar has to analyze carefully all the documents at his disposal. It is not recommended that one simply supplement the external source with information from the Old Testament.

The story of Sennacherib's siege of Jerusalem in 701 BCE provides a fine example of biblical information that is immediately comparable to an external source. We have information about the campaign of Sennacherib against Hezekiah of Judah from Sennacherib's own annals, composed almost immediately after the king's return to Assyria, and from the Old Testament in 2 Kings 18:13–19:37 and in Isaiah 36–37, which is almost identical to the version in 2 Kings. A comparison between the two sources may be useful, although in this case, the comparison should be limited to the factual information in 2 Kings 18:13–16 and Sennacherib's annals.

Without any doubt, both documents refer to the same event. Sennacherib the king of Assyria attacked Hezekiah and conquered and destroyed all his cities, apart from Jerusalem, which was for some reason spared. The two documents include a fair amount of minor differences. Thus it is important to Sennacherib to emphasize that the tribute from Judah was sent on to Nineveh, Assyria's capital. In 2 Kings 18:14–16 it is recorded that Hezekiah paid the tribute on the spot. The size of the tribute is also different. According to 2 Kings, Hezekiah got a better deal than that recorded by his Assyrian counterpart. There is no reason to doubt that Sennacherib really destroyed Hezekiah's kingdom from one end to the other and was proud of his deed. Archaeologists found on the wall of Sennacherib's palace a series of pictorial presentations of Sennacherib's siege on Lachish, which at the time was the largest city in Hezekiah's possession. The information is confirmed by modern excavations at Lachish.

In this case the short note in 2 Kings 18:13–16 must be reckoned a historical source as far as the events of 701 BCE are concerned. It is possible to compare this source with external evidence that confirms the basic historicity of the biblical information. It must be concluded on this basis that external evidence in the form of inscriptions—and in the case of Sennacherib also pictorial information—may prove certain information in the Old Testament to be historical. The case of 701 BCE also proves that there are limits to the kind of information that may be confirmed by external evidence.

According to 2 Kings 18:16, Hezekiah paid his tribute without any delay, but Sennacherib claims that it was delivered only after he had returned to Nineveh. Which document tells the truth? Sennacherib's version finds support in the ensuing events as related by the Old Testament. According to 2 Kings, the king of Assyria received the tribute at an early stage of the campaign. In spite of this he continued to lay siege to Jerusalem. Before the gate of Jerusalem the Assyrian general gave a pep talk to the Judeans in Hebrew ("Judahite"), recommending capitulation as the clearest way to escape total extinction. Impressed by this speech, King Hezekiah prayed to his God and promised to better his ways. Several things happened. Thus the king of Nubia attacked the Assyrians. The prophet Isaiah was activated and supported in his prophecies Hezekiah's cause. In the end, Yahweh interfered in the cause of history and had his angel kill 185,000 Assyrians in the camp during the night (2 Kgs. 19:35). After this disaster Sennacherib returned to Nineveh. Here he was killed by his sons twelve years later (2 Kgs. 19:37).

Although some of the information in the second part of the biblical narrative about Sennacherib's campaign is confirmed by other evidence, such as the note about the death of the Assyrian king, this narrative is mostly made up by legendary embellishments and ends with a miracle that saves Jerusalem. Many scholars have tried to harmonize this narrative with Assyrian references. But that is impossible without willful changes of both sets of documents. Nothing indicates that any disaster struck the Assyrian army as recorded by 2 Kings 19:35. Sennacherib was definitely not defeated by anybody—not even God himself—in Palestine in the year of 701 BCE.

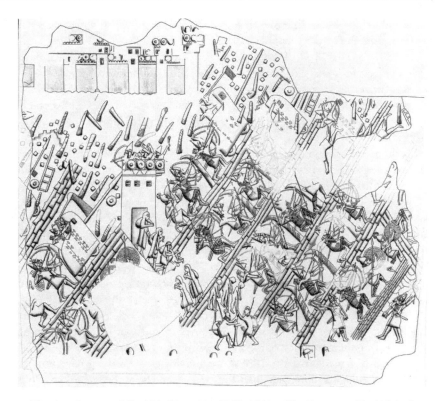

2. The Assyrians attack Lachish (From David Ussishkin, *The Conquest of Lachish by Sennacherib* [Tel Aviv: Tel Aviv University, 1982]. Courtesy of the Institute of Archaeology, Tel Aviv University.)

Archaeological "External Evidence"

The episode of Sennacherib's campaign to the west in 701 BCE is especially important because it demonstrates how important external evidence really is, even if we are no longer talking about written documents. Since the end of the nineteenth century, Palestine has been the center of perhaps the most intensive excavation campaign ever conducted in any part of the world. Hundreds of archaeological expeditions have literally dug through the country from one end to the other.

Archaeological activity in the Middle East did not begin in Palestine but in Mesopotamia and Egypt, both providing ample opportunities for the most spectacular discoveries. The archaeologist only had to put his hand into the sand, so to speak, and marvelous pieces of art, not to say inscriptions, turned up almost by themselves. In Palestine archaeological interest concentrated around Jerusalem, the central scene of archaeological activity since the nineteenth century. The end of the nineteenth century saw general archaeological interest spreading from Egypt especially to Palestine, and soon German as well as British expeditions dug at Megiddo in northern Palestine, at Jericho in the Jordan Valley, and at Gezer in western Palestine, among many other sites.

During the First World War, these activities were temporarily stopped. Now Palestine became a scene of warfare between the British and the Turks, for several centuries the masters of the Middle East. After the war, archaeological activities started again on an even grander scale, since now Palestine had become a part of the British mandate under the League of Nations. American archaeologists also now began serious excavations. Among the many spectacular excavations from this period, we may mention the American and later British at Samaria, the British in Jericho, the French at Ai, the American at Megiddo and Tell Beit Mirsim (identified as biblical Debir), and the British at Lachish. Troubles related to the insurrection of the Palestinian Arabs against the mandate's power in the middle of the 1930s (the so-called "first intifada"), leading among other things to the murder of the leader of the Lachish excavations; the outbreak of the Second World War and Jewish rebellion against the British after the war; and the Israeli war of independence in 1948–49 all effectively put an end to this excavation activity. In the early 1950s excavations started again, now dominated by Israeli archaeologists.

It would be a hopeless project to try to list all the excavations conducted during the last fifty years. However, some ought to be included in a short list. Among the more important excavations we find the British excavations in Jericho in the 1950s and in Jerusalem in the 1960s, methodologically breaking new ground. Israeli archaeologists soon made their appearance, and from the end of the 1950s conducted by far the most extensive campaign ever at Hazor in northern Israel. Other important Israeli excavations are Beersheba in the 1960s and 1970s, Lachish in the 1980s, and Beth-shan, Hazor, and Megiddo in the 1990s and in the early years of the third millennium. American archaeologists were active at Shechem and Gezer in the 1960s and in the beginning of the 1970s. Lately, American archaeologists have been digging at Ekron and Ashkelon.

What kind of archaeology are we talking about in this connection? The technical part of archaeology is not intended in this question, for during the twentieth century archaeologists developed and refined their methodology into a highly technical science. However, just as important are the ideological motives directing the search of the archaeologists, ideologies that cannot be separated from the institutions paying for the excavations. Archaeology is a costly enterprise, and there is never enough money. It is exceptional if public funding is enough to pay for a major archaeological excavation. In recent years, only Israeli archaeologists have had access to extensive public funding, and even this is not enough. Most archaeologists from the United States and Europe are forced to obtain financial support from private institutions and sponsors, although, to be honest, American sponsors have generally been more willing to pay than European ones.

Who has paid for the excavations? When private persons are involved, they normally will have a personal interest in the results of archaeological activity, and they expect the archaeologists to bring home artifacts and knowledge that may be of interest to themselves and the groups they represent. When archaeological excavations in Palestine (but also the excavations in the nineteenth century in Mesopotamia and Egypt) are involved, the most treasured fruit of such expeditions are items that would throw some light on biblical issues, primarily the Old Testament, and to a lesser degree the New Testament.

The general intellectual orientation of the nineteenth century also involved archaeology. The nineteenth century centered on a positivistic interest in history, and it was in this period that the principles of historical-critical biblical scholarship were formulated. Scholars discussed the historical information in the Old Testament and had to make clear sometimes that the historical reality was not always what one found on the pages of the Old Testament. In the eyes of many believing people, this outcome of archaeological and historical activities was most disturbing, especially because they were touched by the general intellectual orientation of their own time, which had changed the biblical story to history, and by history they meant *real* history—as it really was.

The appearance of Christian fundamentalism at the end of the nineteenth and in the beginning of the twentieth century originated in this intellectual orientation toward the historical correctness of the Old Testament historical narrative.[6] Fundamentalism—in recent time more neutrally and perhaps more correctly called evangelicalism—has since its beginning fostered the idea that the Bible is always right. This implies that whenever historical-critical scholarship is at odds with biblical information, the Bible must, as the true word of God (verbal inspiration is a precondition of fundamentalist belief), always be right, because God makes no mistakes.[7]

At first, Christianity inspired by fundamentalism saw archaeological activity in the Middle East in the nineteenth century as a major contribution to the forwarding of biblical truth. It seemed that archaeology proved what the historians were believed to have disproved. The Bible was—in spite of numerous historical analyses based on controversial source criticism—true, and the historians had only started an unending conflict involving as their adversary the testimony of the biblical text. A public confronted for the first time with pictorial depictions like the Assyrian drawings of Sennacherib's siege of Lachish must think, Yes, here we really see how it was. The Bible is after all right!

As a consequence it would be correct to classify most archaeological activity in Palestine as *biblical archaeology*. Archaeology was not considered to be an independent discipline that had its own rules. Archaeologists dug with the spade in one hand and the Bible in the other, as it is often argued, by some with pride, by

---

6. Christian fundamentalism started among Presbyterian theologians at Princeton Theological Seminary in the United States at the beginning of the twentieth century and was named after the movement's publication, *The Fundamentals*, which appeared between 1910 and 1915.

7. It is doubtful that the biblical authors would all agree with this dictum. Somehow, the God who brought the flood because he found humankind evil, had to realize that he made a blunder when after the flood he stated that humankind is and will remain evil. A polemical but still very readable account of fundamentalism can be found in James Barr, *Fundamentalism* (London: SCM, 1977).

others with disgust.[8] Private funding has often depended on the ability of the archaeologist to provide information likely to confirm biblical truth.

American biblical archaeology has, with William Foxwell Albright as its most important representative, been outspoken in its programmatic defense of the motives behind its excavations. It was the task of biblical archaeology to provide an alternative to the then-dominant German school of Old Testament historical-critical scholarship, which was, according to Albright and his students, too speculative if not destructive. The way to counter German source criticism was by providing external evidence in support of the biblical version over against its critics among the historians—mostly revisionists, if not nihilists.

The biblical archaeologists had no problem finding external evidence, because that was what they were looking for. Many a layperson is convinced that archaeology excavating real items found in the ground must be an exact science. However, any person with a little field experience knows that this is hardly the case. Whatever the archaeologist discovers while digging is in itself a "fact," but this "fact" does not necessarily deliver its information by itself. Archaeological facts begin to speak only when first the archaeologist and subsequently other scholars try to understand and explain the meaning of the discovery. The results of archaeology are always *results that have been interpreted;* they are never *das Ding-an-sich,* in Kant's famous expression. If the archaeologists want to make an impression on their pious sponsors, or if they are themselves members of a conservative religious community—as was the case with Albright and many of his students—their interpretation of their findings will most likely tend to be conservative and believed to support biblical historiography.

A survey of the history of the archaeology of Palestine during the last century will show that more often than not archaeological interpretation has had a certain conservative flavor. Many discoveries have been seen as proving the Bible is right, after all, and if doubts arise and new discoveries seem to discredit the historical truth of biblical historiography, the tendency has invariably been to support the Bible against archaeology. This tendency is found not only among archaeologists from North America, but also among Israeli as well as British and French archaeologists.

The last few decades show a change of attitude with the appearance of a number of archaeological schools. Some of these are very conscious of the problems created by the link between biblical studies and archaeology. Instead, they argue in favor of archaeology as an independent discipline that has to escape the entanglement of biblical notions and ideas. Only an independent archaeological discipline will be able to produce results that are useful for historians in their reconstruction of the ancient past.

This new orientation is undoubtedly correct. The mixing of archaeology and Bible in the traditional cocktail called biblical archaeology represents a clas-

---

8. Among the laity, literature best classified as fundamentalistically inspired, popular science has always been admired. The most famous example of this genre may still be Werner Keller, *The Bible as History* (1955, with many reprints—the book boasts of having sold more than 10,000,000 copies).

sic logical problem: mixing different categories introduced to confirm each other. It is, however, a difficult task to separate the Bible from archaeology. The example of the North American biblical scholar and archaeologist William G. Dever is telling. Dever has in many publications advocated the separation of biblical studies from archaeology, but at the same time he has ended up as a defender of a very traditional, if not conservative, historical-critical reading of the Old Testament.[9]

If archaeological procedure is strictly followed—and there are many examples that this is actually on the agenda of many archaeologists—archaeology may in the future provide much valuable information of great help to the student of the history of this part of the world. In this way, archaeology may also pave the way for a better understanding of the biblical text and its relationship to the real history of Palestine in ancient times. Archaeology has developed quite a bit, from being mere treasure hunting to serving as a partner in the reconstruction of cultures and participant in a discourse also shared by professional historians and social anthropologists. This assembly of disciplines creates a forum for the interpretation of ancient cultures and allows for every kind of material pertinent to ancient society to be combined into an organic combination, allowing the scholar to study and understand the processes at work in these societies. It will be possible, to some degree, to write a history of these cultures, although it will never result in a detailed reconstruction. Such historical reconstruction is possible only if we have ample documentation in the form of written sources properly understood.

This is not to suggest that a century of archaeological activity in Palestine is of no value—although it has little to offer the biblical scholar who asks for support for the biblical historiography. The archaeologist has always been part of a process of trial and error, learning successively from its mistakes as it progresses. When the archaeologist leaves his or her field of excavation, it is in principle a wasteland, utterly destroyed. It is destruction for no reason, as the late Kathleen Kenyon maintained, if it is impossible to use the material in a reconstruction of ancient society because the technique was insufficient. Wrong technology has resulted in incorrect dating of even major constructions that have covered many hundreds of years. Thus a certain dominant structure belonging to the defense works of ancient Jerusalem (the so-called Macalister's tower) was, at the beginning, dated to the second century BCE. More recent reinterpretation has moved the date back to the Late Bronze Age or the Early Iron Age.

A final overview of archaeological activity that combines archaeology with historical-critical scholarship shows that in spite of their definite biblical orientation, the archaeologists have provided an arsenal of arguments that, taken together, point to a reconstruction of the history of Palestine in ancient times that is very different from the proposal made by biblical authors.

---

9. As illustrated in his *What Did the Biblical Writers Know and When Did They Know It? What Archaeology Can Tell Us about the Reality of Ancient Israel* (Grand Rapids: Eerdmans, 2001).

HISTORICAL CRITICISM

It has already been said that until recently biblical historians preferred to dismiss theoretical discussions. These historians were, on the one hand, entangled in the net of the hermeneutical circle, "imprisoned" by an assertion from which they found no escape—as if this lack of reflection could act as an excuse for remaining within a scholarly position that is logically untenable. On the other hand they were, because of their immanent positivism, in no doubt that they would be able to penetrate the biblical narratives by applying source criticism and get back to the real world, the world of ancient Israel reflected by the texts of the Old Testament. Maybe they should have paid more attention to Plato, more precisely, to his story of the cave, in the fifth book of *The State*. In this cave the inhabitants' only impression of reality outside the cave is the shadows on the wall. If they had read and understood this parable, they would have realized that historical reality will never be able to speak for itself. Historical reality will always appear in the form of a text, a story created by modern historians, who may in their telling of the story pay attention to ancient documents and archaeological discoveries.

Even if we apply the "logical" system created by traditional historical-critical scholarship, we should understand that it contains so many contradictions that the hermeneutic alone because of this must break down. The following paragraphs have to address this set of problems, although the settlement with the historical-critical paradigm had to start from within the paradigm itself. Scholars who, say, thirty years ago, wanted to dismiss the historical-critical paradigm without entering a serious dialogue with its representatives were simply ignored, although in retrospect they might have been right.[10]

In some ways the following overview of past scholarship may seem superfluous. After all, this should be "history," a thing of the past. Perhaps, however, readers will understand the motivation for the conflict that tore Old Testament scholarship apart, and how it happened. The survey will begin with the period of the patriarchs and continue to postexilic times. This is the logical way of handling the topic, not only because it follows the narrative layout found in the Old Testament historical books, but also because the criticism started with the patriarchs and step by step moved down to the Persian and even the Hellenistic period.

The Time of the Patriarchs

It has for a long time been a source of disbelief how even serious historians continue to speak about the time of the patriarchs as though it represented a historical stage in the development of ancient Israel. However, even today it is not

---

10. The clearest example is the previously mentioned sad story of the German scholar Bernd Jørg Diebner, who in splendid and self-inflicted isolation—in spite of his publishing of the *Dielheimer Blätter zum Alten Testament*—formulated scores of ideas that many times showed the fallacy of historical-critical research. Although he was nominated close to his retirement as honorary professor at

uncommon to find support for the idea that the patriarchs are historical persons, although the historians may paraphrase the biblical narrative presenting the patriarchs as representing ethnic groups that they imagine to have existed in Palestine in prehistoric times.

Thus the unquestionably most influential history of Israel in North America in the last century, written by John Bright,[11] is introduced by an extensive chapter about the age of the patriarchs. Bright opens with a description of the historical situation of the patriarchs and the Middle Bronze Age (according to Bright 2000–1750 BCE) and follows it up with a review of biblical traditions, in order to make it clear that these traditions include historical information. Now that he has "established" that the patriarchs really lived and belonged to the earliest history of Israel, Bright proceeds to place these biblical figures within the compass of the ancient Near East, which he has in fact just constructed. Now he has no problem turning the biblical information into real history and so describes the patriarchs as individual persons and ancestors to ethnic groups whose early history is reflected by the patriarchal narratives.

The belief that there really existed such a period of the patriarchs was also found outside of North America. The conservative German history of Israel written by Siegfried Herrmann includes a less ambitious survey of the history and time of the patriarchs.[12] Herrmann nevertheless defends a position very close to that of John Bright. The real defense of historicity was, however, published by the leading French biblical scholar Roland de Vaux in his comprehensive but unfinished history of Israel.[13] De Vaux considers the role of the patriarchs as decisive for the development of later Israelite-Jewish identity.

The procedure followed by these scholars was discredited more than a hundred years ago by the then-leading German historian of the ancient world, Eduard Meyer (1855–1930). Meyer, who without doubt was one of the most learned people of his time, wrote a history of the ancient world in several volumes.[14] In connection with his studies of the ancient Near East, Meyer also contributed to the study of Israelite history. When he studied the contributions by his colleagues in biblical studies, he had to denounce much of what they had written as meaningless (although he was not able to fully liberate himself from their procedures):

the University of Heidelberg, his criticism was only occasionally discussed by other German scholars. Outside of Germany, especially in the Anglo-Saxon world, he was virtually unknown—not least because of language problems.

11. John Bright, *A History of Israel* (1959; 4th ed., Louisville: Westminster John Knox, 2000). On its origin, see Burke O. Long, *Planting and Reaping Albright: Politics, Ideology, and Interpreting the Bible* (University Park: Pennsylvania State University, 1997), 55–59.

12. Siegfried Herrmann, *Geschichte Israels in alttestamentlicher Zeit* (Munich: Chr. Kaiser, 1973); ET, *A History of Israel in Old Testament Times* (Philadelphia: Fortress, 1981).

13. Roland de Vaux, *Histoire ancienne d'Israël des origines à l'installation en Canaan* (Paris: Gabalda, 1971); ET, *The Early History of Israel* (Philadelphia: Westminster, 1978]).

14. Eduard Meyer, *Geschichte des Altertums*, 5 vols. (1884–1902; many reprints; no ET).

> Besides, then and now I regard every endeavor to be futile and beyond dis-
> pute, which tries to answer these questions or even to translate the Israelite
> sagas into history according to widespread practice. Generally, they deliber-
> ately skip—without considering how fantastic the enterprise is—half a mil-
> lennium and deal with the narratives as suitable historical sources,
> irrespective of their youth and after they have brushed them up by ratio-
> nalistic means. They even consider these sources to be the imperturbable
> basis of Israel's nationality and religion.[15]

Meyer was right. It will be difficult to find another way of describing the studies of the patriarchs by Bright and de Vaux as anything except rather naive rationalistic paraphrases of the biblical patriarchal narratives. Although the procedure
chosen by Bright and de Vaux might seem reasonable—that is, to begin with the
historical environment of the patriarchs and in this way to create a historical
background for these stories, and then to place the patriarchs as historical characters within this scenario—this is not a legitimate scientific approach. The biblical narratives about the patriarchs, at least in the form in which they have been
transmitted to modern readers, are more than a thousand years younger than the
age of the patriarchs. To use the patriarchal narratives as historical sources, even
after a source-critical analysis that distinguishes between "story" and "residue" (to
use two of Droysen's terms), is—as maintained by Meyer—a foolhardy enterprise. The equivalent would be to use Greek legend or the Homeric poems as
sources for the history of the Bronze Age in classical studies or, in a Scandinavian
context, to accept Saxo's description of Frode the Peacemaker (Fredegod) as a useful source for Danish history in, say, the seventh or eighth century CE.

Apart from some conservative authors, no serious Old Testament scholar will
nowadays accept the age of the patriarchs as a historical period. German scholarship understood that as long as two hundred years ago,[16] and the point was
clearly made by Martin Noth, who placed the tradition of the patriarchs among
the stories from the past treasured at the amphictyony, the sacral league of the
Israelite tribes in the period of the judges. In a North American context, the
deadly blow to the idea of a historical patriarchal age was delivered by two scholars, Thomas L. Thompson and John Van Seters, who in two monographs published almost at the same time, in 1974 and 1975, attacked the historicity of the
patriarchs from two different angles, Thompson mostly on the basis of a historical analysis, and Van Seters mostly because of a literary analysis.[17] These two
scholars showed that Bright's method for pleading the historicity of the patriarchs
could at best be called a "bluff." The patriarchs cannot be placed within a defi-

---

15. Eduard Meyer, *Die Israeliten und ihre Nachbarstämme. Alttestamentliche Untersuchungen* (Halle,
1905; reprint, Darmstadt: Wissenschaftliche Buchgesellschaft, 1967), 50. Author's translation.

16. See the marvelous introduction by Wilhelm Martin Lebrecht de Wette, *Beiträge zur Einleitung in das Alte Testament* (Halle: Bey Schimmelpfennig, 1806–7).

17. Thomas L. Thompson, *The Historicity of the Patriarchal Narratives: The Quest for the Historical Abraham,* BZAW 133 (Berlin: de Gruyter, 1974); John Van Seters, *Abraham in History and Tradition* (New Haven, CT: Yale University, 1975).

nite historical context. The image created of the ancient Near East at the beginning of the second millennium by some conservative scholars never existed. It is cobbled together by uniting cultural phenomena from around two thousand years of development in the ancient Near East. Van Seters proceeds to show that the patriarchal narratives are not old documents or "residues." The patriarchal narratives should be dated to the exilic period, in the middle of the first millennium. There is no need for a long tradition history preceding the reduction of these narratives into writing.

In light of these two studies of the patriarchs, it is difficult to find critical biblical scholars who still "believe in the patriarchs." Scholars are not normally ready just to give up an old and obsolete thesis. More often they decide to moderate the thesis that it may survive, if need be, in a new disguise.

Such a remolded hypothesis may declare that although the patriarchs themselves are not historical persons, the stories about them nevertheless include information about Israel's oldest history in Palestine, perhaps between 1250 and 1000 BCE. This sometimes happens in the study of Israelite religion, when the patriarchal narratives are supposed to present information about private religion in ancient Israel, as happens, for example, in the German Old Testament scholar Rainer Albertz's *History of Israelite Religion*.[18]

The problem is the same as before. It is impossible to place the information about religion and society in patriarchal narratives within a certain period. We find information belonging to very different periods, and much that cannot be dated at all. From a logical point of view, scholars have for generations, in order to deduct relevant information from the patriarchal narratives, utilized two important criteria: the terminus a quo and the terminus ad quem. These two concepts are of fundamental importance for all historical analysis. The terminus a quo refers to the first time a certain phenomenon occurs but says nothing about the period it spans. The terminus ad quem, on the other hand, refers to the last occurrence of a certain phenomenon but says nothing about how old it is. Babylonian cuneiform writing seems to have come into being about 3000 BCE or shortly before. A document written in cuneiform cannot be older than the earliest occurrence of this system of writing. But it cannot be younger than the second century CE, the time from which the youngest specimens of tablets written in cuneiform derive. A certain clay tablet including cuneiform writing may therefore be dated initially to between 3000 BCE and 200 CE. Then it is possible to use a series of methods and criteria to calibrate this date more precisely.

The information about culture and religion within the patriarchal narratives in Genesis covers a very long period of time. The calibration of each single element within this data set points to very different times. It is impossible to point to a certain time that fits everything, except the moment when these narratives were written down. Thus there is no reason to date the information about patriarchal

---

18. Albertz, *A History of Israelite Religion*. See also his *Persönliche Frömmigkeit und offizielle Religion. Religionsinterner Pluralismus in Israel und Babylon* (1978; reprint, Atlanta: SBL, 2005).

religion to the earliest possible moment of Israel's history. If these narratives do not belong to the period 1250–1000 BCE, but, rather, about 500 BCE, as argued by Martin Noth, it would be more appropriate to talk about these narratives reflecting a kind of religion known in the middle of the first millennium BCE, but also in the following centuries.[19]

Exodus and the Wilderness

When we move from the patriarchal narratives to the period of the exodus and the sojourn of the Israelites in the desert, we move down in biblical time. The matter remains the same. Are we speaking of a historical period or about narratives about the past that do not have a historical background? Did this exodus out of Egypt ever happen, and did Moses ever establish a meeting between Israel and its God on Mount Sinai in the middle of the peninsula carrying the same name?

The story in the Old Testament of all of Israel numbering several million people who left Egypt was already brought into disrepute by the German scholars of the Enlightenment Herrmann Samuel Reimarus (1694–1768) and his communicator Gotthold Ephraim Lessing (1729–81), who in a pointed way made it clear that according to the number presented by the Old Testament, the first Israelites would have entered Canaan a long time before the last Israelites had left Egypt, even if they marched in ranks of six persons each. This had scholarly consequences, as it has often been argued that although the exodus did not involve millions of people, it still happened, with not nearly as many persons involved. In the end it became popular to mean that only a few persons were engaged in these events.

Apart from the argument that from a numerical point of view the exodus, as described by the Old Testament, is impossible, the total number of people living in Egypt in ancient times hardly surpassed one million. From a historical-critical angle, many critical scholars considered the story about the exodus and the wilderness to belong to the sacred traditions of the tribal league. These stories should not be considered a historical source but were, in the language of Droysen, a narrative—*Bericht*. Thus many scholars were of the opinion that it was hardly worth the effort to study the historical side of the exodus and wilderness traditions. Martin Noth's intelligent analysis of the figure of Moses and his relations to the traditions of the Pentateuch should be heard in this connection: we do not have any real information about Moses, apart from the fact that he may have existed and was buried somewhere east of the Jordan River.[20]

Few other texts in the Old Testament have been so intensively discussed. The reason is the status of the exodus as a foundation myth. Sometimes it is argued that Moses is so important for the development of Israelite religion that he must

19. In his *Der Gott der Väter*, Albrecht Alt used Nabataean texts from the first and second century CE as illustrations of his idea of the patriarchal religion.

20. Martin Noth, *Überlieferungsgeschichte des Pentateuch* (Stuttgart: W. Kohlhammer, 1948), 172–91.

have lived, and if there never was a Moses, ancient historiographers would have had to invent him. The answer is of course, And so they did![21]

As a consequence, and in order to escape from a multitude of discussions of historical substance, it would be more appropriate to concentrate on the relations of the exodus narrative to the history of Egypt. An event of this scale should be reflected in Egyptian tradition about the time when the exodus, according to the scholars who still believe in its historicity, took place, that is, the second half of the second millennium BCE. The traditions of Israel in the desert hardly present a promising starting point for historical investigations. Israel's stay in the desert is placed, so to speak, outside of space and time. The desert is essentially a place where nothing happens and nothing changes.

We therefore leave the investigation to Egyptologists, to see how they evaluate the tradition about Israel's exodus from Egypt. In connection with the exodus (according to the biblical narrative), a pharaoh perished together with his army. The history of Egypt is subdivided into three great periods; the Old Kingdom (third millennium BCE), the Middle Kingdom (the beginning of the second millennium BCE), and the New Kingdom (the end of the second millennium BCE). Between these kingdoms we find so-called intermediary periods, infested with political and social troubles. The New Kingdom was succeeded by a long period of decline that never ended, although the culture of ancient Egypt persisted and inspired awe a long time after the Persians, and following them the Greeks and the Romans, had conquered the country.

According to Egyptian tradition, the first intermediary period led to social unrest that turned the structure of society upside down. The slave became master, and the master became slave. The Middle Kingdom represented—according to later tradition—a return to normalcy. The Middle Kingdom succumbed to the massive invasion of the Hyksos people—this is at least what later Egyptian tradition suggests—from Asia, who invaded northern Egypt and became its master. The New Kingdom reestablished the greatness of Egypt. First and most important, the pharaohs destroyed the Hyksos rule in northern Egypt and expelled them to Asia. Thereafter Egypt invaded Asia and created an empire that at its greatest extent included all territories between Egypt and the Euphrates. For some centuries the Egyptians were the master of the "world," until renewed unrest and more invasions led to a reduction of the reign of the pharaohs and later to the removal of the indigenous dynasties of pharaohs, who were replaced by foreign rulers.

It may be discussed how far this history coincides with reality. This, however, is in this connection not very important. Here the interesting question is, is there in Egyptian documents of the New Kingdom any reference to anything that may be identified at least with a core tradition about the exodus of the Israelites? The Old Testament considers the exodus a great victory for Israel and a fearful defeat of Egypt, whose pharaoh perished in the Sea of Reeds together with his army. It

---

21. Remembering the Italian adage: *Si non è vero, è ben trovato*; If it is not true, it is an excellent invention.

is hardly to be expected that the Egyptian annalists would invest much interest in an event like this. Most official Egyptian inscriptions from this period celebrate the great victories of pharaoh. Defeats were "forgotten," and should such unhappy backlashes ever occur, they were more often than not transformed into great victories.[22] The decisive argument against the historicity of the exodus is not that no official Egyptian source mentions it; this was hardly to be expected. The decisive argument is that an exodus on the scale approaching the biblical description of the event would have had serious consequences for Egyptian society at large.

The decisive argument is that the exodus as described in the Old Testament does not fit any historical scenario from the period supposed to have witnessed the exodus. This period is normally assumed to be the New Kingdom, between about 1539 and 1075 BCE. It is still debated when it began and when it ended. Ramesses II's long reign (ca. 1278–1213 BCE) has especially attracted the interest of scholars, not only because he is the most spectacular pharaoh of this period—his enormous monuments litter the Egyptian landscape—but especially because an inscription from the time of his successor Merneptah (ca. 1213–1204 BCE) mentions an Israel in Palestine beaten and destroyed by this pharaoh. Immediately after its publication,[23] Old Testament scholars jumped to the conclusion that we here have a date of the Israelite migration into Palestine, which must logically have happened before Merneptah defeated Israel in Palestine. Given that the Old Testament mentions a long stay of the Israelites in the desert after the exodus, this event belongs to the reign of Ramesses II.

The problem is only that Ramesses II did not find his grave at the bottom of the Sea of Reeds, but in the National Museum in Cairo, where his mummy, discovered more than a hundred years ago in southern Egypt, is kept together with most of the mummies of the pharaohs of the New Kingdom. Ramesses II, who reestablished the grandeur of Egypt after a short period of decline about 1300 BCE, is probably the least likely pharaoh to play the role of opponent of Moses in connection with the flight of the Israelites from Egypt.

No other period of the New Kingdom is likely to encompass an event on the scale of the biblical exodus, apart from the earliest times, when Egyptian rulers based in Thebes in southern Egypt fought the Hyksos kings residing in the delta of the Nile and expelled them. Nobody advocating the historicity of the exodus will date it as early as that, that is, in the middle of the sixteenth century BCE.

22. Paradigmatic is the Egyptian way of handling the battle at Kadesh about 1275 BCE. There are pictorial reports, as well triumphant inscriptions, showing this great victory of Pharaoh over the Hittites. However, the Hittites were not really convinced that they had experienced a major defeat. Later Hittite tradition was even able to make fun of the Egyptian insistence on the major feats of their victorious Pharaoh. On this battle, see K. A. Kitchen, "Pharaoh Ramesses II and His Times," in J. J. Sasson, ed., *Civilizations of the Ancient Near East* (New York: Scribner's, 1995), 2:763–74. See also Kitchen's translations of the Egyptian version in *COS* 2:32–40. On the Hittite reception, see Mario Liverani, "Hattushili alle prese con la propaganda ramesside," *Orientalia* NS 59 (1990): 207–17.

23. W. Spiegelberg, "Der Siegeshymnus des Merneptah auf der Flinders-Petrie Stele," *Zeitschrift für Ägyptologie* 34 (1896): 1–25.

From Merneptah's victory stele[24]

> The (foreign) chieftains lie prostrate, saying "peace." Not one lifts his head among the Nine Bows.
>
> Libya is captured, while Hatti is pacified.
>
> Canaan is plundered, Ashkelon is carried off, and Gezer is captured.
>
> Yenoam is made into non-existence; Israel is wasted, its seed is not; and Hurru is become a widow because of Egypt.
>
> All lands united themselves in peace. Those who went about were subdued by the king of Upper and Lower Egypt . . . Merneptah

Most important is the lack of reference to Israel in any source predating Merneptah's inscription from the end of the fourteenth century BCE. Thus the Amarna letters, a collection of about 350 clay tablets containing correspondence between the court of pharaoh and foreign princes—many of them from Palestine—between about 1350 and 1335,[25] includes no reference to the presence of an Israel in Palestine in this period, and the information in these letters about political and social conditions does not point to the presence of a major group of tribes united in a kind of tribal league.

The conclusion must be that the exodus is most likely legendary, constructed by Old Testament historiographers in order to create a "national" foundation myth for the Jewish people. There is no external evidence that makes it likely that the Israelites migrated from Egypt as the book of Exodus relates. It is, however, possible that late Egyptian tradition about the end of the Hyksos and the expulsion from Egypt, as found in the writings of the Egyptian priest and historiographer Manetho from the third century BCE and preserved in the writings of the Jewish historiographer Josephus from the first century CE, might have influenced the formation of the exodus narrative.[26] Manetho brings forth a series of adventurous stories about the expulsion of the Hyksos. Josephus does not agree with his review. According to Josephus, Manetho must speak about the Israelites. It is known from other Hellenistic sources that Jews living in Egypt were acquainted with the exodus tradition.[27] It is therefore likely that the exodus narrative represents a Jewish reinterpretation of the Egyptian tradition about the Hyksos, a

---

24. Trans. James K. Hoffmeier, in *COS* 2:41.

25. The classical edition of the Amarna letters is J. A. Knudtzon, *Die El-Amarna-Tafeln*, 2 vols. (Leipzig: J. C. Hinrichs, 1915). A complete modern translation is William L. Moran, *The Amarna Letters* (Baltimore: Johns Hopkins, 1992).

26. Josephus, *Contra Apionem*, II.26–31 (227–87).

27. Thus in Alexandria in the second century BCE, Ezekiel, a Jewish tragedian, wrote a piece based on the story of exodus, the *Exagoge* ("The bringing out"). The extant material is translated by R. G. Robertson in James H. Charlesworth, ed., *The Old Testament Pseudepigrapha* (New York: Doubleday, 1985), 2:803–19.

tradition still in circulation among Egyptian intellectuals among whom we should search for Manetho more than a thousand years after the expulsion of the Hyksos kings at the beginning of the New Kingdom. Nonetheless, this remains a hypothesis that cannot be established as a fact. We can say for sure only that Josephus, living about 250 years after Manetho, made the link between the exodus story and Manetho's version of the Hyksos tradition. He might have as his sources Hellenistic Jewish authors such as Hecataeus from Abdera, about 300 BCE, who connects the exodus with the expulsion of the Hyksos.[28]

Thus the story of the exodus is about as legendary as the patriarchal narratives. It definitely has a different topic, but when it comes to the historical content, these two biblical traditions are on the same level.

As has already been suggested, the setting of the stories of Israel in the wilderness yields no evidence to historical analysis. The main character is Moses, who brings Israel out of Egypt, arranges for the confrontation between Israel and Yahweh at Sinai, and leads Israel through the desert. His name is probably Egyptian and part of a well-known combination of names.[29] It is impossible to say which Egyptian god Moses was the "son" of, whether it might have been Thutmosis, Amenmosis, Ramosis (Rameses), or somebody else. Many proposals have been put forward. They all have this in common: they may all be possible, but they cannot be proven (or falsified). There is no external source with information that allows for an identification of Moses—if he is indeed a real person. In a serious historical-critical analysis of the exodus and wilderness traditions in the Old Testament, these narratives may be considered the constructions of biblical historiographers. It is impossible to decide whether there is any historical background for them. It is, therefore, no credit to modern biblical scholars when they translate the biblical myths into secular history by rationalistic paraphrase.

The Conquest

The following two periods in Israel's history as related by the biblical historiographers, the period of the conquest and the time of the judges, were traditionally regarded as historical periods. Again scholars focused on the tribal league and its institutions as the place where these traditions were transmitted from one generation to the next. The distance between the events and their reduction to writing was relatively short, and the biblical records were likely to carry some historical information, or so it was believed.

The conquest was considered a historical fact, although scholars disagreed on the character of this conquest, whether it was by peaceful immigration followed by an extensive process of assimilation between the Israelite tribesmen and the local Canaanite peasants, or by a violent conquest. Irrespective of their position

---

28. Hecataeus's writings are only preserved as fragments in works by later Hellenistic-Roman authors, epsecially Diodorus Siculus (1st century BCE).
29. See p. 427–28.

on such matters, all scholars of the time agreed that the Israelites came from outside of Palestine, as argued by the Old Testament.[30]

A third theory about the Israelite conquest made its appearance in the 1960s,
when some North American scholars argued that it never took place, or reduced
the Israelite immigration to the question of a small number of people who, led
by Moses, had escaped from Egypt and who brought the "gospel" of Yahweh's
deliverance with them to destitute peasants of Canaan, a society where great differences existed between the rich and the poor. Israel's history did not begin with
an immigration of Israelite tribes; it began with a *revolution*, when suppressed
Canaanite peasants gathered around the worship of Yahweh and its message of
freedom and equality.[31]

It is for good reasons impossible to unite the hypothesis about the Israelite
revolution with any preserved tradition about early Israel found in the Old Testament. This fact never deterred proponents of the revolutionary hypothesis, who
stressed that two circumstances spoke in favor of their hypothesis and against the
previous migration hypotheses, whether peaceful or violent.

The first circumstance in favor of the revolutionary hypothesis, arguing in
support of seeing the Israelite conquest as a result of an internal development
within Palestine, leading to a settlement between the local population and its tor-
mentors, had to do with "external evidence." Many scholars following Albright
argued that there was ample evidence in the form of archaeological remains which
proved a major foreign population had arrived, and the violent character of their
conquest could be studied in the many destruction layers from the time found
in excavations of Palestinian cities spread throughout the country. Other scholars were convinced that such a conquest by a foreign people could not be traced
in the available archaeological evidence. From an archaeological point of view,
the Israelites are invincible. As Mario Liverani expresses it, it is as if the Israelites
migrated into Palestine and occupied it as you might occupy a fully furnished
apartment or house.[32]

Archaeological studies do not point in the direction of a conquest. They indicate that a totally different process took place leading to the destruction of the
urbanized Canaanite lifestyle toward the end of the Late Bronze Age. Some cities
were destroyed by force, some were just forsaken when their inhabitants moved

---

30. On this point there is absolutely no disagreement between the two classical histories of Israel
from the middle of the twentieth century, Martin Noth's (1950) and John Bright's (1959). On all
other points they disagreed. Bright supported the idea of the conquest and saw the description of it
in Joshua as a fair description. Noth disagreed and followed his teacher Albrecht Alt's idea of a peaceful immigration; see Alt, "Die Landnahme der Israeliten in Palästina" (1925), in his *Kleine Schriften
zur Geschichte Israels* (Munich: Beck, 1953), 1:89–125; ET, "The Settlement of the Israelites in Palestine," in Albrecht Alt, *Essays on Old Testament History and Religion* (Oxford: Blackwell, 1966),
133–69.

31. G. E. Mendenhall, "The Hebrew Conquest of Palestine," *Biblical Archaeologist* 25 (1962):
25–53, later vastly expanded in Norman K. Gottwald, *The Tribes of Yahweh: A Sociology of Religion
of Liberated Israel 1250–1050 BC* (Maryknoll, NY: Orbis Books, 1979).

32. In his "Le 'origine' d'Israele progetto irrelizzabile di ricerca etnogenetica," *Rivista Biblica Ital-
iana* 28 (1980): 9–31, 20.

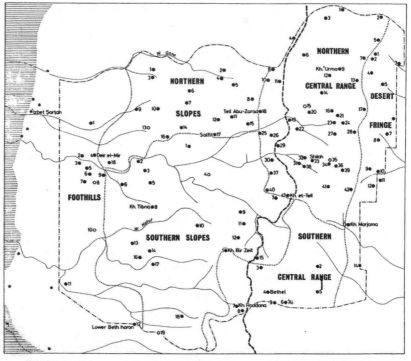

3. Israelite settlements in Bronze- and Iron-Age Palestine
(From Israel Finkelstein, *The Archaeology of the Israelite Settlement* [Israel Exploration
Society, 1988], 189. Courtesy of Israel Finkelstein.)

to other places. Urban culture, not only in Palestine but also in other parts of the
Near East, experienced a definite setback about 1200 BCE and was replaced by
a flowering village culture (mainly in the mountains of Palestine).[33] The period
definitely witnessed a move from the cities to the countryside. According to some
biblical scholars, this development reflects a changing social reality created by the
Israelite revolution.

It is beyond dispute that this move from city to countryside really happened. It
is also beyond dispute that the new village culture was mainly a continuation of the
previous urban civilization of the Late Bronze Age. As time went by, new elements
were introduced, for example, within the ceramic repertoire. These changes did not
happen immediately after the demographic changes but in the course of time.

The increase of the population in the mountains of Palestine may best be
understood by studying the chart produced by Israel Finkelstein. It shows how in

---

33. This development was first described in details by Israel Finkelstein, *The Archaeology of the
Israelite Settlement* (Jerusalem: Israel Exploration Society, 1988).

the Early Iron Age five settlements going back to the Late Bronze Age in the northern part of the mountains of central Palestine were supplemented by scores of new settlements. This graphic presentation is based on surface surveys used by archaeologists who travel through an area from one end to the other to study the pattern of settlement by collecting ceramic remains. The pottery is then studied to investigate when a site was inhabited. The method is not faultless, but useful if the statistical material is so comprehensive that it allows conclusions to be drawn. Of course a demographic change like this one does not say why it happened, and there is no need of a big bang like a *revolution* to explain it. Other circumstances may have provoked such a move from city to countryside—like new agrarian techniques, changing political conditions, climatic changes, health conditions.

Another argument in favor of the revolution hypothesis is the appearance in the Old Testament of the term "Hebrews" meaning "Israelites." In the traditions about the Israelites in Egypt, they are called Hebrews. In 1 Samuel, the Philistines refer to the rebellious Israelites as Hebrews who have revolted against their masters. Abraham is called a Hebrew, and the prophet Jonah describes himself as a Hebrew when he runs away from God. Moreover, some laws refer to Hebrews.

A review of the places where the Hebrews are mentioned in the Old Testament makes it clear that this term, with a few exceptions, always refers to the Israelites in confrontation with foreigners. Moreover, it is clear that these references are not meant to be kind. The Hebrews may be referred to as fugitives, criminals, or rebels, in short, destitute slaves rebellious against their true masters. *Hebrew* in the Old Testament always refers to Israelites, but always to Israelites in difficult circumstances.

In itself this is not enough to legitimate a hypothesis saying that early Israel came into being as the outcome of a social revolution where the "slaves," that is, the Hebrews, revolted against their master, the Canaanites, and became free men. It is, however, a fact that the revolution hypothesis came into being when scholars connected the Hebrews to the social term *ḫabiru*, which in the second millennium BCE referred to dislocated people all over the ancient Near East, refugees who had fled from their homes to seek safety in other places.[34] The term became so common that it was used as a nickname for any person who revolted against his master. This use of *ḫabiru* is often seen in the Amarna letters from Palestine, Lebanon, and Syria.

These and many other references to the *ḫabiru* in the Amarna letters from the middle of the fourteenth century BCE do not prove that a social revolution led to the demographic changes in Palestine more than a century after the closure of the Amarna Age in Egypt. The examples quoted here do not point to general social unrest but involve only local discontent directed against individuals—as regarding the ruler of Lachish who was murdered, or concerning the Egyptian domination of the southern Levant.

34. This is not the place to include a full discussion of the *ḫabiru* vis-à-vis the Hebrews. For an overview, see the articles by this author on the Hebrews and the *ḫabiru* in *ABD*, 3:6–10, 95.

Hebrews in the Old Testament

Abraham

Gen. 14:13:   Then one who had escaped came and told Abram the Hebrew,
                     who was living by the oaks of Mamre the Amorite . . .

Joseph and his brothers

Gen. 39:14, 17:   [Potiphar's wife] she called out to the members of her household
                     and said to them, "See, my husband has brought among us a
                     Hebrew to insult us! He came in to me to lie with me . . ." [17] and
                     she told him the same story, saying, "The Hebrew servant, whom
                     you have brought among us, came in to me to insult me. . . ."

Gen. 40:15:   [Joseph said] "For in fact I was stolen out of the land of the
                     Hebrews."

Gen. 41:12:   [in the report about Joseph in prison] "A young Hebrew was there
                     with us, a servant of the captain of the guard."

Gen. 43:32:   They served him [Joseph] by himself, and them [Joseph's brothers]
                     by themselves, and the Egyptians who ate with him by themselves,
                     because the Egyptians could not eat with the Hebrews, for that is
                     an abomination to the Egyptians.

The Israelites in Egypt

Exod. 1:15–19:   The king of Egypt said to the Hebrew midwives, . . . [16] "When you
                     act as midwives to the Hebrew women . . ." [19] The midwives said
                     to Pharaoh, "Because the Hebrew women are not like the Egyptian
                     women . . ."

Exod. 2:6–7:   . . . and she took pity on him. "This must be one of the Hebrews'
                     children," she said. [7] Then his sister said to Pharaoh's daughter,
                     "Shall I go and get you a nurse from the Hebrew women to nurse
                     the child for you?"

Yahweh, the God of Israel

Exod. 3:18:   [Yahweh said to Moses,] "They will listen to your voice; and you
                     and the elders of Israel shall go to the king of Egypt and say to
                     him, 'The LORD, the God of the Hebrews, has met with us . . .'"
                     (cf. Exod. 5:3; 7:16; 9:1, 13; and 10:3)

Why Moses had to flee from Egypt

Exod. 2:11–13:   One day, after Moses had grown up, he went out to his people and
                     saw their forced labor. He saw an Egyptian beating a Hebrew, one
                     of his kinsfolk . . . . [13] When he went out the next day, he saw two
                     Hebrews fighting . . .

The Law of the Hebrew Slave

Exod. 21:2:   When you buy a male Hebrew slave, he shall serve six years, but in
                     the seventh he shall go out a free person, without debt.

(continued)

Hebrews in the Old Testament (*continued*)

Deut. 15:12:	If a member of your community, whether a Hebrew man or a Hebrew woman, is sold to you and works for you six years, in the seventh year you shall set that person free.
Jer. 34:8–14:	The word that came to Jeremiah from the LORD, after King Zedekiah had made a covenant with all the people in Jerusalem to make a proclamation of liberty to them—⁹ that all should set free their Hebrew slaves, male and female, so that no one should hold another Judean in slavery. . . . ¹² The word of the LORD came to Jeremiah from the LORD: ¹³ Thus says the LORD, the God of Israel: I myself made a covenant with your ancestors when I brought them out of the land of Egypt, out of the house of slavery, saying, ¹⁴ "Every seventh year each of you must set free any Hebrews who have been sold to you and have served you six years; you must set them free from your service."

The Hebrews during the Philistine wars

1 Sam. 4:6, 9:	When the Philistines heard the noise of the shouting, they said, "What does this great shouting in the camp of the Hebrews mean?" . . . ⁹ (The Philistines said,) "Take courage, and be men, O Philistines, in order not to become slaves to the Hebrews as they have been to you; be men and fight."
1 Sam. 13:3, 7:	Jonathan defeated the garrison of the Philistines that was at Geba; and the Philistines heard of it. And Saul blew the trumpet throughout all the land, saying, "Let the Hebrews hear!" . . . ⁷ Some Hebrews crossed the Jordan to the land of Gad and Gilead.
1 Sam. 13:19:	Now there was no smith to be found throughout all the land of Israel; for the Philistines said, "The Hebrews must not make swords or spears for themselves."
1 Sam. 14:11:	So both of them showed themselves to the garrison of the Philistines; and the Philistines said, "Look, Hebrews are coming out of the holes where they have hidden themselves."
1 Sam. 14:21:	Now the Hebrews who previously had been with the Philistines and had gone up with them into the camp turned and joined the Israelites who were with Saul and Jonathan.
1 Sam. 29:3:	. . . the commanders of the Philistines said, "What are these Hebrews doing here?"

Jonah

Jonah 1:9:	"I am a Hebrew," he [Jonah] replied.

Ḥabiru in the Amarna letters

EA 73:26–33:	[The king of Byblos to an Egyptian official] "When he [the king of Amurru] wrote to the men of Ammiah: 'Kill your masters!' They became *ḥabiru*."

(*continued*)

Ḫabiru in the Amarna letters (*continued*)

	Thus say the mayors: 'Do like us!' and every country becomes *ḫabiru.*
EA 144:24–30:	[The king of Sidon to Pharaoh] "All the cities which the king has given into my charge become *ḫabiru;*
	But the king must give into my charge one of his men who shall come leading the soldiers of the king and demand that the cities, that became *ḫabiru,* to be returned into my hand."
EA 148:41–45:	[The king of Tyre to Pharaoh] "The king of Hazor has left his city and joined up with the *ḫabiru.* . . ." The king's country becomes *ḫabiru.*
EA 288:43–44:	[The king of Jerusalem to Pharaoh] "See Zimrida of Lachish: the subjects/slaves have killed him and become *ḫabiru.*"

It is nevertheless a safe conclusion that the question of the *ḫabiru* was so important that the term could develop a second meaning as indicated here. Taken together, documents mentioning the *ḫabiru* from the second millennium BCE are evidence of serious social problems, when people in great numbers fled their countries. We also possess examples of the ideology or propaganda often related to such circumstances, when unscrupulous persons are abusing the need of poor people for their own advantage. Thus the king of Byblos complains to a pharaoh that the king of Amurru behaves improperly against Byblos and promises the citizens of Byblos freedom and wealth in abundance:

> Do not be inattentive to your servant. See, *ḫabiru's* war against me is serious . . . our sons and daughters are gone, because they have been sold in Jarimuta to provide rations that we may stay alive. 'My field has become like a woman without man, because nobody tills it!' All my cities in the mountains . . . or at the sea have joined the *ḫabiru.* Only Byblos and two more cities remain mine. After having captured Šigata, Abdi-Aširta said to the men of Ammiah: 'Kill your masters and become like us; then you will have peace.' They have acted according to his words and become like *ḫabiru.* (EA 74)

The end justifies the means: there is no reason to doubt that the king of Amurru is acting on his own behalf. However this may be, there must be a background for propaganda like this, some kind of social unrest.

It remains a problem for the advocates of the revolution hypothesis that there is no absolute consensus among scholars concerning whether or not the *ḫabiru* can be identified with the Hebrews of the Old Testament. Moreover, documents from the ancient Near East indicate that the term *ḫabiru* went out of use toward the end of the second millennium BCE. Most scholars consider the biblical evidence to be much younger. The question is therefore how the term might have been transmitted to biblical writers; perhaps they found it in traditional literature in Mesopotamia, or it survived in the society of Palestine in the first millennium, perhaps as a remembrance of the origins of their society in a revolution of the past. It is impossible to decide what happened or how it happened. It is, on the other hand, a safe assumption that *ḫabiru* cannot be identified with a specific ethnic group, and the presence of the *ḫabiru* in the Amarna letters does not allow for the theory that there was ethnic continuity between the *ḫabiru* of the Amarna Age and the Hebrews of the Old Testament. We can only talk about a social continuity that says both the term *ḫabiru* and the term "Hebrew" tell us about remaining social problems involving not only Palestine but the entire Middle East.

All of this suggests that the revolutionary hypothesis may not be baseless. It is regrettable that with one important exception every document from the second millennium may be a hundred years older than the demographical development placed in connection with the alleged revolution. The exception is an inscription of Sethos I (ca. 1290–1279) from Beth-shan that records the activity of the *ḫabiru* in connection with some tribesmen.[35]

Finally, it must be said to the distress of scholars who advocate the revolution as well as another explanation of the Israelite conquest that they have forgotten one minor but inconvenient fact: Egypt was still the master of Palestine when the Israelites are supposed to have arrived/rebelled. Furthermore, the Egyptian rule was not weakened under the nineteenth dynasty, the dynasty to which Ramesses II belonged. Ramesses and his successors seem to have strengthened the Egyptian grip on the country. Instead of a situation of chaos and insecurity—always a good starting point for social unrest—Palestinian society may have stabilized and security been restored, a situation probably reflected by the unfortified character of the new settlements in the mountains.

However it may be, it still remains certain that the Israelite conquest of Canaan as related by the book of Joshua lacks every historical foundation. Old Testament scholarship has to accept this. The basic assumption of the Old Testament, that Israel was a nation which came into being outside of Palestine, has no bearing on the reality of historical conditions in the second millennium BCE.

The Period of the Judges

The continuation of Egyptian rule in Palestine after 1200 BCE, and the fact that the Egyptian presence was felt more than a hundred years later, shows that the idea of an Israelite conquest of Canaan at the end of the thirteenth century is impossible. The realization of the political conditions of Palestine after 1200 BCE must also influence our idea of the period of the judges. This period was, in traditional historical-critical scholarship, believed to have lasted from about 1200 to about 1000 BCE.

35. *COS* 2:27–28.

It was formerly the conviction of almost every Old Testament scholar that the period of the judges was the time when Israel strengthened its grip on the country. It was often assumed that the divergent story of the conquest in Judges 1 included historical information that qualified the impression of a total conquest gained from the book of Joshua. According to this chapter, Israel did not manage to subdue all of Canaan. Large pieces of land were still independent Canaanite enclaves. Some of them succumbed to Israelite rule at the beginning of the period of the judges; others—like Jerusalem—became Israelite at a much later date.

The second important idea related to the period of the judges, until a generation ago, was the assumption that the center of Israel in the period of the judges was the tribal league, the amphictyony.[36] Here the representatives of all twelve tribes of Israel met on a regular basis and worshiped their common deity, Yahweh. In this way the tribes of Israel kept their individuality without losing their Israelite identity. They were also able to unite against foreign enemies within the context of the league.

According to Martin Noth, the amphictyony consisted of a complicated structure. It had a common sanctuary and a common priesthood attached to the sanctuary. It had a common juridical organization and a common foreign policy. As the theory of the amphictyony grew older, it was used to explain almost every single incident, every single condition of life relevant to the early existence of the Israelite tribes in Palestine, including the idea expressed by all Old Testament writers that only Yahweh was the God of Israel. The amphictyony promoted the idea of Israel as obliged to worship Yahweh and no other deity. The priesthood at the center of the amphictyony was the guardian of the sacred national traditions of ancient Israel. German Old Testament scholarship of that time especially regarded the amphictyony as the proof that the common Israelite traditions about the past were reduced into writing at a very early stage in the history of the Israelite people in Palestine.

The judge was supposed to be the leader of the Israelite amphictyony. "Judge" is the normal way of translating the Hebrew word *šophet*, which also has the meaning "one who decides" and may in some connections be translated as "ruler" or "governor." Now Judges records the life and deeds of many such "judges." Some of them appear in stories about Israel fighting foreign enemies, while others are listed without much information about their life. Scholars therefore divided the judges into two groups, the "major judges" and the "minor judges." The major judges appear in the book of Judges as the champions of Israel in wartime, while the minor judges appear only in two short lists, Judges 10:1–5 and 12:8–15. It was also recognized that the major judges hardly governed all of Israel. They are related to events only on a local scale. Thus, when Ehud of Benjamin murdered the fat king Eglon of Moab, this deed was important only for his own tribe (Judg. 3:12–30).

Accordingly, the major judges were regarded as local chieftains. The minor judges were, on the other hand, the leaders of the amphictyony. Looking for an analogy to the office of the judge, a person not found in the alleged Greek model

36. See pp. 73–74.

for the amphictyony, scholars finally turned to medieval Iceland, to the institution of the central administrator of law, the "lögsögumaðr" (lit. "The speaker of law"), who was the leading juridical official in Iceland attached to the function of the Alþingi, the parliament.[37]

The narratives of Judges end with the conclusion that because there was no king in Israel, all could do as they pleased (Judg. 21:25). Scholars were on this point in total agreement: the tribes did not normally act together, with one exception, when eleven tribes made war on the twelfth, Benjamin, because of a sexual transgression committed by members of that tribe of Benjamin (Judg. 19–20). This was, or so it was believed, a "holy war," and the intention was to purify the tribal league by removing the offenders. Greek conditions were believed to offer an analogy, because the Greek sacral league of the amphictyony had to act against a member that committed sacrilege against the central shrine of the league more than once (this member had occupied the sacred area of Delphi and confiscated the treasures kept there by the other members of the Delphic Amphictyony— definitely a proper reason for a war).[38]

In most cases the activities of the tribes were very limited in scope. Only minor segments of the tribes were normally involved. The campaign against the Canaanites in Judges 4–5 involved more than one tribe, but several tribes earned a reputation by not participating at all.

The thesis of the Israelite amphictyony in the period of the judges may be considered one of the absolutely central ideas of historical-critical scholarship of the twentieth century. By constructing the amphictyony, Old Testament scholars believed themselves to possess an answer to almost everything related to early Israel. The idea that the biblical tradition about the very earliest times originated under the protection of the amphictyony was commonplace. Moreover, because of the amphictyony, it was now possible to speak about the period of the judges as part of historical times. The amphictyony remained the Alpha and Omega for belief that Israelite identity and its exclusive Yahwistic religion were rooted in this period.

The sad end of the hypothesis of the amphictyony showed how fragile the edifice of the scholars had been. Old Testament scholars had *constructed* the amphictyony rather than *re*constructed it on the basis of available sources. It still remained an unconfirmed assertion. Scholars had used this construction as the basis of many related hypotheses about Israel's fate in the period of the judges, without truly realizing that their argumentation was, from a logical point of view, extremely weak.

---

37. Alt and Noth, who proposed this analogy, may have had a limited knowledge of the institution and its role, which was not limited to Iceland. Such a person was attached to most Nordic local "parliaments" in the early part of the Middle Ages. Another indication of their limited knowledge of the institution is their omission of the Icelandic tradition that it was this person who around 1000 decided that Iceland should become Christian. This would have been a fine analogy to the establishment of Yahwism as the supreme religion within the confines of the Israelite sacral league.

38. On the holy war, see Gerhard von Rad, *Der heilige Krieg in alten Israel* (Zurich: TVZ, 1951); ET, *Holy War in Ancient Israel* (Eugene: Wipf & Stock, 2000).

The hypothesis about the Israelite amphictyony didn't break down because scholars realized that it rested on faulty argumentation; it fell apart because it had become too "heavy" and could no longer stand on its own legs. It was not new methodological advances that brought it down but traditional historical-critical methodologies, in essence not much different from the ones used to put the hypothesis together.[39]

These investigations, carried out on the basis of a traditional historical-critical methodology, made it clear that in the biblical literature concerning the period of the judges, and generally believed to contain historical information, there were absolutely no references to any sacral league uniting all the Israelite tribes. First and foremost, it was impossible to point to any Israelite central sanctuary. There were almost too many sanctuaries spread over the entire country of Israel, the local religious centers of nearby tribes. There was, in the Israelite amphictyony, no center, if this was not identified with the ark of the covenant, symbolizing the presence of Yahweh, which according to the Old Testament was constructed in the desert, carried into the land of Canaan, deposited in Shiloh, and finally brought to Jerusalem by David.

Second, the amphictyony never was a centralized institution calling upon all the Israelite tribes when Israel was threatened by foreign enemies. The single example of cooperation occurred in connection with Benjamin's sin (Judg. 19–20). Otherwise, the Israel described by the book of Judges was an Israel ridden by internal strife and even civil war. At one point the tribe of Manasseh even tried to establish a kingdom, which, however, did not survive for long (Judg. 9).

In this connection it is only of secondary importance that the Greek analogy to the Israelite tribal league, the Delphic Amphictony, was not established until several hundred years after the closure of the period of the judges. The arguments already considered are more than enough to show that any basis of the theory about this league has disappeared among biblical scholars. Around 1975 scholars began to formulate theories about Israel in the prestate period, that is, before the period of kings, that totally disregarded the previous popular amphictyonic hypothesis that was almost totally forgotten.

Scholars limited their settlement with the amphictyonic hypothesis to history only. For a long time they did not acknowledge that the dismissal of this theory meant that the traditions about early Israel had lost their place in the sanctuary of the league of Israelite tribes. Some scholars realized that the disappearance of the amphictyony also meant the disappearance of the period of the judges as a historical period. Now the idea of an Israelite "twelve tribe people" bound by the same religion and fighting its enemies had nothing to do with the prestate period; it could hardly predate the introduction of the monarchy, a period still believed to have originally involved all twelve of the Israelite tribes.

39. A study of relevant literature from this period proves this to be true, including Andrew D. H. Mayes, *Israel in the Period of the Judges*, SBT, Second Series 29 (London: SCM, 1974), and this writer's epitaph over the theory, "'Israel in the Period of the Judges'—The Tribal League in Recent Research," *Studia Theologica* 38 (1984): 1–28.

The period of the judges changed character from a historical period to a *literary* one. Scholars began to refer to the stories about the deeds of the judges as heroic tales similar to heroic narrative found in other cultures, like—to list some of the better known—the Homeric epics, the Icelandic sagas, the poem of Roland, the Nibelungenlied, the legendary tales about King Arthur, and more. The period of the judges had disappeared from history; it no more represented a historical stage in the development of ancient Israel.

The Empire of David and Solomon

The changing understanding of the period of the judges has as a consequence that scholars have been looking to the early Israelite monarchy—especially the days of David and Solomon—as a substitute for the amphictyony and suggesting that this young kingdom, embracing all of the Israelite tribes, may also have kindled the idea of early Israel as found in the Old Testament. From the vantage point of the Old Testament, this period, when Israel was united under one and the same authority, seems the last chance for the biblical idea of the twelve tribes ruling all of Palestine and the western part of modern Jordan to have any bearing on historical conditions. After Solomon the kingdom was split into two parts, and only the northern part carried the name of Israel. It seemed impossible that the notion of the twelve tribes, all descendants of the patriarch Jacob, would have come into being at a time without political coherence between all those tribes. Such a political situation was not to appear again after the breakdown of the Davidic-Solomonic state.

Another precondition for the formation of the tradition of the twelve tribes has to do with the need of an empire like the one supposed to have been created by David: a major bureaucracy centered in the capital of Jerusalem. When David and Solomon created close links to the national worship of the God Yahweh—David by bringing the ark of God to Jerusalem (2 Sam. 6) and Solomon by building God's temple at Zion as part of his palatial complex (1 Kgs. 6–8)—the civil servants of the royal administration and the priests at the central sanctuary would have had plenty of opportunity to elaborate on ancient traditions, some of which may only have a segment of the Israelite tribes in mind, and form them into a common Israelite tradition useful as royal propaganda directed toward part of the kingdom that might not have been too happy about the new political establishment. In the light of a scenario like this, propaganda aimed at uniting people of different origins, by arguing that they all belonged together, because of their common history reaching far back in time, would have been very useful.

The stories about Saul, David, and Solomon contain many details. Sometimes they allow the reader to follow the king into his bedroom. Classic historical-critical scholarship considered this a testimony not only that the author was physically close to the royal court but also that the author was a contemporary of the events described. Scholars were seriously discussing the identity of this author or authors who was supposed to have witnessed the events described. Thus many scholars were of the conviction that the author of the so-called succession narrative, the story about the struggle to become David's successor (2 Sam. 8–1 Kgs. 2), was authored by the priest Abiathar, who was forced to retire early after Solomon's succession to the throne, because he had supported Solomon's competitor Adonijah.

Saul, David, and Solomon created the Israelite empire—at least this is what the Old Testament says. It began with Saul, although he was killed in battle against the Philistines at Gilboa in northern Palestine. David brought victory to Israel wherever he sent his army and forced all of Israel's enemies to submit to his rule—the Philistines, the Moabites, the Ammonites, and the Arameans. David also reduced the few remaining Canaanite enclaves still left among the Israelites, among them Jerusalem, chosen by him as the future capital of Israel. Solomon completed the work of David and created a central royal administration to govern it. At the same time, cracks began to appear threatening the whole structure of his empire. The traditional enemies of Israel began to raise their heads. Toward the end of Solomon's rule, the process of dissolution of the empire, including a diminishing economic foundation, had gone so far that it had been necessary to place ever growing burdens on the shoulders of the Israelites, leading to the complete breakup of Solomon's kingdom after his death.

Seemingly this narrative makes sense and most scholars have accordingly been of the conviction that at least its main parts must be historically correct. This has, however, not deterred other scholars who have dared to express doubts as to the historical content of these narratives. The most important argument against the very existence of an Israelite empire at this time, the tenth century BCE, is that it ought to be reflected in contemporary documents or at least in monumental buildings belonging to the time of David and Solomon. Ancient kings whose rule extended over half of western Asia, an empire reaching from the border of Egypt to Tadmor (Palmyra) in central Syria, must have commanded triumphant inscriptions to be placed at any important point in the realm in order to impress their subjects because of their imperial splendor. Any ancient Near Eastern king worth his salt would have ordered great palaces and wonderful temples to be built in his name. However, about the two great kings of Israel there is complete silence. Not a single inscription has been found from their time, not a single fragment of an imperial construction. Not one contemporary document from the ancient Near East mentions either of these two imperial monarchs. The closest support of their existence would be the Tel Dan inscription,[40] which may include a reference to "the House of David," but this inscription is not from the tenth century BCE. It belongs at the earliest to the ninth century BCE, removed by a century from the glorious days of David.

From the perspective of the tenth century, David and Solomon are invisible. It is as if they never lived. In spite of this, Old Testament scholars, relying solely on the Bible, argue that the argument against the assumption that there ever was

40. See pp. 113–15.

a Davidic-Solomonic empire is an *argumentum ex silentio*, an argument from silence, which is logically a false argument. From a formal point of view, it seems to be a false conclusion. The opposing party often refers to the fact that "absence of evidence is not evidence of absence." Although this may look like a valid position, it is based on mistaken assumptions. The advocates of this position make the logical mistake of mixing two categories, a text and physical reality. In the biblical narratives, David and Solomon are great kings who ruled Palestine and most of Syria. This narrative is not affected by the lack of physical evidence of the presence of these kings in the real world. The Old Testament still tells the story of two great kings. The problem arises at the moment when the content of the biblical narratives is considered to have historical implications as well, because here other factors rule. Here the narrative content of the stories of the books of Samuel and Kings must be considered secondary and physical remains from the tenth century BCE primary. If the primary evidence speaks against the presence of a mighty Israelite empire in the tenth century, the biblical narrative has little to do with the historical conditions of the tenth century BCE. It belongs in a different period and should be understood in the light of the period when it came into being.

This conclusion is supported by archaeological activity relating to the tenth century BCE. However it may be, archaeology seems not to support the biblical idea of an Israelite empire. Two "schools" of archaeologists compete, mostly over conditions in Jerusalem.

One school maintains that in the tenth century BCE Jerusalem was a city, although quite small, covering only a few hectares, apart from the royal residence, and by no means densely populated. The number of citizens in Jerusalem at this time hardly surpassed 1,500 to 2,000 people, which means—the average size of a family in those days taken into consideration, allowing for nuclear families of six persons—that Jerusalem housed no more than 250 to 300 adult men, hardly the number necessary for the maintenance of an empire. In comparison, the total territory of Judah hardly accommodated more than 10,000 to 15,000 people, and all of Palestine definitely fewer than 500,000 people.[41]

The second archaeological school is more radical and argues that until this day not a single trace of Jerusalem being settled in the tenth century has been found—not a single shard.[42]

---

41. The calculation of population in antiquity is always less than certain. Scholars may apply different methods for their calculations, such as the number of people per hectare found in traditional Near Eastern cities of today. The numbers will always be different from place to place and dependent on the method applied. Another method of calculation has to do with the ability of a certain territory to feed a population by traditional agricultural techniques. Modern technology can support perhaps ten times as many people per hectare as traditional farming techniques.

42. The first school centers around the Hebrew University in Jerusalem but is also supported especially by North American archaeologists. The second school is found at the University of Tel Aviv. A recent review of the opinions of this school is presented by Israel Finkelstein and Neil Asher Silberman, *The Bible Unearthed: Archaeology's New Vision of Ancient Israel and the Origin of Its Sacred Texts* (New York: Free Press, 2001).

The conclusion seems to be inevitable: as was the case of the stories about the judges in the book of Judges, the narratives about the first kings of Israel in the books of Samuel and Kings are not history. They do not allow the historian to reconstruct the history of Israel in the period around the year 1000 BCE. We do not know if future archaeological discoveries may change this situation. We do not know for sure if there really existed not two great kings "once upon a time" but two minor chieftains roaming the mountains of Judah in the tenth century BCE.[43] The Bible does not say so, and we have no other traces of their presence that may allow us to identify these "chieftains."

This conclusion leads to serious consequences for the biblical tradition about the unity of the Israelite tribes dating back to the earliest times of their history. There is at the present no period in the reconstructed Israelite history that allows for the compilation of this tradition into a national epic. The consequences are even more compelling when we move onward to the following periods in Israel's history.

The Divided Kingdom

The Old Testament says that the Davidic-Solomonic empire came to a most ignominious end, when Solomon's son and successor on the throne, Rehoboam, was forced to run away from a meeting in Shechem with the delegates of the northern tribes (1 Kgs. 12). Now followed two centuries of never-ending conflict and war between the former two parts of Solomon's kingdom. This conflict ended only when the Assyrians conquered Samaria, the capital of Israel, in 722 BCE and put an end to the independence of Israel. The kingdom of Judah survived almost for another 150 years until the successors to the Assyrians, the Neo-Babylonians, finally extinguished the last traces of the former great kingdom of David and Solomon.

It is safe to assume that the sources relating to the first part of this decline toward total oblivion have about the same historical value as the sources pertaining to the united kingdom of Israel. If the description of the mighty Davidic-Solomonic empire represents biblical historiographers' attempt to paint a golden image of the past, a past that never existed, it is just as likely that the narrative about the disruption of this empire has as little historical value as the description of the empire itself. If David's and Solomon's kingdom never existed, there was nothing to divide. In order to get to authentic history, the modern historian has to move forward in time.

There is no reason to doubt that a small kingdom existed in Palestine in the ninth century BCE. It was known by different names, the most common in inscriptions being "the house of Omri" (Akkadian *Bit Ḥumriya*). Other names were Samaria and Israel. Now we have at last a few external sources referring to

---

43. This is becoming an increasingly popular assumption. See, e.g., Israel Finkelstein and Neil Asher Silberman, *David and Solomon: In Search of the Bible's Sacred Kings and the Roots of the Western Tradition* (New York: Free Press, 2006).

Near Eastern inscriptions referring to the kingdoms of Israel and Judah

The Mesha stele from Moab, 9th century BCE	The King of Israel Omri tortured Moab in his and half his son's time
T. Dan Stele (Hazael?), 9th century BCE?	NN King of Israel
Assyrian texts	
Shalmanassar III, 853 BCE[44]	Ahab of Israel participates in the battle at Qarqar against the Assyrians
Shalmanassar III, ca. 830 BCE	Jehu the son of Omri pays tribute
Adadnirari III, ca. 800 BCE	Title: The conqueror of Omri's land
Tiglath-pileser III, ca. 740 BCE?	Azariah of Judah pays tribute
Tiglath-pileser III, ca. 735 BCE	**Menahem of Samaria pays tribute**
Tiglath-pileser III, ca. 735 BCE	The booty . . . from Samaria
Tiglath-pileser III, ca. 735 BCE	**Menahem submits to Assyrian rule and pays the tribute of the house of Omri.** **Pekah is overthrown and Hosea made king by Tiglath-pileser III**
Tiglath-pileser III, ca. 730 BCE	Joahaz of Judah pays tribute
Sargon II, ca. 721 BCE	**The conquerer of Samaria and all of the house of Omri**
Sargon II, ca. 721 BCE	**The conquest of Samaria and the deportation of 27,280 inhabitants**
Sargon II, ca. 721 BCE	**The conquest of Samaria and the deportation of 27,290 inhabitants**
Sargon II, ca. 721 BCE	**The conquest of Samaria and all of the house of Omri**
Sargon II, ca. 721 BCE?	Samaria rebelled . . .
Sargon II, ca. 714 BCE	**Deportation and forced settlement of Arab prisoners of war in Samaria[45]**

(continued)

44. This date builds an Assyrian record of a solar eclipse in the same year.
45. This source harmonizes with the Old Testament only insofar as mentioning the forced settlement of foreign persons. According to 2 Kgs. 17:24 the Assyrians moved citizens from Babylon, Cuthah, Avva, Hama, and Sepharvaim to Samaria.

Near Eastern inscriptions referring to the kingdoms
of Israel and Judah

Sargon II, ca. 710 BCE?	A *jamani* (i.e., "Greek") urges the ruler of Judah to rebel
Sargon II, ca. 710 BCE?	Title: The conqueror of Judah
Sennacherib, 701 BCE	**Hezekiah of Judah's rebellion and Sennacherib's attack**
	The king of Ekron is released from Jerusalem
Sennacherib, 701 BCE	**Sennacherib destroys Judah and subdues Hezekiah**
Asarhaddon, ca. 680 BCE?	Manasseh of Judah delivers noble timber, etc., to Nineveh
Asarhaddon, ca. 680 BCE?	Mentions the city of Apku in the vicinity of Samaria
Assurbanipal, ca. 669 BCE	Manasseh of Judah pays tribute
Assyrian document, ca. 700 BCE	Tribute from the people of Judah
Neo-Babylonian sources	
Nebuchadnezzar II, 697 BCE	**The conquest of the city of Judah**
Nebuchadnezzar II, before 662 BCE?	Supplies delivered to Jehoiachin, the son of the king of Judah
Nebuchadnezzar II, 595 BCE	Possible mentioning of Nebo-Sarse-kim, a high courtier on the service of the king (Jer. 39:3) [46]

Only the lines in **bold** are directly related to information in the Old Testament.

this state, and some of them can be related to information in the Old Testament. Thus some parts of the biblical narrative seem to have a historical background. Although cases are few, there may be good reason to put some trust in historical information in the books of Kings as we move down to the middle of the ninth century BCE. The kingdom of Judah is invisible in these documents until the late eighth century BCE. Only from about the time of the fall of Samaria does it begin to appear in external references to political conditions in Palestine. There is only one exception, the possible mention of "the house of David" in the Tel Dan inscription.

46. According to a cuneiform tablet "discovered" in 2007 in the British Museum.

A review of the inscriptions from the ancient Near East shows that the account of the history of Israel and Judah in the Old Testament is not invented as far as the general outline is concerned. We have no external source that relates to the early history of Judah, while the first document referring to Israel can be dated to 853 BCE. In this year Ahab was part of a coalition of mostly Aramean states fighting Assyria. Although the Assyrian scribe could not spell Israel correctly—he calls it Sirlaya—it certainly dates Ahab to the middle of the ninth century BCE. In contrast, the reference in the famous Moabite Mesha inscription to Omri, Ahab's father, is more uncertain. It may be a reference not to the person of Omri, but rather to the other name of Israel, the house of Omri.

The Mesha inscription is without doubt the most important monumental inscription found in Jordan or Palestine. It sheds an excellent light over the many problems involved in the interpretation of such documents. Mesha is a well-known character from the Old Testament. According to the narrative in 2 Kings 3, King Jehoram of Israel, in an alliance with King Jehoshaphat of Judah, campaigned against Moab and conquered most of the country, apart from Kir-hareseth, where Mesha resides. The campaign stops when Mesha sacrifices his son on the wall of Kir-hareseth, "and great wrath came upon Israel" (2 Kgs. 3:27). According to the biblical chronology, this happened ca. 850 BCE, which seems to square well with the information presented by Mesha in his inscription, which is, nonetheless, totally silent about the events narrated by 2 Kings 3.

The Mesha stele says that Omri reigned over Israel and oppressed Moab, and that the same happened in his son's (here Ahab's name ought to have been mentioned) time, although Mesha defeated him and destroyed his country. Now, considering the fact that according to Assyrian information Ahab was one of the mightiest kings of his time and moreover allied to the Arameans, it seems hardly likely that little Moab should have "destroyed" Israel. Maybe Mesha bragged of a small and insignificant local advance and made it into a great victory. As already said, Near Eastern royal inscriptions always include propaganda favoring the king who put up the inscription. The Mesha inscription is certainly no more faithful to historical truth than biblical historiography in general.

This impression is confirmed when Mesha moves on to speak about Omri's residence at Madeba in all his time and in half of his son's time, altogether forty years. "Forty" is not an exact number but appears frequently in different connections—forty days, forty years, forty miles—in popular tales from many places. It is an important number and means "a lot of" days/years/miles, and so on. The contrasting number is seven, meaning "a few" years/days/miles, and so on.[47] The date given by Mesha in his inscription about the duration of Israelite rule is not exact. It only says "for a long time." The decisive point is, however, that Omri ruled Madeba in half his son's time. How should he be able to do that? The explanation

---

47. On these numbers in the Old Testament, see Niels Peter Lemche, "Pragnant tid i Det Gamle Testamente," in Geert Halbäck and Niels Peter Lemche, eds., *"Tiden" I bibelsk belysning* (Copenhagen: Museum Tusculanum, 2001), 29–47; ET pending.

The Mesha stele[48]

I am Mesha, the son of KMŠYT, the king of Moab from [2]Dibon. My father was king of Moab for thirty years, and I became [3]king after my father, and I made this high place for Kemosh in QRḤ [4]because he saved me from all the *attackers*[49] and because he let me be victorious over all my enemies. [5]Omri was king of Israel and he oppressed Moab for a long time because Kemosh was angry at his [6]country, and he was succeeded by his son, and he said: "I will oppress Moab." In my time he said [this] [7]but I won over him and his house, and Israel is for ever destroyed. But Omri had conquered the whole land [8]Mehadeba, and he stayed there in his time and half his son's time, for forty years, [9]but Kemosh allowed it to return in my time, and I built Baalmaon and made a cistern in it, and I built [10]Qiriatain. The people of Gad had lived in Atarot since ancient time and the king of Israel [11]built Atarot for them. I made war on the city and captured it and killed all the people [12]of the city (as a) satisfaction for Kemosh and Moab, and I brought the altar for its DVDH and [13]dragged it in front of Kemosh in Qiriat, and I settled in it the people from Sharon and the people from [14]MḤRT. Kemosh said to me: "Go and conquer Nebo from Israel," and [15]I left in the night and made war upon it from early morning to midday and I [16]took it and killed everyone in it: seven thousand men and foreign men and women and foreign [17]women and slaves because I had put a ban on them because of Ashtar Kemosh, and I took from there the [18]vessels of Yahweh and dragged them in front of Kemosh. The king of Israel had built [19]Jahas and he lived there during his campaigns against me, but Kemosh drew him away in front of me, and [20]I took two hundred men from Moab, all its elite soldiers, and I brought them up to Jahas and took it [21]in order to attach it to Dibon. I built QRḤ, the walls around the parks and the walls around its [22]acropolis, and I built its gates, and I built its towers and [23]I built the royal palace, and I constructed the wall around the water cistern in the middle of the [24]city. There was no well in the middle of the city of QRḤ, and I told all the people: "make [25]each of you a well in your house!" I dug the moat around QRḤ with the help of prisoners [26]from Israel. I built

Aroer and I made the road at Arnon. [27]I built Bet Bamot, because it was destroyed. I built Beser because it was in ruins. [28][. . . with] fifty men from Dibon, because all Dibon obeyed, and I [29]was king . . . hundred in cities which I had annexed to the country, and I [30]built [Mahade]ba and Bet Dinlatain and Bet Baalmaon, and I erected there . . . [31]the small cattle of the country, and Horonain, in it lived . . . [32][and] Kemosh said to me: "Go down and make war against Horonain," and I went down . . . [33] . . . and Kemosh [lived] there in my time . . . [34] . . . and I . . .

is that Omri in the Mesha inscription is more than a reference to the king of this name. Rather it involves the royal dynasty of Israel, the house of Omri. It is important that Mesha does not mention the name of the son of Omri—without doubt it should be Ahab—who was not a "Mr. Nobody" in his time. Now it is possible to relate the content of this inscription to minor acts of Mesha east of

48. Translated from the text as presented in H. Donner and W. Röllig, *Kanaanäische und aramäische Inscriften* (Wiesbaden: Harrassowitz, 1962), 1:45, no. 181. Other editions include John C. L. Gibson, *Textbook of Syrian Semitic Inscriptions*, vol. 1: *Hebrew and Moabite Inscriptions* (Oxford: Clarendon, 1971), 74–75, and Andrew Dearman, ed., *Studies in the Mesha Inscription and Moab* (Atlanta: Scholars, 1989), 93–95.
49. Or "kings"; see Dearman, *Studies*, 94.

the Jordan River, but it is not possible to harmonize the content of the inscription with biblical historiography, in spite of its preservation of Mesha's name in 2 Kings 3.

Inscriptions of this kind from the ancient Near East were composed to honor the king who commissioned them. They were not supposed to inform a posterity that lived a long time after an inscription was put in place about "how it really was." Such inscriptions allow for a few glimpses of light, but hardly form the basis of more detailed reconstructions of, say, the histories of Israel and Judah. The closest parallel between a biblical passage and a document from the ancient Near East dates to the time of King Sennacherib of Assyria, when Sennacherib tells the story of his campaign against Hezekiah. However, not even this text is simply to be paraphrased by the modern historian.

Now returning to the question of biblical historiography, it must be maintained that this historical narrative is *interpreted* history. It is a kind of historiography intending to impress on its readership the *meaning* of history. It has no problem manipulating the information presented in it—historical or legendary or invented as it may be—in such a way that the meaning, the interpretation may be understood.

The way the biblical historiographer manipulates the information in his possession relating to a certain event known from history is easy to perceive from his handling of the information about Sennacherib's campaign against Judah in 701 BCE. We have both biblical and Assyrian evidence that, although different at places, clearly includes very much the same information.[50] The exact course of the events narrated by Sennacherib and by 2 Kings 18:13–16 is difficult to establish. It may be that neither of these versions is totally correct. The biblical historiographer does not care if his reconstruction is absolutely correct from a plain historical point of view. He is far more interested in the speech of the Assyrian officer in front of Jerusalem's gate. Here the historiographer expresses his ideas about the arrogant Assyrian ideology of war (2 Kgs. 18:17–35). This speech forces Hezekiah to turn for help to Yahweh, whose spokesperson Isaiah pronounces doom over Sennacherib (2 Kgs. 19:20–34). In the end, Yahweh's angel destroys the Assyrian army.

The historiographer was not interested in the exact reconstruction of the events of 701 BCE. He was interested in the meaning of this event and invented a series of scenes illustrating this meaning. His procedure concurs well with other ancient historiography. Historical events were in themselves of no importance. Their meaning—their interpretation—was. The author of a historical narrative was allowed to manipulate his information, even to add to or subtract from it as he liked, if it helped him to write a more inspiring account. When the narrative was about something that just happened, the idea was to present an interpretation of the event to the people who might themselves have lived at the time it happened. When the historiographer addressed a later generation, the interpretation

50. See p. 117.

An Assyrian text and a biblical text

Tiglath-pileser III	2 Kings 15:29–30
The House of Omri . . . all its inhabitants and its possessions I brought to Assyria. They overthrew their king Pekah, and I installed Hosea to be their king. I received ten talents of gold from them and 1,000 talents of silver and brought them to Assyria.	In the days of King Pekah of Israel, King Tiglath-pileser of Assyria came and captured Ijon, Abel-beth-maacah, Janoah, Kedesh, Hazor, Gilead, and Galilee, all the land of Naphtali; and he carried the people captive to Assyria. 30 Then Hoshea son of Elah made a conspiracy against Pekah son of Remaliah, attacked him, and killed him; he reigned in place of him, in the twentieth year of Jotham son of Uzziah.

was for the benefit of this later generation. The interpretation was always directed to an author's contemporary readership and presented an interpretation of the past to be used in the present with an eye to the future.

Near Eastern documents indicate that the history of Israel and Judah—at least between about 850 BCE and 587 BCE—is not totally an invention. Although we do not normally see uniformity between external evidence and the biblical narrative, as is the case of Tiglath-pileser III's rearrangements in 732 BCE, including the replacing of Pekah on the throne of Israel with Hosea, Tiglath-pileser's puppet king, the information about kings of Israel and Judah and their order of succession is certainly not invented. There is a general harmony between the biblical narratives of 2 Kings and ancient Near Eastern documents. They agree, for example, that Hezekiah ruled before Manasseh. Sennacherib mentions Hezekiah, while his successor Esar-haddon and his successor Ashurbanipal mention the son and successor of Hezekiah, Manasseh.

The books of Kings sometimes refer to their sources, "The Chronicles of the Kings of Israel" and "The Chronicles of the Kings of Judah." We have no concrete evidence about their status or their content. Perhaps they were short year lists, mentioning in few words the events of a year. Such lists are known from Mesopotamian documents. At this point we don't know if something similar existed in Palestine. If such chronicles were in circulation, the authors of Kings might have had access to them. Maybe they found a basis for their reconstructed chronology in such lists. Even if these lists were available—and we still don't know for sure—then the information gained from them would be very short, and we can hardly use such nonavailable information to assert the historicity of the main parts of the books of Kings.

The conclusion is that it is possible to write a short history of Israel and Judah from the ninth to the beginning of the sixth century BCE. The biblical historiographers have not invented all but may have relied on short notes like the ones cited here from Mesopotamian sources. Here they at least had an outline for their

Mesopotamian chronicles

Excerpt from the Neo-Babylonian Chronicle

Belibni's first year: Sennacherib destroyed the cities of Hirimma and Hararatum.

Belibni's third: Sennacherib went down to the country Akkad and removed the booty from Akkad. They brought Belibni and his noble men in chains to Assyria. Belibni was king three years in Babylon. Sennacherib placed his son Assurnadinshumi on the throne in Babylon.

Assurnadinshumi's first year: Hallushu, the brother of Ishtarhundu, the king of Elam, fetched him [Ishtarhundu] and closed the door before him. Ishtarhunda was king eighteen years in Elam. Hallushu, his brother, sat on the throne of Elam . . .

Excerpt from Esar-haddon's Chronicle

In the month of Adar, on the eighteenth day, the Assyrian army conquered the country of Shuprisa, and removed the booty from it.

Tenth year: In the month of Nisam the Assyrian army went to Egypt. In the month of Du'uzu, on the third day a battle was fought in Egypt.

Eleventh year: The king of Assyria killed many of his leading officials.

Twelfth year: The king of Assyria went to Egypt. He became ill underway and died on the month of Arashshamnu, on the tenth day. Esar-haddon was king over Assyria for twelve years.

historiography. Apart from that, they might have made use of other kinds of sources. Potentially numbered among such sources are the tales about the adventures of the prophets Elijah and Elisha, anecdotes, and more. The problem is only that the moment we refer to such sources—as was already the case of the alleged royal chronicles—we are no longer in control. Often such references to sources lead to futile discussions about what is present and what is not. Such discussions are futile, because we are in no position to decide on the basis of available evidence. From a methodoloical point of view, it is foolhardy simply to paraphrase the stories of the two books of Kings in order to write a consistent and modern history of the two kingdoms. The story told here is definitely an interpreted history including a perspective of history that was not part of possible ancient sources but constructed by the historiographers themselves. Although the chronological framework—at least for the latter part of the history of these two kingdoms—may be reliable in outline, it serves the program of the historiographer.[51] This perspective of the historiographer is not a part of the historical framework; it is an interpretation of it that informs its meaning. Perhaps the perspective is not totally wrong, but it is also possible that the perspective on the history of Israel and Judah presented by the historiographer has as little to do with history as was the case of the traditions of the earlier parts of Israel's history.

51. More on this in chap. 7, "The Constructed History," pp. 186–211, esp. 209–11.

The Exile

It is just as important to keep the correct perspective on history in mind when the Old Testament historiographer writes about Israel's exile in Babylon. It is obvious that the notion of the exile is a kind of scarlet thread that runs through biblical historiography from one end to the other. This thread, so to speak, binds the history together, and without this perspective the history of Israel as told by the Old Testament would be meaningless.

The notion of exile was deeply rooted in the ancient Near Eastern mind. Assyrian rulers had arranged for large-scale deportation for hundreds of years, some of them on a much larger scale than the one mentioned in the Old Testament, although the numbers presented by Assyrian inscriptions may perhaps sometimes need to be reduced. When it comes to Assyrian politics in Palestine, they had already, before the fall of Samaria in 722 BCE, deported a part of the population in northern Palestine, and more deportations followed the fall of Samaria. Judah was spared this ordeal until the assault of Sennacherib in 701 BCE. Now Sennacherib boasts of having carried away 200,150 persons from the cities of Hezekiah and made them his booty—many times more than ever lived in this tiny part of Palestine in antiquity.

More deportations followed after the Neo-Babylonian kingdom replaced the Assyrian, to whose downfall between 612 and 605 BCE it had contributed. In 597 BCE, in connection with the first Babylonian conquest of Jerusalem, a fair share of the population of Jerusalem was carried away to Mesopotamia. This event is recorded in the Old Testament in this way:

> He carried away all Jerusalem, all the officials, all the warriors, ten thousand captives, all the artisans and the smiths; no one remained, except the poorest people of the land. [15] He carried away Jehoiachin to Babylon; the king's mother, the king's wives, his officials, and the elite of the land, he took into captivity from Jerusalem to Babylon. [16] The king of Babylon brought captive to Babylon all the men of valor, seven thousand, the artisans and the smiths, one thousand, all of them strong and fit for war. (2 Kgs. 24:14–16)

The Babylonian Chronicle does not mention this deportation in connection with its report of the year 597 BCE (see p. 116). The passage in 2 Kings 24:14–16 is not totally clear. Does it describe one or two deportations, one including 10,000 persons, and a second involving only 7,000? Or do we here have two notes about one and the same event, each with its own number? This might be important, because it seems that the historiographer has a certain interest in boosting the number of persons exiled. Since the deportation(s) is (are) not mentioned by the Babylonian Chronicle, it could be that only the royal family and a few leading officials were exiled at this time.

From the perspective of the historiography in the Old Testament, it is important that the decisive Babylonian exile began ten years before the final destruction of Jerusalem. The book of Ezekiel is based on this information, arguing that the prophet Ezekiel was among those who went into exile in 597 BCE and from

his position in the exile became a witness to the final destruction of his homeland. In this way the book of Ezekiel is framed by two opposite "events." At the
beginning of the book we have the destruction of Jerusalem and its temple and
at the end (chaps. 40–48) the prophet's vision of the new Jerusalem standing on
the ruins of the old and destroyed temple.

It may be that the only result of the Babylonian conquest of 597 BCE was the
abduction of the king and his family and the enthronement of a Babylonian puppet king, who had to pay a tribute to his master but was left in peace to govern
his country as a Babylonian vassal.

The suspicion that the description of the first part of the exile in 2 Kings
24–25 includes less historical information than often supposed is supported by
the description of the deportation after the fall of Jerusalem in 587 BCE, mentioned only in the Old Testament:

> In the fifth month, on the seventh day of the month—which was the nine-
> teenth year of King Nebuchadnezzar, king of Babylon—Nebuzaradan, the
> captain of the bodyguard, a servant of the king of Babylon, came to
> Jerusalem. [9] He burned the house of the LORD, the king's house, and all the
> houses of Jerusalem; every great house he burned down. [10] All the army of
> the Chaldeans who were with the captain of the guard broke down the walls
> around Jerusalem. [11] Nebuzaradan the captain of the guard carried into exile
> the rest of the people who were left in the city and the deserters who had
> defected to the king of Babylon—all the rest of the population. [12] But the
> captain of the guard left some of the poorest people of the land to be vine-
> dressers and tillers of the soil. (2 Kgs. 25:8–12)

There is not the slightest hint in this passage as to the number of people
involved in this deportation. We hear that only the poorest part of the population were left in the country, which is hardly amazing as they, according to
2 Kings 24:14, already were the only ones left in Jerusalem and Judah after the
deportation(s) of 597 BCE. This does not imply that the "whole population"
could not flee to Egypt shortly afterwards when the Babylonian governor
Gedaliah was murdered (2 Kgs. 25:26).

The account of the destruction of Jerusalem in 587 BCE does not stand alone
in the Old Testament. The book of Jeremiah includes an extended version of the
period from the fall of Jerusalem in 587 BCE to the murder of Gedaliah in 582
BCE (Jer. 39–43). These chapters are especially concerned with the murder of
Gedaliah, which is described in detail, and the following flight to Egypt. The
deportation in 587 BCE and the destruction of Jerusalem get less space. Jeremiah's presentation of the details of this destruction and the deportation is, however, no more precise than the account found in 2 Kings. The books of Chronicles
are even less interested in such precise numbers, perhaps because the Chronicler's
idea is that everyone was carried away and the country remained a desert for seventy years (2 Chr. 36:17–21).

The Old Testament has almost no information about life in the exile. Only a little information has survived from other sources, such as a couple of administrative

documents mentioning that the sons (the documents say five, without mentioning their names) of Jehoiachin, who is called both "King of Judah" and "the son of the King of Judah," receive provisions from the palace; something that is described in another document also mentioning eight unnamed persons from Judah.[52]

It is asserted that Judean personal names appear in Neo-Babylonian documents. Even if we think of a Babylonian exile after the deportations of 597 and 587 BCE on a far smaller scale than normally believed, it is certain that a number of Judeans lived in Mesopotamia, in the sixth century the center of the world. One of the documents that includes a reference to the provision for Jehoiachin also mentions people from Tyre and from Lydia, while another document mentions provisions for people from Arvad and Byblus in Phoenicia and for Greeks.

The lack of information about the Babylonian exile in and outside of the Old Testament means that we know almost nothing about this exile. At some point the scholar has to ask himself, was this exile real? Could it be an ideological construction created at a later date to legitimize the right of the Jews to Palestine in spite of the fact that they were not the only ones whose ancestors had lived in the country? According to the Old Testament, no people lived in the land for seventy years. Seventy years is another loaded number and not a precise indication of time; it says only "for more than a generation" (which would be "forty years"). Archaeological discoveries in modern times have shown that although the country was devastated, it was not empty of people, as the Bible suggests.[53]

The Persian Period

It follows in the ideology of biblical historiography that the description of the return from the exile involved tens of thousands of people, precisely 42,360, not including slaves (Ezra 2:64–65; repeated in Neh. 7:66–67), to be exact. The number is based on a "precise" counting of people who returned, family by family.

The return is described as a liberation made possible by the personal intervention by the Persian king, Cyrus (559–539 BCE), who ordered the return of the Jews in 539 BCE, leading to the official date of the return in 538 BCE. Cyrus's decree of liberation is quoted in Ezra 1:2–4:

> Thus says King Cyrus of Persia: The LORD, the God of heaven, has given me all the kingdoms of the earth, and he has charged me to build him a house at Jerusalem in Judah. [3] Any of those among you who are of his people—may their God be with them!—are now permitted to go up to Jerusalem in Judah, and rebuild the house of the LORD, the God of Israel— he is the God who is in Jerusalem; [4] and let all survivors, in whatever place they reside, be assisted by the people of their place with silver and gold, with

52. These texts are translated in Pritchard, *ANET*, 308.
53. New vistas on the history of this period are found in Oded Lipschits, *The Rise and Fall of Jerusalem: Judah under Babylonian Rule* (Winona Lake, IN: Eisenbrauns, 2005), and in Oded Lipschits and Joseph Blenkinsopp, eds., *Judah and the Judeans in the Neo-Babylonian Period* (Winona Lake, IN: Eisenbrauns, 2003).

goods and with animals, besides freewill offerings for the house of God in Jerusalem.

The text of this royal decree is, together with similar decrees in Ezra and Nehemiah, often reckoned to be a genuine official Persian document. A comparison with similar official documents from the Persian Empire reveals that the content and structure of Ezra 1:2–4 are the same as found in such sources. A closer look at the biblical specimen reveals, however, that even if the text of Ezra 1:2–4 is based on such a Persian royal decree, it has been edited by the biblical author of Ezra. The final passage about the gifts for those who decide to return, paid by the local population, seems to be a truth that is better than fiction. It might also be doubted that mighty Cyrus, the ruler of an empire that in the east bordered on India and in the west on Egypt, would attribute his power to Yahweh's providence.

The problems confronting the historian who studies the Persian period are not very different from the ones met by the students of any period in the history of Israel. In some way the problems are even more acute than before. We have no official Persian document that mentions the events in Jerusalem and Judah like the biblical narrative about so-called postexilic times. We possess a variety of documents from less official channels from which we have some information about the conditions in Palestine, especially in the fifth century BCE. Among the more important documents is a series of letters in Aramaic from Elephantine in Egypt. The people who wrote these letters were Jews belonging to a colony of mercenaries in southern Egypt. Here they had their temple of Yahweh. Thus a letter dating from 407 BCE includes a petition from the inhabitants of Elephantine who named themselves "Judeans"—if not simply "Jews"—to Bagoas the governor of Judah. They ask for support for the rebuilding of their temple for the God of Heaven in Egypt.[54] This letter also mentions the names of the sons of the governor in Samaria, Sanballat, who could be the same person mentioned in Nehemiah as Nehemiah's bitter opponent (Neh. 4–5). Some scholars are, however, of the opinion that there might have been more than one Persian governor of this name in Samaria.

The scholar dealing with the Persian period who wants to include biblical sources has been caught by the same kind of circular argumentation that infested studies of Israelite history from before the exile. Basically scholars suppose that the information found in the Old Testament is historically sound, and they use this assertion to reconstruct the history of this period, but find little support in external evidence.

It is often asserted that Persian rule was more liberal than the former Assyrian and Babylonian ones. This assertion is based on an inscription from the days of Cyrus—the so-called Cyrus cylinder. In his inscription the king of Persia boasts of being the generous ruler who cares for the welfare of his subjects. The inscription in question is not singular in content. Rather, it reflects royal inscriptions

54. The letter is translated in Pritchard, *ANET*, 491–92.

The righteous king (see also the prologue to the Codex Hammurabi, p. 84)

Tukulti-Ninurta I (ca. 1241–1206 BCE)[55]

When Assur, my Lord, elected me legally to worship him, and entrusted me with the scepter of my task as herdsman and gave to me the staff for my office as herdsman and provided me with heroic power in order to crush my enemies and to subdue them who do not fear me and put the crown of rulership upon me, I placed my foot solidly on the neck of the countries and let the widespread blackheads graze like cattle!

From the Cyrus cylinder[56]

I am Cyrus, the king of the world, the great king, the mighty king, the King of Babylon, the King of Sumer and Akkad, the king over the four corners of the world, the son of Cambyses, the great king, the King of Anshan, the grandson of Cyrus, the great king, the King of Anshan, the great grandson of Teispes, the great king, the King of Anshan, an eternal royal seed whose rule Bel and Nabu love and whose government they adorn for the happiness of their hearts.

When I in peace entered Babylon, I established my royal residence in the royal palace with hilarity and delight. Marduk, the great lord, (turned) the magnanimous Babylonians [to me] . . . and I participated each day in his worship. My numerous troops moved around in Babylon in peace. I did not allow anybody to frighten all of Sumer and Akkad. I looked for the welfare of Babylon and all its cities. From the inhabitants of Babylon . . . the disgraceful yoke was removed. Their houses which were in decay I repaired and removed their ruins. Marduk, the great lord, rejoiced because of my acts and blessed me, Cyrus, the king who worships him, and Cambyses, my son, and all my troops with gracious words, and we all standing in front of him are praising his greatness.

---

from Mesopotamia going back at least a millennium. Such royal inscriptions include the praise of the king as the good and gracious ruler who alone acts on behalf of the welfare of his people. Cyrus's inscription has no bearing on his system of rule. We find no support in the extant sources for the assertion that Persian rule was especially mild and benevolent.[57]

The idea that one of Cyrus's first acts as king of Babylon—a city he captured in 639 BCE—was to allow the Jews to return home is probably a myth, nourished by Old Testament historiographers and historians of the present who just paraphrased

55. Translated after the text in Ernst Weidner, *Die Inschriften Tukulti-Ninurtas I. und seiner Nachfolger*, Archiv für Orientforschung 12 (Graz: Erich Weidner, 1959), 1.

56. Translated after the text in P.-R. Berger, "Der Kyros Zylinder mit Zusatzfragment BIN II Nr. 32 und die akkadischen Personennamen in Danielbuch," *Zeitschrift für Assyriologie* 64 (1975): 192–234. The newest edition of this text is Hanspeter Schaudig, *Die Inschriften Nabonids von Babylon und Kyros des Großen, samt den in ihrem Umfeld entstandenen Tendenzschriften. Textausgabe und Grammatik*, Alter Orient und Altes Testament 256 (Münster: Ugarit-Verlag, 2001).

57. This view of the implication of the Cyrus cylinder goes back to Amélie Kuhrt, "The Cyrus Cylinder and Achaemenid Imperial Policy," *JSOT* 25 (1983): 83–97.

the biblical history. We have little evidence of the immediate consequences of the Persian takeover for the people deported from Palestine and Syria to Mesopotamia.

The "survey" of history following the Babylonian exile is limited to three incidents. The first one, normally dated to the beginning of the rule of Darius I, concerns the rebuilding of the temple of Jerusalem. The sources are Ezra 3–6, the book of Haggai, and Zechariah 1–6. The inauguration of this temple is normally dated to 516 BCE, exactly seventy years after the destruction of the first temple. The second incident has to do with Ezra's activity in Jerusalem, and the third concentrates on Nehemiah's stay in Jerusalem. There is no external evidence that may help to elucidate any of these events.

The building of the temple is supposed to have been commissioned by Cyrus in his previously mentioned decree of liberation, but according to the information in Ezra 4, it was not finished in the days of Ahasuerus, that is Xerxes, and Artaxerxes. It was finished only in the days of Darius. The chronology presented by this source is hopeless. Xerxes ruled 486–465 BCE, and Artaxerxes I 465–424/3 BCE, while Darius I—if it is Darius I—ruled 522–486 BCE. Perhaps it is better to think of Darius II, who ruled 423–405, although this will lower the date of the inauguration of the rebuilding of the temple by another century. It would also force a breakdown of the entire scholarly chronological reconstruction and the history of Jerusalem and Judah in the Persian period will fall apart. Few Old Testament scholars are prepared to accept this.[58]

The problems pertaining to this period surface in a paradigmatic way when the subject is the relation between Ezra and Nehemiah. According to the book of Ezra, Ezra arrived in Jerusalem after the inauguration of the new temple, but before Nehemiah, whose stay in Jerusalem is dated to Artaxerxes' twentieth year of rule. According to Nehemiah 1–6, which is often reckoned to be his autobiography, written by himself as a report concerning his arrangements in Jerusalem, Nehemiah found a Jerusalem still in ruins. He began in conflict with the aforementioned Sanballat, the governor of Samaria, then rebuilt the city. This part of the book of Nehemiah has nothing to say about Ezra.

Many scholars are of the opinion that Ezra must postdate Nehemiah. If Ezra traveled to Jerusalem in the days of King Artaxerxes, this Artaxerxes need not be the first king of Persia of this name, and it need not be the same Artaxerxes who sent Nehemiah to Jerusalem. There were three kings of Persia bearing this name: Artaxerxes I (465–424/3), Artaxerxes II (405–359), and Artaxerxes III (359–338). It has therefore been proposed that Nehemiah arrived in Jerusalem in 445 BCE and Ezra no earlier than 398 BCE, during the time of Artaxerxes II.

All of this is best classified as educated guesswork. The basis is the conviction that Nehemiah 1–6 was really written by Nehemiah himself and is therefore an

---

58. See, however, Diana Edelman, in her study *The Origins of the "Second" Temple: Persian Imperial Policy and the Rebuilding of Jerusalem*, The Bible and Its World (London: Equinox, 2005). She is of the conviction that the temple was completed only in the days of Artaxerxes I.

authentic source. The form of this narrative, the autobiography, has convinced many scholars that it must be so, although fictive autobiographies were well known in the ancient Near East. We have several specimens of autobiographies of famous persons written many years after they died. This has to be taken into consideration whenever a text like the book of Nehemiah comes to mind.

The problems concerning the historicity of Ezra and Nehemiah are more serious. According to Ezra 7:1–5, Ezra son of Seraiah, son of Azariah, son of Hilkiah . . . son of Aaron went to Jerusalem in the days of Artaxerxes. The problem is that his father, Seraiah, was killed by Nebuzaradan after the Babylonian conquest of Jerusalem in 587 BCE (2 Kgs. 25:18–21), and Hilkiah was the high priest who assisted King Josiah during his reform of the temple cult in Jerusalem (2 Kgs. 22). No matter how scholars intend to reconstruct the chronology of the period, and no matter whether they want to date Ezra to the time of Artaxerxes I or Artaxerxes II or perhaps III, he would have been an extremely old gentleman when he arrived at Jerusalem. The consequence is that biblical authors may have invented a hero of Jewish faith by the name of Ezra who is the person who recites the Law of Moses to the people and completes an ethnic cleansing of the Jewish nation. Ezra is the true father of Judaism, although he seems to have no family and an invented genealogy. Otherwise he would have been at least 200 years old when he came to Jerusalem. Apart from this, nobody knows for sure when he may have arrived. Finally, the book of the Hebrew Bible carrying his name is perhaps the latest part of this collection.[59] This person without a family and without a history was turned by biblical writers into the great national hero of Judaism.

The information included in the book of Nehemiah seems better founded in history, although the account of the Persian period in the Old Testament is at best confused. The chronology is in disorder, and the historiographers had no idea about the correct sequence of Persian kings. The presence of several kings of the same name—Darius and Artaxerxes—seems to be the cause of this confusion. Perhaps it is simply the case that in Nehemiah we find information about living conditions in Jerusalem about 450 or 400 BCE. If this is correct, Jerusalem during Nehemiah's time was definitely a city still in ruins. If the temple was really reestablished as the center of Judaism in 516 BCE—and there is good reason to doubt it—it was of no importance before Nehemiah's time. If the deported people returning from Babylon really came to this Jerusalem, it looks as if they had deserted it again and gone back to Babylon a long time before the arrival of Nehemiah. New results of Israeli archaeological activity also indicate that the story about the end of the exile and the return to Jerusalem has little basis in reality. The surveys carried out by these archaeologists show that there were no major demographical changes in the area of Jerusalem before the end of the fifth century BCE, about a hundred years after the official end of the Babylonian exile.

59. Some will date the present Ezra as late as the first century CE. Moreover, the Hebrew version of the book represents only one version of it. There are other versions, each displaying a number of peculiarities.

The leading Israeli historian of this period, Oded Lipschits, also argues that there was no city worth the name of Jerusalem in the Persian period.[60]

THE LOGICAL PROBLEM: THE THREE (FOUR) DIFFERENT "ISRAELS"

A kind of scarlet thread throughout this chapter is that although it is at times possible to place information found in the Old Testament within a historical framework known from the ancient Near East, such cases are generally isolated. They do not establish a systematic pattern. It has to be maintained that the story of ancient Israel in the Old Testament from Abraham to Ezra and Nehemiah is about a history that never happened. It is not possible to reconstruct a *real* history that has much in common with the story told by biblical historiographers.

We may be closest to a real history in the period of the two kingdoms of Israel and Judah. We know that there was a kingdom of Israel, although in its own time perhaps it was better known as the house of Omri or Samaria. Quite a few kings of Israel and Judah also turn up in documents from the ancient Near East and, as far as it is possible to control the information about them, are placed by biblical historiographers in the corrected historical context.

The conclusion must be that the historiographer writing the story of the kingdoms of Israel and Judah possessed some exact information as short annalistic notes. The historiographer was hardly in possession of much additional material. It probably was of little importance to the historiographer, who was not shy about rewriting his information into legendary tales. The best example—an example that can be examined by modern historians—is the story of Sennacherib's attack on Judah in 701 BCE. Here a short note (2 Kgs. 18:13–16) of definite historical importance has, at the hand of the historiographer, been vastly expanded into a fairy tale about God's deliverance of his beloved city (2 Kgs. 18:17–19:37).

The situation of biblical historiography concerning the most recent periods, the Babylonian exile and the Persian period, is not different from the historiography of the earlier periods. The Old Testament has nothing important (from a historical angle) to say about the exile, and its description of the Persian period is both confused and misleading. Only a person already of the conviction that the Bible tells the truth and nothing but the truth, in spite of all problems, may endorse a reconstruction of the history of ancient Israel with its many details as told by the biblical historiographer.

It is not possible to reconstruct the history of Israel in ancient times on the basis of the information in the Old Testament. This circumstance has not

---

60. Oded Lipschits, "Achaemenid Imperial Policy, Settlement Processes in Palestine, and the Status of Jerusalem in the Middle of the Fifth Century B.C.E.," in Oded Lipschits and Manfred Oeming, eds., *Judah and the Judeans in the Persian Period* (Winona Lake, IN: Eisenbrauns, 2006), 19–52, 31. See also Lipschits's *The Fall and Rise of Jerusalem*, 234–36.

deterred scholars from writing such impossible histories. The question is only, why do they continue to produce such histories?

In a monograph from 1992 about the many absurdities of Old Testament scholarship, the British Old Testament scholar Philip R. Davies proposed to find not only one "Israel" but at least three editions of "Israel" in Old Testament scholarship.[61]

According to Davies it is important to distinguish between historical Israel, biblical Israel, and ancient Israel. *Historical Israel* is the Israel of the real world that was destroyed by the Assyrians in 722 BCE. The second Israel, *biblical Israel*, is a nation that appears only in biblical Scripture. This nation descended from Abraham, went to Egypt, left Egypt again, and conquered Canaan. Later it established a huge empire but was thereafter divided into two minor kingdoms. In the end, this Israel went into exile in Babylon, but returned and reestablished its cult of Yahweh in Jerusalem. This biblical Israel has little in common with historical Israel. The only convergences concern a few personal names and the name "Israel" itself. Finally, *ancient Israel* is the Israel constructed by Old Testament scholars by mixing historical and biblical Israel together in a kind of cocktail that cannot be identified by either of its components but is solely the brainchild of historical-critical scholarship. Ancient Israel is the invention of the present.

Ancient Israel depends on a logical assertion mixing of several categories, each of them legitimate subjects of investigation. The moment they are mixed together, problems arise. In the future, Old Testament scholarship is obliged to study each edition of Israel for its own sake. Each of them should be allowed to speak for itself; each of them has its own story to tell. The fate of historical-critical study of Israel is identical to the fate of biblical archaeology. Here archaeology ended up as the handmaid of biblical studies, or so it was believed. At the end, biblical archaeology became its own worst enemy and destroyed its favorite subject: the historicity of the Bible. The distance between what archaeologists found in the ground and what is related by biblical historiography became so large that archaeologists had to demand to be released from their duty to confirm the Bible. In the same way historians must demand to be able to study their subject, Palestinian history in the second and first millennia BCE, without interference from biblical scholars; vice versa, biblical scholars should continue their study of biblical literature without always having to look for historical elements in this literature.

It is, however, necessary to supplement Davies's analysis on two counts. His category ancient Israel may not be totally clear. It may be too general. There are many editions of ancient Israel in circulation, probably as many as there are historical-critical scholars. Every scholar has created his or her image of ancient Israel, although these images are of course interrelated in many ways.

The second supplement has to do with Davies's description of biblical Israel, because we find in the Old Testament not one biblical Israel but two, on one side the *Israel of the old covenant* and on the other the *Israel of the new covenant* (see

---

61. Philip R. Davies, *In Search of "Ancient Israel,"* JSOTSup 148 (Sheffield: JSOT, 1992).

Jer. 31:31–34). Perhaps the real subject of biblical historiography is not the first one but the second, the new Israel. Indeed, perhaps the story of old Israel is told as an example not to be followed by the members of the new Israel.

Now in order to come to terms with the author(s) who invented the idea of biblical Israel, we will have to return to the historical Israel in order to put biblical Israel in the right perspective. What was Israel in ancient times? What role did it play? How can a history of this Israel be written? What is the purpose of the historiography found in the Old Testament? What did the historiographer have to prove? What did he have to legitimate and to whom? What is really the intention of biblical historiography?

PART III
FROM HISTORY AND
BACK TO THEOLOGY

Introduction

The Text and Its Author
or the Text and Its Reader

Biblical studies are at present divided into two main camps. One of these builds on the results gained by classical historical-critical scholarship and on the refined methodologies born of the attacks on this methodology during the last twenty-five years. We may simply call it critical scholarship. Critical scholarship should, in the future, still aim at a critical analysis of the Old Testament, although the limitations of this scholarship as indicated by the name of its forerunner, historical-critical scholarship, have been removed. *Historical* indicates a predominance of historical interest. This is not to suggest that historical topics are no longer in evidence. On the contrary, the scholar may still be interested in history, although that should no longer be the primary, not to say exclusive, concern. When we decide to present a plea for the continuation of critical studies, this aims at a distinction between critical analysis and fundamentalist naive paraphrase.

Future critical scholarship must be less ambitious when it comes to the historical question. It must escape being caught by the methodological mistake of classical historical-critical research, that is, logically circular argumentation disguised as the hermeneutical circle. By focusing on history, scholars fell into the trap of stressing the referential importance of biblical texts. They became too obsessed with endeavors to trace the historical reality behind the text, and they used this construed reality to interpret their texts.

To mention one example, scholars considered the books of Kings to be the product of the time they are writing about, Israel in the period of the kings. The prophetical books were read in the light of the chronological information in the introductions to the prophetic books and in the light of the historical narrative in the books of Kings. Psalms were understood to be part of a religious and cultic tradition scholars had created for themselves.

The previous part of this book presented criticism of the kind of scholarship that led to a proposal for its abolishment. This does not, however, mean that all critical analysis of the Old Testament is vetoed at the same time. On the contrary, it should lead to a renewed and refined analysis. Historically oriented scholars will never accept that the Old Testament is removed from history. The modern reader is still convinced that the Old Testament is an old book whose origins go back to ancient times. This reader will still consider the contextualization of Old Testament literature in its historical situation of central importance and will try to analyze the text based on its general historical milieu.

The reader in question should not begin his investigation by reconstructing the alleged historical context of his text before he has even read it properly. It is a most difficult enterprise to present a definitive date for most parts of the Old Testament. We could even say that it is impossible, because the biblical text includes no precise information that allows for such precise dates. Some may believe that the chronological information in the introductions to prophetical books may serve as an indicator of the time when these prophets were active, but such information is provided by the collectors of this literature and is a reflection of the collectors' dating of his collection.

Before the appearance of the Dead Sea Scrolls, little concrete, that is, physical evidence existed that had any bearing on the problem of dating biblical books. The discovery of these texts has created a totally new situation that allows for a far more detailed reconstruction of the emergence of Old Testament literature.[1] The discussion of the date of the collection of biblical literature will follow later, together with other evidence for the existence of the text of the Old Testament, or perhaps better, for the existence of the individual parts of the Old Testament.[2]

The next step in the analytical procedure will be to read the relevant texts in the Old Testament in order to study the idea of the history of Israel proposed

---

1. The literature on the Dead Sea Scrolls is too enormous to list. There exists a plethora of translations into English. The most complete may be Florentino García Martínez, *The Dead Sea Scrolls Translated: The Qumran Texts in English* (Leiden: Brill, 1992). The official edition, published by the Dead Sea Scroll Foundation in Jerusalem as *Discoveries in the Judean Desert*, began to appear in 1955 (list available at http://orion.mscc.huji.ac.il/resources/djd.shtml). Biblical texts and fragments are collected and translated in Martin Abegg, Peter Flint, and Eugene Ulrich, *The Dead Sea Scrolls Bible* (San Francisco: Harper, 1999). For the importance of these texts for the textual history of the Old Testament, see the authoritative treatment by Emanuel Tov, *Textual Criticism of the Hebrew Bible* (2nd rev. ed., Minneapolis: Fortress/Assen: Van Gorcum, 2001).

2. See chap. 11, pp. 276–80.

here. The so-called historical books from Genesis to 2 Kings and the Chronicler's literature, including the books of Ezra and Nehemiah, present history as it was understood at the time when these books were written down. A new critical study of this literature must begin with the interpretation of history in the Old Testament and consider this interpretation a reconstruction that may have relatively little to say about the past "as it really was," but constructs a past as the author believed it to have been. It is also a safe assumption that this reconstructed history was meaningful for its original readership. This critical analysis is therefore mainly concerned with reading the text handed down to modern times rather than a text-archaeological exercise intending to discover the "reality" behind the text in question.

The second part of the Old Testament canon, the Prophets, will have to be read and analyzed in light of its self-testimony. A series of questions have to be addressed to this literature: What kind of society is the subject of the prophetic literature? To whom did the collectors address their books? How far may we speak of an agreement between the prophetic books and the historical literature? Do the prophetic books stand on their own legs, or do they represent the other side of the biblical historical construction? Do the prophetic books represent an independent testimony to the history of Israel, or are they dependent on the idea of Israel found in the historical books?

Some of the same questions may be directed to the books of the third part of the Hebrew Bible, the Writings, though the content of this part is most diversified and its books should be analyzed without regard for their scriptural context. The books of Psalms is definitely a subject of analysis, especially because the Psalms are often considered as the most authentic expression of religious life and sentiment of ancient Israel. Here it will be important, if it is possible, to show that the collection of Psalms in the Old Testament is closely related to ideas about the fate of Israel and about its religion, as found in the prophetic books and in the historical literature. When we move on to analysis of individual psalms, it also has to be acknowledged that these sometimes may have had a "life" before they were incorporated into the collection known as the Psalter.

Wisdom literature has its own problems, mostly because it is generally impossible to date or to localize, in spite of the fact that some of these books have been attributed to King Solomon. It may be problematic to look for connections between the ideas expressed by the authors of the Wisdom literature and their colleagues who wrote the historical and prophetical books. Maybe enough can be said to show that they contribute to the general impression of the cultural background for the collectors of other parts of the Old Testament.

The renewed critical analysis of biblical texts must allow the texts to speak for themselves. It is necessary to stress that in this literature authors living in ancient times speak to us. This must be said in contrast to another way of reading biblical texts that has gained in importance during the last generation. Our alternative way will, with some right, argue that the renewed critical reading includes elements of circular argumentation. Classical historical-critical scholarship concentrated on the

real history as a backdrop to the production of biblical literature. Renewed critical scholarship will prefer to concentrate on the person of the author or collector.
The danger is that this author is no more than another reconstruction, which is
then used as the basis of textual reconstruction. Even if the variables are different,
the method is very much the same, or so it might be argued.

Such critics will prefer to make use of that variety of modern literary criticism
that stresses the text as in itself an incomprehensible array of symbols that asks
a reader to create coherent meaning out of such symbols. The text will emerge
only when the symbols are confronted by a reader who can "interpret" their
meaning, that is, "read them." In order to understand the interpretation of texts,
it is necessary to concentrate on the person of the reader and study his or her
background, which will always be very different from that of the original author.
Hence, in this approach the reader, not the author, will be the center of attention. Such contemporary readers may well argue that it is impossible to reconstruct the past on the basis of texts from the past—such reconstruction is no more
than a modern one based on modern prepositions far removed from the prepositions of ancient authors—but it is equally impossible to reconstruct an ancient
writer and his public.

This trend resembles certain orientations within advanced modern natural science that stress the importance of the instrument for the result obtained during
the analytic process. Different instruments may produce different results. It is
also possible to experiment in such a way that even basic natural laws like the law
of gravity are suspended. If we compare the reader to the instrument, different
readers, like different instruments, will produce different results. This is quite a
commonplace assertion, and anybody who, like this writer, has been examining
his or her students year after year will understand this quite clearly. No two examinations are the same. The reader, the candidate, will have present a reading and
an analysis that are his or her own, and it will always be different from the reading of other candidates. Every candidate will have different qualifications. How
well has the candidate studied his texts? How good a reader is this candidate?

It is impossible for people of the modern era to remold themselves as people
of the ancient world. It is therefore impossible to read an ancient text on its own
conditions. Modern human beings have only a peripheral knowledge of these
conditions. In the end the modern scholar has created a monstrosity, another
example of modern human beings' obsession with history as it was supposed to
have been.[3]

The discussion about the importance of the author in any attempt to understand his literature is not a new one. Within general literary studies it is more
than a hundred years old. In its classical form, the argument is, is it necessary to
know the identity of the author to understand a piece of literature, or will the literature in question alone be a sufficient basis of analysis? This discussion has never

---

3. An excellent example of such a monstrosity may be the invention of the redactor, or editor. Cf.
above 45n2.

ended, but it builds on another discussion going much further back, about the author's ability to control his own writings. This discussion is exemplified in the classical anecdote about the Roman poet Virgil's death. On his deathbed Virgil obliged his friends—among them the poet Horace—to promise him that they would burn his unfinished *Aeneid* after his death. The fear that unknown and uninformed persons would get hold of his masterpiece had plagued the poet for many years. Now his control over his poem could no more be exacted, so it would be better to burn it; this would be the poet's final and decisive control over his work. As is well known, his friends broke their oath to Virgil, and the *Aeneid* turned into the national epic of the Roman Empire.

Another example of how important this discussion is has to do with Shakespeare's plays. Very little is known about Shakespeare's life, although he was declared the best author of the whole millennium at the end of the second millennium. This lack of knowledge has not prevented an enormous literature dealing with his life. However, looking over such literature, one is free to ask, has such study forwarded the interpretation of his plays? It will hardly be easier to understand *Hamlet* on the basis of the many reconstructions of the author's life and whereabouts; not even the history of England in Elizabethan times will be of much help. It is often maintained that his dramas are timeless, beyond time and space and including eternal truth, a truth for every subsequent period to come to terms with.

Many faithful readers of the Old Testament will be of the same opinion. The fateful historical narrative—some will call it a national epic—running from Genesis to 2 Kings is somehow removed from time and space like Shakespeare's dramas. We here have a narrative that was once upon a time written for the benefit of a specific audience. This audience is, however, unknown to us and for that reason not relevant for our appreciation of this literature. We, the still living, are alone responsible for the way we read a text from ancient times. We are the persons who have to create a meaningful context for our reading, and we are the people who make this literature important, even today—if it still is important.

Like general literary studies, this is not a new phenomenon. As a matter of fact, before the breakthrough of modernism more than 200 years ago, this was the normal way of reading texts. The modern breakthrough and its consequences were the subject of an earlier part of this book. Here it is only necessary to stress that it represented a radical departure from a traditional Christian and Jewish way of reading texts. Christians from antiquity and the Middle Ages were hardly interested in the past, except to the degree that it was relevant to them. Christian literature of the first several centuries showed little understanding of the Old Testament as a book for Judaism. On the contrary, it was generally held that the Jews had distorted the Bible and their readings were mistaken. The Christians held the only valid key of understanding the Bible, that is, christological interpretation of the message of the Bible. The Old Testament was important because of its message about the coming of the Christ.

The crisis for the position of the Old Testament within Christian tradition emerged at the moment this christological interpretation was replaced by historical-critical research. Soon theologians began to question the idea of having an Old Testament as part of the Christian canon. As a textbook of religious history the Old Testament includes too many things that are, from a Christian point of view, of no importance. Conservative Christians have often argued that historical scholarship has in the main confirmed the historicity of Old Testament historiography. Especially the excavations in Palestine and neighboring countries have contributed to the verification of the biblical version of Israel's history. However, as the late British Old Testament scholar James Barr argued, it is probably only a very few evangelical-fundamentalist Christians who are really so interested in knowing so much about the ancient Near East as historical-critical scholarship has been able to provide in cooperation with other branches of scholarship.[4] The question is now whether we are in a situation where a reading of the Bible, which in the eyes of traditional historical-critical scholarship would be condemned as "unscientific because of its lack of interest in historical-critical matters," might be able to change the status of the Old Testament within theology in general. This will be the subject of the fourth part of this book, about the Old Testament and biblical theology.

Before we get that far it will still be worth the effort to investigate whether a critical (rather than historical-critical) reading of the Old Testament might produce information about those who actually wrote the literature found in this collection of books. It might still be interesting and probably revealing if we were able to narrow down the time frame in which the biblical literature came into being. It has been argued many times that classical historical-critical scholarship was a house of cards built on circular argumentation. The question is whether it is possible to get behind such circular argumentation and still produce falsifiable, that is, valid or legitimate critical results.

This is a choice that has to be made in light of the aforementioned debate about the person of the author and its influence on the interpretation of his or her writings. We could say that the person of Shakespeare is of no importance to his dramas, but this does not say that his dramas are not important for the person of Shakespeare. We know this gentleman mainly through his writings. In the same manner, it can be said that although we know next to nothing about the identity of the biblical writers, we know a lot about them from their writings.

---

4. James Barr, *Fundamentalism* (Philadelphia: Westminster, 1977), 132. Barr's remark is especially directed against the so-called fundamentalist form of Christianity and conservative, not to say evangelical, biblical scholars and their often minute exploitation of everything from the ancient Near East supposed to have even the slightest relevance for Old Testament matters.

Chapter 6

Written or Oral Transmission of Literature

A Renewed Critical Study of the Old Testament I

CANONICAL, RELIGIOUS TEXTS IN ANCIENT TIMES— OUTSIDE OF THE OLD TESTAMENT

Most important religions of today are in possession of collections of written texts officially acknowledged by these religions as their holy scripture, as their canonical inheritance. It has not always been so. Nothing indicates that the Greeks accepted a common canon with an absolutistic demand to control beliefs and ethics. The Homeric epics—according to tradition written by a blind poet who lived a long time before the classical period[1]—were greatly respected in the Greek world and often quoted, but they were not considered an authoritative canon, and they were not accepted as religious guidelines. In the Hellenistic period they were part of a kind of literary canon, but were never a generally acknowledged religious canon.

---

1. Homer is normally dated to the end of the eighth century BCE. The present form of his poems was considered for a long time to have been the result of editorial work in the time of the tyrant Peisistratos at the end of the sixth century BCE. This date is now contested. Other proposals for the final redaction suggest the Hellenistic period.

Comprehensive collections of religious texts were in circulation in the ancient Near East. Such collections have survived, especially from Mesopotamia, but also from Egypt, where a great many religious texts have been found. Among the better known Mesopotamian religious compositions we might mention the so-called Epic of Creation or *Enuma Elish*,[2] which approaches the concept of a canonical religious text and was utilized as part of the ritual at the Akitu festival in Babylon. This poem tells about the fight between the god Marduk and the chaos monster Tiamat and includes, in this way, a description of the creation of the world and the tale of Marduk's ascendancy to the position as high god of Babylon.

Enuma Elish is, however, only one among a multitude of preserved epics from Mesopotamia with religious content. When combined, they constitute a remarkable collection, as demonstrated by modern editions.[3] We nonetheless have to stress that we are talking about modern collections; these ancient texts were never collected into a canon in ancient times.

Egyptian religious texts may be just as diversified as Mesopotamian ones, with one exception: no great religious epic has been preserved from Egypt. Egyptian religious literature includes many poems but is especially interested in the hereafter. Famous among its religious compositions is the Book of the Dead, which goes back to the time of the New Kingdom (second half of the second millennium BCE) and was in use until Hellenistic-Roman times. It has been preserved in about 500 copies, placed in the grave together with the mummy of the deceased person, and written as a personal address to this person. Nothing suggests that it functioned as a canonical text.[4]

From Syria we have the already mentioned epics from Ugarit dating back to the second millennium BCE. The discoveries at Ugarit also include several ritual texts.[5] Most previous research considered the epic cycle of poems relating to the life and death of the god Baal especially to be religious texts relating to the cultic year of ancient Ugarit, and the religion of Ugarit was reconstructed mainly on the basis of these poems. The different phases in the life of Baal were considered to represent the different seasons of the year. The rain god Baal ruled in the wet season during wintertime but was destroyed by Mot, the god of death, at the time of the corn harvest.[6] The study of ritual texts from Ugarit, however, indicates that the religion of this place was very different from the impression of it gained by

2. Translations, e.g., *ANET*, 60–72, and *COS* 1:390–402.

3. Like Benjamin Foster, *Before the Muses: An Anthology of Akkadian Literature*, 2 vols. (Bethesda, MD: CDL Press, 1993). These two volumes cover about 900 pages.

4. Translation in *COS* 1:27–30. Studies including translation: Erik Hornung with David Lorton, *The Ancient Egyptian Books of the Afterlife* (Ithaca, NY: Cornell University, 1999). The classic edition is Sir E. Wallis Budge, *The Book of the Dead: The Papyrus of Ani in the British Museum* (London: British Museum, 1895).

5. The ritual texts are translated in Dennis Pardee, *Ritual and Cult at Ugarit*, SBLWAW 10 (Atlanta: SBL, 2002).

6. A few titles from this research: Flemming F. Hvidberg, *Weeping and Laughter in the Old Testament* (Copenhagen: Arnold Busk, 1962); Johannes C. de Moor, *The Seasonal Pattern in the Ugaritic Poem of Baʿlu according to the Version of Ilimilku*, Alter Orient und Altes Testament 16 (Neukirchen: Neukirchener Verlag/Kevalaer: Verlag Butzon & Bercker, 1971).

modern scholars from the epic presentations. Maybe the epics from Ugarit were no less and no more than epics, and not canonical religious literature. In this function they are close to similar compositions from the classical world, especially the Homeric epics, and certainly very different from authorized canonical texts like the Jewish or Christian Bibles or the Qur'an.

WRITTEN AND ORAL TRADITION

There may be many reasons why canonical collections of religious literature appeared relatively late. One reason may be that ancient societies normally were not bound by the kind of standard religion that became usual at a later date. No religion was the official one, to be adhered to by every member of society. Consider, for example, Mesopotamia, which in historical times was only occasionally united into one state. The ancient states might have their official religion, the worship of their main deity. Thus the divine master of the Assyrian kings was the god Ashur, originally the city god of the city of the same name, the historical center of the Assyrian Empire. There is, however, little evidence that Assyria exported the religion of this deity to conquered countries or demanded that subjects of Assyria worship this state god. It was one thing that the king and his officials regarded the worship of Ashur as the official religion of the state, and something very different that the populace at large worshiped. We have no sign from pre-Hellenistic times of the kind of mental control exercised by the great world religions for the last two thousand years. The closest analogy might be the short-lived religious rearrangements of Pharaoh Akhenaten in fourteenth-century-BCE Egypt. These reforms lasted only as long as the king lived and were almost immediately abolished after his death. Moreover, Akhenaten's reforms did not reflect the wish of his people; they were rather the outcome of the king's settlement with the priesthood of the god Amun of Thebes.

Another reason might have to do with the status of writing in the ancient Near East. The oldest systems of writing—in Mesopotamia cuneiform writing and in Egypt hieroglyphics—appeared around 3000 BCE. At the time when the books of the Old Testament were written down, people had been familiar with writing for at least two thousand years, perhaps even longer than that. There is little indication that writing was widespread in Palestine before the first millennium; what remains of ancient examples are a few fragments of cuneiform written in Akkadian and some tablets written in the Ugaritic alphabet. The many Amarna letters from the fourteenth century from the petty kings of Palestine and Syria to their great master, the king of Egypt, cannot be used to postulate a widespread practice of writing in Palestinian society. When the king of Gezer wrote a letter to Pharaoh, it meant that a scribe with his base at Gezer was possibly placed there by the imperial Egyptian administration in order to facilitate communication with the imperial center. This scribe might well have been the only person in Gezer who could read and write, and his obligations were solely administrative.

The Amarna letters offer some idea of the function of writing in Palestine in the Late Bronze Age. They are composed in the official international language of that time, Akkadian, but it was a barbarous version of Akkadian, a kind of mixture of the grammar of the local Amorite language spoken at that time in Palestine and Akkadian dictionaries. This says that the scribe was a local Amorite-speaking person with a limited scribal education. This does not prevent some of the letters from including some interesting addresses at the end of the letters. Some of the letters from Abdi-Ḫeba, the king of Jerusalem, end in this way:

> To the scribe of the king, my lord: Thus Abdi-Ḫeba, your servant: Bring nice words to the king, my lord. All the king's lands are lost! (EA 286)

> To the scribe of the king, my lord: Thus Abdi-Ḫeba, your servant: I throw myself before your two feet. Bring nice words to the king, my lord. (EA 287)

If we try to reconstruct the communication between Abdi-Ḫeba and his Egyptian master, the Pharaoh, we most likely have a local ruler who could not write or read. In order to communicate with the king of Egypt, he had a scribe with a limited scribal education at his disposal. Abdi-Ḫeba dictated his message to Pharaoh in Amorite to his scribe. This message was put into "Akkadian" that could not be read by either Abdi-Ḫeba or Pharaoh. After the completion of the message, it was placed in an envelope of clay. On this envelope another copy of the message could be written. The scribe—the real sender of the message—dictated orally the content of the message to a messenger who brought it to Egypt. Here the messenger delivered his message to a subordinate Egyptian official employed by the central administration, most likely accompanied by an oral résumé of the message. The Egyptian official most likely placed the message in the archive, never read, but he conveyed to his superior its message in the form he had received it orally from the messenger, most likely translated into Egyptian. Maybe, but only maybe, the message reached the attention of Pharaoh after another few intermediaries. Pharaoh was not interested in seeing the message, because Pharaoh did not read or speak Akkadian.

The letter remained in the archive, perhaps as a guarantee in case it might be necessary to look for attestation if a controversy arose between the Egyptian administration and their local representatives. When the archive was full, it was emptied and its tablets thrown out. There was no historical interest in preserving the content, now without any practical importance.

Obviously it was a good thing that letters could be written and exchanged, but the written word was not alone of decisive importance. The more important part of an exchange of messages was the personal communication when two persons (almost) became acquainted. The written word was reserved for officials. The sender and the receiver used, chiefly, oral messages for their personal interchange, but normally exchanged written versions of their messages through middlemen and messengers. In sociological terms, in these times the society of Palestine included a minute substratum able to communicate in writing, the scribes. The elite, the ruling class, had no need of writing. They had at their ser-vice people who did the necessary recording. The lower stratum, which in an ancient society comprised at least 90 percent percent of the total population, had no use for writing. It received no formal education and was mainly illiterate.

THE ALPHABET AND MISSING INSCRIPTIONS FROM PALESTINE IN THE IRON AGE

The introduction of the alphabet, that is, a system of writing so simple that it is accessible to anyone, led to a democratization of the art of the scribe and a widespread use of written messages. The two previously predominant systems of writing, cuneiform and hieroglyphics, were ponderous systems, difficult to mas-ter, and demanded an education lasting for several years. They included literally hundreds of signs and combinations. Such systems were never likely to develop into a common vehicle for written communication between all the members of a society.[7]

The invention of the alphabet, a system where there is only one sign for a pho-netic sound, did not happen overnight. Ugarit offers us fine testimony as to when and how it happened. The texts from Ugarit dating from the fourteenth century BCE are written in a kind of cuneiform very different from Akkadian cuneiform. Ugaritic scribes used a cuneiform alphabet, although—as in Hebrew—vowels were not included in the writing system. Moreover, it seems likely that the inven-tors of the Ugaritic alphabet tried to adapt it to the shape of characters otherwise only attested from Syria, Lebanon, Palestine, and Jordan in the Iron Age. It is therefore likely that the script otherwise called Phoenician—some say paleo-Hebrew—and the forerunner of the later Greek and Latin alphabets was already established in Syria in the Late Bronze Age. It was therefore not unexpected when an abecedary was found in Palestine in 1977 in a stratum from the eleventh cen-tury.[8] More have followed since then. The ʿIzbet Ṣarṭah abecedary includes all the characters found in similar abecedaries from Ugarit, although the Ugaritic one includes some characters not preserved in Phoenician abecedaries.

It is a remarkable fact that we have no evidence that the introduction of the alphabet automatically led to an increased production of literature in Syria, Lebanon, Palestine, or Jordan. The reason may be that nothing has been pre-served. A small quantity of official inscriptions is known from all these countries, and the inclusion of literary motives in them shows that the people who com-posed the text of these inscriptions were familiar with literature. Another remark-able fact is that so far no major official inscription has been found from the kingdoms of Israel and Judah.

---

7. Although it must be remembered how complicated modern systems of writing, such as the ones found in China and Japan, may be.

8. In ʿIzbet Ṣarṭah about thirteen miles northeast of Tel Aviv.

Ugaritic Alphabet

The sequence of letters in the Ugaritic Abecedary:[9]

ʾ, b, g, ḫ, d, h, w, z, ḥ, ṭ, y, k, š, l, m,
ḏ, n, ẓ, s, ʿ, p, ṣ, q, r, ṯ, ġ, t, i, u, ś

The Paleo-Hebrew (Phoenician) alphabet

The sequence of letters in Hebrew (and Phoenician)

ʾ, b, g, d, h, w, z, ḥ, ṭ, y, k, l, m, n, s, ʿ, p, ṣ, q, r, ś, š, t

4. The Ugaritic and the Paleo-Hebrew Alphabet

Most inscriptions from the territories of Israel and Judah are rather insignificant. Most are found on inscribed potsherds (ostraca) and are of administrative
interest. Short letters have appeared, as well as lists of provisions, names on seal
impressions, and more. There can be no doubt that the alphabet was known and
widely used. One inscription is a little different, the Siloam inscription, which
describes the breakthrough during the construction of the water channel from
the spring of Gihon to the Siloam pool. This water channel is not dated but is
normally attributed to the construction work of King Hezekiah (2 Kgs. 20:20).
The inscription must therefore be considered as at least somewhat official, as it
was placed at the point where the workers from both sides met. Nonetheless, until
now, in spite of intense archaeological activity for more than a hundred years, it
is the only genuine inscription from the Iron Age discovered so far in Jerusalem.[10]

9. Stanislav Segert, *A Basic Grammar of the Ugaritic Language* (Berkeley: University of California,
1984), 23.
10. It must be stressed that it is genuine in light of recent "discoveries." Historical and archaeological studies relating to Palestine's ancient history are at present plagued by forgeries like the so-
called Jehoash inscription. Literature reflecting the intense debate concerning the last-mentioned
inscription can be found on the Internet (http://www.orientalisti.net/ioash.htm).

The Siloam inscription[11]

[This is] the breakthrough, and the conditions of the breakthrough are these: While the stone masons were still [swinging] the hacks, one man against the other, and there still remained three cubits to break through, [one heard] the voice of a man shouting to his fellow, because there was a rift in the rock from south to north. On the day of the breakthrough stone masons hacked against his fellow, hack against hack, and the water ran from the spring to the pool, one thousand and two hundred cubits, and there were a hundred cubits of rock over the head of the stone masons.

Of direct relevance for the question of the early stages of the formation of the Hebrew canon are some silver amulets found in a priestly grave in Jerusalem dating from the end of the seventh or the beginning of the sixth century BCE. The text of these two amulets, which may be somewhat younger than the grave itself, includes most of what is known as the Aaronite blessing from Numbers 6:24–26 and is without question the oldest direct evidence so far of the existence of a text now part of the Old Testament.

The Aaronic blessing

Ketef Hinnom Text 1	*Ketef Hinnom Text 2*
Yahweh bless you	Yahweh bless you
And keep you,	And keep you,
Yahweh make his face to	Yahweh make his face to
shine upon you,	shine upon you, and give you
and be gracious to you	peace[12]

Numbers 6:24–26
The LORD bless you and keep you;
the LORD make his face to shine upon you,
and be gracious to you;
the LORD lift up his countenance upon you,
and give you peace.

11. The Siloam inscription, now in the Archaeological Museum in Istanbul but set to appear on loan in Jerusalem, courtesy of the Turkish government, is here translated following the edition in Herbert Donner and Walter Röllig, *Kanaanäische und aramäische Inschriften* (Wiesbaden: Harrassowitz, 1962), 1:34, no. 189.

12. The text of two amulets follows the edition by Johannes Renz, *Die althebräischen Inschriften* (Darmstadt: Wissenschaftliche Buchgesellschaft, 1995), 1:452–55.

This text is a well-known prayer to Yahweh. It is impossible to say how old it may be, but the fact that it appears on amulets in a context that links it to the priesthood of Jerusalem means that the prayer must have been part of the cultic repertoire there. It is more than likely that priests continued reciting the prayer after the Babylonian destruction of Jerusalem and thus preserved it for later incorporation in Old Testament literature as a prayer attributed to the epical ancestor of this priesthood, Aaron, Moses's brother. The text of these amulets thereby creates an important link to the persons responsible for the collection of traditions in the Pentateuch.

WHO WROTE THE OLD TESTAMENT?

The Art of Writing in Palestine in the Iron Age

Who wrote the Old Testament? is the most common question asked of Old Testament scholars and the most difficult to answer. We simply do not know, because the authors never tell us who they are. It has been commonly accepted for a long time that the traditional authors of Old Testament books, like Moses, Samuel, and David, have nothing to do with the real authors of these books. We have to accept the fact that this literature is anonymous and will remain so.

It must, on the other hand, also be accepted that when we have a text, there must also be an author of this text (see the introduction to this part). That being the situation, the author of a text is not absolutely anonymous. He or she has disclosed—at least in part—his or her identity in the writings. This section is therefore devoted to the task of tracking down their identity without speculating too much about the time when they were supposed to have lived or their precise identity.

At least 90 percent of the population in the ancient Near East were illiterate. In a remote and insignificant corner of that world like Palestine the number can easily be raised to 95 percent or more.[13] Communication, whether from official agents of the state to ordinary people or between ordinary people, must therefore have been predominantly oral. The majority of people living in this corner of the world in ancient times would have considered written messages meaningless and would have paid absolutely no attention to them. If the author of an official decree or a writer of literature wanted to get in touch with ordinary people, it would be in the shape of oral communication. This means, briefly put, that more than 90 percent of the total population had nothing to do with the composition of the books now part of the Old Testament.

---

13. The French biblical scholar André Lemaire has in his book *Les écoles et la formation de la Bible dans l'ancien Israël* (Fribourg: Éditions universitaires/Göttingen: Vandenhoeck & Ruprecht, 1981) tried to paint a picture of a widespread literacy in Palestine in the Iron Age. A survey of existent inscriptions tells a different and much more negative story.

Officers of David and Solomon

2 Samuel 8:16–18 (David):

Chief of the army:	Joab
Recorder:	Jehoshaphat son of Ahilud
Priests:	Zadok, Ahimelech
Secretary:	Seraiah
Chief of the guard:	Benaiah

2 Samuel 20:23–26 (David):

Chief of the army:	Joab
Chief of the guard:	Benaiah
Forced labor:	Adoram
Recorder:	Jehoshaphat son of Ahilud
Secretary:	Sheva
Priests:	Zadok, Abiathar, Ira

1 Kings 4:2–6 (Solomon):

Priest:	Azariah the son of Zadok
Secretaries:	Elihoreph and Ahijah
Recorder:	Jehoshaphat son of Ahilud
Chief of the army:	Benaiah
Priests:	Zadok, Abiathar
Chief of the governors:	Azariah the son of Nathan
The king's friend:	Zabud the son of Nathan
Chief of the court:	Ahishar
Forced labor:	Adoniram

This does not imply that there were no traditions or stories from ancient times that survived among this illiterate population. Orally transmitted stories, sagas, and legends were definitely in abundance. It is, however, impossible to trace such traditions or to control them.

We have narrowed down the number of people who could read and write to less than ten percent. Three groups might have had an interest in written literature: officials, merchants, and priests.

The officials, the administrators, formed the most important group. The size and education of this group was dependent on the complexity of the society which they administered. The tiny Palestinian states were mainly rather uncomplicated structures, each having a small town as its center, surrounded by a territory of no great extent and including a population of limited size. If we apply a model of the number of people in the capitals of these minor Near Eastern city-states in comparison to the number of people living outside the capital, that is, about 20 percent inhabiting the capital, and 80 percent living outside of it, then few Palestinian states would have included more than 10,000 people. The central administration needed for servicing such small societies would have counted only a few officials. There is little information about the administration in the Old Testament, but the information provided by the books of Samuel and Kings shows that the historiographers describing the imperial administration of David and Solomon were not even able to imagine how such an administration would have looked, and it is of no consequence if they built on historical knowledge or simply invented these lists. Civil officers would have been few in number. They might, because of their education, have been able to communicate internally via written messages, but so far we have no evidence of any interest in other literary activities.

Another group who may have needed the ability to write consisted of merchants—not the local grocers but the merchants who traveled the world. They would need to prepare accounts for their business and to write contracts with other merchants. The sources from the Iron Age describing the activity of these merchants are few—compared to the abundance of evidence available from the Late Bronze Age. With their base in the north along the Lebanese coast, Phoenician tradespeople sailed all over the Mediterranean; but it is unknown to what degree Palestinian traders may have participated in this activity. Palestine is less endowed with good harbors than Lebanon. However, these tradespeople were hardly interested in writing down literature. Writing was reserved for business; it was not for pleasure.

One group of people remains, the priests. Scholars' interest has for a long time focused on this group as possible authors of biblical stories. In the Iron Age, some of the priests might have been able to read and write. Some activities centering on the temples would have been very much of the same character as those of other official sectors of the society, including the need for accounts. It is, on the other hand, a rather premature supposition to argue that writing was widespread among this group in Palestine in the Iron Age. Nothing has survived in the form of written documents except the aforementioned amulets from Ketef Hinnom. We have no administrative, not to say religious, documents and almost nothing relating to cult and ritual. We know nothing about cultic or liturgical matters in any of the many temples that existed in Palestine in this age. We don't know if ritual texts were written down or handed down orally. Furthermore, the many separate temple units were of such a limited size that there was hardly any need for an elaborate administrative apparatus at any of them.

Writing and reading mean schools. As far as Palestine in the Iron Age is concerned, we have absolutely no information about the existence of such schools. The only thing at the scholar's disposal is by analogy from other societies, especially from Mesopotamia and Egypt. Here the educational systems were well developed, and the education both of long duration and demanding, because of their cumbersome writing systems. The alphabet, however, put no such demands on the intellectual ability of the student. It is therefore hardly relevant to transfer the establishment of an elaborate school system in Mesopotamia to Syrian or Palestinian conditions. The idea that Syrian and Palestinian scribes received a yearlong education like their Mesopotamian colleagues is far-fetched. It was mainly about learning the alphabet and correct spelling, which means that the student should be able to distinguish between the root consonants—the backbone of any Semitic language, including the Hebrew used in Palestine in the Iron Age. Local inscriptions reveal at least this much: normally the spelling is correct.

The Iron Age as the Background for the Writing of History in the Old Testament

To summarize the previous paragraphs about writing in ancient Palestine: Palestine does not seem to have been a fruitful environment for the production of written literature. Nothing has survived. It is therefore impossible to say that written literature did not exist. The references in the books of Kings to various chronicles may indicate the presence of official year lists like the ones known from Mesopotamia, but their form and content is impossible to reconstruct.

Classical historical-critical scholarship was for a long time of the conviction that the production of literature began in earnest in the tenth century BCE at King Solomon's magnificent court. Here we found the intellectual environment and the people capable at writing wonderful stories like those present in the Yahwist document in the Pentateuch. In more recent times, few scholars still believe in the splendor of the Solomonic age and therefore in the early beginning of Israelite literature. After all, the empire of David and Solomon, the precondition of Solomon's marvelous court, is no more. As seen so often in Old Testament studies, scholars had created the splendor of Solomon on the basis of biblical texts, whereupon they dated this text to the period already constructed on the basis of the same texts.

The knowledge that it is no longer possible to use Solomon's court as the home of the so-called oldest stratum of the narratives in the Old Testament, however, does not mean that scholars have given up their circular argumentation. They have only moved down to other periods. At the present the era of Josiah has come into focus, and many scholars now believe that Josiah's time at the end of the seventh century BCE would have produced the literature found in such biblical strata as the Yahwist.

There is more than one reason for this reorientation. Old Testament scholarship has, for many years, seen the Josianic period as the era of literary production. While scholars were of the opinion that literary production began in the days of David and Solomon, they reckoned the historical literature from Joshua to 2 Kings to be the production of an intellectual movement that blossomed in Jerusalem in the seventh century BCE, the so-called Deuteronomistic movement, the intellectual precondition for the appearance of the Deuteronomistic

History.[14] This historical narrative, ranging from Joshua to 2 Kings, got its name from the fifth book of Moses, Deuteronomy, ideologically quite similar to the history itself. Deuteronomy, as well as the Deuteronomistic History, displays a definite interest in the fate of the old, no longer existing, kingdom of Israel. This interest is markedly different from the one in the books of Chronicles, which are totally indifferent as to the whereabouts of the kingdom of Israel,

Chronicles is therefore supposed to reflect a negative, Judean attitude to apostate Israel. When this was the attitude of the Judeans, how can it be that the Deuteronomistic History is so different? The standard explanation has been that following the Assyrian conquest of Samaria in 722 BCE, some intellectuals fled to Jerusalem and found shelter here. In Jerusalem they were left in peace to develop their ideas about the correct worship of Yahweh, and their version of the history of Israel. During the seventh century this small group of refugees from the north developed into an elite in backward Judah. They implanted their northern tradition in the memory of the Judeans and at the end of the seventh century their religious activity provoked the religious reforms of King Josiah. Under their influence Josiah also saw himself as the new David, who, through conquest of the north, should reestablish the Davidic empire. It was a short-lived dream that was brutally crushed by Pharaoh Neco in 609 BCE, when he killed Josiah "the moment he saw him."[15]

Josiah's reform of the temple and cult in Jerusalem was—according to the biblical narrative provoked by the discovery of an ancient law book during the restoration of the temple complex. It was common to see Old Testament scholars accepting the central part of Deuteronomy (esp. chaps. 12–26) as reflecting the content of this law book. This law book might have been "planted" in the temple to be restored by descendants of the refugees from Samaria.

Some archaeologists are of the conviction that it is possible to point to physical remains that may support this thesis about the Deuteronomistic elite that created Israelite—or to be more correct, Judean—historical writing. At the beginning of the Iron Age, Jerusalem was hardly more than a local town in the highlands of Judah. Few people lived there, hardly more than 2,000. In the eighth century it started to grow. At the end of the eighth century and in the seventh century, in Hezekiah's days, it exploded in size. New quarters were added to the territory of the city, and much energy was invested in the repair of the fortifications, including the construction of a new water system (which has already been mentioned above). The possibility cannot be excluded that refugees from the north were among the increased population of Jerusalem.

The hypothesis about the origin of Deuteronomism and the Deuteronomistic History and its dating to the time of Josiah is a classical specimen of a scholarly

14. See above pp. 92–94. In spite of much criticism, the hypothesis of the Deuteronomistic History still belongs to the standard repertoire of Old Testament studies.

15. The NRSV's "but when Pharaoh Neco met him at Megiddo, he killed him" may not reflect the Hebrew of 2 Kgs. 23:29 very well.

house of cards. One assertion builds on the presence of another that builds on a third and so forth. So far there is absolutely no physical evidence of the alleged flight from the north. Everything depends on the story of the discovery of the law book in 2 Kings 22, whether or not it tells a true story or is invented by the historiographer. The whole construction is very weak.

It may be doubted that refugees from the north made a great impression on Judah after 722 BCE and that in the end they made up a special elite at the royal court with enough power to change the general ideology prevailing at this court, including the idea of the king as the future David. It is not an impossible hypothesis—but there is not one scrap of evidence for it, apart from the biblical narrative. No word about such a movement can be found in the Old Testament. On the contrary, the Old Testament historiographer stressed that the population of the former kingdom of Israel was deported to remote corners of the Assyrian Empire (2 Kgs. 17:6), and the authors of the books of Kings make much out of distancing the Judeans from the population now living in the territory of Israel, mostly imported from other parts of the world.

The second argument against this theory has to do with the political and demographic situation in Judah after Sennacherib's attack on the country in 701 BCE. During his campaign the king of Assyria conquered and destroyed virtually every city in Hezekiah's kingdom and spared only Jerusalem. Sennacherib boasts of his conquest, and archaeological excavations have confirmed his claims. It would be reasonable to link the drastic increase of the population of Jerusalem at this time to an internal migration within Hezekiah's kingdom, when homeless people from the destroyed Judean cities moved to the capital to find shelter and a new home.

The thesis about the emergence of historiography in the Josianic era is beset with the same kind of problems as the former hypothesis that saw historiography as the child of the Solomonic period. The narrative in the Old Testament about Josiah is used to construct this historical vision within the framework of its own narrative. Of course it is still mainly a circular argumentation.

The continued quest for the identity of the compiler of the historical tradition in the Old Testament will have to change methods. We need fewer hypotheses and different arguments. There is only one way open, the Old Testament itself, at the end of the second millennium BCE supplemented by other literature relating to its narrative. It is the conviction of this author that it is still possible to construct a profile of the authors of Old Testament literature on the basis of their understanding of Israel's fate in history and Israel's importance as the people of God.

Chapter 7

The Constructed History

*A Renewed Critical Study
of the Old Testament II*

THE HISTORICAL LITERATURE, ITS AIM AND PURPOSE

It is normal to see the historical literature, which is the main part of the narrative prose in the Old Testament, divided into three major works of ancient historiography that have already been the subject of a preliminary discussion in the earlier parts of this work: the Pentateuch, the Deuteronomistic History, and the Chronicler's History. In recent times, much traditional analysis of these works, building on literary criticism (the so-called higher criticism), form criticism, redaction history, and tradition history, have been exchanged for different kinds of "integrated" readings. Doing this kind of reading, the analyst tries to understand biblical historiography—at least from Genesis to 2 Kings—as one coherent narrative of the fate of humankind and the history of Israel from creation to the destruction of Jerusalem. Modern critics are not necessarily of the opinion that earlier historical-critical analysis is a wasteland, but they stress that in spite of many differences and redactions we have a red thread binding all of these books with their long story together into one narrative unit.

Accepting that the relation between Old Testament historiography and real history ("what really happened") is minor, it is obvious that the authors of this historiography, many or few as it may be, and in spite of many minor differences, were in basic agreement about the content and aim of their narrative, but also that they wanted to express their story of Israel to their readership in the most meaningful way. Nothing indicates that the historiographers were very interested in the past as it really was.

In this chapter it is our intention to present the red thread that holds the narrative together. Thereafter the emphasis will change to questions relating to the readership of this narrative. Who were they, and who did the authors think they were—or ought to be? In what way does this readership differ from other people? There are many legitimate approaches to the historical literature of the Old Testament; however, this is the one chosen for this analysis.[1] Perhaps it will help to identify the authors and present their profile, irrespective of when and where they wrote their history.

THE MEANING OF HISTORY

The Obligations Placed on Humanity

The extended historical narrative from Genesis to 2 Kings includes a series of markers explaining to the reader the meaning of this story. At the center of history we find the fate of the Israelite people, which ended as apostate Israel was destroyed and banished from its homeland.

Israel was not present at the creation. When Yahweh ordered Israel's first patriarch to leave his home in Mesopotamia and travel to Canaan, humankind had already been instructed concerning its destiny:

> "Be fruitful and multiply, and fill the earth and subdue it; and have dominion over the fish of the sea and over the birds of the air and over every living thing that moves upon the earth." (Gen. 1:28)

The first part of the history of humankind, the primeval history in Genesis 1–11, has as its subject the way humankind lives up to this demand of God. It is hardly a story of success, as violence and killings accompany the progress of humankind. The first part ends with the destruction of humankind in the deluge. Only one, Noah, together with his close family, is spared. The second part opens with the same demand to humanity about being fruitful and multiplying (Gen. 9:1). Thus the history of humankind really begins in Genesis. Humankind again lives up to its duty to multiply, symbolized by the "genealogy" of the nations of the world in Genesis 10. In its new self-sufficiency, humankind challenges God by building the tower of Babel, intended to provide it with access to the world of God. God thwarts their plans and disperses them over the face of the earth.

---

1. A more comprehensive explanation of the aim of Old Testament historiography is presented by Thomas L. Thompson, *The Bible in History: How Writers Create a Past* (London: Jonathan Cape, 1999).

Moreover they now get different languages and will no longer be able to communicate and cooperate. God's project has partially succeeded. Humankind has occupied the world but hardly in the way envisaged by God. History demands a new beginning.

The Promise to the Patriarchs

If God really had a plan for humankind, it seems a total fiasco. God has to try again. When all of humankind was united in fulfilling God's plan, it only led to rebellion against God. Now humankind has been dispersed and cannot contribute to the fulfillment of God's plan. God has to choose a new strategy, demanding a narrowing of his perspective: one people, Israel, is elected, and in the future God's promises are directed to this people, although at the beginning only to its three ancestors, the patriarchs Abraham, Isaac, and Jacob. In a series of promises Yahweh addresses these three persons and promises them a great future for their descendants. Here follows the promise to the first patriarch, Abraham:

> "I will make of you a great nation, and I will bless you, and make your name great, so that you will be a blessing. [3] I will bless those who bless you, and the one who curses you I will curse; and in you all the families of the earth shall be blessed." (Gen. 12:2–3)

This promise is a rather general one but serves as a bridge between the previous universal history and the particular Israelite history. If God had a plan for humanity, it has not been replaced by the promises to Abraham. It is still there: In you all the families of the earth shall be blessed. The road to prosperity for humankind is now in Israelite hands.

After this, the content of the promise becomes more specifically addressed to the future of Israel, and the perspective now points at Israel's future history:

> "Know this for certain, that your offspring shall be aliens in a land that is not theirs, and shall be slaves there, and they shall be oppressed for four hundred years; [14] but I will bring judgment on the nation that they serve, and afterward they shall come out with great possessions. . . . To your descendants I give this land, from the river of Egypt to the great river, the river Euphrates, [19] the land of the Kenites, the Kenizzites, the Kadmonites, [20] the Hittites, the Perizzites, the Rephaim, [21] the Amorites, the Canaanites, the Girgashites, and the Jebusites." (Gen. 15:13–14, 18–21)

> "And I will make my covenant between me and you, and will make you exceedingly numerous." [3] Then Abram fell on his face; and God said to him, [4] "As for me, this is my covenant with you: You shall be the ancestor of a multitude of nations. . . . [6] I will make you exceedingly fruitful; and I will make nations of you, and kings shall come from you. . . . [8] And I will give to you, and to your offspring after you, the land where you are now an alien, all the land of Canaan, for a perpetual holding; and I will be their God." (Gen. 17:2–8)

Now here is an opening to the following narratives in the story of Joseph (Gen. 37–50) and of the exodus (Exod. 1–15), but also to the later conquest of Canaan, perhaps even to the Davidic kingdom, which, according to some indications in the Old Testament, is said to include all the countries between Egypt and Mesopotamia (1 Kgs. 5:1).

However, no promise comes without a threat, as the following quotation shows may be read "between the lines":

> "You shall keep my covenant, you and your offspring after you throughout their generations." (Gen. 17:9)

In this passage the covenant is presented in its physical form, symbolized as circumcision, and the demand made has to do with obeying its demands:

> "Any uncircumcised male who is not circumcised in the flesh of his foreskin shall be cut off from his people; he has broken my covenant." (Gen. 17:14)

Isaac also receives a promise:

> "Do not go down to Egypt; settle in the land that I shall show you. [3] Reside in this land as an alien, and I will be with you, and will bless you; for to you and to your descendants I will give all these lands, and I will fulfill the oath that I swore to your father Abraham. [4] I will make your offspring as numerous as the stars of heaven, and will give to your offspring all these lands; and all the nations of the earth shall gain blessing for themselves through your offspring, [5] because Abraham obeyed my voice and kept my charge, my commandments, my statutes, and my laws." (Gen. 26:2–5)

New in this connection is the warning against traveling to Egypt—in contrast to the earlier promise to Abraham that included a prophecy that Israel will stay in Egypt for a while (Gen. 15:13). New here also is the explanation for Yahweh's wish to fulfill his promise to Abraham: Abraham's loyalty toward him and the covenant.[2]

The promise is renewed when Jacob travels into exile in Haran, and after his return. Both occasions happen in Bethel:

> "I am the LORD, the God of Abraham your father and the God of Isaac; the land on which you lie I will give to you and to your offspring; [14] and your offspring shall be like the dust of the earth, and you shall spread abroad to the west and to the east and to the north and to the south; and all the families of the earth shall be blessed in you and in your offspring. [15] Know that I am with you and will keep you wherever you go, and will bring you back to this land; for I will not leave you until I have done what I have promised you." (Gen. 28:13–15)

---

2. See Gen. 15:6: "And he believed the LORD; and the LORD reckoned it to him as righteousness." The meaning of the Hebrew text is more likely that Abraham trusted Yahweh, rather than that he "believed" in him.

[11] "I am God Almighty: be fruitful and multiply; a nation and a company of nations shall come from you, and kings shall spring from you. [12] The land that I gave to Abraham and Isaac I will give to you, and I will give the land to your offspring after you." (Gen. 35:11–12)

[3] "I am God, the God of your father; do not be afraid to go down to Egypt, for I will make of you a great nation there. [4] I myself will go down with you to Egypt, and I will also bring you up again; and Joseph's own hand shall close your eyes." (Gen. 46:3–4)

The first two promises have nothing new to say in comparison with the earlier ones, although the promise to Jacob while he was traveling to his relatives in Mesopotamia, that God will lead him back to his home, may be important from a later perspective, since Jacob is also Israel (Gen. 32:29), the apical ancestor of the nation and the nation itself. The second promise is the same as that formerly presented to Abraham, that he will become the ancestor of mighty kings. The third promise announces to Jacob that he can be confident and travel to Egypt. Yahweh will not desert him there, but a great people will arise after him. Yahweh will bring Jacob, who is Israel, home again.

When summarized, the promises to the patriarchs include these main points:

- Yahweh will conclude a covenant with Israel;
- Yahweh is the God of Israel—even in a foreign country;
- Israel will become a great people—in a foreign country;
- Israel will live in the land given to it by Yahweh.

Another subject is here present; that when there is a covenant between Yahweh and Israel, Israel is obliged to keep it unconditionally, but it does not play a major part. The period of the patriarchs is the time of promises and not of threats. The patriarchs—especially Abraham—are paragons of the righteous God-fearing person. Abraham was just, not because he was perfect—he was far from that, never really understanding what God demanded from him—but because he always trusted Yahweh.

This theme is present from the very beginning of the story of Abraham. The moment Abraham arrives in his future homeland, together with the woman who shall give birth to his children, the ancestors to the great nation promised to him, he leaves his country at the first occasion because of a drought and flies to Egypt, where he sells his wife to Pharaoh. This is really the merciless message of the story in Genesis 12.

Yahweh has to save Abraham and Sarah personally. However, Abraham is hardly back in Canaan before he is about to hand it over to his nephew Lot (Gen. 13:1–13), who was asked to choose his part of the country first. Again Abraham is saved, however, this time by Lot, who chose the seemingly most inviting part, the valley of the Jordan, which would soon become the place of death after the destruction of Sodom and Gomorrah (Gen. 19).

Abraham's (and Sarah's) lack of understanding does not stop here. When Sarah seems not to be able to give birth, Abraham provides for himself an heir by the Egyptian slave Hagar. Although God visits Abraham in person and promises him a son, the old couple have little faith in this promise (Gen. 18).

Now, in spite of Abraham's and Sarah's skepticism, Sarah gives birth to Isaac. Finally Abraham is convinced that God is always right, and when God orders him to sacrifice Isaac, he immediately obeys and travels with his son to Moriah to sacrifice him there. Only God's personal act of salvation prevents Abraham from effectively destroying the promise given to him about a son and a nation coming from him (Gen. 22). Abraham never understands the ways of God because they are much too subtle for him. Abraham always tries his best but never succeeds. God never deserts him, because he is always faithful to God.

This faith in God is essentially the most important part of the promises to the patriarchs. There is no question of questioning the authority of God. It is not a crime to be stupid, and Abraham's stupidity is proverbial. After all, Abraham is only human. It is a crime to disobey God. In the historical narrative in the Old Testament, the patriarchs serve as paragons for later Israel, not because they were something special but because their faith in God, unlike the faith of later Israel, never wavered.

From Egypt to Canaan

Søren Kierkegaard is supposed to have said that we must experience history as something in front of us, but understand it backwards. Nothing better could be said about the history found in the books of Exodus through Deuteronomy. Kierkegaard's aphorism might characterize the red thread leading through these biblical books. The course of the narrative has already been presented in the prolegomena to this book. Here we will follow the sayings of God which accompany Israel on its way to the border of Canaan.

> Then the LORD said, "I have observed the misery of my people who are in Egypt; I have heard their cry on account of their taskmasters. Indeed, I know their sufferings, 8 and I have come down to deliver them from the Egyptians, and to bring them up out of that land to a good and broad land, a land flowing with milk and honey, to the country of the Canaanites, the Hittites, the Amorites, the Perizzites, the Hivites, and the Jebusites." (Exod. 3:7–8)

The first occasion when Yahweh addresses Israel, this time to the person of Moses, is from the burning bush at God's mountain of Horeb (Exod. 3). The quotation refers to the idea of the promised land in the promises to the patriarchs but supplements its description of Canaan as the country flowing with milk and honey. This supplement will be repeated several times as recapitulations of the promise. In a later speech, this part of the promise about salvation from Egypt is more specific, arguing that Yahweh will save Israel because of the covenant with the patriarchs, including the promise of the land (Exod. 6:1–8).

The purpose of these sayings is quite narrow: the liberation from Egypt. Canaan is the next target, and it is not specified how Israel will get to this country. Before Israel arrives at Sinai, the problem is not how Israel will get back to Canaan but how it will get out of Egypt.

When this goal is achieved and Israel has arrived at Sinai, Yahweh returns to his promise about the country to be inherited by the Israelites. The promise is included in a long speech that also contains a threat:

> I am going to send an angel in front of you, to guard you on the way and to bring you to the place that I have prepared. 21 Be attentive to him and listen to his voice; do not rebel against him, for he will not pardon your transgression; for my name is in him.
> 22 But if you listen attentively to his voice and do all that I say, then I will be an enemy to your enemies and a foe to your foes.
> 23 When my angel goes in front of you, and brings you to the Amorites, the Hittites, the Perizzites, the Canaanites, the Hivites, and the Jebusites, and I blot them out, 24 you shall not bow down to their gods, or worship them, or follow their practices, but you shall utterly demolish them and break their pillars in pieces. 25 You shall worship the LORD your God, and I will bless your bread and your water; and I will take sickness away from among you. 26 No one shall miscarry or be barren in your land; I will fulfill the number of your days. 27 I will send my terror in front of you, and will throw into confusion all the people against whom you shall come, and I will make all your enemies turn their backs to you. 28 And I will send the pestilence in front of you, which shall drive out the Hivites, the Canaanites, and the Hittites from before you. 29 I will not drive them out from before you in one year, or the land would become desolate and the wild animals would multiply against you. 30 Little by little I will drive them out from before you, until you have increased and possess the land. 31 I will set your borders from the Red Sea to the sea of the Philistines, and from the wilderness to the Euphrates; for I will hand over to you the inhabitants of the land, and you shall drive them out before you. 32 You shall make no covenant with them and their gods. 33 They shall not live in your land, or they will make you sin against me; for if you worship their gods, it will surely be a snare to you. (Exod. 23:20–33)

There can be no doubt about the content of these promises. The angel of Yahweh will protect Israel on its road to the promised land. Yahweh will guarantee that this country belongs to Israel, a country that reaches from Egypt to the Euphrates. A special part of this speech has to do with the expulsion of the peoples of Canaan already present in the country. It will not happen overnight, but bit by bit. This seems to contrast with the main story of the conquest in Joshua, because the conquest here seems to be a total one. All of Canaan is conquered and its territory divided between the tribes of Israel. The closest parallel to this description in Exodus 23 may be the first chapter of Judges, listing, as it does, those parts of Canaan not conquered by Israel. Perhaps Exodus 23 is referring to this second impression of the conquest rather than to the one found in Joshua.

The threat to Israel is hardly pronounced and not at all specific, not yet. If the Canaanites will remain in Israel's land, Israel will desert its God and worship

Canaanite gods, and this will be a "snare" to Israel. Soon this second theme will become a dominant one in comparison to the theme of the conquest.

Soon we hear about the dangers of letting the Canaanites live (Exod. 34:10–16). It will lead Israel to sharing its sacrifices with the Canaanites and its daughters marrying Canaanite men who will entice them and lead them away from Yahweh. Israel is obliged to destroy without mercy all forms of Canaanite religion, their altars, pillars of stones (the "massebahs"), and their Asherah poles, symbolizing the worship of Baal, the main adversary of Yahweh, and Asherah, the divine consort of Canaanite El:

> Take care not to make a covenant with the inhabitants of the land to which you are going, or it will become a snare among you. [13] You shall tear down their altars, break their pillars, and cut down their sacred poles [14] (for you shall worship no other god, because the LORD, whose name is Jealous, is a jealous God). [15] You shall not make a covenant with the inhabitants of the land, for when they prostitute themselves to their gods and sacrifice to their gods, someone among them will invite you, and you will eat of the sacrifice. [16] And you will take wives from among their daughters for your sons, and their daughters who prostitute themselves to their gods will make your sons also prostitute themselves to their gods. (Exod. 34:12–16)

In Leviticus the possession of the country is related to Israel's keeping of God's law:

> The LORD spoke to Moses, saying: [2] Speak to the people of Israel and say to them: I am the LORD your God. [3] You shall not do as they do in the land of Egypt, where you lived, and you shall not do as they do in the land of Canaan, to which I am bringing you. You shall not follow their statutes. [4] My ordinances you shall observe and my statutes you shall keep, following them: I am the LORD your God. [5] You shall keep my statutes and my ordinances; by doing so one shall live: I am the LORD. (Lev. 18:1–5)

Here in Leviticus we are confronted by the most outspoken warning so far against breaking the law and not obeying it (Lev. 26). If Israel will be faithful and keep its contract with God in its future homeland, this land will remain fertile and Israel shall "live securely in [its] land" (Lev. 26:5). If Israel disobeys the law and breaks the covenant with Yahweh, Yahweh is going to afflict Israel with all sorts of plagues and will let the enemy loose on Israel's land. The land will lose its fertility, and the enemy will settle in the land. Israel will be dispersed among the many nations of the earth, while its land will be deserted. The most interesting part here is not the section on punishment but the one on the salvation that will follow after punishment. Now the future exile is implied:

> Yet for all that, when they are in the land of their enemies, I will not spurn them, or abhor them so as to destroy them utterly and break my covenant with them; for I am the LORD their God; [45] but I will remember in their favor the covenant with their ancestors whom I brought out of the land of Egypt in the sight of the nations, to be their God: I am the LORD. (Lev. 26:44–45)

The time of punishment is limited to only a few years, although the majority of the Israelites are going to perish. However, the few who repent will find hope at the end of darkness because Yahweh is—in spite of his anger—always faithful to his covenant.

The last admonition to Israel follows when it has already arrived in the plains of Moab opposite Jericho, ready for the conquest (Num. 33:50–56). It has nothing new to say but stresses the importance of driving out all of the Canaanites, that they shall not become "as barbs in your eyes and thorns in your sides" (Num. 33:55).

Deuteronomy presents itself as one long speech Moses gave to Israel on the plains of Moab. This speech includes several reflections on the relations between Israel and its future homeland. Most of these themes are already known from the previous part of the Pentateuch: Israel must keep the Law. Israel shall not worship other gods and make idols. The most famous admonition is probably the Shema:

> Hear, O Israel: The LORD is our God, the LORD alone. [5] You shall love the LORD your God with all your heart, and with all your soul, and with all your might. [6] Keep these words that I am commanding you today in your heart. [7] Recite them to your children and talk about them when you are at home and when you are away, when you lie down and when you rise. [8] Bind them as a sign on your hand, fix them as an emblem on your forehead, [9] and write them on the doorposts of your house and on your gates. [10] When the LORD your God has brought you into the land that he swore to your ancestors, to Abraham, to Isaac, and to Jacob, to give you—a land with fine, large cities that you did not build, [11] houses filled with all sorts of goods that you did not fill, hewn cisterns that you did not hew, vineyards and olive groves that you did not plant—and when you have eaten your fill, [12] take care that you do not forget the LORD, who brought you out of the land of Egypt, out of the house of slavery. [13] The LORD your God you shall fear; him you shall serve, and by his name alone you shall swear. (Deut. 6:4–13)

Yahweh's protection against the enemy is a certain fact when Israel "observe[s] this entire commandment that I am commanding you" (Deut. 11:22), and the land will become a mighty kingdom reaching as far as the Euphrates (Deut. 11:24). Israel's possession of its land is, on the other hand, not a given fact that will last forever. It is certainly a possibility that Israel will break the covenant. At its worst, this will mean exile:

> The LORD will single them out from all the tribes of Israel for calamity, in accordance with all the curses of the covenant written in this book of the law. [22] The next generation, your children who rise up after you, as well as the foreigner who comes from a distant country, will see the devastation of that land and the afflictions with which the LORD has afflicted it— [23] all its soil burned out by sulfur and salt, nothing planted, nothing sprouting, unable to support any vegetation, like the destruction of Sodom and Gomorrah, Admah and Zeboiim, which the Lord destroyed in his fierce anger— [24] they and indeed all the nations will wonder, "Why has the LORD

done thus to this land? What caused this great display of anger?" [25] They will conclude, "It is because they abandoned the covenant of the LORD, the God of their ancestors, which he made with them when he brought them out of the land of Egypt. [26] They turned and served other gods, worshiping them, gods whom they had not known and whom he had not allotted to them; [27] so the anger of the LORD was kindled against that land, bringing on it every curse written in this book." (Deut. 29:21–27)

The perspective is clear: the future exile means the end of history. The alternative is obvious: Israel must worship Yahweh alone in its country or be driven into exile.

If some should gain the impression from the last quoted passage that this is not a prophecy but a reflection based on events that have already happened, he is hardly totally wrong. Somehow Israel is leaving its country even before it has entered it. The passage looks like a commentary on a history that already belongs to the past. The last passage from Deuteronomy only confirms that this impression is correct, because it refers not only to the Babylonian exile, that is, the "official" closure to "Israel's history" as related by the historiographers who wrote Genesis to 2 Kings; it also has a wider meaning and refers to the Jewish Diaspora, the "dispersal," the existence of Jewish communities all over the Persian and Hellenistic world, in Mesopotamia, Egypt, Syria, and other places:

When all these things have happened to you, the blessings and the curses that I have set before you, if you call them to mind among all the nations where the LORD your God has driven you, [2] and return to the LORD your God, and you and your children obey him with all your heart and with all your soul, just as I am commanding you today, [3] then the LORD your God will restore your fortunes and have compassion on you, gathering you again from all the peoples among whom the LORD your God has scattered you. [4] Even if you are exiled to the ends of the world, from there the LORD your God will gather you, and from there he will bring you back. [5] The LORD your God will bring you into the land that your ancestors possessed, and you will possess it; he will make you more prosperous and numerous than your ancestors.

[6] Moreover, the LORD your God will circumcise your heart and the heart of your descendants, so that you will love the LORD your God with all your heart and with all your soul, in order that you may live. [7] The LORD your God will put all these curses on your enemies and on the adversaries who took advantage of you. (Deut. 30:1–7)

This passage includes not only historical perspective of the future; it also stresses the importance of a new human being who will, among the future people of God, be the partner of Yahweh. In this respect Deuteronomy 30 seems very close to the quotation from Jeremiah that opened this study (Jer. 31:31–34). This similarity is not incidental, nor unwanted. This will be clear when we turn in the next chapter to the prophetic literature.

In conclusion, the perspectives concerning Israel's future history from the exodus to the conquest of Canaan include the following main themes:

- Yahweh will act in accordance with his covenant with Abraham, Isaac, and Jacob.
- Yahweh will lead Israel's way out of Egypt to Canaan, a land flowing with milk and honey.
- Yahweh (or his angel) will destroy the Amorites, the Hittites, the Perizzites, the Canaanites, the Hivvites, and the Jebusites.
- The Canaanites shall not be allowed to live in Israel's land.
- Israel must not enter a covenant with the Canaanites and their gods.
- If the Canaanites remain in the country, Israel will worship their gods and suffer the consequences of disobeying Yahweh.
- The altars of the Canaanites must be destroyed, their sacred pillars smashed, and their Asherah poles cut down.
- Israel must obey Yahweh's laws and commandments.
- If Israel obeys, it will live for long in its land. If it does not obey, destruction and exile will follow.
- Even in exile Yahweh will remember Israel and pardon it and bring it back to its land as a renewed Israel.

The Lost Possibilities: From Conquest to Exile

Now the question is, will the following section—the so-called Deuteronomistic History—include any differences as to the relations between the author's commentaries and the events included in the long story of Israel's fate from the conquest to the exile? Will the following sections also refer to the conditions placed before Israel during its wanderings through the wilderness?

When Joshua is about to begin his campaign in Canaan, Yahweh has one more instruction to deliver (Josh. 1:1–9). The motto for Joshua is to keep the Law of God in one hand and the sword in the other.

The book of Joshua introduces a new theme. Until now, either God or his angel or Moses commissioned by God has presented God's plans. In the book of Joshua, it is Joshua who acts in this capacity. In the books that follow, this role will be taken over by Samuel and following him several other prophets—in one case a prophetess (2 Kgs. 22:16–20). The first example is Joshua's instructions to the Israelites just before they cross the Jordan River. Here Joshua refers to God's promise that he will drive out the Canaanites, the Hittites, the Hivvites, the Perizzites, the Girgashites, the Amorites, and the Jebusites (Josh. 3:10). Later he refers to Reuben and half of Manasseh that obeyed the command of God (Josh. 22:3). This role of Joshua dominates the last two chapters of his book (Josh. 23 and 24).

Joshua opens his speech in Joshua 23 by confirming that the Canaanites who have not already been driven out by the Israelites will be expelled by God himself after Joshua's death. Hereafter follows a series of well-known admonitions to Israel about obeying everything included in Moses's law book, and not entering into any kind of relationship with the former inhabitants of the land or worshiping their gods. They must only worship Yahweh. The speech ends with this harsh caution:

> "If you transgress the covenant of the LORD your God, which he enjoined on you, and go and serve other gods and bow down to them, then the anger of the LORD will be kindled against you, and you shall perish quickly from the good land that he has given to you." (Josh. 23:16)

The theme is taken up again in the following chapter, however, in connection with a second motif, which places Joshua 24 in a special position. Israel has a choice. It need not accept Yahweh's covenant with all its obligations. It is too difficult for Israel to keep the covenant, but Israel has itself agreed to obey Yahweh's covenant. This covenant was given and not dictated to Israel. If Israel fails, Yahweh is not to be blamed:

> But Joshua said to the people, "You cannot serve the LORD, for he is a holy God. He is a jealous God; he will not forgive your transgressions or your sins. 20 If you forsake the LORD and serve foreign gods, then he will turn and do you harm, and consume you, after having done you good." 21 And the people said to Joshua, "No, we will serve the LORD!" 22 Then Joshua said to the people, "You are witnesses against yourselves that you have chosen the LORD, to serve him." And they said, "We are witnesses." (Josh. 24:19–22)

When Joshua dies, the generation that was part of the exodus from Egypt has finally died out. This is marked by the author of Judges at the beginning of his book. Now Israel's problematic history is about to begin, and Yahweh may not be too confident of Israel's ability to keep on the right track. His reproaches are already plentiful:

> "I brought you up from Egypt, and brought you into the land that I had promised to your ancestors. I said, 'I will never break my covenant with you. 2 For your part, do not make a covenant with the inhabitants of this land; tear down their altars.' But you have not obeyed my command. See what you have done! 3 So now I say, I will not drive them out before you; but they shall become adversaries to you, and their gods shall be a snare to you." (Judg. 2:1–3)

The condemnation of Israel put into the mouth of the angel of God is based on the enumeration at the beginning of Judges of the Canaanite enclaves not yet conquered by Israel. Judges 1—one of the more problematic parts of the historical narrative in the Old Testament, because it includes several traditions that are in opposition to the main thrust of this literature[3]—is often regarded as a special

---

3. The idea that several Canaanite enclaves were not conquered by Joshua is in opposition to the main line of the book of Joshua that almost every Canaanite was either killed or expelled from the country. Older scholarship often regarded Judges 1 as presenting a more realistic version of the Israelite conquest than the book of Joshua.

tradition included in the Deuteronomistic History;[4] but it is a necessary part of the picture of Israel's land painted by the rest of Judges. If the conquest had followed a course as laid out in Joshua, not much would have remained to be done in the period of the judges. The condemnation of Israel for not having obeyed the word of God and expelling all Canaanites would also have been meaningless. Only in light of Judges 1 are these words of reproach against Israel meaningful and a proper introduction to the following tale of Israel's history in the period of the judges:

> Then the Israelites did what was evil in the sight of the LORD and worshiped the Baals; [12] and they abandoned the LORD, the God of their ancestors, who had brought them out of the land of Egypt; they followed other gods, from among the gods of the peoples who were all around them, and bowed down to them; and they provoked the LORD to anger. [13] They abandoned the LORD, and worshiped Baal and the Astartes. [14] So the anger of the LORD was kindled against Israel, and he gave them over to plunderers who plundered them, and he sold them into the power of their enemies all around, so that they could no longer withstand their enemies. [15] Whenever they marched out, the hand of the LORD was against them to bring misfortune, as the LORD had warned them and sworn to them; and they were in great distress. (Judg. 2:11–15)

In comparison with the catalog of possible transgressions presented by the many instructions to Israel during its wanderings in the desert, the stress in this passage is put on idolatry caused by the continuous presence of the Canaanites in the land. If the Canaanites were allowed to stay in the land, the Israelites would follow them and worship their gods. This would make Israel's survival in Canaan highly problematic.

When Joshua died, the Israelites almost immediately forgot Yahweh and worshiped the gods of Canaan. Yahweh punished Israel because of its transgressions (Judg. 3:7–8; see also 3:12; 4:1–2; 6:1–2; 8:33–35; 10:6–8; 13:1), but later pardoned it and sent a "savior," a judge.[5] This is the often repeated pattern of the narrative in Judges.

Another way to emphasize the differences between the admonitions, warnings, and condemnations and the historical narrative in which they are embedded in the Pentateuch and in the Deuteronomistic History has to do with the perspective of their authors. In the Pentateuch, but also in Joshua, these admonitions and warnings are generally about Israel's fate in its land. The future is in the center. The perspective changes in Judges: now there is a direct link between the warnings and the story about Israel's transgression, punishment, and salvation. Now it is not about the future; Israel is part of the future, and the future has turned into the present.

---

4. Thus by Noth, *History*, 58.

5. The Hebrew word *šophet* meaning "judge" has a wider semantic field than English "judge." It also means "administrator," "regent." The verbal rool *špṭ* may mean "to decide."

Although we may speak of a seeming change of compositional strategy, there is no break between the earlier narrative that brought Israel to the borders of Canaan and the following description of Israel's stay in its land.[6] It is true that the admonitions and warnings in the Pentateuch address the future while those in Judges and the books of Samuel are aimed at the present (but also—as will be shown—at the future). This change should not be attributed to the activity of different authors; it is a consequence of the progress of the narrative. This is important in connection with the question placed at the beginning of this chapter: Are these speeches and commentaries an integral part of the narrative, or are they secondary elaborations of the narrative? The answer must be that they are a necessary part of the narrative. Warnings and narrative are both parts of this kind of historiography. Without these warnings, it is impossible to see any coherent meaning in Judges.

Judges was therefore compiled with the special idea of demonstrating how tribally organized Israel ended up in a moral morass that made a new way of organization necessary. Otherwise Israel would soon be banished from its land. Although Yahweh many times reestablishes peace and harmony by sending his saviors, the intervals between periods of peace and periods of tribulation caused by Israel's transgressions grow shorter and shorter. Also the judges and saviors become increasingly problematic; the infantile Samson, caught by the Philistines, overturns their temple, killing himself and more Philistines than he had as a judge (Judg. 16:30). Although a brave act, it was hardly a recommended procedure if Israel intended to stay in its land.

The period of the judges ends as a lawless time when Israelites are fighting Israelites (Judg. 17–21). Having failed to expel the remaining Canaanites, the Israelites enter into hopeless civil war, because "in those days there was no king in Israel; all the people did what was right in their own eyes" (Judg. 17:6; see 18:1; 19:1; 21:25). Historical-critical scholars have often considered the last four chapters of Judges secondary, because they believed the content of these chapters to be in opposition to the main line of narrative in Judges. It is hardly so; rather, they build the bridge between the judges and Israel's kings.

At the beginning of the story about the kings of Israel and Judah, the function of the commentaries changes again. The first series of commentaries is more interested in the future than in the past and present.

When Samuel reacts against the demand of the Israelites to have a king, Yahweh answers him, "Just as they have done to me [Yahweh], . . . they are doing to you [Samuel]" (1 Sam. 8:8). They have deserted him and now worship other gods. In his farewell speech to the Israelites Samuel includes this admonition:

6. In older historical-critical scholarship, some scholars, like the important German scholar Gerhard von Rad, placed the cut between the books of Moses and the Deuteronomistic History between the book of Joshua and the book of Judges. These scholars preferred to talk about a Hexateuch ("six books") instead of a Pentateuch. Other scholars placed the cut between Numbers and Deuteronomy and talked about a Tetrateuch ("four books"). The problem of where to place this cut will probably be decided by the ongoing discussion about the very existence of the Deuteronomistic History.

"See, here is the king whom you have chosen, for whom you have asked; see, the LORD has set a king over you. [14] If you will fear the LORD and serve him and heed his voice and not rebel against the commandment of the LORD, and if both you and the king who reigns over you will follow the LORD your God, it will be well; [15] but if you will not heed the voice of the LORD, but rebel against the commandment of the LORD, then the hand of the LORD will be against you and your king." (1 Sam. 12:13–15)

This comes at the culmination of a speech that includes a long résumé of the history of Israel from Egypt to Samuel's own time, and the emphasis is on Israel disobeying Yahweh and Yahweh's loyalty toward Israel. The speech ends with another admonition to the Israelites about worshiping Yahweh and a threat that describes the consequences of disobeying him.

The long narrative about Saul and David proceeds until David's installment as king over Israel in Jerusalem without being interrupted by admonitions or historical reviews (1 Sam. 13–2 Sam. 6). The last part of this narrative (1 Sam. 16–2 Sam. 6) is often regarded as one coherent story called "David's Ascent to the Throne." When David rules all of Israel from his throne in Jerusalem, it is time for the prophet Nathan to announce his vision of the eternal dynasty (2 Sam. 7:5–17). In David's ensuing prayer to Yahweh, he stresses that the introduction of the kingdom of David means that Yahweh has "established your people Israel" (2 Sam. 7:24).

After the narrative about how David became king comes a section describing his period as king over Israel, a story normally dubbed the Succession History after the German *Thronfolgegeschichte*.[7] The main theme of this story is the struggle within the family of David about his successor. This story is totally free of any commentary or admonition of the kind encountered on many previous occasions. The focus is on the turbulent process that leads to Solomon's ascension to the throne after having removed the last of his rivals. This succession story, like the preceding one, has little to do with the fate of the people of Israel. It is interested only in the power game between the acting characters in the story. Whether the Israelites obey Yahweh is immaterial to the course of the narrative.

The situation is different when we get to the story of King Solomon. In the historical narrative in the Old Testament, the glorious first years of Solomon constitute the dividing line. In the Old Testament tradition David is always the good king, although the stories about him do not always present him as an ideal king. Here David seems to be another Abraham. As human beings they are far from perfect, but Yahweh never withdraws his support, because they never desert Yahweh and worship other gods. Solomon is different. Although he builds the temple, he is also the king who brings disaster on Israel, although it is postponed until after his death.

---

7. Leonhard Rost, *Die Überlieferung von der Thronnachfolge Davids* (Stuttgart: Kohlhammer Verlag, 1926), reprinted in Leonhard Rost, *Das Kleine Credo und andere Studien zum Alten Testament* (Heidelberg: Quelle-Meyer, 1965), 119–244.

At this decisive moment in the story of Israel's fate in its land, the commentaries become extremely important. The first example is found in the "dialogue" between Solomon and Yahweh in his nocturnal oracle at the sanctuary at Gibeon (1 Kgs. 3). This passage begins with Solomon praising Yahweh because of his faithfulness toward his promise to David about a successor. Because of this, Solomon asks Yahweh to give him an "understanding mind"[8] that his rule may be just and righteous. Yahweh answers in the oracle:

> "Because you have asked this, and have not asked for yourself long life or riches, or for the life of your enemies, but have asked for yourself understanding to discern what is right, . . . [14] [i]f you will walk in my ways, keeping my statutes and my commandments, as your father David walked, then I will lengthen your life." (1 Kgs. 3:11, 14)

The following chapters, until the inauguration of the temple, have as their subject the wisdom and wealth of Solomon, who is the epitome of the blessed king who succeeds in everything. The main part of the story about King Solomon in 1 Kings, however, is dedicated to his construction of Yahweh's temple in Jerusalem and culminates in Solomon's prayer at the inauguration of the temple (1 Kgs. 8). In his prayer Solomon praises Yahweh—as he had in Gibeon—because of his loyalty to his covenant and the people that worships him, including the royal house of David. After this, Solomon prays for Yahweh's righteousness and charity in connection with sin and guilt, defeat, drought, and hunger. He also prays for Yahweh's mercy toward the strangers who might visit the temple to worship Yahweh. The last and most comprehensive part of the prayer relates to people being exiled from Israel:

> "If they sin against you—for there is no one who does not sin—and you are angry with them and give them to an enemy, so that they are carried away captive to the land of the enemy, far off or near; [47] yet if they come to their senses in the land to which they have been taken captive, and repent, and plead with you in the land of their captors, saying, 'We have sinned, and have done wrong; we have acted wickedly'; [48] if they repent with all their heart and soul in the land of their enemies, who took them captive, and pray to you toward their land, which you gave to their ancestors, the city that you have chosen, and the house that I have built for your name; [49] then hear in heaven your dwelling place their prayer and their plea, maintain their cause [50] and forgive your people who have sinned against you, and all their transgressions that they have committed against you; and grant them compassion in the sight of their captors, so that they may have compassion on them [51] (for they are your people and heritage, which you brought out of Egypt, from the midst of the iron-smelter)." (1 Kgs. 8:46–51)

This place, more than most others, shows that the exile constitutes the decisive perspective for the history of Israel as related in the Old Testament. The passage is about exile in general and is not limited to a special occasion like the Babylonian

---

8. Thus the NRSV, which is a very weak translation of the Hebrew *leb šōmēᶜa* "a listening heart."

exile. It is about people who live in dispersion, a prayer about forgiveness. The following commentaries in the books of Kings confirm the impression gained from this passage. They relate to the tragic fate of the people of Israel, who were seduced by their kings who did not walk in the steps of David. In spite of all his merits, Solomon—the builder of the temple—is the one who personally opens the road to perdition. Yahweh's warnings are not to be mistaken, combining the usual themes of transgression and idolatry with punishment and destruction:

> The LORD said to him [Solomon], "I have heard your prayer and your plea, which you made before me; I have consecrated this house that you have built, and put my name there forever; my eyes and my heart will be there for all time. [4] As for you, if you will walk before me, as David your father walked, with integrity of heart and uprightness, doing according to all that I have commanded you, and keeping my statutes and my ordinances, [5] then I will establish your royal throne over Israel forever, as I promised your father David, saying, 'There shall not fail you a successor on the throne of Israel.'
> [6] "If you turn aside from following me, you or your children, and do not keep my commandments and my statutes that I have set before you, but go and serve other gods and worship them, [7] then I will cut Israel off from the land that I have given them; and the house that I have consecrated for my name I will cast out of my sight; and Israel will become a proverb and a taunt among all peoples. [8] This house will become a heap of ruins; everyone passing by it will be astonished, and will hiss; and they will say, 'Why has the LORD done such a thing to this land and to this house?' [9] Then they will say, 'Because they have forsaken the LORD their God, who brought their ancestors out of the land of Egypt, and embraced other gods, worshiping them and serving them; therefore the LORD has brought this disaster upon them.'"
> (1 Kgs. 9:3–9)

First Kings proceeds: Solomon would not listen but collects a harem of foreign women coming from all the nations with whom the Israelites are not allowed to have relations. According to the logic of the narrative, it is unavoidable that Solomon, seduced by his foreign women, introduces the worship of these foreign nations' deities in Jerusalem (1 Kgs. 11). Yahweh's punishment follows soon and is plain and clear, although it is temporarily postponed in order to spare Solomon—a theme that is resumed in connection with King Josiah (2 Kgs. 22:19–20):

> Then the LORD was angry with Solomon, because his heart had turned away from the LORD, the God of Israel, who had appeared to him twice, [10] and had commanded him concerning this matter, that he should not follow other gods; but he did not observe what the LORD commanded. [11] Therefore the LORD said to Solomon, "Since this has been your mind and you have not kept my covenant and my statutes that I have commanded you, I will surely tear the kingdom from you and give it to your servant. [12] Yet for the sake of your father David I will not do it in your lifetime; I will tear it out of the hand of your son. [13] I will not, however, tear away the entire kingdom; I will give one tribe to your son, for the sake of my servant David and for the sake of Jerusalem, which I have chosen." (1 Kgs. 11:9–13)

Solomon's idolatry has as its consequence the dissolution of the kingdom of David. Now the dynasty of David is allowed to keep only a minor part, the territory of one and a half tribes (1 Kgs. 12:1–19). Following the dissolution of the kingdom, two golden calves are placed in Bethel and Dan. Although they represent Yahweh—"Here are your gods, O Israel, who brought you up out of the land of Egypt" (1 Kgs. 12:28)—they nevertheless represent a transgression of the commandment that forbade the Israelites to make idols.[9]

After Solomon, the historical narrative is accompanied by minor commentaries, each of which puts matters in place, leading to the final judgment of Israel and Judah in 2 Kings 17. These commentaries normally have this content, at first in connection with the kings of Israel:

> About Nadab: Nadab son of Jeroboam began to reign over Israel in the second year of King Asa of Judah; he reigned over Israel two years. [26] He did what was evil in the sight of the LORD, walking in the way of his ancestor and in the sin that he caused Israel to commit. (1 Kings 15:25–26)

> About Baasha: In the third year of King Asa of Judah, Baasha son of Ahijah began to reign over all Israel at Tirzah; he reigned twenty-four years. [34] He did what was evil in the sight of the LORD, walking in the way of Jeroboam and in the sin that he caused Israel to commit. (1 Kgs. 15:33–34)

Jehu, who exterminates the dynasty of Omri and destroys the temple of Baal at Samaria, is followed by a sulky commentary, although in the eyes of the commentator Jehu was a well-behaving Israelite:

> But Jehu did not turn aside from the sins of Jeroboam son of Nebat, which he caused Israel to commit—the golden calves that were in Bethel and in Dan. [30] The LORD said to Jehu, "Because you have done well in carrying out what I consider right, and in accordance with all that was in my heart have dealt with the house of Ahab, your sons of the fourth generation shall sit on the throne of Israel." [31] But Jehu was not careful to follow the law of the LORD the God of Israel with all his heart; he did not turn from the sins of Jeroboam, which he caused Israel to commit. (2 Kgs. 10:29–31)

The commentaries have a wider variety when we turn to the kingdom of Judah. Some of its kings are villains, but other kings are evaluated with more kind words. Two kings, Hezekiah and Josiah, are almost as good as David.

> About Rehoboam: Judah did what was evil in the sight of the LORD; they provoked him to jealousy with their sins that they committed, more than

9. The narrative about King Jeroboam's golden calves relates to the story of the golden calf set up by Aaron in Exodus 32. This calf is also presented as "These are your gods, O Israel, who brought you up out of the land of Egypt!" (Exod. 32:4). The primacy of 1 Kings 12 over Exodus 32 is shown by the reference to "your gods." In Exodus 32 there is only one calf! Another reflection of the tradition of the golden calf is the similarity between the names of Jeroboam's and Aaron's sons: Nadab and Abihu (Abiah).

all that their ancestors had done. [23] For they also built for themselves high places, pillars, and sacred poles on every high hill and under every green tree; [24] there were also male temple prostitutes in the land. They committed all the abominations of the nations that the LORD drove out before the people of Israel. (1 Kgs. 14:22–24)

About Jehoshaphat: Jehoshaphat son of Asa began to reign over Judah in the fourth year of King Ahab of Israel. [42] Jehoshaphat was thirty-five years old when he began to reign, and he reigned twenty-five years in Jerusalem. . . . [43] He walked in all the way of his father Asa; he did not turn aside from it, doing what was right in the sight of the LORD; yet the high places were not taken away, and the people still sacrificed and offered incense on the high places. (1 Kgs. 22:41–43)

About Jehoram: In the fifth year of King Joram son of Ahab of Israel, Jehoram son of King Jehoshaphat of Judah began to reign. [17] He was thirty-two years old when he became king, and he reigned eight years in Jerusalem. [18] He walked in the way of the kings of Israel, as the house of Ahab had done, for the daughter of Ahab was his wife. He did what was evil in the sight of the LORD. [19] Yet the LORD would not destroy Judah, for the sake of his servant David. (2 Kgs. 8:16–19)

The tragic story of Israel goes on until the fall of Samaria (2 Kgs. 17), after which follows a very long commentary on the fate of Israel, including the well-known catalog of its transgressions. Although it is long, it is worthwhile to quote the whole:

This occurred because the people of Israel had sinned against the LORD their God, who had brought them up out of the land of Egypt from under the hand of Pharaoh king of Egypt. They had worshiped other gods [8] and walked in the customs of the nations whom the LORD drove out before the people of Israel, and in the customs that the kings of Israel had introduced. [9] The people of Israel secretly did things that were not right against the LORD their God. They built for themselves high places at all their towns, from watchtower to fortified city; [10] they set up for themselves pillars and sacred poles on every high hill and under every green tree; [11] there they made offerings on all the high places, as the nations did whom the LORD carried away before them. They did wicked things, provoking the LORD to anger; [12] they served idols, of which the LORD had said to them, "You shall not do this." [13] Yet the LORD warned Israel and Judah by every prophet and every seer, saying, "Turn from your evil ways and keep my commandments and my statutes, in accordance with all the law that I commanded your ancestors and that I sent to you by my servants the prophets." [14] They would not listen but were stubborn, as their ancestors had been, who did not believe in the LORD their God. [15] They despised his statutes, and his covenant that he made with their ancestors, and the warnings that he gave them. They went after false idols and became false; they followed the nations that were around them, concerning whom the LORD had commanded them that they should not do as they did. [16] They rejected all the commandments of the LORD their God and made for themselves cast images of two calves; they made a sacred pole, worshiped all the host of heaven, and served Baal. [17] They made their sons and their daughters pass through fire; they used divination and augury; and they sold themselves to do evil in the sight of the LORD, provoking him to anger. [18] Therefore the LORD was very angry with Israel and removed them out of his sight; none was left but the tribe of Judah alone.

[19] Judah also did not keep the commandments of the LORD their God but walked in the customs that Israel had introduced. [20] The LORD rejected all the descendants of Israel; he punished them and gave them into the hand of plunderers, until he had banished them from his presence.

[21] When he had torn Israel from the house of David, they made Jeroboam son of Nebat king. Jeroboam drove Israel from following the LORD and made them commit great sin. [22] The people of Israel continued in all the sins that Jeroboam committed; they did not depart from them [23] until the LORD removed Israel out of his sight, as he had foretold through all his servants the prophets. So Israel was exiled from their own land to Assyria until this day. (2 Kgs. 17:7–23)

The résumé only introduces one new idea: Israel should have understood its destiny. There are no more excuses, because the prophets of Yahweh had warned Israel and its kings about the consequences of their transgressions. These prophets are of course first and foremost the ones mentioned in the books of Samuel and Kings: Samuel, Nathan, Ahijah from Shiloh, especially Elijah and Elisha, and many more. When we read their warnings, these are mostly about kings who abuse their power and follow a road different from Yahweh's. There is little about Israel being disobedient to Yahweh. It is possible that the reference in 2 Kings 17:13–14 to the activity of these prophets has a wider perspective than the historical narrative. We shall return to this issue in the next chapter on prophetism. Here the tragic end of the kingdom of Judah is still pending.

The LORD said by his servants the prophets, [11] "Because King Manasseh of Judah has committed these abominations, has done things more wicked than all that the Amorites did, who were before him, and has caused Judah also to sin with his idols; [12] therefore thus says the LORD, the God of Israel, I am bringing upon Jerusalem and Judah such evil that the ears of everyone who hears of it will tingle. [13] I will stretch over Jerusalem the measuring line for Samaria, and the plummet for the house of Ahab; I will wipe Jerusalem as one wipes a dish, wiping it and turning it upside down. [14] I will cast off the remnant of my heritage, and give them into the hand of their enemies; they shall become a prey and a spoil to all their enemies, [15] because they have done what is evil in my sight and have provoked me to anger, since the day their ancestors came out of Egypt, even to this day." (2 Kgs. 21:10–15)

In the eyes of the historiographer King Manasseh is without doubt the most abominable creature ever to have ascended to the throne of Judah—or perhaps he was more of a scapegoat. The historiographer accordingly invests a lot of energy in describing his cruelty. There is hardly any religious crime that Manasseh has not committed, and as expected, this godforsaken tyrant "shed very much innocent blood, until he had filled Jerusalem from one end to another" (2 Kgs. 21:16). The cup is full and the fate of Judah sealed. This is the verdict of the historiographer, who again stresses the fact that Yahweh's prophets had told this to the king of Judah and his people many times. Judah and Jerusalem will be punished as were Israel and Samaria. After Manasseh follow Josiah, who "did what was right in the sight of the LORD, and walked in all the way of his father David; he did not turn aside to the right or to the left" (2 Kgs. 22:2), and another prophet (this time the prophetess Huldah, 2 Kgs. 22:14–20), who announces the fall of the kingdom. Her only promise to Josiah is that he shall be spared the ordeal of seeing his kingdom destroyed.

The end arrives without any further comment. The notes about Nebuchadnezzar's settlement with Jehoiakim are short but include the standard themes of warnings by the prophets, Yahweh's punishment because of Manasseh's transgressions, and Yahweh's decision not to forgive the Israelites any more (2 Kgs. 24:2–4). The story of Jerusalem's destruction, the exile of the Judeans, and the fall of the Davidic dynasty follows without any further comment. These events speak for themselves.

SUMMARY

The meaning of history as related by the biblical historiographers from Genesis to 2 Kings is univocal. It is one long and tragic narrative about how the human race rebelled against its God and creator. In this respect there is no difference between the prelude, the so-called primeval history (Gen. 1–11), and the following story about the cruel fate of the Israelite people.[10] The only difference is the change of perspective from world history to a national history.

The creation of humankind was no blessing to God. The first human couple disobeyed a direct order from God, seduced by a serpent. The result was banishment from God's presence in paradise. In its exile, humankind continued to rebel, until its total dispersal over the surface of the earth, after the futile attempt to build the tower of Babel. The long story of the people of God that follows also ends with dispersal, exile, and the removal of God's presence from his temple in Jerusalem. The nature of the crime is stressed several times and consists of the transgression of God's law and commandments as stated in the covenant between Yahweh and Israel. The transgression can be narrowed down to the worship of other gods. Israel's remaining sins and transgressions—among them their failure to exterminate the Canaanites but allowing them to live among the Israelites— were not decisive; the decisive impact of this failure was the possibility given to the Canaanites to corrupt the Israelites, to turn Israel away from its God.

---

10. On the Israelite history as presented by the Deuteronomistic History as a tragic story compared to the tragic perspective of classical history writing, e.g., in Herodotus's *Histories*, see Flemming A. J. Nielsen, *The Tragedy in History: Herodotus and the Deuteronomistic History,* JSOTSup 251 (Sheffield: Sheffield Academic Press, 1997).

This motif of corruption has no place in the first part of the history of Israel, the time of the patriarchs. There is no hint that the descendants of the patriarchs are going to desert Yahweh. The first period covers a relationship between Yahweh and his chosen ones characterized by harmony, although the internal affairs of the patriarchal families are far from harmonious.[11] One text alone mentions the possible punishment of members of Abraham's household who are not circumcised (Gen. 17:14).

The second phase of Israel's history, Israel in Egypt and in the wilderness, includes a series of commentaries and admonitions centering on the obligation of Israel to leave Egypt and return to Canaan. At first these admonitions are not accompanied by threats of punishment, but as soon as Israel enters the covenant with Yahweh at Sinai, such threats become a common feature of the admonitions: Israel must not enter any relationship with the Canaanites. Israel must exterminate the Canaanites; otherwise they will be caught in the trap and worship their gods. Several motifs and narratives belonging to the complex of stories about Israel in the desert allude to this as a problem for Israel, as Israel continues to disobey the words of God, whenever their leader is absent or inattentive.

Here we will refer to only three such traditions. The first concerns a repeated motif of the stories of the sojourn in the desert, the grumbling people who have no confidence in Yahweh and his servant Moses: "If only we had died by the hand of the LORD in the land of Egypt, when we sat by the fleshpots and ate our fill of bread; for you have brought us out into this wilderness to kill this whole assembly with hunger" (Exod. 16:3). The second incident is the golden calf of Aaron (Exod. 32); its relation to the story of Jeroboam's two golden calves has already been mentioned. The third example concerns the transgressions of the Israelites at Shittim, where Moabite women seduced Israelite men to participate in their sacrifices and worship their gods (Num. 25).

Sometimes the perspective is broadened to include not only the dangers awaiting Israel in its future country, but also the consequences of Israel breaking its covenant in the future, including destruction and exile (Lev. 26:30–34; Deut. 30:1–14). In the final admonition in Deuteronomy, the audience is already exiled and living in the Jewish Diaspora: "Even if you are exiled to the ends of the world, from there the LORD your God will gather you, and from there he will bring you back" (Deut. 30:4). More than any other, this last quotation shows that the history narrated by the complex of books from Genesis to 2 Kings is a history of the past. The historiographer is not writing for a public living in Israel's land, but for a public living in the Diaspora. The theme of the narrative is not the conquest of the land as related by the book of Joshua, or

---

11. See Abraham's sale of his wife to Pharaoh (Gen. 12), Isaac's relation to Jacob, and Jacob's to his brother Esau (Gen. 27–28; 33), Jacob's relation to his uncle Laban (Gen. 29), and the enmity between Joseph and his brothers, who attempted to kill him (Gen. 37).

Israel's fate living in the land of promise as narrated in Judges, 1 and 2 Samuel, and 1 and 2 Kings.

As long as Joshua leads Israel in its conquest of Canaan, Israel is safe. It is a consistent part of these narratives that as long as strong and pious men (and sometimes women) are leading Israel, the people are protected and living in security. The importance of Joshua's death, told twice (Josh. 24:29–30; Judg. 2:8–9) can hardly be overrated. When there is no leader, Israel deserts Yahweh, and the new leaders sent by Yahweh, the judges, are hardly ideal. Israel is still likely to be the victim of every possible temptation.

It was already mentioned that there is a progress in the moral deterioration of the leaders of Israel in the period of the judges, stretching from Othniel, about whom we know nothing but who ruled for forty years (Judg. 3:7–11); to Ehud, who killed the fat Moabite king while he was in the privy (Judg. 3:12–30) and established a period of peace for Israel lasting eighty years; to Barak and Deborah, who defeated the Canaanites in a big battle (Judg. 4–5); to Gideon who rejected the offer to become king (Judg. 8:22–23), but did not want personally to kill his enemies but left it to his son, and is taunted for this (Judg. 8:20–21); to Abimelech, who was definitely not sent by Yahweh to deliver Israel but who killed his own family and continued to slaughter his fellow countrymen instead of Israel's enemies—a habit already inaugurated by his father Gideon (Judges 8:13–17)—but was killed by the hand of a woman (Judg. 9). The college of judges ends with Jephthah, the son of a whore, who without discrimination murders Israelites as well as foreigners (Judg. 11), and Samson, who had more strength than brains and who killed Philistines at will but was caught by the treachery of a woman (Judg. 13–16).

The verdict over Israel in the period of the judges already expressed at the beginning of the narrative about this period (Judg. 2:11–15) is merciless, and Israel survives only because of Yahweh's actions. A new endeavor is made to provide Israel with proper leadership that is able to protect it against itself. This leadership is entrusted to the hands of kings, who are originally chosen by Israel in the person of Saul; then, when Yahweh rejects Saul, he asks his prophet Samuel to anoint the shepherd boy David from Bethlehem. The introduction of kingship is accompanied by a new series of admonitions to keep the covenant and warnings against breaking it and to stay away from the gods of Canaan. Nathan's promise to David of an eternal dynasty (2 Sam. 7:11–16), repeated later to Solomon (1 Kgs. 8:25), suggests that the kings are now responsible for the people. By choosing a king, the people of Israel have demonstrated that they prefer a king to Yahweh their God and his prophet Samuel (1 Sam. 8:7).

The admonitions soon change to threats following the apostasy of Solomon. Now Israel is similar to its kings and heading toward destruction and exile. Now almost every king of Israel and Judah is condemned. The kings fail as leaders of the people of God. The people of Israel has lost all hope of survival, and the end comes when Israel is forced to leave its land and when Yahweh has to live in exile after the destruction of his home, the temple of Jerusalem.

WHO WROTE THE GREAT HISTORICAL NOVEL
ABOUT BIBLICAL ISRAEL?

One thing is obvious: the many commentaries on the history of Israel presented as promises, threats, judgment, and more are not secondary additions to this history, attached to it post-factum. They are an integral part of this history and constitute the red thread that binds many different sorts of traditions and heterogeneous narratives together. The commentaries develop as the narrative progresses, but this progress has to do with the place in the narrative where the commentary is found. The historiographer elaborates in his commentary on the place in the narrative where he placed his commentary. In this way the narrative and its commentaries develop side by side as one organic entity. Without these commentaries—and the idea of history expressed herein—there would be no history of Israel as related in the Old Testament. The narrative illustrates the points made by the commentaries, and the commentaries present the structure of the narrative. In this way the commentary and the narrative are two sides of the same coin. They cannot exist without mutual support.

The consequence must, on the one hand, be that the historiographer invented his history of Israel. The narrative is the creation of the historiographer, a constructed history. It is obvious from the previous part that the biblical version of Israel's history "never happened." There was never a historical development of the kind narrated by the biblical historiographer.[12] We hardly have to spend more time on this issue.

This does not automatically mean that everything found in the biblical historiography is invented, that is, written for the context where it is now found. The historical narrative displays many examples of a heterogeneous origin of its individual parts, among them many problematic passages often in internal conflict. Traditional ways of reading biblical texts may not be totally obsolete because of a different form of understanding these texts from the one in existence when these methods developed. The really important thing is that these texts are basically not about the "real" past but parts of a narrative following its own laws and ideas.

The survey presented here of the handling of these commentaries is evidence of the methods employed by the historiographer to establish coherence among various traditions. It is not that the narratives contradict the commentaries—the historiographer is much too skilled to make such blunders—but they are sometimes allowed to develop according to their own internal narrative logic.

The clearest example of this may be the Succession History (2 Sam. 8–1 Kgs. 2) where there is hardly any commentary at all. The story proceeds almost like a classical tragedy, including incest, rape, fratricide, rebellion against the father, tragic deaths, revenge, and accidents. The many analyses of this narrative, since its existence was demonstrated by the German scholar Leonhard Rost in 1926,[13] are all

---

12. See chapter 5.
13. *Die Überlieferung von der Thronnachfolge Davids.*

valuable as far as the literary composition of the material is concerned, although classical historical-critical scholarship made the usual mistake of including in its analysis the usual circular hermeneutical argumentation.

Judges presents another and very different example of the way the historiographer handled traditions in his possession. The composition of Judges is disgraceful. The first part of the book is made up of a series of heroic tales placed within a narrative framework very similar to the one used in the books of Kings. The problematic part is the lack of coherence in these stories, which are sometimes contradictory or simply misleading. Thus we find in the narrative about Gideon a reference to events used to explain a part of the narrative without being a part of the book itself.[14] In the story about Abimelech, the historiographer has tried, without any success, to harmonize two absolutely conflicting traditions concerning the strategy used by Abimelech to conquer Shechem (Judg. 9:31–45).[15]

It is in this connection a spectacular fact that there are no commentaries in the complex of prophetic legends about Elijah and Elisha (1 Kgs. 17–2 Kgs. 9), apart from those short notes relating to dynastic changes. Considering the assertion of the historiographer that Yahweh had addressed the kings of Israel through his prophets, one would expect Yahweh to use Elijah and Elisha to speak about the future of Israel, but this is not the case. Elijah condemns Ahab and envisages the fall of his dynasty, but the perspective in these narratives is confined to this dynasty and does not relate to Israel's fate in general. It may well be that the historiographer simply uses the material available to him and places it in a context chosen by him. There is hardly any trace of elaborate editing. These prophetic stories are relevant only in connection with the dynasty of Ahab. They have hardly anything to do with the idea of the continuous warning of Israel and its kings by Yahweh's prophets.

This analysis may lead to two results. The first has to do with the material available to the historiographer. If this historiographer is dated to Persian or Hellenistic times, this dating has evidently little bearing on the problem of dating the individual parts of the narrative. Each tradition and each narrative must be evaluated on its own. All of them are components of a major narrative, but they do not present a date for this narrative, although a section dating from, say, about 300 BCE indicates that the context in which it is found cannot precede this date. It has, until now, been impossible to present such assured dates. The individual parts of the Pentateuch and the Deuteronomistic History are anecdotes, novellas, short stories, heroic legends—the scholar is actually free to decide.

The second outcome of the analysis presented here says that the historiographer who combined narrative with commentary was not himself part of this his-

---

14. Judges 8:18–21, where the killing of Gideon's two brothers at Tabor is mentioned as the reason for executing some Midianite chiefs, although this event cannot be found in Judges or in any other part of the Old Testament.

15. The first strategy is to arrange a surprise attack on the city at sunrise, when the gates open. Here the attacking force must be in place before sunrise. The second strategy involves a concentric attack on the city from three different angles, however, fully visible to the inhabitants of the city.

tory. The historical narrative from Genesis to 2 Kings is a story about the past, and its events all belong to the past. The historiographer has no part in biblical Israel's destiny, but presents the consequences of the history as he describes it. His public consists of people sharing his situation and his opinions, his despairs and hopes. The historiographer presents to his readership a history that would have identified them with the fate of biblical Israel. In short: The Jewish Diaspora constitutes the context of the historiographer and his public, not only the exile in Mesopotamia but the dispersal of Judaism in the Persian or Hellenistic world.

Chapter 8

The Prophets as the Spokespersons of Yahweh

A Renewed Critical Study of the Old Testament III

THE PROPHETIC BOOKS

Within the context of ancient Near Eastern literature the biblical prophetical books are unique. We have nothing comparable from other places. However, what precisely is a prophetic book? A collection of prophecies from Israel's past? A collection of sundry prophecies attributed to a certain prophet from the past? A sermon to unfaithful Israel? An explanation of the tragic fate of biblical Israel? There are many questions and even more answers. The postmodern person's acceptance of the role of reader in the interpretation of literature has rarely been more relevant.

In early historical-critical scholarship, dominated as it was by German Protestant scholars, the prophets were considered authors who in the books named after them published their sermons to the people of Israel. This Protestant scholarship more or less considered the prophets to be (Protestant) lay preachers who addressed their contemporaries with threats of punishment and doom and announced Yahweh's dissatisfaction with the existing immoral times illustrated by his people's idolatry. Titles like "Hosea's Spiritual Background" and "How Did Micah from Moresheth Understand His Prophetic Office?" were expressions of the biographical interest in the prophets and the role they played in Israelite society.[1]

This scholarship was especially interested in the connection between the prophet and his (since the named prophets are all men, we will use masculine pronouns) preaching (and it often used the word "preaching" in this context) and used the prophetic sermons in their studies of Israelite religion in the period of the kings. The prophets were generally believed to represent the old Israelite religion with roots reaching back to the period in the desert. The prophetic religion represented the nomads from the desert and was supposed to be seen in contrast to Canaanite religion. The nomads were supposed to place more emphasis on ethical issues than Canaanite peasants, who were more interested in the fertility of their fields and animals. At the end, this kind of scholarship almost denied that prophets were prophets, people who could inform about the future. The prophet of Protestant scholarship was not a prophet in the narrow sense; he was a reporter who was commenting on the religious affairs of his own time.

In this light, Isaiah (or at least the first part) should be evaluated as a commentary on the events of Isaiah's own time, and Jeremiah as presenting a personal impression of the last years of the kingdom of Judah. Although most historical-critical scholars were of the opinion that the prophetic books as they have been handed down to posterity were not the creation of the prophets who gave their names to these books, but had been revised by later editors, they still considered the prophets to be preachers and not prophets.

THE CONCEPT OF PROPHETISM—
IN A NEAR EASTERN CONTEXT

We have already seen that the historical context within which previous historical-critical scholarship placed the prophets was predominantly fictive and created by biblical historiographers. The intention of this section is to place the prophets within a Palestinian and Near Eastern religious context.

Prophet is the usual English translation of the Hebrew word *nabî*ʾ, derived from the verbal stem *nb*ʾ, the translation of which is less than clear. Scholars often refer to Akkadian *nabû*, meaning "to call," "pronounce," and consider the prophets to be spokespersons. Sometimes Hebrew *nabî*ʾ is considered to have a passive meaning, "the one who is called." Because of the context in which some of these prophets are found in the Old Testament, it has sometimes been assumed that *nabî*ʾ originally referred to ecstatic prophets (1 Sam. 10:10–13), although there also seem to be older names for prophets such as *ḥozeh* and *roʾeh*, meaning

---

1. Both titles refer to articles by the German scholar Hans Walter Wolff: "Hoseas geistige Heimat," *Theologische Zeitschrift* 81 (1956): 83–94; "Wie verstand Micha von Moreschet sein prophetisches Amt?" VTS 29 (Leiden: Brill, 1978), 393–417.

"the one who sees" (see 1 Sam. 9:9: "for the one who is now called a prophet [*nabî*] was formerly called a seer" [*roʾeh*]).

Prophets were known in every part of the ancient Near East. There were several different categories of prophets, but the available sources hardly make it possible to draw a sharp distinction between the different categories. Basically two main types existed, prophets in public service, normally at sanctuaries or at the royal court, and prophets who were acting on their own behalf, "freelance prophets," who were not authorized by a public institution but acted on behalf of the deity supposed to have called them. Another way to differentiate between prophets would be to divide them into ecstatic prophets and soothsayers who formulate their prophecies inspired by certain signs and omens.

The function of the prophet was—when we discount the biblical evidence— to tell what was going to happen in the future, and this was the normal reason people addressed prophets. In this capacity prophets had to compete with other categories of soothsayers.

It is sometimes said that the most importance difference between modern and ancient humans is their ability to control the future. On the personal level, modern people may visit their doctor or bank advisor, in short, any person who can tell you something about your expectations of the future. On a public level, we have economic experts, meteorological experts, and experts who can explain just about everything. Ancient people had few possibilities to get advice from such expert persons. The general opinion was that nothing happened that had not been decided by the gods. So people looked for specialists who could tell them about the intentions of the gods.

Now several categories of specialists were at the disposal of the public in those days. The best information comes from Mesopotamia. The information from other parts of the ancient Near East is more sporadic and rare. In Mesopotamia, specialists could tell the future from studies of the intestines of sacrifices or because of the flight of birds. Other specialists might make inquiries among the dead. Astrologers knew about the future from the position of the stars and planets. Many of these specialists were highly regarded experts with a lengthy education behind them. Thus, sacrificial priests who prophesied on the basis of intestines built on a recorded tradition reaching back many centuries, if not millennia. They were in possession of books to be consulted when something extraordinary appeared and were definitely not regarded as charlatans.[2]

The lowest ranking group of soothsayers was undoubtedly the prophets, because they had received little formal education. Sometimes they were considered to be inspired by a deity, but in other cases by a demon. The prophets could not rely on previous experience in the form of a written tradition. Their prophesying was spontaneous and incontrollable.

---

2. Among more recent studies devoted to the theme we may mention Frederick H. Cryer, *Divination in Ancient Israel and Its Near Eastern Environment: A Socio-Historical Investigation,* JSOTSup 142 (Sheffield: JSOT Press, 1994).

Mesopotamian liver omens

> If the gall bladder is loosened and is attached to the gate of the palace, if the two liver flaps lean against each other [it means]:
>
> Enmity will break out; a fire will be lighted; a break of a dam will break through; the house of a man will be destroyed; the person who walks out through your gate will not meet the enemy, a magnate will run away; the king will be killed in his palace; the city of the king will be surrounded, and it will be destroyed . . .

In comparison to the extensive omen literature, reports about prophets are few—perhaps another indication of their low status. Two areas of prophecy are, however, considered important, the first from Mari at the Euphrates, dating from the eighteenth century BCE, and the second from Neo-Assyrian times, dating to the seventh century BCE.

The prophecies from Mari, which were discovered in connection with excavations at this place that began in 1929, soon attracted the interest of biblical scholars. It was the first major collection of prophecies ever discovered, but another important factor was the context of these prophecies, which was compared to biblical conditions. Finally, Mari was considered especially important by Old Testament scholars because of the assumed similarity between the society of Mari and that of early Israel, both considered to have nomadic origins. In this way the acts of the prophets from Mari were regarded as archetypal also for Israelite prophets.[3]

We do not possess the actual wording of any prophecy from Mari. They are all preserved in reports mostly written by officers of the state of Mari for the benefit of the palace. However, in consideration of the importance placed on such prophecies, it is likely that they have been reported as faithfully as possible.[4]

When reading a report like the one translated here, several issues are worth noting. It is a simple message. The god does not argue for his case. He makes complaints and asks the king to change his ways. If the king does as he says, he will succeed. The prophet and the deity through him interfere with the affairs of the king, and the king is asked to pay attention to this deity which was among the most important in the kingdom of Mari. The final paragraph about the hair and seam of the dress is repeated in many such reports. By confiscating these items, the sender would be able to control the person in question, as both items were useful as remedies in magical procedures directed against the owner. This procedure was deemed necessary in case the prophet was not already known—here we only hear that the prophet is a "man from Šakka"—because nobody could say if he was a true representative of the god or acted on behalf of evil demons.

---

3. Jean-Claude Margueron, "Mari: A Portrait of a Mesopotamian City-State," *CANE* 2:885–99.

4. A translation of these letters can be found in Martti Nissinen, *Prophets and Prophecy in the Ancient Near East*, SBLWAW 12 (Atlanta: SBL, 2003).

Prophecy at Mari: A letter from Itur-Asdu to Zimrilim[5]

Say to my lord: Thus Itur-Asdu, your servant: On the day when I sent this letter to my lord, Malik-Dagan, a man from Šakka, came to me and said this: "In my dream I intended together with a man from the district of Sagaratum in the Upper District to travel to Mari. In my vision I wanted to enter Terqa, and when I entered, I entered the temple of Dagan. When I prostrated myself, Dagan opened his mouth and said this: 'Have the king of the Benjaminites[6] and their soldiers made peace with the soldiers of Zimrilim?' I (answered) thus: 'They have not made peace!' Before I left, he said this to me: 'Why are Zimrilim's messengers not sitting constantly in front of me? Why does he not inform me about his plans? Otherwise I would a long time ago have delivered the kings of the Benjaminites to Zimrilim. Now, leave! I send you! Thus you shall say to Zimrilim: Send your messengers to me and tell me all your plans! Then I will let the kings of the Benjaminites sprawl in the casket of the hunter and place them before you.'" This man saw this in his dream and he told it to me. Now I have written to my lord. My lord must decide what is going to happen with the dream. Besides—if my lord allows it—my lord should inform Dagan about all his plans and my lord's messenger should always be on their way to Dagan. The man who told this is going to sacrifice an animal to Dagan. (Therefore) I do not send him, but because this man is an express messenger, he carries neither his hair nor the seam of his dress.

A similar situation is known from the Old Testament and lies behind Elijah's settlement with the prophets of Baal at Carmel (1 Kgs. 18) and Micaiah the son of Imlah's quarrel with the prophets belonging to the court of Ahab (1 Kgs. 22). The last mentioned narrative also suggests what may have happened to a prophet whose message disturbed the king or was considered unreliable: "Thus says the king: Put this fellow in prison, and feed him on reduced rations of bread and water until I come in peace" (1 Kgs. 22:27).

The second group of prophecies consists of Neo-Assyrian specimens. Most of them relate to the reign of King Esar-haddon of Assyria. From a formal point of view they are totally different from the Mari examples. They are all collected by Assyrian scribes, but the only information provided about their origins is the name of the prophet or (in most cases) prophetess who delivered the prophecy.

Compared to biblical prophecy, these prophetic sayings from the ancient Near East are short and laconic. They do not contain complex messages or reports of transgressions. Although a prophet may occasionally comment on a contemporary situation and include the god's dissatisfaction, we never find any expression of dissatisfaction with lawless people or a nation devoted to the worship of foreign gods.

A comparison between the prophecies of the Old Testament and the other ancient Near Eastern examples rather emphasizes the distance between them than

---

5. Translated according to the text as presented in George Dossin, *Revue Assyriologique* 42 (1948): 125–34. Zimrilim was king of Mari in the eighteenth century BCE.

6. It is uncertain whether there are any relations between these Benjaminites (in Akkadian *binu-jaminu*, more often written as DUMU^MEŠ *iaminu*) and the biblical Benjaminites.

Neo-Assyrian Prophecy[7]

Do not be frightened, Esar-haddon! I am Bel. I speak to you. I guard the beams of your heart. When your mother gave birth to you, sixty mighty gods stood together with me and protected you. Sin was at your right side and Šamaš at your left. Sixty gods stood around you and have girded your loins.

Do not trust people. Raise your eyes and look at me. I am Ištar from Arbela. I have made peace between Aššur and you. I guarded you as a child. Do not be frightened! Praise me!

Did any enemy attack you while I was silent? The future will be like the past. I am Nabu, the lord of the writing pen. Praise me!

From the woman Baia from Arbela.

creates a link between them. The prophetic literature in the Old Testament remains unique. With their emphasis on moral disorder and social injustice, the biblical prophets are still more lay preachers than prophets in the proper sense.

NEW VISTAS ON THE PROPHETIC LITERATURE AND THE PROPHETS IN THE OLD TESTAMENT

In spite of the fact that the view of prophecy in the Old Testament has changed during the last twenty years—a consequence of the diminishing faith in the history of Israel as related by biblical historiography—it would be an exaggeration to argue that interest in the prophets and the prophetic literature has vanished. On the contrary, the prophetic literature is still regarded as an important source for the reconstruction of preexilic and exilic Israelite religion.

The discussion about the composition of the prophetic books has sharpened, and much scholarship devoted to the topic considers their history of tradition as very complicated. Formerly, scholars worked with the assumption that a prophetic book included a comprehensive nucleus that might go back to the prophet who gave his name to the book. This original prophetic material was later elaborated and commented on by a series of redactors. Today, many scholars are more hesitant when it comes to attributing certain passages to prophets who might have lived several centuries before their books achieved the shape in which they have been handed down to posterity.

If we use Jeremiah as an example, it might at first glance seem an important way to grasp the nature of Israelite prophecy. Jeremiah includes major biographical passages describing the life and whereabouts of this prophet at the end of the independent history of the kingdom of Judah. Jeremiah is also characterized by an extensive use of a style of prose that seems very close to Deuteronomistic

7. Translated following the text in Nissinen, *Prophets and Prophecy*, 105.

phraseology in, for example, the books of Kings. It was also believed that Jeremiah's scribe Baruch the son of Neriah was supposed to have written down Jeremiah's prophecies (see Jer. 36) and therefore the book was an important source of information since it was based on eyewitness testimony, making it possible to reconstruct the career of Jeremiah from his call as a prophet to his exile in Egypt.

However, some dissenting voices appeared toward the end of the twentieth century. The late Robert P. Carroll's studies in Jeremiah represent a kind of turning point. His analysis of Jeremiah shows the book to be the result of extended discussions in exilic and postexilic Jewish circles, including the construction of the prophet's life and career. Much of this construction might only be literature, and the handling of Jeremiah's biography in his book might be compared to the way early Christianity elaborated the traditions about Jesus, resulting in the present construct of his life in the Gospels.[8]

Another study of the same character is by the German scholar Otto Kaiser, whose analyses of Isaiah were a watershed. In Kaiser's view, the first part of this book (chaps. 1–39) includes a few sayings about the destruction of the kingdom of Judah, which may belong to the period when Jerusalem was destroyed, but it was edited and published only in the fifth century BCE in an edition highly influenced by Deuteronomistic theology. After its first publication, more redactions followed, all the way down to the fourth century BCE.[9]

A similar study of Micah by the Danish scholar Knud Jeppesen presents a view of this book not very different from Carroll's and Kaiser's ideas about prophetism. Jeppesen reckons with a nucleus of prophecies in the seven chapters of this book, which may go back to a historical prophet of the name of Micah from Moresheth—we can never be absolutely sure that they really belong to this prophet. Although the exilic editors of Micah's book declined to present a biography of their prophet, they have nevertheless embedded much material from many hands, presenting Micah as a kind of collage, an expression also used by Carroll about Jeremiah.[10]

Another study from the same period—Hosea—ought to be included in this context. In this study the Finnish scholar Martti Nissinen, based on his extensive knowledge of ancient Near Eastern prophecy, proposed that we understand Old Testament prophetic literature as the outcome of a kind of a series of rewritings (he uses the German word *Fortschreibung*). This period of rewriting spanned several phases of editing of the many minor prophecies that were traditionally attrib-

8. Robert Carroll's most important studies on Jeremiah are *From Chaos to Covenant: Uses of Prophecy in the Book of Jeremiah* (London: SCM, 1981) and his commentary on Jeremiah, *Jeremiah: A Commentary*, OTL (London: SCM, 1986).

9. Kaiser developed his ideas about the book of Isaiah over a period of more than twenty years. Thus the first edition of his well-known commentary on Isaiah was absolutely traditional: *Der Prophet Jesaja Kapitel 1–12*, Altes Testament Deutsch (Göttingen: Vandenhoeck & Ruprecht, 1960). In the fifth edition, from 1980, we encounter a completely new view on the composition of this book: ET, *Isaiah 1–12: A Commentary*, 2nd ed., completely rewritten, OTL (Philadelphia: Westminster, 1983).

10. Knud Jeppesen, *Grader ikke saa saare: Studier I Mikabogens sigte* I–II (Århus: Aarhus Universitetsforlag, 1987).

uted to the prophet Hosea and were very similar to the kind of prophecy found in Neo-Assyrian documents.[11] These basic prophecies were worked over in several phases in such a way that they represented the sentiments and ideas of the time of their reworking rather than their original situation.

This kind of study, with an open mind to the possibilities of a totally new understanding about the character of the prophetic literature of the Old Testament, allows the scholar to establish a more realistic image of the role of biblical prophets. It cannot be denied that there were prophets around in ancient times, but it is reasonable to imagine Palestinian prophets to have functioned in a way similar to other prophets in other parts of the ancient Near East. Prophets were not preachers but simply prophets, people believed to be divinely inspired and possibly the media of the divine will. People went to the prophet not to hear about present conditions but to obtain knowledge about the future. The assembly of prophets did not act like the folk of London's Hyde Park Corner, each of them standing on his soapbox lecturing to the passersby.

This is one side of this case. The other side involves the prophetic books and says that these were not the result of early prophetic activity—with a few secondary additions. On the contrary, they were the result of their own redaction. This idea of the prophetic books therefore makes it likely that their origin was similar to that of the historical literature, the result of the work of one or more collectors who constructed "the history of Israel" as a story about the past adopted by his readership as its history. This does not suggest, though, that no part of the prophetic books goes back to earlier times. As was the case of the historical literature, it is highly likely that some prophetic sayings may really belong to the prophet supposed by the biblical books to have formulated them in the first place. We can never know for sure. As once put by Knud Jeppesen, the distance between the question, "Wasn't it Isaiah who said?" and the assertion, "It was really Isaiah who said!" is very short. The prophets were respected figures from the past and were therefore able to serve as the gathering point for many traditions from various places and times that may originally have had nothing to do with them. This is not very different from other personalities of the Old Testament who had books ascribed to them, such as Moses and Samuel (who dies in chapter 25 of his first book!).

WHY WAS THE PROPHETIC LITERATURE WRITTEN DOWN, AND FOR WHOM?

Many historical-critical scholars of the past believed firmly in the idea that at least some of the prophetic books were collections created by editors who in many ways considered themselves intellectually related to the prophets from Israel's period of the kings, for example, Isaiah, Micah, and Hosea. They sometimes

11. Martti Nissinen, *Prophetie, Redaktion und Fortschreibung im Hoseabuch: Studien zum Werdegang eines Prophetenbuches im Lichte von Hos 4 und 11* (Neukirchen: Neukirchener Verlag, 1991).

talked about these collectors as the physical disciples of these prophets (eventually likening them to the disciples of Jesus). This did not mean that these scholars were blind to the fact that the perspective of these prophetic books did not always relate to the time of the prophets themselves. They understood that the intended reader of prophetic books might have been a person who either lived at the time of Jerusalem's destructions in 597/587 BCE or in the subsequent period of exile.

But in the last part of the twentieth century Old Testament scholarship became more and more interested in the period of the exile as the background for not only the historical literature in the Old Testament but also for the compilation of the prophetic literature, as the prophets were supposed to have announced to the Israelite people the impending exile since ancient times.

This scholarship was on the right path. Without an exile—irrespective of how and when it took place—the content of the historical and prophetic literature is meaningless. The idea of an exile understood to represent Yahweh's punishment of his unfaithful people is central to both the historical and prophetical books in the Old Testament. The question is, what kind of exile does this literature talk about? It is obvious that the direct referent must be the Babylonian exile, which according to the Old Testament and its modern interpreters began in 587 BCE—if not already for some in 597 BCE. Nevertheless, we may question this interpretation and speculate about what is really going on. Do these biblical books speak about only one exile, the Babylonian one?

> On that day the LORD will thresh from the channel of the Euphrates to the Wadi of Egypt, and you will be gathered one by one, O people of Israel. [13] And on that day a great trumpet will be blown, and those who were lost in the land of Assyria and those who were driven out to the land of Egypt will come and worship the LORD on the holy mountain at Jerusalem. (Isa. 27:12–13)

> Therefore, the days are surely coming, says the LORD, when it shall no longer be said, "As the LORD lives who brought the people of Israel up out of the land of Egypt," [15] but "As the LORD lives who brought the people of Israel up out of the land of the north and out of all the lands where he had driven them." For I will bring them back to their own land that I gave to their ancestors. (Jer. 16:14–15)

> But I will spare some. Some of you shall escape the sword among the nations and be scattered through the countries. [9] Those of you who escape shall remember me among the nations where they are carried captive, how I was crushed by their wanton heart that turned away from me, and their wanton eyes that turned after their idols. Then they will be loathsome in their own sight for the evils that they have committed, for all their abominations. (Ezek. 6:8–9)

The first text, from Isaiah, speaks about the Israelites lost in Assyria and Egypt. The first group could consist of deportees after the Assyrian destruction of the kingdom of Israel in 722 BCE. These Israelites were deported to Assyria. In the assumed context of Isaiah's prophecies, this prophecy would be likely. However, the second group, the refugees in Egypt, makes no sense in this context. The first group of "Israelites" who fled to Egypt might have been the same that included Jeremiah and left Palestine for Egypt after the murder of Gedaliah in 582 BCE (Jer. 42–43).

In the context of the eighth century BCE, this quotation from Isaiah makes no sense. However, it would be of no help to move the date down to the fall of Jerusalem in 587 BCE. This time there was nobody who was deported to "Assyria," because there was no more Assyria, the last traces of which were extinguished by Nebuchadnezzar in 605 BCE.[12]

Furthermore, the Judeans deported by Nebuchadnezzar were not settled in former Assyrian territory but in Tel-abib in central Mesopotamia, close to the ancient city of Nippur (Ezek. 3:15). In Isaiah 27:12–13, Assyria is hardly a reference to the ancient kingdom of Assyria. It is more likely a metaphor for the north (as Egypt may be a metaphor for the south). The meaning may be that Yahweh will bring home the Jews from the Diaspora, whether they are in the north or in the south.[13]

Is Isaiah really talking about people who are living in exile in the technical sense of the word? Are these people really deportees from Jerusalem? Maybe this prophecy addresses persons now living in Mesopotamia or in Egypt, in the north or the south. The two other passages quoted here speak of the return of the Israelites and Judeans from every country of their dispersal.

The perspective of such quotations may not be the exile, although the Babylonian exile was considered in the historical literature the end of Israel's old abominable history. The authors of texts like the ones just quoted may have intended them for use among people of their own time. In this context the Babylonian exile is already "history," just like exodus and conquest, all great events that are examples of Yahweh's greatness. Also the prophetic literature agrees: Yahweh does all of this to show that he is God. It is questionable that these texts have anything to do with a literal exile based on deportations from Palestine in the past, although the historical referent may be such an exile. These deportations, the exile of the "fathers," were to be remembered by the "sons," the Jewish communities of the Diaspora. It would hardly be a surprise if the talk in the Old Testament of an "exile" and the threats of exile were intended to be read, not by people who were living in exile, but by people belonging to the Jewish Diaspora who were in danger of forgetting their origin in the homeland.

The North American scholar Morton Smith argued more than a generation ago for the idea that the Old Testament is the result of the debate between

---

12. The fall of Assyria occurred between 612 and 605 BCE. In 612 Nineveh, its capital, was destroyed. In 605 the last survivors met their fate at Carchemish. The Neo-Babylonian Empire really tried to extinguish any trace of Assyria by not even mentioning it in official documents. They used the term Subartu for the former territory of Assyria. In this way, any memory of the evil empire of Assyria was to be forgotten, although Assyria lived on not only in biblical but also in Greek tradition.

13. Isaiah 27:12–13 is part of the so-called little apocalypse (Isa. 24–27), normally considered the latest part of the whole book of Isaiah.

different factions living in Palestine, among them the already mentioned "Yah-weh alone movement," a group of fanatical worshipers of Yahweh who saw them-selves in opposition to everyone who did not share their beliefs and were therefore regarded as "unbelievers" or godless people.[14] This theory was formulated in 1971 in a period totally dominated by the classic historical-critical paradigm. Because he wrote when he did, Morton Smith traced the origins of this movement to the preexilic period and kept much of the historical tradition in the Old Testament, which he paraphrased, however, in a new manner.[15]

The question is really if he was quintessentially right. It is also a question of the perspective of the exile and return and the rhetoric that relate to this devel-opment within the Old Testament literature. To answer such questions, it is important to get a clearer idea of the people who wrote these texts, in opposition to other contrasting groups who might not have shared their idea of history. The central text in such a discussion may be Isaiah 5:8–24, the subject of which is the conflict between irresponsible people and the followers of Yahweh's Torah. This passage may be supplemented by Isaiah 6:8–10, the passage about the deaf and blind, and Isaiah 6:11–13, about the remnant that shall remain.[16]

> Ah, you who join house to house,
>   who add field to field,
> until there is room for no one but you,
>   and you are left to live alone
>   in the midst of the land!
> [9] The LORD of hosts has sworn in my hearing:
>   Surely many houses shall be desolate,
>   large and beautiful houses, without inhabitant.
> [10] For ten acres of vineyard shall yield but one bath,
>   and a homer of seed shall yield a mere ephah.
>
> [11] Ah, you who rise early in the morning
>   in pursuit of strong drink,
> who linger in the evening
>   to be inflamed by wine,
> [12] whose feasts consist of lyre and harp,
>   tambourine and flute and wine,
> but who do not regard the deeds of the LORD,
>   or see the work of his hands!
> [13] Therefore my people go into exile without knowledge;
>   their nobles are dying of hunger,
>   and their multitude is parched with thirst.

14. Morton Smith, *Palestinian Parties and Politics* (see p. 86n26, where there is also a reference to the subsequent use of this theory in the works of the German scholar Bernhard Lang).

15. This feature was quite common in those days. Thus the Danish scholar Eduard Nielsen, in his *Shechem: A Traditio-Historical Investigation* (Copenhagen: G. E. C. Gad, 1955), dates the texts showing a conflict between Jerusalem and the north, embodied in the city of Shechem, mostly to the early history of Israel. Today many scholars would prefer to see them as reflections on the enmity between Jerusalem Jewry and the Samaritans (Shechem is the holy city of the Samaritans). The demise of Noth's amphictyony really removed the basis for an early dating of the biblical tradition.

16. A more complete discussion can be found in Niels Peter Lemche, "'Because They Have Cast Away the Law of the Lord of Hosts'—Or: 'We and the Rest of the World.' The Authors Who 'Wrote' the Old Testament," *SJOT* 17 (2003): 268–90.

[14] Therefore Sheol has enlarged its appetite
    and opened its mouth beyond measure;
the nobility of Jerusalem and her multitude go down,
    her throng and all who exult in her.
[15] People are bowed down, everyone is brought low,
    and the eyes of the haughty are humbled.
[16] But the LORD of hosts is exalted by justice,
    and the Holy God shows himself holy by righteousness.
[17] Then the lambs shall graze as in their pasture,
    fatlings and kids shall feed among the ruins.

[18] Ah, you who drag iniquity along with cords of falsehood,
    who drag sin along as with cart ropes,
[19] who say, "Let him make haste,
    let him speed his work
    that we may see it;
let the plan of the Holy One of Israel hasten to fulfillment,
    that we may know it!"
[20] Ah, you who call evil good
    and good evil,
who put darkness for light
    and light for darkness,
who put bitter for sweet
    and sweet for bitter!
[21] Ah, you who are wise in your own eyes,
    and shrewd in your own sight!
[22] Ah, you who are heroes in drinking wine
    and valiant at mixing drink,
[23] who acquit the guilty for a bribe,
    and deprive the innocent of their rights!
[24] Therefore, as the tongue of fire devours the stubble,
    and as dry grass sinks down in the flame,
so their root will become rotten,
    and their blossom go up like dust;
for they have rejected the instruction of the LORD of hosts,
    and have despised the word of the Holy One of Israel.
                        (Isa. 5:8–24)

It is clear that the author of this text from Isaiah did not consider himself a member of the people condemned in this passage. The condemned people mentioned here have rejected the law and order of Yahweh. The author—in this prophetic book represented by Isaiah—has not. The other group, the condemned, are described as people who do not care at all about justice and righteousness. They get drunk early in the morning, despise God, and think that they are wise without help from God. Who is not included in this group except the author and his party, and they are few, as we shall soon hear?

The fate of the condemned ones will be exile, in this passage identified with death, including imagery with roots in ancient Near Eastern religious poetry.[17]

17. Cf. the description of Mot, the god of death at Ugarit, who swallows up Baal: *KTU* 1.5 ii. Translation, e.g., N. Wyatt, *Religious Texts from Ugarit: The Words of Ilumilku and His Colleagues,* The Biblical Seminar 53 (Sheffield: Sheffield Academic Press, 1998), 120.

However, what have they really done? Are they villains, criminals? Are they condemned for the sole reason that they have rejected the law of Yahweh? Are they unjust because they don't pay attention to the words of God, or have they rejected God's law because they are unjust? The characteristics of the condemned group of people may provide an answer to these questions. They seem to be like most people enjoying a good life. Their only crime is their rejection of Yahweh's law, that is, their disobeying the Lord. Here they are opposed to the author and his followers, who have chosen another path.

If this is a correct observation, the decisive factor in deciding who is righteous and who is not is Yahweh's law. The two other Isaiah passages mentioned in this context do not elaborate on this theme but stress that the prophet's endeavor to make people repent of their evil ways is doomed to failure, because the eyes supposed to see cannot see, and the ears supposed to hear cannot hear. Only a remnant will survive, a decimated one, but this is a "holy seed" (Isa. 6:13). From the perspective of such passages, the thesis of Morton Smith and Bernhard Lang about a "Yahweh alone movement," a prophetically inspired Yahwistic minority group, may seem justified. The principal argument is that we, the righteous ones, are few, and the godless people are many! The question is now whether this "minority" group was active before the exile or is a result of the experience of exile and dispersal.

The central concept that creates a distinction between the just and unjust is the law of Yahweh, the *tôrā*, also meaning "teaching" and "instruction." The unjust have rejected the *tôrā* and the righteous have accepted it. Passages similar to Isaiah 5 are present in other parts of the prophetic literature, and the wording is often very similar to that of Isaiah 5. The technical expression meaning "to reject," Hebrew *māʾas*, is often used in the Old Testament about Israel rejecting—apart from Yahweh's teaching or law—his instructions, his commandments, or even Yahweh as their God. It can also be used of Yahweh rejecting Israel.

Before we can proceed, it is necessary to comment on the meaning of the Hebrew word *tôrā*, which should not always be translated as "law" but, for example, as "instruction," as in the NRSV's translation of *tôrā* in Isaiah 5:24. The different translations of *tôrā* in passages whose content may seem almost identical may seem somewhat inconsequential.

The etymology of the word is related to education, and the Hebrew verbal stem *yrh* means "to teach" and "to instruct," and the participle may simply mean "Teacher." *Tôrā* means "teaching," or "instruction." In Jewish tradition *tôrā* means "the Law," alias the five books of Moses. However, the translation of *tôrā* as "law" in the forensic sense has a long history within Christianity, since the days of Paul who spoke of "the curse of the law" (Gal. 3:13), from which the Christian has been redeemed through Christ. In its early confrontation with Judaism, Christianity emphasized the importance of distinguishing between the Law—Judaism—and the Gospel—Christianity.

"Law" is a translation of Hebrew *tôrā*, which covers only a minor part of the semantic field of the Hebrew word. Historical-critical scholarship realized this very soon, but because its Protestant background led to a desire to separate itself from Judaism, it created a division between prophetism and regular Judaism. The prophets were believed to represent the ancient preexilic Israel that knew nothing of the "Law," the written Law of Moses in the Pentateuch.[18] The prophets predated the appearance of the Law. In this way the prophets was considered to be "proto-evangelists" and their religion much closer to Christianity than later Judaism.

According to this line of scholarship, the prophets used the word *tôrā* without the connotations that became part of its semantics in Judaism. This is the reason for the many times when, even in the NRSV, *tôrā* is translated as "instructions" in texts believed to belong to preexilic prophets, and as "law" in texts considered "Jewish." The distinction is absolutely fictive and misleading. It also distorts the real meaning of *tôrā* in the Old Testament, and for that matter also in early Judaism.

The book of Amos has one reference to the Israelite people's rejection of the Law of Yahweh. Although the essential parts of Amos are regarded by most historical-critical researchers as preexilic and from the eighth century BCE, it is also seen as handed down in a Deuteronomistic redaction either during the exile or shortly afterwards. The passage about *tôrā* is therefore considered a part of this redaction.

> Thus says the LORD:
> For three transgressions of Judah,
>   and for four, I will not revoke the punishment;
> because they have rejected the law of the LORD,
>   and have not kept his statutes,
> but they have been led astray by the same lies
>   after which their ancestors walked.
>   (Amos 2:4)

Amos uses the motif of the rejection of the *tôrā* in its word of judgment against Judah as early as the beginning of the book.[19] The crime of Judah is that the Judeans have rejected Yahweh's *tôrā*. The fathers were led astray by lies, meaning foreign gods. The accusation is no more precise than this; neither is the punishment presented in any details: "a fire on Judah" (Amos 2:5). Most of the words of doom in Amos are directed against Israel, whose magnates suppress the poor and worship false gods. At the end these accusations create problems for Amos, who clashes with the high priest at Bethel. Amos has no offer to Israel except death, destruction, and deportation "beyond Damascus" (Amos 5:27). It is impossible to say with any certainty when this prophecy was formed, in preexilic or exilic times.

Amos includes more passages that may be of interest in this connection. In his accusations against carefree Zion, the prophet threatens Zion with a punishment worse than Israel's: "Therefore they shall now be the first to go into exile" (Amos 6:7). This prophecy may not need to be a *vaticinium ex eventu*, a prophecy

---

18. This is a basic assumption in Julius Wellhausen's famous *Prolegomena zur Geschichte Israel* of 1878, which for generations dominated within Protestant Old Testament scholarship.

19. The Hebrew wording is almost the same as found in Isaiah 5:24.

that comes after the event, because in another context Amos addresses the final destiny of the people in exile:

> On that day I will raise up
>   the booth of David that is fallen,
> and repair its breaches,
>   and raise up its ruins,
>   and rebuild it as in the days of old;
> 12 in order that they may possess the remnant of Edom
>   and all the nations who are called by my name,
>   says the LORD who does this.
>
> (Amos 9:11–12)

Most historical scholars will traditionally reckon this passage to be secondary. It was previously the rule to think of prophets like Isaiah, Amos, Hosea, Micah, and Zephaniah as prophets of doom, who did not include prophecies of hope for the future. If there is a positive prophecy, it must be secondary. In modern times, scholars are more reluctant to accept such a line of division between threats and promises. Whether or not this passage is a secondary part of Amos, it ends with a subject that is different from the main theme of the book, the ultimate fate of Israel. It is not difficult to find passages about the reestablishment of the house of David in prophetic literature, but such passages seem a little out of their way in the specific Israelite context as found in Amos. It presupposes a view on the history of Israel in the time of its kings as present in the books of Samuel and Kings, the original and golden period—something that never existed in real time.

Hosea, purportedly written by the prophet of this name, a contemporary of Amos, mentions the rejection of Yahweh's *tôrā* a couple of times:

> Yet let no one contend,
>   and let none accuse,
>   for with you is my contention, O priest.
> 5 You shall stumble by day;
>   the prophet also shall stumble with you by night,
>   and I will destroy your mother.
> 6 My people are destroyed for lack of knowledge;
>   because you have rejected knowledge,
>   I reject you from being a priest to me.
> And since you have forgotten the law of your God,
>   I also will forget your children. (Hos. 4:4–6)

> 1 Set the trumpet to your lips!
>   One like a vulture is over the house of the LORD,
> because they have broken my covenant,
>   and transgressed my law.
> 2 Israel cries to me,
>   "My God, we—Israel—know you!"
> Israel has spurned the good;
>   the enemy shall pursue him.
>
> (Hos. 8:1–2)

5. Deported inhabitants of Lachish—the Assyrian version
(Detail from pl. 70 in D. Ussishkin, *The Conquest of Lachish by Sennacherib* [Tel Aviv: Tel
Aviv University, 1982]. Courtesy of the Institute of Archaeology, Tel Aviv University.)

The first passage is part of a fictive court scene involving the case of Yahweh
against Israel, a motif favored by other prophetic literature.[20] The accusation
against Israel is that there is no knowledge of God in this country, a favorite
expression in Hosea. Because of this lack of knowledge, Israel's land is full of all
sorts of crime and about to perish. The case involves the leaders of the people,
the prophet, and especially the priest because he has rejected (*ma‘as*) the knowledge of God and forgotten God's *tôrā*. Playing on the favorite metaphor used in
Hosea about Israel's idolatry, Hosea concludes: "For a spirit of whoredom has led
them astray, and they have played the whore, forsaking their God" (Hos. 4:12).

The second passage from Hosea includes a direct link between the breaking
of the covenant, the inability to keep Yahweh's *tôrā*, and exile. This verdict is followed by accusations of having transgressed the command that forbids idolatry.
Because of its transgressions, Israel will have to go to Assyria (Hos. 8:9), and they
are to return to Egypt (Hos. 8:13)—a recurring motif in Hosea.

Hosea copies Amos by including at its end a series of hopes for the future, when
everything becomes as it was in the beginning, when Yahweh has "healed" Israel
(Hos. 11:3), and the harmonic relationship between Yahweh and Israel has been
restored (Hos. 11–14). In Hosea 11 we have the usual imagery: Israel was called
from Egypt by Yahweh, but it worshiped the Baals and sacrificed to idols. This
image is in agreement with the picture painted by the warnings against idolatry in

20. The best example is Isaiah 1.

the Pentateuch and the prophecies about impending doom in the commentaries in the Deuteronomistic History. The punishment is the same, exile, although in Hosea it is followed by a return to Egypt and a submission to Assyria.

In the last part of Hosea 11, Yahweh repents and promises to forgive Israel and not to destroy Ephraim a second time (Hos. 11:8–11). The people in exile shall return. It is interesting to see from which places they are homebound. In Hosea's time, exile would normally be the consequence of a deportation by force; the Assyrians used this method extensively but described it as a blessing for the defeated nations.

> They shall go after the LORD,
>   who roars like a lion;
> when he roars,
>   [11] his children shall come trembling from the west.
> They shall come trembling like birds from Egypt,
>   and like doves from the land of Assyria;
> and I will return them to their homes, says the LORD.
>   (Hos. 11:10–11)

Earlier studies in prophecy regarded the first part—eventually the whole passage—about those who return from the west as a secondary addition.[21] It has no meaning if the historical context is supposed to be Hosea's. If exiled Israelites were to return home from the west, they had first to go there, and the Old Testament has nothing to say about such a migration. In this way the supplement to chapter 11 might belong to the time of the Jewish Diaspora, or so it was believed. It did not belong to the period immediately following the end of the exile in Babylon; it must be much later, perhaps from the third century BCE. It is evident that if we are less likely to date the essential part of Hosea in the eighth century BCE, we have less reason to reckon this part to be secondary.

The thesis presented here seems well founded. In its way of handling the problem of exile, prophetic literature as handed down to posterity is not necessarily the product of the preexilic period, the exilic period, or the period following immediately the official closure of the exile. It might address a much later period. It may be in order not to speak about an exile in the narrow meaning, understood to be caused by forced deportations from Palestine. "Exile" may have a wider meaning. Its very existence may be considered the punishment inflicted on the inhabitants of "Israel" for not respecting their God, but not in the past—rather, when the collectors of the prophetic literature were active.

A study of the last so-called preexilic prophet, Jeremiah, will provide a confirmation of the value of this thesis. In Jeremiah we have three passages directly involving Israel's rejection of Yahweh's law. Here is the first one:

---

21. Thus still Jörg Jeremias, *Der Prophet Hosea*, Altes Testament Deutsch (Göttingen: Vandenhoeck & Ruprecht, 1983), 147.

Hear, O earth; I am going to bring disaster on this people,
    the fruit of their schemes,
because they have not given heed to my words;
    and as for my teaching [*tôrā*], they have rejected it.
(Jer. 6:19)

The wording is very much the same as that found in Isaiah 5:24 and Amos 2:4 (*ma'as* is used in all three places). It is placed in the same forensic context we encountered in previous prophets where Yahweh accuses his people of having broken his covenant with them and worshiped other gods. This introduces a prophecy about the mighty enemy to the north. This enemy will attack and destroy the country. The daughter of Zion, that is, Jerusalem, and Judah are the recipients of the prophecy of doom. As such this prophecy would not be out of place in connection with the events that led to the Babylonian conquest of Jerusalem in 597 or 587 BCE.

Here is the second passage from the book of Jeremiah:

> Who is wise enough to understand this? To whom has the mouth of the LORD spoken, so that they may declare it? Why is the land ruined and laid waste like a wilderness, so that no one passes through? [13] And the LORD says: Because they have forsaken my law that I set before them, and have not obeyed my voice, or walked in accordance with it, [14] but have stubbornly followed their own hearts and have gone after the Baals, as their ancestors taught them. [15] Therefore thus says the LORD of hosts, the God of Israel: I am feeding this people with wormwood, and giving them poisonous water to drink. [16] I will scatter them among nations that neither they nor their ancestors have known; and I will send the sword after them, until I have consumed them. (Jer. 9:12–16)

Jeremiah is characterized by the extensive use of prose narrative. Other prophetic books include passages composed in prose, but nowhere on such a scale as in Jeremiah, more than half of which is in prose. This change between passages in prose and poetry was early in the history of historical-critical exegesis seen as the result of a redaction of the prophecies of Jeremiah that involved a running commentary on his prophecies, including his "biography." The classic version was proposed by Sigmund Mowinckel, who distinguished between four strata in Jeremiah:[22]

- a collection of Jeremiah's oracles
- a collection of stories about the life of the prophet
- sundry speeches
- prophecies of salvation found in Jeremiah 30 and 31

---

22. Sigmund Mowinckel, *Zur Komposition des Buches Jeremia* (Kristiania: Dybwad, 1914).

Mowinckel was especially interested in the relationship between the speeches and Deuteronomism as represented by the historical literature.[23] Later scholarship has built upon Mowinckel's theory but has to an even larger degree supported his theory of a Deuteronomistic origin of Jeremiah in the late preexilic, exilic, and early postexilic periods. And Robert Carroll's aforementioned Jeremiah studies builds on the foundation laid by Mowinckel, although Carroll is less certain about the amount of old tradition going back to a historical prophet of the name of Jeremiah.[24]

When we turn to the passage from Jeremiah 9 quoted here, this commentary has more or less the same content as similar commentaries in the books of Kings. Israel has rejected Yahweh's *tôrā* and worshiped other gods, "as their ancestors taught them." Therefore they will be spread among the nations. Some questions remain.

First of all, we have to ask about the meaning of the sentence "I will scatter them among nations that neither they nor their ancestors have known" (Jer. 9:16). Is this a reference to the Babylonian exile *stricte sensu*, or is it a general reference to the Jewish Diaspora? Do we have here an expression of the same expectations as already seen in Hosea concerning the end of the exile? The first questions leads to the next, which is a bit more problematic: Who are the "ancestors" (Heb. "fathers") in such prophecies? Who are these "fathers" and—implicit—who are the "sons"?

The answer to the first question points in the same direction as the earlier examples. It is a part of the composition of Jeremiah that indicates a time of origin in a period when there was a Jewish Diaspora, that is, the late Persian or the Hellenistic period.

It is equally important but more complicated to answer the second question. There are many references in the Old Testament to the "fathers" ("ancestors") who sinned against Yahweh. In some cases the fathers are the patriarchs, in others the generation that participated in the exodus from Egypt. In other examples, the "fathers" simply indicate the old generation whose sin and transgression led to the exile. Often this destitute generation is compared to the present (the "sons"), with a constant warning to the sons of not following in the footsteps of their fathers, as in the famous saying in Jeremiah 31:29: "The parents have eaten sour grapes, and the children's teeth are set on edge."

The accusation in Jeremiah 9 is directed against the "sons" who have been taught by the "fathers" to act against God and worship other gods. Who are these sons really? It can only be the generation that is addressed by the author of Jeremiah 9:11–15. This says that the idolatry mentioned here belongs not to the past but the present generation, the author's contemporaries. It has nothing to do with the Babylonian exile as such, which is considered the time of punishment because of the transgressions of the fathers. It has to do with a later, so-called postexilic

---

23. It must be remembered that Mowinckel's study of Jeremiah appeared almost a generation before Noth formulated his theory of the Deuteronomistic History.

24. See p. 218.

situation where transgression—basically idolatry in its many forms—still dominates and will lead to God punishing the present generation.

Here is the last passage from Jeremiah to be mentioned in this context:

> Therefore, the days are surely coming, says the LORD, when it shall no longer be said, "As the LORD lives who brought the people of Israel up out of the land of Egypt," [15] but "As the LORD lives who brought the people of Israel up out of the land of the north and out of all the lands where he had driven them." For I will bring them back to their own land that I gave to their ancestors. (Jer. 16:14–15)

Even clearer than the previous passage from Jeremiah, this quotation expresses the hope of a future Israel that will assemble to live again in its land, brought back from all the "lands" among which they had been dispersed. In Jeremiah 23, with almost exactly the same words, this hope is combined with the theme of the new king of the house of David—another recurrent motif in prophetic literature, probably best known from the book of Isaiah.[25]

Classical historical-critical scholarship regarded this hope for a new king of David's dynasty as another expression of the expectations nourished among the people exiled from Jerusalem for their future, when their ancient kingdom with its dynasty would be reestablished. Such ideas were traced back to Judean royal ideology in the period of the kings and formed the link to later Jewish messianic expectations. There is no reason to expand on this theme here. The only point to be made here is that the lowering of the date of the compilation of prophetic literature argued here may be an indication that such messianic expectations were already a governing motif when this literature came into being.

This leads to the decisive passage in Jeremiah about the future, Jeremiah 31. Here it is made clear for whom this book, and perhaps even the prophetic literature in general, is composed. I opened the prolegomena of this book by quoting Jeremiah's words about the new covenant (Jer. 31:31–34).

Jeremiah 31 consists of two parts. First we have a long passage in poetry linking up with Jeremiah 30. Here the return of the people in exile is described:

> For thus says the LORD:
> Sing aloud with gladness for Jacob,
>   and raise shouts for the chief of the nations;
> proclaim, give praise, and say,
>   "Save, O LORD, your people,
>   the remnant of Israel."
> [8] See, I am going to bring them from the land of the north,
>   and gather them from the farthest parts of the earth,
> among them the blind and the lame,
>   those with child and those in labor, together;
>   a great company, they shall return here.

---

25. Especially Isaiah 7:11–17, the prophecy about the birth of Immanuel; 8:23–9:6, the wonderful king who is going to rule in the future; and Isaiah 11, the new David and the new paradise.

> [9] With weeping they shall come,
>   and with consolations I will lead them back,
> I will let them walk by brooks of water,
>   in a straight path in which they shall not stumble;
> for I have become a father to Israel,
>   and Ephraim is my firstborn.
>
>   (Jer. 31:7–9)

This passage includes several themes already mentioned in other parts of Jeremiah, including Yahweh bringing the refugees back from the countries of the north and other remote countries, a theme similar to that of being exiled to countries unknown to the people.

The next part of Jeremiah 31, up to the passage about the new covenant, describes the exuberance following the return of the dispersed part of the population. Hereafter the central part, Jeremiah 31:31–34, follows. The new covenant is something absolutely new; unlike the Sinai covenant, it cannot be broken, because it has been written not on stone but on the hearts of human beings. Historical-critical scholarship tended to view this passage as secondary and late, summing up the ideology not only of Jeremiah but of much prophetic literature in general. It is about the Israel of the future, with a covenant that cannot be broken: "I will be their God, and they shall be my people" (Jer. 31:33). Everyone knows Yahweh, in contrast to the old Israel, which forgot the covenant as well as their God. Jeremiah 31 ends with a prophecy of the restoration of Jerusalem and opens up a theme that is far more important in Ezekiel, with its vision of the new temple (Ezek. 40–48), and played a major role within early Judaism (cf. Isa. 4) and later Christianity, exemplified by Revelation's vision of the heavenly Jerusalem (Rev. 21:9–27).

> On that day the branch of the LORD shall be beautiful and glorious, and the fruit of the land shall be the pride and glory of the survivors of Israel. [3] Whoever is left in Zion and remains in Jerusalem will be called holy, everyone who has been recorded for life in Jerusalem, [4] once the Lord has washed away the filth of the daughters of Zion and cleansed the bloodstains of Jerusalem from its midst by a spirit of judgment and by a spirit of burning. [5] Then the LORD will create over the whole site of Mount Zion and over its places of assembly a cloud by day and smoke and the shining of a flaming fire by night. Indeed over all the glory there will be a canopy. [6] It will serve as a pavilion, a shade by day from the heat, and a refuge and a shelter from the storm and rain. (Isa. 4:2–6)

> [22] I saw no temple in the city, for its temple is the Lord God the Almighty and the Lamb. [23] And the city has no need of sun or moon to shine on it, for the glory of God is its light, and its lamp is the Lamb. [24] The nations will walk by its light, and the kings of the earth will bring their glory into it. [25] Its gates will never be shut by day—and there will be no night there. [26] People will bring into it the glory and the honor of the nations. [27] But nothing unclean will enter it, nor anyone who practices abomination or falsehood, but only those who are written in the Lamb's book of life. (Rev. 21:22–27)

SUMMARY

The major part of prophetic literature is "exilic literature." This does not mean that it must be dated to the period of the Babylonian exile in the sixth century BCE. It means that it addresses a public living "in exile" over the world. To live in exile does not mean that one is forced to live there. It is rather an expression referring to the mentality of not living in one's real homeland. The slogan among Jews living in the Diaspora has been for centuries "Next year in Jerusalem!" Jerusalem represents a dream, a hope for the future, and therefore symbolizes the fulfillment of God's intentions for this world, when all the holy ones belonging to God will assemble on Zion in the kingdom of God.

These and similar ideas control the compilation of the main body of prophetic literature as this corpus has been handed down to posterity. It does not imply that all the prophets of the Old Testament—or rather their books—are in total agreement. Historical-critical scholarship has at least achieved this: it has demonstrated the existence of many different ideas and attitudes within this body of literature. Not everything is about Israel's exile and return. Thus Jonah, as already mentioned, is hardly a prophetic book in the usual sense of the word. It is a burlesque about a prophet who makes the Gentiles repent their evil ways and turn to Yahweh, although Jonah expected to be killed by the same heathen. The book has nothing to do with exile and return.

The differences within prophetic literature are most apparent when it comes to the third part of Isaiah, so-called "Trito-Isaiah" (Isa. 56–66). This collection is not about exile and return. It is concerned with the maintenance of the Sabbath, admission to the temple, and similar questions, which have long ago been placed by historical-critical research in connection with early Judaism and the discussion among Jews living in Jerusalem and Palestine about who is a God-loving Jew and who is not.

The thesis of Morton Smith and Bernhard Lang about the Yahweh alone movement has already been discussed. They traced the origin of this movement to the period of the kings. This is a variation of the old idea about the origin of the Deuteronomistic movement as a reform movement active in Jerusalem in the last century before the city was destroyed by the Babylonians, between Sennacherib's attack on the city in 701 BCE and Nebuchadnezzar's conquest of it in 587 BCE. It is impossible to reject this thesis, but it is also impossible to prove it. We have no sources demonstrating that this movement ever existed, although its advocates would stress that the Old Testament itself proves its existence—which is clearly a circular argument. Smith and Lang may be right, and many scholars are prone to accept their idea as a simple explanation of the religious changes from a polytheistic religion dominating the period of the kings to later monotheistic Judaism. However, this represents only one among many possible explanations.

On one point Smith and Lang are evidently right: such a movement existed when the corpus of prophetic literature came into being, because it is a governing idea in this literature that the people of Yahweh are few in number but the enemies of God are many. It is evident that the compilers of this literature identified themselves with the people of Yahweh—best expressed by a text like Isaiah 5:8–24, which condemns the whole world because it has in the eyes of the "prophet"/compiler rejected Yahweh's *tôrā*. Because of the way the compilers are identifying themselves with the people of God, in contrast to the many who are not members of their community, it would be obvious to talk about a sectarian movement. The members of this sect are in possession of the correct faith in God. The rest of the world is condemned to destruction and death.

The rejection of Yahweh's *tôrā* is followed by the breaking of the covenant, idolatry, injustice, improper behavior; in short, every possible evil is remembered by the prophets and their compilers. This is the idea of a minority group, or so the compilers saw it. In his monograph Morton Smith argues for variety and cites Old Testament texts that speak in favor of the presence of several competing Jewish factions or parties in the postexilic period. The prophetic literature seems to confirm his theory. Sectarian movements have been convinced that they alone are right and everybody else is a sinner. We find expression of this on almost every page of the Old Testament.

This does not mean that there are no traces of older literature and traditions in the prophetic books. Because of a lack of evidence, it cannot be denied that fragments of prophecies may originate—as proposed by, for example, Martti Nissinen—in the time of the kingdoms of Israel and Judah. Whether such fragments go back to prophets like Isaiah or Hosea is basically a question that cannot be answered. It is probably also a question of no real importance. The scholar has to base his or her ideas on the evidence in his or her possession, and only this material—not the multitude of ideas and theses proposed by scholars—will be capable of providing answers. As it is, the corpus of prophetic literature can be linked to a situation of exile or, rather, to the Diaspora. It is related to the construction of the history of biblical Israel already discussed. It is an expression of how writers construct a history as expressed by Thomas L. Thompson.[26]

Now what remains is to see how this thesis works in connection with the remaining parts of the Old Testament, and here the collection of the Psalms is especially important. Perhaps this collection will provide more answers as to the identities of the compilers who were responsible for the creation of Old Testament literature.

---

26. See the subtitle to his monograph, *The Bible in History: How Writers Create a Past*.

Chapter 9

The Writings in
the Intellectual Context
of the Old Testament

A Renewed Critical Study
of the Old Testament IV

The third part of the Old Testament, the Writings, consists of a sundry collection of books of many kinds. Basically we find three genres of literature included: historical literature, including Chronicles, Ezra and Nehemiah, and Esther (although literary critics will probably reckon Esther as a novella); Psalms and similar poems, including the Song of Songs and Lamentations; and Wisdom literature, including Job, Proverbs, and Ecclesiastes (the Preacher).

THE PSALMS OF DAVID

The two most important books belonging to this collection are indisputably the Psalms of David and Job. They are as different as one can imagine, and only the Psalms are of relevance in this context. After all, the compiler of Psalms has linked his or her collection to a historical person known from the historical books. Several psalms are said to be the compositions of David, and two are attributed to his son and successor Solomon (Pss. 72 and 127). Other psalms are considered the work of Asaph (Pss. 50; 73–83) and the sons of Korah (Pss. 42–49; 84–85; 87–88). And Moses too has his psalm (Ps. 90). Other psalms are provided with anonymous authors. Some psalms refer to events—known or unknown—belonging to the life and career of David. Some psalms are dated because of their content, such as Psalm 127, reckoned to be composed by Solomon because of its reference to the building of the temple, and Psalm 72, where the king is described as the son of a king, and David was definitely not a son of a king, so the psalm must be Solomon's.

The principle of the collection of the psalms seems to be shrouded in mystery and a challenge to modern scholarship. They represent a variety of genres, and their content may be very different from one psalm to the next. The order of psalms may also seem rather casual. It is, on the other hand, obvious that the beginning and the end of the collection are a close match.[1]

The lack of transparency when it comes to composition may be illustrated by listing the first fifteen psalms:

Psalm 1   Wisdom psalm about the pious and the godless

Psalm 2   Royal psalm about the installment of the Messiah on Zion

Psalm 3   Psalm expressing trust in God

Psalm 4   Lamentation

Psalm 5   Psalm expressing trust in God

Psalm 6   Lamentation

Psalm 7   Psalm expressing trust in God

Psalm 8   Hymn

Psalm 9   Thanksgiving

Psalm 10   Psalm expressing trust in God

Psalm 11   Psalm expressing trust in God

Psalm 12   Psalm expressing trust in God

Psalm 13   Lamentation

Psalm 14   Wisdom psalm

Psalm 15   Psalm for the pilgrimage or a psalm expressing trust in God

And it goes on in the same way, although there are in some sections greater unity, especially in the group of Hallelujah psalms, Psalms 104–6; 110–18; 135–36; 146–150; and in the psalms of pilgrimage, Psalms 120–34.

There is no heading to Psalm 1. There is no indication of an author. It is reasonable to suppose that this psalm reflects the view of the collector of himself (we

---

1. See pp. 23–24.

treat the collector as masculine) and his adversaries—the psalm was quoted earlier in this book, but for the sake of clarity we will repeat it here as it contains the key to the understanding of the collection:

> Happy are those
> who do not follow the advice of the wicked,
> or take the path that sinners tread,
> or sit in the seat of scoffers;
> ² but their delight is in the law of the LORD,
> and on his law they meditate day and night.
> ³ They are like trees
> planted by streams of water,
> which yield their fruit in its season,
> and their leaves do not wither.
> In all that they do, they prosper.
>
> ⁴ The wicked are not so,
> but are like chaff that the wind drives away.
> ⁵ Therefore the wicked will not stand in the judgment,
> nor sinners in the congregation of the righteous;
> ⁶ for the LORD watches over the way of the righteous,
> but the way of the wicked will perish.

In this introductory psalm the collector expresses his view of human nature. Humanity can be subdivided into two kinds of people, and there is no middle ground between them. On one side we have the godless and on the other the people who fear God, or simply the righteous. The righteous one is characterized at the beginning of the psalm as a person who has nothing in common with the godless. He or she is also described as the only one who is interested in Yahweh's *tôrā*.

The two contrasting kinds of human life will have totally different outcomes. The godless will perish in the middle of life. The God-fearing will stand firmly in the middle of Yahweh's road. The righteous person is the tree standing at the stream of water. He or she drinks from the perennial source of life. The unjust person is like the chaff carried away by the wind, barren and without descendants; but the just person acts according to God's wisdom.

After having presented the contrast between the God-fearing person and the godless one, the collector introduces in the second psalm the context of his collection. Psalm 2 was formerly regarded as a royal psalm belonging to the rituals of the enthronement of the Davidic king in Jerusalem. Although it cannot be ignored that the psalm may once have played such a role, that is not the reason it is included in the collection in this prominent position. The key word appears already in the second verse: "The kings of the earth set themselves, and the rulers take counsel together, against the LORD and his anointed." "His anointed" is a translation of Hebrew *mešîḥô*, or simply messiah. The first time the king is mentioned in Psalms is in the form of the messiah. This is not casual; it belongs to the same context in which the several references to the hope for a new David appear in the prophetic literature. It is not a reference to the past history of biblical Israel but expresses a hope for the future, when Israel is again ruled by a king of David's house, that is, the messiah.

This is why the first two psalms have no headings. They themselves function as the heading to the collection of Psalms, introducing on the one hand the sorts of persons one finds in the Psalms and on the other the messiah. We have a kind of triangle. On the lower level we have humans, the godless and the God-fearing, and on the top level we have God. We also have the purpose for the collection of Psalms: the expectation of messiah's kingdom. In this way the psalms address the contemporaries of the collector and have a message for that generation. The solution to all problems will not be in this age, which is evil and nasty, but in the future, when "David" rules the world.

When Psalms is set in such a context, its different elements all find their place. Thus when Psalm 36 is introduced by a lamentation because of the success of the godless, that godlessness is soon explained in the light of Yahweh's providence; and so we are introduced to one of the best known lines from Psalms:

> Your steadfast love, O LORD, extends to the heavens,
>   your faithfulness to the clouds.
> ⁶ Your righteousness is like the mighty mountains,
>   your judgments are like the great deep.
>   (Ps. 36:5–6)

After this comes a motif very popular in this collection, in which Yahweh is described as the savior who received the righteous in his temple, where "you give them drink from the river of your delights" (Ps. 36:8). Psalm 36 ends with a prayer to Yahweh asking him to be faithful to the righteous and to punish the godless.

Only God-fearing people are granted admission to the temple, although they have to pass an examination, as recorded by the choreography of Psalm 24:

> Who shall ascend the hill of the LORD?
>   And who shall stand in his holy place?
> ⁴ Those who have clean hands and pure hearts,
>   who do not lift up their souls to what is false,
>   and do not swear deceitfully.
> ⁵ They will receive blessing from the LORD,
>   and vindication from the God of their salvation.
> ⁶ Such is the company of those who seek him,
>   who seek the face of the God of Jacob.
>   (Ps. 24:3–6)

This text and the related Psalm 15 are often believed to represent special liturgies enacted at the entrance to the temple (they are often described as Torah liturgies). Whether or not this evaluation is correct, the psalm gives a good impression of the expectation of the righteous. It is hardly an accident if the reader recalls the wordings of the Ten Commandments here. This attitude is very much the same as that found in several places in the prophetic literature where Yahweh rejects sacrifices but demands a pure heart.

What to me is the multitude of your sacrifices?
    says the LORD;
I have had enough of burnt offerings of rams
    and the fat of fed beasts;
I do not delight in the blood of bulls,
    or of lambs, or of goats.
. . . .
[16] Wash yourselves; make yourselves clean;
    remove the evil of your doings
    from before my eyes;
cease to do evil,
    [17] learn to do good;
seek justice,
    rescue the oppressed,
defend the orphan,
    plead for the widow.

(Isa. 1:11, 16–17)

The passage from Isaiah may be supplemented by many similar passages in other prophetic books.[2] It is hardly surprising that similar passages are also included in the collection of Psalms, in, for example, Psalm 40:6 and Psalm 50:7–15. The wording of Psalm 50:7–15 is especially important in this connection:

"Hear, O my people, and I will speak,
    O Israel, I will testify against you.
    I am God, your God.
[8] Not for your sacrifices do I rebuke you;
    your burnt offerings are continually before me.
[9] I will not accept a bull from your house,
    or goats from your folds.
[10] For every wild animal of the forest is mine,
    the cattle on a thousand hills.
[11] I know all the birds of the air,
    and all that moves in the field is mine.

[12] "If I were hungry, I would not tell you,
    for the world and all that is in it is mine.
[13] Do I eat the flesh of bulls,
    or drink the blood of goats?
[14] Offer to God a sacrifice of thanksgiving,
    and pay your vows to the Most High.
[15] Call on me in the day of trouble;
    I will deliver you, and you shall glorify me."

---

2. E.g., Amos 5:21–26; Hos. 6:6; Jer. 6:20; 7:21–23; Mic. 6:6–8.

The text of Psalm 50 follows the criticism of the cult in the prophetic literature. The essence is the same: Yahweh does not care about bloody sacrifices; he prefers sacrifices of thanksgiving and the fulfillment of vows. Therefore the author is allowed to say:

> [6] Sacrifice and offering you do not desire,
>   but you have given me an open ear.
> Burnt offering and sin offering
>   you have not required.
> [7] Then I said, "Here I am;
>   in the scroll of the book it is written of me.
> [8] I delight to do your will, O my God;
>   your law (*tôrā*) is within my heart."
> (Ps. 40:6–8)

We are no longer among the unjust in Psalms. The author addresses, in contrast to the prophets, not the godless with an admonition to change their ways. The author addresses the just, who do not need such a warning but see the godless as the enemy. The different recipients of the prophetic literature and the Psalms may constitute the major difference between these collections. The prophets address the unjust directly, demanding that they repent and hope for Yahweh's salvation. The Psalms see the unjust from the perspective of the righteous. They know the end of the wicked: they have no admission to the glory of God and no place in Yahweh's congregation, and they are expelled from the people of God. The recipient of the Psalms is the just, God-loving person. We may say that Psalms represents the inner façade of the God-loving community, the true people of God; while the prophets represent the façade of the outside world. The intellectual situation is the same in both parts. Whether we talk about prophetic literature, Psalms, or the historical literature, all three parts relate to the expectation in early Judaism of the future glory of Yahweh's kingdom administered by his chosen messiah.

The rule of the messiah is still to come. The people of God are still longing for its appearance. When it comes, it will be a mighty kingdom as described in Psalm 72, a kingdom where the king rules according to the statutes of God and cares for the welfare of his people. The king is also going to rule over all of the world, to the benefit of the poor and destitute. In the collection of Psalms, these expectations are not presented as a narrative but more like a kaleidoscope that casts light over the central motifs from every possible angle.

WISDOM LITERATURE AND THE AUTHORSHIP
OF THE OLD TESTAMENT

When we move on to the next category of literature within the Writings, Wisdom literature, the situation is somewhat different. It has often been noted that the attitude of this literature to issues like Israel and its history is absolutely neutral. There are many parallels outside of the Old Testament to Wisdom literature.

Thus Proverbs has many parallels, especially in Egyptian and Mesopotamian collections of proverbs. Also the theme of Job is, at least in part, known from other places. The skepticism of the Preacher is, however, unparalleled in ancient Near Eastern literature.

A significant difference between Wisdom literature and other parts of the Old Testament is the missing division of humankind into the God-fearing people and the godless.

Wisdom literature includes, on the other hand, extensive discussions about the difference between the fortunate person and the unfortunate person, between the person afflicted by disease and misfortune and the person who is successful in all that he or she does. And the Old Testament has more than one answer to such questions.

Proverbs includes an extensive discussion about such themes, especially in chapters 10–22—generally in short sentences, technically "proverbs." The basic idea is that the industrious person will always succeed, but the foul will fail. God supports the diligent, and happiness and success follow him or her. The person whose life is in ruins is so because punished by God. God remains with the righteous, and several parts of Wisdom literature discuss justice seen from this perspective, although Job seems to question this "philosophy."

The many parallels to Wisdom literature in the Old Testament discovered in ancient Near Eastern documents include in one case a direct borrowing, in Proverbs 22:17–24:22, where a translation of an Egyptian wisdom book, the *Admonitions of Amenope*, has been incorporated into the biblical texts. It is clear that Wisdom literature came into being in an internationally oriented environment. The question is, where exactly did it originate? And why is it a part of the Old Testament? Its main thrust seems to be quite different from that forming the center of other parts of the Old Testament.

Both Job and the Preacher are magnificent pieces of literature. Without doubt they were composed by authors of a high intellectual status with an extensive education behind them. The short proverbs of Proverbs are also parts of a collection of sayings of high value, but they are not exceptional and are limited to one intellectual environment. Proverbs existed in every culture at all times, most often examples of "popular wisdom," although written down by educated people.

People like those who created the Wisdom literature in the Old Testament had received their education in schools. They formed a limited class—very few could read and write—they were very well educated. Most information about the educational system comes from Mesopotamia. The impression is that there existed a system of education not dissimilar from the ones found at later Arabic and European universities. Apart from the basic (but complicated) art of writing, the students were engaged in astronomy (for astrological purposes), mathematics, medicine, law, philosophy, and literature. Nothing was foreign to this education.

The educational process lasted for many years and created a self-assured class of scribes, that is, administrators, whose members, like the later Chinese mandarins, considered themselves the elite of their society. They controlled all

Wisdom literature

Proverbs 22:17–21	*Amenope Chapter 1*[3]
The words of the wise:	Give thy ears, hear what is said,
Incline your ear and hear my words,	Give thy heart to understand them.
and apply your mind to my teaching;	To put them in thy heart is worthwhile,
[18] for it will be pleasant if you keep them within you,	(But) it is damaging to him who neglects them.
if all of them are ready on your lips.	Let them rest in the casket of thy belly,
[19] So that your trust may be in the LORD,	That they may be a key in thy heart.
I have made them known to you today—yes, to you.	At a time when there is a whirlwind of words,
[20] Have I not written for you thirty sayings of admonition and knowledge,	They shall be a mooring-stake for thy tongue.
[21] to show you what is right and true,	If thou spendest thy time while this is in thy heart,
so that you may give a true answer to those who sent you?	Thou wilt find it a success;
	Thou will find my words a treasury of life,
	And thy body will prosper upon earth.

written communication within and between their societies. This self-assuredness is present not least in Egyptian collections of wisdom sayings, especially when compared to other occupations.

One qualification has to be made: the system did not include a critical awareness of problems. There were no critical sciences as in modern educational systems. The process of learning consisted mainly of repetition. Observations belonging to natural science, mathematics, medicine, and also law were collected into educational textbooks. These textbooks presented such observations mostly as lists to be learned by heart by every generation of students. The same applied to literature as well, although it was presented in a different, narrative format. In this way the student learned not only sciences but also writing.

We have no clue as to the quality of education outside the two centers of learning in Mesopotamia and Egypt. The introduction of the alphabet in Syria and Palestine meant that education could be considerably reduced in time, but we don't know if this happened.

The authors of Old Testament literature might have received their education in one of two places: they might have been educated in Palestine, for example, in Jerusalem. Old Testament scholarship has invested a lot of energy in proving that

3. Trans. John A. Wilson in *ANET*, 421–22.

Excerpts from the instructions of Cheti
the son of Duauf to his son Pepi

I don't see a calling like it of which this saying could be said. I'll make you love scribedom more than your mother, it makes its beauties stand before you; it's the greatest of all callings, there is none like it in the land.

But I have seen the smith at work at the opening of his furnace; with fingers like claws of a crocodile he stinks more than fish roe.

The carpenter who wields an adze, he is wearier than a field-laborer; his field is the timber, his hoe the adze. There is no end to his labor. He does more than his arms can do, yet at night he kindles a light. The jewel-maker bores with his chisel in hard stones of all kinds; when he has finished the inlay of the eye, his arms are spent, he's weary; sitting down when the sun goes down, his knees and back are cramped.

See, there's no profession without a boss, except for the scribe; he is the boss. Hence if you know writing, it will do better for you than those professions I've set before you, each more wretched than the other.

Lo, I have set you on God's path, a scribe Renenet is on his shoulder on the day he is born. When he attains the council chamber, the court. . . . Lo, no scribe is short of food and of the riches of the palace.[4]

a system of education was attached to the royal temple complex in Jerusalem based on Mesopotamian models. However, these authors might also have been trained outside of Palestine, most likely in Mesopotamia, although Egypt cannot be dismissed as an alternative.

The first option is supported by the number of sources in the Old Testament that in a direct way point toward Palestine by showing a definite knowledge of the geography and society of this land. Thus many historical traditions refer to the ancient kingdom of Israel. How did they survive in consideration of the lapse of time between the downfall of this Israel and the reduction of the traditions about it to writing in the Deuteronomistic and Chronistic literature?

The second option is supported by a series of points of contact between Mesopotamian, Egyptian, and Old Testament traditions, some of these so direct that the version in the Old Testament is almost a reference to the existence of the ancient Near Eastern tradition from which it borrows. Thus the primeval history in the first eleven chapters of Genesis includes not only many associations and references to Mesopotamian motifs, but also a reproduction of one of the central parts of the Mesopotamian epic of Gilgamesh, the story of the flood.[5] The similarity between the biblical version of the story of the flood and the one found in

---

4. Trans. Miriam Lichtheim in COS, 1:123–24.

5. There are many excellent translations of the Gilgamesh epic in existence, among them Ephraim A. Speiser's in ANET, 72–99, and Stephanie Dalley, Myths from Mesopotamia: Creation, the Flood, Gilgamesh, and Others (Oxford: Oxford University, 1989), 39–135. The story of the flood in Gilgamesh is translated by Benjamin R. Foster in COS, 1:458–60.

Gilgamesh is so striking that we may be allowed speak about one and the same story in two versions. Since the epic of Gilgamesh has a prehistory that reaches far back in history, to at least the third millennium BCE, and since another Mesopotamian epic also contains the story of the flood,[6] there can be no doubt about the origin of this story, in Mesopotamia.

The biblical narrators have simply rewritten the Babylonian epic in such a way that it fits the context in which it appears in the primeval history. They also include a direct (however ironic) reference to the epic of Gilgamesh, when they decide that Noah shall first send out a raven (Gen. 8:7). The raven never returns but flies around for weeks. Hereafter Noah sends the pigeon three times. The raven in the Old Testament is an unclean bird and can never be accorded the honor of having found the earth dry again. In Gilgamesh three birds are sent out: the pigeon, the swallow, and a raven. The raven never returns, "It ate, it cried, it flew away with food in its beak and did not come back" (Gilgamesh XI:155).

The primeval history begins in Mesopotamia, in Eden, long ago recognized as an Akkadian loanword in Hebrew; and it ends with God driving humanity away from Babel because of their plan to build a tower. The story of the first sin is unthinkable without its relation to Babylonian religious motifs and associations. Finally, the family of Abraham comes from Ur in Chaldea, in southern Mesopotamia, to Haran, and from Haran Abraham travels to Canaan. The perspective in this first part of the Bible is directed toward Mesopotamia. Israel's roots are, according to the Old Testament, found there.

If this orientation of the primeval history points toward Mesopotamia as the intellectual home of the authors who wrote it, other parts of the Old Testament point in the same direction. Here we may mention the introduction to Moses's Law, Exodus 21–23. The complex of Moses' Law (Exod. 20–Num. 10) opens with the Decalogue. Hereafter the first collection of laws follow, the book of the covenant (Exod. 21–23) which itself is a combination of two collections, a series of "secular" laws (Exod. 21:1–22:18) and another of "religious" rules (Exod. 22:19–23:19).

It has for a long time been accepted that the first collection, the secular laws, are related to Mesopotamian legal tradition. The similarity between the book of the covenant and, for example, Hammurabi's famous law codex from the eighteenth century BCE is striking. This first part of the book of the covenant squarely belongs to this Mesopotamian tradition, which is known from many collections dating from the third millennium to Neo-Assyrian and Neo-Babylonian times.[7] The book of the covenant is not identical to any of these Mesopotamian collections and introduces a series of rules and amendments to the Babylonian laws, as illustrated here with the example of the law of the goring ox:

---

6. The epic of *Atra-Ḥasis*, published and translated in W. G. Lambert and A. R. Millard, *Atra-Ḥasis; The Babylonian Story of the Flood* (Oxford: Oxford University, 1969). There are several excellent English translations, among them Benjamin R. Foster's in *Before the Muses: An Anthology of Akkadian Literature* (Bethesda, MD: CDL, 1993), 1:158–201.

7. See Martha T. Roth, *Law Collections from Mesopotamia and Asia Minor*, SBLWAW 6 (2nd ed., Atlanta: SBL, 1997).

The law of the goring ox

Exodus 21:28–32, 35–36	Hammurabi's law §§250–252 [8]	Eshnunna laws §§53–55 [9]
When an ox gores a man or a woman to death, the ox shall be stoned, and its flesh shall not be eaten; but the owner of the ox shall not be liable. [29] If the ox has been accustomed to gore in the past, and its owner has been warned but has not restrained it, and it kills a man or a woman, the ox shall be stoned, and its owner also shall be put to death. [30] If a ransom is imposed on the owner, then the owner shall pay whatever is imposed for the redemption of the victim's life. [31] If it gores a boy or a girl, the owner shall be dealt with according to this same rule. [32] If the ox gores a male or female slave, the owner shall pay to the slaveowner thirty shekels of silver, and the ox shall be stoned.	When an ox gores a man to death when it walks in the street, there is no reason for a process. §251 If a man's ox is known to gore, and his city has told him, and he does not cut its horns and control his ox, and this ox gores a man to death, he shall pay 1/2 mina of silver. §252 If it is a man's slave, he shall pay mina of silver.	When an ox gores a(nother) ox to death, the owners of the oxen shall share the value of the living ox and the cadaver of the dead. §54 If an ox is (known as) a gorer, and the city has told its owner, but he has not looked after his ox, and it gores a man to death, he shall pay 1/3 mina silver. §55 If it gores a slave to death, he shall pay 15 shekel silver.
[35] If someone's ox hurts the ox of another, so that it dies, then they shall sell the live ox and divide the price of it; and the dead animal they shall also divide. [36] But if it was known that the ox was accustomed to gore in the past, and its owner has not restrained it, the owner shall restore ox for ox, but keep the dead animal.		

8. The translation follows the text in Martha T. Roth, *Law Collections from Mesopotamia*, 128.
9. The translation follows the text in Roth, *Law Collections from Mesopotamia*, 67.

It is very interesting that the Mesopotamian legal collections did not play the role originally attributed to them. We have literarily thousands—if not tens of thousands—of documents from the daily life of the court from the time of Hammurabi, without any indication that this collection had any importance here. It seems isolated from the practical distribution of justice in real life. This has induced Assyriologists to reconsider the importance of these collections of law which are today generally regarded as representing an academic discussion and not as directly related to actual practice at the courts of Mesopotamia. As an academic tradition, these collections may represent a kind of forensic Wisdom literature, discussed at educational institutions for thousands of years.[10]

The collectors of the laws included in the first part of the book of the covenant must have borrowed from this Mesopotamian academic tradition and provided it with their own commentaries and expansions. They also used their version of the Mesopotamian tradition to introduce a far-reaching collection of religious legislation. This indicates that these collectors had received their educations at institutions colored by the Mesopotamian academic tradition, most likely in Mesopotamia itself.

The legal tradition found in the Old Testament is therefore another indication of where we should look for the intellectual background of the authors who created this literature: not in ancient Palestine, but much more likely at Mesopotamian educational institutions, whose tradition they turned into a "Jewish" one. It will still be necessary to discuss when this happened and how old the incorporation of Mesopotamian tradition is. We should most likely look for a postexilic date but cannot totally exclude an earlier one. After all, Mesopotamian influence was a fact even in the Iron Age.

However, the observations presented here, in combination with the earlier analysis of the historical literature, the prophetic literature, and especially the Psalms, point in the direction of a Judaism whose roots may lie, in its external manifestations, in Palestine but intellectually belong to Mesopotamia. The relations with Mesopotamia were not cut in connection with the official end to the exile in 538 BCE. On the contrary, relations were strengthened in the Persian and Hellenistic periods.

THE "ETHNOGENESIS" OF ANCIENT ISRAEL[11]

The realization of belonging to a special "nation," a special ethnic group, demands that there are at least two groups of people present with distinctive marks. This

---

10. An overview of this discussion among Assyriologists is presented in Roth, *Law Collections from Mesopotamia*, 4–7. The first to recognize this special role of the law collection might have been F. R. Kraus, "Ein zentrales Problem des altmesopotamischen Rechts: Was ist der Codex Hammurabi?" *Genava* 8 (1960): 283–96.

11. This paragraph is based on the more complete discussion in Niels Peter Lemche, *The Israelites in History and Tradition* (Louisville, KY: Westminster John Knox, 1998), chap. 4: "The People of

forms the basis of any modern scholarly discussion about the subject of nationality and ethnicity leading up to the following definition of a people:

- a biologically self-perpetuating group
- a group sharing common cultural values
- a group that constitutes a forum for communication and interaction
- a group whose membership defines itself, and whose members can also
  be identified by human beings not themselves members of this group

This definition, which in its present form goes back to the Norwegian social
anthropologist Fredrik Barth,[12] is very important when we finally turn to the
question of the relationship between the appearance of the books of the Old Testament and ancient Judaism. It is normal for the Old Testament that in all its
parts there is a fundamental distinction between godless people and the God-
fearing ones—between two groups of people, on one side the Israelites and on
the other the "Canaanites."

The analysis of the narrative of the history of Israel in the Old Testament
showed this to be a constructed history. Thus we have to reject, from a historical
point of view, the notion in the Old Testament of an ethnic and historical difference between Israelites and Canaanites. Although contrast to the Canaanites
appears in many places in the books of the Old Testament, this contrast is the
creation of the authors of these books. There is no historical foundation for it in
Palestine in the Iron Age. The inhabitants of Palestine in the Iron Age were never
divided into two clearly distinctive ethnic groups based on differences of religion
as argued by the biblical writers. The historiographer used the Canaanites as
archetypal crooks and made the Israelites into the heroes of his narrative—at least
until they were corrupted by the Canaanites.[13]

Opposed to the Canaanites we find the Israelites, God's chosen people. In the
Old Testament the real Israel is simply the people of God, Abraham's children.
The condition for those who decide to join this people is that they keep the
covenant and the command of the Decalogue: "you shall have no other gods
before me" (Exod. 20:3).

Now two criteria are in place for deciding who is a true Israelite: common origin and common religion—every member of this people must worship Yahweh
alone. One more criterion must be included, a common land, the land of promise
given by Yahweh to the ancestors of Israel. True Israel therefore includes three elements: common blood, common religion, and common land.

God: The Two Israels of the Old Testament," 86–132, and the shorter version in Niels Peter Lemche, "Israel og dets land," in Niels Peter Lemche and Henrik Tronier, eds., *Etnicitet I Bibelen* (Copenhagen: Museum Tusculanum, 1998), 12–22.

12. First formulated in Fredrik Barth, "Introduction," to Fredrik Barth, ed., *Ethnic Groups and
Boundaries* (Oslo: Universitets forlaget, 1969), 10–19.

13. On this literary construction see Niels Peter Lemche, *The Canaanites and Their Land: The
Traditions of the Canaanites* (2nd ed.; JSOTSup 110; Sheffield: Sheffield AcademicPress, 1999).

This is a short repetition of the criteria set up by the narrators of the books of the Old Testament as obligatory for those wanting to belong to this people. A true Israelite must descend from Abraham; that is, he must know his genealogy and be able to prove his right to belong here, or he will be the subject of ethnic cleansing as exemplified by the book of Ezra (Ezra 10). A true Israelite worships Yahweh and no other god. If one transgresses this commandment, there is no future for him as a member of God's chosen people. Finally, you must, as a true Israelite, live in the land of your fathers, in Israel's land, the gift of Yahweh to Israel.

This definition of the people of God as found in the Old Testament shares two criteria with the classical one presented by Herodotus in the fifth century BCE: a people must share common blood, a common religion, and a common language,[14] although Herodotus does not really say religion in the narrow sense of the word as understood by modern Western people; he says culture or civilization. The modern distinction between religion and a secular society did not exist in antiquity; it is a phenomenon that came into being after the French Revolution in 1789, which separated the church from the state.

Language is not a criterion in the Old Testament for defining a nation, and for good reasons. The language, Hebrew, was nothing special for the "Israelites." Hebrew belongs to a family of languages called Amorite, or more technically Northwest Semitic. It had been spoken in large parts of the ancient Near East for millennia when the books of the Old Testament were written down. Although in the first millennium BCE it was hard pressed by Aramaic, a closely related language, it was still the language spoken by the Phoenicians of Lebanon. In Palestine it would have been impossible to distinguish a member of the people of God from nonmembers on the basis of language.

The two other criteria forming part of the ancient definition of ethnicity are valid and used by biblical writers to construct the notion of "ancient Israel" or the people of God as a national ideology.[15]

The notion of the people of God is inflexible as formulated by the biblical authors. As already noted, it is also a construction based on something that never existed in reality in Palestine in the Iron Age. The peoples of Palestine never showed the ethnic differences assumed by biblical writers.

The study of Palestine in the Iron Age leaves an impression of the cultural, religious, and political conditions that are absolutely in opposition to the one formulated by the study of the Old Testament. In the appendix to this book there is an overview of the history of Palestine from ancient times to the present. Technical details will be taken up there. In this place it is only necessary to maintain that in the Iron Age there were many small states in this country, each of them in sharp competition with the others. Ethnic markers, elements that allow the

14. Herodotus, Book VII, 144: "There is the Greek nation, the common blood, the common language, the temples and the religious rituals, the whole kind of existence we understand and are part of."
15. In this they have never been alone. It is interesting to see how Herodotus's definition of a nation is still dominating much modern debate about ethnicity, especially in Europe.

The prohibition against idols in the Old Testament and the zealous God

> You shall not make for yourself an idol, whether in the form of anything that is in heaven above, or that is on the earth beneath, or that is in the water under the earth. [5] You shall not bow down to them or worship them; for I the LORD your God am a jealous God. (Exod. 20:4–5 = Deut. 5:8–9)
>
> [13] You shall tear down their altars, break their pillars, and cut down their sacred poles [14] (for you shall worship no other god, because the LORD, whose name is Jealous, is a jealous God). (Exod. 34:13–14)
>
> [23] So be careful not to forget the covenant that the LORD your God made with you, and not to make for yourselves an idol in the form of anything that the LORD your God has forbidden you. [24] For the LORD your God is a devouring fire, a jealous God. (Deut. 4:23–24)
>
> [14] Do not follow other gods, any of the gods of the peoples who are all around you, [15] because the LORD your God, who is present with you, is a jealous God. The anger of the LORD your God would be kindled against you and he would destroy you from the face of the earth. (Deut. 6:14–15)

historian to distinguish between different ethnic groups, do not exist. Nothing indicates that the population was divided into two main parts, on one side the Israelites (including the Judeans) and on the other the rest of the population.

Now the first criterion forming part of the biblical definition of ethnicity has gone: the idea of a special bloodline uniting every Israelite together as the children of Abraham. Religion, or, according to Herodotus, civilization, is the next criterion.

According to the Old Testament, belief in Yahweh is the decisive criterion for belonging to Israel. It is the decisive distinction between the Israelites and the Canaanites. No God-loving person should worship any other god. Yahweh resides in heaven but at the same time—according to the opinion of those days—in his temple: There is, or so it was maintained, no real difference when in the presence of God, because where God is, the temple is—and where the temple is, God is. Yahweh can never be represented by an idol, because he is not a "tame" God; he is a zealous God (or jealous God), in Hebrew an ʾel qannâ.

In contrast to this expression in the Old Testament of the unity of God, we find a religious scenario in Palestine in the Iron Age that is absolutely different and definitely not in accordance with the demands made by the Old Testament. Idols existed in plenty, and other deities were worshiped. Archaeologists have found several images of deities depicted both as human beings and as animals, often in the shape of figurines from private cults or as seal impressions. There may even have been pictures of Yahweh.

This obscene image dating from the end of the ninth century or the beginning of the eighth century BCE from a jar excavated at Kuntillet ʿAjrud in the

6. Kuntillet ʿAjrud ostracon
(From Z. Meshel, *Kuntillet ʿAjrud: A Religious Centre from the Time of the Judean Monarchy on the Border of Sinai* [Jerusalem: Israel Museum, 1978], fig. 12. Courtesy of Zeev Meshel.)

northern part of the Sinai Peninsula is believed to represent a "popular" version of Yahweh, although its interpretation is anything but clear. Specialists name such images Bes-figures after the way the Egyptians depicted the god Bes. It cannot be finally decided therefore if this figure is Yahweh or somebody else, but an inscription on the same jar has the following reference to Yahweh:

> [. . .] says: Say to YHK[. . .] and to JV ʿŠH: I bless you by Yahweh from Samaria and his Asherah![16]

Another inscription from the same time and place has this text:

> *ᵓMRJV* says to my lord: Are you well? I bless you by Yahweh from Teman and by his Asherah. He blesses you and preserves you and protects my lord![17]

The exciting part of these inscriptions is not their references to Yahweh. After all, this was to be expected in an inscription from a place so close to Palestinian territory. The amazing part is the reference to "his Asherah," Yahweh's Asherah. Who is she? We have met the name of Asherah in many texts in the Old Testa-

16. Translated from the text in Tilde Binger, *Asherah: Goddesses in Ugarit, Israel and the Old Testament,* JSOTSup 232 (Sheffield: Sheffield Academic Press, 1997), 102.
17. Translated from the text in Johannes Renz, *Handbuch der althebräischen Epigraphik* 1:62–63. See also Binger, *Asherah,* 103.

ment denouncing Canaanite religion. In these two texts she is related to Yahweh: in the first instance, to Yahweh from Samaria, in the second, to Yahweh from Teman, a place in Edom (cf. Ezek. 25:13). In the description of the setup of the temple of Jerusalem in 2 Kings, Asherah also appears in connection with Josiah's reformation. Here she had her pole, that is, idol, and a whole section devoted to her, including women weaving clothes for her (idol) (2 Kgs. 23:6–7).

Although it would, from a methodological point of view, be a mistake to transfer this text from 2 Kings into the realm of religion in the Iron Age—when we have argued here that the books of Kings may lead astray the reader who tries to paraphrase them as reports of what really happened—it is remarkable that this text places Asherah in the immediate context of Yahweh. In Syria and perhaps also in other places, Asherah was the consort of the most high God, and the queen of the divine world. In the two inscriptions from Kuntillet ʿAjrud she and Yahweh are coupled together.

The author(s) of the inscriptions from Kuntillet ʿAjrud may not have been alone in his confession of Asherah as the divine consort of Yahweh. Second Kings says the same, and now also another inscription, this time from southern Palestine, about a century younger than the previous ones, from Khirbet el-Kom near Hebron:

> ʾUrīyāhû, the rich man, wrote this: Blessed be ʾUrīyāhû by Yahweh, who has saved him from his enemies by his Asherah . . .[18]

It is not only clear that there were other deities than Yahweh in Palestine in the Iron Age—the polemic against foreign cult in the Old Testament says the same—but the Yahweh of the Iron Age was hardly the Yahweh supposed to be worshiped by the Israelites. Furthermore, the Israelites were not the only people who worshiped Yahweh, who in one of these inscriptions is related to Teman, a place in Edom, which may have had its own local version of Yahweh.

The first two parts of the ethnic definition of "Israel" in the Old Testament are constructions created by the biblical authors. They are part of the fictive image of ancient Israel in the Old Testament. Therefore it is reasonable to assume that the third part, the special country reserved for this fictive Israel, is also a part of the fiction. The "ethnogenesis" of the Israelites was created by biblical authors. It is present in the historical books but also in the prophetic literature. It is a safe assumption that it also dominates the collection of Psalms, which, from an intellectual perspective, is close to the two previously mentioned collections.

SUMMARY

Who wrote, then, the Old Testament? The question that was formulated at the beginning of this part may have found an answer. We do not know any names of

---

18. Translated from the text in Renz, *Handbuch*, 207–11. The following three lines make little sense.

authors but have established a "profile" of these authors that can also be related to the period when they were active.

In their own eyes the authors were God-loving Jews, if we understand a Jew of those times as a person devoted to the study of the *tôrā*, who considered himself or herself a member of a religious community totally devoted to the worship of only one God, Yahweh, the creator of heaven and earth. Such persons considered themselves unique and in opposition to all other people not sharing their devotion to God's instruction. Such people were the representatives of a godforsaken society. In this religious image of the world there is no middle way. Either you belong to us, or you are against us. Either you are a member of Yahweh's party, or you belong among the godless multitude, doomed to extinction.

Although these God-loving people may be described by the modern term "religious fanatics"—almost like modern Islamists—they were well-educated people who borrowed from many sources. They had at least initially their intellectual background in educational institutions most likely situated in Mesopotamia, where Judaism had centers of learning for many centuries. Judaism in Mesopotamia disappeared only in modern times, when the modern state of Israel brought the Mesopotamian Jews to the new Jewish state in the beginning of the 1950s.

It is likely that the religious movement represented by the biblical authors at an early date—perhaps around 400 BCE—found another home in Palestine and Jerusalem, understood to be the center of the world and the city chosen by God, which was to reemerge as the golden city. With this "golden" city in mind, they turned, in their writings, to their counterparts in all parts of the world with a message like "Next year in Jerusalem!" They considered the presence of the Jewish Diaspora in the Persian and Hellenistic periods as a sign of Yahweh's punishment of unfaithful Israel, understood by them to be the Israel of their fathers, the people of the old covenant. They could not accept the idea that many of their kin preferred to live comfortably in other countries, in Egypt, Mesopotamia, and elsewhere.

We do not know to what degree they were the spiritual heirs of an ancient Yahweh alone movement. It cannot be denied that such a movement may have existed, for example, in Jerusalem in the seventh century BCE, with the temple as its spiritual home. However, it is likewise impossible to prove this hypothesis, which remains only an assertion. The thesis is unnecessary to explain the development from a polytheistic milieu as found in Palestine in the Iron Age to early Judaism's monotheism.[19]

19. We often encounter the idea that the religion of ancient Israel was not monotheistic but monolatrous. The existence of other gods was accepted but had no importance for true Israelites. I have to express my dissatisfaction with such ideas. Religion in Iron Age Palestine was polytheistic. The Old Testament is dominated by a clearly monotheistic theology, leaving no room for any other deity in its religious universe. It should not be a surprise that monotheism in the Old Testament is expressed in many different ways, some of these having their origin in a polytheistic environment such as Psalm 82. After all, the Old Testament embraces some of the earliest ways of formulating monotheism, a way of imagining God not previously known. It must have been a period of trial and error. Thus Deutero-Isaiah, arguing that Yahweh also created evil (Isa. 45:7), may be considered such an early way of defining absolute monotheism, allowing not even for the existence of an evil "god" like the later Satan.

There is more reason to connect the Yahweh alone movement, understood to be an early Jewish religious trajectory, with the growing monotheism of the ancient Near East, which was destined to dominate religion there ever after. The movement toward monotheism can be followed in Mesopotamia, where some gods became more and more important and other, minor gods were regarded as manifestations of the major ones. Thus Marduk, the city god of Babylon, acquired the status of Bel (the Akkadian form of Baal), meaning "Lord."

A similar trend was in evidence in Egypt, and the same seems to have been in evidence also in Syria, where local gods assumed the position of the highest god, such as the city god of Tyre, Ba'alšamem, "the Baal of heaven."[20]

Judaism as a monotheistic movement did not emerge in a religious vacuum. In the form in which we encounter it in the Old Testament it was more radical than other expressions of monotheism in those days, but it was not the only one. We may, with some right, argue that the Near East began a course toward exclusive monotheism that still dominates that part of the world.

When such a radical religious movement appears, one thing is a safe assumption: that its contrast will also be there, in the form of people who do not share the religious sentiments of the fanatics. We meet them in many places in the Old Testament as the godless, the wicked enemies of God's kingdom, and in the disguise of "Canaanites," as expressed at the end of Zechariah: "And there shall no longer be Canaanites[21] in the house of the LORD of hosts on that day" (Zech. 14:21).

The influence of the "Canaanites" on early Judaism may have been more important than first realized. The division of Judaism into many parties as explained by later Jewish writers may have its origin in such early contrasting religious groups. Being a sectarian movement, Judaism definitely possessed the "genes" that forwarded separation, because in the consciousness of a sectarian group there are only two categories of humans: the believers and the nonbelievers.

If we get the impression that the insistence on following the *tôrā* of Yahweh may sound almost pharisaical, it does not mean that there were Pharisees around in the technical meaning of the word or that Pharisees wrote the story of ancient Israel as they saw it. It is, however, possible that the Pharisees had very old ancestors.

Not everything fits this hypothesis. This should not be an obstacle to our progress forward. The labile character of many sects, which constantly expels dissenting members, makes it in theory possible to identify a countless number of factions and parties within early Judaism. The presence of many dissenting voices in the literature of the Old Testament may point in this direction, and it did not end here but traces of the discussion can be found in other Jewish documents, as found among the Dead Sea Scrolls. Early Judaism was not a monolith, but included many factions constantly in conflict.

20. On Syria and the Levant, see Herbert Niehr, *Der Höchste Gott: Alttestamentlicher JHWH-Glaube im Kontext syrisch-kanaanäischer Religion des 1. Jahrtausend v.Chr.*, BZAW 190 (Berlin: De Gruyter, 1990).

21. The NRSV has "traders" because of an obsolete understanding of the Canaanites of the Old Testament. The Hebrew text has "Canaanites."

PART IV
OLD TESTAMENT AND
BIBLICAL THEOLOGY

Chapter 10

What Are We Talking About?

JOHANN PHILIPP GABLER

It is often suggested that biblical theology in the modern sense, understood to be a special discipline within the academic study of the Bible, like other disciplines such as the history of Israel, the geography of Palestine, and exegesis, was born on March 30, 1787. On this day the German biblical scholar Johann Philipp Gabler (1753–1826) held his first lecture as professor at the University of Altdorf, "De justo discrimine theologiae biblicae et dogmaticae regundisque recte utriusque finibus" ("On the Proper Distinction between Biblical and Dogmatic Theology and the Specific Objectives of Each").[1]

We may well ask what Gabler's real subject was, and no hasty perusal or reading of his lecture is sufficient, because of the very apparent intellectual differences between his age and ours. However, most interpreters argue that Gabler spoke in favor of a separation of exegetical and systematic disciplines within theology.

---

1. A handy English translation of Gabler's Latin lecture can be found in Ben C. Ollenburger, ed., *Old Testament Theology: Flowering and Future*, Sources for Biblical and Theological Study 1 (Winona Lake, IN: Eisenbrauns, 2004), 499–506.

Exegesis and systematic theology have their specific tasks to fulfill, and each of them has its limitations vis-à-vis the other. The borderline between them should not be confused.

Ever since Gabler's lecture, theologians—mainly exegetes—have discussed the real thrust of Gabler's program. Gabler is here of little use. After his lecture, he never wrote anything of lasting importance, although his influence grew as he rose to the position of a full professor at one of the then-dominant German universities, at Jena. Neither did he have any precise idea about the future of biblical studies in the period following him. Many of the ideas formulated in his lecture may therefore seem a bit curious to modern readers trained in historical-critical methodologies.

In spite of these limitations, Gabler's lecture is still and correctly considered the point of departure for the debate about the task of biblical theology within the larger field of biblical studies. It has, for more than a hundred years, been summarized as demanding a division within biblical studies between historical-critical scholarship and systematic-dogmatic interpretation based on the studies of historical-critical scholars. Here Gabler is outspoken. He fully understands the importance of the difference between the present and the past. He is convinced that the past must be studied on its own and not by modern standards. He also admits that the past cannot control the present. The task of dogmatic theology is therefore to hand down and translate the intentions of the biblical writers in modern terms. Here he especially stresses that modern people may not necessarily follow the prescriptions of the Law of Moses, and that Paul's ideas about the dress of women in church may not be relevant to present conditions.

From a classical theological viewpoint Gabler only suggests that there are different ways to read the Bible, a historical one and a systematical-dogmatic one, and they should not be confused. It has always been like that. There never was only one way to read the Bible. There were always competing methods, for instance, in the early church the conflicting readings of the Antiochene and Alexandrine schools, the first favoring a literal reading and the second an allegorical one. In the Middle Ages the allegorical reading dominated and was regarded as preferable to the literal, because the latter would never be able to disclose the secrets embedded in the text of the Bible. Finally, the Reformers chose the literal reading in contrast to the allegorical interpretation of the Catholic Church, regarded as misleading and uncontrollable.

After the Reformation, literal reading dominated the Protestant branch of Christianity, however, not in the historical-critical sense. It was certainly not a historical reading; it was centered on Christ. Luther always demanded that the Old Testament should be interpreted on the basis of the witness of Christ in the New Testament. This christocentric reading of the Old Testament had led to many "biblical theologies." As late as a few years before Gabler's lecture a major one in several volumes was published by Gotthilf T. Zachariae,[2] but during the

---

2. *Biblische Theologie oder Untersuchtung des biblischen Grundes der vornehmsten kirchlichen Lehren*, 5 vols. (Göttingen u. Kiel: 1771–86).

Enlightenment, changing intellectual standards led to a renewed discussion about hermeneutics forming the background of Gabler's separation of "science from theology." Early biblical criticism was inaugurated in European tradition by the philosopher Baruch Spinoza in the seventeenth century, but it was only toward the end of the eighteenth century that biblical criticism became so important that some of the historical problems involved in the biblical narrative became obvious—such as the problem of the exodus, which is still debated. Here Hermann Samuel Reimarus's verdict is famous (or infamous if you prefer). With the number of Israelites reported in Exodus to have left Egypt, the head of the column had already reached Canaan before the last had left Egypt, even if they walked in ranks of four plus four.[3]

Historical-critical scholarship in the true sense of the word appeared first in the generation that followed Gabler. Here scholars like Karl David Ilgen (1763–1844) and Wilhelm Martin Leberecht de Wette (1780–1849) would have numerous critical ideas about the history of the Old Testament. Gabler belonged to the Enlightenment and his fight for the independence of biblical theology, seen as the synthesis of biblical studies liberated from its systematic-dogmatic prison, must be seen in light of the critiques of religion of his age, including Immanuel Kant's *Die Religion innerhalb der Grenzen der bloßen Vernunft*, which appeared in 1793, just a few years after Gabler's lecture (Gabler didn't like it very much), along with Rousseau's idea of the "noble savage," and sympathy for a religion of reason and natural theology.

Gabler described the difference between religion and theology by defining religion as spontaneous and unsophisticated religiosity, in contrast to theology, which received its impulses not only from the Bible but also from many other sciences. He especially mentions philosophy and history. Gabler's biblical theology is not a simple reading of the biblical narrative along the lines of "the Bible interprets itself." His idea of theology suggests exactly the opposite: biblical theology consists of a sophisticated analysis of biblical literature. The difference between a biblical and a dogmatic theology—to use Gabler's own way of presenting his case—has to do with the independence of biblical theology from Christian dogmatics foreign to it.

In the German tradition the de facto separation of the history of religion from theology was a consequence of Gabler's division of theology into biblical and systematic parts. This was not Gabler's own idea but a result of the development of historical-critical scholarship in the generation that followed him. Biblical studies also bifurcated into the two branches of Old and New Testament studies. This separation of the Old from the New Testament had severe consequences for the status of the Old Testament as a theological discipline. The Old Testament was not the subject of biblical theology as Gabler understood it, but was soon reduced to a textbook

---

3. Hermann Samuel Reimarus (1694–1768) lived and taught in Hamburg his whole life. He was known because of his often very sharp remarks about the Old Testament, but he never published anything. After his death Lessing published a selection from his writings.

of the history of religion. Here scholars could study ancient Israelite religion. True biblical-theological analysis was left in the hands of New Testament exegetes.

It was to be expected that the developments within historical-critical scholarship would lead to a clear division of the tasks of theology and the history of religion. The students of the history of religion would study the physical dimension of ancient Israelite religion. It would soon turn into phenomenology of religion. Old Testament theology has as its aim the study of the content of the beliefs of the ancient Israelites as expressed in their literature. The student of religion would be interested in all sorts of evidence, written sources, imagery, anything relating to the cult. The student of the theology of the Old Testament had only one source, the Old Testament itself.

Although this division of tasks for both disciplines seems obvious, the separation between them never really came into being. An overview of theologies of the Old Testament and histories of Israelite religion from the twentieth century makes this very clear.

Gabler had opted for methodological transparency in his procedure for studying the Bible. The exegete must begin his analysis by applying historical and philological methods. This should lead to a clarification of the intentions of the different books. The next part of the procedure consisted of the production of a biblical theology based on exegesis. Finally, a systematic arrangement of this theology would translate the theology of the biblical books into modern terms.

How did biblical theology develop? Was Gabler's program of lasting importance? Have subsequent biblical scholars been able to fulfill his intentions? Many scholars, especially Old Testament theologians, answer the last question with a no: biblical scholars have never succeeded in separating the different parts of their studies. Gabler's program remained important for the sole reason that almost every critical scholar has accepted that he was right. In this way Gabler lived on as the bad conscience of biblical scholarship, because subsequent scholarship never succeeded in following his program.

What went wrong? Gabler held his lecture almost immediately before the breakthrough of the modern concept of history in the earliest part of the Romantic period. We should never underrate the implications of the shift said to have taken place in Goethe's way of referring to the narratives of the Bible. Young Goethe, who was only a few years older than Gabler and who survived him (1749–1832), described the biblical stories as *die Geschichte sind* (the stories are), but old Goethe as *die Gechichte ist* (history is). The stories had changed character and had become history, *the history*. The development of this changing concept of history can be followed during the Enlightenment, when some of the most entertaining historical works, like Edward Gibbon's (1737–94) *The Decline and Fall of the Roman Empire* (1776–88) appeared. History gained a new importance in connection with the French Revolution of 1789, when historians were committed to proving the legitimacy of the new kingless state, showing the people that it was a unified people because of its common history, not because it was ruled by a king.

The narrative of the Old Testament ceased to be a narrative; it became reality. The biblical stories were really speaking about *real* events. The nature of the biblical text was transformed. They were no longer stories about ancient times but documents for the study of ancient times, and more precisely, documents for the study of the history of a single nation, Israel. Ancient Israel emerged in the Romantic period as a consequence of this new understanding of history. This had important consequences for Old Testament theology. It had as its task to explain to the biblical scholar the intentions of biblical writers, that these intentions might be "translated" into modern terms for modern times. When the narratives become historical documents, the theological emphasis changes and moves from narrative to reality, that is, reality as understood in the modern age.

From now on, God's acts were not a part of a narrative; they happened in history. For this reason the most important job of the researcher was to reconstruct this history as carefully as possible. Nobody could have, at the beginning of this development, envisaged that historical studies would lead to a situation that history and story had to separate. The scholars focused on a historical-critical analysis of the narratives of the Old and New Testaments. Influenced by the then-governing ideas about positivistic scholarship, students of biblical history saw their task as providing as much knowledge of real history as possible in order to achieve a correct theological understanding of the content of biblical narrative, the only really important corpus of documents relating to Israel's history.

It was not considered a problem for the idea that biblical theology began with history, as long as there were only minor discrepancies between the history as related by biblical writers and real history. For two hundred years historical-critical analysis intended to create a kind of harmony between biblical stories and reality. Biblical scholars, of course, understood that there are new laws when you move from narrative to history. In the real world, the rules of reality govern. A scholar of European origin was bound by his tradition to the development of the fundamental European scholarly concepts from Aristotle to Thomas to Kant to Hegel. The history of reality happens within the confines of space and time. There is no room for miracles. The supernatural has no say.

The biblical narratives accept the supernatural as a decisive factor; so biblical scholars of the modern age had a problem. How should they translate the biblical stories as history? How is it possible to unite the many stories in one and the same history? How is it possible to transfer this history to real history? History was the important issue; biblical narrative only came in second. In order to achieve the desired harmonization, biblical scholars made use of rationalistic paraphrases of biblical narratives. Their paraphrases simply removed the supernatural from the narratives, including God's miracles such as his dividing of the waters in front of the Israelites fleeing Egypt. Some scholars wasted energy in trying to find natural causes, for example, in connection with the ten plagues of Egypt, simply because of their conviction that it must have happened because it is written, although tradition may have distorted what really happened. After all, this tradition belonged to an age dominated by a mythical and magical perception of reality.

As described in the first part of this book, historical-critical scholarship lived on and developed for two hundred years. There can be no doubt that the historical-critical paradigm was well constructed (and perhaps it also says something about its representatives, who allowed it to exist for so long). After all it is based on the assertion that the narrative reflects reality, and a reality that the modern scholar can reach, although he has to separate chaff from grain.

This development had important theological consequences, because history and not theology dominated biblical scholarship. The first result was the "discovery" of the peculiarity of the Old Testament in comparison to the New Testament. The second result consisted of the ascription of the narratives of the Old Testament to the people or nation who is the center of these stories, that is, ancient Israel. Nobody really realized that the argumentation was circular (or they ignored the problems involved). Thus members of the ancient Israelite nation wrote Old Testament books. They were the ancestors of later Jews but not themselves Jews, most of them living in the Iron Age. It is evident that there was a later Jewish redaction of much of the literature in the Old Testament—most markedly represented by the P source in the Pentateuch. However, the original narrative was pre-Jewish, and this original part was considered the essential part of the traditions of the Old Testament (following one of the Romantic period's mantras: the original is unique, whether a piece of art or a piece of music or a new scientific discovery).

In this line of thinking, Judaism only had a marginal influence on Old Testament literature, which, from a normal perspective, would reasonably be considered "Jewish." The Old and New Testaments were not only separated by a long span of time, in many cases by more than five hundred years, but they also belonged to two absolutely distinct cultures. From both an Old Testament and a New Testament perspective, there was no *original* relationship between the two testaments, although such an *original* relationship was supposed to be very important from the viewpoint of modernity. However, when there is no historical relationship, how can there be a theological one? Here we may say that biblical theology broke down. The development of the study of Israel's history led to a breakdown of the relation between the Old and the New Testaments.

In spite of this, Gabler's program lived on—at least in theory—and found a special role in the Anglo-Saxon world, which could not see any difference between theology and religion. Theology was considered to be religion, and Old Testament theology the religion of ancient Israel. It was already mentioned earlier that as late as 1992, when the *Anchor Bible Dictionary* was published, there was no entry titled "Israelite religion" or "the religion of ancient Israel." The concept of the history of Israel did not create any problems, and there are a considerable number of historical textbooks from this part of the world, but very little in the way of a history of Israelite religion. Religion is theology, at least in the case of ancient Israel. History is a substitute for exegesis, or exegesis's main task is to dig out historical information that may allow the scholar to draw conclusions about the religion of Israel, supposed to follow a course identical with historical developments.

The alliance between history and theology survived for many years, although Old Testament scholarship moved on, colored by changing theological orientations like liberal theology at the end of the nineteenth and the beginning of the twentieth century, and dialectical and existentialist theology in the twentieth century. The theological debate about the relevance of the Old Testament sharpened during the twentieth century, mostly because many scholars ignored Gabler's warnings against confusing the various sectors of biblical study. A perusal of the theologies of the Old Testament from the last century shows that few scholars realize what a history of Israelite religion is, compared to a theology of the Old Testament. Scholars doing biblical theology are just as interested in phenomenology, studying the religious institutions—temple, Sabbath, and cult—as part of their biblical theological writings. Perhaps, then, we should speak about Israelite theology instead of Old Testament theology.

Another development within Old Testament studies in the twentieth century also demanded the attention of the theologians. As time went by, it became more and more clear that it was no longer possible to harmonize biblical narratives with real history. At the end of the century the history of ancient Israel as retold by rationalistic paraphrase of the biblical narratives simply collapsed. Only the most conservative and evangelical segments of the scholarly community still believed in this history.

Theologians had to accept that, at most, they could establish only a few points of convergence between the biblical story and history; or, rather, perhaps it was now time that they realize this to be the case. The crisis of history has resulted in a series of developments, including from the conservative party, some conventional theologies of the Old Testament like the one by Horst Dietrich Preuß, where no progress forward has been made,[4] along with canonical theology, and postcolonial biblical theology.

Most scholars have adopted a more flexible approach to Old Testament theology, realizing the supremacy of history over theology; they have asked theology to submit to the results of historical investigation. Theology constitutes the malleable party in the relationship between history and theology. Without a doubt the most important theology of the Old Testament written from such a perspective is Gerhard von Rad's *Theology of the Old Testament*, which appeared in German between 1957 and 1960.[5] Von Rad is of the conviction that the Old Testament should be regarded as the way Israel rendered account of its history. We will return to von Rad's theology of the Old Testament later. It can, however, be stressed already in this place that we may here have a starting point for a better understanding of the relationship between the biblical text and theology, because von Rad prepares the way for a liberation of the biblical text from history.

4. Horst Dietrich Preuß, *Theologie des Alten Testaments*, 2 vols. (Stuttgart: Kohlhammer, 1991–92); ET, *Old Testament Theology* (Louisville: Westminster John Knox, 1996).

5. Gerhard von Rad, *Theologie des Alten Testaments*, 2 vols. (Munich: Chr. Kaiser, 1957–60); ET, *Old Testament Theology*, 2 vols. (London: Oliver & Boyd, 1962–65).

A third way out of the collapse of history is to sacrifice the idea of a basic agreement between the biblical narrative and real history. Such reflections are found not least among North American theologians who have accepted the separation of biblical narrative from history. Instead of accepting an alliance between text and history, they operate with a view of the biblical text that stresses the relationship between a text and its reader.

A final way out can be found in the political application of biblical theology, especially in the third world. Here a series of new tendencies are present, including postcolonial (also ethnic) criticism of Eurocentrism, feminist theology, and liberation theology.

AN OVERVIEW OF THE FOURTH PART

In this part I intend to discuss most of the problems facing Old Testament and biblical theology mentioned here, including new proposals for the use of the Old Testament within theology. More traditional contributions will also be discussed.

The criticism directed against classical historical-critical scholarship by contemporary scholars and not least by the members of the Copenhagen School is obviously correct. If this school has achieved anything, it is in having paved the way for an alternative theological way of handling the Old Testament, on a scholarly foundation but liberated from a dominating Eurocentric paradigm. Historical-critical scholarship received its fatal blow when it neglected *the* basic logic of scholarly communication and turned to circular argumentation. For two hundred years it relied on circular argumentation.

The criticism of the embodiment of historical-critical scholarship in a Christian, white, male, and European/North American world also makes sense in light of its many mistakes relating to a world different from itself. The issue of "orientalism" was raised by the late Edward Said (1935–2003), born in Jerusalem but active in New York, where he taught at Columbia University for many years.[6] Orientalism implies the distorting and insensitive manner in which the European spectator views the Near East. Orientalism touches only the tip of the iceberg. The European, who might just as well be described as a white Protestant male, created his own image of the Orient and its peoples in which his own European background was clearly expressed. He did not accept a hermeneutic that would lead into a foreign world not sharing his ideas and culture. In this context the Old Testament had become a European book to be read through European lenses. Any other path to the biblical text was understood as misleading and insufficient.

To mention only one example, it was considered a major advance for exegesis of the Old and New Testaments when the Reformation gave up allegorical

---

6. Edward Said, *Orientalism* (New York: Vintage Books, 1979). See also the splendid use of this concept in Steven W. Holloway, ed., *Orientalism, Assyriology and the Bible* (Sheffield: Sheffield Phoenix Press, 2006).

interpretation or at least placed it second after the literal reading, which was, over the following centuries, to develop into historical-critical research. It is, however, a remarkable fact that the evangelist Mark, the first time he has Jesus interpret one of his parables, makes use of an allegorical explanation (Mark 4:13–20). Allegorical reading was something quite normal in antiquity and in those societies where the Old and New Testaments came into being. This implies that it is reasonable to ask whether the writers really wrote texts to be read literally, as was so often assumed by European scholars of the past, disregarding the evidence of ancient interpretation as it points in the direction of a different understanding. Maybe the ancient church was right when it argued that although it is possible to read a text as it stands, this is only a superficial reading. The real meaning is embedded in the text. So perhaps the form of the text—the only thing accessible to a literal reading—is misleading. Maybe there are more layers than normally assumed. Maybe the maxim of the Swedish author Jan Guillou is also valid in this case: what you see is not what you see!

It speaks in favor of European scholarship that it often perceives where it fails. Maybe one of the most important "discoveries" of modern European man—and we should emphasize the meaning of the word *man* in this connection—is that *he* is not alone in this world but has to compete, not only with European women, but also with people from many other cultures, who may not be as convinced as our European of the excellence of his culture. This discovery opens the door to some obvious theological possibilities for alternative but meaningful readings of the Bible. Although some modern theologians, for example, of the third world, may express the opinion that European exegesis, apart from being imperialistic, is also misleading, it is far from certain that we should speak about an either-or. Earlier biblical interpretation allowed for an allegorical reading as well as a literary one. One method does not exclude others.

When talking about biblical theology and discussing the theology of the Old Testament as part of this subject, we should not too willingly give up our own tradition of biblical studies. If the Old Testament is regarded as an old *Israelite* book that was later usurped by Judaism and turned into a Jewish collection, only even later to be usurped by Christianity and turned into a Christian book, the logical consequence must be that the secondary editions, the Jewish and the Christian ones, in many ways may have distorted the original Israelite tradition. If this is the case, the distance between the Old Testament and the New Testament might grow to such a length that there is no reason to have any illusions about the unity of the Bible. Maybe it would be better to follow Marcion's proposal, 1,800 years old, and give up the Old Testament as part of Christianity's Bible.

The real tragedy of historical-critical scholarship is that it has created a gap between the Old and the New Testament that is extraordinarily difficult to bridge. In recent times the tendency has been to diminish the importance of the Old Testament in comparison with the New. Previously the two testaments were reckoned to have roughly the same status, with a slight edge going to the Old, as it was considered impossible to understand the New Testament without the Old.

The New Testament authors made extensive use of the Old Testament, but according to historical-critical scholarship they often distorted its meaning. The Old Testament does not speak about the messiah of Christianity but about the Jewish hope for a future king belonging to the house of David, who shall again rule over David's empire. The Old Testament does not speak of the kingdom of God as a kingdom of heaven. It is a worldly empire. When Isaiah, in his famous encounter with King Ahaz, says that the young maiden will become pregnant and give birth to a son, it is not Jesus or the messiah; it is the heir to Ahaz's throne, addressed to a historical context of the late eighth century BCE, that is, more than 700 years before the birth of Christ.

What use can there be of the Old Testament in a Christian theological context, if this is true? Even many Old Testament scholars have difficulty finding a place for the Old Testament within biblical theology. Many may entertain the idea that the Old Testament is relevant only for the study of the Old Testament and has no meaning for a theologically oriented analysis of the New. The Old Testament has turned into an auxiliary discipline of New Testament studies. There are many such auxiliary disciplines, so why should we pay special attention to the Old Testament? Why should we keep it as part of our canon? In what way is it more important for the understanding of the New Testament than, say, Greek literature and philosophy?

If there is no way to create a direct link between the Old and the New Testament that establishes them as one theological and Christian unity, the Old Testament will have no future in a Christian context—except among fundamentalists, who will always believe that everything written in the Old Testament must have happened. The classical historical-critical study of the Old Testament created this gap. It will be the task of a renewed critical study to see if it is possible to bridge the gap without sacrificing what we know about the historical context of both testaments.

We have to move on cautiously in order to reach any resolution concerning the issues presented here. What do we really intend to say when we talk about the Bible including the Old Testament as well as the New Testament? The archetypal German professor is supposed to have introduced a lecture in this way: "Well, ladies and gentlemen, this looks very simple, but now I am going to explain to you how it really is!" We all know what we are talking about, or so we believe. The Bible consists of the thirty-nine books of the Old Testament and the twenty-seven of the New Testament. But does it? If one follows the Lutheran tradition and buys a Bible, it may also include eleven books belonging to the apocryphal literature. Are these books a part of the canon? They are often bound in the same volume as the Old and New Testaments. They are, according to Luther, who found them useful, still not canonical literature. There were nevertheless translated and placed between the two canonical testaments in Luther's complete translation of the Bible from 1545. It seems that Luther's way of handling the canonical question was less restrictive than the one popular among his followers.

The apocryphal books are, on the other hand, *canonical* literature in the Orthodox church. Here they are not put together in a kind of appendix to the Old Testament but have been placed in such contexts within the Old Testament as deemed relevant. Furthermore, the Orthodox tradition includes more apocryphal books than the Bibles belonging to the Western European tradition do, for example, 3 and 4 Maccabees.

The following chapter will discuss canon as a concept within Christianity and—as far as the Old Testament is concerned—in Judaism. How important is it for theology in general that the early church formed its doctrine on the basis of a Greek Bible larger and different from later Western European Bibles? How important is it that first the Catholic Church and then the Reformers, especially Luther, chose to translate as the Old Testament a Jewish tradition from the Middle Ages?[7] Is this reorientation from a Christian point of view a legitimate one? Should we return to the praxis of the church before the Reformation? Finally, it is one thing that Christianity accepts a Bible that has two parts, but another thing that it includes in its canon a Jewish collection of Jewish writings. So we may ask about the status of this collection within Judaism. Does Judaism possess a canon like the Christian one? If so, when may it have accepted one? And if so, will this canon have any theological implications in a Christian theological debate?

Having, then, worked on the concept of canon, the discussion here may proceed to the debate about Old Testament and biblical theology in the twentieth century. We might have started this overview in 1787, as every contribution since Gabler may be considered relevant to this discussion. However, in practice the discussion sharpened during the twentieth century, making it relevant to include only contributions from the last century. Even here, there are so many contributions that it is hardly possible to include every aspect of the discussion. There is help at hand in the shape of the British scholar James Barr's (1924–2006) recent overview.[8] We are therefore allowed to concentrate on the more important and typical theological contributions to Old Testament theology.

The following two chapters will discuss the consequences of "the collapse of history." We have already described the phenomenon, but the discussion in these chapters will penetrate further into these consequences. First, some endeavors to repair the damage caused by the collapse will be the subject of discussion. Is it possible to replace biblical history, now that it has been shown to be an illusion, a story about something that never happened? Is it possible to replace the biblical history with real history, as proposed by the German scholar Rainer Albertz, and change the history of religion into theology and identify the study of religious history with theological studies?

7. The Bible of the Catholic Church, the Vulgate, is in Latin, but the Old Testament was translated by Jerome in the fourth century CE from Hebrew.

8. See James Barr, *The Concept of Biblical Theology: An Old Testament Perspective* (London: SCM, 1999).

Albertz's position may represent a faux pas, not because of a lack of clarity in the biblical narrative, but because of European scholars' misreading of this literature, believing it to be the basis of historical studies, the preferred pastime of European scholarship for two hundred years. It might be that the reaction to the collapse among scholars from other parts of the world is more honest, as it may also be among so-called postmodern readers of biblical texts.

It will be clear from this discussion that this author entertains great respect for these new and alternative approaches to the Old Testament. One may hope that New Testament studies are experiencing the same plurality of accesses, although one might suspect that too many New Testament scholars spend too much time on questions like the content of the Q document and the historical Jesus (now that Bultmann seems to have been pacified and new questers of the historical Jesus are at work).

It might be conceivable to stop the discussion here in order to study the alternative approaches alone. However, the next few chapters are devoted to the classical debate about biblical and Old Testament theology, beginning with canonical theology as represented by Brevard S. Childs, James Sanders, and Rolf Rendtorff. This kind of theology has been under fire from the pen of James Barr for a long time.[9] It will in this context be relevant to discuss Barr's theological standing compared to those of his opponents. All representatives of the canonical approach are Protestant biblical scholars, mostly following in the tradition of Luther. As Barr says of Childs, he accepts three church fathers, Augustine, Luther, and Karl Barth (in ascending rank). Barr's background is at first the Presbyterian Church, then the British Anglican Church. He has less respect for the Lutheran tradition and is only to a limited degree interested in the Lutheran doctrine of *sola scriptura*. Maybe this is the principal reason for Barr's rejection of canonical theology, and also for his interest in natural theology.

Canonical theology is a kind of theology that builds primarily on the Protestant Evangelical Lutheran German tradition of Old Testament theology, which will in the first place imply Gerhard von Rad's theology of the Old Testament. This theology is at the center of two chapters, the first one discussing the mainly German tradition from Walter Eichrodt to Otto Kaiser. The second chapter sharpens this discussion when we turn to von Rad's famous concept of "salvation history." Does the Old Testament contain such a history? Or would it be better, following Franz Hesse, to speak of a "history of misfortune"? If Hesse is right, and he has a strong case, what would then be the theological importance of the Old Testament? How can we formulate an alternative to von Rad's salvation history? The suggestion will be that the New Testament is already present in the Old, as it has been handed down to us. The Old Testament includes many indications that point in the direction of the New Testament uniting both testaments into

9. See James Barr, *Holy Scripture: Canon, Authority, Criticism* (Oxford: Oxford University, 1983), appendix II: "Further Thoughts on Canonical Criticism," 130–71; *The Concept of Biblical Theology*, chap. 24, "Child's Theologies," 401–38.

one whole and without which the New Testament would make little sense. It may, in a programmatic way, be formulated in this way: the Old Testament is in the New, and the New Testament is in the Old. I will later return to a New Testament angle on this discussion.

Before that, the question about the relevance of the Old Testament has to be settled. Dialectical theology, with its preaching of God's direct revelation in the New Testament, has little use for the Old Testament, including its theology of creation. This is an important part of the modern rejection of the Old Testament; although tolerated, the Old Testament has nothing important to contribute.

Would we have a New Testament without the Old Testament? This question is not very ingenious, since the very name of the New Testament makes it clear that we also have the Old. However, is it likely that a collection of writings like those present in the New Testament would ever have come into being if they were not able to benefit from the presence of Old Testament literature? It is likely that the revelation would never have had any impact if it was not promoted by Old Testament ideas. The revelation of God cannot be limited to the pages of the New Testament. Christian theology would be a poor subject without the Old Testament. It is legitimate to ask: what would come of the Western idea of humankind without the Old Testament?

Chapter 11

Our Text

Canonical History and Theology

THE HEBREW BIBLE OR THE GREEK BIBLE?

Before we can proceed we have to establish the foundation on which to build an Old Testament and biblical theology. Some may think that this is a simple issue: the biblical text. However, which text are we talking about? There are many different Bibles in circulation. Then many will answer, the original text. But how do we define that? Often it will be assumed that the original text will be a certain text in its original language, in the case of the Bible, Hebrew, Aramaic, and Greek. This original text is not identical to the first version of the text, which will be the first version of a biblical text, for instance, Isaiah. However, what is this first version? The idea of a first version, entertained by exegetes for generations, has been badly received within the last generation. The first text should form the basis of any and all subsequent editions. However, any part of Isaiah may have existed in a first version, but this version may in some cases have existed before it was put together with other parts to form Isaiah (as this book consists of three parts, Proto-Isaiah, Deutero-Isaiah, and Trito-Isaiah, often considered to be separated by centuries).

Because of this, we may argue that the original text of the Old Testament on which all modern translations are based will be the edition of the Hebrew (and in some passages Aramaic) text of the Hebrew Bible as presented by *Biblia Hebraica Stuttgartensia*.[1] The newest edition of the Hebrew Bible, *Biblia Hebraica Quinta,* is based on the same Hebrew manuscript as *Biblia Hebraica Stuttgartensia*, that is, the so-called Leningrad Codex or Codex Leningradiensis, which is a questionable decision, because the main part of the Old Testament is now available in a form that predates Codex Leningradiensis by a hundred years.

Codex Leningradiensis is a Jewish manuscript dating from 1008 or 1009 CE and preserved in St. Petersburg in Russia.[2] Since the first part of the twentieth century this manuscript has functioned as *the* text of the Hebrew Old Testament. Before scholars had access to Leningradiensis, they had to rely on a different and younger tradition, still used in the third edition of Rudolf Kittel's *Biblia Hebraica*.[3] The basis of Kittel's earlier edition was a rabbinic manuscript dating from the Renaissance, the Bomberg Bible, published in 1525.[4] The basis of older English translations, like the King James Version, is therefore not the same as that used by modern translations.

The editors of *Biblia Hebraica Quinta*, which began to appear in 2004, choose to retain Leningradiensis as their foundation because of its completeness. The older manuscript, Codex Aleppo, is incomplete, since a part of the manuscript was lost in riots in Aleppo in 1948.[5] The preserved parts of Codex Aleppo form the textual basis of modern Israeli scholarly editions of the Hebrew Bible.

The decision to retain Leningradiensis as the basis of the new *Biblia Hebraica Quinta* may be questioned. When Luther translated his Old Testament from Hebrew, he chose the best available printed edition from his own time. His and subsequent translators' idea was that the *Biblia Hebraica* must be the basis of a translation of the Old Testament. This is a generally accepted procedure. The text in its original language will normally be preferable in comparison to translations, which cannot be anything other than a filtered version of the original, because the meaning of the original has to be transferred to another language. The decision to translate the Hebrew Bible as part of the Christian Bible is, however, not unproblematic, as every Hebrew manuscript was a *Jewish* manuscript and reflects Jewish interpretation of the text of the Old Testament.

This is not a minor issue. To mention only one example, the name of God, Yahweh, which cannot be pronounced, according to Jewish tradition (modern English translations keep this tradition alive, following a Christian tradition with roots going back to the Septuagint), is rendered by the Septuagint as κύριος,

---

1. Or *BHS*. *BHS* was published by the German Bible Society in Stuttgart between 1967 and 1977.

2. The manuscript is accessible in a modern facsimile edition: David Noel Freedman, ed., *The Leningrad Codex: A Facsimile Edition* (Grand Rapids: Eerdmans, 1998).

3. Or *BHK* (3rd edition, Stuttgart: Deutsche Bibelgesellschaft, 1937).

4. The Bomberg Bible may be downloaded from the Internet at the following address: http://www.christianhospitality.org/benchayyim.htm.

5. A facsimile was published by Moshe H. Goshen-Gottstein, *The Aleppo Manuscript* (Winona Lake, IN: Eisenbrauns, 1976). The Hebrew text can be found on the Internet at http://www.mechon mamre.org/i/t/t0.htm. A facsimile edition is in the course of publication on the Internet: http://alep pocodex.org/images/x4/1.jpg.

"Lord," and Jerome also decided to stay within this tradition when he translated his Vulgate and rendered the divine name as *Dominus*. Many Protestant theologians have, for some hundred years, decided not to follow this tradition of hiding the name of God—although they for many years, especially in the Anglo-Saxon world, used a distorted version, "Jehovah," a creation dating from the Middle Ages brought to life by mixing two Hebrew names for God: *YHWH*, the name of God himself, and *ʾadonai*, "Lord." Modern Bible translators have generally decided to remain within this tradition as well. Because of tradition, versions of translated biblical texts using "Yahweh" as the name of God look somewhat odd. These translations might do for textbooks for students of the history of religion, but will hardly be accepted by church congregations.

Luther's decision to use a Jewish text as the basis of his translation is acceptable. A Jewish manuscript from the Middle Ages or Renaissance might be as good as any version of the Bible. The question is only, how adaptable is such a text for a Christian theological evaluation of the content of the Old Testament?

I will return to the relevance of a theology of the Old Testament that is disconnected from biblical theology. However, here it must be said that to use a medieval text as the basis for a discussion of a connection between the Old Testament and the New Testament supposed to have existed since ancient times is probably less reasonable. No part of the theological discussion in the early church reveals any special interest in the Hebrew Bible, which only a few Christians had any access to (and very few read Hebrew). The authors of the New Testament who quote from the Old Testament never use the Hebrew text or make their own translation. They quote from extant Greek manuscripts, especially the Septuagint.[6]

Most Christian translators of the Bible were not of the opinion that they were translating a *Jewish* text to be used within a Christian context. This is clear because of the arrangement of the Christian Old Testament, which follows a tradition very different from the Hebrew one. This Christian tradition allows us to have an Old Testament that ends in this way:

> Lo, I will send you the prophet Elijah before the great and terrible day of the LORD comes. [6] He will turn the hearts of parents to their children and the hearts of children to their parents, so that I will not come and strike the land with a curse. (Mal. 4:5–6).

In this way the otherwise unnoticed prophet Malachi became the final Old Testament harbinger of the good news to appear and hands off the torch to a new Elijah (although the irony of the remark of the Jews in connection with the crucifixion is obvious: "This man is calling for Elijah": Matt. 27:47; Mark 15:35).

In modern Hebrew Bibles, Malachi is followed by Psalms (in Codex Leningradiensis and Codex Aleppo, however, by 1 Chronicles). Here there is no special theological emphasis on the sequence between the end of the collection of

---

6. Though see the important work of Hans Hübner, *Biblische Theologie des Neuen Testaments*, 3 vols. (Göttingen: Vandenhoeck & Ruprecht, 1990), for a contrary viewpoint.

prophetic literature and the opening of the last part of the Hebrew Bible. The priority of the different parts of the Hebrew Bible has already been discussed: placing the Torah above all other parts of the Bible, and placing the Writings in a position that may, to a certain extent, be likened to the status of the Apocrypha in the Christian Bible.

Some theologians, including the Danish New Testament scholar Mogens Müller, have argued for many years that the present situation is, if not intolerable, at least unfortunate.[7] The authors of the New Testament refer to the Septuagint and not to the Hebrew Bible. The first Bible of the church was not the Hebrew Bible but a Greek translation of Jewish writings including much that is not a part of the Hebrew Bible. This extended version of the Old Testament formed the basis of Christian doctrine.

Mogens Müller's proposal is to replace the Hebrew Bible with the Septuagint as the Old Testament of the church in our time as well, or at least to place the Septuagint on an equal footing with the Hebrew Bible. The proposal may at least be worth trying although it is not without problems as the authorized modern church Bibles based on the Septuagint would include the supplementary books of the Septuagint as canonical literature, not only the Apocrypha but also some of the Pseudepigrapha, such as 3 and 4 Maccabees, the *Odes of Solomon,* and the *Psalms of Solomon.* The sequence in which such books are placed in the Septuagint creates no problems, as the Septuagint here follows the traditional Christian sequence.

Another problem is the fact that the New Testament never refers to the Old Testament as a book or a collection of books. Sometimes the reference is to "the Law and the Prophets," or so it is normally assumed.[8] If it is really the Old Testament that is meant by such references, this has nothing to do with the traditional Christian Bible; it's a reference to the Jewish tradition of placing the Torah and the Prophets before other parts of the Hebrew Bible. By mentioning "the Law and the Prophets," the authors of New Testament literature refer to a Jewish tradition that may or may not yet be complete. This may indicate that there was in those days no Old Testament as we know it, secondly, that only a part of the later Hebrew Bible was considered authoritative. There was no Old Testament canon, and it is equally doubtful if a complete Greek version of the Old Testament, including the Writings, existed when, for example, the Synoptic Gospels came into being.

THE CANON

To proceed with the issue of the textual basis of biblical theology, it is necessary to discuss the concept of canon and the appearance of our canon.

7. Cf. Mogens Müller, "The Septuagint as the Bible of the New Testament Church: Some Reflections," *SJOT* 7 (1993): 194–207; *The First Bible of the Church: A Plea for the Septuagint,* JSOTSup 206 (Sheffield: Sheffield Academic Press, 1996).

8. See further on this in chap. 18.

It is common to speak about the canon and the canonical books of the Bible. κανών is Greek and may be translated as "staff." Perhaps the best translation would be "ruler," and κανών does often refer to a tool. In figurative speech κανών means "rule" or "standard," for example, within art and grammar. The Greeks did not use the word κανών to denote a privileged and authoritative collection of writings, regarding everything not part of the canon as second rate.

Whatever the meaning of the Greek κανών, the word is now used by theologians to mean a selection of privileged writings. Many think that this indicates the books included in the canon are better than other books. This is likely to be a secondary meaning of the word, and it must be remembered that even Luther, in spite of his respect for the canon, rejected James, calling it a letter of straw, while he at the same time held the Apocrypha in high regard.

In the Protestant tradition the principle of *sola scriptura*, "scripture alone," became enormously important for the development of the modern concept of canon. The canon did not play nearly the same role before the Reformation. One bit of evidence for the lack of importance of the canon is the disinterest in allowing the laity to read the Bible. The Bible and especially the New Testament was important because of its testimony about Christ; the Old Testament was important because it prophesied about the coming of Christ. This does not mean that theology and doctrine as expressed in the ancient confessions of Nicaea and Chalcedon were totally dependent on the testimony of the New Testament, since it has little to say about the doctrine of the two natures of Christ and nothing to say about the Trinity.

A biblical theology that was dependent on the Bible alone, and was ignorant of all other testimonies and dogmatic decisions from a multitude of councils and synods, would have had little chance of survival before the Reformation, which brought in the concept if not the dogma of *sola scriptura*. Then everything changed. The status of the Bible became a totally different one.

As a theologian, often recognized as a radical one, I am often asked the question, do you believe in the Bible? It is normally easy to dismiss the question as imprecise and meaningless, because it makes little sense. What is intended? Does one believe in the content of the Bible? Then we have to ask additional questions about the meaning of the word "content." Do we intend to say the whole content, or only a minor (however important) part of it? Should we believe that the hare belongs among the cud-chewing animals, because it is written in the Bible? Does one believe in the New Testament gospel about salvation? Or is everything "the truth"?

After the Reformation, the Bible became a fetish, almost an idol to be worshiped and used for ceremonies. Every part of the Bible must be true because it is part of the Bible. "You shall not make for yourself an idol, whether in the form of anything that is in heaven above, or that is on the earth beneath, or that is in the water under the earth. You shall not bow down to them or worship them; for I the LORD your God am a jealous God" (Exod. 20:4–5). In the pious tradition of religious people, the truth of the Bible can be used against the sinner. People summoned to North American courts swear with their hand on the Bible. The

Bible has become a magic stone that can punish the one who commits perjury. The Bible has become an idol, an image of God.

This happened to the Bible shortly after the death of the Reformers, in the time of Lutheran orthodoxy. In this period the Bible changed from being a source of inspiration to a doctrine about God to something that was true from the first to the last page. Now the Bible no longer spoke about God; it was God's own word from one end to the other. The Bible de facto turned into Law, a development like that which changed the Jewish concept of the Torah, meaning instruction, into juridical binding law.

We are no longer allowed to burn our theological opponents. This is a shame, as this would put an end to many theological "oracles." It would also fill the empty churches if the service was followed by a really awful *auto-da-fé*, the burning at the stake of the disbeliever. There may be conservative religious people around who would still react in this way if someone dared to doubt their interpretation of the Bible and its truth. The reason for this attitude was the conviction of Protestantism that the Bible, as *the* authority, decided everything even remotely relevant to faith. The magic of the Bible was astonishing and followed the Christian from birth to grave. The Bible was always within reach and also followed the condemned to the place of execution. The Bible became God.

In recent times the importance of the Bible is diminishing. People still read the Bible—at least some people do. Reading is no longer compulsory, and the Bible's authority is not the same anymore. It is understood that reading is a personal matter, and that every person will do his own reading and interpretation. Nobody forces you to believe that the Bible is something extraordinary and more important than other literature. Nobody tells you that the Bible represents better literature than, say, William Shakespeare's plays. We are more likely to encounter the opposite attitude, and should remember that the work of Shakespeare became practically canonical when he was selected the greatest author of the second millennium.

It is not true that no one believes in the Bible anymore. Such an assumption is nonsense and wrong. Today too many people still "believe" in the Bible and worship it like an idol. The person who believes in the Bible decides if he or she really does so. Nobody decides for you.

James Barr devoted several publications to the status of the Bible in present times. The most important contribution was perhaps his *The Bible in the Modern World*.[9] Barr mentions here the problems created by modern liberalism for the reception of a Bible that is no longer the authority, but may be authoritative like an authoritative source used by a journalist. The Bible is the authority only for people who have decided to consider it their authority. Barr's position is without doubt correct, and we often see people—journalists and others—who might not consider themselves to be believers and yet refer to the Bible as an authority among others.

This new position of the Bible is in fact rather old. The Bible is no longer— even in a Protestant environment—unique as far as dogma is concerned. In light

9. James Barr, *The Bible in the Modern World* (Philadelphia: Westminster, 1973).

of this renewed understanding of the Bible, the concept of canon breaks down. Every source—an image, a piece of literature, or music—may achieve a canonical status with or without the Bible. The new ideas about the status of the Bible may have important theological consequences, because they allow the Bible, so to speak, to cooperate with other literature and kinds of theology very different from traditional Christian dogma. It would be wrong in this changing world just to reject the image of God presented by, say, the Qur'an, although this may only lead to an extension of our canon to include the Qur'an. According to Muslim tradition, the Old Testament, the New Testament, and the Qur'an are holy writ and therefore enjoy a status not given other literature.

THE COMPILATION OF OUR CANON

Until now we have discussed the idea of canon only in Protestant theology. In this tradition canon developed to be a stone that never changed, with everlasting ideas and sentiments. The many translations since the days of Martin Luther may have to some degree changed this impression of a Bible that cannot change. No two translations are alike, and this is true of old translations as well as the most recent ones. Now the skepticism regarding the concept of canon expressed here may be a help when we consider the issue of the formation of the Old Testament canon.

The phenomenon called "canon" is accepted not only as a guideline within Protestant theology; it is simply the rule that limits the extent of the theological analysis of the Old Testament. It is not uncommon to find Protestant theologians of the opinion that the canon has always been the canon, although the Jewish scholar Frederick Greenspahn has made some interesting observations about the Christian concept of canon and argues that nothing similar is known within Jewish tradition. He argues that the idea of a Jewish canon is a Christian invention.[10] The Jewish concept of canon is very different from the Protestant Christian one. Another Jewish scholar has described it in this way: "In the Jewish tradition this book known as the Tanakh or the *Miqra'*, is properly placed alongside the Talmud, Midrash, and medieval rabbinic commentaries. These books . . . establish a pluriform yet bounded context of interpretation for the Tanakh."[11]

The background for this difference between the Christian and the Jewish concepts of canon is most likely a semantic one. As we have seen, the word *canon* has many meanings, including the understanding of canon as a guiding rule and as an exclusive collection of texts. In antiquity Judaism had its Torah, identical with the five books of Moses. This did not prevent a collection of laws from being

10. Frederick E. Greenspahn, "Does Judaism Have a Bible?" in Leonard Jay Greenspoon and Bryan F. LeBeau, eds., *Sacred Text, Secular Times: The Hebrew Bible in the Modern World*, Studies in Jewish Civilization 10 (Omaha, NE: Creighton University, 2000), 1–12.

11. Jon Levenson, "The Hebrew Bible, the Old Testament, and Historical Criticism," in Jon Levenson, *The Hebrew Bible, The Old Testament, and Historical Criticism* (Louisville, KY: Westminster John Knox, 1993), 1–32, 1.

established although not part of the Pentateuch but represented, for example, by the temple scroll from Qumran.[12]

Because of the importance attached to the concept of canon in post-Reformation Protestant theology, when the canon became the guiding rule for Christian doctrine and theological discussion, the discussion of canon entered a new phase, understanding the Bible in a very different way. Before the Reformation, canon meant limitation, a limitation of the literature accepted for the Bible or other literature. Membership in this exclusive club of canonical literature did not automatically mean that canonical books were better than other books. Such an attitude would lead to the absurd consequence that 2 Peter, James, and Jude should be considered masterpieces of world literature. The Bible had, for obvious reasons, authority, but it shared its authority with other writings, not least the writings of the church fathers, and among these, especially Augustine.

How did the canon emerge as a historical fact? By way of introduction, the process that led to the formation of the canon of the Hebrew Bible was a very complicated one, and it is difficult to achieve an overview of the various parts of the process. This process not only involves the dating of the different books of the Hebrew Bible, which may be more than 500 years apart; but it also has to do with the criteria for the selection of books allowed to enter the collection known as the Hebrew Bible.

There is no reason to dwell on the issue of dating the individual books of the Hebrew Bible in this context. To mention Isaiah as an example of the proceedings that led to its formation, we would have to speak about a complicated process, as the book consists of at least the three major units normally believed to be originally independent prophetic writings, which were put together in one book at a later date, Isaiah 1–39; 40–55; and 56–66. Classical historical-critical scholarship dated the basic content of the first part to the end of the eighth century and the beginning of the seventh century BCE. The second part was believed to go back to an anonymous prophet who lived during the Babylonian exile in the sixth century BCE, and the last part indicates that the exile is over and the exiled back in their country of origin. It also presupposes the existence of a temple and may date to the fourth or third century BCE.

A modern dating of this book's individual parts will use a method that may look as if it has been borrowed from archaeology. It is a kind of textual archaeology that seeks the youngest part of the book. If the latest section dates from, say, the third or second century BCE—and it is commonplace to think of the so-called little apocalypse (Isa. 24–27) as no older than that—then it is a safe assumption that the present Isaiah cannot be older than its youngest component.

All these sophisticated scholarly endeavors to date the literature of the Hebrew Bible become futile when they are confronted by the clear criterion for selecting

12. Published by Yigal Yadin, *The Temple Scroll,* I–III (Jerusalem: Israel Exploration Society, 1977). Text and translation, Florentino García Martínez and Eibert J. C. Tigchelaar, *The Dead Sea Scrolls: Study Editon,* vol. 2 (Leiden: Brill, 1998), 1228–1289.

the books accepted for inclusion in the collection. The traditional Jewish idea about the date of the collection is that the compilation of the books of the Hebrew Bible ended when Ezra read the Law in Jerusalem in the time of King Artaxerxes (Neh. 8). It is immaterial whether or not this ever happened. According to traditional Judaism, Ezra's lecture constituted the end of the formation of their holy literature, and this happened sometime during the fifth century BCE. After Ezra, there was no need of any more prophets or any more laws. No later literature would be accepted as part of the collection. Thus in the case of Isaiah, the only reason why Trito-Isaiah made it into the Hebrew Bible was because of the incorporation of these chapters into Isaiah, and Isaiah was supposed to be absolutely pre-Ezran and therefore acceptable. If the true identity of Trito-Isaiah had been known, it is a safe assumption that this part of Isaiah would never have survived as part of the biblical corpus.

Jewish scholars must have understood the problem at an early stage of the formation of their Bible. This may well be the reason why a series of biblical books are considered the works of historical figures all of whom lived before Ezra, such as Moses, Samuel, David, and Solomon. Because the authors were old, the books ascribed to them also had to be old. To mention a couple of examples, some psalms are definitely very late, later than Ezra's appearance in Jerusalem. However, because they belong to a composition carrying the name of David, they must be old; otherwise David would not have been in the position to compose them. The same applies to such books as the Song of Songs, Ecclesiastes, and Proverbs, ascribed by Jewish tradition to the wise King Solomon.

For Ben Sira there was no help, because the publisher of this book mentions his visit to Egypt in 132 BCE, and attributes the book itself to the pen of his grandfather. However "orthodox" the content of this book is, it would never have gained access to a collection like the *Biblia Hebraica*. Daniel, which is younger than the main body of Ben Sira, claims that its author, the prophet Daniel, lived in the time of Nebuchadnezzar and the first kings of Persia. It was accepted without problems.

The case of Ben Sira shows that it was not decisive whether a certain book was composed in the Hebrew language (or Aramaic, like the central part of Daniel). Ben Sira was not left out because of language, as it existed in a Hebrew version.[13] The discovery of the Dead Sea Scrolls around the middle of the twentieth century also shows that several writings not accepted as part of *Biblia Hebraica* existed in a Hebrew version, such as Ben Sira, Tobit, and the Letter of Jeremiah, according to Protestant tradition all parts of the Apocrypha; and *Jubilees,* an important Pseudepigraph. From the way the manuscripts were organized at Qumran, it is clear that there were no special sectors reserved for biblical manuscripts. Most of the caves contained biblical as well as other manuscripts. Furthermore, when we

---

13. The Hebrew manuscript of Ben Sira was found in a synagogue in Cairo in 1895 and is easy to access in the edition of Israel Lévi, *The Hebrew Text of the Book of Ecclesiasticus*, Semitic Study Series (Leiden: Brill, 1904).

speak about popularity, *Jubilees* appears here in as many manuscripts as many of the biblical books and in greater quantity than some.

So far one thing seems certain—there were no overriding principles behind the selection of writings accepted on one hand for the Hebrew Bible and on the other for the Christian Old Testament, which indicates that the Western tradition of the Old Testament based on the Hebrew Bible is preferable to other traditions. From a historical point of view ("the first Bible of Christianity") there is no reason to value the Hebrew Bible more than the Septuagint.

There was no Hebrew Bible in the time of Jesus. Neither is it likely that all of the books of the Greek Bible were in existence at that time. The Septuagint in some way presupposes the existence of a Jewish collection that also includes the third part of *Biblia Hebraica*, the Writings.[14] This observation suggests that it is of the utmost importance that we establish the date of the Hebrew collection before it is possible to discuss the date of the Christian one.

Previous scholarship often talked about a meeting of the rabbis, a synod, in Jamnia about 90 CE, as the place and time when the content of the Hebrew Bible was finally established. Modern scholarship has shown that the Hebrew Bible was not a central topic at this meeting. Jewish scholars of that time would need another century in order to get to a consensus about what to include and what to exclude in their collection.[15]

This is, from a historical point of view, not very problematic. It cooperates well with ideas concerning the emergence of the Christian canon; the appearance of a normative Christian canon was not one of Christianity's first manifestations. It is a reasonable argument that the invention of the book in the form of a codex, that is, an assembly of single sheets, as a substitute for scrolls, made the idea of a canon meaningful, but this invention happened no earlier than the third century CE. *Bible* comes from the Greek βίβλος (originally βύβλος) and means book. It says nothing about the form of this "book," whether a codex or a scroll.

It may therefore be the case that the idea of the Bible as a closed collection of holy writ was something that came into the mind of Jews and Christian no earlier than the second and third centuries CE. But the following many different editions of the Bible shows that nothing was really settled in those days.[16]

14. This presupposes that the rabbinic editors or collectors of *Biblia Hebraica* did not possess the collection contained in the Septuagint and simply deleted from their collection those parts of the Septuagint that did not fit their criteria of selection.

15. On Jamnia, see Mogens Müller, *The First Book of the Church*, 30–31. See also Jack P. Lewis, "Jamnia Revisited," in Lee Martin McDonald and James A. Sanders, eds., *The Canon Debate* (Peabody, MA: Hendrickson, 2002), 146–62. On the discussion among the rabbis about the Hebrew Bible, see Jack N. Lightstone, "The Rabbi's Bible: The Canon of the Hebrew Bible and the Early Rabbinic Guild," in McDonald and Sanders, *The Canon Debate*, 163–84.

16. To take one illustrative example, the book of Psalms: The Hebrew Bible counts 150 psalms and is followed by modern Western tradition. The Greek Bible has also 150 psalms, but has added one more (sometimes known as Psalm 151). In order to keep the accepted number of psalms, two psalms are joined together as one. This additional psalm also appears in the principal Psalms manuscript among the Dead Sea Scrolls (11QPs^a), together with other apocryphal psalms. The same happens in the Peshiṭta, although the additional psalms here are not the same as found in the Qumran manuscript. The Syriac translation is from the same period as the Vulgate, the fourth century CE.

The New Testament includes a number of references to "the Law and the Prophets," but none to "the Writings."[17] When the Gospels were reduced to writing, there must have been Jewish collections around identifiable as "the Law" and "the Prophets." The Law must have existed in a form that was more or less the same as the one included in medieval Jewish Bible manuscripts, and the same applied to the Prophets, with one notable exception: Daniel did not belong in the Jewish collection of prophetic literature as it has survived in Hebrew manuscripts. There were theological reasons for this omission. Rabbinic Judaism, which in the course of the first centuries of the Common Era decided what belonged to the Hebrew Bible, had little interest in the apocalyptic idea of history expressed by Daniel. The rabbis probably would have preferred to omit it, but Daniel's prestige as one of the ancient wise men (together with Noah and Job, Ezek. 14:14) was of a character that excluded such an action against his book. It might be that Daniel at a time was regarded in Judaism as a prophetic book, but was removed from that position to a less important one among the Writings. The position of Daniel in the Septuagint may speak in favor of Daniel being originally considered a prophetic book in Judaism.

When the Gospels came into being, there was probably no Hebrew Bible, but at least two Jewish collections of such importance that they stood out from the rest and thus were sources of quotations for New Testament authors. Aside from these collections, there may well have been other collections of Jewish literature hard to reconstruct today. A selection of such manuscripts was eventually included in the Hebrew Bible as "the Writings." When we, like Mogens Müller, speak of the first Bible of the church, there is reason to speculate about the size and character of this first Bible.

HOW IMPORTANT IS CANON?

We will later return to a group of modern theologians totally absorbed with the idea of the canonical relationship between the Old and the New Testaments. The best known among them, the late Brevard S. Childs, was undoubtedly of the conviction that the canon was the only legitimate basis of biblical theology. The question is, however, what canon are we talking about? If we discuss the question on the basis of a historical-critical approach, there was no Old Testament in existence when most of the New Testament came into being. There existed some forerunners of a Jewish authoritative collection of books, the Torah and the Prophets. Probably the priority of the Law (ranking, as it did, higher than the Prophets) already existed. It is also likely that the Prophets also included, as it did in later Jewish tradition, the historical books from Joshua to 2 Kings. Should we therefore want to discuss the canonical approach of Childs and his colleagues on this basis, the resulting theology would not be one that paid any attention to the

17. Luke has one reference to the Psalms (Luke 24:44).

canon as it exists today—in its Protestant form—as this canon came into being almost 1,500 years after the Gospels were first published. It would also be necessary to exclude the third part of the Hebrew Bible, including Daniel, which was not accepted by the rabbis as a prophetic book.

The canon is no more than a historical accident, the result of a series of choices made by ancient theologians. When Jesus lived, there was no Old Testament or, more precisely, no Hebrew Bible. There was in circulation a series of Hebrew manuscripts that were at a later date incorporated into the Hebrew Bible, and there were Greek translations of these and more books around. Moreover, there was more than one Greek version of a good many "biblical" books, and New Testament authors do not always quote from the Septuagint. Furthermore, translators did not always base their translation on a version of the Hebrew books later incorporated into the Hebrew Bible.

The last assertion depends on one of the blessings of the discovery of the Dead Sea Scrolls. In the century leading up to the Common Era, books that later were part of the Hebrew Bible existed in more than one form. Several versions competed. Specialists argue that the so-called proto-masoretic manuscript tradition dominated even then, but it was not the only one. The differences between the different versions may have been considerable. It is possible, on the basis of the Dead Sea Scrolls, to study the different versions of Isaiah; but it is also possible to make comparative studies of the versions of biblical books in the Hebrew Bible and the Septuagint. Sometimes the Septuagint may be a translation from a manuscript not belonging to the proto-masoretic tradition. Thus Jeremiah in the Septuagint is very different from the version included in the Hebrew Bible.

How important is, then, the canon within the context of biblical theology? First of all, the canonical connection between the testaments is a secondary one. At the beginning of Christianity, there was neither an Old Testament nor a New Testament. The New Testament includes references not only to the Law and the Prophets but also to several other books of the Old Testament. When we argue that the Jewish collection of holy books cannot be older than, say, 100 CE and probably in its present shape may be considerably younger, we are not suggesting that the books later included in the Hebrew Bible were not in existence a long time before their inclusion. This also involves the writings included in the Hebrew Bible's third part. It was stated above that the Jewish tradition held that no books were younger than Ezra. Some books are likely younger than Ezra, but they are all—or almost all—from before the Common Era. Every book of the Old Testament—except Esther—is represented by manuscripts found at Qumran, and it is unlikely that any of these manuscripts postdate the first century BCE.[18]

---

18. I have no intention of getting involved in the sometimes acid discussion about the dating of the Dead Sea Scrolls. The old system of dating these manuscripts was based on paleographic observation, and saw some of these manuscripts predating the first century BCE; but modern neutron-activated analysis points to the first century BCE as the most likely date. See Greg Doudna, *4Q Pesher Nahum. A Critical Edition*, Journal for the Study of the Pseudepigrapha Supplement Series 35 / Copenhagen International Series 8 (London: Sheffield Academic Press, 2001), 675–82. On modern

If we still wish to discuss "canonical" theology, we have a problem. I will return to this as well as other problems below. From a historical-critical perspective, this theology is meaningless if it is supposed to build on the Bible in its entirety. If this were really the case, canonical theology would have no interest in the theology of the early church, although the time of the great fathers from the second and the third centuries CE may be of interest.

This is a serious objection to anyone who may hold the idea that the Bible was important for the development of early Christian doctrine. It is more than likely that the central parts of Christian doctrine came into being without paying much attention to the Bible. It has already been mentioned that the New Testament does not include any doctrine of the two natures of Christ or of the Trinity. This does not imply that there is reason—at least not on this basis—to question accepted theses about the dating of the books of the New Testament. It does not say that from a theological perspective it is unimportant that the evangelists and Paul on several occasions refer to Jewish writings that are now part of the Hebrew Bible.

The implication is—if we should stay with the illusion of a canonical theology founded on historical considerations—that this canon would be a canon within the canon: not all the Bible is "canon," but only selected parts of it. In the history of Christianity this was often the solution, when unwanted parts of the Bible were put aside and in reality expelled from the canon. This makes sense as every period will look for relevance in the Bible—whether based on serious reflection or governed by instinct. It is easy to understand that a quote like "Happy shall they be who take your little ones and dash them against the rock!" (Ps. 137:9) may not be met by any sympathy in the modern world. Most people will reject this passage as abominable. But perhaps it was different for the people who committed genocide in Rwanda ten years ago.

Every living member of Western civilization—whether a believer or a nonbeliever—will have his or her own canon: passages from the Bible, but also from elsewhere, considered personally important. This has to do with the observation that the BIBLE (in capitals) is no more *the* authority, but only authoritative. It also suggests that it is possible to discuss canonical theology, although not on a historical basis. The present (post)modern world allows for individuality. It demands that every person make his or her own choices and defend such choices against the opinion of other people. It is such a choice to decide that the canon as we have it, for example, in a Protestant Lutheran context, based on Luther's final edition of his translation from 1545, is *our* canon. This choice and the resulting theology will be deemed important for people who accept the choice and identify with its consequences. It is of course also possible to choose another

---

methods of dating, see also I. Carmi, "Radiocarbon Dating of the Dead Sea Scrolls," in L. Schiffman, E. Tov, and J. VanderKam, eds., *The Dead Sea Scrolls Fifty Years after Their Discovery* (Jerusalem: Israel Exploration Society, 2000), 881–88; Kåre L. Rasmussen, and more, "The Effects of Possible Contamination on the Radiocarbon Dating of the Dead Sea Scrolls I: Castor Oil," *Radiocarbon* 43 (2001): 127–32.

canon, as for example the one in the Leningrad Codex's Hebrew text as presented by the *Biblia Hebraica Stuttgartensia* (and soon also the *Biblia Hebraica Quinta*), or the Greek text of Erasmus's *Textus Receptus*, as recreated by Kurt Aland's Institute at Münster and presented in the Nestle-Aland version of the Greek New Testament, now in its twenty-seventh edition. It is also possible to choose the text of the Septuagint as the basis for the study of the Old Testament; after all, this is the version of the books of the Old Testament most often quoted by New Testament authors. Every choice will have consequences for the theological process. If one prefers a historical angle, this decision is final, and the results of the theological analysis will be judged on a historical basis.

If we choose to use, for example, the New Revised Standard Version from 1989 as our canonical foundation, this choice also has historical implications. There was no such Bible before 1989. A canonical theology based on this edition of the Bible must take the year of 1989 into consideration as a historical fact. It will be a canonical theology that has the year of 1989 as its historical point of departure. At any rate there are many possible versions of canonical theology. The only requirement is that the foundation of every version be as clear and precise as possible.

Also the decision to apply a modern literary approach to biblical theology is a historical decision. The person who chooses such an approach is also a historical fact, part of the categories of time and space.

Chapter 12

Old Testament Theologies of the Twentieth Century

THE OLD TESTAMENT AS PART OF THE BIBLE

The German Old Testament scholar Ernst Knauf once presented a personal "thesis" about the special character of German scholarship: "There are two compartments in heaven: a big one, advertised as 'heaven,' where you are going to meet just about everybody, and a small one with a huge billboard reading 'Introduction to the Theory of Heaven.' There you'll find the Germans." Up until recent times, Old Testament theology was a subject almost totally dominated by German scholars.[1]

An overview of theologies of the Old Testament from the twentieth century shows that the vast majority of these were German. It also shows that most German theologies are rather traditional as far as their concept of a theology of the Old Testament is concerned. These theologies followed the development within historical-critical scholarship and have few questions of this kind of scholarship. Most theologies were written by Protestant scholars, especially scholars with a

---

1. Ernst Axel Knauf, "From History to Interpretation," in Diana Vikander Edelman, ed., *The Fabric of History; Text, Artifact and Israel's Past*, JSOTSup 127 (Sheffield: JSOT Press, 1991), 26–64, 26.

Lutheran background. Authors from other parts of Christendom, like the late James Barr, may have produced important studies on theological subjects relating to the Old Testament, but these were mostly essays. The North American Old Testament scholar Walter Brueggemann's *Theology of the Old Testament* from 1997 is an exception,[2] but is also vastly different from the theologies belonging to the German tradition. We will return to Barr and especially Brueggemann later in this part.

When we inquire concerning the reason for the multitude of theologies of the Old Testament in the German language in the past century, it is necessary to understand the position of the discipline of Old Testament studies within theology at the beginning of that century. In his famous book on Marcion from 1921,[3] the great German church historian Adolf von Harnack (1851–1930) characterized the position of the Old Testament within the Christian church in this way:

> It was a mistake to reject the Old Testament in the second century, and the church was right in rejecting this mistake. The decision to keep the Old Testament in the 16th century was a destiny from which the Reformation could not yet escape. However, to preserve the Old Testament since the nineteenth century as a canonical document for Protestantism is the result of a religious and intellectual paralysis.[4]

Harnack continues with a recommendation to Protestantism that it should concentrate on the truth of the Christian creed and teaching ("der Wahrheit in Bekenntnis und Unterricht die Ehre zu geben") and he ends this section with the observation that it may already be too late, something almost imaginable in light of the present position of the Old Testament within university theology, especially in Protestant Europe, where the Old Testament has been marginalized from being a major subject to become a side discipline of New Testament studies.

Old Testament scholarship is itself the main reason why this happened. It was Old Testament scholars who paved the way for an evaluation of the Old Testament like Harnack's, and it was Old Testament scholars who, for most of the twentieth century, broadened the gap between the Old and the New Testament. Even as late as at the end of the twentieth century, many Old Testament scholars still opposed the idea of the Old Testament as an entirely *Jewish* book, while an independent Jewish scholarship would help liberate their Hebrew Bible from the clutches of Christianity.

---

2. Walter Brueggemann, *Theology of the Old Testament: Testimony, Dispute, Advocacy* (Minneapolis: Fortress, 1997).

3. Adolf von Harnack, *Marcion: Das Evangelium vom fremden Gott,* Eine Monographie zur Geschichte der Grundlegung der Katholischen Kirche (Leipzig: Hinrichs, 1921). Marcion (110–60) was against the inclusion of the Old Testament as part of the Christian canon.

4. "Das Alte Testament im 2. Jahrhundert zu verwerfen war ein Fehler, den die große Kirche mit Recht abgelehnt hat; es im 16. Jahrhundert beizubehalten was ein Schicksal, dem sich die Reformation noch nicht zu entziehen vermochte; es aber seit dem 19. Jahrhundert als kanonische Urkunde im Protestantismus noch zu konservieren ist die Folge einer religiösen und kirchlichen Lähmung" (Harnack, *Marcion*, 127).

I have already commented on the basic problem. The Old Testament developed in the course of the nineteenth century from being a Christian canonical part of the Bible to become a textbook for studies in the history of religion. When the concept of history changed—from being a story to history—the Old Testament lost its *Sitz im Leben* in the Christian canon. Only one thing "rescued" the Old Testament (apart from conventions as indicated by Harnack); that very much the same thing happened to the New Testament.

Apart from this, it is possible to argue that around 1900 the Old Testament was no longer a part of the Christian canon. The connection between the two testaments was no longer considered of primary importance, in comparison to the relations between the Old Testament and the society assumed to produce the books of the Old Testament. Another factor became important: an increasingly conservative attitude as far as historical issues was concerned. While it was at the beginning of historical-critical scholarship not uncommon to find the Old Testament—or parts of it—dated to the Hellenistic period,[5] developments within Near Eastern disciplines belonging to the nineteenth century and their many spectacular discoveries had changed the general attitude of the public. At the end of the nineteenth century the Iron Age, the period between about 1200 and 600 BCE, was widely considered the period within which the writings of the Old Testament came into being.

Now the Old Testament was no longer a *Jewish* book. Most Old Testament scholars found this unproblematic, although we cannot totally disregard the possible influence of the growing anti-Semitism of the early twentieth century. When the origin of the Old Testament was moved back into the Iron Age, the Old Testament became an *Israelite* book. Its relationship to the New Testament and Christianity became of secondary importance and was the invention of New Testament authors who had distorted the true meaning of the books of the Old Testament. The New Testament authors read the Old Testament very naively without any regard for its historical origin in "ancient Israel," whose history is related by the Old Testament in contrast to the "new Israel," the Christian church. A historical-critical reading of, for example, Paul's discussion of the children of Hagar in Galatians (4:21–31) shows Paul's exegesis as a conscious distortion of the story of Hagar as presented by the Old Testament, because of his allegorical way of reading Genesis 16 and 21.

No one has defined the new role of the Old Testament as clearly as Julius Wellhausen (1844–1918) in his famous manifesto: *The Prophets come before the Law.* The prophets are considered the representatives of the faith of ancient Israel, while the Law represents later Judaism. Since the Law is seen in light of the Christian definition of the law of the Jews, its meaning for Christianity is totally negated. The prophets remain as the exalted expression of the true faith in one

---

5. We may think of Ilgen's dating of the Song of Balaam to the Hellenistic period (see p. 38).

God before Christianity, and a source to understand the essence of God and the meaning of the world.[6]

We have to ask, how long was this fraudulent interpretation of the Old Testament going to last? For how long a time would the Old Testament be accepted as a part of the Christian canon, when it had long before ceased to be "the word of God" (with or without the "doctrine" of verbal inspiration)? It was seemingly only a testimony about beliefs in God in a remote ancient society that had disappeared centuries before the coming of Christ. Old Testament scholarship was confronted by questions like these, and had problems finding proper answers.

If we review the landscape of biblical studies outside of Germany, which still dominated Old and New Testament studies at the beginning of the twentieth century, we realize that these scholars were generally not interested in qualified answers to these problems. In a later chapter we will move on to the North American biblical theology movement, at the center of which were problems created by the discrepancy between biblical history and real history. Inspired by the mentor of this school, William Foxwell Albright, the supporters of this branch of biblical theology tried to remove such discrepancies by harmonization. One example of this kind of harmonization is Albright's *From the Stone Age to Christianity*;[7] another is his student John Bright's *A History of Israel*,[8] still used in many North American seminaries as their textbook on this subject.

In spite of the presence of some of the most important Old Testament scholars of the twentieth century, Scandinavia produced very little in the way of a reflection on the importance—or lack of importance—of the Old Testament for theology. Although some wrote important studies of value for the study of the theology of the Old Testament, their direct subject was the history of religion. The work by a Scandinavian scholar that may have been closest to the demands of a theology of the Old Testament was probably by the Danish scholar Johannes Pedersen, whose major opus was *Israel I-IV*, which appeared between 1920 and 1934.[9] The many impulses from both Sigmund Mowinckel and the so-called Uppsala school were mostly related to the history of religion.

Which brings us back to the Germans, although it would be impossible in a restricted space to include all of them, but also unnecessary as others have done this before me. Here the description of German contributions will follow the typology of their theologies presented by James Barr, but also place the development

---

6. See also Jon Levenson's justified criticism of Wellhausen and his idea of Judaism in *The Hebrew Bible, the Old Testament, and Historical Criticism* (Louisville, KY: Westminster John Knox, 1993), 10–15.

7. William Foxwell Albright, *From the Stone Age to Christianity: Monotheism and the Historical Process* (New York: Doubleday, 1940; 2nd ed., 1957).

8. John Bright, *A History of Israel* (Philadelphia: Westminster, 1959; 4th ed. Louisville: Westminster John Knox, 2000).

9. Danish edition *Israel I–II. Sjælaleliv og Samfundsloiv* (Copenhagen: Poul Branner, 1920; 3rd ed., 1958); *III–IV. Hellighed og Guddommelighed* (Copenhagen: Poul Branner, 1934; 2nd ed., 1960); ET, *Israel: Its Life and Culture*, I–II and III–IV (Oxford: Geoffrey Cumberlege, 1964).

of the theologies of the Old Testament in contrast to the general development dividing theology into dialectic and existentialist branches. I will return later to the contributions of both directions to the discussion of the status of the Old Testament within the Christian canon.

According to Barr, theologies of the Old Testament from the twentieth century can be distributed between five—maybe only four plus one—main categories.[10] The first category may be summarized as confessionally oriented theologies. The theology of the Old Testament follows the pattern of Christian dogmatics. At the end this might lead to a proper biblical dogmatic. The German scholar Friedrich Mildenberger published such a dogmatic as late as the 1990s.[11] Barr in this context mentions not Mildenberger but Ludwig Köhler, whose theology of the Old Testament appeared in 1935 but has been often reprinted, perhaps because it is short and therefore "digestible" for students of theology.[12]

LUDWIG KÖHLER

Köhler's theology is divided into three main parts. The first is about God, the second about humanity, and the third about judgment and salvation. The part about God is introduced by this bombastic assertion: "The assumption that God exists is the Old Testament's greatest gift to mankind."[13]

According to Köhler the Old Testament is unique because it never questions the existence of God. God is always presupposed. This is a correct observation. The Bible does not open with a discussion about the existence of God but with the acts of God, his creation of heaven and earth.

Hence, the section on God is subdivided into three paragraphs. In the first Köhler deals with the anthropomorphism of the Old Testament; in the second he turns to the *Gottestypen*, the way God appears; and in the third paragraph the subject is God as lord. Thereafter follows a rather stereotypical but exhaustive listing of the names of God in the Old Testament. The last part of the section devoted to God concerns "God in history." Now Köhler's theology begins to change from a systematic arrangement to one oriented toward history. In his paragraph titled "Die Tatsache der Offenbarung" (The reality of the revelation), the subject is still the revelation as part of the narrative in the Old Testament, but now follow paragraphs dominated by historical ideas: the image of God during the Israelite settlement and the religion of the Israelite state. In spite of his systematic arrangement of subjects, history is never out of his mind. Elements of Old Testament theology can be placed within the context of Israel's history as

---

10. *The Concept of Biblical Theology: An Old Testament Perspective* (London: SCM, 1999), 27.

11. Friedrich Mildenbergen, *Biblische Dogmatik*, 3 vols. (Stuttgart: Kohlhammer, 1997).

12. Ludwig Köhler, *Theologie des Alten Testaments*, Neue theologische Grundrisse (3rd ed., Tübingen: Mohr, 1953); ET, *Old Testament Theology*, Library of Theological Translations (Cambridge: Lutterworth Press, 2002).

13. Köhler, *Theologie*, 1.

outlined by the Old Testament. The paragraph on God ends with a discussion devoted to the forms of the revelation of God and the importance of the spirit.

The section on humanity opens with three paragraphs devoted to humans as living beings, followed by a historically oriented paragraph on life within the human family and in society, and ends with a discussion of original sin and the (self-)liberation in the cult.

It is hardly a surprise that the last part about judgment and salvation ends with a paragraph called "Heil durch Erlösung" (Salvation through redemption), which again ends with a section "Der leidende Messias" (The suffering Messias). Old Testament theology exists only on conditions decided by Christian theology.

In summary, Köhler has presented a theology acceptable to Christian theology in his theology of the Old Testament. The historical part, although present, does not play a decisive role, and allusions to the historical-critical scholarship of his era are not much in evidence. The factor that decides the content of a theology of the Old Testament is Christian dogmatics.

THEODORE C. VRIEZEN

Theodore C. Vriezen's theology of the Old Testament, which appeared in Dutch in 1949 but was soon translated into German and then into English,[14] is related in outline to Köhler's theology. Barr characterizes it as Christian dogmatics. It opens with a chapter titled "The Christian Church and the Old Testament." The first sentence of this chapter says:

> Historically and spiritually Christianity stands on the shoulders of Judaism. Like St. Paul and almost all the authors of the New Testament, Jesus Christ was an Israelite. He lived by the Hebrew Holy Scriptures which were, for him as well as His disciples, the Word of God.[15]

A few pages later the following remark can be found:

> The Jewish Christians at the beginning of the apostolic age also lived fully in the Old Testament.[16]

Vriezen has no doubt about the fundamental importance of the Old Testament for the early church. The connection between the Old and the New Testament is seen as a vital basis of Christian belief. More than a third of Vriezen's theology is devoted to this issue.

---

14. *Hoofdlijnen der Theologie van het Oude Testament* (Wageningen: H. Veenman & Zonen nv, 1949; 2nd ed., 1954). Here the English translation is used: *An Outline of Old Testament Theology* (2nd ed., Newton, MA: Charles T. Branford, 1970).
    15. *An Outline of Old Testament Theology*, 11.
    16. Ibid., 13.

Vrizen's second part explains the content of the theology of the Old Testament as seen through the encounter between God and humankind, that is, in the revelation. This part is good reading because it builds on the text of the Old Testament exclusively and is not dependent on questions that may not be part of the text. There is also a discussion about natural theology, which is a natural choice when the Old Testament alone, and not the New Testament, is the focus. Nobody who starts reading the Old Testament from the beginning can be in doubt about the fundamental importance of creation as an expression of God's plan for the world he created. This is a long way from the position held by much Protestant theology of the twentieth century, which argued that humankind is informed about the plan of God only through the revelation in Christ. Like Köhler, Vriezen opens this part of his theology with a discussion about God in the Old Testament. Hereafter he turns to humankind in a chapter called "The Community of God." Now one's impression of the book changes, because of the author's fundamentally conservative perspective on the history recorded in the Old Testament. His theology is fitted into this conservative historical framework and placed in paragraphs about the social system seen from a historical perspective about the community of law, Moses, and more.

Vriezen's dependence on history is of no help when he warns against identifying the idea of patriarchal religion or of the religion of Moses with the historical patriarchs and the historical Moses, because it is a presupposition of the discussion in these paragraphs that the patriarchs and Moses were really living persons. Thus Abraham, that is, the historical Abraham, cannot have known Yahweh, the God of Israel, because it is written (as Vriezen states it) that God revealed his identity only to Moses (Exod. 3). There is, hence, really reason for asking about the level of the discussion: is the basis a literary or historical one?

The following part makes it clear that the historical reconstruction of the community of God is used as the foundation for the discussion about the beliefs and ethics of this community. Vriezen simply identifies the people of God of the Old Testament with historical Israel. He never questions the historical reconstruction or the connection between the—in theory—historical background and its manifestation in the stories of the Bible.

Reading through Vriezen's theology of the Old Testament, one will many times be reminded of Bernd Jörg Diebner's already-quoted maxim: You cannot prove it . . . but it is a fact; for example, when he speaks about the connection between the religion of the patriarchs and Moses's religion. He opens with a confession: we don't know anything. Then follows his statement that "Otto Eissfeldt may have been correct when he assumed that Moses was the person who created a link between Yahweh religion and the faith of the patriarchs."[17] The next part of the discussion builds on this assertion—and it still remains only an assertion, irrespective of how many times the argument is repeated. Before long, we have a complete history of Israelite religion based on such assertions.

17. Ibid., 363.

The last chapter in Vriezen's theology is devoted to the community of God and its place, that is, the place of the Christian church, in modern society. Now it is evident that Vriezen, in his argumentation, is totally dependent on Paul's distinction between the old and the new Israel. Vriezen's theology appeared only a few years after the Holocaust. The new "Israel" had, in its own way, found a solution to the problem of old "Israel." With such in mind it is remarkable that it is possible to write about the community of God in our time without paying any attention at all to the present.

The community of God is a religio-ethnic concept. It is related to *ethnicity*, however, not as defined by contemporary sociologists and social anthropologists like Fredrik Barth, that is, as a social way to organize cultural difference.[18] Cultural differences are described as societal differences among people who are different as far as culture is concerned. However, the theological difference between the old Israel and the new Israel is organized as an ethnic difference between those who belong to the old people of God and those who have membership cards to the new people of God. None of these peoples of God can exist without the presence of the other one. When you play football, there must always be someone on the other half of the field, or there would be no game.[19] Vriezen's omission of the other part, which is at the same time the part you play with, places the people of God in an impossible position—at least until a new opponent can be found, which in a European, Christian, and postwar connection means the secularized society.

Although Barr reckons Köhler and Vriezen as authors of two different although related types of theologies of the Old Testament, it is perhaps more reasonable to place them in the same category: church-oriented theologies of the Old Testament, not ready to sever the connection between the Old and the New Testament.

WALTER EICHRODT

The two most important theologies of the Old Testament of the twentieth century, that of Walter Eichrodt (1890–1978), which appeared between 1933 and 1939 (but was reprinted in new editions until the mid-1960s),[20] and that of Gerhard von Rad (1900–1971), published between 1957 and 1960,[21] are basically in agreement with Vriezen insofar as the connection between the Old and the New Testaments is accepted as of fundamental importance. Barr places these two theologies in two different categories and for good reason. In spite of their common

18. Cf. Fredrik Barth, "Introduction," in Fredrik Barth, ed., *Ethnic Groups and Boundaries* (Oslo: Universitetsforlaget, 1969), 9–37.

19. This passage was written during the football world championships in the summer of 2006, so I hope to be excused for this simile.

20. Walter Eichrodt, *Theologie des Alten Testaments*, 3 vols. (Stuttgart: Ehrenfried Klotz / Göttingen: Vandenhoeck & Ruprecht, 1933–39); ET, *Theology of the Old Testament* (Philadelphia: Westminster, 1967).

21. Gerhard von Rad, *Theologie des Alten Testaments*, 2 vols. (Munich: Chr. Kaiser, 1957–60); ET, *Old Testament Theology*, 2 vols. (Louisville: Westminster John Knox, 2001).

background, the then-dominant German paradigm of Old Testament scholar-ship, they are very different.

In classical physics, there existed a major divergence between how Isaac New-ton and James C. Maxwell defined light: is light a point or a wave? A point is a static identity, absolutely different from a wave. The answer arrived at by the researcher depends not on the item under discussion, that is, the light, but on the instrument used to observe this item.[22]

We will not continue with a discussion about disagreements within classical physics. The example has only one purpose, to illustrate the difference between two fundamentally different theological concepts. Eichrodt searched for the cen-ter of the Old Testament, a pivotal point for its theology. In contrast, von Rad was interested in the "wave," in his eyes the history of Israel as related by the books of the Old Testament.

Eichrodt's pivotal point is the *covenant*. The first part of his theology—more than half of his theology—is devoted to the concept of the covenant in the Old Testament as seen from every possible point of view. The covenant's character as the pivotal point is illustrated by the way every part of biblical theology revolves around this concept. Eichrodt opens with a discussion of the history of the covenant in ancient Israel, after having described the covenant as a theological and *historical* concept. One of his first paragraphs concerns the history of the con-cept of the covenant. In Eichrodt's own words:

> It is therefore no wonder that in the whole long process of adjusting the Mosaic religion to the environment of Canaanite religion and culture it is round this crucial issue that the struggle fluctuates to and fro, now assimi-lating, now rejecting, striving in part toward distortion, in part toward new understanding and sharper definition of the covenant concept. A glance at the history of the concept is therefore indispensable if it is to be properly understood.[23]

The hermeneutical circle has been a widely debated subject within exegesis. Eichrodt's argumentation here is a perfect example. In order to arrive at a pro-found understanding of the concept of the covenant, we must know its history. This history is presented by the Old Testament where we find the concept of the covenant, and according to Eichrodt this history produced the idea of the covenant between Yahweh and Israel. This line of argumentation moves from the concept of the covenant as presented in the books of the Old Testament back to a historical reality that is not part of the Old Testament, whereupon the argu-

---

22. My thanks to my former student Mrs. Ingrid Salinas for advice in connection with this "simile."
23. "So ist es kein Wunder, daß in dem großen Prozeß der Auseinandersetzung der mosaischen Religion mit der kanaanäischen Kultur- und Glaubenswelt auch an diesem Punkt der Kampf in Assimilation und Abstoßung hin- und herwogt und teils zur Verzerrung, teils zu einer Erfassung und schärferer Abgrenzung des Bundesgedankens treibt. Ein Blick *auf die Geschichte der Bundesidee* ist daher zu ihrem vollen Verständnis unerläßlich (*Theologie*, 1:15; ET, 1:45).

ment returns to the Old Testament in order to explain its content. No external phenomenon—that is, no event absent from the Old Testament—is allowed to interfere. The circle is a perfect one. However, it explains nothing.

Having found a place for the concept of the covenant in history, Eichrodt has no problem finding a place for every phenomenon linked to it, among these the importance of the concept of the covenant for the development of Israelite justice and cult.

There may be good reason to wonder if the concept of covenant is really the pivotal point of Eichrodt's theology of the Old Testament. Perhaps it is simply a more conventional usage, *covenant* being utilized as a kind of catchall term. In his next chapter, Eichrodt presents a rather conventional overview of the appearance of God in the Old Testament without referring to the covenant, opening with a discussion of the names of God ("The Names of the God of the Covenant") and following it with a discussion of the character of God ("The Identity of the God of the Covenant").

Reading through the pages of the first volume of Eichrodt's theology, we meet history again in the next chapter, which concerns the institutions of the covenant and includes his discussion of Moses, prophecy, the judges, prophetic ecstasy, and more. Placing the covenant at the center, Israel's answer to different challenges is studied as presented by the literature of the Old Testament.

It is unnecessary to continue with a prolonged review of Eichrodt's theology, which of course embraces far more subjects than the few mentioned here. The essential thing has already been mentioned, and Eichrodt's idea of the covenant as the center of the Old Testament is far from unreasonable. If we were looking for such a center, few things would be more central than the covenant. In his comprehensive theology of the Old Testament, which appeared toward the end of the twentieth century (1991–92), Horst Dietrich Preuß (1927–93) places the idea of God's choice of Israel as the center of the Old Testament.[24] Preuß, however, is even more dependent on the link between theology and real history than Eichrodt.

This connection with real history had important but devastating consequences for Preuß's theology because of the changes within the study of this history that belonged to the same period that also saw his theology published. The collapse of history left a theology like Preuß's—and for that matter Eichrodt's—hanging in the air. This is a pity, as Preuß's idea of the importance of the concept of God's election of Israel may have been a bridge between Eichrodt's relatively stable concept of covenant and von Rad's idea of "salvation history" in the Old Testament. The notion of election is far more dynamic than the concept of covenant, and this dynamic element is necessary for the idea of history as a theological process, as well as the meaning of history as the forum of the election.

---

24. Horst Dietrich Preuß, *Theologie des Alten Testaments*, 2 vols. (Stuttgart: Kohlhammer, 1991–92); ET, *Old Testament Theology*, 2 vols. (Louisville, KY: Westminster John Knox, 1996).

The theology of the covenant changed character when, in the middle of the 1950s, the North American scholar George E. Mendenhall published two popular articles about the origin of the idea of the covenant.[25] Mendenhall attempted to achieve harmony between the narrative about the conclusion of the covenant at Sinai and history by arguing that the covenant at Sinai was structured according to Hittite suzerainty treaties considered contemporary with Moses. The historical Moses borrowed from the way Hittite treaties were organized in order to structure his own covenant.

Irrespective of the rather primitive form in which Mendenhall presented his thesis, it became very popular and was able to dominate Old Testament scholarship for many years, until the end of the 1960s, when the German scholar Lothar Perlitt, using traditional historical-critical methodologies, showed that the idea of the covenant appeared in ancient Israel only at a relatively late date. It had no relation to the time of Moses.[26]

It is really remarkable how a discussion that basically ought to be a theological one ended up as an exclusively (tradition-) historical one. If we look at Gabler's project (explained earlier), his project was about to collapse toward the middle of the twentieth century. Scholars were generally not able any longer to make a distinction between theology and history. Theology had turned into a slave of history. Theology was totally dependent on history, understood to be real history, and this history was decisive for theological reflection. More than anything else, this illustrates the problem related to the change of the concept of history in the generation that followed Gabler.

Somehow it was necessary that Old Testament scholars make a compromise with history. It was unavoidable that they entered a more conscious relationship with real history. Gerhard von Rad's theology of the Old Testament provided an answer.

GERHARD VON RAD

Von Rad changed the center of the theology of the Old Testament into something dynamic. The idea of history became central to his idea of theology. The Old Testament has a story to tell. This might appear to be an acknowledgment of the central part of the Old Testament as historical, but von Rad explains it in this way: Israel's history as related in the Old Testament represents the way in which Israel retold its history. Von Rad was a staunch supporter of traditional German Old Testament scholarship; tradition history therefore plays a decisive role in his theology. The history of Israel in the Old Testament is not one history

---

25. George E. Mendenhall, "Ancient Oriental and Biblical Law," *Biblical Archaeologist* 17/2 (1954): 26–46, and "Covenant Forms in Israelite Tradition," *Biblical Archaeologist* 17/3 (1954): 50–76, both reprinted in Edward F. Campbell and David Noel Freedman, eds., *The Biblical Archaeologist Reader* (New York: Doubleday, 1970), 3:3–53.

26. Lothar Perlitt, *Bundestheologie im Alten Testament*, Wissenschaftliche Monographien zum Alten und Neuen Testament 36 (Neukirchen: Neukirchener Verlag, 1969).

but many histories. We do not possess one "canonical" history of Israel but many different ones. By asserting this, von Rad is close to the modern concept of a "rewritten Bible," that is, a Bible that never stiffened in one format but was rewritten time and again according to the sentiments and ideas of different times and places. This notion has, as explained earlier, become especially popular within prophetic scholarship. A prophetic book had to change according to the circumstances, in order to stay relevant.

In von Rad's perspective, Israel's history reflects the many layers of tradition. In this von Rad's theology is solidly ensconced in German scholarship. Each layer represents different ideas about the history of Israel at different times. This notion of tradition history creates few problems. It is also flexible, far more flexible than imagined even by von Rad himself.

If history in the Old Testament is understood to be a story—and this is absolutely within von Rad's horizon—the story is still dependent on a reality that is not itself part of the narrative. Once upon a time there was somebody who narrated the history of Israel in the way it is written in the Old Testament. We may even say that reality dominates the story, an idea not so far removed from the notion of the historical covenant found in Eichrodt's theology. If we concentrate on von Rad's theology as he saw it, we will find that there was no great distance between the story about Israel and its real history. In von Rad's theology, we may say that story and history are linked closely together.

Apart from this limitation (which has to do with von Rad's spiritual background in German Old Testament scholarship), his theology opens for its reader many possibilities that will be discussed later in this part. His theology does not establish a fixed dividing line between history and story. It is not, for example, that 70 percent of the story can be directly converted into history, or 60 percent or more or less. It is in principle possible that no part of the story has to do with historical events. The story remains even if nothing like it happened in real life.

With this in mind we may now proceed to place the content of the story of Israel in the Old Testament in focus. It is of little or no importance whether it reflects any historical event or is totally fictive. From this perspective, von Rad's theology remains important. When one reads through the story of Israel in the Old Testament, it becomes clear that this is a story about God's acts in history. In this light the history of Israel is "salvation history," a history of the story of Yahweh's many beneficial acts toward his chosen people. We shall later discuss in more detail the concept of salvation history. This is rather problematic, but it creates links between the Old and the New Testaments.

The second point where von Rad's theology stands out in comparison with older theologies is his tradition-historical approach to the Old Testament. While older theologies from Köhler to Eichrodt mainly studied the theology of the Old Testament as the theology of one book only, von Rad accepts that there are many theologies in this "book" or, rather, collection of books. In the first volume of his theology, von Rad discusses the theology of Israel's historical traditions, the theology of Old Testament narratives from the primeval history to the conquest of Canaan. In this way von Rad pays special attention to the theology of the Pentateuch—or in von Rad's case, the Hexateuch, as he reckoned Joshua as part of the complex of the books of Moses. The theologies of the Deuteronomistic History and of the books of Chronicles receive less attention.

In his second volume, von Rad turns to the prophetic narratives and thinks of the prophetic traditions as a special source of information about Israel's life and religion. This part is less coherent than his discussion of the books of Moses and must be so, although there is still a kind of red thread. However, this thread is more historical than literary. We will therefore see von Rad dividing the prophetic tradition into periods that follow the biblical subdivision of Israel's history, assigning Amos, Hosea, Isaiah, and Micah to the eighth century BCE, Jeremiah to the seventh century BCE, and Ezekiel and Deutero-Isaiah to the time of the exile in Babylon, and finally Trito-Isaiah, Haggai, Zechariah, Malachi, and Jonah to the postexilic period.

We will later return to von Rad's theology in order to discuss it in more detail. Both von Rad's and Eichrodt's theologies of the Old Testament remained influential, and especially von Rad's theology is still highly regarded, especially because of his students, some of them now important theologians.

No more major theologies of the Old Testament appeared in German for more than thirty years. To be sure, more compact theologies were published, mostly for the benefit of theological students, like those of Claus Westermann,[27] Walther Zimmerli,[28] and Antonius H. J. Gunneweg.[29]

These shorter theologies are dependent on the "great masters." Zimmerli's theology is close in outline to Eichrodt's theology, and Westermann's to von Rad's. They are, however, all easy reading. They have not contributed much to the development of Old Testament theology as a discipline. I will return later to another German contribution, that of Erhard Gerstenberger, whose *Theologies of the Old Testament*[30] represents a new direction, although Gerstenberger's dependence on von Rad's theology is noticeable. Gerstenberger, together with Rainer Albertz, will be the subject of the following chapter.

OTTO KAISER

One major German contribution to the theology of the Old Testament remains to be discussed, that of Otto Kaiser, which was published between 1993 and

---

27. Claus Westermann, *Theologie des Alten Testaments in Grundzügen*, Grundrisse zum Alten Testament 6 (2nd ed., Göttingen: Vandenhoeck & Ruprecht, 1985); ET, *Elements of Old Testament Theology* (Atlanta: John Knox Press, 1982).

28. Walther Zimmerli, *Grundriß der alttestamentlichen Theologie*, Theologische Wissenschaft 3 (Stuttgart: Kohlhammer, 1972); ET, *Old Testament Theology in Outline* (Edinburgh: T. & T. Clark, 1978).

29. Antonius H. J. Gunneweg, *Biblische Theologie des Alten Testaments: Eine Religionsgeschichte Israels in biblisch-theologischer Sicht* (Stuttgart: Kohlhammer, 1993).

30. Erhard S. Gerstenberger, *Theologien im AT. Pluralität und Synkretismus alttestamentlicher Gottesglaubens* (Stuttgart: Kohlhammer, 2001); ET, *Theologies in the Old Testament* (London: T. & T. Clark, 2002).

2003.[31] With its more than 1,100 pages, Kaiser's theology is by far the most comprehensive theology around today. Kaiser's theology, which Barr describes as outspokenly Lutheran in its outlook, is about God. Its title, *Der Gott des Alten Testaments* [The God of the Old Testament], covers well its subject. The first volume may be considered a kind of prolegomenon. It opens with a discussion of hermeneutical problems, whereupon follow chapters on the Old Testament as part of the heritage of the church, and on the Old Testament as a problem for the church in light of the progress of historical-critical scholarship.

Following this part, Kaiser turns to the background of Old Testament theology in the religion of ancient Israel, following it in its various stages until the Persian and Hellenistic periods. After this survey, Kaiser, following the tradition of von Rad, takes up the theology of the individual parts of the Old Testament, beginning with the Pentateuch, the Deuteronomistic History, and the Chroniclers. Then he proceeds to the prophets. Neither is Wisdom literature forgotten. His first volume ends with a long paragraph on the Torah as the center of the Old Testament. Eichrodt is not forgotten.

The second volume carries the subtitle, translated, "Yahweh the God of Israel, the Creator of the World and of Humanity." In many ways it follows previous theologies, with its emphasis of the identity of Yahweh, on the names of God, on the people of God, and especially in its discussion of creation, including the biblical concept of humanity as created in God's image.

The third volume has the subtitle "Yahweh's Justice." It opens with a discussion of the covenant, and moves to the law of Yahweh, his judgment of the nations and Israel, his salvation of Zion, and finally his Messiah. In the last part the justice of Yahweh is compared to the foolishness of humankind. Here a discussion about the justice of God in Job is included, as well as the skepticism of Ecclesiastes and Jesus ben Sira. Finally, the concept of monotheism is discussed after an overview of apocalyptic and the book of Daniel, and this major theology ends with a treatise on the Old Testament as *Existenzauslegung* or the interpretation of existence.

THEOLOGY DEPENDS ON HISTORY: SUMMARY

An overview over Kaiser's comprehensive theology of the Old Testament shows that all the problems of the German theological discourse are still in existence. Von Rad was probably closest to a solution of the fundamental problem as set forth by Gabler, although he still refers to real history and regarded his salvation history, the story told by the Old Testament, as a reflection based on real history. Nevertheless, von Rad may have presented a formula that may help his successors to break away from their dependence on history.

---

31. Otto Kaiser, *Der Gott des Alten Testaments. Theologie des AT,* 3 vols. (Göttingen: Vandenhoeck & Ruprecht, 1993–2003).

Other German theologians are still stuck in the morass of history, not the history as narrated by the Bible, but real history. This especially includes Otto Kaiser, who has presented the most comprehensive description of the relation between the Old Testament and real history, and whose theology in many ways cannot be considered a theology in the narrow sense of the word. It is more a history of the development of human thought, as it is reflected by the stories of the Old Testament.

The situation of the theology of the Old Testament as represented by many theologies of the Old Testament in the German language cannot last. Also German biblical scholarship has been hit by the crisis of history so evident in many parts of international Old Testament scholarship. It was previously so confident that it was correct that it simply saw no reason for change, although everyone understood that Gabler's project still remained unresolved.

Scholarship will always be a reflection of the era that produced it. In the modern world, the trend is toward a multicultural society. Former eras' nationalistic and often Protestant self-assuredness has been replaced by the acceptance of the existence of other forms of theology and, furthermore, of the existence of other religions (including their theology). It is also mandatory that a dialogue shall exist between these theologies. When this writer studied theology in Copenhagen forty years ago, I for a time spoke of Jewish theologians. That was a big mistake, and I was soon corrected by one of my professors: Judaism has no theologians. They may have learned people who know the Scriptures, wise persons, people who know their law, but they cannot have true knowledge of God. Only a real theologian will have that knowledge, through the revelation found in the New Testament (the professor in question was a specialist in the New Testament).

Now only one of the five categories of Old Testament theologies mentioned by James Barr remains, canonical theology. It will have its own chapter.

Chapter 13

History, Theology, and/or the History of Religion

The Collapse of History:
The Theological Consequences I

THE COLLAPSE OF HISTORY

Inasmuch as the mainly German-oriented theology of the Old Testament was bound up with a history of ancient Israel that was really supposed to have happened, this theology would be in dire straits if this history had never happened or had "collapsed" (as expressed by the North American scholar Leo G. Perdue, although Perdue's idea of the collapse of history may be different from this author's).[1] Perdue writes about the collapse of history from a postmodern rejection of the historical referent behind the text. This writer talks about the collapse of history as the loss of connection between the biblical narrative and real history. The result is that theology will be left suspended in the air without an anchor in the real world. Why should we speculate about the historical development of the concept of covenant in the Old Testament as a reflection of the development of covenant theology in ancient Israel, if a covenant was never concluded between God and Israel at Mount Sinai?

---

1. Perdue's idea of the collapse of history and its consequences will be discussed in the following chapter.

299

I have already described in which way the theologian's dependence on real history that is supposed to be virtually identical with written historical narrative represented a series of mistakes, one of the more important being the change in the early Romantic period of the general concept of history. Because scholars of that age created this new understanding of history and at the same time forgot the previously prevailing notion of the Enlightenment, they never understood the real intentions of Gabler's project. As a consequence, and because of the next century's intensive historical investigations, theology ended up with an Old Testament and a real history which were increasingly difficult to harmonize into only one story. In the end, the Old Testament had to leave theology to itself.

Old Testament scholars of the last two centuries invested enormous energy in the study of the history of ancient Israel. They only helped to sharpen the crisis, as the gulf between real history and biblical story continued to widen. Many Old Testament scholars tried in vain to stop this development. Instead of accepting modern historical research, they used the method of the ostrich and argued that nothing had happened that damaged in a serious way the impression of ancient Israel found on the pages of the Old Testament. For too long scholars maintained that the history of ancient Israel and the story of biblical Israel in the Old Testament were more or less identical, as far as the big picture was concerned. We only need accept the biblical story as real history. For many years scholars have tried to convince the laity that there is no danger. The Bible's story and real history are the same. They did not see that they were building a palace on sand. Real history, following its own rules, would sooner or later break down the edifice, and the consequence could well be that the laity would simply regard the Old Testament as a book of lies.

In the first part of this book I described the progress of historical-critical research from its beginning to its collapse. In an appendix I will return to the subject of history and present a history of the landscape variously known as Palestine, the land of Israel ("Eretz Israel"), and the Holy Land—without the Old Testament. The first version of this appendix was written in 2001. After that the Italian Assyriologist Mario Liverani published his version of a history of "Israel" with the title, translated, *On the Other Side of the Bible.*[2] Liverani's history of Israel consists of two parts, "A Normal History" and "An Invented History." The normal history can be identified with the concept of "real history" used here, while the invented history is the biblical history. I shall return to Liverani's history in the last chapter.

When Perdue writes about the collapse of history, he may be speaking prematurely. The rationalistic paraphrase of biblical narrative, morphing it into real history, may be dead or ought to be a thing of the past. This does not mean that the subject of history is taboo to biblical scholars. It is, however, mandatory that students of the Old Testament follow methodologies that are generally acceptable to the discipline of general history. It is important, as pointed out by Liv-

---

2. cf. 282–83.

erani (and this writer), that we distinguish between history and story, between real history and the biblical story. There is a vast and irreconcilable gap between these two. Because the reconstructed (paraphrased) story of the Bible has collapsed as real history, it does not imply a collapse of the biblical story. The collapse involves Old Testament scholars' *assertion* that there exists a correspondence between real history and invented story.

It was the argument of the previous chapter that the formerly dominant German theological tradition regarded Old Testament theology as narrowly linked to other sectors of German Old Testament scholarship, including both history and the history of tradition. Two German scholars from this period stand out, Abrecht Alt (1883–1956) and his student Martin Noth (1902–68). Among North American theologians they were often regarded as radicals, even nihilists—the "minimalists" of that time—but they created the foundation for theologies not only of the caliber of von Rad's and Walter Eichrodt's, but also for all ensuing theologies in the German tradition. It is not uncommon today to hear German colleagues "whisper": "they were *die großen Hypothesesmacher*" (the great inventors of hypotheses), because they used the hypothesis as a heuristic tool to establish the connection between the theology of the Old Testament understood to represent Israelite religion and real history. It is absolutely true that these scholars were exceptionally skillful in their endeavor to formulate great hypotheses in order to construct the house of cards of classical historical-critical scholarship.

This is said without disrespect for these scholars. It is, however, important to stress this to an audience of North American scholars, whose "ancestors" made condescending remarks about their German colleagues. Both the German and North American scholars dominated by Albright followed the same lead. The real difference was the fact that at least sometimes the German scholars succeeded in liberating their ideas from the embrace of the biblical story. North American scholars almost never forgot their biblical background. It is an eye-opening fact that many students of the disciples of Albright have virtually joined the German school and express ideas originating from the pen of Alt and Noth.

Who had the best understanding of the problem, Alt and his students or Albright and his students? Albright entertained the most precise understanding of the problems involved. The history of ancient Israel as reconstructed by historical-critical scholarship is truly a house of cards. If one withdraws one single card from the edifice, the whole construction tumbles down. No history is left. This is the reason why Albright and his followers so avidly persecuted all attempts at "revisionism"—another word used for dissenting colleagues used at present of the "minimalists."[3] Alt and Noth were of the conviction that the building would remain standing, although some elements were unreliable. In this connection von Rad's theology was perceived to be liberating among his students. In spite of historical analysis which pointed in another direction, they were able to keep the

---

3. The true impact of the word *revisionist* has to do with its meaning within general history where it is used about historians like the notorious David Irving, declaiming the reality of the Holocaust.

version of this history as preserved by the Old Testament, understood to be the recounting of believing people of their own history.

The changes occurred where the story of ancient Israel and the real history of ancient Palestine diverged. First, scholars had to give up the idea of a patriarchal age. The separation of the patriarchs from real history began two hundred years ago in a German context and became acute in the work of Julius Wellhausen. Neither Alt nor Noth reckoned the patriarchs to be historical persons, and accordingly they did not see the promise to the patriarchs in Genesis as a fundamental part of patriarchal religion, which they reconstructed as the religion of the fathers, that is, as something belonging to a cultural stage represented by the patriarchal narratives.[4]

The attacks from Albright and his disciples soon followed, and they were very precise, because Albright understood that this did not involve the patriarchs alone, but the whole subject of Old Testament theology—which in a North American context was the same as the religion of ancient Israel. When Thomas L. Thompson more than thirty years ago attacked Albright's defense of the historicity of the patriarchs and showed how Albright wavered in his defense of the historical part of that tradition,[5] he was ostracized by North American divinity schools. However, the impact of Thompson's study was the way he showed Albright to have changed like a chameleon, that is, he presupposed that the patriarchs were historical persons and changed his mind every time his previous arguments became obsolete.

When we talk about the collapse of history, its representatives in the North American school come first. The arguments in favor of the basic historicity of the biblical story as proposed by North American theologians did not survive the onslaught of new arguments and evidence pointing in a different direction. It is of course possible to deny that anything happened, but at a certain moment the arguments against the historical content of the biblical narrative demolished the whole structure. It is normal in this world to see such a collapse followed by total disbelief. It is also normal that previously historically oriented Old Testament scholars, like an endangered species, tried to escape from the collapse by looking for alternatives.

Within Old Testament scholarship few will subscribe today to the ideas of Albright about the early history of Israel. Exceptions would be theologians of a very conservative orientation, who curiously consider Albright a liberal, which he was not. However, when it comes to the evangelical subculture of scholarship, nothing would induce it to change its mind.

---

4. See Albrecht Alt, "Der Gott der Väter" (1929), in *Kleine Schriften zur Geschichte Israels* (Munich: Beck, 1953), 1:1–78; ET, "The God of the Fathers," in *Essays on Old Testament History and Religion* (Oxford: Blackwell, 1966), 1–77.

5. Thomas L. Thompson, *The Historicity of the Patriarchal Narratives: The Quest for the Historical Abraham*, BZAW 133 (Berlin: De Gruyter, 1974). It is a revelatory fact that the first North American edition of this work did not appear as a reprint until 2002 (Harrisburg, PA: Trinity Press International).

In summary, many modern scholars see the history of Israel as narrated by the authors of the Old Testament's historical literature as collapsed, at least in parts. The history was never identical with the story. Many will therefore be of the conviction that Gabler's project is impossible. We have no history to play with. It is another matter altogether that the misery has been caused mostly by an anachronistic reading of Gabler.

How does scholarship react to this belatedly recognized misreading that created so many historical problems for theologians? There are as many different ways of answering the question as there have been different reactions, some of which will be the subject of the remainder of this chapter and the following chapter.

A typical human reaction when something happens with which we do not agree is to pretend that nothing has happened. The best defense would of course be a counterattack. However, if such an operation is impossible because the opponent (and his arguments) is too strong, Old Testament scholarship sometimes displays a strange kind of amnesia.

Fifteen years ago my teacher Professor Eduard Nielsen warned me that the members of the Copenhagen School would end up being forgotten like the French scholar Maurice Vernes, who at the end of the nineteenth century published a thesis claiming that the Old Testament was a Hellenistic book.[6] After the respected Danish scholar Frantz Buhl (many will know him for his edition of Gesenius's dictionary) had likened Vernes's thesis to a shot from a pistol—"The Old Testament came out of the Hellenistic Period like a shot from a pistol"—nobody paid any attention to Vernes and his theories.[7] The expected reaction among biblical scholars when confronted by unpleasant ideas and discoveries is simply to ignore radicals. We will never enter into a discussion with them. The religious viewpoint is normally of a rather traditional mood, and there is for that reason no cause to fear that really new ideas will have a chance among the laity, if only the university theologians shut up. Excommunication is unnecessarily dramatic, because it creates interest about the person excommunicated, as the public realized when the Scottish Old Testament scholar William Robertson Smith (1846–94) was removed from his posts within the church because of his exegetical ideas. Today the main reason why Robertson Smith is still known is not because of what he wrote but because of what other people did to him. It is an ironic fact that something similar happened to Frantz Buhl, who was considered too liberal for the chair at the theological faculty in Copenhagen. He served as professor of Semitics for many years and became the teacher of Johannes Pedersen, who became the teacher of Eduard Nielsen, this author's teacher.

---

6. Eduard Nielsen, "En hellenistisk bog?" *Dansk Teologisk Tidsskrift* 55 (1992): 161–74. See Maurice Vernes, *Précis d'histoire juive depuis les origines jusqu'à l'époque persane (V^e siecle avant J.-C.)* (Paris: Librairie Hachette et Ci^e, 1889).

7. Frantz Buhl, *Det Israelitiske Folks Historie* (6th ed., Copenhagen: Gyldendal, 1922), 12.

If we do not use the tactics of the ostrich, there are still two ways out of the problem. We can choose to follow the mainstream, or we can fight against it. If we follow the mainstream, it will be because we realize that the collapse of history opens something new worth exploring. We will soon return to those who saw the collapse of history as a source of inspiration and a possibility for creating a totally new universe of biblical studies. Here we will study the other response and see how scholars who were fighting for the old historical paradigm decided to act.

The foundation of historically oriented theology is the doctrine that God acts in history. The precondition is that there is a history within which God can act. Behind this rather naive argumentation we find many of the problems for modern theology that have to do with the change of the concept of history in the Romantic period. The change led to a change of mind also among the laity, who became principally historically oriented. The most important criterion—and one often heard even today—is, is this true or false? Translated into historical terms, it means, did it really happen? Now applied to the "truth" of the Bible (and truth in quotation marks, because of the many meanings of this concept in the modern world) it meant, did it really happen as written in the Bible? When the Bible has something to say, it must have happened in order to be "truth."

SALVATION HISTORY AND HISTORY

More than twenty years ago John Strange, a senior lecturer at the University of Copenhagen, published a study, "Salvation History and History," in a Danish theological journal.[8] Strange, a biblical scholar who had been concentrating on archaeology, that is, material subjects, had became acquainted with so-called synchronic readings of the Bible in studies by the British social anthropologist Edmund Leach (1910–89) and the Canadian literary critic Northrop Frye (1912–91), who preferred to read biblical narrative as mythology rather than history.

If the Bible includes mythological narratives it means—to quote Strange— that the Bible has no more to do with salvation than, say, the fairy tales of the Grimm brothers or Tolkien's *The Lord of the Rings*. If something said to have happened according to the Bible never happened, how important can it be? What will become of Christianity if there was no crucifixion and no resurrection?

Strange claims that there must be a relationship between the biblical history— in his eyes salvation history—and real history. Otherwise, the narrative carries no weight, or we end up in a situation with a "double truth," as found in dialectical theology postulating that the Bible is the word of God. In Strange's words, "One

---

8. John Strange, "Frelseshistorie og historie. Et synspunkt på bibelsk teologi," *Dansk Teologisk Tidsskrift* 48 (1985): 225–37. It was translated into German as "Heilsgeschichte und Geschichte. Ein Aspekt der biblischen Theologie," *SJOT* 2 (1989): 100–113. In its German version it was followed by a short discussion between Strange and Niels Peter Lemche.

will look right through the historical into the spirit of the Bible, which is the eternal spirit."

Strange stresses (with a certain correctness) that it is impossible, if one is an honest person, to read the Bible *kata sarka*, that is, historical-critically, and, simultaneously, *kata pneuma*, that is, with theological or spiritual lenses. An analysis of the narrative about King David, for example, of the story of his transference of the royal sanctuary to Jerusalem (2 Sam. 6) must be a historical-critical analysis or a synchronic reading which focuses on the text as literature and theology. There must be symmetry between salvation history and real history, or we end up with a *sacrificium intellectum*.

As a consequence of the understanding of real history as salvation history, there is no biblical theology understood as a systematic discipline. Biblical theology is the history of religion and general history.

THEOLOGY OR HISTORY OF RELIGION

The German Old Testament scholar Rainer Albertz has, from time to time, expressed ideas similar to the proposal set forth by Strange. This is interesting, because Albertz is a student of von Rad and especially of Claus Westermann. In spite of this heritage, Albertz proposes to exchange the theology of the Old Testament for the history of Israelite religion.[9] In his article Albertz lists a series of problems relating to traditional theologies of the Old Testament:

1. There are too many and too diversified theologies around. Each author is too occupied with his own subjective ideas.
2. What is the meaning of "theology of the Old Testament"? Is it about the contribution of the Old Testament to theology, that is, a subjective genitive, or is it about the way we read the Old Testament as a book of theology, that is, an objective genitive?
3. What is the context of interpretation? Do we perceive the Old Testament as an old book or a contemporary book?
4. The concept of theology is decisive, because it is this concept that demands a systematic arrangement of a theology of the Old Testament. According to Albertz, the theologies of Kaiser, Preuß, and Gunneweg are close to being history of religions.
5. Systematic theology demands a focus in the analysis of the Old Testament that leads to a narrowing of perspective.

---

9. Rainer Albertz, "Religionsgeschichte Israels statt Theologie des Alten Testaments! Plädoyer für eine forschungsgeschichtliche Umorientierung," in *Jahrbuch für Biblische Theologie* 10: *Religionsgeschichte Israels oder Theologie des Alten Testaments?* (Neukirchen: Neukirchener Verlag, 1995), 3–24.

6. The concept of theology in the Western world leads to a reduction of the spiritual and ideological content of the Old Testament.
7. The theological demands of the Old Testament result in an emphasis on the unique character of the religion in the Old Testament compared to other Near Eastern religions.
8. When the Old Testament is reduced to a side discipline of New Testament studies, it will be read as a Christian book.

Albertz also lists a series of advantages if we replace Old Testament theology with the history of Israelite religion:

1. Although the history of the religion of Israel is also a subjective enterprise, we should be able to control this subjectivism.
2. There is a clearly defined method, the historical one.
3. This will lead to the correct placement of Israelite religion within the world to which it belonged.
4. The history of Israelite religion follows a clear diachronic pattern, the history of Israel.
5. There is room for all kinds of divergences as seen from a synchronic as well as a diachronic perspective.
6. There is room for comparison between the religion of Israel and Near Eastern religion in general.

Albertz's proposal (and Strange's) may sound attractive. Because of his historical point of departure, Strange must stress the importance of the salvation history identified as the biblical narrative concerning salvation. If this story has little to do with real history, we must make a choice between biblical story and real history. Albertz's language is less bound by theological phraseology, and so he will not talk about salvation history. He will only change focus to the religion as described by the Old Testament, liberated from the Christian dogmatic censure normally found active in theologies of the Old Testament. We might think that Albertz—and that is probably also his opinion—has taken up again Gabler's project of 1787 by drawing a line in the sand between historical and dogmatic studies. When Albertz speaks in favor of an Old Testament history of religion without dogmatic interference, he definitely follows the line of Gabler, or so he believes. We saw, however, that he, as well as many other biblical scholars, may have misread Gabler, because he has a different idea of history, an idea that came into being after Gabler's famous lecture and therefore was not present in Gabler's original program.

Albertz draws a conclusion from the unholy mixing of theology and history in almost every theology of the Old Testament that appeared during the twentieth century. He correctly sees how confusing this mixture really is, both when it comes to the concept of history and in its mixing of different categories of argumentation. It is, however, somewhat frustrating that he uses the same mix as a legitimization of his own project, arguing that if Kaiser, Preuß, and Gunneweg mix theology with the history of religion, he is allowed to take things one step further and replace theology with the history of religion.

His list of problems involved for traditional theologies of the Old Testament includes several important observations. It is important to note the problematic character of a Christian reading of a document dating from before Christianity, that is, the Old Testament. The concept of theology involved is not only "Christian"; it is white, male, and European. The theological debate about the status of the Old Testament has until recently been the prerogative of the white European (including the white North American) male theologian. The male has nowadays been supplemented (if not replaced) by the female. Furthermore, our classical concept of theology is predominantly Protestant and extremely narrow, as a consequence of the settlement of dialectical theology with natural theology, claiming that God speaks to us only in his revelation (with or without the Old Testament—we will return to this subject later).

Even in a European context, where "European" indicates a special form of "ethnic" biblical exegesis that in the future will have to compete with other forms of ethnic exegesis, there is reason to revise our concept of theology, leaving room for a theology with many (European) faces. James Barr pleaded for the return of natural theology. Otherwise we have little use for the Old Testament or, for that matter, the first part of our creed. Othmar Keel and Silvia Schroer (both of Catholic theological orientation) have clearly shown in their recent book *Creation: Biblical Theology in the Context of Ancient Near Eastern Religion* another *new* theology.[10] In their book on creation, they not only discuss the way the Bible speaks about creation, but they also stress the connection between biblical and ancient Near Eastern concepts of creation. They include not only cosmological comparisons but also ontological notions of the place and tasks of human beings in a world created by God. Their references to the ancient Near East do not involve only external manifestations but also its notion of the divine and of humanity.

A study like that by Keel and Schroer on creation lives up to the demand made by Albertz for a new form of Old Testament "theology," and they show how important it is to introduce new and revised ideas about theology at this time. It is impossible to proceed with any discussion of the merits of previous contributions to the theology of the Old Testament without such a rethinking of our concepts. It is in this context suggested that the interested study the contributions on this to the von Rad-100-year symposium in 2001, published by Manfred Oeming, Konrad Schmid, and Andreas Schüle.[11] Only a few years ago, such a title would have been

---

10. Othmar Keel and Silvia Schroer, *Creation: Biblical Theology in the Context of Ancient Near Eastern Religion* (Winona Lake, IN: Eisenbrauns, 2007), translated from *Schöpfung: Biblische Theologien im Kontext altorientalischer Religionen* (Göttingen: Vandenhoeck & Ruprecht/Freiburg: Universitätsverlag, 2002).

11. Manfred Oeming, Konrad Schmid, and Andreas Schüle, eds., *Theologie in Israel und in den Nachbarkulturen*, Altes Testament und Moderne 9 (Münster: Lit Verlag, 2004).

impossible. Here we may mention the contribution of Andreas Schüle (himself a systematic theologian) to a reorientation of the concept of theology:

> Moreover theology belongs to the absolutely elementary results of spiritual activity: Human beings perceive the world in which they live not only as it is but they form an image of it, interpret it and act accordingly. So far the *practically oriented interpretation* of the world on this level must be the primary task of theology. The specific *theological* element in contrast to other kinds of interpretation consists of the fact that the understanding of the world presupposes the existence of the gods and their acts in this world.[12]

Here is clearly an opening to a very broad definition of the concept of theology, allowing us to live in a multicultural world where no part is in possession of the "truth." Here there is room for many images of God, and there is space for religions other than the Christian one. This does not say that we cannot favor our own religion and claim that we are right—when have we seen a Christian religious faction that did not consider itself as possessing the "truth"?—but we are right in the same way as a Jew or a Muslim is right. We will have to accept that as human beings we are interpreting the world in which we live. This is our interpretation, and it is first and foremost of importance for us. If other people agree with us, so much the better. If they disagree, we will have to accept that their interpretation is different from ours but still legitimate. As already mentioned, it is no longer possible to burn one's opponents at the stake.

The Christianity we meet in the rather naive form denoted "evangelicals," but certainly also among theologians belonging to a different school like dialectical theology, will disagree, because of God's revelation in Christ. This is as it must be, and it is normal that religious people entertain such convictions. As a young student heading the council of students, I was invited to a dinner given by the faculty of theology in Copenhagen for one of its professors who was retiring. This professor's colleague made a speech claiming that the difference between him and his retiring colleague was that he had *a* theology while his colleague had *the* correct theology. Too many are in possession of the correct theology, an attitude that may prevent a fruitful exchange of ideas and interpretations. Happily, the general development of the modern multicultural society, at least in Europe, prevents an exclusive idea of the correctness of only one religion from surviving.

I will end this chapter with three examples that in very different ways illustrate the way Albertz's program may be a blessing to theology.

---

12. "Vielmehr gehört Theologie zu den ganz elementaren Vollzügen geistiger Tätigkeit: Menschen finden die Welt, in der sie leben, nicht einfach vor, sondern machen sich ein Bild von ihr, deuten sie und bringen ihr Handeln in Einklang damit. Insofern ist auf dieser Ebene die *Praxisbezogene Deutung* der Welt die grundlegende Aufgabe von Theologie. Was sie als spezifisch *theologisch* von anderen Deutungen unterscheidet, ist die Tatsache, dass sie das Verständnis der Welt wesentlich von der Präsenz der Götter und deren Handels her erschließt" (Andreas Schüle, "Deutung, Reflexion, Überlieferung. Die Ebenen eines konzeptionellen Theologiebegriffs. Zugleich eine Erinnerung an Gerhard von Rads Verständnis alttestamentlicher Theologie," in Oeming, Schmid, and Schüle, *Theologie,* 1–16, 2–3).

RAINER ALBERTZ AND THE HISTORY
OF ISRAELITE RELIGION

My first example is Albertz's major opus, his *A History of Israelite Religion in the Old Testament Period*.[13] His program is quite simply stated: the history of Israel's religion is the focus of attention, instead of the theology of the Old Testament.

Albertz follows his own program to the letter. But his history of Israelite religion is based on historical-critical scholarship, and there is no excuse for following this old methodology. The history of religion as reconstructed by Albertz is de facto a history of Israel, where the history of religion and the real, reconstructed history are interwoven. Albertz's reconstruction of the general history strictly follows the German tradition—with one addition. Albertz grew up with the concept of social history, which was a dominant trend within general historical studies at the end of the twentieth century. Previous German scholarship had mainly ignored it, although it is commonplace today.

Because of his sociological approach, Albertz is able to retain the patriarchal era as a historical period. He has no intention of bringing Abraham, Isaac, and Jacob back to life, but it is possible for their religion, considered to be the oldest Israelite one, the religion of the fathers, to be reconstructed. The same procedure may be followed in the study of subsequent parts of Israel's history. A sociological analysis of Israelite society at different times will disclose information about its religion.

It is remarkable how traditional historical-critical scholarship dominates Albertz's history of Israelite religion. It is hardly the case that he uses his sociological history to formulate new ideas about the history of Israel. In a manner not very different from, for example, Preuß's, he builds on a very traditional view of Israelite history and has his history of religion follow a layout that might have been constructed fifty years ago. We may ask why Albertz proposed to replace theology with the history of religion. His history of religion has the same historical-critical foundation as German theologies of the Old Testament published during the twentieth century. Because of this, Albertz's project is in trouble the moment his historical construction breaks down. Or perhaps we should say that such a collapse would liberate his project from the invented history of the Old Testament and let it loose to develop into something really important.

Albertz does not pay attention to such developments but goes up to the Hellenistic period. He sees no reason to continue in order to establish any link between the Old and the New Testaments. There is reason to question whether Albertz's program would really satisfy a "salvation historian" like Strange. The history of religion, understood as a secular scholarly enterprise, has little to do with theology. It does not desire to "prove" anything. Although general historians have

---

13. Rainer Albertz, *A History of Israelite Religion in the Old Testament Period*, 2 vols. (Louisville: Westminster John Knox, 1994); German original: *Religionsgeschichte Israels in alttestamentlicher Zeit*, 2 vols., Grundrisse zum Alten Testament 8/1–2 (Göttingen: Vandenhoeck & Ruprecht, 1992).

tried to establish the "laws" of historical development, they do not plead any kind of determinism as far as this development is concerned. Humans belong to an unruly race, which will always be looking for its own individualistic and subjective ways. If Alexander had died young, the course of Near Eastern history would have been very different. The fact that Alexander survived at a time when up to 90 percent of children died was a decisive factor in a historical development that in itself will always be unpredictable.

When confronted with a theology like von Rad's, the theologian will argue that there is no need for Albertz's proposal. If we speak about salvation history, it must be teleological. It must be directed at something specific. It cannot be accidental. History has a reason and needs a *prima causa*, which is God. God is an assertion, an assertion of no use to general history, and it is immaterial whether the historian believes in the presence of a divine power.

ERHARD GERSTENBERGER AND THE THEOLOGIES

It may be that this last issue governed another contemporary German biblical scholar, Erhard Gerstenberger, when he published his *Theologies of the Old Testament*. He is definitely at odds with the German tradition. The problem of salvation history is a nonissue to Gerstenberger. He, very much like Albertz, is interested in social history, and so he writes a social history and relates theology to this history.

In his social history Gerstenberger moves between the different social strata, between the religions of the family, the clan, the village, the tribe or tribal league, and proceeds via the theology of the period of the kings to the theology of the exilic and postexilic "believing society." In contrast to Albertz, Gerstenberger includes an interesting chapter in which the theologies of the Old Testament are placed in a contemporary perspective. The last part of the book consists of an appendix: "God in Our Time."

If we compare Albertz's and Gerstenberger's attitude to Gabler's original project, it has already been pointed out that Albertz does not consider it relevant at all. It is more difficult to say what the attitude of Gerstenberger to Gabler really is, although it might well be that his proposal of an Old Testament theology(ies) is closest to Gabler's idea, in spite of the concluding part of Gerstenberger's theology, which places his "theologies" in a context far more comprehensive than just the world of the Old Testament.

HANS JØRGEN LUNDAGER JENSEN AND THE RELIGION OF THE OLD TESTAMENT

My third example of a theology of the Old Testament or history of Israelite religion building on the collapse of history will be by a scholar unknown outside of a Scandinavian context, the Danish historian of religion Hans Jørgen Lundager Jensen's *Old Testament Religion*.[14] As early as the preface, Lundager Jensen exposes a definite lack of interest in historical issues in the narrow sense of the word. This is the reason for the title of his book, *Old Testament Religion* instead of *A History of the Religion of Israel*. His interest is in themes and structures. It is important, as it was with Albertz, that the religion of the Old Testament is not identical with the Israelite religion as maintained by previous scholarship, but a religion "related to the religions of the ancient Near East." Lundager Jensen presents his interpretation of Old Testament religion by arguing that it is different from other descriptions of this religion because of his emphasis on subjects neglected by other scholars (while he neglects many popular themes found in histories of religion written by other scholars: the historical part).

History is not totally neglected in this book, although history is found in a chapter with the title "Narratives," and qualifies as "Bible history." The narratives dominate at the expense of history. History alias the story is not the main interest of the book, which is chiefly concerned with basic theological concepts like the divine, creation, blessing and curse, death, and wisdom.

Lundager Jensen's thesis is that the religion of the Old Testament has as its center the preservation of the world and the blessed life of human beings. Rituals and their place in the cult are therefore accorded a dominant role, as is—in contrast to almost every theology of the Old Testament—the priestly theology. Prophecy of course also has its place in this study of Old Testament religion.

It is likely that this way of handling the problem of religion in the Old Testament comes closer to the concept of an independent study of the stories of the Old Testament than any previous book on the subject. Whether Lundager Jensen is right in everything he writes about the religion (or theology) of the Old Testament is a different matter. He prefers to work with the semiotic structures of the transmitted texts and considers these structures as decisive for the meaning of these stories. It is, however, a question whether the author is so bound up in his interest in structures and their relation to the subject of the preservation of the world that he neglects the scarlet thread running through the story of the Old Testament from creation to exile and further on. The motif of "Israel's salvation," understood as a narrative theme, may be too important to be neglected.

Another problem with the studies of Albertz, Gerstenberger, and Lundager Jensen has to do with the intended reader of the stories relating to the religion of the Old Testament/ancient Israel. Who wrote these stories and for whom? This question is even more interesting when we move to canonical theology. When Lundager Jensen claims that the religion of the Old Testament is about the good life, we have to define what a good life really is and for whom. Lundager Jensen sees the good life as the safe life in one's own country. Is this really the subject of

---

14. Hans Jørgen Lundager Jensen, *Gammeltestamentlig Religion* (Frederiksberg: Anis, 1998). It is a pity that this valuable book, which has for the last decade served as a textbook at our Danish theological faculties, has not yet been translated into English.

biblical narrative? Perhaps it is more about how this good life was lost and why it was lost.

The societal stratum that was able to read and write was very narrow, most likely not even 5 percent of the total population. Any written religion is the religion of the elite. In that sense, Old Testament religion is the religion of an elite.

Any history of religion or theology of the Old Testament that neglects this and describes this religion or theology as the theology of the majority distorts how religion really was. Any socially oriented scholar—including Albertz—knows this.[15] It is a kind of self-deception if one reads about the religion of the Old Testament and believes this to represent the beliefs of ancient Israel. The text as we have it represents the theological outlook of the *Jewish* elite; it is *their* narratives about God, the past, their present, and the future. Popular religion is not found among the pages of the Old Testament; evidence about it comes from archaeology, and that is a different story.

---

15. Evidence of this is Albertz's previous volume, *Persönliche Frömmigkeit und Offizielle Religion* (1978; reprint, Atlanta: SBL, 2006).

Chapter 14

Alternative Theologies

The Collapse of History:
The Theological Consequences II

HISTORY AND ITS COLLAPSE

There are two sides of the idea of the collapse of history. On one side, traditional historical-critical scholarship is in trouble when the connection between the story of the Bible and real history breaks down, because not much of the story of the Bible has survived the onslaught of historical-critical investigation; not much remains that can be the subject of a process of falsification. On the other side is a hermeneutical change: history has collapsed because it no longer has any *normative* importance.

The modern concept of history arose at the same time as the nation-states of Europe came into being, about 1800. History writing is older that that date, but in the form of chronicles, collections of historical anecdotes, tales, and stories, without any interest in the development of critical procedures leading to the establishment of modern historiography.

The need for writing history became even more relevant when the old symbols were crushed in the wake of the French Revolution. Before 1789 it would be inaccurate to talk about nation-states in Europe. There existed many kingdoms and principalities ruled by one person and one family, almost like a patronage system, with the king or queen as the patron and everyone else as his or her clients.

The ruler owned the country, and when territories were gained or lost, it was an exchange between rulers. One would increase his or her territory, the other lose a part.

As the notion of "the people" or "the nation" developed through the nineteenth century—paving the way for the cruel wars of the twentieth century—authorities turned to the historians to create national histories in order to prove the antiquity of the new nations. It mattered little in what form and under what circumstances this history was invented. The task of the historians was clear, and they lived up to expectations.

In this way history became an extension of nationalism. Then came the idea that each nation is unique. A nation needed a history of its own, and it was supposed to be greater and nobler and have a higher morality than any other nation. In this connection the German writer Moritz Arndt (1769–1860) became famous (or infamous) because of his insistence on the superiority of the German nation. We are here close to the later idea of the supreme Aryan race. Mixed with a considerable amount of anti-Semitism in Arndt's writings, this ideology turned into a deadly cocktail for classical European civilization.

Now relations with other nations became problematic. Already a problem in Europe, nationalism in the wider perspective turned into Eurocentrism. European ideas of nationality turned into an imperialistic enterprise that in the course of the nineteenth century colonized most of the known world.

We will not consider the many consequences of this intellectual development but concentrate on one element, which has already been mentioned earlier, *orientalism*, an expression coined by the late Edward Said in order to characterize the image created by Europeans of the outside world, which was understood to be inferior to European civilization.

In a discussion of concepts like nationalism and ethnicity, the "other" plays a decisive role. Fredrik Barth's definition of ethnicity as a social way to organize cultural difference must be remembered. There must be at least two different ethnicities present. The concept of orientalism provides this "other," making it possible for the European to make a distinction between himself and the surrounding world.

During the process of colonization, the European met many "Orientals," people of a different culture. Because Europeans were convinced of the superiority of their own civilization, the European was bound to consider other people as inferior or, in the worst case, dispensable. The fact that most people from other parts of the world were not Christians also prevented the European from accepting foreign habits and ideas.

THE BIBLE AS A TEXTBOOK FOR COLONIALISM

As a result of this situation, the Bible and especially the Old Testament gained in importance, because it has a story to tell that is our story, the history of a Christian nation—or so it was believed. Because we are the representatives of the new Israel, the Bible tells *our* history, not the history of the Jews, who are the representatives of old and rejected Israel.

This created a change probably similar to the one that in ancient times separated the members of the Jewish Diaspora and the local inhabitants of Palestine. We can read more about this separation in Ezra and Nehemiah. The real Israelites were forced into exile. The land was empty for "seventy" years. From a logical point of view, this implies that the population present in the land when the Jews returned from exile (or the Diaspora) represented foreign intruders. This population should be chased away (best to kill them, with the book of Joshua in one hand and the sword in the other).

The modern "translation" of this ideology formed the intellectual background of the Jewish return to Palestine in the nineteenth and twentieth centuries, now with the sword replaced by a gun. The Arab population, whether Muslim or Christian, had to be viewed as foreign intruders without any right to the country. The Bible turned into a tool for suppressing other people and for ethnic cleansing, as expressed by no less than Albright:

> It was fortunate for the future of monotheism that the Israelites of the Conquest were a wild folk, endowed with primitive energy and ruthless will to exist, since the resulting decimation of the Canaanites prevented the complete fusion of the two kindred folk which would almost inevitably have depressed Yahwistic standards to the point where recovery was impossible. Thus the Canaanites, with their orgiastic nature worship, their cult of fertility in the form of serpent symbols and sensuous nudity, and their gross mythology, were replaced by Israel, with its pastoral simplicity and purity of life, its lofty monotheism, and its severe code of ethics.[1]

Following this, Albright compares the Israelite conquest of Canaan and the genocide that followed on the heels of the Roman destruction of the Punic—originally "Canaanite"—civilization, carried out by a people "whose stern code of morals and singularly elevated paganism remind us in many ways of early Israel."[2]

The story of the "morally supreme people" that defeats and exterminates another, inferior nation was part of the ideological baggage of European imperialists and colonizers throughout the nineteenth century. It was also carried by European Jews who, since the first part of the nineteenth century, in ever increasing numbers, migrated to Palestine to inherit their ancestral country, and it was also popular among the many who fled from the European Holocaust to Palestine to create a state of their own in that place. In this modern version of the biblical narrative, the Palestinian population turned into "Canaanites," supposed to be morally inferior to the Jews, and of course the Arabs were never considered

---

1. William Foxwell Albright, *From the Stone Age to Christianity* (New York: Doubleday, 1940; 2nd ed., 1957), 281.
2. Ibid.

their equals technologically or culturally. The Bible was the instrument used to suppress the enemy.[3]

This development did not begin with Romanticism and its new concept of history, but has been present, some might say, since the first impulses toward evangelization inculcated in early readers of the New Testament and their descendants ever since. The conquistadores, the Spanish conquerors of Latin America, followed biblical principles in their gruesome treatment of the local Indians, and very successfully at that, as can be seen from the simple fact that the language of the region became (with the important exception of Brazil) Spanish. The Christian church became totally dominant in this part of the world.

The Anglo-Saxon colonization of North America was about as successful as the Spanish conquest of Central America and South America. Although a few French-speaking enclaves in Louisiana and Canada continued to exist, English became totally dominant, and a Protestant European white elite and its ethics have for centuries dominated North American society. The original population was forced to make a choice between assimilation and extinction.

Many other parts of the world experienced a similar kind of Europeanization. The European colonists found in the Bible legitimation for their acts. Since they belonged to the new Israel, everyone else must belong to old Israel. The option for all non-Europeans was simply to join the Europeans or perish! A chapter like Joshua 9 played an important role in this context. This chapter has as its subject the story of a group of Canaanites that concluded a covenant with Israel and were allowed to live, although in the role of servants to the temple. They were allowed to live but could never rise to important positions within Israelite society. The message to subdued people in more recent times was this: Do as these Canaanites and convert, and we will certainly allow you to live. Do not count on being our equals. You are allowed to live, but on our terms.

Imperialism met serious opposition only in parts of Asia, where they were confronted by well-organized political structures like that of China, which boasted of a history much older than the European one. The Chinese have often been said to despise European culture, which is about 2,000 years old, while their own is more than 5,000 years old. In Asia the only areas colonized by Europeans were on the periphery. Furthermore, Europeanization involved primarily the elite, as was the case, for example, in Indochina. The Japanese chose a different path, remaining more or less immune to European influence, but accepting the technology of the foreigners.

THE BIBLE AND LIBERATION THEOLOGY

"The collapse of history" means, according to some third-world theologians, that the historical narrative in the Old Testament has lost its importance as a legiti-

3. On this role of the Bible see also Keith W. Whitelam, *The Invention of Ancient Israel: The Silencing of Palestinian History* (London: Routledge, 1996), and several publications by the late Michael

mation of European (and North American) colonialism. It is not because they, like many theologians who grew up with historical-critical scholarship, are of the opinion that this history never happened. It is because of the changing attitude toward history as a concept in the postmodern world.[4]

This is not the place to discuss postmodernism as such. Many people can explain this phenomenon better than the present writer. Postmodernism as such is not at issue here. However the postmodern concept of a "privileged" text, as opposed to other nonprivileged texts, is important. For 1,800 years the Bible was the privileged text within Western civilization (and its position within an Orthodox context was not very different). The Bible is the authority, which means that the interpretation of the Bible by Western theologians, whether Catholics or Protestants, created this authority. The church and the state were in alliance from the days of Constantine the Great and formed the background of later Western colonialism and imperialism.

This alliance has broken down today, or so the argument goes. The Bible is no longer *the* authority rising above all other authorities, although it must be admitted that many believing Christians still think so. Although there may be a movement in parts of Western Christianity toward a reinstallation of the Bible to its former position, the Bible has authority only among people who believe so. It is no longer a generally privileged text.

As a consequence, we have seen over the last forty years a series of new orientations within theology benefiting from the fact that the Bible has lost its paramount authority. When this happened, Western civilization also lost its status as the authority among many other traditions formerly considered inferior to it. Now other stories could be told, and new identities of Christians found to replace the former Western identification with the principal players of the biblical narrative, the Israelites.

There are many forms of postcolonial theology. Here we will include only liberation theology in several of its many incarnations: feminist theology, North and South American liberation theology, and postcolonial and ethnic studies in Africa and Asia.[5]

FEMINIST THEOLOGY

When it was decided to include feminist theology under the rubric of liberation theology here, it was for good reason. Common for all sorts of liberation theology

---

Prior, summarized in his *The Bible and Colonialism: A Moral Critique*, The Biblical Seminar 48 (Sheffield: Sheffield Academic Press, 1997).

4. This process has been evaluated by Leo G. Perdue, *The Collapse of History: Reconstructing Old Testament Theology* (Minneapolis: Fortress, 1994). See also John J. Collins, *The Bible after Babel: Historical Criticism in a Postmodern Age* (Grand Rapids: Eerdmans, 2005).

5. Leo G. Perdue, *Reconstructing Old Testament Theology: After the Collapse of History* (Minneapolis: Fortress, 2005), formed the background of this choice of subjects. See also Collins, *The Bible after Babel*, chaps. 3–5, pp. 53–130.

is the liberation of theology from a discourse that is white, male, and European. Supporters of feminist theology believe that traditional exegesis from antiquity to the present has been dominated by men, while the voices of women have generally been silenced or marginalized.

From a historical point of view, this is definitely true and an excellent basis for an alternative theology, although it must also be realized that the male domination of exegesis goes back to the authors of biblical literature, who were men. It was not subsequent exegetes who marginalized the feminine part of humanity; it had already happened when the stories of the Bible were written down. Therefore we are in need of an exegetical instrument able to show how the suppression of women in the biblical literature functions. In this connection Elisabeth Schüssler Fiorenza's idea of *a hermeneutic of suspicion*[6] may be the most serious attempt at creating a method that without sacrificing historical-critical scholarship incorporates modern hermeneutical ideas, including the modern discussion about the relationship between subject (event), text, and reader.

The basic thesis of this theological methodology is that when a text omits the female or reduces it to a shadowy existence as subject—the narrative of Judges 19–20 provides perhaps the best (or worst) example of all in the Old Testament—it is the deliberate choice of the author. A methodical, comparative, and critical analysis of such texts may reveal a pattern that may tell us why the authors react in this way. A text that does not mention women may after all include them "between the lines." Feminist theology may in this way develop into a demonstration of male phobias. What is it that men fear, and why have they excluded women?

From a historical-critical point of view, it is not too difficult to find a reason for the problematic relationship between men and women in biblical texts. A prime example of this is probably the religious changes that occurred in the ancient Near East during the first millennium BCE, when a generally patriarchal monotheistic religion replaced the ancient polytheistic one. In the first millennium, the Near East became largely monotheistic—although in many different forms.[7] Hereafter it never gave up its monotheism. However, monotheism was definitely a male affair in most places. It was dominated by men and by male metaphors about the Divine. The religious language became male. It was probably different in earlier, polytheistic times. Here the Divine world included a multitude of gods and goddesses; even Yahweh had his consort, Asherah, as we know from inscriptions from Palestine from the Iron Age.[8] In Judaism Asherah has been banished. According to the biblical narrative, the preexilic temple of Jerusalem included a whole compartment and a staff placed at the disposal of Asherah (2 Kgs. 23:7); in the second temple she was no more.[9]

---

6. Elisabeth Schüssler Fiorenza, "Toward a Feminist Critical Method," in Elisabeth Schüssler-Fiorenza, *In Memory of Her: A Feminist Theological Reconstruction of Christian Origins* (London: SCM, 1983), 41–60, 64–67.

7. See pp. 253.

8. See pp. 250–51.

9. Among the many books about Asherah, we need mention here only Tilde Binger, *Asherah: Goddesses in Ugarit, Israel and the Old Testament*, JSOTSup 232 (Sheffield: Sheffield Academic Press, 1997),

Everything indicates that the reduced importance of women originated in the second half of the first millennium BCE, and the Hellenization of the east only hastened this process. The Greek attitude to females was—if possible—even more dominated by "macho" ideas than the Near Eastern one. When women in some narratives of the Old Testament still have a say, it is normally women belonging to the elite. This involves royal actresses like Bathsheba in the David narratives, who plays an important role—if not the decisive role—in the election of her son Solomon as king of Israel, and the Tyrian princess and queen of Israel Jezebel, who plays the role of the evil fairy whose acts lead to the fall of the house of Omri. Active women may, however, also include foreign women such as the Kenite woman Jael, who kills one of Israel's enemies with a tent stake (Judg. 4:17–22), and the Moabite woman Ruth, who sleeps with a relative of her dead husband in the field and forces the man to marry her. This foreign origin may also be the case with Tamar in the story in Genesis 38, who might be a Canaanite (although this is not said expressly), and who begets a child with her father-in-law. All three women are considered a blessing to Israel, but they are all foreign women. A nice Israelite girl would never behave in such a way!

If we look for the rehabilitation of women in the Old Testament, we look in vain. Any kind of exegesis desiring to find such a thing will fail, because there is nothing that can change the prevailing biblical concept of women, that is, that they must, because of original sin, submit to the will of their husbands. In the story in Genesis everyone is punished: woman, man, and the serpent. The punishment of the man is as severe as the punishment of the woman, but men do not give birth, and the woman still has to obey her husband.

If the Bible provides any explanation for the assumed inferiority of women, it may be the story of the creation and man and wife in Genesis 2, where the woman comes second and is formed from a rib taken from the man, although this text says something more: that the woman was created because the man needed a companion, an assistant like him. The creation of humankind in Genesis 1 is of little help, because it is here more the creation of the principles of the male and female than the creation of man and woman as living beings. Humanity is, according to Genesis 1, created in the image of God as man *and* woman. Even in the perfect world of Genesis 1, humanity is twofold, male and female.

A feminist theology of liberation will have as its task—and here it is of no consequence whether it belongs to the Western hemisphere or to the third world—to use this hermeneutic of suspicion to the end. By following such a procedure, it will create a forum for a feminist theology that is not interested in just deploring the sad state of affairs in the Bible. Moreover, the procedure must be neutral. It makes little sense after more than 2,000 years to attack the authors of these texts because of their antifeminism and male chauvinism. A more positive way forward is to expose the extent to which male concepts have dominated the view of humanity expressed by the Bible. Gabler, in his pre–historical-critical consciousness,

and Paolo Merlo, *La dea Ašratum—Atiratu—Ašera. Un contributo alla storia della religione semitica del Nord* (Rome: Pontificia Università Lateranense Mursia, 1998).

understood that it was perhaps not a very good idea to accept Paul's ideas about the role of women. His note on this could have been sufficient: the Bible should not dictate to the present age its male-dominated idea of the world. The Bible cannot legitimize the suppression of the female half of humanity. That the Bible includes suppression of this kind is only another example of it being an ancient book with a perspective limited by the sentiments and ideas of the ancient world. When this is fully realized, the way is paved for adjustments. The idea of the position of woman in the Old and New Testaments belongs to the periphery. It has no consequence for modern times.

Feminist theology includes a settlement with a theology dominated by men that has misunderstood its duty to translate the Old Testament into modern theological terms. Feminist theology is not different from the attitude to the Old Testament that has forced us to reject, for example, the ideology of violence included in a book like Joshua. If we as soldiers followed this ideology today, we would soon be seated next to other war criminals at the international court in The Hague; and the excuse that "we just followed orders"—in this case the orders of the Bible—would be of no avail. No sensible person will accept today the suppression of women expressed by the stories of the Old and New Testaments and use them as a guide for modern ethics. It is only evidence of how the Bible is linked to the period that created it. Modern ethics have to liberate itself from the embrace of the Bible; a well-executed feminist theology will tell us this.

LIBERATION THEOLOGY—*STRICTE SENSU*— AND POSTCOLONIAL EXEGESIS

We may follow a similar procedure with any other manifestation of liberation or contextual—or ethnic—theology. Liberation theology had its origins in South America in the 1960s as a local reaction to the dominant Spanish elite and their suppression of minorities, including poor agricultural laborers. It feels a little odd that Leo G. Perdue, in his recent book on Old Testament theology after the collapse of history, almost totally neglects this part of liberation theology and almost exclusively concentrates on its North American exponents,[10] including Spanish-speaking immigrants in the United States. The point of departure for this kind of liberation theology is the story of the exodus in the second book of Moses. The story of the enslavement of the Israelites in Egypt and Yahweh's subsequent liberation of his chosen people is a story about God caring for the poor—by no means a minor subject in the Old Testament. Whether or not this liberation ever happened in real history is of little concern for liberation theologians. After all, liberation theologians have to change the elements of the story. Liberation theologians in South America are addressing the Spanish elite that goes back to the

---

10. There is a short description of South American liberation theology in Perdue, *Reconstructing Old Testament Theology*, 77–80.

time of the conquistadores, while North American theologians turn against the supremacy of the white North American elite of European origin. However, in the story of the exodus, the Israelites are the immigrants suppressed by the local elite, represented by Pharaoh. Somehow everything is turned upside down. The North American use of the story is easy to understand if we identify the Israelites of the exodus story with illegal immigrants from Hispano-America, but in the case of the original North American population of Indian origin, the situation is the same as in South America. In both cases the immigrants are the suppressors. Such historical minutiae are, however, immaterial, as liberation theologians are generally not interested in historical correctness.

Instead of being bothered by historical details, liberation theologians turn to those parts of the Old Testament used as a legitimation of the suppression of the destitute original population or, in the case of North America, the often deplorable situation of immigrants of Hispano-American origin. The moral superiority of the white conqueror as formulated by, for example, Albright (and it should not be forgotten that Albright's parents were missionaries in Chile) is linked to biblical notions about the superiority of the Israelites compared to the Canaanites and the satisfaction of belonging to a superior race (the white) chosen by God. Such sentiments resulted in a suppression that lasted for hundreds of years, although people within the Catholic Church even in the sixteenth century raised their voices against slavery, not believing that it was exactly what God intended by creating humankind.

How are third-world theologians to deal with such an apparent abuse of an ancient text? Our immediate reaction to this situation ought to be anger and contempt. Third-world theologians react by rejecting the "exegesis" of the white male, and ultimately by totally rejecting the theological interpretation of the West. This reaction is understandable and even useful if it is followed at the same time by a political and economic liberation from Western interests—perhaps even a utopia in this globalized world, if globalization means a new way to detach the third world from its role as suppliers to Western economies. In the present situation, little indicates that utopia is near.

It is possible to propose a biblical history that does not follow the usual Western story, pointing at postmodernism and its settlement with the privileged reading of the Bible belonging to the Western world. However, the Western world as it is today has little interest in people in the third world who have a story to tell that is different from the Western one. Such alternative groups will be isolated as long as they only tell a story. If they also try to act, they may potentially be considered terrorists.

The way out is to attack Western tradition where it is weakest, that is, in its understanding of itself, and here the Bible provides excellent material because of the Western world's insistence of building on biblical values. Here there can be no doubt that liberation theologians are right. In its way of handling the Bible, the Western world has made many wrong decisions. One reason the Bible is so difficult to understand for people belonging to the European and North American tradition has to do with the way people of our world read texts, that is, literally and historically. If there is any other meaning, it is not seen. I have already mentioned the possibility of understanding the biblical text in ways other than the literal one. Although the Reformers preferred literal interpretation, they did not totally abolish the allegorical interpretation, neither did they understand the literal reading to be historical and critical. Their exegesis still belonged to the form of exegesis popular among theologians of the Middle Ages. Here the literal reading was the first choice, but it was far from the most important sort of exegesis. Other possible kinds of readings were allegorical, typological, and anagogic. In the case of Luther, we normally speak about the primacy of christological interpretation.

A reading of the exegesis of antiquity, which was far from literal, will find specimens of typological as well as allegorical interpretation, for example, in the Dead Sea Scrolls. Here the prophecies of the Old Testament are without ado considered relevant for the present. And we also have allegorical and especially typological interpretation of the Old Testament in the New.

I addressed the issue of the Western lack of understanding of the biblical text in a lecture given at the University of Stellenbosch in South Africa in 1996, at a conference that discussed the juridical consequences of the breakdown of the apartheid rule.[11] I suggested there that, as a member of the Western elite, the archetypical Western professor of theology will sometimes have little sympathy for the way the Bible is understood by theologians from other parts of the world—including the way biblical writers might have understood their own texts. The idea that these writers and their original readers understood their text in a literal sense is bound up with Western standards and is just one more example of Eurocentricism.

My primary example came from the story of the flood as we have it in the Old Testament and in the epic of Gilgamesh. In the epilogue to the version of the story in Gilgamesh—and as mentioned previously it is almost exactly the same story as narrated by the Old Testament—we find an encounter between the gods, who are not very happy about what has just happened and who are attacking the god who caused the flood, Enlil. In the dialogue here the two gods, Ishtar and Ea, simply call the flood a mistake:

> Ishtar: "Behold, O gods, I shall never forget (the
> significance of) my lapis lazuli necklace,
> I shall remember these times, and I shall never forget.
> Let other gods come to the *surqinnu*-offering
> But let Enlil not come to the *surqinnu*-offering,
> Because he did not consult before imposing the flood,
> And consigned my people to destruction!"
> As soon as Enlil arrived
> He saw the boat. Enlil was furious,
> Filled with anger at the Igigi gods.

11. Published as "Are We Europeans Really Good Readers of Biblical Texts and Interpreters of Biblical History?" *Journal for the Study of North-West Semitic Languages* (Studies Hannes Olivier) 25 (1999): 185–99.

"What sort of life survived? No man should
have lived through the destruction!"
. . . .
Ea made his voice heard and spoke,
He said to the warrior Enlil,
"You are the sage of the gods, warrior,
So how, O how, could you fail to consult, and
impose the flood?
Punish the sinner for his sin, punish the criminal
for his crime,
But ease off, let work not cease; be patient, let not [. . .]
Instead of your imposing a flood. Let a lion come
up and diminish the people . . ."[12]

The interesting line in this passage is: "Punish the sinner for his sin, punish the criminal for his crime." A collective punishment is of no avail. God cannot punish the wicked together with the just. We also have this motif in the biblical version of the story when God sees that Noah is a righteous person in a generation of criminals and decides to spare his life, only at the end of the story to declare that nothing has changed and humanity is as wicked as before. In the second story of the flood in the Bible, when God let it rain not with water but with fire from heaven over Sodom and Gomorrah (Gen. 19), the story opens with the negotiation between God and Abraham, who argues that God cannot punish the righteous together with the wicked. Abraham trades like one would in a Near Eastern bazaar and makes God reduce to ten the number of just people necessary to save Sodom, although to no avail, as there are not ten just people in Sodom. However, the one just person there, Lot, is spared, together with his family.

Maybe the point of a story like this is that it is not what we think it is, that is, a story about the flood. Maybe the real point has to do with justice. Collective punishment is pointless. The wicked must suffer because of their wickedness. It is possible, in fact, that the long narrative about the flood is sheer entertainment. The true meaning is somewhat hidden between the lines.

The example was meant to show the limits of traditional European interpretation of biblical texts. Modern Europeans have little understanding about what such texts really mean. I have already introduced the Danish scholar Hans Jørgen Lundager Jensen and his discussion of code systems embedded in the text of the Old Testament.[13] The discovery of such systems may show many hidden meanings of ancient texts, invisible to the modern eye. The same can be said about the late Fredrick Cryer, who, in his discussion of ancient magic, has described ancient society as a magic society.[14] Once Frederick Cryer told his colleagues that he had

12. Trans. Stephanie Dalley, *Myths from Mesopotamia*, 114–15.
13. See above, pp. 310–11. In this connection his dissertation should also be consulted (although, alas, so far only in Danish): *Den brændende ild: Strukturelle analyser af narrative og rituelle tekster i Det Gamle Testamente* (Århus: Aarhus Universitetsforlag, 2000).
14. Frederick H. Cryer, *Divination in Ancient Israel and Its Near Eastern Environment: A Socio-Historical Investigation*, JSOTSup 142 (Sheffield: JSOT Press, 1994).

introduced the concept of a magic society in his teaching a class of students from the third world. Until the moment when he introduced this topic, the class had shown little interest in what was described; they had little chance of understanding the basically European sort of interpretation presented. The moment he suggested that ancient Israel was a magical society, magic happened: now they understood that ancient Israelite society was very much like their own at home.

These students from the third world suddenly realized that their own reading of the Old Testament at home might represent a more accurate interpretation than the European academic tradition to which they had been introduced.

A *hermeneutic of suspicion* may be an essential part of third-world exegesis. In this case the suspicion should involve not the biblical text but the European style of exegesis of that text. It should be fairly easy to present a series of criteria capable of elucidating the main problem that European and North American tradition has moved so far away from the situation of the biblical narratives and created a totally different culture, that it is impossible to reenter the world of these biblical texts. Now third-world theologians should be able to go one step forward and show how the imperialism linked to the European tradition of understanding the Bible represents an abuse of the biblical text. Hereafter it will be possible in the third world to keep the Bible as its literature, freed from the domination of European exegesis.

Here the importance of the so-called Copenhagen School of Old Testament studies becomes self-evident. Because of its demolition of the story of the Old Testament believed to represent real history, it has liberated the Old Testament from history. The first two parts of this book were devoted to the history of historical-critical scholarship, from its inception to its becoming increasingly obsolete. The demonstration of the distance between the narrated story and real history is important because it lays open the degree of "misprision" within Western academic tradition: misprision meaning deliberate misunderstanding, deliberate distortion of the meaning of biblical texts.

After 1800 Europeans became historical beings, in the sense that they were obsessed with history. The criterion for what is true and what is false changed from, is this true or false in an ethical and moral sense? to, is this true or false from a historical point of view? Meaning, did it really happen? This change represents, when applied to biblical narrative, a false alternative, based on a misapprehension of the intent of the biblical story, which was written under the influence of the old criterion for truth: is this morally and ethically true? The meaning was not hidden away in the past and the events of the past. This implies another settlement with the imperialistic European tradition of reading the Bible. The Bible is not about ancient times. Its importance lies in the present, not because of its historical narrative, but because of its theology.

Such a reorientation would provide theologians of the third world with an important tool for creating an independent theology. This theology should not be considered an alternative to the European model and its usefulness for political projects. It is about proposing new theologies which can replace old models, and such alternatives may well represent a better understanding of the meaning of biblical texts. The triumph of third-world exegesis in such a context will not involve a rejection of the European tradition as being imperialistic and colonizing; it will be the demonstration of the insufficiency of the European way of handling the Bible.

Because of their generally superior philosophical arsenal of tools for research, European scholars should be in a position to take advantage of such a situation. When it is clear that our tradition has led us astray, European scholars will have to accept that their exegesis represents only one kind of ethnic theology, one voice among a multitude of voices heard at present.

Recent developments show that we are still far away from acknowledgment of this state of affairs. In general, the European and North American white population still has a long way to go before it accepts that it is not alone in the world. The present application of Christian clichés to world politics demonstrates the sorry state of affairs. We talk about bringing democracy to the rest of the world and recommend our way of living compared to their barbarian ideas, forgetting that *Barbarian* was a Greek way of characterizing nations not speaking Greek.

Globalization includes two elements that function at the same time: acculturation and deculturation. Acculturation is the name of a process of assimilation between—in our case—two or more civilizations. This process takes place in every corner of the earth: everyone speaks English or ought to. Somehow English is believed to remove the problem of linguistic division born at the tower of Babel. We are supposed to be able to communicate. But we do not.

Deculturation is the name of the opposite process, that is, when two civilizations move apart and new differences appear. At present this process is remarkably successful and has led to a confrontation between two world religions, Christianity and Islam, that may, if the development is not impeded, result in a new world war. Islam recognizes, essentially, the revelations of Judaism and Christianity, Jews and Christians being along with Muslims "the people of the book." It is fundamentally a liberal religion. Acculturation between the West and the East in the twentieth century did not involve a better understanding of the respective religious traditions. As late as a hundred years ago, Christianity was still in a strong position in the Middle East, including 20–60 percent of the total population. Now it is a shadow of its former greatness, in some quarters almost annihilated. Only in Lebanon do we see a large segment of the Arab-speaking population that is Christian in orientation.

When the European arrived in the Middle East with his form of Christianity, Near Eastern Christianity was doomed. The first reaction of Near Eastern Christians was to embrace the European Christians as brothers and sisters. Soon a violent reaction from the Muslim population followed. "Liberation theology," here in an Islamist disguise, may be unnecessarily violent because it is fighting against a phenomenon, Christian European colonialism, which is in itself violent. As a result of such developments, the world today is dominated by the confrontation between two great religions, both claiming to inculcate "peace." However, radical elements within both religions are planning a global confrontation and in preparation describe the other as "the great Satan." We may say about those who have done nothing positive to improve biblical theology that they are like the representatives of the "white terror" that struck France after the fall of Napoleon: They have learned nothing and forgotten nothing.

Chapter 15

Canonical Theology

Previously, in chapter 11, the second chapter of this part, I discussed some of the problems connected with the concept of canon, among them the manner in which modern Christian ideas about the Bible were transferred to antiquity and used as a standard for understanding the formation of the canon. The view of the Hebrew Bible within the Jewish tradition is only one part of this problematic concept of canon within modern Christianity. This chapter will continue this discussion by including an evaluation of a special "branch" within modern Protestant biblical studies, the so-called canonical theology, as represented by its three best-known spokesmen, James A. Sanders, Brevard S. Childs, and Rolf Rendtorff.

All three of these theologians will advance a biblical theology that relies mainly on a synchronic reading of biblical texts. This means that they prefer to read the Bible as it is, not as it may have been at an earlier stage during the history of its formation. Furthermore, they prefer to discuss the Bible in its totality, which in the case of Sanders and Childs means the totality of the Old and New Testaments considered as one book. Rendtorff appears to prefer to speak about the Old Testament alone.

Their choice means a deliberate ignoring of tradition history (at least in theory, and maybe only in theory). Another consequence of their choice is disinterest in other historical issues—and again this is perhaps more theory than reality. All three of them are unified in their rejection of the strong reliance on the history of religion found in previous theologies of the Old Testament.

The central concept here may be "in theory." It is probably correct to say that historical considerations have never influenced any of these scholars. The condition, if one intends to pursue canonical theology, is the existence of a canon. Now, if this is an exclusively modern enterprise, it makes sense that we actually have a canon—or, better, many such canonical collections of biblical writings. Here it is a problem for both Sanders and Childs that they want to move back to early Christianity to study the canon of the early church from a synchronic orientation, although there may not have been any canon in those days. To be sure, they even intend to go behind the existence of the canonical books. In this way we may speak of a canonical theology on a historical foundation, but somehow this sounds like a contradiction.

JAMES A. SANDERS

James A. Sanders thinks of the canon as the product of the community of believing people in its life with the Divine. Canon has its origins within such a community, consisting at first of Jews, then of Christians (who were of course originally Jews). Although this is only an assertion, it is meaningful. As Sanders puts it:

> The canonical shaping took place in a community determined by how the tradition being shaped functioned in community. The tradition or text that was moving toward canonicity was always in dialogue with the community. The community shaped the text as it moved toward canon, and the text or tradition shaped the community as it found its way along its pilgrimage to canon.[1]

Sanders here wants to say that the tradition in its dialogue with the community moved toward a canonization that materialized in a text. As its background the tradition has the Law, in Sanders's view the basis of Israel's tradition about the past and God's acts in history (i.e., in the tradition). The implication is that Sanders's idea of the development of canon is very close to the one expressed by Gerhard von Rad based on tradition history. It will later be clear that with some modifications, Sanders's position is not fundamentally different from the one held by the present writer.

It is, on the other hand, not easy from a historical point of view to accept Sanders's absolutely traditional background. Because of his standing within traditional historical-critical scholarship, his point of departure may be considered just another specimen of the usual rationalistic paraphrase of the Old Testament's story about ancient Israel. He dates the decisive part of the canonization of the "bibli-

---

1. James A. Sanders, *From Sacred Story to Sacred Text* (Philadelphia: Fortress, 1987), 163.

cal history" to the time of the Babylonian exile and the postexilic period. Here he combines the traditional Jewish idea of canonization, that it was completed by Ezra with "Pan-Deuteronomism," a concept very popular at the end of the twentieth century: It was the Deuteronomists who *created* the traditions in the Old Testament about the history of Israel and transformed it into the concept of the people of God, God's chosen people. Basically Sanders's version of the history of Israel is founded on tradition-historical analysis which somehow makes his preference for the final edition of the canon questionable. It is contradictory because his tradition-historical and historical analysis points to an intellectual and literary movement that led forward to a stage when the tradition stiffened to one form only. He here tries to unite what cannot be united, the point and the wave.

Hereafter we are entitled to say that his canonical theology is impossible, because the only reason for the existence of the canon must be the personal choice of the believer. We need only briefly refer to what has already been said, that the canon of the Old Testament found its final form very late. If we speak about the Hebrew Bible, we may well be into the early Middle Ages before the canon hardened and became "unchangeable." If we intend to operate with a canon past change, it will be this late canonical shape of the Hebrew Bible that should be the guide for the *canonical* theological enterprise. When we return in two subsequent chapters to von Rad's idea of salvation history, we will have to realize that the *movement* toward an end based on this salvation history is preferable to Sanders' *hardened* tradition, which demands a *sacrificium intellectum*, because it presupposes a situation that never was and represents no more than an individual choice of a tradition that may have existed only in an imaginary moment.

Sanders's belief is a beautiful dream: that ancient Israel, God's chosen people from its earliest times, followed a tradition defined as the Torah, worshiping only one God, in contrast to the many idols of the heathen, and transforming their beliefs into true biblical *and* canonical monotheism. The only problem is that this never happened. There is really no reason to dwell on this.

This does not mean that the story of Israel as narrated in the Old Testament becomes irrelevant for the theology of the Old Testament. It only means that the foundation of canonical theology is moved from the world of history to the world of literature. It must necessarily be so: history represents the wave that moves through time. The story is a point fixed in time, in the moment when it was put into writing by its authors, intended to be read and heard by his original public.

This is another reason to reject Sanders's idea of canon as the result of how a believing community handed down its tradition. This is based on a common misunderstanding originating in modern conditions. It shows a definite lack of apprehension of how written traditions developed in ancient conditions. If we speak about oral tradition, which for generations of biblical scholars became a chimera, we must introduce some amendments to the theory. Oral tradition is of no use if it cannot be confirmed by other sources that may affirm the content of the tradition. It is unreliable, because it cannot be controlled without external testimonies. If a scholar prefers to use oral tradition as an argument, he is in a position to assert everything but will never be able to prove that it was really so. Oral tradition is a gratuitous concept. The scholar is in no danger of losing anything, but he does not gain anything.

Written tradition is different because it can be controlled. Information in a written document is linked to the document in question and may be submitted to an analysis of the scholar's choice. When Sanders argues that the formation of the traditions of the Old Testament—and let's for a moment forget that there perhaps never was a canonical *Jewish* Bible—gained momentum during the exile and in the postexilic period, his argument is based on facts, the written documents of the Hebrew Bible. Hereafter the historical-critical scholar may proceed from this point with his analysis; there are sources.

This does not imply that Sanders is right about the time of the formation of the biblical tradition. It is likely that he is wrong. After all, he bases his ideas of the establishment of canon on a view of ancient society far removed from reality. As demonstrated beyond doubt by Philip R. Davies, a written tradition is the tradition of the elite, the few who were able to communicate in writing.[2]

Monotheistic Judaism did not originate in a nonliterate early Jewish society as an expression of beliefs in such a society. This is a romantic idea nourished by European scholarship of the nineteenth and twentieth centuries. Judaism originated among the few, the elite who considered themselves the people of God, and who looked with contempt on any person who was not a member of their group. When and where this group was active may be discussed—although not in this place, because here the issue is of little consequence for the general theme. I have already described how Jewish monotheism is linked to a far greater movement toward monotheism present in the ancient Near East in the first millennium BCE.[3] Monotheism was something, and difficult to handle. In the Old Testament we have some very interesting specimens of early formulations of monotheism, not least about the relationship between good and evil, when the concept of a personalized devil had not yet come into being. One such example is Isaiah 45:6–7:

> I am the LORD, and there is no other.
> [7] I form light and create darkness,
> I make weal and create woe [Heb: רעה—"evil," not "woe"!];
> I the LORD do all these things.

The problem of theodicy became of paramount importance for theology for centuries, and the ancient solution was to introduce the devil as God's adversary. The gnostic solution was different: The gnostics introduced a demiurge who had created this evil world in opposition to God's world, not part of this dimension.

None of this has to do with canonical theology strictly speaking, as formulated by Sanders and his colleagues. Canonical theology is based on the Bible *as*

---

2. Philip R. Davies, *Scribes and Schools: The Canonization of the Hebrew Scriptures*, Library of Ancient Israel (Louisville, KY: Westminster John Knox, 1998), 15–17.
3. See pp. 253.

we have it. In light of what is known today, we may doubt that canonical theology will have any future if it is based on historical arguments.

BREVARD S. CHILDS

Such arguments are no problem for other canonical theologians like Childs and Rendtorff. In his *Biblical Theology of the Old and New Testaments* Childs produces what today would pass as a parody of a history of the canon.[4] According to Childs, the canon of the Old Testament—the Hebrew Bible—was completed about 100 CE, or perhaps even as early as the time of Jesus. As a consequence, the canon of the Old Testament in this scenario would have been able to influence the formation of the New Testament canon. Childs, who has, as a matter of fact, published several important studies on the Old Testament not directly related to canonical theology, knows very well that his theory is beset with historical problems and simply bends the truth to keep the foundation of his system. One thing we can say for sure: there was no Hebrew canon of the Old Testament in existence at the time of Jesus.

Apart from this, the ideas of Childs and Sanders about the formation of the canon are very similar. Both scholars belong within traditional Old Testament scholarship, and both follow a program created by German scholars in the first half of the twentieth century. They have both inherited the same theological problem because they are forced to work with a tradition history that, according to their *Vorlage,* lasted for a thousand years. Childs knows this and is forced to find new criteria for his study of the biblical text. He cares little for the school of religious history that saw biblical traditions as sources for Israel's history.

From a theological point of view he is right. It was certainly so—as already explained—that this school of religious history had changed the books of the Old Testament into sources for the study of the history of religion. The question is, how do we change this situation and bring back the Old Testament as history? Childs knows the answer, or so he presumes. He proposes to divide the study of the Old Testament into two main parts. He will, on one hand, with his basis in traditional historical-critical scholarship, not give up historical-critical scholarship in general. He will, on the other, as a theologian study the texts of the Old Testament as testimonies about the faith of Israel through the ages.

On this there is a complete agreement between Childs and Sanders. Childs's definition of his concept of testimony is almost an exact copy of Sanders's talk about the Old Testament as the product of a believing society's formulation of its historical tradition. The criticism formulated here against Sanders's idea of tradition history is just as valid when we turn to Childs's concept of testimony. It is obvious that texts with such an expressive idea about one faith only—the faith

---

4. Brevard S. Childs, *Biblical Theology of the Old and New Testaments: Theological Reflection on the Christian Bible* (Minneapolis: Fortress, 1993), 55–57.

of monotheistic Yahwism—as found in the Old Testament are testimonies about the faith among those people who wrote these books. They say far less about faith among ordinary people of their own time.

Like Sanders, Childs is of the opinion that Israel was a monotheistic society from its inception. Therefore the Old Testament is a testimony about how this monotheistic faith developed through time. When he arrives at the period of the kings, Childs simply denies the idea that Yahweh had a consort, Asherah, as based on too little evidence. As mentioned earlier, it is, however, clear because of recent discoveries, including some inscriptions from Palestine dating to the Iron Age invoking Yahweh and his Asherah, that Yahweh was in those days not a bachelor but had at his side the queen of heaven.[5] I have already introduced Elisabeth Schüssler-Fiorenza's concept of a hermeneutic of suspicion as a vehicle of feminist theology. I can think of few places where this hermeneutic would do better than in the case of Yahweh's consort.

The image gained from the study of the history of popular religion as well as official religion in Palestine in the Iron Age is difficult to harmonize with the biblical impression of this religion. The image created by this study of religion contrasts with the description of monotheistic Yahwism in the Old Testament, in the same way that the study of history has created a contrast with biblical history. In the case of Israel's religion, an approach like Childs's operates with a picture of Israelite religion that in its essence never changes. The reason is that the faith of Israel goes back to God's revelation to Israel.

Inasmuch as it is reasonable, we may speak of the texts of the Old Testament as testimonies of faith. These testimonies have nothing to do with the past (from the authors' perspective). They are testimonies about the faith of those people who created the literature of the Old Testament. The decisive quality of the texts of the Old Testament does not rely on any history of tradition understood to be expressions of how Israel formulated its faith through the ages. The decisive element is their testimony of faith among their authors. Instead of this, later Jewish tradition, including its understanding of Scripture, and internal discussion should be considered the true expression of "Israel's" faith—although from his exclusive Christian point of view, Childs would hardly be interested in this tradition. As a consequence it must be stated that the history of Israelite religion cannot serve as a testimony for faith. Ordinary history does not contain a salvation history in the biblical sense. Neither does the history of religion.

This does not mean that the history of religion has nothing to contribute to theology. Every single expression of religious sentiment in Palestine and its neighboring cultures is relevant, because practically all expressions of the Divine found in the Old Testament will find parallels outside of the Old Testament. It is possible to write a history of the theology of the ancient Near East, not restricting religious studies to a phenomenology that concentrates on the external expressions of religion like the cult, the sacrifice, and rites. More than thirty years ago

5. See pp. 250–51.

an Italian team under the supervision of Sabatino Moscati created a magnificent work, *L'alba della Civiltà* [The Beginning of Civilization]. The last part, concerning the theology of the ancient Near East, has the title "La concezione dell'universo" [The Idea of the Universe].[6] In a similar fashion this writer, in a book published ten years ago, discussed theology as expressed in literature from ancient Syria in the Bronze Age.[7] Of course people of ancient times also had ideas about the world in which they lived and understood the events of their life to have been caused by deities. Such sentiments are clearly of theological interest, placing them in a kind of system. In this way we may reconstruct not only their religion but also their beliefs and hopes, their life expectations—in short, everything categorized as theology.

When we talk about testimonies of faith from ancient times, we need not follow Childs's concept of testimonies, which is solely connected to earlier stages of Christian beliefs. Childs's view of the ancient world is clearly reductionistic, because it excludes the meaning of ancient "testimonies" for the religion of the Old Testament. His ideas have as their background his theological "backup," which consists of his three "Church fathers," Paul, Martin Luther, and Karl Barth. His ideas are also reductionistic because they effectively limit the biblical-theological discussion to the two testaments and their relationship. Here the Old Testament is decisive for the development of New Testament concepts, at the expense of ideas from other backgrounds that may have been influential when Christian doctrine was first formulated.

An overview of the table of contents in Childs's *Biblical Theology* shows how dependent he is on the traditional historical paradigm as presented by the Old Testament, beginning with the primeval history and moving step by step forward through Israel's canonical history to the prophetic tradition and the apocalyptic world of the late biblical book of Daniel. Apocalyptic creates problems for Childs's theology, as the Old Testament in the canonical form in which it is accepted by Childs has very little to say about apocalyptic. We may rather say that the Hebrew Bible is antiapocalyptic. It is likely that the book of Daniel found a place in the Jewish collection of books because of the prestige of its assumed author, Daniel, although in the Hebrew Bible it is relegated to the Writings. There is apocalyptic literature elsewhere, such as the last section of Ezekiel (Ezek. 40–48), which is a vision of the temple and represents an early stage in the development of the visions of the new Jerusalem so popular within Hellenistic-Roman Jewish literature,[8] and parts of Revelation in the New Testament. Isaiah also

---

6. Sabatino Moscati with Paolo Matthiae, F. Mario Fales, Pelio Fronzarolle, Giovanni Garbini, Mario Liverani, Franco Pintore, and Carlo Zaccagnini, eds., *L'Alba della Civiltà*. I: *La Società*; II: *L'economia*; III: *Il Pensiero* (Torino: Unione Tipografico-Editrice Torinese, 1976). The chapter on the idea of the universe is written by Mario Liverani, 3:439–516.

7. Niels Peter Lemche, *Prelude to Israel's Past: Background and Beginnings of Israelite History and Identity* (Peabody, MA: Hendrickson, 1998).

8. There are numerous manuscripts among the Dead Sea Scrolls relevant to this subject. For a translation, see Florentino García Martínez, *The Dead Sea Scrolls Translated: The Qumran Texts in English* (Leiden: Brill, 1994).

includes an apocalyptic text, Isaiah 24–27, sometimes described as the little apocalypse, normally dated to the Hellenistic period.

This creates difficulties for Childs's canonical theology, because it is evident that apocalyptic influence is marked in the New Testament. Much of this has no background in the Old Testament, which says that the authors of the New Testament found inspiration for their apocalyptic theology not in the Old Testament but in literature that Childs would never consider "canonical." Maybe this is a reason for reconstructing another edition of the canonical Bible, different from Childs's and other canonical theologians' mixture of the Jewish Hebrew Bible and the Christian New Testament. Our Bible is not really an integrated canonical collection of holy writ. This we find in the Greek Bible, the first truly *Christian* Bible. Here Daniel is found among the prophets. Although most scholars think of this as the original place of Daniel, dissenting voices have recently been heard. The possibility cannot be excluded that Daniel owes it present place (since the Middle Ages) to rabbinic antiapocalyptic activity.

It would be more correct to study canonical theology on the basis of the Orthodox Bible, including the complete Septuagint as well as the New Testament in Greek. Christian doctrine—as far as it is dependent on the Bible—relied on this Bible and not anything like modern Bibles, which are (as already suggested) the result of an early historical-critical consciousness among the Reformers. Such a solution is, however, not the one followed by Childs and his colleagues.

ROLF RENDTORFF

The third main representative of canonical theology considered here is the German Old Testament scholar Rolf Rendtorff, the author of the latest major contribution to this form of biblical theology, *The Canonical Hebrew Bible: A Theology of the Old Testament.*[9] Rendtorff has less ambition than Childs and declines to write a *biblical* canonical theology. He limits himself to the Old Testament. It is remarkable that the New Testament is of little interest to Rendtorff's theology. Unlike many previous theologies of the Old Testament from German authors, which include at least a chapter on the relations between the Old and the New Testaments, this subject is not discussed in Rendtorff's theology. Rendtorff's theology is definitely a canonical theology of the Old Testament alone. Here he is unique. It is hard to see Sanders and Childs following him. The question is, are Jewish theologians like Jon Levenson ready to subscribe to Rendtorff's approach. Somehow it is doubtful.

Rendtorff uses paraphrase of the Old Testament as the vehicle for his theology, and the first half of his theology is a very long paraphrase of the books of the

---

9. Rolf Rendtorff, *The Canonical Hebrew Bible: A Theology of the Old Testament*, Tools for Biblical Study (Leiden: Deo Publishing, 2005); German original, *Theologie des Alten Testaments. Ein kanonischer Entwurf,* 2 vols. (Neukirchener: Neukirchener Verlag, 1999–2001).

Old Testament from one end to the other. The second part is devoted to a "thematic development," including a discussion of some of the central themes of the Old Testament: "the world as created by God," the covenant and the election of Israel, the patriarchs, and more.

As far as the paraphrase is concerned, the advice in my *Ancient Israel* from 1988, that instead of presenting another paraphrase of, for example, the books of Kings, one should read the books themselves, is the same I would offer to Rendtorff. In spite of Rendtorff's meticulous paraphrase, it might be preferable to read the Bible. This has to be said because there is nothing new here. Rendtorff's paraphrase does not provide new light on biblical texts.

The point of departure for Rendtorff's canonical theology is the following statement: "The Old Testament is a theological book. An account of the 'Theology of the Old Testament' therefore scarcely requires special justification."[10]

This sounds good, but does it say anything? Perhaps the quote only suggests that Rendtorff argues that the Old Testament is a theological book. Does every person who reads the Old Testament have to agree with Rendtorff? What does such a programmatic statement imply, more than that Rolf Rendtorff is convinced that the Old Testament is a theological book? The questions are really, who is the intended proselyte to be converted to this view on the Old Testament, and why does he want to convert said person?

For the representatives of canonical theology, the Old Testament is a theological book (whatever this means). The main character of the book is definitely the God of Israel, and the main subject has to do with the relationship between this God and his chosen people. As such, the Old Testament is of course a book of theology. However, the collection of literature included in the Old Testament is not limited to theology *stricte sensu*; emphasis might just as well be put on its aesthetical qualities, its pedagogical strength, its moral teaching. Rendtorff still owes his reader an explanation as to why this book is predominantly "theological." It would be easy to point to many other books that might be called "theological books" with equal right, such as John Milton's *Paradise Lost* or Dante's *Divine Comedy*. It is also a question whether it says something about a book's quality that it may be called "a theological book." The theology found here could be intolerable or even worthless. Rendtorff's characterization of the content of the Old Testament is of little help.

A study of Rendtorff's hermeneutical reflections in the introduction to his theology soon makes it clear that he, in spite of his canonical approach to the reading of the Bible, ends up in the same situation as his predecessors, including Gerhard von Rad. Rendtorff has the same problems as the other canonical theologians in separating a synchronic analysis from an diachronic one. Rendtorff intends, like Sanders and Childs, to present a synchronic exegesis of biblical texts

---

10. *Theologie*, 1:1. "Das Alte Testament ist ein theologisches Buch. Darum bedarf eine Darstellung der 'Theologie des Alten Testament' keiner besonderen Rechtfertigung." (*Theologie*, 1:1) ET, *Canonical Hebrew Bible: A Theology of the Old Testament* (Leiden: Deo, 2005), 1.

on the basis of a diachronic historical foundation. Biblical theology is not the place where these two concepts are united. Rendtorff never makes a choice between them.

From a methodological point of view, Rendtorff intends to present his theology as a new edition of von Rad's, although without tradition history. His theology is based on the present and final canonical form of the texts. So naturally we will have to ask if he is really a new von Rad? Maybe this is just an example of how the tradition of Old Testament theologies after von Rad are divided into two main streams. One of these streams leads to a position like Rainer Albertz's, with an emphasis on the position of tradition history and the history of religion as theology. Another stream leads in the opposite direction and ends in a position like Rendtorff's, where tradition history solidified and became canonical theology. Von Rad's theology of the Old Testament and Old Testament theology in general have a problem, because it has always been their intention to unite two incommensurable concepts, the point and the wave.

This problem becomes evident numerous times when one reads Rendtorff's paraphrase and is nowhere so obvious as in his paraphrase of Isaiah. Here Rendtorff operates with the concept of "the canonical process." It sounds like a procedure close to the talk of Sanders (and Childs) about a tradition, handed down by a community of believers, but it also implies that the tradition history is a "canonical" tradition history. As a consequence the argument must be that in the case of Isaiah the canonical process started the first time a pen was put to a piece of paper (papyri) that was to become the biblical book of Isaiah. There may be more than one way to understand Rendtorff's position. His use of "canonical" in this context may be only a cliché, saying no more than that the final result of the process was the canonical book of Isaiah. From this perspective any process that ends with a canonical biblical book may be called canonical.

Canonical process may, however, also have normative implications. Here the process as such is canonical, that is, authoritative. Now it is no more a historical process following the uncontrollable laws of history; it is a process that from its inception is governed by its character of being "canonical." What does this really say? Well, it might be a new way to express the ancient idea of a text (verbally) inspired by God. The argumentation is also circular: a text is canonical because it is authoritative, and it is authoritative because it is canonical. However, too often theologians have been indifferent to such illogic.

CANONICAL THEOLOGY: AN EVALUATION

It should be evident by now that the project of a canonical theology on a historical basis makes little sense. The problem with canonical theology is in this respect similar to the one of the relationship between biblical theology and the history of Israel's religion. Biblical theology is part of a text that may be studied in a synchronic or diachronic way, as a process that went on for a long time, that is, a historical process, or as the final product, the present Bible—irrespective of the edition of the Bible the theologian based his theology on. If the theologian chooses to study the process that led to the present Bible, he will soon end up with another process, the one of the history of religion. At the end the student of the Bible will have to make a choice between two options: the process linked to the history of religion, or the process linked to the history of the development of thought or reason.

There are many indications from theologians who in serious ways work with biblical theology as canonical theology on a historical foundation that they are really just as interested in the development of human thought: the historical development of the biblical concepts of God and Israel. They are all convinced that these concepts developed over a long period, and here they build on traditional historical-critical scholarship—in spite of especially Childs's many attacks on it. It is a problem for canonical theology of this sort that so many objections have been raised against its *historical* foundations.

We saw how problematic Albertz's approach is, because in spite of his profound sociological understanding of ancient society, he is not ready to draw conclusions relating to the society in which biblical monotheistic Yahwism developed. Childs, Sanders, and to some degree also Rendtorff speak about a "believing society" as the place where the biblical tradition was formed. Philip Davies correctly rejects this concept, indicating that the "believing society" consisted of a literate elite, whose religious ideas survived because of their monopoly on communication and became normative for posterity, probably because, as time went by, this theological elite also formed the political elite of their society.

In the final chapter we will return to the question of how the elite understood itself. From a religious and sociological perspective, it was definitely a sectarian one: We are God's chosen people, and everybody else is a poor godforsaken creature. We know God. Nobody else knows God! Our history is the history of God's way of handling his people. The infidel has no part in this history (except as godless enemies to be exterminated). If we describe such persons, mutatis mutandis, as Taliban, we may not be too far from the mark, although in a biblical context it would perhaps be better to speak about the Maccabees.

This is perhaps not too far removed from the talk of Childs, Sanders, and Rendtorff about the community of believers. We may hope so, and it is a far cry from the age-old notion among biblical scholars of the "people," that is, the people of Israel, which for decades dominated Old Testament scholarship. A people are more than one person. No people share the same opinion. Just as many (or more) opinions will be present as there are people present. However, in the case of the people of God in the Old Testament, this is not so. They are all united in the same belief in God, because they study the law of God day and night (Ps. 1).

Is canonical theology meaningless? If we discuss it in the version formulated by Childs, Sanders, and Rendtorff, it is meaningless. If we turn to Gabler's old differentiation between biblical studies and systematic theology, none of the three theologians listed here is able to overcome the problems that have haunted every biblical student since Gabler's time. Thus there is little that separates, for example, the theologies of von Rad and of Childs. Childs's emphasis is on the final product, the canon, while von Rad is mainly interested in the process that led to this canon. Both accept the same history behind the process of canonization. The themes presented by Rendtorff in the second part of his theology are almost identical to the themes presented by more traditional German theologies of the Old Testament.

But perhaps the most serious objection to canonical theology has to do with its manipulation of history to mold it into a historical base for canonical theology. Childs and Sanders argue in favor of a unity of the two testaments that never existed before the Reformation. Nothing indicates that the canonical Hebrew Bible had any importance for the authors of the Greek New Testament. It would be easy to propose a working hypothesis that suggests that the Septuagint was considered canonical, while the Hebrew Bible represents a Jewish and rabbinic reaction against the Christian usurpation of the Septuagint. The Christian canon exists in many different editions; who knows, perhaps, just perhaps, the canonical theologians have not chosen the best one.

Does this criticism imply that canonical theology is dead? This is far from the case. Canonical theology in its present form may represent a crude example of how to circumvent Gabler's distinction between a historical and a systematic theology in recent times. They change history to a systematic concept—although still maintaining that it is history—and mix the two categories of text and event. This is a classical historical-critical issue. Canonical theology has done nothing to overcome this methodological problem.

It is, of course, possible to proceed with a canonical biblical theology. It is, however, necessary to concentrate on the final product in the form chosen by the theologian who wants to proceed with this kind of theology. Canon—whatever form it takes—is a product of history and represents a historical process at its (temporal) end. The process and the final product are not identical. The final product is not a given from the logical outcome of the process. The final product, the many forms of the Christian canon, exists, and may be submitted to historical, theological, and aesthetical analyses. The question remains, how are we to proceed?

Chapter 16

Salvation Theology and Gerhard von Rad

Theologies of the Old Testament I

TEXT AND EVENT

Up to this point, this review of the theological debate about Old Testament and biblical theology in the twentieth century has included traditional theologies following the German paradigm for such things. It has moved from there to modern forms of theology including postcolonial forms of theology and liberation theology of different sorts. Finally, a modern misconception represented by the canonical thelogy of Childs, Sanders, and Rendtorff was the subject of investigation.

This chapter will return to a form of theology of the utmost importance for the theological environment of the modern (postmodern) Western world. Although we belong to a globalized world and are members of a (in some cases) growing multicultural society full of challenges, it is still important to compare ideas exported from elsewhere with local ones. There is no reason to reject, for example, contextual biblical theology. It is my hope that we have here shown that this is hardly an issue. There is, on the other hand, no reason simply to capitulate to the onslaught of new ideas and theologies. Although the tradition of the Western world may have reached an impasse, this does not mean that it is worthless and has no future. Although this writer has for thirty years campaigned against traditional historical-critical scholarship, this does not suggest that historical-critical methodology is rejected at the same time. It is only necessary to look for a change of procedure in a critical way because of the changing intellectual environment that is causing traditional historical-critical scholarship to be no longer either critical or historical.

In this and the following chapter we will discuss the concept of salvation history already mentioned in connection with von Rad's theology of the Old Testament. In the following chapter its meaning for the North American biblical theology movement will be scrutinized. The general outline of von Rad's theology has already been presented. There is reason to go further with this theology because of its status as unquestionably the most important contribution to the subject from the twentieth century. The concept of salvation history as explained by von Rad is misleading. Franz Hesse's criticism of the concept—to be discussed later—is without doubt correct when seen in light of von Rad's argument. But the concept of a salvation history may not be misleading if it is founded on better premises than first proposed.

German theologies of the twentieth century were in trouble when it came to separating the task of the theologian from the task of the historian. Without exception, these theologies always ended up being built on a historical foundation. Until the end of the century, scholars had problems separating fact from fiction, that is, separating the text from the event. It was generally assumed that the text of the Bible was built on facts, based on something that really happened (although not always in the form found in the biblical text). Most scholars stressed the referential value of the biblical stories. Old Testament exegesis saw as its main task to create harmony between the text of the Bible and the event supposed to be reflected by the text.

This process did not consist of a naive harmonization of differences in various biblical texts. The texts were, however, "edited" in such a way that they fit the historical event, and historical events and archaeological data were manipulated to conform to biblical stories.

European Protestant biblical scholarship has, since the Enlightenment, been part of the historical game of historical-critical scholarship, applying such rules and methods as were deemed legitimate for scholarship of sundry kinds. The most marked part of this process was the rejection of divine influence on history. In the narratives of the Old Testament, God is the prime mover in history. He had to leave. Scholarly analysis must, if it wishes to be called "scholarly" ("scientific"), be independent, freed from the interruption of a God who is himself not part of history.

As an aside: conservative Christians, evangelicals or simply fundamentalists, have never understood or accepted scholarly argument. For more than a hundred years they have tried to circumvent the methods of scholars by applying a logic that a child (if not from an evangelical environment) would be able to unmask. While these conservatives on one hand describe the methods of scholars as "ideology"—at the same time trying to cover up their own problems, especially in a

North American context, where "ideology" is often translated as a "false perception of reality"—they on the other hand pretend to be part of the scholarly enterprise. Their argument is simple: if there is a God, this God must be active in history, and it is reductionistic in the scholarly sense to exclude God from history. This argument has been repeated several times recently, for example, in a recent discussion of historical methodology by Jens Bruun Kofoed.[1]

The argument is a bluff, no more or less than that. It does not recognize the real problem as agreed on by theologians of the last two hundred years: God is and will remain an assertion. There is not a scholarly method that can bring God back. He can never be part of a process of falsification. The argument that God is present in history is an assertion that has no place in a scholarly debate of history.

When historical-critical scholarship realized this, it created its own narrative, one of a rationalistic paraphrase of the Old Testament. Biblical texts were cleansed of the supernatural, whereupon they were considered valuable sources for ancient history. As shown in the first two parts of this book, such a paraphrased history was doomed when it was demonstrated that the historical nucleus of these texts might be like the core of Peer Gynt's onion: there is none.

GERHARD VON RAD, HISTORY, AND TIME

Now let us move to critical scholars and see how they, from their methodological point of view, handled the problem of the confrontation of the biblical texts with an assumed reality behind them. The contribution of Gerhard von Rad reigns supremely.

Gerhard von Rad, together with his contemporary Martin Noth, was probably the finest student of the history of Israel in the twentieth century. Both scholars had as their foundation the work of the old master of German Old Testament scholarship, Albrecht Alt. Younger German scholars sometimes refer to them as the great inventors of hypotheses. They have recognized that their formidable reconstructions of both history and literary history have as their foundation an extensive use of rationalistic paraphrase. These scholars, together with innumerable less important but nevertheless very professional European scholars, built up a historical construct, "ancient Israel," that formed the basis of the historical part of the theologies of the Old Testament, as is evident not only in von Rad's theology but in all subsequent German theologies of the Old Testament, whether by Preuß, Kaiser, or Rendtorff, to mention only the major ones.

The links to the historical analyses included both the history of religion and tradition history. The reconstruction of the history of Israelite religion followed the same paraphrasing procedure as was the case of the construction of Israel's history. The reconstructed history of religion may be considered a revision of the

---

1. Jens Bruun Kofoed, *Text and History: Historiography and the Study of the Biblical Text* (Winona Lake, IN: Eisenbrauns, 2005).

history of Israel's faith as related by biblical writers. Israel's religion was at the same time considered to be something special compared to other ancient Near Eastern religion. This was not based on a study of all available material for the construction of religion; it was founded on the testimony of the biblical narrative.

The history of tradition made it possible to trace the development of biblical narrative back almost to the events themselves narrated by Old Testament storytellers. Both von Rad and Noth belonged to the group of the most respected representatives of tradition history, those who wrote central theses about the formation of the biblical tradition and whose work is still accepted by many scholars and often quoted in the literature of today. Noth's best-known theory is the one concerning the Deuteronomistic History including the books from Joshua to 2 Kings.[2] It is ironic that von Rad never subscribed to Noth's hypothesis.

As already mentioned, von Rad described the history of tradition as the study of the way Israel told its history from one generation to the next. The different stages of the development of the tradition reflected a continuous rewriting of the basic tradition. In this way it is possible to follow the changes in the view of Israel's history and religion that was part of Israel's life in its land. It remains the task of the theologian to study how Israel spoke about God throughout its history.

It has already been discussed how historical-critical scholarship used text archaeology to recover the different strata of tradition. The famous four-document hypothesis of the formation of the Pentateuch is the most exquisite example of such a methodology. Thus von Rad dated the earliest stratum, the Yahwist, to the tenth century BCE, and the youngest to the postexilic period, probably the fifth or fourth century BCE. Each stratum represents one period of Israel's history and may therefore be considered a testimony of the notions of God current in, say, the tenth century, and successively down to the postexilic period. Thus the Yahwist includes a colorful image of God who dines with Abraham, while the God of the Elohist is a remote God who communicates with his chosen ones through media like his angels. The exalted creator of the world is the God of the Priestly writer.

Tradition history was one means by which to create a distance between preexilic, Israelite religion and postexilic Jewish law. Judaism was, in those days, considered a secondary form of religion in comparison to the original Israelite one. Judaism represented a *degenerated* Israelite religion. Out of the fresh, almost gospel-like, Israelite religion of preexilic times came the Jewish law-religion with its formalized cult and its narrow-minded system of religious rules. The Israelite religion turned into legalism—almost echoing Paul's language about the dead letter of the law. From the angle of tradition history—or so it was tacitly understood—there was a direct link between the original Israelite religion as expressed by the Yahwist and Luther's Protestant religion of the sixteenth century.

---

2. The hypothesis of the Deuteronomistic History was first published as Martin Noth, *Überlieferungsgeschichtliche Studien* I. *Die sammelnden und bearbeitenden Geschichtswerken im Alten Testament* (Königsberg, 1943), but reedited more than once (e.g., Tübingen: Max Niemeyer, 1957). ET, *The Deuteronomistic History*, JSOTSup 15 (Sheffield: JSOT Press, 1981).

This preexilic Israelite and pre-Jewish religion placed special emphasis on history. This was, at any rate, how von Rad and his contemporaries saw it. Yahweh was the God of history, and the worldview of the Israelites was both historical and linear. Old Testament theologians regarded the Israelite religion (as found in the Old Testament) as something special in comparison not only to other ancient Near Eastern religions but also to contemporary Greek religion. Thus the Israelite notion of time was linear, in contrast to other cultures, whose concept of time was cyclic. In his apology, Socrates describes his understanding of time, arguing that it is likely that the same persons will stand in the same place in another aeon and will be involved in the exact same activities. Time moves in circles from creation to the end of the world, which is nothing more than a new creation.

The same happened according to ancient Near Eastern beliefs, or so it was argued. The original time was also the final time, as expressed programmatically by the title of Hermann Gunkel's famous dissertation *Schöpfung und Chaos in Urzeit und Endzeit*.[3] The history of the world was counted in ages, cycles of time. The popularity of the idea is not so difficult to understand. Even in modern times, it sometimes surfaces, for example, in the shape of the 1,000-year kingdom, with roots going back to the book of Revelation in the New Testament.

However, things were different in ancient Israel. The concept of time was linear. There is a beginning of time and an end to it. At the beginning of time, God creates the world, and at the end of time, the world comes to an end (but somehow the idea of changing ages survives, now in the form of eternal life: after this miserable life on earth, the kingdom of God replaces it). Like the world with its beginning and its end, the history of Israel has a beginning and an end. At the beginning God chooses Israel as his people; at the end he rejects his chosen people, which is sent into exile.

Two concepts are here combined; a linear concept of time and a teleological idea of the meaning of time. History is not neutral. God has a plan for history. The biblical idea of time seems in accordance with the modern notion that history constantly moves forward. It never goes back. Now it is easy to combine the two concepts of time and history in a religious synthesis. When we have a history based on a linear concept of time, the religious reaction is likely to be that it is God who directs this history.

An overview of historical research during the last two hundred years will confirm the impression gained here. The religiously oriented "historian" will not accept a history that moves on without a purpose. A secular historian is not likely to accept the casual character of history but will try to find "laws" for historical development. While the religious will say that God is the law of history,

---

3. Hermann Gunkel, *Schöpfung und Chaos in Urzeit und Endzeit: Eine religionsgeschichtliche Untersuchung über Gen 1 und Ap Joh 12* (Göttingen: Vandenhoeck & Ruprecht, 1895). The text of the German original can be downloaded at the following address: http://library.case.edu/ksl/ecoll/books/gunsch00/gunsch00.html. It was more than a hundred years before an English translation of this important work was published as *Creation and Chaos in the Primeval Era and the Eschaton: A Religio-Historical Study of Genesis 1 and Revelation 12* (Grand Rapids: Eerdmans, 2006).

the secular historian will look for "laws." Thus, as perhaps the clearest example, Marxist historians will stress the importance of the organizing power of economics. Other historians are likely to follow the school of Les Annales, approaching a kind of ecological determinism, because most things in history are decided by external conditions; there is little room for the genius.

In his theology, von Rad profits from this basically Western and European idea of history with its two bases in, on one hand, a religious interpretation of history and, on the other, the secular Western idea of a history that moves forward and is never repeated. We might say that in his theology von Rad follows three interconnected legs, each of them placed on a historical, diachronic axis.

Secular history, the first leg of his investigation, concerns the secular history of Israel from the earliest periods to postexilic Judaism.

In tradition history, the second leg, it is supposed that the biblical story more or less follows the developmental lines of secular history.

The third leg has to do with the Israelite interpretation of God's acts in history.

If anyone has entertained doubts about the strength of the classical historical-critical paradigm, he should by now be convinced of its resiliency. These three legs are bound together in such a way that one is always supporting the other two. The historical-critical scholar opens his studies with an analysis of "the history of Israel," as related by the biblical authors. This has to do with the many times mentioned "rationalistic paraphrase": God is removed from history. On this basis the scholar reconstructs the tradition history of the biblical text, making it follow the historical stages already distilled from the same texts. Logically the argumentation is of course circular: A supports B that supports A. A is here the secular history of Israel, and B tradition history. Having established this axis between A and B, the historical critical scholar moves to the next stage, the history of Israel's religion from early times to Judaism. The scholar reconstructs the mental history of ancient Israel, how Israel's concept of God and the world developed through the ages. It would, from this perspective, be correct to say that von Rad's theology of the Old Testament is definitely a kind of mental history and not a traditional theology of the Old Testament. The argumentation is still circular, although a new element has been introduced: C, the theology of the Old Testament. The historical-critical paradigm may then be said to be a synthesis between A, B, and C.

In the following chapter we will show how North American scholarship introduced a D to this edifice (D signifying the study of the history of ancient Palestine through archaeology). In spite of this, it must be repeated: the Old Testament has, in its historical-critical phase, been dominated—for two hundred years—by argumentation that from a logical point of view is questionable, not to say abominable. Now the final question is, when we have to give up a paradigm because of such faulty argumentation, do we also need to reject a theology that is related to this paradigm? Is it possible to point at new beginning also for biblical theology? More on this in due course.

GERHARD VON RAD AND SALVATION THEOLOGY

How does von Rad unfold this "trinity" of history, history of literature, and history of thought in his theology? The main outline of it has already been presented: the first part had to do with Israel's historical tradition, and the second with the theology of the prophetic tradition. Von Rad's separation of the historical tradition from the prophetic has been well received, because it is a signal that his theology is primarily based on historical tradition and is not a Procrustean bed that every theology based on Old Testament literature has to conform to. It is, however, remarkable that wisdom tradition plays no role in his theology. It would be hard to argue that the book of Job has no importance for the theology of the Old Testament! Von Rad compensated for this omission in his last work, published at the end of his life, on Wisdom literature.[4]

Von Rad discusses the first part, the secular history, in an almost-one-page overview of the history of Israel from the earliest times to "the constituting of the post-exilic cultic community." It is remarkable—but absolutely in line with the lack of interest in Judaism common among Old Testament scholars of this period—that postexilic Judaism gets only about seven pages. Even after the end of World War II, Christian theologians showed little interest in linking the Old Testament to Judaism and according Jewish authors a decisive role in the production of Old Testament literature.

The historical introduction is subdivided into five chapters, following the normal arrangement of the history of Israel among historical-critical scholars, beginning with the time before the conquest of Canaan, the settlement in Canaan, the period of the judges and the monarchy, endeavor to revitalize ancient Yahwism, and finally postexilic Judaism. This section in concluded with a chapter about the offices in ancient Israel, divided into two groups, the sacral offices and the charismatic offices.

The history follows the one in Martin Noth's classic *A History of Israel*, which appeared shortly before the publication of the first volume of von Rad's theology,[5] although von Rad concentrates on the history of thought rather than on general history. Here he combines two parts of the aforementioned trinity, secular history and the history of thought, in a synthesis that is then used as the basis of his history of theology.

The main part of the first volume of von Rad's theology, "the theology of Israel's historical traditions," also concentrates on the synthesis, not between secular history and the history of thought, but between the history of literature, tradition history, and theology (or history of thought). He uses tradition history, together with the results of German higher criticism with its division of the

---

4. *Weisheit in Israel* (Neukirchen: Neukirchener Verlag, 1970); ET, *Wisdom in Israel* (London: SCM Press, 1972).

5. Martin Noth, *Geschichte Israels* (Göttingen: Vandenhoeck & Ruprecht, 1950).

Pentateuch into four strata, as the point of departure for his history of theology. Every tradition and every source gets its place in this development.

New to this section is the introduction of the concept of "salvation history," in German *Heilsgeschichte*. Salvation history has already been mentioned a number of times. Salvation history is identical with the history that is the theme of the historical literature in the Old Testament but already present in the oldest strata of the Israelite tradition.[6]

One famous expression of salvation history is, according to von Rad, found in the credo-like text of Deuteronomy 26:5–9:

> You shall make this response before the LORD your God: "A wandering Aramean was my ancestor; he went down into Egypt and lived there as an alien, few in number, and there he became a great nation, mighty and populous. [6] When the Egyptians treated us harshly and afflicted us, by imposing hard labor on us, [7] we cried to the LORD, the God of our ancestors; the LORD heard our voice and saw our affliction, our toil, and our oppression. [8] The LORD brought us out of Egypt with a mighty hand and an outstretched arm, with a terrifying display of power, and with signs and wonders; [9] and he brought us into this place and gave us this land, a land flowing with milk and honey."

Von Rad dates this "confession," often called "the little historical credo" (*das kleine geschichtliche Credo*) to the oldest stratum of tradition. It is a fragment of an ancient tradition that was at a later stage incorporated into the first sources of the Pentateuch. Hereafter he builds on this credo in an analysis that intends to trace the development of the credo in subsequent tradition. His thesis is that the credo was used from a very early stage of the traditions of ancient Israel to show how Yahweh directed its history and intervened whenever the people of Israel found itself in trouble. The historical literature of Israel is, in this way, one long confession of belief in Yahweh as the Lord of history. Its fundamental core is the conviction that God saves Israel.

In this salvation history, the exodus is of central importance. The exodus is used in several places as Yahweh's self-legitimation; "I am the LORD your God, who brought you out of the land of Egypt, out of the house of slavery" introduces the Decalogue in Exodus 20 and Deuteronomy 5. Israel was in trouble in Egypt and cried to Yahweh for help. He sent Moses and saved his people. This theme is repeated several times and forms the backbone of the book of Judges; Israel is in trouble and cries to Yahweh, who sends a savior, a judge, who liberates Israel, and so forth.

The covenant plays a decisive role in the administration of salvation history. Thus von Rad provides his chapter on the theology of the Hexateuch[7] with the

---

6. The thesis was originally formulated in his thesis, *Das formgeschichtliche Problem des Hexateuch* (Stuttgart: Kohlhammer, 1938), reprinted in his *Gesammelte Studien zum Alten Testament*, Theologische Bücherei 8 (Munich: Chr. Kaiser, 1958), 9–86. On the credo, see 11–16.

7. As already mentioned, von Rad was no supporter of Noth's Deuteronomistic hypothesis but considered the book of Joshua a part of the Pentateuch, which in this way became the Hexateuch (the "six books").

subtitle "The Time-Division of the Canonical Saving History by means of the Covenant Theology,"[8] and places the revelation at Sinai in the center of tradition. The covenant, which in Walter Eichrodt's theology formed the pivotal point, becomes a dynamic force in von Rad's theology. Israel's history revolves around the covenant, and at the center of the covenant we find the so-called covenant formula: Yahweh is Israel's God and Israel is Yahweh's people. The preservation of the people of God is the same thing, then, as the maintenance of salvation history.

Salvation history is not identical with secular history. It represents a theological reflection based on this secular history, as put down into writing in the course of Israel's secular history. However, salvation history also influenced the secular history, because its essentials were considered important for ancient Israel, whose reaction to the secular history should be linked to its belief in the salvation history.[9]

THE TRAGIC HISTORY OF ISRAEL

It is possible to attack von Rad's concept of salvation history from many sides. One of the most important engagements with this theological concept was by the German theologian Franz Hesse, who is of the opinion that the attempt to understand the history of Israel in the Old Testament as representing salvation history is beset with difficulties.[10] When that history has reached its end, there is no longer any land of Israel. The relationship between Yahweh and Israel is dissolved, finished by the same God who promised to save Israel. The historical books from Joshua to 2 Kings do not say much about the salvation of Israel but concentrate on its destruction. The subject of the historical literature is Israel deserting its God, or Israel disobeying Yahweh by worshiping idols. At the end of the story Yahweh has had enough of Israel and cancels his salvation project. Israel's history is, in Hesse's view, not a salvation history, it is a "reversal-of-salvation history" (*Unheilsgeschichte*). There is no optimism in the historical literature of the Old Testament related to any kind of salvation history. It is a tragic story resulting in destruction and exile. The land of Yahweh/Israel is desolated, destroyed by the enemy, and Yahweh's people carried away into exile, his temple robbed and burnt down, symbolizing that Yahweh too has deserted his country.

Hesse's criticism of the concept of a salvation history is correct—at least if the concept is narrowly defined. Israel's history, as it is in the Old Testament, is a history of disaster now over. However, is this really the end of history, even in the Old Testament? A historically oriented exegete like von Rad would undoubtedly

---

8. *Old Testament Theology*, 1:129.

9. For a positive evaluation of salvation history, see Robert Gnuse, *Heilsgeschichte as a Model for Biblical Theology: The Debate concerning the Uniqueness and Significance of Israel's Worldview* (Lanham, MD: University Press of America, 1989).

10. Franz Hesse, *Abschied von der Heilsgeschichte*, Theologische Studien 108 (Zurich: TVZ Verlag, 1971).

say this: Ancient Israel ceased to exist in 587 BCE when Nebuchadnezzar conquered Jerusalem (we forget for a moment that historical Israel was destroyed by Assyria in 722 BCE). From this perspective, salvation history as a concept belongs to ancient Israel; the idea that God acted in history in favor of his chosen people was part of the creed of ancient Israel. The destruction of Jerusalem and its temple was the anticlimax of this history.

This impression of salvation history as part of Israel's faith from its early times is confirmed by the prophets of the Old Testament, in the prophets of doom. These prophets preached death and destruction to faithless Israel. Von Rad discusses prophetism in the second volume of his theology, using the usual text-archaeological procedure of digging for the original sayings of the prophets. Such prophets of doom include the original Isaiah, Amos, Hosea, and more, and their message was one of despair and hopelessness. However, in his view—a view of prophetism he shared with most scholars of his time—all of these prophets belonged to the time of ancient Israel, the eighth through sixth centuries BCE, and are testimonies to the importance of the concept of a salvation history already in their time.

THEOLOGY OR THE HISTORY OF THOUGHT?

Now the remaining question is, what should we do with this paradigm of biblical studies and biblical theology? The argumentation supporting it is basically circular. It moves within a closed circle and should have been abandoned long ago, although it is hard to say that this has really happened within Old Testament scholarship. When confronted with too harsh attacks on the prevailing paradigm, biblical scholarship will look for a loophole or will simply ignore dissenting voices.

Such a loophole might be the hypothesis of the Yahweh alone movement previously mentioned. Bernhard Lang, who proposed this theory following the lead of Morton Smith, is absolutely aware of the difference between religion in Palestine in the Iron Age and Israelite faith as presented by the biblical authors. People in general "worshiped many gods." They were hardly happy "mono-Yahwists." Only few reckoned Yahweh to be the only God around—not to mention Asherah, Yahweh's consort.

How did the biblical authors get the idea of "Yahweh alone"? Lang and scholars like him would say that the God of Israel was from the very beginning one and only one. This is one of the many idiosyncratic notions about ancient Israelite religion provoked by the taciturn acceptance of the biblical history of Israel. The Old Testament asserts that Yahweh alone is God, and Christian theologians are ready to follow: God is one and cannot be divided into many deities. The point of departure must be that the religion of Israel was, from the very beginning, monotheistic. The traces of polytheism that pop up in many places in the Old Testament are the result of a syncretism that resulted in the amalgamation of Israelite monotheism with Canaanite polytheism.

According to the hypothesis, the Yahweh alone movement presented an alternative to this syncretistic polytheism evidenced in the eighth and seventh centuries BCE. The spokespersons of this movement were the prophets of the Old Testament.

To analyze von Rad's theology on the basis of a traditional historical foundation, we will have to ask, is this really theology? If there is a theology here, it is one of a static idea of God, and we actually have such a concept of an unchangeable God in the Old Testament. The God of Israel is one and the same from beginning to end, although this does not mean that the biblical concept of God is a simplistic one. In von Rad's reconstruction of the development of religion based on tradition history, which has here been described as a piece of the history of thought, Israelite religion moved from henotheism and monolatry (the worship of one God alone, although other gods are believed to be present) to monotheism. Tradition history has an answer to all kinds of questions.

We may therefore ask if von Rad's theology is a theology of the Old Testament or a history of Israel's religion. If a history of religion has as its subjects only the external manifestations of religion, if it is no more than phenomenology, von Rad's theology is a *theology*. However, if the study of religion involves also beliefs and ideas, then von Rad's theology is a history of Israelite religion without phenomenology, although the phenomenology is there.

I have already mentioned that Rainer Albertz, at least for a while, studied in Heidelberg, the home of von Rad. I have also argued that it is a personal choice whether one accepts Albertz's religion history of the Old Testament as a proper history of religion or thinks of it as historical theology. When the table of contents in von Rad's theology is compared to the one in Albertz's history of religion, the similarity between the two is striking. This also places Albertz's proposal to replace Old Testament theology with the history of Israelite religion in the correct perspective. Like von Rad, Albertz belongs to the classical German tradition of Old Testament studies. Both work with tradition history and a diachronic reconstruction of Israel's faith through the ages. The only real difference between the two is Albertz's reliance on sociological analyses.

Von Rad's theology stands or falls together with the view of tradition history exposed here. From the perspective of the Copenhagen School of Old Testament studies, it has fallen. The tradition history, along with the basis proposed for it by von Rad, has little to do with the realities of ancient Palestine. The same has to be said about his proposal for a history of thought based on biblical evidence. The religion practiced in ancient Palestine, including in the two small states of Israel and Judah, was not monotheistic, whether we talk about official state religion or popular religion among ordinary people. Furthermore, there is no evidence from the Iron Age that a change of religion was underway. The religion was a polytheistic one.

In spite of such objections, one important element of von Rad's theology remains: the Old Testament's version of Israel's history represents "Israel's"—it would be more correct to say early Judaism's—version of its history, as seen by its author and his public. The concept of the only God of the Old Testament who created the world is a reflection of religion in the time of the author who wrote these stories about God. It is clear that there exist variations within the general image of God presented in the Old Testament. This is to be expected when theologians get together. It is also ridiculous to imagine that a dogmatic kind of theology already existed but was not to be discussed. On the contrary, differences in outlook show that different opinions were present. They mainly agreed on one thing: Their God is God.

If we concentrate on the authors and their product, an important step forward is taken. The authors of the literature of the Old Testament had a special idea about the Divine, and this idea is present on every page they wrote. This is a literary image of God. This is not a history handed down from one generation to the next. It is the story of the history that we carry with us. The Old Testament does not deceive us. It says very much the same:

> Hear, O Israel: The LORD is our God, the LORD alone. [5] You shall love the LORD your God with all your heart, and with all your soul, and with all your might. [6] Keep these words that I am commanding you today in your heart. [7] Recite them to your children and talk about them when you are at home and when you are away, when you lie down and when you rise. (Deut. 6:4–7)

And furthermore:

> When your children ask you in time to come, "What is the meaning of the decrees and the statutes and the ordinances that the LORD our God has commanded you?" [21] then you shall say to your children, "We were Pharaoh's slaves in Egypt, but the LORD brought us out of Egypt with a mighty hand. [22] The LORD displayed before our eyes great and awesome signs and wonders against Egypt, against Pharaoh and all his household. [23] He brought us out from there in order to bring us in, to give us the land that he promised on oath to our ancestors." (Deut. 6:20–23)

The history in the Old Testament is a narrative (as all history is), and its religion or theology is also a narrative. As a consequence, there is nothing that intervenes between history and story. There is no reason to confront a secular history with this narrative. As a narrative it is thoroughly autonomous.

This is not the same as saying that there are no internal differences between the two parts of the historical narrative in the Old Testament. There are many, and it will be a personal choice of the modern scholar whether he intends to use such differences to argue in favor of different levels of tradition or the presence of different authors.

The theological study of the Old Testament is the study of literature. Biblical theology must be seen in this light.

Chapter 17

From the Biblical Theology Movement to Postmodernism

The North American Scene:
Theologies of the Old Testament II

From a theological point of view North America may be called the land of extremes. The most conservative expressions in theology are heard here, as well as the most radical reformulations of Christian doctrine, including everything from primitive doomsday movements to mass suicide to deeply engaged liberation theology. Liberation theology has been discussed previously and will appear only sporadically in this connection. We will ignore the doomsday/apocalyptic movements.

The subject of this chapter will be two theologies originating in North America that can be used to characterize theology in this part of the world by dividing the theological discourse into two sectors. The first subject will be the biblical theology movement, although many North American theologians of today reject its presuppositions. The second subject will be the most extensive theology of the Old Testament yet to appear here, that of Walter Brueggemann, which represents a postmodern approach to biblical theology. Both subjects (biblical theology and postmodernism) are representative for the periods in which they came into being, the biblical theology movement in the years following the end of the Second World War, and postmodern exegesis in the aftermath of the Vietnam War. The relationship between historical-critical scholarship and these two directions is not

351

really a happy one. Both directions entertain rather critical ideas about historical critical scholarship, although for different reasons. The biblical theology movement saw itself in opposition to historical-critical scholarship as it developed especially in a Protestant European (especially German) university environment. It tried to domesticate it and turn its results into a conservative formula supported by the members of the movement. Postmodern exegetes have, for their part, also been combating historical-critical scholarship, however, for hermeneutical and philosophical reasons.

THE BIBLICAL THEOLOGY MOVEMENT

The rise and fall of classical historical-critical scholarship formed the subject of the two first parts of this book. This direction within biblical scholarship took its point of departure from the Enlightenment and the new scientific image of the world established at that time, created an artificial construction called "ancient Israel," and based its construction on a positivistic idea of scholarship.

Immanuel Kant had made it clear that science would have to work within the two parameters of time and space. Building on the philosophical tradition from Descartes to Hegel, there was, in the scientific image of the world, no room for any god. Miracles and wonders, everything that reminded people of God's presence in history, had to be eliminated from history. Biblical criticism also began in this period, although at first hardly very impressively. Not everything in the Old Testament would survive scholarly scrutiny. This critical attitude included more than just minor issues like the identity of the wife of Cain, or the status of the hare; it also embraced central issues like the authorship of biblical books.

It would be wrong to say that the rise of critical scholarship was welcomed by the masses. As late as at the end of the nineteenth century, a respected biblical scholar like Frantz Buhl was rejected as professor at the University of Copenhagen, and had to move to Semitic philology. The fate of the Scottish scholar W. Robertson Smith has already been mentioned. Julius Wellhausen too had to give up his theological chair and move to humanities to escape (as Melanchthon had put it in his time) the rabies of the theologians.

The North American Christian world reacted rather sharply to the—it must be admitted—until then rather insignificant contribution of American critical scholarship. The year 1910 saw the first edition of a series of volumes called *The Fundamentals*, which gave its name to a whole theological trend. Fundamentalism is a modern historically oriented branch of theology that is fighting, at any cost and without much subtlety, against historical critical scholarship—as a matter of fact against every critical trend within Christianity that may express a critical attitude to the biblical truth. In principle every word and every sentence in the Bible must be true, because it is God's own word.

There is no reason to waste more time on this phenomenon. James Barr wrote four hundred pages about fundamentalism, only to conclude that it was not worth the effort.[1] It is, however, important to understand the essentials of fundamentalism when we move on to the biblical theology movement, because, although this direction within biblical studies is not fundamentalist, its rhetoric and demagogical procedures seem borrowed from evangelical circles.[2] Many members of the movement also come from a fundamentalist environment. The biblical theology movement may therefore be considered an answer to proper fundamentalism, arguing that not everything is as "bad" as proposed by historical critical scholars, while at the same time it is definitely attempting to rescue the Old Testament from being irrelevant to theology.

We will return to this later. Already the principal voice of the biblical theology movement, the North American biblical archaeologist G. Ernest Wright (1909–74), spoke of the spread of Marcionism in recent times. Marcion was renowned for his attempt to remove the Old Testament from the Christian Bible. In his attack on Marcionism, Wright was definitely also aiming at European scholarship, which he considered to be rejecting the Old Testament as part of the Christian heritage.

As Wright put it:

> Surely, if the New Testament is not proclaimed as the fulfilment of the Old, if the gospel as proclaimed by Jesus and by Paul is not the completion of the faith of Israel, then it must inevitably be a completion and fulfilment of something which we ourselves substitute—and that most certainly means a perversion of the Christian faith.[3]

On this basis Wright opens his crusade in favor of keeping the Old Testament as a Christian book. The Old Testament is the best defense of Christianity against paganism, or so it is maintained.

The central assertion of this movement suggests that God acts in history, especially Israelite history as narrated by the Old Testament, and that this is the very history in which God acts. We have heard that before. Von Rad might use the same words but in the sense that God is acting in the historical narrative, in the Israelite interpretation of history, while Wright means that it is in real history, not in the history that hides behind the narrative. The task of the theologian, historian, and archaeologist (Wright united all three in one person) is therefore to confirm the correctness of the version of Israel's history in the Old Testament as far as it is possible.

1. *Fundamentalism* (Philadelphia: Westminster, 1977). Barr's religious background was a very conservative Presbyterian environment from which he had "escaped." He also wrote a book titled *Escaping from Fundamentalism* (Philadelphia: Westminster, 1984). Fundamentalists are in general not pleased with Barr, although probably only a few of them have ever read him.

2. It should be noted that the term *fundamentalist* is increasingly replaced by *evangelical* and *fundamentalism* with *evangelicalism*. This may make sense in a North American context. However, in Protestant northern Europe, *evangelical* is misleading, as the Lutheran churches are generally called "evangelical Lutheran" without being fundamentalist. Thus also this writer is "evangelical," but definitely in the European meaning of the word.

3. G. Ernest Wright, *God Who Acts: Biblical Theology as Recital*, SBT 8 (London: SCM, 1952), 17.

Wright was a student of William Foxwell Albright, already mentioned here a number of times, and in those days—at least in North America—considered the greatest Orientalist and archaeologist ever. Albright was not himself a member of the biblical theology movement, but his students were its main representatives, and he published several works that had a fundamental importance for the movement, not least his *From the Stone Age to Christianity*, which appeared in 1940.[4]

As indicated by its title, this work covers the history of the ancient Near East from the Stone Age to the rise of Christianity. It is introduced by a discussion of the various disciplines helpful for the study of Near Eastern cultures, especially archaeology and epigraphy. Then follows a chapter "Toward an Organismic Philosophy of History," which, in accordance with the spirit of the time and with great respect for the work of the British historian Arnold Toynbee and his philosophy of history, proposes to see meaning in history: history is purposeful and directed by "laws."[5]

The next four chapters of his book are devoted to the history of the ancient Near East with the four telling titles: "Praeparatio," "When Israel was a Child . . .", "Charisma and Catharsis," and "In the Fulness of Time . . ." "Praeparatio" includes an overview of the history of the Near East from early times to the middle of the second millennium BCE. From here the Old Testament takes over. The chapter "When Israel was a Child . . ." is a well-formulated defense of the historical Moses and the originality of Mosaic monotheism. In the following chapter we find the history of Israel from Joshua's conquest of Canaan—and Albright still believed in a violent conquest—to the fall of Israel and the exile. The final chapter is about Judaism and Hellenism but ends with a section "Jesus the Christ." Christ is the fulfillment of history.

It is obvious that the biblical theology movement presupposes this "organismic" idea of history as expressed by Albright: Christ is the center of history, which is an accepted and traditional doctrine of the church. Everything that precedes Christ finds its explanation in the incarnation. The study of secular history is supposed to confirm this impression, and it is the historian's/theologian's task to look for this confirmation.

We saw a similar attitude behind von Rad's theology oriented toward tradition history. Von Rad built on critical biblical scholarship as it had developed over more than a century. He considered the division of the Pentateuch into four source documents as indisputable. He was of the opinion, along with his contemporary Martin Noth, that although it was possible to study many episodes from the history of ancient Israel on the basis of biblical literature, there were also periods that the historian could not reach. This attitude found its best expression in Noth's history. Here the traditions about the patriarchs, the exodus, and the revelation at Sinai belong among the sacred literature of the sacral league, Noth's amphictyony or twelve-tribe league.

4. See p. 287.
5. Arnold Joseph Toynbee (1889–1975) was a British universal historian, whose main opus, *A Study of History*, 12 vols. (Oxford: Oxford University, 1934–61), was devoted to the cyclic course of history, following history through different stages from greatness to decay.

To Albright this was blasphemy. He, and especially his students, used violent language when characterizing their German opponents as "nihilists." Without a historical period of the patriarchs and without the historical exodus and revelation at Sinai, not much would be left of the history that led to Christ. The answer from the members of the biblical theology movement was not a theological one but an archaeological one, and it found it main expression in John Bright's *A History of Israel* from 1959, which basically follows the layout of Albright's *From the Stone Age to Christianity* although Albright's "In the Fulness of Time" is reduced in Bright's version to an appendix at the end, "Toward the Fullness of Time."

In their time, Albright and his students dominated the American scene until the 1970s. Albright died in 1971 and hereafter his authority soon disappeared. But until then—or at least oral tradition says so—the members of the biblical theology movement were known to react in a most forceful if not violent way against any opponents not so convinced of the correctness of Albright's arguments. The impact of the biblical theology movement on the North American theological landscape is still felt. Bright's history is still used as a textbook in many North American colleges—not because it is the best available, but because of its attitude to the study of the biblical history: it is still the task of the historian to confirm this history, an aim definitely supported by conservative theologians.[6]

In spite of such successes, it must be said that the biblical theology movement failed. Wright and his allies were of the conviction that archaeology would be able to confirm the historicity of biblical events. They dug for many years in the soil of Palestine to find evidence of Joshua's conquest, the existence of the historical David, everything pertaining to the biblical history of Israel, always referring to their grand master, Albright, as the master of Palestinian archaeology.

Archaeology fought back. The insistence on the importance of archaeology had severe consequences when its representatives in increasing numbers had to question the accuracy of the biblical tradition. Unable any longer to create confidence among the public, the situation led to an increasing distrust in the historicity of the biblical narrative.

THE COLLAPSE OF HISTORY AND THE BIBLICAL THEOLOGY MOVEMENT

This change of attitude, caused by archaeologists who were unable to confirm the historical exactness of biblical storytelling, should not be forgotten when we are discussing the previously mentioned "collapse of history," an expression in the context of Old Testament studies coined by Leo G. Perdue.[7] Perdue and scholars of the same perspective speak about the collapse of the modern scientific paradigm

---

6. The most recent edition of Bright (with a preface by William P. Brown) is the fourth (Louisville, KY: Westminster John Knox, 2000).
    7. See above p. 299.

from the viewpoint of epistemology and because of philosophical speculation. The discourse within such sectors has led to a change from modernity to the postmodern world. It should, however, not be forgotten that although the intellectual elite of today has turned "postmodern," the majority is still very much "modern." Among the general public, nothing has really changed. They are still as historically oriented as before the breakthrough of postmodernism, and have little interest in the hermeneutics of history. They believe something—in the Bible or elsewhere—to be either true or false. There is no third choice! By true or false they mean, did it happen or did it not happen? The truth of the Bible is a historical one. If there was no Abraham, no Isaac, no Jacob, then the Bible is a lie. This is admittedly a primitive but useful point of view, and modern conservative and evangelical contributions to this debate demonstrate that at least conservatives are well aware of this state of affairs.

Although the biblical theology movement should be dead by now, it still survives as far as its hermeneutics are concerned among the laity as representing the majority's approach to "historical" literature. Ideas of biblical theology expressed by John Strange and Rainer Albertz may be close to the orientation of the biblical theology movement, although both scholars are aware of the changes in historical research that have occurred since the 1950s.

Perdue is not interested in the collapse of biblical history. His interest is in the changing attitude toward the interpretation of texts as part of the postmodern process. In his settlement with historical-critical scholarship Perdue aims at its intellectual background. He is not interested in its results. As a matter of fact he seems—like many other scholars sharing his ideas—to accept most of them. In spite of a general rejection of historical-critical scholarship as such, he accepts a version of the history of Israel that may be called mildly conservative. This has no real importance to Perdue, because in his theological recommendations he moves toward liberation theology and other related subjects. However, this attitude creates problems for a "self-proclaimed" postmodern theologian like Brueggemann, although Brueggemann is hardly aware of their existence.

At the center of the postmodern project as seen from the viewpoint oriented toward the Bible we find the concept of "truth." Truth has changed from something external to the biblical text to something that has to do with the encounter between the text of the Bible and its reader. There are many ways to describe this change. However, to be brief, Western philosophy has, through its history, had two poles, the subjective and the objective (sometimes called "positivistic"). The basic question is, does an objective truth exist, or is truth a subjective issue? Is it possible to reach back to the ancient history of Israel and its religion in a positivistic way, or is this quest just another expression of the arrogance of the Western mind?

Historical-critical scholarship was objective insofar as it was seeking positivistic results. The biblical theology movement was based on such a foundation, which formed its raison d'être, and ended in a serious crisis when its foundation

was shaken. When a historical-critical scholar of the past studied prophetic literature, he might be interested in knowing what the text under scrutiny is about.
However, the meaning of the text was linked to its original situation. Thus the
famous example of the prophecy about the birth of Immanuel in Isaiah 7:1–20
was studied in the context of a historical event assumed to have taken place about
734 BCE. It could therefore not have anything to do with the birth of Christ,
although the story was used for such a purpose by later writers.

The truth did not belong to the text of the Bible. It was part of the world
reflected by this text. This kind of logic dominates critical commentaries dating
from before 1970. After 1970 something new began to appear, especially in
North American exegesis. The child has many names, depending on the viewpoint of the reader, according to the hermeneutic of "reader response" exegesis.
It has to do with the answer provided by the text of the Bible when it is read by
a modern reader. Seen in this light, Isaiah's prophecy about Immanuel would not
be important because it belonged to the context of 734 BCE but because the
modern reader saw it as important. The modern reader will still be dependent on
the knowledge he or she had acquired, meaning that a Christian reader would
perforce see Isaiah 7:14 in the light of the New Testament. A Jewish reading
would be different. The conclusion is that interpretation of a text like Isaiah 7:14
is subjective, linked to the reader and no one else.

Over the following decades, North American theology witnessed the tri-
umphal forward march of reader-response related exegesis. At the end of the
twentieth century, this kind of biblical interpretation has almost ousted previous
historical-critical exegesis. Historical-critical interpretation had, as a child of the
Enlightenment, developed into a dominating "hegemonistic" (a favorite expression among postmodern theologians) method demonstrating the superiority of
the European male to the rest of the world. Postmodern exegetes believed themselves to have been liberated from historical-critical exegesis and saw themselves
as representing liberation theology, ignoring the fact that the liberation of biblical studies began two hundred years ago, when historical-critical scholarship
broke with a reading of the Bible dictated by the church.

From the point of view of the history of the intellectual development—at least
among North American theologians—the postmodern project is beset with problems. The laity have not accepted it. Rather, it has weakened the acceptance of
theology and humanistic studies in general among the public. Today the concept
of the truth as established by natural science is totally dominant and is, in the
eyes of the laity, simply *science*—although a great part of the believing community in North America is still "prescientific," which means that it is not interested
in historical-critical advances. Natural science has won simply because it does not
normally include the subjective element always present in humanistic studies.
Newton explained the fall of the apple toward mother earth by introducing the
law of gravity. The apple will always fall down. It is possible to repeat the experiment, and the result will remain the same. Natural science is modern (although

some may say that nuclear physics may sometimes approach postmodernism) and remains modern. An attack by theologians against the intellectual breakthrough of the Enlightenment, which had as one of its main intentions the appearance of modern natural science, will only be ignored by the public of today.

A reader's letter in a local newspaper included the following story, which shows the humanist's dilemma: The writer traveled by train in northern Sweden with a Swedish scholar on the subject of the Eskimo. The writer had recently visited Greenland and liked the place. He asked the professor if he had visited Greenland and how he liked the place. The professor told him that he had visited Greenland briefly, but really didn't like the place. He preferred to stay home and read and write about the Eskimos. Now the writer understood the essence of humanistic studies: stay home and write books based on what other people wrote!

When Perdue and his colleagues describe postmodern exegesis as liberation, some caution is necessary. Although postmodern exegesis considers itself a liberation from historical-critical scholarship, the real liberation happened, as was also stressed by the late James Barr, centuries ago.[8] It is possible that postmodernism creates a status of serfdom for biblical studies, subjected to the tastes of the individual. The individual becomes more important than anything, maybe more important than Christ. Remember the very existence of Christ is, from a postmodern perspective, something that exists only in the encounter between the modern reader and the text of the New Testament. If there is no reader, there is no Christ.

Nevertheless, much that is positive may also be said about postmodern exegesis. The problem with historical-critical scholarship can best be characterized by another story, related by a Danish systematic theologian: A young man is traveling by train between Copenhagen and Aarhus, a city some 200 miles northwest of Copenhagen. He writes a letter to the woman he loves. After several years this letter ends up in the hands of a historical-critical scholar who begins his analysis of the letter by acquiring all kinds of information about the travel, the ticket, fare, the weather, and more. But he never sits down to read the text of the letter.

This story does not give a totally false impression of historical-critical scholarship as it used to be. This kind of scholarship often ended up buried in details without recognizing the major subjects under study. Like the biblical theology movement, it reacted toward criticism in an apologetic way, trying to preserve what could no longer be preserved. In spite of its repeated attacks on plain fundamentalism, it was essentially not totally foreign to it. Some subjects were not studied and some questions never asked. Historical-critical scholarship often limited itself to scratching the surface and remained in the dark when issues popped up like the historicity of King David or the historical Moses.

8. See Barr's critical attitude to Brueggemann's theology (see below) in *The Concept of Biblical Theology*, 553–54, and his general settlement with postmodernism and postmodern exegesis in his *History and Ideology in the Old Testament: Biblical Studies at the End of a Millennium* (Oxford: Oxford University, 2000), 141–62 and 163–78.

WALTER BRUEGGEMANN AND GOD'S TRIAL

Brueggemann's "postmodern" theology of the Old Testament is the most comprehensive study of Old Testament theology on a nonhistorical foundation, and so far the only one.[9] Brueggemann tries to place the many expressions in the Old Testament of God and his interaction with his chosen people in a number of boxes. He has no interest in the historical referent, that is, what lies behind the text as we have it, but concentrates instead on the direct testimony of the text and its interface with its modern reader.

It is a comprehensive book, as Barr stresses, of no fewer than 777 pages. It is subdivided into five sections, introduced by a prolegomenon split between two tasks: First, Brueggemann presents a survey of the development of Old Testament theology up to the end of the historical-critical era. Then he describes the task of a theology of the Old Testament in the future. This discussion continues in the fifth part of the book, where Brueggemann presents a series of ways to make the theology of the Old Testament relevant to a contemporary multicultural society.

The main section of the book centers on a "metaphor," a case in court, chosen because Brueggemann has no interest in absolute certainty. He has only contempt for the quest since the Enlightenment to reach the "truth." He decides not to follow such a course and explains his choice of venue for his theology. When a juridical case goes to court, many things are unknown. The circumstances involved are only vaguely known. During the process testimonies will be presented. First we have the basic testimonies, aimed at a characterization of the person whose acts are being scrutinized by the court. After this introduction the cross-examination follows. Now the integrity and motives of this person are questioned. Then we have a third phase—or so Brueggemann believes—when some witnesses say more than they intended to say, when they leave the role they have been assigned by the prosecutor or the defense.

The metaphor is a bit strained and may not be correctly used. After all, as argued by James Barr in his critique of Brueggemann, it is the task of the court to find out what happened and make decisions based on the knowledge supposed to be in the possession of the court.[10] It sounds like an old-fashioned historical-critical project.

In spite of such criticism, the choice of the court case is not a bad one. We may say that God plays a much more prominent role in Brueggemann's theology than in any other theology we have discussed. It is not the God who acts in history—Brueggemann has absolutely no sympathy for the essential quest of the biblical theology movement—but the God who is at the center of the testimony of the text of the Old Testament. For that reason the first part of Brueggemann's theology has the very appropriate title "Israel's Core Testimony." How does the

---

9. Walter Brueggemann, *Theology of the Old Testament: Testimony, Dispute, Advocacy* (Minneapolis: Fortress, 1997).

10. Barr, *Concept of Biblical Theology*, 548–49.

Old Testament speak about God? "What is the grammar of this text?" is actually a favorite expression of Brueggemann's. He uses grammatical elements to guide his reader through the various texts of the Old Testament relevant to the process of expressing God. First, he discusses verbs. He opens paragraphs with verbal sentences and looks for the Hebrew verbs used in connection with the activities of God, for example, the creation. The primary expressions of God's acting here are בָּרָא and עָשָׂה, but other verbs are also used like כּוּן, "to establish," יָצַר, "to shape," קָנָה, "to create," or in connection with God as the one who promises something, שָׁבַע, "to swear," נָתַן, "to give," and בָּרַךְ, "to bless." God as the one who liberates is characterized by the verbs employed, for example, in Yahweh's self-legitimation in Exodus 6:6: "Say therefore to the Israelites, 'I am the LORD, and I will free (יָצָא) you from the burdens of the Egyptians and deliver (נָצַל) you from slavery to them. I will redeem (גָּאַל) you with an outstretched arm and with mighty acts of judgment.'"

Other themes are mentioned but it is, according to Brueggemann, a remarkable fact that this "grammar" of the verbs leads the reader through every central theme of the Pentateuch as identified by Martin Noth and Gerhard von Rad.[11] The expressions listed here are not casual but central to the testimony of the Old Testament about its God as the God of Israel. However, Brueggemann also stresses that it is impossible to create a systematic connection between the different verbal expressions:

> Israel does not offer a finished portrayal of Yahweh. Israel only provides the materials out of which a coherent account of Yahweh, *in any particular setting*, might be presented. Israel offers odd, incidental, concrete, episodic case studies, whereby material is given from which the listener may do constructive work.[12]

This is Brueggemann's way of saying that we find no systematic theology in the Old Testament, only proposals for such a theology—hardly a sensational observation. Every traditional theology of the Old Testament will agree.

Second, Brueggemann moves from verbs to adjectives. What kind of adjectives are used in connection with Yahweh? He opens his analysis with Exodus 34:6–7 where a series of adjectives is used to characterize the essence of God:

> "The LORD, the LORD, a God merciful (רַחוּם) and gracious (חַנּוּן), slow to anger (אֶרֶךְ אַפַּיִם), and abounding in steadfast love (רַב־חֶסֶד) and faithfulness (אֱמֶת), [7] keeping steadfast love (נֹצֵר חֶסֶד) for the thousandth generation, forgiving (נֹשֵׂא) iniquity and transgression and sin, yet by no means clearing the guilty, but visiting the iniquity of the parents upon the children and the children's children, to the third and the fourth generation."

Brueggemann mentions the method of using adjectives in this passage: it opens with a series of positive characterizations that lasts until the final part of verse 7,

---

11. Brueggeman, *Theology of the Old Testament*, 205.
12. Ibid., 206.

when it turns and Yahweh is presented as the God who punishes. The verbs are used to characterize the acts of God, but the adjectives describe God's nature.

The third grammatical element included here comes as no surprise: the nouns. They can be found in a chapter titled "Yahweh as Constant." It is clear that when we speak about Yahweh by using nouns, we are speaking a metaphorical language. Brueggemann therefore includes a discussion about the concept of metaphors as he sees them. Metaphors are "nouns that function in Israel in order to give access to the Subject of verbs, who is endlessly elusive." They are also "nouns used to characterize the Subject, God." The metaphor is not identical with God, and the example quoted shows this: "Yahweh is my shepherd." Yahweh is God, not a shepherd.

There is another way of using metaphors in the Old Testament, in opposition to idolatry and pointing toward monotheism. Finally, as Brueggemann's fourth point, metaphors are used to characterize the nature of Yahweh "because no single name is adequate." The nature of God cannot be expressed by only one image.

The following pages are dedicated to a systematization of the metaphors about God in the Old Testament, showing him to be the God who reigns, who judges, who acts as a king, a warrior, and a father. There seems—or so Brueggemann thinks—to be a kind of contradiction here. The metaphors show Yahweh to be a gracious and loving God, but they also have another story to tell of Yahweh as an awe-inspiring power. We also see metaphors that describe Yahweh as an artist, a healer, a gardener, a mother, and a shepherd.

An review of the language of metaphors shows an image of God with many colors. This image is not always in internal harmony. Sometimes there is an unmitigated transfer from one aspect of the image to the other. Brueggemann also stresses the originality of this image, although he is probably exaggerating a little: many of the metaphors used in the Old Testament have been used in other religious literature from the ancient Near East.

Well, at the end of the day it must be admitted that Brueggemann's "grammar" gives a remarkable and comprehensive impression of the God of Israel. Verbs, adjectives, nouns (metaphors)—together they tell a multifaceted story about God according to the "testimony" of Israel. Now it is time for the cross-examination; now it is time to modify or even reject the testimony of God's nature already presented. God is called to defend himself. The concepts used here are "the hidden God," "the ambiguity of God," and the dark side of God's nature/acts. Israel has questions to put to its God.

There are many ways of organizing such questions. We may open with the question, how long? as in Psalm 6:3: "My soul also is struck with terror, while you, O LORD—how long?" a question that is repeated a number of times in the Psalms. "How long?" is followed by a "why?" as in Psalm 10:1: "Why, O LORD, do you stand far off? Why do you hide yourself in times of trouble?" and a "where?" as in Psalm 42:3: "My tears have been my food day and night, while people say to me continually, 'Where is your God?'"

Such questions are expressions of hopelessness when Yahweh has forsaken those who believe in him. They express doubts about Yahweh's power. The absence of Yahweh or the hidden Yahweh is constantly a problem for his faithful, a problem familiar to Israel—according to Brueggemann. This also implies the ambiguity of Yahweh, whose acts according to the Old Testament may not always be considered "ethical." Sometimes Yahweh abuses, cheats, and seduces. The story of Micaiah son of Imlah in 1 Kings 22 is a cruel example of how Yahweh entices the king of Israel to attack Aram, where he is killed.

This part, including the cross-examination of God, has, of course, more to offer. The image of God presented by the Old Testament includes many contradictions, and the Old Testament itself is a story about how Israel in its testimony had to cope with such contradictions.

The final part of the interrogation is about—in Brueggemann's words—"unsolicited testimony." This part of the court procedure involves "unwanted" or "unintended" testimonies where a witness says too much. The defense or the prosecutor will instruct his witness to say only what fits the defense or the prosecution. However, the witness often goes further and includes extra information not asked for. We also have such extras in the testimony of Israel about its God. The codeword in this part of Brueggemann's theology is "partner." Who is Yahweh's partner? First and foremost, Israel, then the individual human being, then the nations—in a positive sense when the Gentiles are united in praise to the God of Israel, and in a negative sense when Yahweh makes use of foreign powers to punish unfaithful Israel.

Also the world, or in Brueggemann's terminology "creation," may count as Yahweh's partner. Maybe it would have been easier to accept his suggestion if he had said the world as created, which is blessed by God.

There are more facets to the image of God painted by Brueggemann in this theology of his. It is hardly possible or necessary to include every aspect here. It would also be repetitious.

If we ask whether Brueggemann succeeds in writing a theology of the Old Testament that does not follow the layout of traditional theologies, the answer is definitely yes. If we compare his theology to that of Otto Kaiser, published at the same time as his,[13] the similarities and differences are striking. As the title of Kaiser's theology says (*The God of the Old Testament*), God is no less in the center of Kaiser's theology of the Old Testament than in Brueggemann's version. Kaiser also introduces his theology with a prolegomenon, although, in contrast to Brueggemann, Kaiser's prolegomenon is more or less a history of Israel's religion. Kaiser's theology belongs squarely within the German tradition of writing theologies of the Old Testament, building on a historical foundation.

The images of God created by Brueggemann and Kaiser are very much the same. The major difference lies in the tools selected for creating this image, and here there is much that speaks in favor of Brueggemann's approach. Brueggemann's Yahweh is allowed to stand forth in all his multiplicity. Brueggemann does not attempt to

13. See pp. 296–97.

cover up the ambiguous nature of Yahweh as found in the Bible. In Kaiser's theology, the traditional historical paradigm is always lurking in the background and can be called upon to explain differences. Brueggemann's neglect of history means that he abstains from historically oriented explanations of the nature of God as presented by different parts of the Old Testament. He allows such differences to speak for themselves. In his theology one image of God is not replaced by another. All differences are there, undisturbed by historical considerations.

Brueggemann's project has succeeded. It is definitely possible to write a theology of the Old Testament on a synchronic and postmodern foundation, based on the testimony of texts that are relevant for theological analysis. The image of God has never been better exposed than in this postmodern project.

Potential criticism directed against Brueggemann at most involves the paraphernalia. His language is, as remarked by Barr, a kind of "as-if-language." Brueggemann has problems expressing his ideas in clear, plain language. He does not tell you exactly what he is talking about but walks around his themes, trying to make them precise without saying precisely what they are. In this way Brueggemann establishes an unnecessary distance between himself and his readers, or maybe he thinks of the distance as necessary because it always provides him with an opportunity to withdraw. The extensive amount of political correctness here is another way of creating such an escape route.

More serious are the examples of traditional historical-critical scholarship present in this theology of the Old Testament. It is thus necessary to ask Brueggemann about the meaning of "Israel" in his book. What does he mean by "Israel's testimony"? What is this "Israel"? If he said "the Old Testament" there would have been nothing to question; so why "Israel"? The answer might be that Israel is here used to summarize everything in the Old Testament that serves as a testimony about God. If this is the case, there is no problem at all. However, Breuggemann never tells his reader what this Israel really is. Could it be the Israel that appears in the Old Testament, that is, *biblical* Israel? Now it becomes a problematic issue, because there are several parts of the Old Testament where this Israel does not appear, especially in Wisdom literature, which plays an important role in Brueggemann's description of the image of God in the Old Testament.

It might, however, also be that he means *ancient* Israel, understood as the Israel created by modern historical-critical scholarship. There is much in his theology to recommend such a view. If this is a correct observation—and it should not be forgotten that Brueggemann says that he has no intention of rejecting the results of historical-critical scholarship—then we have to ask questions about the character of this theology as a postmodern project. Maybe he is just accepting a historical paradigm uncritically and believes that it is a solution to all problems. In this case Brueggemann's theology becomes somewhat redundant and represents only a new and smart way of saying what has already been said by many other theologians of the past. This may be the reason—but it cannot be proven—for Leo G. Perdue to publish his *Reconstructing Old Testament Theology*, already discussed.[14] Perdue expressed great hopes for Brueggemann's (then) forthcoming theology several years before it appeared. These hopes may not have been fulfilled by Brueggemann's theology as published.

A final remark is in order concerning Brueggemann's choice of writing only a theology of the Old Testament. Brueggemann does not favor biblical theology—especially not its canonical version represented by Sanders and Childs (he didn't know Rendtorff's when he published his theology, since it was not yet published).[15] Brueggemann is dominated by a desire for political correctness that may have persuaded him to ignore—if not reject—Christian elements in the Old Testament. His Old Testament is definitely the Hebrew Bible. Instead of pointing to reasons for including *his* Old Testament in the Christian Bible, he underscores its undeniable Jewish basis, although this is quite absurd for a book with the title *Theology of the Old Testament*. Some say that Brueggemann has written not a theology of the Old Testament but a Jewish theology of the Hebrew Bible. This may be a good compromise, but what is characteristic of a good compromise? No one is satisfied with it! Jewish theologians may recognize Brueggemann for his good intentions, but would perhaps add that no Jewish theologian would limit his theological analysis to the Hebrew Bible. He would study the Bible in connection with his reading of Jewish commentaries, especially the Talmud.

The Christian theologian cannot be satisfied with the few sentences included in Brueggemann's theology about the New Testament and the relevance of the Old Testament for the New. A theology of the Old Testament that is no more than that will, in a Christian context, be no more than a study of the history of thought. No links between the two testaments are established in this way. It might even be said that it helps deepen the differences and may provoke Christian readers to ask questions about the position of the Old Testament within *their* Bible.

14. See pp. 334–36.

15. It is interesting but not totally fair to Brueggemann that Barr places him close to the North American canonical theologians. It may be that the intentions of Brueggemann and Childs are not very dissimilar but the execution is totally different.

Chapter 18

The Old and New Testaments

Elements from the Discussion
in the Twentieth Century

THE OLD AND THE NEW TESTAMENTS
IN CHRISTIAN AND JEWISH THEOLOGY

We have until now discussed only the theology of the Old Testament in its many forms. We have deliberately ignored parts of the discussion, such as the debate among Jewish theologians. The decision not to discuss Jewish contributions is of course not very politically correct, and the often sharp criticism of the Christian usurpation of the Jewish Bible formulated by Jon D. Levenson is both important and in many ways correct.[1] This writer is both absolutely on board with Levenson and at the same time in total disagreement with him. The problems caused by Western Christianity's acceptance of the Hebrew Bible have already been mentioned. The Hebrew Bible did not exist when early Christianity came into being. Thus the Hebrew Bible was not Paul's Bible. It is a rabbinically edited collection of Hebrew (and Aramaic) literature from the time after 70 CE, after the destruction of the second temple and the appearance of pharisaically inspired rabbinic

---

1. In his *The Hebrew Bible, the Old Testament, and Historical Criticism.* See p. 276.

Judaism. The true Christian Old Testament is the Septuagint, the Greek version with all its idiosyncrasies.

Jewish exegesis, understood as the traditional Jewish interpretation of the Hebrew Bible, may be extremely interesting for the student of the Hebrew Bible. It is, however, hardly relevant in a Christian connection, except when it addresses subjects and themes of a common interest to both Jews and Christians. More than one of Levenson's books fulfills this demand.[2]

Levenson's criticism is definitely on the mark when Christian Old Testament theologians focus on the Old Testament alone—even in the shape of the Hebrew Bible—and pretend that this is a Christian and not a Jewish book. Most theologies of the last two hundred years have been based on this false assumption and have deliberately deceived themselves and their readership, because their authors were not ignorant of the fact that this book belongs to a Jewish and not a Christian environment. They, accordingly, forced the content of the Hebrew Bible to agree with Christian doctrine, although it seems likely that the Jewish writings in the Hebrew Bible may have been collected and edited as an antithesis to the Bible of the Christians. It was perhaps not the basis for the development of the Christian Bible.[3]

It is absolutely absurd if, in a Christian context, Old Testament theology is a subject that is studied only on the basis of the Hebrew Bible. If the Hebrew Bible is the only foundation for such a theology, it will turn out to be a *Jewish* theology of the Old Testament, which is a *contradictio in adjectu*, as the name "Old Testament" presupposes the existence of a new one. This is not presumed by the Hebrew Bible.

The growing recognition of the difference between the Jewish Bible and the Christian New Testament led to the alienation of the Old Testament from Christian theology. The first break of the old tradition occurred only few years after Gabler's lecture at Altdorf in 1787, when G. L. Bauer in 1800–1802 proposed to separate biblical studies into two parts, the Old Testament and the New Testament. His proposal was based not on theological but historical considerations and can be seen as one of the first results of the new historical-critical consciousness of the biblical scholar. In this changing intellectual situation the journey of the Old Testament, from representing sacred literature to becoming a textbook of the history of religion, had begun.

From a historical-critical point of view, such a development was unavoidable and legitimate. From a Christian theological point of view, it was harmful to both Old Testament and New Testament studies, including theology. The Old Testament became not only a textbook for the history of religion; it also became a

---

2. Thus his *Creation and the Persistence of Evil: The Jewish Drama of Divine Omnipotence* (San Francisco: Harper & Row, 1988), and *The Death and Resurrection of the Beloved Son: The Transformation of Child Sacrifice in Judaism and Christianity* (New Haven, CT: Yale University, 1993). See also his recent volume, *Resurrection and the Restoration of Israel: The Ultimate Victory of the God of Life* (New Haven, CT: Yale University, 2006).

3. See, e.g., the debate about the place of the book of Daniel, already mentioned earlier, p. 280.

problem for Christianity, the church. We may even say that before the break-through of modern scholarship, neither the Old Testament nor the New Testament in isolation was a problem for Christianity; the whole Bible was. The Catholic Church decided to remove any problem related to the Bible by excluding the laity from reading it, by keeping it in Latin, from the early Middle Ages a language inaccessible to ordinary people. The Irish-Scottish Old Testament scholar Robert Carroll has called the Bible a "wolf in a sheepfold," and it is the duty of clerics to protect their congregations from such a predator.[4] We saw at the end of the twentieth century, when the new millennium was approaching, how all sorts of doomsday movements appeared "based on reading the Bible," completely out of the control of the clerics. When the world turned "modern" and the unity of the two testaments was basically a thing of the past, the New Testament became the book of the church and the Old Testament still remained a problem. Historical-critical scholarship did not possess any means to control the beast. On the contrary, as historical-critical scholarship developed, it became increasingly difficult to keep the Old Testament a part of the canon.[5]

What separates the Old Testament from the New Testament? Let me relate an incident from the life of this writer. Back in the 1980s I taught an introductory university course in Hebrew. Shortly before the examinations one of the best students was missing from class. When he came back, I asked him why he had stayed away for so long. The answer was rather astonishing: "I had to pass an examination in basic New Testament subjects. If it had been the similar course in the Old Testament, I would not have been absent here, because that is easy. New Testament is difficult, because there they demand not only that you know your stuff; you must also believe in it, and that is difficult!"

New Testament scholars have often been in doubt about what to do with the Old Testament. The assertion of traditional historical-critical scholarship, that the Old Testament was a creation of ancient Israel, which ceased to exist in 587 BCE, had created a gap between the time of the Old Testament and the New Testament of, well, 587 years. The realization that Judaism had also played its part in the final redaction of the *Israelite* books was not of much help. It was rather harmful, as Judaism was seen as representing a perversion of true Yahwism as practiced by the ancient Israelites.

Although many biblical scholars tried to build a bridge between the two testaments by applying a tradition-historical approach to their study—we need mention only Gerhard von Rad—it all resulted in Harnack's already quoted rejection of the Old Testament as a book belonging to the Christian church. The only

4. Robert P. Carroll, *Wolf in the Sheepfold* (London: SPCK, 1991). The North American reader seems to have been in need of a pedagogical title: *The Bible as a Problem for Christianity* (Philadelphia: Trinity Press, 1991).

5. The Danish theologian and poet N. F. S. Grundtvig (1783–1872) found a better way to express the difference between the testaments: The New Testament is the book of the church, while the Old Testament belongs in the school. Grundtvig was himself a great reformer of the school system and especially famous for his invention of the free "high school" (cultural institutions without examination) open to everyone.

way out of the dilemma would be to propose a hermeneutic that allowed the Old Testament to be read in a context decided by the New Testament.

RUDOLF BULTMANN
AND THE HERMENEUTICS OF FAITH

The hermeneutics of Rudolf Bultmann (1884–1976) may be an example of how to attempt to solve a problem that cannot really be solved. Bultmann was without doubt one of the most important, if not the most important, New Testament scholar of the last century. His approach to the Old Testament should not have created problems, as he was a student of the then-leading Old Testament scholar, Hermann Gunkel. In spite of his studies of the Old Testament under the supervision of Gunkel, he had to invent a hermeneutical understanding of the Old Testament that was able to remove the historical-critical obstacles between the two testaments.

The subject of Rudolf Bultmann and the Old Testament is enormous, and his contributions to this field spread over his many publications. There is, however, no need to go into further detail here, as the job has been done by the German scholar Karolina de Valerio.[6] The point of departure for most discussions about Bultmann and the Old Testament is the somewhat dubious character of the European attitude to Judaism in the beginning of the twentieth century. As already mentioned, it was common in those days to see ancient Judaism described as inferior to Christianity. Inspired by a somewhat Lutheran reading of Paul and the Christian tradition after him, the theologians of that time stressed the difference between "the dead letter of the Law" and "the living Gospel."

Since Luther, it has been normal within Protestant Christianity that any reading of the Old Testament must be christocentric (in Luther's words, *Christum treiben*). The Old Testament is relevant for Christianity only insofar as the testimony about Christ in the Old Testament is the reason for reading it. Positively this demands a focus on the Old Testament as a book of promise, a prophecy about the coming of the Messiah, fulfilled in the incarnation in the New Testament. In order to understand the incarnation, one must read the Old Testament, especially the prophetic literature.

This sounds familiar to any reader of the Old Testament. Early Christians read the books of the prophets as testimonies about the Christ who would come. If these Christians could read, they would also soon understand that there is more than this in the Old Testament. The Old Testament begins with creation, and so that the reader should truly understand its importance, there are two stories about

---

6. *Altes Testament und Judentum im Frühwerk Rudolf Bultmanns*, BZAW 71 (Berlin: de Gruyter, 1993). This writer, being Danish, also had access to Katrine Winkel Holm, *Det Gamle Testamente som teologisk problem*, Tekst og Tolkning 12 (Copenhagen: Museum Tusculanum Press, 2000). Winkel Holm is positive to the intentions of de Valerio's study and her collection of the relevant material, but critical of de Valerio's lack of overview, which involves her theological conclusions.

creation. The story of original sin sets the parameters for human life. God's originally perfect world is destroyed by disobedient humanity. However, everything
will be restored when Christ is born—in the Jewish tradition, the new King
David. Life in God's world is regulated by the commands of the Decalogue in
particular and the law in general.

The Old Testament includes more than one way to understand God. The first
is through his creation. Yahweh is praised because of his wonderful world, perhaps no better than in the great hymn of Psalm 104. In European tradition this
way to God was understood as natural theology. The Enlightenment was the high
moment of natural theology, because it recommended itself to the rationalism of
this period. Recent Protestantism reacted sharply against natural theology, which
was ostracized after Karl Barth's famous "Nein!" to Emil Brunner, The only way
to understand God is through the revelation in Jesus Christ. It can be said that
this "Nein!" was of little help for the reception of the Old Testament among
Protestant theologians of the twentieth century.[7] Catholic theologians have never
had the same problems with natural theology, which many centuries ago was recognized as a legitimate way to understand God. It is hardly a wonder that modern Catholic theologians in their discussions about the theology of the Old
Testament may refer to natural theology as an appropriate means of understanding God. A fine example of this attitude can be found in the recent book of Othmar Keel and Silvia Schroer on creation.[8]

There is in the Old Testament one more way to know God: the revelation.
God reveals himself to humanity: first to the patriarchs, then to Moses alone in
the burning bush, and finally to all of Israel at Sinai.

Barth's insistence on the unique value of the revelation of Christ in the New
Testament—that this is the only way to God—will perforce lead to a rejection of
the revelation in the Old Testament as of any relevance for Christian belief. This
is in contrast to the Protestant habit since the days of Luther of including in every
catechism the Decalogue, which opens the story of the revelation at Sinai. Christianity is, in this way, becoming even more particularistic than Islam, which
except in its most primitive form has no problems accepting both the Jewish and

---

7. This "Nein!" introduces the famous Barmen Declaration from 1934, which was published as
a response to the pressure from the German Church, the Christian branch of National Socialism.
Barth's text runs: "Jesus Christus, wie er uns in der Heiligen Schrift bezeugt wird, ist das eine Wort
Gottes, das wir zu hören, dem wir im Leben und im Sterben zu vertrauen und zu gehorchen haben."
[Jesus Christ, as he is attested for us in Holy Scripture, is the one Word of God which we have to
hear and which we have to trust and obey in life and in death.] The antithesis runs: "Wir verwerfen
die falsche Lehre, als könne und müsse die Kirche als Quelle ihrer Verkündigung außer und neben
diesem einen Worte Gottes auch noch andere Ereignisse und Mächte, Gestalten und Wahrheiten als
Gottes Offenbarung anerkennen." [We reject the false doctrine, as though the church could and
would have to acknowledge as a source of its proclamation, apart from and besides this one Word of
God, still other events and powers, figures and truths, as God's revelation.] ET: http://www.german-
lutherans-melbourne.asn.au/en/16330e_barmend. shtml.

8. See above, p. 307n10. James Barr's defense of natural theology should also be noted: *Biblical
Faith and Natural Theology* (Oxford: Oxford University, 1993).

the Christian revelation. In Islam, Jews and Christians belong together with Muslims among the "People of the Book."

All of this created problems for Protestant Christianity in the first part of the twentieth century. Historical-critical scholarship had demonstrated that the Old Testament was no more than a textbook for the history of religion. Yes, the authors of the New Testament literature quoted from this textbook. The reason was believed to be their insufficient understanding of what had happened. Furthermore, they were mistaken, or so it was maintained. Why should the prophet Isaiah worry about Christ if Christ was born about 700 years after Isaiah's death? If we follow Barth's rejection, the ties to the Old Testament have been cut. This was hardly Barth's intention; he has few problems including extensive sections of exegesis in his *Church Dogmatics*. However, it became common among the less reflective followers of Barth to isolate his "Nein" from its historical context and ask that the Old Testament be expelled from the Christian Bible. Although Barth's "Nein" was understood to be a strong denial of the relevance of natural theology and its meaning for theology in the eighteenth and nineteenth centuries, it was in reality also a denial of the relevance of historical-critical studies of the Old Testament for Christianity—with serious consequences for the status of the Old Testament within the church.

Many will say that the Old Testament is a remarkable book. It has so much to say, except about Christianity. It is clear that this old book was accepted by early Christians as a source of illustrative quotations. However, it had no important theological message. It was, in a Christian context, simply of no use.

Bultmann belongs to this period but was not prepared to give up his Old Testament, although he had little respect for liberal theology and its characterization of the Old Testament as a textbook for the history of religion. Bultmann was too much of a Christian theologian to accept a total dismissal of the Old Testament. At the same time, he accepted that the Old Testament will be relevant only if it includes a prophecy concerning the coming of Christ. As a historical-critical exegete he had trouble finding such a prophecy, although as a Christian he understood that it must be there.

Bultmann belonged to the theological direction called existentialism. Following the "ideology" of existentialism, he made a number of choices (inspired by Søren Kierkegaard, who had been his interest as a young student) that enabled him to recognize the christological message of the Old Testament. As a historical document the Old Testament has no importance for Christianity. It is one source of the past and past religion, like so many other documents. We mention Plato's dialogues, Greek and Roman philosophy in general, ancient Near Eastern legends, for example, the Babylonian epic of creation *Enuma Elish*, and Pharaoh Akhetaten's hymn to the sun. From a Christian point of view, the Old Testament is an important testimony about Christ. From a Christian standpoint, correct exegesis will be "the exegesis of faith." It is accepted without debate from historical knowledge that evidence of Christ can be found in the Old Testament. Bultmann talked about "jumping" not into the 70,000 fathoms of Kierkegaard, but into the "hermeneutical circle."

From a scholarly historical-critical point of view this is obviously madness. However, from a postmodern perspective it might be meaningful after all. Here the emphasis is on the relationship between a text and its reader, which will always be there. The same cannot be said for the historical-critical assertion of the link between a text and its supposed historical referent. Although "pre-postmodern"— he died just as postmodernism was breaking out—he can probably be seen as someone who paved the way for a postmodern theology. Somehow his argument in favor of his idea of Christian exegesis resembles James Barr's position that the Bible has authority only if its reader thinks so. It is no longer a sufficient argument simply to refer to the Bible.

Bultmann has been accused of being an anti-Semite—at least anti-Jewish, which is definitely not the same. He undoubtedly was anti-Jewish, although this attitude became politically and ethically unacceptable only after the Holocaust, at least in Bultmann's sense. He merely represented a clear and traditional Christian attitude toward Judaism. After all, the New Testament is outspokenly anti-Jewish. Anti-Judaism is, so to speak, the raison d'être of Christianity. Christianity arose in antiquity as a religion that declared itself in opposition to Judaism, and it would be totally naive to doubt that. Christian eyes colored by New Testament sentiments will still regard Judaism as representing "the dead letter of the Law." There is no reason to deny it (to accept it is another matter). This is not the total story about Christianity and Judaism, but it is a fair part of it.

Bultmann's being "anti-Jewish" has, in principle, nothing to do with the political currents of his time. He represents a traditional Christian rejection of Judaism. We should remember that one element supposed to lead to ideas of ethnicity is the presence of at least two kinds of people. For people living alone on an isolated island, any sense of ethnicity will be absent. This is the case of Robinson Crusoe, who sees who he is only when he confronts the cannibals. There is no reason to dismiss Bultmann's position as anti-Semitism in the banal, however catastrophic, meaning of the word. Anti-Judaism is the correct word, but should never be allowed to develop into anti-Semitism, which is exactly what hundreds of years of Christian instruction has led to.

Jewish theologians have objected to this anti-Judaism, but they don't understand the reasons for it as expressed by Bultmann or Karl Barth. They confuse recent European anti-Semitism with a theological Christian orientation almost two thousand years old. The two religions exist side by side in spite of their differences.

It is telling that Bultmann's appeal to a hermeneutic of faith comes from a New Testament scholar, not an Old Testament scholar. No Old Testament scholar has ever taken up this idea. Most are still bound by historical-critical ideas that have been updated several times. Some of these new ideas and proposals may be of interest in this connection.

MANFRED OEMING AND HIS ALL BIBLICAL THEOLOGY

One of the more interesting proposals has been published by Manfred Oeming, a professor at the University of Heidelberg (famous for also having been the home of Gerhard von Rad). Oeming has published a study, *Gesammtbiblische Theologien* [Theologies of the Entire Bible], available for now only in German.[9] His theological reflections on the relationship between the two testaments are summed up in a series of theses or recommendations:[10]

> Biblical theology must trace the process of rewriting during which the most diverse kinds of themes developed as part of the tradition history. [Biblische Theologie muß die Fortschreibungsprozesse verfolgen, in denen die verschiedensten Themen überlieferungsgeschichtlich entfaltet wurden.]

Fortschreibung or "rewriting" is a new way of saying "tradition history." The original, that is, the first version of a text is rewritten time after time until it is locked as part of a canonical, unchangeable text. Each stage is followed by a series of reflections that lead to changes and rearrangements of the original message of the text. The concept of rewriting is rather popular these days but may simply be understood as a new way to say old things. In classical tradition history—especially in its German variety, based on the development of a written tradition—every stage of the development can be traced as examples of a theological reflection. Here Oeming seems very close to von Rad.

> It (biblical theology) must be able to explain the changes of the content of the faith that it experienced in different historical situations and pay attention to their theological implications. [Sie {Biblische Theologie} muß die Wandlungen bewusst machen, die Glaubensinhalte in verschiedenen historischen Kontexten durchlebt haben und die jeweiligen theologischen Implikationen bedenken.]

Put in a formula, this sounds like the understanding of tradition among canonical theologians like Sanders and Childs. Both have emphasized the character of biblical canonical tradition as handed down by a believing community.

> It must recognize the presence of the productive semantic ambiguities that make it possible with a clear intellectual conscience to find traces of elements of the event of Christ in the Old Testament. [Sie muß die produktiven semantischen Unschärfen erkennen, die es ermöglichen, auch im Alten Testament mit gutem intellektuellen Gewissen Elemente des Christusgeschehens angedeutet zu finden.]

---

9. Manfred Oeming, *Gesamtbiblische Theologien der Gegenwart—Das Verhältnis von Alten und Neuen Testament in der hermeneutischen Diskussion seit Gerhard von Rad* (Stuttgart: Kohlhammer, 1987); new edition in his *Das Alte Testament als Teil des christlichen Kanons? Studien zu gesamtbiblischen Theologien der Gegenwart* (Zurich: Pano Verlag, 2001), 41–243.

10. *Das Alte Testament als Teil des christlichen Kanons?* 271–72.

There are two ways to understand this "thesis." One way would be to study those parts of the Old Testament that de facto are in line with New Testament ideas. One may think of the concept of the messiah in the Old Testament. This may be a classical historical-critical task, although it is also possible to present it otherwise, as done by Thomas L. Thompson in his book on the idea of the messiah, that is, thematically and literarily arranged.[11]

The second way would be to follow Bultmann's proposal, the hermeneutics of faith. But let us allow Oeming to speak for himself again:

> [Biblical theology] will have to appreciate how vital {or vitalizing?} the relation to God is. [Sie muß die Lebendigkeit der Beziehung zu Gott zu würdigen lehren.]

> [Biblical theology] must show, on the basis of the concrete thematic areas, how far one testament may influence the other. [Sie muß an den konkreten Themenfeldern herausarbeiten, inwiefern beide Testamente der gegenseitigen Ergänzung bedürfen.]

> [Biblical theology] will have to keep theological reasoning alive in respect to the contemporary dialogue with a tradition on the move. [Sie muß das theologische Denken lebendig halten für den gegenwärtigen Dialog mit einer bewegten Tradition.]

We may think of Oeming's theses as too influenced by traditional theological concepts. The German language is not always easy to understand. However, his theses summarize in an excellent way the present situation of historical-critical scholarship when confronted by the demands of modern theology. As indicated, we almost hear the voice of Bultmann here: the acceptance of the Old Testament depends on faith.

THE OLD TESTAMENT IN THE NEW TESTAMENT

It is time to return to the central topic of this chapter, the Old Testament in the New Testament. In the New Testament's reception of the Old Testament, there are two conflicting connections. On the one hand, the Old Testament represents the past. The Old Testament is the dead letter of the Law, in contrast to the New Testament, which includes the gospel for the future. On the other hand, the Old Testament also includes all the promises and prophecies that point forward to the life of Christ. The New Testament does nothing more than tell that these prophecies have come true.

It is not uncommon for theologians working with the Old Testament to maintain that the New Testament is incomprehensible if left alone. We only have to

---

11. Thomas L. Thompson, *The Messiah Myth: The Near Eastern Roots of Jesus and David* (New York: Basic Books, 2005).

read the introduction to the Gospel of Matthew with its long genealogy to understand why!—or, for that matter, the Christmas Gospel in Luke. If there were no
Old Testament, we would know that Joseph went to Bethlehem because of a census, but we wouldn't know why. The explanation can be found in the Old Testament, along with its connection to Old Testament concepts of the messiah as being
the new David come from Bethlehem. The Bible does not agree with the assertion
of Karl Barth and dialectical theology that God speaks directly to (an unprepared?)
world. On the contrary, the connections between the two testaments emphasize
that God reveals himself to a world that is—finally—prepared to receive his revelation. "In the fullness of time" is seen not as a historical concept, as the biblical
theological movement understood it to be, but as a theological concept.

In this respect the Old Testament functions as a prolegomenon to the New
Testament. So far nothing here speaks against the hallowed understanding of the
hierarchic order between the two testaments. This function of the Old Testament
does not mean that the Old Testament is subordinated to the New. The Old Testament is not a textbook of the history of religion (which it perhaps also is—however in a different context) that is limited to the time before the birth of Jesus, as
if it was a profane history or a history of the development of thought. The Old
Testament paves the way for the New Testament theologically. The Old Testament comes before the incarnation, while the New Testament tells the story of
the incarnation and what followed it.

The present new form of Marcionism is unhealthy for theology, because it
leaves the gospel alone and deserted—and then the assumption is utopian: that
it should be possible from a theological standpoint to go on without the Old Testament. It is possible to follow Marcion in his rejection of the Old Testament only
if one lacks an extensive knowledge of the Old Testament. We cannot read the
New Testament without the Old, because, in spite of Barth's assertion, it is always
there in the baggage. Barth's "Nein" implies that there is something to say no to.
In spite of the assertion of dialectical theology about God's direct address to
humanity in the incarnation, this address is understandable only because we
already know God from his creation (because of natural theology) and because
God has already addressed humanity through revelation in the Old Testament:

> "I am the God of your father, the God of Abraham, the God of Isaac, and
> the God of Jacob." (Exod. 3:6)

> I am the LORD your God, who brought you out of the land of Egypt, out
> of the house of slavery. (Exod. 20:2)

God has his history—or put another way, God is not without a history. This
is also true of the God of the New Testament. God may speak to humans because
they know the God that speaks to them. If we did not have an Old Testament, it
might just as well be the unknown God of Paul's speech at the Areopagus.

Christianity has known this since ancient times. Otherwise, why would there
be a first part of the confession? "We believe in God the Father almighty, maker

of heaven and earth." Christians do not believe in an unknown God and do not use metaphors about this unknown God—neither in the Old Testament nor in the New. This does not mean that there are no problems in the relationship between Christianity and its God. Brueggemann's survey of the metaphors about the absent God who has turned his back on the faithful gives a good impression of the character of such problems.

The New Testament is the conclusion to the narrative of the Old Testament. In this light we should perhaps no longer imagine the Old Testament as a prolegomenon to the New. Indeed, perhaps it would be more correct to describe the New Testament as an epilogue to the Old. It is similar to the ending of a famous fairy tale: when all the problems are over, the prince gets his princess and half the kingdom and they live happily ever after. The tribulations of the hero of the fairy tale often follow a fixed pattern, describing his traveling from the original harmonious place where he grew up to his final place, where happiness awaits him. We may use a similar model for the story of the Bible. Paradise is the place of harmony—we are still in God's perfect world. Travel, with all its temptations and tribulations, starts when humanity is driven out of paradise and ends when the Messiah is born, and we live happily ever after.

The theme of promise and fulfillment creates a harmonic and unbreakable tie between the two testaments. However, there is still the other theme, the Old Testament as the letter of death. Read without its context, this may be understood as a rejection of the Old Testament. This is a misconception, because not all of the Old Testament has been taken into consideration.

We have already discussed the structural differences between the Hebrew Bible and the Septuagint. The TaNaK is divided into three parts, the Law, the Prophets, and the Writings. The Greek Bible has a different structure: Historical literature, the Writings, and the Prophets. The history related here is the history of old Israel. This Israel is no more, because it was destroyed when God finally turned his back on it and delivered it into the hands of its oppressors. The Prophets have a different subject. They are not about old Israel, but have as their center the Israel to come. The prophetic literature is about the new covenant; the historical literature centers around the old covenant:

> The days are surely coming, says the LORD, when I will make a new covenant with the house of Israel and the house of Judah. [32] It will not be like the covenant that I made with their ancestors when I took them by the hand to bring them out of the land of Egypt—a covenant that they broke, though I was their husband, says the LORD. [33] But this is the covenant that I will make with the house of Israel after those days, says the LORD: I will put my law within them, and I will write it on their hearts; and I will be their God, and they shall be my people. (Jer. 31:31–33)

It is clear that the opposition between the extremes of the Old Testament in the New Testament has been decisive for the arrangement of the books of the Old Testament in the Septuagint. The books of Moses and the historical literature represent the history of death, while the prophets speak about the hope for the future and the coming of the kingdom of God. In between come the Writings. In this Christian tradition of structuring the Bible, the Writings play almost the same role as the Apocrypha in a modern Western Bible: They are placed between the two extremes, on one side the old covenant and on the other the new one (not forgetting that the Latin word *testamentum* also means "covenant"). The Writings are good and useful books but have no decisive importance. The Psalms are highly praised, whether in the Jewish or Christian tradition, but they do not have a decisive importance for faith.

The paradox that the Old Testament is both dead law and promise at one and the same time can be solved if we look at the Old Testament as one narrative. The Old Testament is not exclusively dead law; neither is it exclusively promise. It is both at the same time. Law and promise, however, belong to two separate parts of the narrative in the Old Testament about the two covenants of Israel: *The New Testament is in the Old Testament, and the Old Testament is in the New Testament.* Thus there is no reason to remove the Old Testament from Christian theology. The New Testament does not reject the Old. What we find in the New Testament is a rejection of the tragic history of old Israel, the old people of God. This rejection is already expressed by Jeremiah in the saying that is placed just before the passage from Jeremiah 31 already quoted twice:

"The parents have eaten sour grapes,
and the children's teeth are set on edge."
(Jer. 31:29)

THE OLD TESTAMENT IN THE NEW TESTAMENT:
ACCORDING TO THE SCRIPTURES

We will return in the last chapter to Jeremiah 31 in order to be more precise about the identity of the people who might have entertained such ideas about the two peoples of the two covenants. Here we will only reflect on the testimony in the New Testament about its reception of the Old Testament.

It is not our task here to discuss the many contributions of New Testament scholars to this discussion; neither will we trace every single reference to the Old Testament in the New. I will limit the discussion to one classic, the British theologian Charles Harold Dodd's (1884–1973) little study *According to the Scriptures*.[12] Dodd's thesis is simply that the Old Testament was important for the authors of the New Testament not only as a source of quotations from the Old Testament serving as *Prüftexte*, that is, proofs of the place of the incarnation in history. Among New Testament scholars it had long been popular to think of such quotations as coming from collections (so-called "florilegia") including those parts of the Old Testament considered to be most relevant. Such excerpts

12. (London: James Nisbet & Co., 1952), with the important subtitle: *The Substructure of New Testament Theology.*

have been found among the Dead Sea Scrolls, although Dodd may not yet have known about their existence when he published his little study in 1952.

In the New Testament, especially in the Gospels, we find a series of texts from the Old Testament that must have been considered especially important—a kind of canon within the canon (although there was hardly any fixed edition of the canon in existence when Christianity came into being). Such texts were used to organize the Gospel literature.

A text like Jeremiah 31:31–34 is of course very important and is quoted in extenso in Hebrews (8:8–12). There are also allusions to this passage in other places, like 1 Corinthians 11:25 and 2 Corinthians 3. Isaiah 6–9 is just as important and is quoted a number of times in the New Testament. Dodd mentions in this discussion other texts as well, including some from Daniel with its apocalyptic visions.

The decisive point is not that New Testament authors quote from the Old Testament here and there. The decisive point is that how they use the quotations from the Old Testament reveals that they are aware of the context of such quotations within the Old Testament. Thus it is possible in the case of the last of the Servant Songs in Deutero-Isaiah (52:13–53:12) to find so many quotations in the New Testament that practically every part of the song is quoted somewhere in it. The way this text is quoted may be different from time to time (Dodd includes a survey, pp. 92–94), but the whole text is preserved here, not just some selected passages removed from their contexts.

The same is the case of some of the Psalms. In order to illustrate the importance of Dodd's observation, we will refer to the use of Psalm 22:

v. 1	"... *lema sabachtani?*" Mark 15:34; Matt. 27:46
v. 6	"despised by the people." Cf. Isa. 53:3; Mark 9:12
v. 7	ἐξεμυκτήρισαν (Heb: יַלְעִגוּ "laugh"),
	Luke 23:35, ἐκίνησαν κεφαλήν, Mark 15:29
v. 8	"let him rescue the one." Matt. 27:43
v. 18	"they divide my clothes among themselves." Quoted as γραφή
	John 19:24; cf. Mark 15:24
v. 20	μονογενής John 1:18
v. 22	"I will tell of your name ..." Quoted in Heb. 2:12
v. 24	"but heard when I cried to him." Cf. Heb. 5:7
v. 26	"The poor shall eat and be satisfied." Luke 6:20–21
v. 28	"For dominion belongs to the LORD." Rev. 11:15 (cf. Matt. 6:10)

The use of this psalm isn't arbitrary. In early Christianity the psalm belonged in its total to the most respected texts from the Old Testament.

This is only a sample but should be enough to show that talk about rejecting the Old Testament as irrelevant to Christianity has no basis in the New Testament, which even the supporters of Marcion never countenanced. The Old and the New Testaments are interwoven in such a fashion that theologians like Manfred Oeming see it as the task of a biblical theology to show how the two testaments are interrelated and to define the degree of interdependence.

When this is said and we remember the main point—that we, without the Old Testament, wouldn't have had a New Testament, and without the New Testament *and* the Old Testament there would be no Christianity, one question still remains unanswered. Is this thesis dependent on a "hermeneutic of faith," or can it be seen as independent of it?

When Bultmann spoke about leaping into the hermeneutical circle, it is impossible that an excellent exegete like him could be in doubt about the fundamental relationship between the two testaments. We don't need the hermeneutics of faith to see this. Historically oriented theology is totally capable of defining the character of this relationship. The New Testament authors did not quote from the Old Testament in any arbitrary fashion because they knew that there were prophecies in that book about the coming of Christ. Instead they consciously incorporated selected passages from the Old Testament and quoted them in their own writings. It may even be true that some parts of the narrative in the New Testament were written in such a way as to conform to the layout of Old Testament texts, or they were dependent on a tradition also based on Old Testament literature. The use of Psalm 22 in the story of the passion may be an indication of such a literary strategy. Maybe the Roman soldiers would never have divided Jesus' clothes among them if it had not been written in Psalm 22.

Chapter 19

The Contribution
of the Copenhagen School

THE STUDY OF THE BIBLE—BIBLICAL THEOLOGY

To summarize, where are we? Gabler's lecture from 1787 formed the point of departure. Gabler demanded the separation of biblical theology from dogmatic theology, including the liberation of biblical theology from the control of the church. His project never succeeded. There are many reasons for this failure. First, the nature of biblical studies changed fundamentally in his lifetime. The change in the concept of history has already been discussed a number of times, but other differences also arose.

Gabler's definition of biblical theology was different from, for example, that of Childs and the one utilized by other theologians of today. When Gabler talked about biblical theology he meant biblical studies in general, not only the limited part of such studies devoted to the theology of the Bible in the narrow sense. Gabler's plea was that biblical studies should be an independent discipline and follow its own course. Dogmatic theology should not decide the content of biblical studies. Students of the Bible should proceed without dogmatic interference. When they have finished, it is time for systematic theology to take over.

After this the representatives of biblical studies never looked back, but they soon translated Gabler's concept of "biblical theology" to biblical studies, the study of the Old and the New Testaments, without the dominance of the church, and they based these studies on the fundamental historical-critical observation that the two testaments have different origins. Before long it was established that, as previously mentioned, the central part of the Old Testament belonged to the period before the destruction of the first temple in 587 BCE. There was accordingly a historical gap between the two testaments of more than half a millennium. Although things did not develop in antiquity with the speed of modern times, 500–600 years is a long time. In comparison, people of today would be back in the fifteenth century if things had developed at the same rate then as now.

This creates many obstacles for a biblical theology in the narrow sense. One solution is to choose Bultmann's option and plead for a hermeneutic decided by faith. This will definitely involve a *sacrificium intellectum*, because it would then be necessary to forget what we already know. Another course would be to accept that the authors of the New Testament found their reasoning in a very old book, in an Old Testament with roots that stretched back at least five or six hundred years or more and belonged to a world that had not been in existence for hundreds of years. It seemed most important to remove the Old Testament from being embraced by Judaism and to deal with it as if there had never been an important Jewish redaction of its content in the postexilic period. Whenever the Jewish element had to be accounted for, it was in the shape of the "dead letter of the Law."

One Jewish answer to this challenge is to assert that those parts of the Old Testament, such as the Priestly writer in the Pentateuch, which Christian exegetes reckon to be postexilic, are in fact preexilic.

The arguments in favor of such an early date have mainly been of a linguistic kind: The language of the Priestly writer is not different from the language used in Palestine in the Iron Age. Although the issue of language is part of a heated debate, very few non-Jewish scholars are in agreement. Perhaps Jewish scholars arguing in favor of an early date of the Priestly writer have not seen another possibility—that the similarity between this writer and the other authors of the Pentateuch, the Yahwist and the Elohist, might be because they were as *late* at their Priestly colleague?

How will the so-called Copenhagen School of Old Testament studies be able to help theology find a new kind of unity between the two testaments? When we say Copenhagen School, what does this name imply, and why are we talking about a school? One reason is of course that the main representatives of this school come from the University of Copenhagen. A third member of this group of "musketeers" comes from the University of Sheffield. There is a high degree of commonality among these scholars. They all date Old Testament literature late. Philip R. Davies would say to the Persian period, this writer to the Hellenistic period, and Thomas L. Thompson to the Hellenistic-Roman period. They also share a definite skepticism concerning the historical content of the story about Israel as presented by the books of the Old Testament, and do not care much for the many types of rationalistic paraphrase of this story found in histories of ancient Israel from the last two centuries. Apart from that, there is little commonality among their choices of subjects. This also involves their place within postmodernism. Here Davies may be more of a postmodern scholar than his two colleagues.

Two recent monographs by Thompson may, in some way, be regarded as post-modern: *The Bible in History: How Writers Create a Past* and *The Messiah Myth: The Near Eastern Roots of Jesus and David*.[1] They are rather modern, not because Thompson writes a modern form of historiography (this he did elsewhere),[2] but because he is still interested in the historical referent of his texts: how do ancient authors talk about the past? Although Thompson does not (any longer) discuss dating, he is far from representing a reader response position.

THE COPENHAGEN SCHOOL AND HISTORY

If we return to the two central issues discussed by the members of this school, we will see that both of them have theological consequences.

If we see the story in the Old Testament about ancient Israel as primarily a narrative written for the benefit of readers living at the time in which this story was drafted and with a message for this public, and not as report about what really happened in the past, the usual salvation history based on the biblical narrative is in jeopardy. Whether we speak about von Rad's salvation history or about the version found among the members of the biblical theology movement, both have lost their *Sitz im Leben*. Their basis has simply disappeared. Von Rad's notion of salvation history was based on tradition history, representing a kind of rewritten Bible following the course of history reconstructed by von Rad's contemporaries, especially Albrecht Alt and Martin Noth. However, much of their reconstruction of "real" history was wrong; if there never was a Davidic empire or a great king by the name of David, then the idea that the birth of Jesus is the fulfillment of all the expectations of the birth of a messiah presented by the Old Testament authors has no historical foundation. This is only one—important—example among many possible ones.

The consequence for von Rad's North American opponents is even more disastrous. Any hope of being able to create a situation of harmony between biblical history and real history is lost when there is nothing to harmonize. Real or secular history and Bible history are two stories that cannot meet.

In short, there is no salvation history that builds on real events of the past. The only thing left is a narrative, which may include a salvation history. In this case the reason such a narrative was written was very different from what previous biblical scholarship assumed to be true.

---

1. *The Bible in History* (London: Jonathan Cape, 1999); *The Messiah Myth* (New York: Basic Books, 1999).

2. See Thomas L. Thompson, *Early History of the Israelite People: From the Written and Archaeological Sources*, Studies in the History of the Ancient Near East 4 (Leiden: Brill, 1992).

If there is no more reason to concentrate on the events behind the text, what is left? The theologian may simply read his text. If this theologian is convinced that the historical method is advantageous and to be preferred, he might proceed with a historical analysis of the classical sort. Such a procedure is not without merit. To take my previous example of the love letter never read by the historical-critical scholar,[3] this scholar may never get down to reading the text of the letter, but perhaps he will find out that there was no train that day and the whole setup of the letter is a fake. The Old Testament presents, for example, the time of King David and King Solomon as one of great prosperity. However, when he studies the historical remains of Palestine in the Iron Age, he will be struck by the simplicity of the culture reflected by archaeological discoveries. Never in the ancient world was there such a destitute and simple culture. It is poor and marginalized. There is little in common between what is found in the ground and what is found in the stories of the Bible. The historical text of the Bible does not relate to any known past of the country.

Why is this an important observation? It suggests that even the production of a historical narrative like that in the Old Testament is in itself a theological process. The historiographers operated with a salvation history that was broken off at a point. However, Yahweh's promises to his people and his subsequent withdrawal had little to do with the events of the secular world. It represents an invented and constructed history, the meaning of which is not hidden in the past but belongs to the construction itself. There is definitely a kind of "dialogue" between the history of Palestine in the Iron Age and the biblical story. The biblical historiographer "speaks" with the past and describes it in his own words. He simply constructs it.

THE HISTORY OF PALESTINE AND THE HISTORY OF ANCIENT ISRAEL

Some scholars have addressed the subject of the "dialogue" between real history and invented history. So far, the two most outspoken have been Mario Liverani and Thomas L. Thompson. A few years ago Liverani published his previously mentioned history of Israel, *Oltre la Bibbia: Storia Antica di Israele*.[4] Liverani's history is not a normal textbook of the history of ancient Israel. It is split into two parts. The first part is devoted to—in Liverani's words—the "normal history," while the second part has the "invented" history as its subject. The first part is about an insignificant part of the ancient Near East in the Iron Age known to us under many names: Palestine, Israel, and so on. The second part describes how

---

3. See p. 358.
4. *Oltra la Bibbia* (Rome-Bari: Laterza, 2003); ET, *Israel's History and the History of Israel* (London: Equinox, 2005).

the authors of the historical literature in the Old Testament invented a history as their answer to the real history.

The story of the past has to provide answers to people living in the postexilic period. Thus the patriarchs were invented because of problems that arose after the exile between the part of the Palestinian population that had never been in exile and those who returned from Mesopotamia. This strained relationship is also reflected in the conquest stories and the governing ideology behind them. The stories of the judges were written in order to put a halt to a discussion about having a king in postexilic "Israelite" society, and so on.

Liverani has undoubtedly chosen the correct method, but we still have to question its execution, at least in parts. He is still too much of a historical-critical scholar in the old sense. In his history the biblical story decides the parameters of the dialogue with the secular history. Furthermore, he has not exhausted the possibility of characterizing the theology of history that is presented by the historiographers of the Old Testament.

Thomas L. Thompson moves further in his *The Bible in History* in the direction of the liberation of the historical narrative from the embrace of historical-critical scholarship, although its grip on Thompson's history is still there. This book consists of three parts. The first is about how texts begin as explanations of the past. The titles say a lot. The first chapter is called "History and Origins: The Changing Past." The paragraphs are named "When texts are confirmed by texts," "There is nothing new under the sun," "Stories of conflict," and "The Bible as survival literature." The second chapter is called "Confusing Stories with Historical Evidence." The last paragraph has the title "A collapsing paradigm: The Bible as history."

This part includes a clear and sharp settlement with historical-critical scholarship. Its great mistake consisted of confusing the text with the history. It constantly made the mistake of confusing categories and blended text with event. There is no reason to dwell on this now.

Thompson's second part, "How Historians Create a Past," is more problematic, because we here find a history of ancient Palestine—although without the Bible like Liverani's version. This secular history is included to provide a basis for a discussion of the dialogue between the history as retold by biblical writers and real history.

The third part is more interesting in this connection. Here Thompson deals with the texts of the Old Testament as historical texts: "The Bible's Place in History." The first chapter may be characterized as a mixture of old and new: "The Bible's Social and Historical Worlds." Here we find everything, including a survey of the nations of ancient Palestine, not dissimilar to the one found in Keith Whitelam's work,[5] a discussion of "the theology of the way" and of Judaism: "Many Judaisms," and "The 'Jews' according to Josephus."

---

5. Keith W. Whitelam, *The Invention of Ancient Israel: The Silencing of Palestinian History* (London: Routledge, 1996).

After this comes a series of important paragraphs. Thus, chapter 11: "The Bible's Literary World," where Thompson explains his methodology; and three chapters devoted to the theological world of the Bible: "How God Began," "The Myth of the Sons of God," and "Israel as God's Son." Chapter 12 is about God, "How God Began." The subtitles are equally meaningful: "What the Bible knows and doesn't know about God," "Yahweh as God in Genesis," "Yahweh as god-father," and "How Yahweh became God." Such titles indicate the theological directions of the Copenhagen School. This also includes the following "theological" chapters on "the birth of the son of God and the sending of a savior," and "The role of Immanuel and the son of God."

The last chapter directly addresses the present theological discussion and includes paragraphs such as "Theology as critical reflection," and "The Bible and the theologians."

Thompson's book was not well received in North America. Here it was met with violent opposition, especially from (former) members of the biblical theology movement who again used language similar to that employed by Albright and his students against German scholars like Gerhard von Rad, Martin Noth, and Albrecht Alt. Furthermore, the North American publisher made the mistake of "translating" the title of the British edition from *The Bible in History* to *The Mythic Past*. *Myth* in an American context is often understood as the opposite of "truth." In this way Thompson was seen as one who claimed that the Bible was a lie from one end to the other, which of course everyone—though perhaps not members of the biblical theology movement or evangelicals—will understand as an absurd accusation.

Thompson's book is bedeviled with some of the same problems as Liverani's history. The secular history plays too significant a role here. Thompson is in possession of all the tools necessary for writing a postmodern analysis of the story of Israel as found in the Bible. Had he decided to concentrate on this subject, it might have been an advantage among a public heading in a postmodern direction—although the attacks from the conservative quarter would have been even more violent.[6]

The history of ancient Israel is dead. It has nothing to contribute to theology. The story of biblical Israel in the Old Testament stands on its own feet. It is in no need of a historical backdrop. Thus the Copenhagen School has helped the Bible by liberating it from (real) history, and has shown the basic fallacy of traditional Old Testament theology, which still relies on the story of the Bible as if it were real history. We are, from a theological point of view, in no need of this real history as described by the historical-critical interpretation of the stories of the Old Testament. We still have the stories unmolested.

---

6. The late James Barr in his last book, *History and Ideology in the Old Testament* (Oxford: Oxford University Press, 2000), demonstrated an outspoken lack of understanding of the changing situation for historical studies, without realizing it playing into the hands of evangelical Christianity and its endeavors to circumvent historical-critical scholarship.

WHO WROTE THE OLD TESTAMENT, AND WHEN?

In case we decide to stay with a modern and not a postmodern project, it might still be relevant to ask questions about the identity of those who wrote the Old Testament. The only way to find an answer will be through the biblical texts. No external source provides any information—although in the case of the Septuagint there circulates a myth about its origin as a translation of the books of the Hebrew Bible, including a date for this translation, which was finished by seventy sage Jews (some sources says seventy-two) in the course of seventy days, each working in isolation, and each translation an exact copy of the other. Thus it must have been God who did the translation.[7]

There is no such legend about the Hebrew Bible (more evidence for the claim that its status within Judaism is different from that of the Christian Bible). Here we have only the texts and their internal evidence of authorship. There is nothing to pick up in the history to which this text is said to refer. We only have the testimony of its authors: What did they know? What are their intentions? How do they see the world? How do they understand God?

Before we go further into this, we will have to discuss another central focus of the Copenhagen School, the dating of the text of the Old Testament. Most of what we have rests on circular argumentation. The Bible tells a story about a certain era. This era is reconstructed by the historian on the basis of its description in the Bible. Now the Bible—or the relevant parts—are dated to this era, although such a dating rests purely on a biblically inspired construction. Although it has often been suggested by historical-critical scholars of the past that this circular argumentation is a necessity, we still have to ask: Why is it so? And is it really so?

The existence in real time of the biblical books was the point of departure for a late dating of the biblical literature.[8] The first copies (mostly fragments) of biblical books belong to the late second and the first centuries BCE, and are included among the Dead Sea Scrolls. Here all the books of the Hebrew Bible are present, apart from Esther. When we start discussing the dates of biblical books, the point of departure must therefore be the second and first centuries BCE. If there is no reason to go further back and it is not possible to find traces of this literature in earlier contexts—for example, because of the existence of a variant manuscript tradition—any argument in favor of an early date is baseless and unnecessary. It is sometimes opined that the content of many of the biblical books does not fit

7. Some years ago I heard in Damascus a lecture by a so-called "liberal" imam. He told us that for more than twenty years he had been a member of a committee with the task of investigating if the Qur'an was really the word of God, or if it was written by human beings. After twenty years the committee arrived at the "surprising" conclusion that only God would be able to write a text like the Qur'an. Religious books often have a magical origin.

8. Further on this in Niels Peter Lemche, "The Old Testament—A Hellenistic Book?" *SJOT* 7 (1993): 163–93; revised edition in Lester L. Grabbe, ed., *Did Moses Speak Attic? Jewish Historiography and Scripture in the Hellenistic Period*, JSOTSup 317 (Sheffield: Sheffield Academic Press, 2001), 287–318.

the Hellenistic period.[9] How do we know this? The argument presumes that we know everything about the Hellenistic period, which we certainly do not. If this literature does not fit in with what we know about the period, it could be that we know too little and will have to broaden our knowledge by including the testimony of the Bible.

The basic impression is that the *books* of the Old Testament do not need to be older than the period from which the oldest manuscripts come, although it would be foolish to argue that every line and every story is as late as that. Thus a text like Psalm 82 may seem a little out of place in a monotheistic context, and we still wonder why it was included—perhaps because of a popular melody?

The societal context of the literature of the Old Testament is a Jewish one. It is also a monotheistic context, definitely sectarian in orientation.[10] The world is divided not into Israelites and foreigners but into the faithful ones and the disbelievers. If there is only one God, the religiously oriented man or woman will seek only this God. Then the conclusion is an easy one: I know God. Any person who disagrees with me doesn't know God. Not knowing God is the same as being dead (although not yet knowing it).

Another characteristic of sectarianism is the tendency of a sectarian movement to split. It is often believed that the word *sect* comes from the Latin *seco*, "to cut," and that a sect thus represents something cut out of something. As a matter of fact, *sect* comes from the Latin *sequire*, "to follow," and characterizes the members of a sect as the followers of somebody or something. One of the characteristics of the new form of religion, monotheism, which in the course of the first millennium BCE came to dominate religious life in the ancient Near East, involves the many sectarian movements that originated in this period. Judaism was only one among these.

The attitude toward foreigners in the Old Testament is a sectarian one. On one side we have the people of God, Israel, and on the other everybody not belonging to this people. There can be no middle way. Either you are a member of the people of God, or you are rejected by God. There is no other choice. God is the godfather, the patron, the boss, and this patronage language dominates the pages of the Old Testament. God even has his hit man, the angel of Exodus 23, who smooths the way for Israel, and Israel's relations to God are regulated by the stipulations of a covenant dictated by God and to be obeyed without question.[11]

---

9. E.g., in Rainer Albertz, "An End to the Confusion? Why the Old Testament Cannot Be a Hellenistic Book!" in Grabbe, ed., *Did Moses Speak Attic?* 30–46. Also in the same volume, Barstad, "Deuteronomists, Persians, Greeks, and the Dating of the Israelite Tradition," 47–77.

10. The use of *sect* in this book is based on the mainly European and Protestant understanding of the concept as referring to a minor religious group which has broken off from a larger and more established religious group. The connotation, often met in Christian orothodox literature, that sects are heretical has no place here.

11. See also on patronism in the Old Testament Niels Peter Lemche, "Kings and Clients: On Loyalty between the Ruler and the Ruled in Ancient 'Israel,'" *Semeia* 66 (1995): 119–132; "From Patronage Society to Patronage Society," in V. Fritz and Philip R. Davies (eds.), *The Origins of the Israelite States,* JSOTSup 228 (Sheffield: Sheffield Academic Press, 1996), 106–120.

However, because the covenant regulates the relationship between God and humanity, the transgression forms the single most important theme of the story line. These two things go together: the covenant and breaking the covenant.

The idea of society in a sectarian movement is sometimes utopian. A sect is more a dream than reality, the dream about a world where the members of the sect are saved while evil humanity perishes. The language used is in such cases violent and warlike. The God of the Old Testament demands that every Canaanite must be killed, and Joshua and Judges suggest that although the Israelites tried to obey, they failed miserably. The Canaanites were allowed to survive; the biblical Israelites perished.

When a sectarian movement establishes itself, it may need a myth about its origins. Here the demands of ethnicity play a role, seeking a reason for the identity of a certain group. It is necessary to see oneself as something special, and membership in the biblical people of God is definitely related to the concept of ethnicity. According to the Old Testament, the people of God have two enemies. The first is of the Canaanites, who in the literature of the Old Testament belong primarily to the past, although they are still the main opponents, worshiping other gods.[12] The second enemy is understood to be a thing of the past as well: old Israel, which perished when Nebuchadnezzar conquered Jerusalem and destroyed its temple. After this catastrophe seventy years followed (according to Jeremiah). Old, rejected Israel died in exile. The sons and daughters returned to their old country as a renewed Israel.

Now this people of God of the Old Testament are in possession of two myths about its origins. The first is the exodus from Egypt, the second the return from Babylon. The exodus led to the constitution of old Israel, who received the covenant of God inscribed in stone as emphasized both by the story of the Sinai covenant in the book of Exodus and by Joshua 24. The second covenant, which is inscribed in the hearts of human beings, is without external symbols. It is a personal covenant between every single human being and his or her God.

Monotheism tends to lead to a personalized relationship to God. The Old Testament speaks extensively about the people of God; however, it is the individual who chooses to be a member of this people. Perhaps the prophetic preaching about mending one's way seems to be directed at a collective, and perhaps the author of such texts thought so. However, conversion is often a personal matter.

The Old Testament expresses a sectarian understanding of society understood to form the people of God. The reality of this people is separated from secular reality. The people of God lives in God. Nonmembers may sometimes be considered the enemies of God. However, the true believers will at the end of the day all meet at Zion under God's direct protection (Isa. 4), when the new messiah, the new David, has been born.

---

12. See Niels Peter Lemche, *The Canaanites and Their Land: The Idea of Canaan in the Old Testament*, JSOTSup 110 (Sheffield: Sheffield Academic Press, 1991; 2nd ed., Sheffield: Sheffield Academic Press, 1999).

Humanity seems to have embraced the idea of a tripartite understanding of time as far back as written sources reach. We still divide time into three phases: the past, the present, and the future, as indicated by our verbal system. In our mythical universe, these three kinds of time are more than just time. They also have different qualities. The past was a golden age, the present is evil and cruel, but the future will see the golden age return. This may be a personal matter, or it may involve the group to which we belong.[13]

The idea of history in the Old Testament, its narrative theology, is linked to this sense of time. The past was golden, and increasingly golden as we move back in time. God dines with Abraham, David's prophets keep him on track, the king always knows the will of God. We, say the authors and their public, live in the present, and we have got the bad teeth of Jeremiah 31:30; however, we also embrace the hope for a golden future, when the kingdom of David is re-established.

In short, we may discuss when the books of the Old Testament came into being, and we may discuss the identity of their authors. It would, however, be difficult to discuss their spiritual identity as members of a religious sectarian group. As far as dating is concerned, it is impossible to suppose that this literature came into being before the destruction of Jerusalem at the hands of King Nebuchadnezzar of Babylonia and the subsequent exile of the elite of Judah to Mesopotamia. This is the pivotal point around which everything turns.

LAW AND GOSPEL—PROMISE AND FULFILLMENT

There are two main thrusts of Old Testament theology: a static one, concentrating on correct ritual, the observation of the Sabbath, and the Law of God; and a dynamic one, concerning the acts of God in "history," the positive as well as the negative. The static part concerns institutions—the most important of which is the temple—and the good life in the land given to Israel by God. The second thrust is about the golden future or is fulfilled in this golden future.

The future became a most important theme in ancient Judaism. It is part of its self-consciousness. It is common that a sectarian movement is at odds with its environment, which will always be bigger than the sect in question. There is more than one way to answer this challenge. One possibility is to migrate to a country where a gentler reception may be hoped for. The history of America provides many examples of this. For instance, America welcomed many sectarians of European origin, almost depopulating large stretches of Scandinavian territory. Another more recent example is the Taliban takeover of Afghanistan, where they intended to establish the kingdom of God. The violent potential of a sectarian movement has been amply illustrated by the actions of the Taliban.

13. This sense of time is virtuously used by Mario Liverani in his analysis of the correspondence of Rib-Adda, the king of Byblos, in the Amarna archive. See Mario Liverani, "Rib Adda. Giusto sofferente" (1974); ET, "Rib-Adda, Righteous Sufferer," in *Myth and Politics in Ancient Near Eastern Historiography*, ed. Zainab Bahrani and Marc Van De Mieroop (London: Equinox, 2004), 97–124.

Another escape route is the flight into the future. The best-known example is undoubtedly the Jehovah's Witnesses and their dependence on the book of Revelation in the New Testament. Originally they believed that only the 144,000 people mentioned in Revelation were going to survive the battle of Armageddon, and those 144,000 consisted of the members of Jehovah's Witnesses. The remainder of humanity was doomed to extinction. The blessing you get from God must be seen in contrast to the discomfort brought on other people: "You prepare a table before me in the presence of my enemies" (Ps. 23:5).

The greatest joy is malice. The thought that the enemy, the godless, is placed in a situation without hope finds expression in Psalm 23, where the enemy is left outside, almost like children pressing their noses toward the window, staring at the goodies found inside, so close and yet inaccessible.

Ancient Judaism enjoyed many prospects of the golden age. Such expectations may have varied from one group to the next. The future was waiting for them, and apocalyptic literature, of which not much has been preserved in the Hebrew Bible, was a widespread literary genre. Apocalyptic circles developed a special religious interpretation of life and history, and expressed their beliefs in stories about the many visions concerning the future to come at the end of time. The final object remained the establishment of the messianic kingdom of paradise, when David/David's descendant reestablishes Israel and takes his seat at the right side of Yahweh (and in Judaism the high priest).

Historical Judaism in this formative period was in many ways different from the Judaism that united the many scrolls in existence in its Hebrew Bible. This Judaism did not favor apocalyptic ideas and sentiments and did not have a place for the dominating figure of the messiah, although the idea of a messiah was never totally forgotten. Rabbinic Judaism is the result of the "apocalyptic" defeats to the Romans in 66–70 and 132–34 CE, when expectations for the future ran amok and almost led to the total annihilation of Judaism—at least in its Palestinian form. Rabbinic Judaism had roots that can be traced further back, as one of the many "Judaisms" of the last centuries BCE. The many versions of Judaism are of course a consequence of Judaism being originally a sectarian movement.

Josephus divided Jewish society into three religious parties, the Pharisees, the Sadducees, and the Essenes. The Zealots constitute a fourth group. Each of these groups represents its own particular variety of Judaism. Josephus's description of the Jewish society is schematic and written with the well-educated Roman and Greek in mind, persons who wanted to know more about these strange people in a simple way—much like modern well-educated Europeans and Americans. Josephus's three or four groups of Jews cover the spectrum of varieties within Judaism, from the law-abiding party on one end to fanatical supporters of apocalyptic visions on the other.[14]

14. Josephus's description of the Jewish sectarian groups can be found in his *The Jewish Antiquities*, book 18:11.1–23.

What has all of this to do with biblical theology? Maybe everything! We are here speaking of a religious society that in its many forms had created a religious and sacred literature which would in time become part of the various editions of the Old Testament, whether in the form of the Septuagint or as the Hebrew Bible. This society's interpretation of the history of God's acts in history became the history of the old Israel that perished and the covenant that was rejected by both God and his people, but was replaced by the new Israel and the new covenant that is in no need of external proof but is a part of humanity itself. Without it, there is no life: "Let everything that breathes praise the LORD! Praise the LORD!" (Ps. 150:6) With these words the collection of the Psalms of David come to an end. Everything that breathes is alive, because it contains the breath of God (Gen. 2:7). The godless person does not share this gift and so is dead.

When a society as represented here by ancient Judaism looks forward to the coming of a messiah who will establish the kingdom of God on earth, it is inevitable that it will, at some point, see its expectations fulfilled and attach that fulfillment to special persons. We may see such expectations "fulfilled" in the person of Bar Kokhba (the "son of the stars") and his rebellion against the Romans in 132 CE. Similar expectations, but not nearly as violent, may also have induced one Jewish group to choose its messiah in the person of Jesus from Nazareth. It may be only a coincidence that this group had a special role to play in the future, for example, its "doctrines" that could not be reconciled with Judaism in any form.

This must be read as a warning against turning biblical theology into a tool of harmonization. This can never be the intention of a biblical theology. We are certainly in no position to force either Judaism or Christianity to think in the same way. Biblical theology is about how Christianity broke with its Jewish past and created a new synthesis. This synthesis was a necessity if the early church was going to survive. It had to break away from Judaism, but included many important parts of Judaism in its own doctrine.

Christianity used the first element of Judaism mentioned before, the static one, to create distance from its origins. Christianity was never passive or static, but always included a message and a mission that had the whole world as its object. It may be a topic of discussion as to when Judaism became predominantly static—whether it was before or after the destruction of Herod's temple, but there were tendencies even before 70 CE that pointed in this direction.

The late dating of the literature of the Old Testament, current in the Copenhagen School, has further consequences. It not only suggests that the messianic content of Christianity comes from ancient Judaism (which has been common knowledge for many years), but it also emphasizes that this messianism was not something foreign to the so-called ancient Israelite belief. It is already present in the Old Testament and in a much more massive form than sometimes assumed. The two first psalms of the collection of David's Psalms introduce the main characters of the book of Psalms: the faithful, the godless, and God himself. The second psalm also introduces the king, for the first time, in the person of the messiah

(Ps. 2:2): "The kings of the earth set themselves, and the rulers take counsel together, against the LORD and his anointed."

After this introduction follows Psalm 3, a "Psalm of David." The messiah is David in the Psalms.

This has nothing to do with old preexilic Israel; it is part of the religious belief of early Judaism. There might be links to previous religious sentiments related to the king. This is an issue for the historian of religion and of little importance for Christianity as it presents itself in the New Testament.

It is likewise possible to include more examples of the links between ancient Judaism and early Christianity. We may mention Isaiah's prophecy of the birth of the child Immanuel (Isa. 7:14), which is in its present form not a prophecy about the eventual birth of an heir to the throne of Ahaz about 734 BCE. It is a prophecy about the birth of the messiah who should live on milk and honey, the nectar and ambrosia of the Near East, products not touched by humans but nature's—that is, God's—own products.

A discussion of more examples is unnecessary here. The first Christian community was a Jewish sectarian group that had to separate from its origins. This is a normal occurrence whenever a new sect is born out of an old one. From a theological point of view, early Christianity is very close to contemporary Judaism and must have shared the essentials of Judaism. Christianity did not ignore Judaism but incorporated essential parts of it into its teaching. We may even suggest that Christian theology is a form of Jewish theology—however, with a twist.

Biblical theology may, therefore, with a good conscience describe its incorporation of the Old Testament as part of its theological basis as a legitimate development within the broader spectrum of Jewish religious beliefs. Christianity ended up in a religious conflict with Judaism that only sharpened as time went by. This conflict is like many divorces; love is changed into hatred.

Judaism and Christianity are united into the same world of interpretation. Both religions include the same questions and will often deliver similar answers. There are some serious differences. The problem of the blood has already been mentioned. Another related problem is the assertion of the New Testament that Jesus is "the way, and the truth, and the life. No one comes to the Father except through me" (John 14:6). This goes against the grain of Judaism, which has reserved this role for the Law.

Does this mean that Christianity should give up its Old Testament and stay with the New? This would be a decision based on a history that never happened. The discussion here suggests the opposite: that in a postmodern setting the Bible should be allowed to speak in its entirety about God and humankind. The Old Testament has a lot to say about God. As expressed by C. S. Lewis, God is not and will never be a "tame lion." Aslan, Narnia's God, is a wild lion. He comes and goes as he wishes. An analysis of the image of God in the Old Testament will inform the reader that there are many images (or testimonies) of God in this book, but they all say that Aslan is still a wild lion.

The New Testament represents an independent description of the experience of the early Christians as belonging to a Jewish, messianic sect. The Old Testament—or rather, the literature that was to be included in the Old Testament—provides the mental framework for this sect, which would not have survived without it. In this way the group managed to survive the death of its messiah by interpreting it in the light of the last of the Servant Songs in Isaiah.

Appendix

The History of Israel or the History of Palestine?

ORIENTALISM

In his 1996 publication *The Invention of Ancient Israel: The Silencing of Palestinian History*[1] the British Old Testament scholar Keith W. Whitelam discusses the study of the history of ancient Israel during the last hundred years. According to Whitelam, European and North American scholars have, from the Christian point of view, created an image of the ancient Near East that is dominated by the division in the Old Testament between the people of Israel and all the other nations of the East.

Scholars had, as early as the Enlightenment, begun to construe an image that had more to do with the European's view of himself than with the realities of the Orient in their early expeditions to the Orient. This image of the East is today coined orientalism.[2] Orientalism is how Europeans perceive the Middle East. It is "Eurocentric," reflecting only the European idea of the East. It does not give

---

1. Keith W. Whitelam, *The Invention of Ancient Israel: The Silencing of Palestinian History* (London: Routledge, 1996).
2. On this, see Eduard Said, *Orientalism* (Harmonsworth: Penguin, 1985).

The historical periods of Palestine

The Neolithic Period	ca. 8500–4300 BCE
Pre-ceramic Neolithic	ca. 8500–ca. 5500 BCE
Ceramic Neolithic	ca. 5500–4300 BCE
The Chalcolithic Period	ca. 4300–3500 BCE
The Early Bronze Age	ca. 3500–2300 BCE
The Transition from the Early to the Middle Bronze Age	ca. 2300–1900 BCE
The Middle Bronze Age	ca. 1900–1550 BCE
The Late Bronze Age	ca. 1550–1300 BCE
The Transition from the Late Bronze Age to the Iron Age	ca. 1300–900 BCE
The Iron Age	ca. 900–600 BCE
The Neo-Babylonian Period	ca. 600–539 BCE
The Persian Period	539–331 BCE
The Hellenistic Period	331–63 BCE
The Roman Period	63 BCE–ca. 300 CE
The Byzantine Period	ca. 300–640 CE
The Arab Period	640–1525 CE
The Turkish Period	1525–1918 CE
The British Mandate	1918–1948 CE
Israeli Period	1948– CE

due attention to the way people living in the East look upon themselves and their societies.

Within modern social anthropology, there is a dividing line between *emic* and *etic* testimonies. Whenever a social anthropologist begins his work in the field, changing his place of living from a Western university to some village or tribe in the third world, he must remember to make a distinction between what he is told by the members of the society which he studies and what nonmembers tell him about this society.[3] If this social anthropologist fails to separate the two types of evidence, his study might end up as one-sided and monochromatic. The *emic* ideas of a society might differ a lot from the *etic* ones.

Thus there is a vast difference in the Middle East between the view of Bedouins among Bedouins and how they are looked upon by non-Bedouins. The Bedouins may consider themselves to be masters of bravery; other people may think of them

3. From linguistics phon-emic and phon-etic.

as reckless cutthroats. While the Bedouins may think of their society as following the way of God, other people may believe that they are godless criminals.

Orientalism is an *etic* concept. It is one-sided and one-dimensional because it was formed by scholars who were not from the Near East and who paid little attention to the *emic* testimonies of local people.

This leads to the necessity of studying the construction in its separate elements as proposed by European scholars. There are three basic questions to be answered: When did the concept of orientalism arise? Who produced this image? And what were the preconditions for its construction?

During the Enlightenment and in the Romantic period Europeans began to travel to the Middle East. I have mentioned the Danish expedition from the second half of the eighteenth century. Most such expeditions included important scholars and specialists from many fields. The most famous was without doubt the huge scholarly entourage of Napoleon's campaign in Egypt at the end of the eighteenth century.

Although the frequency of such expeditions increased during the nineteenth century, the basic image of the East was the work of the pioneers from the eighteenth century. It will therefore be necessary to make inquiries about their intellectual background and to scrutinize their education.

European civilization was, as late as the eighteenth century, totally dominated by Christian theology and its requirements. Christian doctrine followed the individual from birth to grave. The first literature to read or listen to would be—apart from fairy tales or the like—the Bible. Additional literature existed, even though accessible only for a few people. The concept of the world was totally dominated by biblical ideas. Another century had to pass before the publication of Charles Darwin's presentation of his theory of evolution. Although critical analysis of the content of the Bible began in the eighteenth century, the stories of the Bible formed the portal of every European individual to the world. The motives of all explorers of the East had this common background, whether they were Catholic or Protestant.

Along with this biblically colored orientation toward the East, the European traveler also nourished the idea of his society and his church as the "new Israel" of the New Testament, the true successor to the ancient Israelites. People of the East—ancient as well as contemporary—were identified as "the other nations," and read through glasses colored by the Bible. The explorer of those days could not escape this fate. Even the best (in a modern sense) among them carried this spiritual heritage with them, thinking of the peoples of the Middle East as—basically—Canaanites. Personal observation in some cases mitigated this biblical influence, but it could never annul it.

THE CORRECT PERSPECTIVE: ISRAEL'S OR PALESTINE'S HISTORY IN ANCIENT TIMES?

This attitude to the Near Eastern world had serious consequences for Palestine and its Arabic-speaking population. The European explorers began to visit this country in greater numbers only during the nineteenth century. Previously the country had been visited mostly by pilgrims looking for its holy places. The impression of the country they visited was not different from the one that governed the view of the Middle East among earlier explorers. The only change was a sharpening of the contrast when Palestine and its population came into focus. The European perception of Palestine and its inhabitants was formed on the background of the biblical image of ancient Israel. Whoever else might have lived here was evaluated in this light. Now scholars began to explore the possibilities of their ideas about the past, Israel, Palestine, and the present. The study of the ancient history of Palestine began in earnest, however, still governed by the idea that we have on the one hand Israel, and on the other the remaining many nations of ancient Palestine. The reason to study the non-Israelite part of the population was the fact that they are listed in the Bible. They had no existence or value of their own.[4]

The stream of histories of Palestine in ancient times has been practically endless. Almost without exception they concentrate on the history of ancient Israel.[5] Their titles may change from "the history of Israel" to "the history of the Israelite people" to "the history of the Jewish people." Israel is, however, always a dominant part of the title. There are exceptions in the form of recent studies of the Philistines, the inhabitants of the coastal plain, even freed from the embrace of biblical narrative. No one has ever attempted to write the history of Palestine in general, except as a (minor) part of a history of Israel.

Of course the reason is the fact that the Old Testament has normally served as the most important source for the history of the area, simply because it is the most comprehensive written source. The number of additional written documents relating to the history of Palestine in ancient times is limited. There is no comprehensive extrabiblical source. From the Hellenistic-Roman period we have the Jewish history of Josephus from the first century CE; however, up to the Hellenistic period, Josephus's history is mostly a paraphrase of the Old Testament.

It is understandable that, even to the nonreligious historian, the Old Testament has been exceedingly important for any construction of Palestine's ancient history. But it is difficult to understand why it continues to play this role. Even a rough draft of the history of Palestine in ancient times shows that the Old Testament perspective on this history is, from a historical point of view, misleading. Apart from the mention in Merneptah's "Israel-stele" from the late thirteenth century BCE,[6] we know of a political constellation called Israel, alternatively "the house of Omri" or "Samaria," only in documents dating from the middle of the ninth to the end of the eighth centuries BCE. Between 722 BCE and 1948 CE there was no Israel in the historical or political sense.

4. The clearest specimen of this type of study may be John Bright's *A History of Israel*, which is introduced by a comprehensive overview of ancient Near Eastern history that is there only to provide a backdrop for the history of ancient Israel from the patriarchs to the Hellenistic period.

5. The only exception to the rule is Gösta W. Ahlström, *The History of Ancient Palestine from the Palaeolithic Period to Alexander's Conquest*, JSOTSup 146 (Sheffield: Sheffield Academic Press, 1993), although even here the history of Israel gets the lion's share of attention.

6. See pp. 131.

This does not mean that there were no people who reckoned them to be Israelites or traditions about something called Israel, both before the formation of this Palestinian state and after its dissolution. However, as a centralized and organized state in the proper sense, Israel existed only between, say, about 900 and 722 BCE—for less than two hundred years.

The territory of this state of Israel was, in this short period, never stable. At its greatest extent it covered an area centering on the northern part of the central highlands of Palestine. The valleys in the north were also likely part of the territory of the kings of Israel in this period, extending as far as the city of Dan in the northeast. Parts of the territory to the east of the Jordan River were in Israelite hands, although they were lost about 850 BCE when Damascus assumed control over these areas. Shortly after 750 BCE, most of the territories to the west of the Jordan River—except the central area around the city of Samaria—were organized as Assyrian provinces.

Even when it was greatest, Israel covered a very small territory of a very limited extent, say 5,790 square miles, a little more than half the size of Massachusetts. After 750 BCE it was only a minor kingdom in a distant part of the world.

The Old Testament compares the kingdom of Israel with the kingdom of Judah, believed originally to have formed one state, which separated into two shortly before 900 BCE. It is certain that there was, from at least sometime in the ninth century BCE, a tendency toward statehood in the southern part of the central highlands, perhaps fully realized around 800 BCE. When the kingdom of Judah was at its highest, it encompassed a territory covering the southern part of the central mountains, the northern part of the Negev desert, and the area to the west of Jerusalem, which reached at least as far as the city of Lachish. It was never bigger than the kingdom of Israel, even when this was diminished by the Assyrians to the insignificant little city-state of Samaria. In 701 BCE, King Sennacherib of Assyria attacked Judah and reduced its territory to something like 368 square miles. It is likely that the kings of the seventh century managed to enlarge their territory, although there are no details. In 597 BCE and perhaps also in 587 BCE (a date attested only by the biblical sources), the Babylonians conquered Jerusalem and turned Judah into a Babylonian province.

Thus the territory of Palestine is hardly larger than 11,580 square miles. Although the western part of the present kingdom of Jordan was at times governed by the kings of Samaria, the territory considered by the Old Testament to constitute the land of Israel will not have been bigger than 17,300 square miles. Even at its greatest extent, the state of Israel didn't cover more than a fraction of this territory.

The history of "historical" Israel only covers a couple of centuries from the first part of the first millennium BCE, and includes only a part of the total Palestinian territory. The history of Palestine, however, goes back to "the dawn of time." There are traces of human activity here that go more than a million years back. The Israelite share of this history is therefore extremely limited. It is limited to the Iron Age. It is clear that the Old Testament perspective of history absolutely distorts the facts. The historiographers of the Old Testament have absolutely no interest in the real history of Palestine in ancient times. They are governed by motives of a very different kind. When we in a theological context study the perspectives of the biblical historiographers, it must also be done on the correct historical background. It is necessary to present at least an outline of the history of Palestine that does not place the narrative of the Old Testament in the position of the *privileged* text.[7] The following historical overview will predominantly concentrate on nonbiblical sources, although the testimony of the Bible will also—sometimes—be called upon.

PRINCIPLES FOR HISTORY WRITING

Prescientific history writing from ancient times to the present concentrates on the unusual. Human beings are always in the center of of the historiographer's interest, whether it is Greek historians like Herodotus and Thucydides from the fifth century BCE, a Roman historian like Livy from the first century BCE, medieval chroniclers like Saxo, historians from the Enlightenment like Edward Gibbon, or from modern times the Swedish historian Carl Grimberg. Ordinary humans are not in the focus of such history writing. Moreover, normal humans enjoy tracking the careers of great individuals like Moses or Napoleon or—for that matter—Hitler or Stalin. Such historians seek the reason for historical events among such individuals and are especially interested in the confrontations between their heroes and their adversaries. There are heroes and villains in history. The historian and his readership identify with the heroes and fight, so to speak, their battles with them.

It is obvious that this way of presenting the past is at the same time a reflection of the way we look upon ourselves in confrontation with the surrounding world: a kind of I—you confrontation. We see ourselves standing on one side, while our opponents and the phenomena opposing us are on the other. Our "personal" history is the story of how we succeed. In recent times the novel and the movie confirm these essential parts of our way of understanding history. Nothing has changed. The individual is placed at the center of the story. Western human beings understand history individualistically.[8]

Although scientific history writing began to appear only some two hundred years ago, it did not arise from nothing. The beginning of historical research still concentrated on the individual. It was only later that historians changed their ways. Perhaps it was not historiography that changed but the critical reflection behind it.

The romantic idea of the nation was another factor of importance for early scientific historical writing. Every nation was unique. The German nation had

7. This appendix was originally written in 2001, a few years before the appearance of Liverani's *Oltra la Bibbia* (see p. 382). Although the perspective presented here and Liverani's "history" are similar, the execution is very different, which warrants a publication also of this appendix.

8. In the 1970s, when there was a tendency to forget the real impact of the Holocaust, Nazi symbols were getting too popular. An American TV series, *Holocaust*, changed all of this—at least for a while—by showing the fate of a single family from Germany to the gates of Auschwitz. Stalin said that the mishap of an individual is a tragedy, but the death of 10,000 is no more than statistics.

these qualities, the Italians some absolutely different from the German ones. Such abstractions made it easy for the historian to write the history of a nation as though it were in fact the history of a single individual with this individual's special qualities. The interest of prescientific historiography in the individual was transferred to the nation, and the nation was personalized. However, the idea of dividing humanity into the good and the bad also continued. Now there were "good" nations and "bad" nations. Some had to play the role of the hero: others became the villains.

The real breakthrough of modern historiography came with historians like Karl Marx, who in the second half of the nineteenth century claimed that history was governed by economics. Now the assumption began to be heard that history is directed by superhuman forces, that is, the economical factor was of much greater consequence than the individual. Now a new horizon of historical studies appeared that was impersonal and supposed to be neutral. Humans may believe that they control history, but in reality this is a false perception. Humans are governed by economic considerations. In this way it is possible to write a history based on economic development. This historiography has no heroes and no villains; its focus is no longer individual human beings or nations; it concentrates on "general development."

The ideas of Marx about the development of human society may not be separated from the publication of the theory about evolution, which also belongs to the second half of the nineteenth century. Marx's economic theory, like the original version of Darwin's theory, is now considered too simple to explain the many facets of history. It was also compromised by being raised to the status of the official "state religion" in the communist world. His theory became an important element in a general materialistic model for the society and its development, which had the misfortune to be tried in real life. A model is always simpler than the original and cannot therefore be used to remold reality. The model will never be able to control the world, for the interpretation of it is in the minds of humans who no longer understand the link between the original and the copy. Economic history is still very important and will remain so, but it is not the only general model for human development from the Stone Age to our time.

Among the different schools of historical thought that appeared in the course of the twentieth century, the French school of *les annals* has played a special role not least in the study of the history of the Near East.

This school builds on a proposal by the French historian Marc Bloch (1886–1944),[9] which he published in the years between the two world wars. After the Second World War, it was developed further by a number of important historians, the best known being Fernand Braudel (1902–85).[10] Within this school, economics plays an important role, but it is not the only important factor deciding the historical development. In the theory of *les annals*, history may

9. Executed as a member of the French Resistance during the Second World War.
10. See Marc Bloch, *The Historian's Craft*, trans. and introduction by Joseph R. Strayer (New York: Vintage Books, 1953). Fernand Braudel, *On History* (Chicago: University of Chicago, 1980).

be subdivided into three perspectives, the long perspective, the middle perspective, and the short perspective.

The *long perspective* is about the geographical framework of historical developments. It is a constant factor, and in the case of Palestine there are some geographical and physical factors that must always be accounted for: its place on the world map and its physical composition. Any historical event relating to the history of Palestine will have to adjust to such conditions presented by geography. Geography is changeable, but changes appear very slowly. They may include changes of climate. The two other perspectives will have to adjust to the conditions of the first and long one.

In order to move from theory to the way it may be used, we will present an example that is neutral and has no direct relevance for the ancient history of Palestine, although it is not totally irrelevant to this history: the case of Anatolia, the central part of modern Turkey. No economic development is possible here without regard for the natural conditions of the area. When a certain development starts and assumes a distinct form that may even be repetitive, this may be related to the possibilities and limits decided by geographical factors. If these factors change, the consequences for the area may be most serious. From the side of nature, Anatolia is a marginal area, in relation to precipitation. Grain is dependent on rain. Changes in the amount of rain will have consequences for the development of Anatolian society.

Anatolia consists of a central plain surrounded by mountain ranges. This physical setup provides opportunities for several types of human life, agricultural pastoralism, village culture, and more. The local frame is a constant factor, but it is not determined in advance how the inhabitants will administer the possibilities offered by nature. Here other factors may have a say, as is also true of areas outside of Anatolia.

Now we move on to the *middle perspective*, which also includes human activity. How do humans react to the challenges of nature? In traditional Anatolia there will, in principle, be three kinds of local human interaction. The inhabitants on the plain may dominate the whole area including the mountains; or people living in the mountains may control the plain. The third solution will be a type of interaction including peaceful symbiosis allowing both sectors to exist. Examples of all three forms of interaction can be found in the long history of Anatolia.

The economic factor, which is part of the middle perspective, may be different according to the shifting political situation, whether the area in question is ruled by mountaineers or a peaceful farming community on the plain. The development in adjacent territories may likewise be important or even decisive. Seen in such a light, the difference between Anatolia in the second millennium BCE and the first millennium BCE rests in control. For a large part of the second millennium BCE, Anatolia was controlled by the Hittite state that originated in central Anatolia.[11]

11. Some literature: O. R. Gurney, *The Hittites* (2nd rev. ed., Harmondsworth: Penguin, 1990); J. G. Macqueen, "The History of Anatolia and of the Hittite Empire," in Jack M. Sasson, ed., *Civilizations of the Ancient Near East* (New York: Charles Scribner's Sons, 1995), 2:1085–1106.

For a time this state was able to dominate most of Anatolia and control the inhabitants living in the mountains. Economy and culture blossomed. The Hittites were also able to send their armies across the borders of Anatolia. Thus they conquered northern Syria and ruled that territory as a part of their empire. Toward the end of the second millennium, the Hittite Empire vanished, because of a series of factors, perhaps the most important being climate change. The area was hit by a century-long drought that at the end of the Late Bronze Age influenced all of the eastern Mediterranean area. The population of the plain diminished, simply because the drought was worse here than in the mountains. The Hittites lost control of the mountains, and at the end, mountaineers overran the defense of the empire and destroyed its mighty capital, Hattushash.

In the first millennium BCE, several kingdoms were in existence in Anatolia, but no great power arose. The local states remained local and only seldom moved across the Anatolian border to Syria or Mesopotamia. The normal picture was to see these states as the victims of greater powers like the Assyrian Empire, until they were incorporated successively into first the Persian Empire, then the Macedonian, and finally the Roman.

The third perspective, the *short perspective*, is about the human factor and can be likened to the classical idea of history as governed by individuals. If we stay with our example, the Hittite Empire in the first part of the Late Bronze Age was a stable and influential state. The period when this state grew into a major power of Asia Minor and the ancient Near East saw the establishment of many important institutions, including a stable monarchy. The development toward the great empire lasted for centuries and was decidedly not a peaceful one. However, in the fourteenth century BCE conditions stabilized and allowed a highly gifted king, Shuppiluliumash I (1344–1322), to conquer and subdue most of Syria.

Shuppiluliumash's closest predecessors had been energetic governors who created the preconditions for his conquests. And his successors were not inefficient rulers. However, none of them was able to expand the borders of the empire beyond its shape as created by Shuppiluliumash. They were at the same time the victims of a historical "coincidence." While in Syria, the army of Shuppiluliumash was stricken by a plague that it carried back to Anatolia. Over the following years a major part of the Anatolian population, including the king himself, fell victim to the plague. Such an event frequently has consequences of lasting importance.

We here see how different perspectives work together. The plague was an indirect consequence of the period of stabilization belonging to the middle perspective, although it was part of the short perspective. Normally such factors may be mitigated by other factors. In this case, however, the long perspective influenced the course of events, making the territory suffer from a protracted drought.

If the rules of the school of *les annals* are used in a rigid form, the result tends to be historical determinism. Here the cause of history is predestined. Everything has to be in accordance with the long perspective. Historical factors belonging to the middle perspective are dependent on factors belonging to the long one, and factors deciding the short perspective are dependent on developments within the middle perspective. Such a rigid application of the theory can sometimes be found in prehistory, when there are no written sources to provide a more diversified picture.

Normally this kind of history writing is part of a sociologically oriented historiography, and here a special branch of social anthropology originating in North America plays a major role. One of the ways to describe this sociology is cultural evolutionism. Cultural evolutionism rests on the assumption that it is possible to subdivide the history of humankind into specific phases. These may represent different systems of economics, such as the gathering and hunting society, agriculture, animal breeding, and industrialization. They may also be divided according to their systems of organization, such as band society, tribal societies, the chiefdom, and the state. According to this anthropological school, each stage has its characteristics or variables, which it is possible to map almost in the same way we have seen medicine creating a map of the human genome. Thus, if a certain society examined by the anthropologist displays some of these variables, the conclusion is that it is organized along already determined sociopolitical lines.[12]

Historians building on sociological method and following the designs of this school will, on the basis of the material at their disposal–mostly nonwritten evidence gained by archaeological excavations and surveys—draw conclusions relating to the type of society under investigation. They might reach the conclusion that a society was on the tribal level or a chieftainship was established here. If further archeological investigations allow it, they might also be able to trace a development within this society, perhaps toward the fully established state.

In this direction the long perspective has little to offer. The method is nonetheless very useful when we move to the middle perspective, about the possibilities provided by a certain area for human exploitation. Sometimes the results have been questioned. Are they too simplistic, and do they reduce this model in such a way that the evidence may fit it? We have no space for an extensive—and largely irrelevant—discussion here. The main objection has to do with the assumption that the human race will always behave in the same manner if confronted with the same set of possibilities (or challenges). It is assumed that the development from one set of variable factors to another is one-dimensional, which is never the case. Cultural evolutionism may often operate with a too simplified model of human behavior, which allows scholars to confirm their results without much respect for the actual circumstances that may speak against the model. The meaning of this is not that sociology and social anthropology are of no importance to the historian of today. The indications here point toward other schools of anthropological thinking as more fruitful. Sociology will never provide the scholar with results that cannot be challenged. Sociology provides the historian with options, presents many new ways of explaining "facts on the ground."

12. The basic ideas of the school of social anthropology were presented in Elman R. Service, *Primitive Social Organization* (2nd ed., New York: Prentice-Hall, 1971) and *The Origins of the State and Civilization: The Process of Cultural Evolution* (New York: Norton, 1975), and Morton M. Fried, *The Evolution of Political Society: An Essay in Political Anthropology* (New York, Random House, 1967).

The problem of deterministic historical scholarship has to do with the disappearance of the short perspective, the human factor. In this way, history becomes a subject for the middle and long perspective only. However, the example presented here from Anatolia shows that all three perspectives may cooperate, and that we should not discount in advance the importance of the short perspective. Theoretically it also means that modern historical reconstructions will have to include classical ideas belonging to the short perspective. None of the three perspectives taken in isolation will be enough to explain a historical development.

The acceptance of this is important for a new trend within general history called virtual history, that is, a history that never happened but *could* have happened. Classical historiography concentrated on the exceptional individual and had a special interest in the exceptional event. This is contrary to the attitude of the *les annals* school, because it stresses the importance of the short perspective at the expense of the two other perspectives. Virtual history is related to this classical procedure by assuming that history might have followed a different course from the one we know of. By creating scenarios, models of a historical course of events that never happened, this kind of "what-if history" may cast new light on what really happened. This method accords well with a historiography interested in the short perspective, but is largely meaningless whenever a superior perspective is called upon.[13]

THE HISTORY OF PALESTINE

The Long Perspective: The Geography and Climate of Palestine[14]

Palestine belongs to the southwestern end of the so-called Fertile Crescent, which includes those parts of the ancient Near East where climate made agriculture possible and where urban civilization came into being. The total area covered by the crescent is less than fifty percent of the total area of the ancient Near East. Its southeastern end can be found at the north end of the Persian Gulf, and it follows a course toward the north and northwest, including Mesopotamia, the northern part of Syria, and the Levant. Here it ends in the arid desert conditions on the northern part of the Sinai Peninsula. Sometimes the Nile Valley is also counted as part of the crescent. From a historical point of view, this is a reasonable decision, as the culture along the Nile exerted great influence on the territories of western Asia and also received much from Syria and Mesopotamia in exchange.

From a geographical view, Palestine is part of greater Syria. Geographically, topographically, ecologically, and ethnically it represents a continuation of Syria.

13. Old Testament scholarship has not really been touched by virtual history. An exception is the volume published by J. Cheryl Exum, ed., *Virtual History and the Bible* (Leiden: Brill, 2000).

14. The following description of the geography, climate, and occupations of ancient Palestine represent an updated version of my description of Palestine in *Ancient Israel: A New History of Israelite Society* (Sheffield: JSOT Press, 1988), 11–27.

There are no natural borders between Syria and Palestine, only occasional political lines of division.

Palestine can also be seen as an isthmus linking Asia to Africa. Any person who intends to travel between these two continents by land will have to pass through Palestine. This geographical factor has had a continuous effect on the fate of the country since antiquity.

The Borders

Palestine covers only a small territory. Agriculture is limited to the area between the sources of the Jordan River in the northeast and the borders of the Negev Desert in the south, a distance of no more than 150 to 200 miles. The distance from the Mediterranean to the Jordan River ranges from 30 miles in the north to 80 miles in the south. From this fertile part of the country must be deducted desertlike stretches reaching as far as the north end of the Bay of Aqaba. All together, the territory covers an area of about 9,650 square miles, slightly larger than, say, Massachusetts.

On more than one side there are no natural borders. The Mediterranean provides a natural border to the west. In the south a strip of desert sixty miles wide separates Palestine from Egypt and may be considered a natural border between Egypt and Palestine.

In the south the Negev extends into the desert of the Sinai Peninsula, and to the east and southeast, the Arabah valley borders the North Arabic Desert. Further to the north the border between the arable land and the desert has always fluctuated. Sometimes the Jordan River has functioned as a natural border when it is impassable because it meanders and because of a rather steep drop (in general in a mile it falls more than 157 inches). It is, however, quite easy to cross this river because of a series of fords. It is also rather narrow. North of the Gennesaret Lake the border between Palestine and Syria is badly defined. Just to the east of Gennesaret the terrain rises into a flat plateau that continues into Syria (the Golan Heights). Mount Hermon in the north is, on the other hand, a remarkable obstacle.

The northern border against Lebanon is badly defined, although mountainous. The Huleh Valley continues as the Beqaa Valley of Lebanon. Further to the west the mountains of southern Lebanon blend into the north Galilean Highlands until they reach the coast of the Mediterranean.

The Physical Landscape

Physically Palestine is split into numerous minor regional enclaves. Moving from the north to the south, the northwestern part is mostly made up by medium-sized mountains. Only at the northeastern border is a major mountain found, Hermon, which attains almost 9,842 feet. Otherwise the mountains of the Galilee are mostly less than 3,280 feet. These mountains are intersected by several deep valleys.

To the west and south of the Galilean mountains we find the plain of Akko, reaching from the borders of Lebanon (Rosh Hanikra) to the Carmel range, and the Jezreel Valley reaching down to the Jordan Valley in the east. South of these valleys the central highlands begin.

South of the Galilee, the landscape become more monotonous. Along the Mediterranean the Plain of Sharon proceeds toward the south until it blends into the Sinai Peninsula. It is only about fifteen to twenty miles broad. In the east it is followed by a low mountain range, the Shephelah, and again by the central highlands, which are mostly below 3,280 feet. As in Galilee, the central highlands are cut by many valleys connected by mountain passes that do not constitute any obstacles of importance.

The Jordan Valley follows the meandering of the Jordan River from the Hermon massif in the north through the lakes of the Huleh (now gone due to extensive irrigation) and the Sea of Galilee (the Gennesaret), and down to the Dead Sea. North of Palestine, it is known as the Beqaa Valley, and south of the Dead Sea, it continues down to Elath in the form of the Arabah Valley. It is a rift valley reaching far below sea level, at the Sea of Galilee about 656 feet below, and at the northern end of the Dead Sea about 984 feet below sea level.

The descent from the central highlands to the Jordan Valley is steep. However, the ascent to the east of the Jordan River is equally steep, reaching a height of about 3,280 feet. Here the ascent ends in a high plain that gradually becomes desert as one moves east.

Climate and Fertility

The climate is a subtropical one. The summers are dry and hot. In the winter an important period of rain begins in September or October—sometimes as late as November—and lasts until February and sometimes March. The precipitation is sufficient in most of the country to allow for extensive agriculture, although some parts of the country are arid areas, like the Negev in the south and the eastern descent toward the Jordan Valley.

The climate is not a stable factor, however. Drought is a common feature when the rain fails. In many areas, agriculture is dependent on water from cisterns, from rivers and springs. The modern landscape has changed because of extensive irrigation projects that have transformed former arid areas into fields.

There is one more possibility of collecting water, wells based on watery layers in the rock. Wells and springs may sometimes give rise to local thriving oases like Jericho in the Jordan Valley and, on a minor scale, En-gedi along the west coast of the Dead Sea.

Precipitation has traditionally helped to divide the country into different zones, some of them fertile, others absolutely arid. The lowlands in the north and the west have always been favored by extensive rain, although malaria has, at times, been a problem in some parts of the country, not least in the Huleh Valley and in parts of the Plain of Sharon. The breadbasket of the country must be sought in the valley of Galilee. In the mountains agriculture is also a possibility, but only when the necessary technical means were available. Thus the western slopes, including the Shephelah, were easily exploited, while the eastern slopes toward the Jordan were arid. The rain brought by the western wind from the Mediterranean makes the difference. East of the watermark, precipitation falls off until there is almost none. East of the Jordan River, the situation is similar. Here the western ascent gets all the rain, and when it fails the desert begins.

This sketch of the climatic conditions is based on contemporary conditions. From the point of climatic history, the present climate is moderately favorable to agriculture. During its postglacial history (although Palestine was not directly affected by the latest glacial period) Palestine experienced periods of drought as well as periods of abundant precipitation. Sometimes such changes were of short duration, but at other times they seriously affected the conditions of life. Thus a long period of drought had severe consequences for the early civilizations of the country around 6000 BCE, followed by almost two thousand years of increasing humidity beginning about 5000 BCE. The people of the third millennium, on the other hand, experienced a climate that became increasingly hostile and reduced agriculture considerably. At the beginning of the second millennium BCE, climate improved temporarily, to be replaced by a prolonged drought toward the end of the Bronze Age. This climatic pattern has continued ever since, although the changes are not so dramatic as in the Stone and Bronze Ages.

The Middle Perspective: Forms of Occupation

The Natural Fauna and Flora and Human Interference

In the ancient Near East human interference with the natural habitat began early and sometimes led to serious changes in the geography of the landscape. Palestine was no exception.

The mountains provide clear examples of this interference with natural resources, changing them into areas suitable for agriculture. A subtropical mountainous zone like the highlands of Palestine would, from the hand of nature, be covered by forests. Documents from the ancient Near East as well as archaeological discoveries indicate that as late as the beginning of the historical period woodlands were still in evidence in this country. As time went on, humans removed most of this woodland and began to grow cereals there. However, without their natural vegetation, highlands would soon suffer from erosion and become infertile rocky areas. The remedy for this deplorable situation was the terracing of the mountain slopes, and there is in Palestine evidence of an early application of this technique.

The fauna in ancient times was very different from the present, as it was then supplemented by animals known only from the savannas of Africa, for example, the lion and the panther. Their presence was a result of favorable climatic conditions before 6000 BCE, when the Sahara was severely reduced in size and allowed a passage for animals from Africa to Asia.

The Use of the Natural Resources
The Pattern of Occupation

Through the ages the pattern of settlement has followed the changing climatic conditions. The demographic centers will always be in the areas most favored by natural conditions and suitable for extensive agriculture. Less favored areas like the highlands might allow peasants to live there, but in smaller numbers than on the plains. Finally, marginal areas that bordered the zones where agriculture was possible but were still not desert became the home of a population mostly engaged in the breeding of animals, primarily goats and sheep.

This general sketch has been modified several times through history by other considerations. Sometimes political conditions have forced people to leave fertile areas and move to the highlands to find protection. Overgrazing and exhausting the soil for agriculture have also had consequences for the settlements. Finally, an ever-changing political and economic balance between different lifestyles, on one hand agriculture and on the other cattle breeding, has also caused changes in the settlement pattern, sometimes forcing farmers to become cattle breeders (nomads) and at other times inducing nomads to settle as farmers.

The special conditions that caused to be sporadically populated some areas we should believe extremely fitted for agriculture, such as the Huleh Valley and the Plain of Sharon, have already been discussed. Here settlement in the form of cities and villages is not as dense as expected. The presence of many important settlements in the Shephelah, however, indicates that people living here may also have exploited parts of the coastal plain. Conditions of health and also the need for protection caused people to live further away from their fields, although this was, in a country of such small dimensions, hardly a major problem. In Galilee the last 5,000 years have seen the presence of an extensive agricultural population, almost without interruption.

The Palestinian highlands, both in Galilee and in the central part of the country, housed a population far smaller than that of the plains. They were nonetheless not deserted areas. The valleys especially became the home of an extended village culture including some minor cities. Some of the best-known localities are found in the mountains—such as Hebron, Jerusalem, Bethel, Shiloh, and Shechem.

Similar conditions ruled east of the Jordan River. Here a series of rivers moving from the east to the west have influenced human settlement. However, when precipitation was absent, humans responded with various strategies: to settle in oases like Jericho, to settle along the fringe between the fertile and arid land, and to supplement some agriculture with animal breeding.

Agriculture and Husbandry; Nomadism

In those parts of the country allowing for agriculture, the most important cereals have traditionally been barley and wheat. The growing of cereals was supplemented by the growing of grapes and olive trees. Here the mountain slopes were especially profitable. Other crops were known, such as the date, although in ancient times hardly of the same importance as today. Ancient people of the Near East did not know the range of citrus fruits available to modern humans, such as the lemon and the orange. Their presence in modern times is due to import, mostly from East Asia. The cultivated apple was a thing of the future; people of that time disposed of the pomegranate.

Most people living in Palestine in premodern times, some 90 percent or more, were engaged in agriculture. Generally this population lived in villages spread around the cities. Although a fair share of the production of the peasants went to the cities, even a part of the urban population was engaged in agriculture.

The nature of the country made some land not usable for agricultural purposes. Such areas were often suitable for animal breeding, and many Palestinian peasants have traditionally also been engaged in the breeding of mostly small cattle. The most important domesticated animals, the goat and the sheep, are flock animals and have always been easy to care for. This led to widespread pastoralism. In ancient Palestine the responsibility for the animals probably rested on professional herdsmen who looked after the flocks of their village or on family members like older boys.

Villages in the mountains profited from the climatic conditions of their area, being more diversified than the climate on the plains. The physical differences allowed a kind of "transhumance" (an expression borrowed from Southern France), meaning that cattle were in the winter kept in the village and in the summer were moved to the mountains by herdsmen, sometimes followed by entire families.

Nomadism is an occupation closely resembling transhumance. Here whole families, lineages, clans, or tribes specialize in animal breeding. This way of life is nomadic and indicates that other occupations like agriculture are less important, although generally not unknown. Nomadism can be found in many varieties, from mountain nomadism, which is almost impossible to separate from transhumance, to the nomads of the desert almost exclusively engaged in the raising of animals. Nomads have often been assumed to be totally different from other sectors of Near Eastern life, such as the peasants and the urban populations. They are not; this is a stereotype created by European travelers of the past. It is better to talk about different strategies available to the people of the Near East, sometimes pursued in isolation, sometimes in different combinations. However, until the end of the Bronze Age, one kind of nomadism was unknown, the life of the bedouin. The bedouin living in the desert have traditionally been totally dependent on the camel. This animal was domesticated only fairly late, shortly before 1000 BCE. The bedouin as known today may be as late a cultural phenomenon as belonging to the first and second centuries CE.

Before the appearance of the bedouin nomadic type, nomads were members of a society that also included agricultural and urban sectors. They lived either among the peasants or in the periphery of the settled area and had an important economic role to fulfill. Animal breeding and agriculture were supplementary strategies for survival and so contributed to optimize the exploitation of a territory like Palestine. This is of course a theoretical statement, as the vagaries of the climate might at any time destroy the symbiotic system normally assumed to be present. One or two successive years of drought would imply a disaster for societies living in a marginal area like ancient Palestine. The small scale of its territory also meant a constant pressure on its resources and a high degree of internal competition for control of these resources. When the factor of the fragmented territory is added to the other factors of climate and economic strategies, the typical Palestinian political situation is easy to understand: a country divided between several local political units, if not governed by a foreign power.

The Differentiated Society

Ancient Palestine's basic agrarian society is often assumed to have been an egalitarian one, that is, a society without great differences between different groups of people, nearly all of them basing their existence on the presence of free peasants living in villages out of reach of the urban civilization with its specialization of crafts. In principle, all people living in the village will be equally ranked—or so many studies based on social anthropology are arguing.

Although it may be doubted that such an egalitarian culture ever existed—it may be no more than a scholarly fairy tale—there was no home for it in ancient Palestine, at least not in the last 5,000 years. There are many reasons for it, and it is impossible today to decide which factor was decisive in each case. One reason was the scanty resources of the country, which provoked competition between its inhabitants; a second was the fact that the country was split into several small enclaves. On top of this, there was basic competition between agriculturalists and animal breeders, whose interests were not always identical (for instance, the animals may destroy crops if not under tight control), and between local communities such as the peasants living in one valley in the highlands and the peasants living in the valley next to them. Competition might be serious in years of famine, when the crops failed because of a drought or because they had been destroyed, for example, by locusts. It was a society where the strongest survived.

One way to reduce the danger of ending up as the losing party in the competition for resources was social integration. People moved together in order to establish a collective defense against intruders. We see no isolated farms dotting the landscape. The dominant way of life in the countryside was as part of a village community. This integration might be supported by fortifications and strongholds: in a village that was chosen as the center of a certain district, extensive defenses were constructed. In such a case the process represented a decisive step toward the establishment of a city. Here a number of functions of common interest would find a home, such as the coordination of the common defense against foreign predators. Generally some kind of leadership would soon appear as part of this process. Now the differentiated society was about to appear, especially because such a leadership would not be able to produce its own food but would have to rely on supplies extorted from ordinary peasants.

What form the process took that resulted in the political and social setup of ancient Palestine is unknown. The fact is that Palestine, from the Bronze Age, was dominated by a system of small- or medium-sized cities surrounded by villages that supplied the specialists of the urban population with food and were protected by the organization of the city. The origins of the city-state system of the Bronze Age should be sought in such a social and political organization. Now the differentiated society was in existence, with a basic difference between people who produced their own food and people who were dependent on others to acquire their provisions. Thus the central city ended up as a place of taxation of the surrounding agricultural zone. It was, however, also the home of the organization that coordinated the tillage of the fields.

When the city was created, a division of crafts based in the city followed. Apart from a military staff at the disposal of the leader of the society, who in historical times mostly was called king, there was at his disposal a series of civil officers who helped the leader to control the territory of the city, including its dependent villages. Trades like pottery making and leatherwork were specialized, and their practitioners were equally dependent on the villagers for the procurement of food.

The differentiated society that has characterized the Near East since ancient times dominated the political scene, although the precise details of its organization may have been different from place to place. In some places economic life may have centered on the existence of free markets where the peasants could sell their products. In other places the surplus productions of the peasants were absorbed by taxation and redistributed by the king and his officials.

Trade

The city was more than just a place where the surplus production was collected. From early times, it also became the center of trade. The city in most cases would have markets for the redistribution of the products of the agrarian zone, where breeders of livestock could sell their products. Here also the villagers might go and buy specialized products that they could not manufacture, at least not in the desired quality, such as tools, pottery, textiles, even luxury products like jewelry. In historical times Palestine was the home of a mixed economy that dominated also the marginal parts of the country.

Archaeological excavations have shown how certain urban centers developed into considerable size—local conditions taken into consideration. There must have been special reasons in some cases for the growth of certain urban centers, while others were left behind. The local exchange between the countryside and the city cannot explain such developments. Somehow some cities must have functioned like magnets for the local population, as well as people from other places, maybe because they offered the best opportunities for earning a living. The obvious way to become rich was trade, not through local barter but through long-distance trade between different urban centers. Palestine offered few possibilities of acquiring objects for superregional trade. Every part of the society possessed the same goods and produced the same kind of artifacts. Every city housed potters, peddlers, and other artisans, and the production shows an amazing homogeneity, although mostly on a very basic artistic level. Food was not an object of long-distance trade. The transport was too costly and the means of preserving the goods absolutely insufficient. Ancient international trade would normally concentrate on the unusual goods, luxury items, and specialized food like wine and olive oil. There were no precious stones, no gold or silver worth exploiting.

Although Palestine is short of natural resources, it still functions as a bridge between continents—or, considering ancient conditions, between two major and rich civilizations, the Egyptian in the south and the Mesopotamian in the north. The comprehensive trade between these two poles of civilization in the ancient Near East would mostly have passed through Palestine, organized as trade caravans. Some sources document that sea trade between Egypt and the Phoenician cities in Lebanon and Syria was also considerable.

The land-based trade followed different routes passing through Palestine. The best-known and most widely used route of trade caravans would follow the sea ("the Road along the Sea"), beginning in the delta of the Nile in Lower Egypt (the northern part of ancient Egypt), and then cross the Sinai Peninsula following a course running close to the Mediterranean. It continued along the sea to the Carmel range, which was crossed via the narrow pass at Megiddo, and entered the Jezreel Valley. Here it split into different routes. One led to the north along the coast to Lebanon; another followed the Beqaa Valley to the northeast. The most important branch went through the Jezreel Valley down to Beth-shan in the Jordan Valley where it crossed the Jordan River and continued toward the east and Damascus and the other great cities of Syria and beyond Syria, Mesopotamia.

A second route between Egypt and Mesopotamia separated from the first in southern Palestine. It traversed the northern part of the Negev to the territories east of the Jordan River and moved to the north through the different territories of the modern state of Jordan. The route is known in the Old Testament as the King's Highway. It followed a course via Amman (ancient Rabbat Ammon) to Damascus.

Finally, a third route went through Palestine from Beersheba via Hebron, Jerusalem, Bethel, and Shechem to the Jezreel Valley. It had mostly only local importance but allowed for detours to the fords of the Jordan River.

The trade routes—especially the route along the coast—provided local communities with an opportunity to tax the transit trade. Characteristically some of the major cities of Palestine were placed along this route: Gaza, Ashkelon, Ashdod, and Megiddo controlling the pass through the Carmel range. Other cities were placed at local branches belonging to this route, like Hazor in upper Galilee.

The presence of these routes opened up other positive as well as negative possibilities. Among the benefits of the international trade that passed through the country was the import of goods from neighboring cultural centers, both material item and cultural borrowings. It also meant that the way of organizing the major centers became known, as well as the intellectual tradition belonging to the great civilizations of that time. In this way Palestine was a part of Near Eastern civilization in general.

The negative effects of trade had to do with the interest of the primary producers in Mesopotamia and in Egypt to control the trade routes. If a great power like Egypt was able to control politically the territory through which trade passed, it would mean not only increased security for the tradespeople but also less taxation and increased profit. This is not only theory. The history of Palestine tells a story of repeated conquest by other nations. The local authorities have most often been unable to maintain the independence from their powerful neighbors. Palestine was often reduced to a politically and economically insignificant province of a foreign power. Furthermore, the trade routes were also the routes that foreign armies followed and where they met in battle. Palestine became a battlefield for foreign powers—hardly to the benefit of its population.

The Short Perspective: The History of Palestine

The Neolithic Period: The Preceramic Period

There is no need to start with primeval history in this place, in this case, the Paleolithic Period and the Mesolithic Period. In Palestine there are traces of human presence hundred of thousands of years old. These human beings belong to the subject of paleoanthropology (the study of human development until the appearance of the Homo sapiens, the Cro-Magnon race of human beings), and not to history in the more narrow sense of the word. The study of the history of Palestine may begin in the Neolithic Period, although scholars must always realize that it is impossible to write a history that moves beyond the middle perspective before the Late Bronze Age. Before the middle of the second millennium BCE there are practically no written sources relevant to the history of Palestine, apart from some indications in Egyptian inscriptions showing an interest in western Asia—an interest also demonstrated by archaeological excavations in southern Palestine.

The border between the Mesolithic and the Neolithic periods is marked by the change from one economic strategy, the gathering and hunting way of life, to a new one including agriculture. As in other parts of the Near East, the introduction of agriculture soon resulted in the appearance of a village culture, with some villages of considerable size, more than a thousand square meters. In one case the village was soon defended by fortifications, as happened in Jericho in the Jordan Valley, in a settlement that dates to the ninth millennium BCE.

It is impossible to put a name tag on the population or the populations of Neolithic Palestine. It is anonymous insofar as there are no written documents attesting the identity of these people. The knowledge of writing was many millennia away. Although this anonymous population had a history, it can be related only in very general terms. It may be that in the future DNA-analyses will allow scholars to trace the identity of this population, showing it to be homogenous or from different parts of the world. Such analyses may tell us whether the population was stable or constantly on the move, whether migrations between Palestine and other parts of the Near East were common. Until such studies are possible, we have very little information these matters or things like political and religious institutions.

Some scholars will use language as a means to penetrate further into the question of the composition of the population. At the beginning of so-called historical times (when written sources are available) most of the area may have spoken a Semitic dialect—in the case of Palestine presumably the one known as Amorite. The Semitic languages constitute a special family of languages strongly resembling the languages of North Africa, including ancient Egyptian (formerly known as Hamitic). The Indo-European languages first appeared in the Near East in the second millennium BCE. The Semitic-speaking population may therefore represent a kind of "original" population, which in spite of many differences lived in an area bordering on the Zagros range in the east and the Mediterranean in the west with its North African extension to the Atlas mountain range in northwest Africa. The separation between the Semitic and the North African languages may be due to the climatic changes resulting in the gradual increase of the arid zones after the Neolithic moist interval, creating physical obstacles to the intercourse between the different regions. It is impossible to say when this development began and how it happened.

The events belonging to this period traced by archaeologists involve only very general conditions like the changes of settlement patterns and the beginning of animal husbandry. The settlement pattern can be linked to climatic conditions, which seem more favorable at the beginning of this period than later. The domestication of animals began in the seventh millennium BCE, when sheep and goats were tamed. The domestication of cattle and other animals belongs to the following millennia, although the horse was late in appearance—the second millennium BCE—and the camel was first domesticated during the transition from the Bronze to the Iron Age.

During the seventh millennium, two major changes of the settlement pattern are in evidence. These changes also affected the neighboring countries. The first crisis seems to be dated to about 6500 BCE, the second at the end of the millennium. Some settlements like Jericho were deserted by their inhabitants, some among them forever. Other settlements survived. There is more than one explanation for these changes, one among them that prolonged drought affected agricultural life. Marginal zones became unsuitable for agriculture, and a certain migration to Palestine from more arid areas outside of Palestine took place.

The image of a reduction of settled life toward the end of the first part of the Neolithic Period is ambiguous. Some of the settlements belonging to this period continued to exist while other settlements disappeared. This may be used as an argument against a prolonged period of drought. If Palestine was affected by such a drought, the settlements that survived probably would have succumbed to worsening environmental conditions. Other theories say that the changes happened because of impoverishment of the soil, which forced the peasants to move to other parts. Also this hypothesis may not explain every case when a settlement has been given up. Thus there is no reason why a settlement like Jericho was deserted, either because of drought or because of the impoverishment of the soil. Jericho is placed in an oasis with plenty of water resources and would still be inhabitable if the climatic conditions worsened.

In such a case, human political activity might have forced the inhabitants of the oasis of Jericho to leave their homes. It is perhaps also reasonable to ask questions about probable political reasons for other changes in the settlement pattern of those times. Here the limitations to our knowledge of this period are evident. We have no information that allows us to describe in any detail what really happened. We may describe the effects, but we do not know the reasons.

Thus we cannot say whether there is a link between this development and the contemporary appearance of a new economic strategy in the form of nomadism as a special branch of life in the countryside.

Previous scholarship often argued that nomadism represents an independent stage in human development, between the hunter-gatherer stage and settled agriculture. The criterion of mobility was deemed decisive. Gatherers and hunters were always on the move and traversed large areas searching for prey. Nomads are always on the move but bring their previous booty with them in the form of domesticated flocks of sheep and goats. Modern studies have demolished this theory about evolution of human societies; animal husbandry came after the introduction of agriculture and represents a specialization of one part of the life of the peasant, the breeding of animals.

The appearance of nomadic culture in its many forms led to a fragmentation of the agrarian population of ancient Palestine because of different categories of occupation. The fertile soil is limited but attractive for all different groups of agriculturalists, whether concentrating on the growing of crops or the breeding of animals. Thus these groups are in constant competition. The fertile soil provides the best fodder for the animals of the cattle breeder; the peasant sees the exploitation of such areas as his prerogative.

In the Near East these economic strategies have mostly existed in a kind of symbiosis, sharing the exploitation of one and the same area. In recent times cattle breeding was under pressure and often reduced to a phenomenon belonging to the marginal areas of the periphery of settled zones. However, there is no reason to transfer these conditions to earlier periods. It is far from certain that the relationship between the different occupants of a certain territory was always a harmonious one.

Symbiosis seems to be the rule when a society is governed by an urban elite, otherwise identified as the leadership of a centralized state that was able to exert police and military control over all sectors of this state. When such centralized political institutions have been absent, the nomadic part of the society has often gained the upper hand and dominated the other sectors. Sometimes they have simply destroyed the conditions for settled life. The role of the Turks after their conquest of the Near East at the beginning of the sixteenth century CE tells the sad story of the consequences of the lack of central interest in Palestine (as well as Jordan and Syria). Because of their lack of interest, the area under Turkish rule experienced a period of "nomadization" that destroyed the village culture of the past. It changed only in the nineteenth century CE when the Ottoman Empire lost its provinces in Europe and began to get involved in Near Eastern affairs.

Hereafter there was a marked increase of settled life that continued until the Turks were forced out of the Near East after their defeat in the First World War.[15]

Irrespective of the real course of events, which can no longer be traced, it seems clear that the period of decline of settled life in Palestine was replaced by new progress as we witness at the beginning of the sixth millennium BCE a tendency toward increasingly growing settlements. Cases are now known from Syria and Jordan of villages covering more than fifteen hectares; Palestinian parallels are somewhat smaller. This phase was gradually replaced by the return of the minor villages.

Neolithic: The Ceramic Period

Something "happened" between about 6000 and 5500 BCE that has always attracted the attention of archaeologists: the invention of pottery making. The hundreds of thousands of years of the Paleolithic and Mesolithic periods saw an increasing sophistication when it came to the refinement of tools made by stone. The basic material—primarily flint stone—remained unchanged although shaped into new forms. This was also the case with other materials like wood and bones. The new pottery technique was unique in the sense that it led to a metamorphosis of the original material, clay, which was formed and burned and became ceramic, having basic characteristics quite different from the original soft material.

The mastering of this new technique spread rapidly, and pottery became extremely popular, creating some variation in an otherwise monotonous world. Since the first pottery makers made their appearance, their products have ever changed form and ornament, not only over time but also from place to place. Because of such changes and variation, archaeologists from this period on have new possibilities of dating their discoveries. Pottery, however, has more to contribute than just dating. By tracing families of pottery it is possible, after having established a date for these families, to look for regional and superregional diffusion. It is now possible to discuss economic exchange between different regions showing the same pottery. It is also possible to speculate about the character of such exchanges, whether exclusively economic or also involving political or family ties. The invention of pottery simply allows the archaeologist and the historian to move at least a few yards into the area of the short perspective, that is, into history.

Sometimes the importance of pottery has been exaggerated, most often because archaeologists have attached ethnic tags to their pottery. Many archaeologists are of the opinion that a certain type of pottery can be linked to a special ethnic group. They presume that there is a commonality between the material culture and the identity of the population sharing this culture. But social anthropologists a long time ago pointed out that such a connection between material culture and ethnic units is not an established fact. The appearance of a certain type of pottery in a certain area does not automatically say anything about the composition of the population, whether it was a fragmented political organization or a centralized

15. The modern situation in the Darfur province in Sudan is another cruel but perfect example of the domination of the cattle breeders.

society with strong leaders. Pottery may have spread in different ways, for example, as containers for goods to be traded, or through the moving around of specialized and popular pottery makers.

With or without pottery, the period between about 5000 and 4500 BCE may be the least inspiring from an archaeological point of view, having little to show. Archaeologists seem to be in disagreement as to the reasons for the poor culture of the time, whether it was a consequence of a diminishing population—although certain places like Jericho were resettled in this period, by a population with a very different material culture, which may say little about its origins and identity, and new religious habits reflected in its burials—or simply an archaeological coincidence. Many settlements dating from this period are invisible, simply because they developed and were "hidden" by the subsequent urbanization of the Chalcolithic Period.

The Chalcolithic Period

The Chalcolithic Period—or the Stone-Bronze Age (*Chalcolithic* is a compound of Greek *chalcos*, "bronze," and *lithos*, "stone")—is a transitory period between the Stone and the Bronze Ages, although stone remained the dominant material for the production of weapons and tools, because copper is too soft a material to be of any practical use for such purposes and far too expensive for ordinary use. When the technical process for changing soft copper to hard bronze was discovered, humans were in possession of a material that could be used, for example, for weapons. From a technological point of view the bronze also represented something fundamentally new: the first attempt to use metal as a material, for example, for jewelry.

We know of a considerable number of settlements from this period, spread over the whole territory from the Negev in the south to the Golan Heights in the northeast. Some of these settlements were small, others quite comprehensive, on the order of about 25 hectares or 60 acres, like Teleilat el-Ghassul, which has given a name to the culture of the Chalcolithic Period in this part of the Levant. A certain pattern also appears when these settlements are reviewed, as a certain hierarchical order seems to have been the rule of the day, showing a hierarchical organization between bigger and smaller settlements and indicating some kind of political centralization. In the interpretation of many archaeologists, this period saw Palestinian society arranged as a series of chiefdoms, with chieftains residing in the major settlements.

This is a reasonable assumption as other factors point toward a beginning of the differentiation of the society. There is evidence of the presence of specialist artisans, some of them working with copper and able to produce quite amazing artifacts, many of them of religious importance. Also painters are in evidence, leaving imposing wall paintings in Teleilat el-Ghassul. There is a refinement of pottery after the invention of the pottery wheel and an increasing variety of ceramic forms. Archaeologists also point to evidence of superregional trade activities.

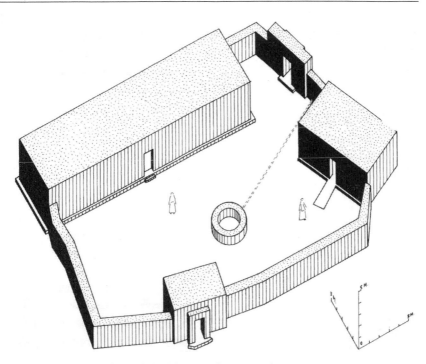

7. A reconstruction of the Chalcolithic temple at En-gedi
(From D. Ussishkin, "The Assulian Shrine at En-Gedi" [*Tel Aviv* 7 (1980): 1–44].
Courtesy of the Institute of Archaeology, Tel Aviv University.)

Religious buildings dating from this period have been excavated, among these the temple complex at En-gedi, close to the Dead Sea. This temple may not be related to any major settlement in its vicinity. This might indicate that it was serviced by a professional priesthood, religious specialists, and also functioned as a place of pilgrimage for people living far away.

It is impossible to say anything precise about the ethnic and historical relationship between the people of the Stone and Chalcolithic ages in Palestine. Some scholars are of the opinion that the Chalcolithic population was new in comparison to the old one, bringing with them a new civilization. Nowadays most scholars, however, consider the Chalcolithic culture a spin-off from the previous one from the Neolithic Period, representing a local Palestinian phenomenon.

There is evidence of relations with the neighboring countries—especially Egypt and Syria, and sometimes even Mesopotamia. This may be evidence of the mobility of the people living here, but it cannot be decided whether people that moved were new settlers or migrant traders.

New habits of burials also began to be seen, with burials outside of the settlements in special reserved graveyards. Such a change may be an indication of the arrival of a new population and has in other places been used for identifying such population elements. In northeastern Europe, and best known perhaps from Denmark, were the so-called "single grave people," also called the "corded ware culture" and the "Battle Axe culture." This group is supposed to have arrived here during the local transition between the Stone Age and the Bronze Age (ca. 2800–2400 BCE) in the shape of Indo-European nomads, although more recently this explanation has been abandoned in favor of theories involving a change of religion rather than a change of population.[16] Changing burial habits point in the direction of changing religious ideas and need not have anything to do with a change of population.

When archaeological discoveries cannot be supported by written sources, it is impossible to present more precise explanations of such changes. Thus it is only a theory that the tendency toward a more centralized society in the fifth and fourth millennia BCE was due to the appearance of chieftainships, of a society governed by "big men." It may be possible to point at other reasons for this, suggesting that the political and economic changes were not primarily linked to the appearance of an elite group of families but were linked to, say, a priesthood who acted not only independently of the society—which may have been the case at En-gedi—but also decided the life of people living here.

For reasons such as these we know little about the development that caused the Chalcolithic Age to change into the Early Bronze Age toward the end of the fourth millennium BCE, although it is evident the changes were considerable for a civilization that had already been in existence for a very long time, leading, for example, to changes that caused to be deserted not only many of the major settlements, but also a religious institution like the temple at En-gedi, which was not only deserted but physically closed down and made inaccessible to the public.

The Early Bronze Age

The same problems for the scholar who intended to find an explanation for the developments belonging to the Chalcolithic Period also affect the decisions of the scholars who study the Early Bronze Age. In spite of a regionally diversified but also remarkable development that can easily be tracked by archaeologists, we know practically nothing about the details of this development and absolutely nothing about the people who caused it to happen.

This is frustrating, especially because of what happened in other parts of the ancient Near East at the same time. Here, shortly before 3000 BCE there came into being important and rich cultures that developed writing as a primary means of communication. Because of the two very different systems of writing that orig-

16. The old, still popular, theory about the identity of this people and culture is still the foundation of this period in the authoritative Johannes Brønsted, *Danmarks Oldtid, Stenalderen* (2nd ed., Copenhagen: The National Museum, 1957), 1:250–64. The revision is evident in the successor to Brønsted's major work, Jørgen Jensen, *Danmarks Oldtid, Stenalder 13.000–2000 f.Kr.* (Copenhagen: Gyldendal, 2001), 455–503. Jørgen Jensen sees the changes caused not by immigration but by a new individualistic family structure.

inated in this period—in Egypt hieroglyphic writing and in Mesopotamia cuneiform writing—modern scholars are now able to attach descriptions to much of what happened here. They are able to identify the names of kings, people, cities, and countries and tell about religious beliefs and practices. A local variant of the cuneiform system of writing appeared in Syria around the middle of the third millennium BCE, known from the archives of the city of Ebla, near Aleppo. In Palestine nothing similar has been found.

This means that from a historical point of view the history of Palestine in the third millennium is still "prehistory." There may be some historical references to Palestine in Egyptian documents dating from this period, although they are relevant only to Egyptian interference in the history of southern Palestine. Such references are both imprecise and very general.

The Early Bronze Age is divided by historians and archaeologists into three or four periods that are characteristically different. Here we need to pay attention only to the so-called Protourban Period or Early Bronze I, about 3300–3000 BCE, and the fully blossoming culture of the Early Bronze Age, about 3000–2300 BCE, alias Early Bronze II and III.

The *Protourban Period* is exactly what the name suggests: a period characterized by the forerunners of later urban societies belonging to the heyday of the Early Bronze Age. Most settlements were still unfortified villages, a reflection of the former life of the Chalcolithic Period. This does not mean that every settlement of this period was a continuation of a previous settlement. Many Chalcolithic settlements were deserted, some of them among the most important from the previous period, and new settlements were founded. Furthermore, the development is not the same in every part of the country. There are obvious regional differences between south and north, between the central highlands and the Galilean Mountains, and the Negev and the Jordan Valley.

Around 3000 BCE some settlements began to develop into small cities fortified by strong walls. These new cities, distributed all over the country, are normally seen as indications of some kind of political centralization. Scholars of this period speak about embryonic kingdoms—city-states following a pattern that is repeated in both the Middle and Late Bronze Age.

We have no secure evidence of the reasons for this development toward a centralized, fortified urban society. One thing is clear: the presence of such fortifications implies that the political situation had changed, making fortifications necessary. There may be several reasons for this change, some local and others having to do with problems originating outside of Palestine.

The Chalcolithic Period saw major settlements appear mostly unfortified. This means that the period was characterized by peace and prosperity. The wealth of this period may have been caused by the Neolithic moist interval after 5000 BCE. After 3000 BCE, everything changed, as the moist interval was replaced by a much dryer period, which must have had serious consequences for the population of the ancient Near East, which saw its resources constantly diminishing.

In light of this development, the appearance of fortified settlements in Palestine may have been caused by the necessity of defending oneself against neighbors. The competition for resources between local communities made such defenses necessary. When there is plenty of everything, there is no need for such restraints.

From the point of view of practical organization, such defense works demand not only extensive human resources but also coordination, that is, a political organization able to direct the work and later on the defense.

Historians talk about "kings" in connection with these new cities, although the term is not very precise here. A fortified city that is the center of a certain region is often considered the center of a city-state, a concept borrowed from the classical world and the Greek *polis* ("city") state. The Palestinian specimens of this type of organization were generally much smaller than their Greek counterparts and as far as organization is concerned very different. Within the city different types of settlements existed side by side, ordinary peoples' houses, the king's palace, sacred and administrative buildings.

The pattern of settlement within these cities is an indicator of substantial and hierarchically arranged differences among the inhabitants. In this connection it is meaningful to describe the rulers as kings, although most of them ruled a very limited area, not major well-organized states.

We may, perhaps, think of a development similar to the one found in early medieval northern Europe leading to an urbanized society, with cities built around the fortress belonging to the elite who resided in the fortress. The owner of the fortress was perhaps not really a king in the precise sense of the word. He was more likely the local *patron*, and the society around him organized in a system of alliances and contracts between him and the rest of the population, his *clients*.

The hierarchical distribution of settlements in the Chalcolithic Period may indicate a similar development toward a separation of the population between the patron and his family on one hand and his clients, the remaining population, on the other. During the Early Bronze Age this system became a permanent one, leading at the end to the appearance of the kingdoms characterizing the ancient Near East in historical times. Here the king still functioned as the supreme patron and all his subjects—important as well as unimportant—as his clients. Some scholars have called the system a despotic one and have talked about oriental despotism, simply because there was only one leader, the patron-king who distributed all the resources of his territory between his subjects-clients.

Thus worsening climatic conditions may have led to advances for civilization in general, affecting the material, the political, and the economic culture. The environmental conditions for life grew worse and demanded a concentration of efforts if the society was going to survive. The more demanding the challenge, the more advanced the answer to it.

It is possible to survive such harsh conditions as long as the fields close to the city can still be used. Problems arise when pressure originating outside of the city forces the inhabitants to stay behind their protective barriers. At a certain point it becomes impossible to defend fields, crops, and belongings, even when hidden behind walls. Then the city will disappear, because it is either deserted by its inhabitants or destroyed by enemies from the outside world. The process is likely to begin when, because of a lack of provisions, some inhabitants choose another place to live. Now the ability of the city to defend itself is weakened. In the end there will be so few inhabitants left that the defense of the city becomes impossible.

Palestinian cities were generally able to support themselves as far as food production was concerned. However, they had one more option. During the Chalcolithic Period there were tendencies toward the appearance of a differentiated society. In the cities of the Early Bronze Age this differentiation sharpened, and the number of specialists grew considerably. Specialists—whether civil or military—had to be supported by the food-producing part of the population.

Specialists make it possible to supplement the income of the city because their products can be traded, not only within the confines of the city and its surrounding countryside, but also with other urban societies. Still this trade, to sustain the speciaists, had to be supported by people who produced the food necessary, whether it was food for local consumption or items for trading, such as wine and olives.

Actually there is evidence of the growing importance of wine and olives in this period. A number of olive presses have been excavated, among other places at Arad in the northern Negev. Since the beginning of the Bronze Age, olive oil has had an important place among goods for trading in the Mediterranean world. It was eagerly asked for by people living in areas not able to produce it themselves, such as Egypt.

An economy like this, based on the production of this kind of merchandise, is vulnerable to changes that affect the market. Without a trade system that reaches beyond the narrow borders of a city-state, in this case Palestine, it will die. Moreover, a product like olive oil will never be of primary interest for local consumption. It will be an element only in food production. If too much stress has been placed on such goods, a crisis affecting the production and trade will have catastrophic consequences for the economy. There is an example much later of the effects of a breakdown of the trade with olives—in Syria, where a whole region was abandoned by its inhabitants in the early Middle Ages. Now only the presence of the many "dead cities" in the Ansariye Mountains tells us about a formerly blossoming civilization there.

When defense works were completed, who was the enemy? There is more than one answer. Most attackers will have been people very much like the defenders, people who lived in Palestine who were looking for booty in the form of food in order to survive, or for a way to enrich themselves. The presence of a great many fortified cities may be evidence of a state of war where one patron/king tried to gain the upper hand over his neighbors. The idea was to defend the little one owned against the colleague who did not own more but wanted to acquire whatever you owned. This is not only theory, but can be traced in historical documents relevant to the history of the Late Bronze Age.

The enemy might also be people not sharing the defenders' way of life, such as roaming tribes living as nomads. It is clear that such a migrating component of the population had a part to play in the development that led to the collapse of urban life at the end of the Early Bronze Age. The nomads were, however, not the cause of the crisis but a consequence of the climatic deterioration that forced peasants to give up tilling the fields and change economic strategies.

Finally, the enemy may be a force originating in territories outside of Palestine, like the Egyptians, who in this period had at least economic interests in southern Palestine. There may also be evidence of their presence in the shape of trade colonies or even military outposts, although most historians are of the opinion that Egypt was not heavily involved in an occupation of the southern part of Palestine as early as the Early Bronze Age.

Civilization in Palestine in the Early Bronze Age developed primarily on a local basis, although there are certainly traces of a beginning orientation toward the international world. Cultural borrowing happened not only from the Levantine coast but also from Egypt and even Mesopotamia.

This is not the place to present an overview of the history of the ancient Near East in general. However, it is clear that the development confronting the historian of Palestine in the Early Bronze Age can be paralleled by similar developments in other places in western Asia, in Lebanon, Syria, and Mesopotamia. There were differences between one place and the next, but the broad perspective says that the development was of the same kind, although the changes were of a different scale outside of Palestine's narrow territory. Thus northern Syria saw a major process of centralization with the city of Ebla, located some twenty-five miles south of Aleppo, as its center. The city of Ebla reached a size much larger than anything found in contemporary Palestine in this period, with a population of perhaps 10,000 to 20,000 people. However, the real difference between Syria and Mesopotamia on one hand and Palestine on the other is the presence of written sources, since these transform Syrian and Mesopotamian prehistory to history. Ebla was destroyed about 2350 BCE. The precise circumstances are not known, although this period was characterized by ambitious Mesopotamian rulers who tried to expand their territories toward the west. The destruction of Ebla was linked to a human factor and not conditioned by deteriorating climatic circumstances, although the consequence of the general more arid climate was also evident in Syria.

The Transition from the Early to the Middle Bronze Age

Documents like those found at Ebla are unknown in Palestine. It is therefore uncertain whether or not the collapse of Ebla and the considerable Syrian community having its center there also influenced the contemporary collapse of urban civilization in Palestine. The subsequent political turmoil probably left a power vacuum in Syria that lasted for more than two hundred years, broke the trading links between Palestine and other countries, and interrupted the supraregional trade between Mesopotamia and Egypt running through Palestinian and Syrian territory.

There are also other ways of explaining the collapse of urban civilization in Palestine toward the end of the third millennium BCE. After about 2300 BCE the dominant urban civilization of the Early Bronze Age was replaced by a much more primitive lifestyle, showing the local population to have largely given up life in protected cities, in favor of a kind of mixed economy including agriculture as well as cattle breeding.

The period was characterized by a kind of subsistence economy that produced hardly any surpluses to be traded. People living in this period produced food in order to survive. There were neither luxury goods, nor specialists, nor the elaborate administrative system of a centralized state.

The pattern of settlement indicates the presence of a population in this intermediary period much more mobile than the previous period. Cattle breeding became more important, whether in the form of nomadism or as transhumance. The economy was based on "risk spreading," implying an economic system that included more than one strategy for survival and thereby used the natural habitat in an optimal way.

In recent times most scholars have considered this development from centralized city-state to a decentralized agrarian society as a consequence of a development within the boundaries of Palestine, although influence from neighboring territories cannot, of course, be ruled out. The open borders of Palestine make it more than likely that the country also attracted people living in even more arid areas to the east and in the south. It is, on the other hand, unlikely that the scant resources of the country in this period would have allowed for a more extensive migration from outside to Palestine.

It was previously popular among historians to explain major shifts of occupation like the one experienced in Palestine toward the end of the third millennium BCE as the result of a massive invasion of foreign people that destroyed the centers of the previous inhabitants and left them at the mercy of the invading hordes. The stories of the Old Testament were used to suggest that these invaders were Amorites living as nomads.

According to the Old Testament, the Amorites lived in the mountains and the Canaanites in the valleys and along the Mediterranean coast (Num. 13:29). In this light, the Amorites were supposed to have been ethnically distinct from other ethnic groups living on Palestinian soil. Palestine was divided between two populations, the Canaanites, who were the old inhabitants of the country, and the Amorites, the nomadic newcomers to the territory.

The Syrian-Arabian Desert was considered the cradle of these Amorites, and the development in Palestine equaled similar developments in other parts of the ancient Near East also affected by Amorite invaders.

Such explanations are considered today too simplistic and misleading. The Amorites did not constitute a new people living in an area previously belonging to another people. There had been Amorites around for centuries, hundreds of years before the collapse of the civilization of the Early Bronze Age. The terminology is also misleading. Amorite is an etic and not an emic term. The name of the Amorites comes from Mesopotamia where, since the middle of the third millennium BCE, it was used to identify people who came from the west, that is, the territories to the west of the Euphrates. *Amorite*, in Akkadian *amurru*, is a derivation of Sumerian MAR.TU, "westerner," and the Mesopotamian scribes did not distinguish between people coming from northern Syria or southern Syria or even Palestine. Their name has, by modern linguists, been used as a name for a group of Semitic languages, the Amorite. It became the dominant language of western Asia in the second millennium BCE, but until then it is mostly known from personal names of "westerners."

It is therefore meaningless to talk about Amorite conquerors of Palestine belonging to the end of the third millennium BCE. Historically the name has nothing to do with the arrival of a *new* population in Syria and Palestine. Neither does the term Amorite indicate the presence of a homogenous population that can be ethnically separated from the remaining part of the Syrian and Palestinian population. It is a foreign name tagged on people living in Syria and Palestine. If the "Amorites" ever conquered Palestine about 2300 BCE, they would have conquered their own land.

Furthermore, the development about 2300 BCE resembles a situation that was also in evidence for a long time before this period, when one form of life was replaced by a different one. Sometimes the tendency toward demographical and political centralization was replaced by the opposite tendency of people moving apart and changing their way of life.

It is common to view such a development on the basis of two interconnected sociopolitical phenomena: *retribalization* and growing nomadism. Neither of these terms is absolutely precise; their use simply reduces a very complex process in order to make it meaningful. They do, however, present at least some kind of answer.

Retribalization means that the political organization changes from centralized systems, based of the presence of fortified cities ruled by kings, to decentralized ones, organized in clans and tribes kept together at least nominally by family ties, either real or imagined.

Nomadization means that the settled life of peasants gives way to an existence based on the ability to move around. It also implies an increasing dependence on cattle breeding.

Both processes cover a much more complex demographic process that has changed from one period to the next and includes many variations, such as different forms of tribal organization with different systems of leadership.

Common for both phenomena is their demonstration of the way a population may change according to the political and economic conditions of its time, allowing people at all times to exploit their territory optimally.

It should therefore not be a surprise when the next many thousands of years of Palestinian history have the same story to tell about changing life habits— sometimes mainly nomadic, at other times attached to the settled life of peasants.

The Middle Bronze Age

The Middle Bronze Age of Palestine, in the first half of the second millennium BCE, is different from earlier periods in one important sense. Now for the first time it is possible to name places and persons, although with a single exception—an Akkadian text found at Hazor in northern Palestine—no inscriptions have turned up dating from this period, and so far nothing in the local language, Amorite.

Documents from Egypt, however, include occasional references to towns and rulers in Palestine in the nineteenth and eighteenth centuries BCE. Those names are found in two groups of execration texts written on clay figurines and probably used in a kind of voodoo ritual cursing of foreign places and their rulers. Here such Palestinian place names as Ashkelon, Shechem, Hazor, and Jerusalem appear. All personal names are Semitic, belonging to the aforementioned family of Amorite languages.

We encounter personal names belonging to this language family almost wherever we go in western Asia in this period. In Mesopotamia, Amorite-speaking rulers established themselves in many places, founding a series of dynasties ruling not only minor localities but also Babylon. The most famous Amorite ruler is without doubt Hammurabi (1792–1750 BCE).[17] From a linguistic point of view, the population of Mesopotamia and Syria and Palestine seems to have been rather homogenous, and the Amorite language dominated the region. Undoubtedly there were local dialectal differences, but as a rule, a person traveling from, say, Aleppo in northern Syria, to Hazor in Palestine would have had few problems understanding the local dialects. Amorite dominated western Asia for most of the second millennium BCE but was still spoken in some parts of the Levant in the first millennium BCE in the shape of Phoenician. It has survived—although revitalized—today in the form of Hebrew.

The universal use of Amorite was not reflected in any political unity. In Syria in the Middle Bronze Age two major states, ruled by Amorite dynasties, dominated the political scene, in the north Yamḥad or Aleppo and in the south Qatna. In addition to these two major powers, a multitude of small states also existed, although subjected to one of the two leading powers. A letter from the royal archive at Mari (see next paragraph) mentions about twenty kings following Yarim-Lim, the king of Yamḥad, while at the same time a king like Hammurabi is followed by only ten or fifteen kings. The political setup seems based on a kind of patron-client system, now embracing not only the local political community but also the international. While most minor kings were patrons in their own societies, they at the same time were the clients of a major prince. This political pattern repeated itself many times in the history of the Near East.

17. There are different chronological systems around, placing Hammurabi at the higher end in the nineteenth century BCE and at the lower end as late as in the seventeenth century BCE. The tendency today favors the so-called middle chronology.

Another important state, Mari at the Euphrates, existed in eastern Syria. The rulers of Mari carried Amorite names and were clearly of Amorite origin. Mari was located on the border between Mesopotamia and Syria. Its royal archive, discovered by French archaeologists in 1929, included thousands of letters exchanged between the royal administration and its officials that allow the student to obtain a remarkably detailed impression of life here at the beginning of the second millennium BCE. Thus several letters address the problem between the central administration and elements of the population not ready to submit to the regular life required by the royal administration. The nomadic *binu-jaminu* or Benjaminites created problems moving through Mari's territory every year.

During the Middle Bronze Age, other population elements became visible, especially in the northern part of Syria and Mesopotamia. The two more important among these newcomers spoke languages not related to Semitic but totally different. The first among these was Hurrian, sometimes related to the Finnish-Ugrian family of languages. It is therefore likely that the language and the people who spoke it came from outside the ancient Near East, maybe from the Caucasus or inner Asia. At the end of the Middle Bronze Age, the Hurrians ruled a major kingdom in northern Syria, Mitanni. Hurrian-speaking peoples were also present in other places. Their memory is preserved in the Old Testament, where they appear as the Horites, one of Canaan's pre-Israelite nations.

The Hittites formed the second major population group that did not speak Semitic. Their language was Indo-European. The Hittites may also have traced their origins to areas outside the ancient Near East. The Hittites were mentioned earlier in connection with their conquest of northern Syria, which happened in the Late Bronze Age, but they were already active there toward the end of the Middle Bronze Age, when Hittite military expeditions not only destroyed Yamḥad and created the preconditions for the establishment of the Hurrian state of Mitanni here. They also went as far as Babylon, which they conquered, removing at the same time the Amorite dynasty of Hammurabi.

Thus the general outline of Syria's history in the Middle Bronze Age is known to modern historians. The same cannot be said about Palestine. The Egyptian execration texts have no further information, apart from the aforementioned personal and topographic names. They indicate that the Egyptians were politically interested in the area but cannot prove that this interest induced the Egyptians to occupy the territory of Palestine, although they definitely have been interested in controlling the trade through the country.

A growing competition between two economic and political powers, Egypt and Mesopotamia, seems evident in this period. Palestine's position as the bridge between western Asia and northern Africa is becoming an important factor for international trade.

The Middle Bronze Age is often characterized by archaeologists as the classical period in pre-Hellenistic Palestine. In this period the material culture reached a level in a blossoming urban civilization of a magnitude far surpassing that of the Early Bronze Age and not to be reached again before the Hellenistic period.

Several factors may have influenced this development, one of them the climatic one, as climate improved after about 2000 BCE, although it never reached the moisture level of the Chalcolithic Period.

Other factors also had a role to play. Trade—the raison d'être of the cities—grew after the consolidation of Egypt, which had also experienced a period of decline toward the end of the third millennium BCE. However, improving conditions along the Levantine coast in general influenced the growth of international trade.

In the third millennium trade stations and cities existed along the coast of the Mediterranean, where for more than a thousand years Byblos had special ties to Egypt and delivered especially timber to building projects in Egypt—among them cedar trees from the mountains of Lebanon. The trading societies of the Levant expanded during the Middle Bronze Age and again in the Late Bronze Age, and several new cities were founded here, such as Sidon, Tyre, Beirut, and, in the north, Ugarit, close to modern Latakia.

This civilization, based on international trade, was not confined to the coastland of modern Lebanon and Syria. The northern part of Palestine was affected as well. Thus Akko belonged among the trading centers of the coast. Somehow the coastal plain north of the Carmel range seemed to have been more Levantine than Palestinian.

In this period the largest city ever in ancient Palestine before the arrival of the Greeks was founded: Hazor in upper Galilee, which at its most expansive encompassed almost 100 hectares or 250 acres and provided room for a considerable population, maybe between 20,000 and 30,000 people. Hazor, like the smaller Dan further to the north, may have been more of a Syrian city than Palestinian. A city-state of this magnitude is otherwise unknown in Palestine.

The development in southern Palestine followed the same track but mostly affected the coastal areas. On the other hand, some of the cities belonging to the central highlands were not resettled in this period, and the Negev remained mostly uninhabited. There may be reasons for this difference. Maybe such desolated places were simply too far removed from the trade routes and therefore not favored by the general economic development.

In this period the cities were strongly fortified strongholds, fortresses surrounded by strong walls often built on artificial slopes (or glacis). Access to these fortresses/cities was through complicated gate structures.

There was in this period, as far as the evidence of the Egyptian execration texts goes, no central political power in Palestine. Every major city had its king and its defenses. Walls and towers were built, not in defense against foreign invaders like Egyptian marauding armies, but mostly to keep the local competitors away. Politically the country was as fragmented as ever. If a superregional power existed here, it cannot be traced in the remains of the period.

Palestine in the later part of the Middle Bronze Age is linked to the fate of northern Egypt, according to Egyptian tradition at this time ruled by the so-called Hyksos-kings, foreign conquerors coming from Asia. The Greek translation of

Hyksos is "shepherd-kings," although the word itself is Egyptian and means "rulers of foreign countries."

Our knowledge of the Hyksos comes from late Egyptian sources, especially the Hellenistic Egyptian historian Manetho (third century BCE) and excavations conducted in the northern and northeastern part of Egypt, including the delta of the Nile. Egyptian sources have a story to tell about the hubris of foreign rulers who were in the end driven out of Egypt by brave Egyptian pharaohs. The Hyksos were an unpleasant foreign element in Egypt that had to be removed so that Egypt might regain its independence.

Modern historians for many years followed their Egyptian sources and considered the Hyksos to have been a foreign conquering nation. This people were sometimes considered Hurrian. The names of the Hyksos people are, however, Amorite and indicate an Amorite background. The Hyksos were most likely a Semitic-speaking population stratum present in Lower Egypt and related to similar people living in Palestine. Their presence was hardly due to a forceful conquest, but an immigration that may have lasted for some hundred years.

The Hyksos in Egypt were organized like their relatives in Palestine into a series of minor political units with strongly fortified cities as their centers. Egyptian sources as well as archaeological discoveries indicate that one of these cities, Avaris, functioned as a kind of Hyksos capital. The precise extent of the rule of the Hyksos is unknown, although some scholars are of the opinion that it also included southern Palestine. Archaeologists speak about a common cultural pattern that unites southern Palestine and northern Egypt in this period.

Thus it also seems likely that the Hyksos state was organized very much like the Syrian states of Yamḫad and Qatna. The king of a major state would reside in perhaps the biggest town in the area—in the case of the Hyksos, most likely Avaris. He played the role of the patron over a number of minor political constructions, each of them organized as a satellite state to the larger one and each with its urban center, where the petty king or patron governed his territory somewhat like the feudal lords of the Middle Ages.

A political system like this is based on the loyalty that unites patron and clients. It is, however, fragile. If the central patron disappears, the whole political structure is likely to collapse. This happened in northern Syria when the Hittites conquered and destroyed Aleppo; this led to a political fragmentation of those parts of Syria formerly under the control of the kings of Aleppo.

The same happened when Egyptian pharaohs in the sixteenth century turned against the Hyksos and, according to Egyptian propaganda, started a war of liberation. The battle concentrated on the possession of Avaris, which was destroyed. Hereafter the realm of the Hyksos fell like dominoes and the way was open for the pharaohs to continue their campaign into western Asia.

The urban civilization of Palestine in the Middle Bronze Age did indeed end in the traditional way: by a massive destruction of urban settlements. Now we do not need to be in doubt as to what caused this wave of destruction. It was not the climate, and it was not tribesmen seeking a better and richer life. Between 1550 and 1500 BCE the Egyptians simply conquered southern Palestine and reduced it to a province under Egypt. In the fifteenth century the remaining parts of Palestine succumbed to Egyptian rule, which when it was strongest reached the borders of the Euphrates in Syria and even surpassed this border in the time of Thutmosis III, who directed his activity in the north against the Hurrian state of Mitanni.

The transition from the Middle Bronze to the Late Bronze Age does not imply a general change of culture in Palestine. It is a political dividing line between—in the case of Palestine—political independence and the status as a province of a major empire.

The Late Bronze Age

It is possible to trace at least the outlines of the history of Palestine in the Middle Bronze Age. In the Late Bronze Age as well, the people living in Palestine are allowed to speak for themselves. Although not all parts of the Late Bronze Age are equally favored by the existence of written sources, and such documents disappear toward the end of the era, it is possible to reconstruct not only the course of history but in some cases also the details of this development.

A great many of the documents relevant to the history of Palestine in this period come from Egypt in the form of reports of the campaigns of the pharaoh in Asia. In these we find mentioned Palestinian individuals and places and the various population groups confronting the Egyptians. Inscriptions listing conquered Palestinian cities decorated the gates of Egyptian temples.

The Amarna letters are the most important source for conditions in Palestine in the Late Bronze Age. These letters came to light in 1888 and have since then been one of the most eagerly studied collections of documents from the ancient Near East. These letters were discussed earlier (p. 131). The letters are named after the modern name of the place where the Egyptian capital was located in the middle of the fourteenth century BCE, Tell el-Amarna, and can be dated to between about 1360 and 1335 BCE, and thus cover only a limited period.

The Amarna period from a religious point of view was a time of religious turmoil in Egypt when a pharaoh, Amenhotep IV or Akhetaten (ca. 1353–1335 BCE), wanted to break with a thousand-year religious tradition and its power structures. For that reason earlier students of this period considered it unique and the importance of the letters restricted to this period only. Because of Pharaoh's occupation with religious problems at home, he had no spare time for his provinces in Asia, which were partly lost to the aforementioned Hittite king Shuppiluliumash I.

Modern scholars have revised their ideas about the Amarna period and the importance of religious reforms in Egypt. Thus they do not generally accept the old view of Pharaoh's lack of interest in Asia. The Egyptians did not stay away from Asia or neglect their provinces. They were simply outgunned by their Hittite adversary.

Amarna Letter 276

Tell the king, my lord, my sun: Message from Yaḫzib-Adda, your slave, the dust before your feet. I throw myself seven times seven in before the feet of my lord the king, my sun. The order which my lord the king, my god, my sun, sent to me, I truly obey before my lord the king, the sun from heaven.

This interpretation seems to be correct. In western Asia the Amarna period was not something special, aside from one important factor: the threats from outside to the Egyptian Empire became acute in this period and led to considerable reductions of its Syrian territories. Otherwise it was business as usual, as demonstrated in the Amarna letters from Palestine.

These letters give the scholar a fair impression of how Palestine was organized as part of the Egyptian Empire. The map of Palestine printed here is based on the information in these letters and provides an excellent overview of the political fragmentation so typical for this country. It is not the case that the map never changed. On the contrary, it is accurate only for a very short span of time in the fourteenth century BCE. It, however, shows that the fragmentation of the political landscape was a normal thing, most likely also traceable in earlier periods. Politically the country was split into innumerable small patronage organizations. Every tiny spot had its center, a small town, where its patron resided.

This patron—according to his own emic conviction a "king" but according to the etic understanding of the Egyptians no more than a "mayor," that is, a minor official in the service of the Egyptian provincial administration—ruled a territory of a very limited extent, restricted to the town and its immediate surroundings. He functioned as the middleman between the Egyptian administration and people living in his territory.

The Egyptians were able to control their provinces without great efforts because of this system of delegation of power. The Egyptian headquarters were located at Gaza in the south and Hazor in the north. Outside of Palestine there were other Egyptian strongholds, like Kumidi in southern Lebanon. From these centers came Egyptian officials whose main task was to collect taxes for Pharaoh. These officials should also ensure that there would be supplies for Egyptian armies moving through the country to the front, at this time located in northern Syria. Apart from the local Egyptian officials, special emissaries might also be sent by the Egyptian royal court.

This system would normally not create problems. Many letters imply little more than "yes, we obey," when a local magnate promised to have done his uttermost to fulfill Pharaoh's requirements. Sometimes the local princes could not resist the temptation to add complaints, normally against their neighbors.

Such letters of complaint have induced many scholars of the past to believe that the Amarna period was characterized almost by a state of civil war in Palestine. This was hardly the case but reflects a political system where the Egyptian overlords asked their subjects to mind their own affairs. The Egyptians were hardly

8. The Egyptian Empire in western Asia at the end of the Amarna period (After W. Helck, *Die Beziehungen Ägypten zu Vorderasien im 3. und 2. Jahrtausend v. Chr.* [Wiesbaden: Harrassowitz, 1962], 191)

Amarna Letter 280

Tell my lord the king, my god, my sun: Message from Šuwardata, your slave, the dust before your feet. I throw myself seven times seven before the feet of my lord the king, my god, my sun. My lord the king let me make war against Qiltu. I made war. Now there is peace in my place. I got my city back. Why did ÌR-Ḫeba write to the men in Qiltu: "Accept the silver and follow me"? Besides: If my lord the king would investigate the case. If I took a man, one ox or a donkey from him, he had the right to do so! Besides: Labayu, who used to take our cities, is dead, but now ÌR-Ḫeba is another Labayu who takes our cities. If only the king took care of his slave because of this act! I will not do anything before the king sends an answer to his slave.

interested in the whereabouts of these local strong men and their local problems. Principally, the Egyptians would act only if the local disturbances interrupted the flow of taxes to Egypt. One local patron resident at Byblos in Lebanon especially wrote many letters of complaint to Pharaoh, who finally reacted—by asking him why he is sending so many letters, more than all the other mayors.

The conditions in the area to the north and south of Jerusalem are most interesting because we here see a pattern which might also be important in subsequent periods. A local patron, Labayu (the name means "the lion"), who in the Amarna letters is linked to Shechem, is described by his neighbors as a constant menace. The mountainous area between Jerusalem and the Jezreel Valley in the north was the center of his dominion. His territory was therefore bigger and more diversified than those that belonged to his colleagues. His whereabouts and the activities of his sons are linked to the *ḫabiru,* the previously discussed substratum of homeless refugees (see pp. 135–38).

There can be no doubt that Labayu intended to expand his territory at the coast of his neighbors. Thus he is being accused by the rulers of Jerusalem, Megiddo, and Gezer of foul play. Once he wrote a letter to Pharaoh describing his loyalty and good conscience, although the letter was sent from Gezer, a city not considered to be legally belonging to Labayu. After his death Labayu was used as a nickname in a controversy between two other petty lords, one of them accusing the other of being a new Labayu.

In the Amarna age the northern part of the Egyptian Empire was lost to Suppiluliumas's army. Palestine was not directly affected by these happenings. The following period saw a tightening of Egyptian control over the remaining parts of their empire in Asia.

This period of consolidation stretching from the end of the fourteenth century well into the twelfth century is often described as the Ramesside period, named after a long series of pharaohs, all of them named Ramesses. Without doubt the most famous among them was Ramesses II, who reigned for most of the thirteenth century BCE (1279–1213 BCE). He succeeded in stabilizing the frontier in Syria by fighting a glorious and eventful battle with the Hittites at

Kadesh on the Orontes River, a feat memorialized by great inscriptions and reliefs on Egyptian buildings. A few years after this battle the Egyptians and the Hittites made peace, probably because of problems for the Hittites, who were under pressure both from growing Assyria and from local tribes living at the fringe of the Hittite Empire in Asia Minor.

Without discussion Palestine remained an Egyptian province. Now it seems that the Egyptians may have interfered more directly in local matters, when they garrisoned troops in selected places like Beth-shan. An inscription from the time of Sethos I (ca. 1300 BCE) describes how Egyptian troops defeated tribes living in the territory surrounding Beth-shan. Not much is known from this period, as written sources dried out during the thirteenth century BCE. We can say with some certainty only that the Egyptians may have controlled the country until ca. 1150 BCE and even continued to have strongholds here until much later.

Archaeological evidence relevant to the Late Bronze Age sheds additional light on the period. It shows how several cities were destroyed at the beginning of the Late Bronze Age but were mostly rebuilt. Maybe the cities were less prosperous than before, but the population seems to have remained basically the same.

The Palestinian society of the Late Bronze Age seems not to have reached the level of its predecessor from the Middle Bronze Age as far as the material culture is concerned. Although the cities destroyed, probably in connection with the Egyptian annexation of the country to their growing empire, were rebuilt, they were not endowed with new and better fortifications. The reason may have been lack of money, now that the local leaders had to pay a considerable tax to foreign occupants. Moreover, their Egyptian overlords would hardly have been interested in the establishment of local strong fortresses.

The Transition from the Late Bronze Age to the Iron Age

Near Eastern society was, in the Late Bronze Age, characterized by international relations between its different regions and by the intensive trade activity that helped the great powers of that time to enter a network of the "good old boys." Here kings called their colleagues "brothers." The king of Babylon wrote to his "brother" the king of Egypt and sent him gold asking for more gold in exchange. Ambassadors traveled among the capitals.

This situation of peace and prosperity did not last for long. At the same time the two by now "old" great kingdoms of Hatti and Egypt made peace, promising to keep the peace for eternity, new problems arose on the horizon. The fall of the Hittite kingdom has already been discussed, caused by a series of events that in the long run could not be controlled by the central administration of the kingdom. At the same time an extended period of drought—by some scholars named the great Mycenean drought—which characterized the last years of the Late Bronze Age and affected all of the eastern Mediterranean basin, pressed foreign migrants toward the east in ever increasing numbers.

Such groups, often of Aegean origins, are called Sea People and their migration is described by some modern scholars as a wave of conquest in the thirteenth century. The name comes from Egyptian sources. Here the march of these roaming people is described until they reached the delta of the Nile, where brave Egyptian soldiers in the time of Ramesses III (ca. 1187–1156 BCE) put an end to their plundering.

The Egyptian description of the Sea People, which also includes pictorial representations, is without doubt tendentious and propagandistic, although there can be no doubt that the clashes between these Sea People and local inhabitants along the Levantine coast were often bloody and violent. The first Sea People, however, appeared in Egyptian sources many years before the invasion. Thus a corps of Sherden, a group belonging to the Sea People, fought in the Egyptian army at Kadesh. Most likely they were mercenaries.

Among the Sea People we also find the Peleset or Philistines, mentioned in connection with the battle in Ramesses III's time in the delta of the Nile. In the Iron Age, the Philistines lived on the coastal plain of Palestine. Previously, scholars reconstructed the course of events that led to the settlement of the Philistines as either the result of a withdrawal from Egypt after their defeat there, or of being settled there forcibly by the Egyptians. Both explanations may be simpler than the actual course of events.

Modern scholarship is less categorical when it comes to the origins of the Philistines and their settlement in Palestine. There is general agreement that this population group had its origins outside of Palestine and consisted of people speaking a language not belonging to the Semitic family. Scholars looked to the Aegean archipelago or the Balkans as their place of origin and named a certain type of pottery after them, because of similarities between this pottery and the types found at Cyprus dating to the same time and related also to contemporary pottery in Greece. It is supposed that the Philistines brought this pottery with them to their new home. Recently some scholars have begun to question this theory, arguing that the pottery may in Palestine predate the arrival of the Philistines.

Apart from these newcomers, the general development looks familiar. A centralized urban civilization is replaced by a more dispersed pattern of settlement. This development had its center in the mountains of central and northern Palestine, and in the northern part of the Negev. Between about 1250 and 1150 BCE a village civilization appeared here, consisting mostly of unfortified settlements (see the map of the central highlands in this period, p. 134). Some cities were destroyed, such as Hazor in upper Galilee. Resettlement in such places was of a different kind than the previous one. At Hazor and in other places, the fortified city of the Late Bronze Age was replaced by an unfortified settlement, often placed at the acropolis of the former city. At Hazor the great city from the Bronze Age was never rebuilt.

The picture is, however, somewhat confusing, and one theory will not suffice as explanation for the development within Palestinian society in those days. Whatever their number, the arrival of the Sea People influenced the development at the coastal plain to the south of the Carmel range. North of this, the development was very different. In Syria the previously important city of Ugarit at the Mediterranean was destroyed about 1180 BCE, most likely as a result of the activity of the Sea People. However, the Lebanese cities along the Mediterranean were left unmolested, and this also included their extension to the south up to the Carmel range. The invasion of the Sea People may have been less comprehensive than sometimes assumed.

It should not be forgotten that the Egyptians still ruled the territory. The appearance of village civilizations in the highlands of Palestine is an indication of a crisis that befell the previous urban civilization of the Late Bronze Age. This crisis may have been caused by the breakdown of international trade toward the end of the Late Bronze Age. The many international crises destroyed the diplomatic system that allowed tradesmen to move around freely in the Near East, and the disappearance of the Hittite Empire created a power vacuum in northern Syria, where the political situation only stabilized after 1000 BCE. The Assyrians were not yet able to take over political control. Their expansion toward the west only started in earnest in the ninth century BCE.

If we put the different factors together, the conclusion might be that a period of drought characteristic of the last part of the Late Bronze Age put stress on the urban civilization of this period. However, it was the resulting crisis for trade that forced the people to leave the cities to find other ways of sustaining themselves. Now the previous urban population settled in the mountains.

The political conditions must have been fair, as the newly founded villages in this period were unfortified. There are two explanations. The first is that Egyptian garrisons stationed in Palestine provided law and order. Thus it was possible to live without physical protection in the form of solid walls and ramps. Simple defensive arrangements like the construction of the houses of the village in a circle would be sufficient to protect the villagers against highway robbers, but they would have been of little avail if the village was attacked by larger gangs of plunderers or by nomads. The second explanation, which does not nullify the first, supposes that the villagers were organized as tribespeople living within the territory of a certain tribe and protected by their relatives against foreign invaders.

Some archaeologists have pointed to a development during the twelfth and eleventh centuries BCE, when several villages disappeared and gave way to bigger and better fortified settlements, which might one day turn out to have become cities. Beersheba provides a fine example of such a development. It was settled in the twelfth century BCE. However, as late as the eleventh century it was a small village consisting of only some twenty houses, housing—if an average family was about six persons—about 120 persons, only about twenty of them being able to oppose an eventual attacker. The houses were placed in a circle around a central square. In the tenth century Beersheba developed into a small town or, perhaps better, a fortress with strong defenses. The number of houses had grown from twenty to seventy-five, giving room for about 450 people, although the number of men capable of carrying arms was still fewer than a hundred.

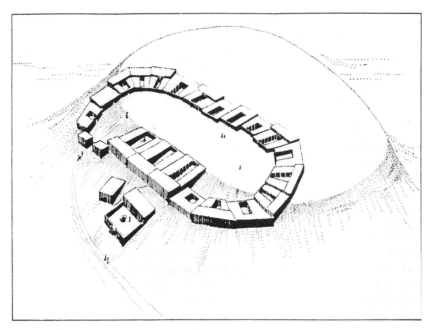

9. Beersheba Stratum VII (11th–10th century BCE)
(From Z. Herzog, *Beersheva* II [Tel Aviv University, 1984], 80. Courtesy of the Institute of Archaeology, Tel Aviv University.)

Close to Beersheba another settlement was located at Tel Masos, whose ancient name is unknown. In the early stages this settlement resembled Beersheba, but when Beersheba began to grow, Tel Masos was deserted.

Due to the special attention of many Israeli archaeologists to the events of the period between 1200 and 1000 BCE, it is possible not only to describe the development in general terms but also to reconstruct the course of events locally. Thus it is in this case possible to describe in detail how conditions developed that were certainly not unique in the long course of the country's history from centralized settlements—in the Stone Age major villages, and in the Bronze Age cities—to decentralized hamlets. It is at the same time possible to trace at least the outlines of a renomadization of some elements of the Palestinian population.

A special phenomenon belongs to this period, although it does not, at the beginning, involve Palestine. When written documents reappear in the course of the tenth and ninth centuries, the population of Syria does not any longer speak Amorite. Its language is now Aramaic, and Assyrian documents from the time of Tiglath-pileser I (1115–1077 BCE) describe the Syrian population as Arameans. In his royal inscriptions these Arameans are his chief enemies to the west.

These Arameans were formerly believed to represent a foreign, newly arrived population that was migrating toward the arable land between 1200 and 1000

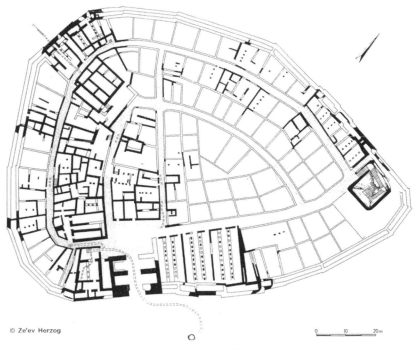

© Ze'ev Herzog

0   10   20m

10. Beersheba Stratum II (10th–9th century BCE)
(From Z. Herzog, *Archaeology of the City: Urban Planning in Ancient Israel and Its Social Implications* [Tel Aviv University, 1997], 247. Courtesy of the Institute of Archaeology, Tel Aviv University.)

BCE. In the tenth and ninth centuries they became organized in a series of states, the most important being Damascus. In Mesopotamia the Arameans were at the beginning of the first millennium BCE already an important substratum of the population, and their language had begun to replace Akkadian as the language of the common people. This development continued for another millennium and made Aramaic the principal language of western Asia until Arabic replaced it following the Arab conquest of the Near East.

Although it still happens that scholars talk about an Aramaic migration, it is more likely that the dispersal of Aramaic was of the same kind as the previous dispersal of Amorite and the Amorite-speaking population some fifteen hundred years before. Tiglath-pileser I speaks about fighting Arameans along his western border, but in spite of claiming to have defeated them, it is likely that a constant "moving in" of Aramaic-speaking people was taking place already in the time of his predecessors and continued after his death. There was no coordinated Aramaic conquest but a gradual Aramaization of the ancient Near East, when the people of the fringe moved toward the population centers and the more fertile areas and finally ended up as the masters of the whole region.

Aramaic is close to Amorite in the the northwest Semitic family of languages. We may assume that this language was not originally an independent Semitic language but developed from the Amorite, a process most likely to have taken place outside of the areas controlled by central political establishments. The process is unknown so far as details are concerned, but early Aramaic may resemble Amorite more than it does in its later stages.

Parts of western Asia remained Amorite-speaking. This includes Lebanon, Palestine, and the provinces immediately to the east of the Jordan River. The change in language had not taken place here before the end of the first millennium BCE and at the beginning of the first century CE and was perhaps never total.

The Iron Age

The Iron Age got its name from the new metal that after 1200 BCE was destined to be of decisive importance for the future. Iron was known previously, as it can be found almost everywhere. However, there had been no reason to exploit this metal, which was far less suitable for utensils and weapons than bronze. Only when steelmaking was invented, in the course of the tenth century BCE, did iron take over.

If iron was an inferior product originally, why was it introduced? At first the introduction of iron was no technological advance. It was probably introduced as an answer to problems that prevented the acquirement of bronze. Bronze is an alloy of either arsenic and copper or tin and copper, depending on the system of international trade of the Bronze Age. Copper was among the most important goods traded by merchants of the Bronze Age. Tin also had to be imported from far corners of the known world. If the trade routes were cut off, the production of bronze would cease. This was the situation at the end of the Late Bronze Age. When it became necessary to find substitutes for bronze, ubiquitous iron was an easy solution.

The term Iron Age is, as far as the early period is concerned, somewhat a misnomer. The use of iron was forced upon people living in this period, who had to invent steel to make it useful. The Iron Age is also the last archaeological period in Palestine. Periods after the Iron Age are named after the historical conditions of Palestine. After the Iron Age come the Neo-Babylonian period—or the time of the exile—then the Persian and Hellenistic-Roman periods. From a technical point of view, we are still in the Iron Age, as there was no technological progress that warranted a change of name.

The Iron Age, up to the time of the Neo-Babylonian Empire, also belongs to the historical periods of Palestine. A series of local inscriptions followed by foreign documents are able to shed light on the history of Palestine between the tenth and the seventh centuries BCE. I have already presented a list of Assyrian and Babylonian references to Palestine (pp. 147–48). On top of this follow a few Egyptian documents—the most comprehensive being Pharaoh Shoshenq's (biblical Shishak, ca. 945–924 BCE) inscription in which he commemorates his campaign in Palestine. This campaign is also mentioned in the Old Testament (1 Kgs. 14:25–26), although the biblical report is very different from Shoshenq's own inscription, showing how difficult it sometimes is to compare biblical evidence to the testimony of ancient Near Eastern inscriptions. The Old Testament says that Jerusalem was the principal objective of Shoshenq's campaign, but Jerusalem is not mentioned at all in Shoshenq's inscription. He was more interested in the coastal plain, with the intention of being able to control the trade that went through this area.

In general, political conditions in the Iron Age resembled most of all the political setup of the Late Bronze Age. Palestine was divided into several minor states, especially on the coastal plain, centering in a series of cities whose names are known also from Assyrian sources. The center of the country had conditions similar to those of the Amarna Age, being dominated by a major political organization named "the house of Omri" (in Assyrian documents *Bît Ḫumriya*) or "Samaria." The Old Testament, like the Mesha inscription from Moab (see p. 150), and the Tel Dan inscription (see pp. 113–14), knows it under the name of Israel.

It was quite normal in this period to see states named like "the house of Omri." Some of the Aramaic-speaking states of Syria and Mesopotamia carried names like Bit-Adana and Bit-Gusi. Such states seem to have been named after the historical or legendary founders, *bît* meaning both "house" and "dynasty." It is more remarkable that the name of Omri may be Arabic, suggesting that his dynasty might have been of foreign origins.[18] If the family of Omri was Arabic, it would have been neither the first nor the last time a foreign family ruled this country, Herod the Great (40/37–4 BCE), an Edomite, being an obvious example.

Judah and Jerusalem appear only in documents from the eighth century BCE, and there are only few such references. The most important is Sennacherib's report about his campaign against King Hezekiah in 701 BCE (see p. 117) and King Nebuchadnezzar's campaign in 597 BCE (p. 116).

The system of governing these states seems to have been more or less the same as found in the Bronze Age: small patronage states with a restricted administration. Most states were of a minute size, although the fragmentation of the country was not quite as marked as in the Amarna Period. The local endeavors to create comprehensive political structures were few in number and mostly limited to the eighth century BCE and linked to the activities of the house of Omri, which for a few years succeeded in establishing a major regional power in central and northern Palestine. Already at the end of the ninth century the Aramean kingdom of Damascus had put an end to the aspirations of this Palestinian state. In the following century this kingdom, like the rest of Palestine, was overrun by the Assyrians.

The few cities that grew to any important size would have only regional importance. The best-known cities of the Late Bronze Age can also be found on a map of Iron Age Palestine. However, the previously mentioned example of

18. The Semitic root behind this name ʿmr is known from the Arab personal name Omar.

Hazor is characteristic. In the Middle and Late Bronze Age, Hazor had been a major city covering about a hundred hectares or two hundred fifty acres, but in the Iron Age, settlement there was restricted to the acropolis and covered only twenty-five hectares or sixty acres. Something similar happened at Megiddo, where new excavations have discovered a large "lower" city below the acropolis, being replaced by a minor Iron Age settlement at the top of the tell of about the same size as Iron Age Hazor. Other important cities of the Iron Age are Lachish and Gezer. We know little about their political affiliation, although Lachish was destroyed by Sennacherib in connection with his actions against Hezekiah.

From a material point of view, Iron Age civilization in Palestine never equaled that of the Bronze Age. Economic activity was low compared to previous periods. The Iron Age was not characterized by any internationalization; it was more a time of regionalism. International trade, the backbone of Bronze Age civilization, never grew to a level known from the Bronze Age, or it bypassed Palestine, because it went either by (Phoenician) ships between Egypt and western Asia or through the desert to the east of Palestine, something made possible by the domestication of the camel shortly before 1000 BCE. Now it was possible for trade caravans to move along routes outside of Palestine, thus escaping the need to pay taxes to local rulers.

The Assyrian conquest in the eighth century had serious consequences for Palestine. Samaria, the capital of Israel, was destroyed in 722 BCE, and a number of its citizens deported to Mesopotamia. The Assyrian sources say as many as 27,290 persons, which is not an unrealistic number. In their place, people from other parts of the Assyrian Empire were settled in Palestine.

Judah and perhaps other parts of the country benefited from the fall of Samaria, but not for long. When he left Palestine, Sennacherib left a wasteland, with Jerusalem as one of the few places left intact. As a consequence, an increasing number of people found a new home in this previously insignificant town in the mountains.

Archaeological excavations have confirmed the impression left by Sennacherib of a society severely harmed by the Assyrian conquest. There is evidence from the eighth century of a state-sponsored economy. A considerable number of fragments of jars with the Hebrew inscription *lmlk*, "to the king," have turned up denoting goods that may have been produced by the king's estates or from segments of trade that were regulated by the royal administration. In the seventh century BCE, inscriptions disappear and are replaced by a different kind of stamps. These are, however, few in number compared to the ones of the previous period, possibly indicating a weakened economy.

Although it is possible to trace a certain reconstruction of Judean society in the course of the seventh century BCE, it would be a mistake to think that it reached that level from before the Assyrian conquest. The cities along the coast, as well as those in the north, survived as Assyrian vassal states or were ruled directly by Assyrian governors as parts of Assyrian provinces. This was also the case with the central highland, which was left unaffected by Sennacherib's attack.

The Neo-Babylonian Period

The Neo-Babylonian period covers only about seventy years and from an archaeological point of view would be hard to separate from the following Persian period. The term is accordingly not based on archaeology but on history.

The Neo-Babylonian period opens with a crisis for urban civilization so typical of Palestinian history. In this period, settled life is at its lowest in the Iron Age of Palestine, with a reduction of settlements of some 50–80 percent. In the region of Jerusalem and in some other parts of the country the reduction reached about 90 percent, compared to the situation in the eighth century BCE.[19] The American archaeologist David Jamieson-Drake describes a total breakdown of Palestinian society at this time.[20]

The Neo-Babylonian Chronicle informs us that the Babylonians, under the command of King Nebuchadnezzar II (604–562 BCE), conquered "the city of Judah" in 597 BCE (see above p. 116). This document breaks off a few years later, and we accordingly have no evidence of a later Babylonian campaign to Palestine under Nebuchadnezzar, apart from the description of the fall of Jerusalem in the Old Testament. Here the historiographer includes a description of the Babylonian conquest of Jerusalem normally dated to 587 BCE. He also includes notes about the deportation of Judeans to Mesopotamia in 597 and 587. The information in the Old Testament may very well be correct, mentioning a total destruction of Jerusalem—not mentioned by the Neo-Babylonian Chronicle in connection with the conquest of 597 BCE. In spite of this, neither the Neo-Babylonian Chronicle nor the Old Testament has any explanation for the almost total destruction of the country in general. Only the central highland north of Jerusalem was spared. Here the local society lived on unmolested and may not have experienced destruction along with the rest of the country.

The Old Testament speaks about Palestine under the Babylonians as "the empty land." It was not empty, especially not its central part. In spite of this, the period witnessed a recession like few others, and to change this would take a lot of time.

The Persian Period

During more than a thousand years, foreign great powers had queued up, asking for permission to occupy Palestine. First came the Egyptians, then the Assyrians and the Babylonians. Now the Babylonians were replaced by the Persians, who in the course of the sixth century BCE established an enormous empire stretching from India in the east to Greece in the northwest and the Libyan Desert in the southwest. In the south the Persian Empire bordered on Sudan.

19. On this, see Oded Lipschits, "Demographic Changes in Judah between the Seventh and the Fifth Centuries B.C.E.," in Oded Lipschits and Joseph Blenkinsopp, eds., *Judah and the Judeans in the Neo-Babylonian Period* (Winona Lake, IN: Eisenbrauns, 2003), 322–76, and Oded Lipschits, *The Fall and Rise of Jerusalem: Judah under Babylonian Rule* (Winona Lake, IN: Eisenbrauns, 2005).

20. David Jamieson-Drake, *Scribes and Schools in Monarchic Judah: A Socio-Archeological Approach,* The Social World of Biblical Antiquity Series 9 (Sheffield: Almond Press, 1991), 145–47.

This empire, according to the most important Greek source, the *Histories* of Herodotus, soon divided into twenty administrative regions, the so-called satrapies, each of them governed by a satrap, a Persian noble who was entrusted by the Persian king to administer his region. Each satrapy was subdivided into provinces ruled by either Persian officials or local magnates. Palestine belonged to the province of Eber Nahri, "the other side of the river" (the area to the west of the Euphrates). The local Palestinian base of a subordinate Persian official was Samaria. Here the office was occupied by the same family for many years, several of its members bearing the good Babylonian name of Sanballat (*Sin-uballit*, i.e., "Sin [the moon god] gives life").[21]

Otherwise, concerning the history of Palestine in the fifth century BCE we are almost totally left in the dark. We have no information about Palestinian officials or magnates involved in any of the political conflicts that harassed the Persian administration until the end of the empire. Thus we do not know if Palestinians took part in the Egyptian rebellion against the empire in the last years of the fifth century BCE.

The Old Testament speaks of the return of many Jews from Babylonia. This cannot be confirmed by other sources. Nothing found in Palestine and dating to the fifth century BCE indicates a massive migration from the east in this period. There was no important increase of settled areas, and no utensils coming from Mesopotamia have been discovered.

The situation began to change during the last century of Persian domination. It is, however, sad that archaeologists have previously paid little attention to this period; although this has now changed, it is not possible in any detailed way to reconstruct the course of events. By and large, Palestine seems in the Persian period to have hibernated, being bypassed by history. We do not know if the country was affected by the Persian conquest of Egypt in 343 BCE or by the contemporary Phoenician rebellion against Persia. Written sources—Greek ones such as Herodotus, Thucydides, and Xenophon, all from the fifth century and early fourth century BCE—have nothing to contribute. Some documents found in Egypt, such as papyri from Elephantine, where there was a colony of Palestinian origins, and ostraca from Palestine and other written material found in caves may provide an occasional glimpse of the state of affairs. But they do not allow for any detailed reconstruction of the history of this period.

The Hellenistic Period

The Hellenistic and after that the Roman period are well known from ancient written sources. Now Palestine reenters the scene of history, although the perspective is still unbalanced. Most of the sources—either the apocryphal books of the Maccabees or the Jewish historian Josephus's writings and other Greek and Roman

---

21. The major opus devoted to the Persian Empire today is without doubt Pierre Briant, *From Cyrus to Alexander: A History of the Persian Empire* (Winona Lake, IN: Eisenbrauns, 2002).

sources—center on the history of the Jews, while non-Jewish parts of the country are only occasionally mentioned.

This restriction on the historian becomes less important as time passes and the Jewish part of the population grows to become the dominating factor in Palestinian life and politics. From the end of the second century BCE until the Roman suppression of the second Jewish rebellion in 135 CE, Judaism seems to have been the dominating factor in the life of the country, although other groups existed, who only occasionally are allowed to speak for themselves. This especially concerns the Samaritans, the people of the central highlands north of Jerusalem, whose history was almost totally different from the one of Judaism, which based its existence of the experience of the exile in Mesopotamia. The information we possess about the history of the Samaritans is heavily influenced by Jewish tradition. This includes the evaluation of the Samaritans in the New Testament. This tradition sees the Samaritans as a pariah group without proper legitimation for its existence.[22]

Another population group mentioned only sporadically by the extant sources, although of no little importance for the history of southern Palestine, is the Edomites, now called Idumeans, with a territory bordering on Judah in a line running between Hebron and Bethlehem. In spite of the source's relative silence, the Idumeans could boast of providing the most important local leader, King Herod, who ruled over the whole territory between 40/37 and 4 BCE.

The Hellenistic period resulted in an unbelievable change of life in the ancient Near East. The politics of integration pursued by Alexander the Great and his successors changed the urban sector on a scale never seen before. Previously the eastern empires used deportations to change the demographic composition of their provinces. The Macedonians stopped that and chose—with great success—another road to integration: incorporating the cities of the Near East in the Greek cultural sphere, influencing them with Greek cultural heritage. This can be deduced from the considerable physical remains of this period. The Hellenistic civilization became a highly developed urban society based on international trade. There appeared cities of a size paralleled only by some of the major Mesopotamian cities of previous times. Hellenistic cities sometimes housed more then half a million people. On top of this a series of new urban settlements were founded in this period, like Alexandria in Egypt, which in its heyday covered about fourteen square kilometers or five square miles and contained between half a million and a million people. Other examples of new cities that grew to enormous proportions are Antioch in Syria, only a trifle smaller than Alexandria, and Seleucia in Mesopotamia, founded close to Babylon, which it replaced. Babylon was simply forsaken by its inhabitants, who moved to the more spacious confines of the new Greek city.

22. For a new evaluation of the Samaritan history and the break between the Samaritans and the Jews of Jerusalem, see Ingrid Hjelm, *The Samaritans and Early Judaism: A Literary Analysis,* JSOT-Sup 303 (Sheffield: Sheffield Academic Press, 2000).

The development in Palestine was, for the first 150 years under Macedonian rule, different from that of Syria, Mesopotamia, and Egypt. The Hellenization of the country went slowly and originally only involved the coastal plain and the valleys in the north. The central highlands were relatively unaffected by the new currents.

This was in accordance with the general trend at that time. Hellenization followed the trade routes, and the Hellenistic cities were founded along such routes. After the situation in such areas became stable, Hellenization spread to more peripheral regions, and the development was repeated here. This means that the Hellenization of the central parts of Palestine began in earnest only in the second century BCE; it was soon met by fierce resistance from the local non-Hellenized population.

The description of the history of Palestine from Alexander's arrival in 332 BCE to Pompey's appearance in Jerusalem in 63 BCE need not be long. After Alexander's death in Babylon in 323 BCE, his empire was split between his generals. Palestine became part of Ptolemy's territory, with Egypt as its center, while another general, Seleucus, ruled Syria and Mesopotamia. Both of these generals established long-lasting dynasties. A third general, Antiochus, ruled Greece and Asia Minor.

The subsequent period was characterized by the rivalry between these rulers, an international political situation very similar to the one of the Late Bronze Age, when three great powers also competed for control of western Asia. This state of affairs, which sometimes resulted in bloody wars, was never allowed to influence in a serious way international trade between competing states. The problems were political, not economic.

Palestine remained under Ptolemaic rule until 200 BCE, when the Seleucids took control. At this time a new great power, Rome, began to make its influence felt in the Near East. In 201 BCE, the Romans had finished their long and hard war against Carthage. During the following century and a half they managed also to incorporate one by one Greece, Asia Minor, the Levant, and Egypt.

During this period the Maccabees revolted against the Seleucids. The rebellion, which started in 167 BCE, led to the establishment of an independent Jewish state under John Hyrcanus (135–104 BCE). The details of this development are not very important. In many ways the politics of the central highlands resemble earlier attempts at achieving political independence.

The new element in the Maccabean revolt has to do with the importance of religious motives. Here Jewish sentiments were seemingly called upon in opposition to the "Hellenizers," a term used in the books of Maccabees without any great precision to denote the supporters of the Seleucid party. However, the name says something about the opposition against Greek influence on the life of the country. The other new element is the degree of foreign involvement in the local political process.

According to the books of the Maccabees, the Maccabees, the leaders of the Jewish rebellion, approached Rome and were well received. Although there are reasons to ask about the real Roman interest in the area at that time, a Roman engagement in the conflict would absolutely have been in accordance with general Roman politics, which was then aimed at reducing the influence of the Seleucid Empire. Thus the Romans defeated the Seleucids in a pitched battle at Magnesia in 190 BCE, and so regulated conditions in Syria at Apamea in 188 BCE. Hereafter the Mediterranean was practically reduced to a Roman lake, the *mare nostrum* as they called it. In 168 BCE in the most arrogant fashion the Romans stopped the Seleucid endeavor to occupy Egypt. This was the famous episode when the Roman envoy, C. Porfilius Laenas, drew a circle around Antiochus IV and demanded that he answer questions before he left the circle; otherwise he would be at war with Rome. The constant Roman pressure on the Seleucid Empire gave the Seleucids little room for maneuvering in cases such as the Maccabean revolt. Internal dynastic conflicts at home also weakened the Seleucids in this period.

John Hyrcanus continued the process toward freedom from the Seleucid Empire and also tried to unite the southern Levant under his dominion. He conquered the territory of the Samaritans and destroyed Shechem in 128 BCE and Samaria a few years later. He expanded his territory to include Idumea south of Jerusalem and occupied parts of the territory east of the Jordan River. His politics was continued by his son Alexander Jannaeus (103–76 BCE), under whom the Jewish kingdom reached its greatest expanse. A few years later the end came when dynastic problems opened the way for direct Roman interference, and the period of eighty years of independence came to an end.

Even when it was strongest, this Jewish kingdom existed under the usual conditions for Near Eastern petty states. Surrounded by competing great powers, it found a niche of independent political activity. This niche was created by the confrontation between Rome and the Seleucid Empire and lasted as long as this conflict existed. As long as political ambitions were limited to the local territory and its immediate periphery, the Jewish rulers could continue without interruption from outside powers. However, the moment one of the great powers decided to end this state of independence, the local ruler would have to obey his masters. The history of Palestine under the Romans makes this very clear.

The Roman Period until 135 CE

In 64 BCE the Roman general Pompey defeated the Seleucid armies in Syria. In 63 BCE he paid a personal visit to Jerusalem, which was never to forget his intrusion into the Holy of Holies in its temple. From this moment and until the last days of antiquity, Palestine remained a Roman, and then a Byzantine, province.

In the first part of the Roman occupation the tendencies of the Hellenistic period continued and were strengthened. The country was dominated by the imperial power that ruled it and was for most of the time governed by an official responsible to the consular province of Syria, led by a Roman senator with the rank of proconsul. Another factor, nationalistic and religious Judaism, brought catastrophe on the country, with everlasting consequence for subsequent Judaism.

These consequences are of little interest in this connection. Here we will concentrate on the general course of events. Pompey reorganized the whole country, reducing the Jewish kingdom of the Hasmoneans to a Roman puppet that included only the central highlands and Galilee. The hellenized cities on the plains and in the valleys were freed from the control of Jerusalem and granted many privileges. In this connection the Decapolis came into being, a union of Hellenistic cities that with one exception were located east of the Jordan River. The exception was Scythopolis, ancient Beth-shan. The political framework looks familiar: along the coast and on the plains a series of independent cities, almost like the city-states of ancient times, and in the mountains local organizations governed by local patrons kept at bay by their imperial masters.

This picture changed for a while in the time of Herod, but only for a while. The reason was the faith the Romans put in Herod as a person. Because he never opposed them but remained faithful to his death, Herod was allowed by Rome to rule over all of Palestine. However, as soon as he was gone, his kingdom was split into several parts, two of them ruled by his sons, although these were soon replaced by Roman prefects, who had to answer to the proconsul of Syria.

Herod's reign led to a consolidation of Hellenism in Palestine. Therefore the Roman period can best be seen as a continuation of the Hellenistic period. Several important cities were founded by Herod, who chose names for them displaying his loyalty toward Rome: Caesarea, named after Julius Caesar, and Sebaste, built on the site of ancient Samaria in honor of Augustus (Sebaste, from Greek *sebastos*, being the same as Augustus, "the most honored one").

The first two centuries under Roman dominion saw an increase in wealth for Palestine in general and a culture reaching a level hardly to be imagined. Life became safe. The Romans, unlike earlier occupants, kept as many as four legions in the country. These could be deployed almost immediately whenever their presence was needed. The Romans also introduced a system of taxation that was in the long run extremely harmful to the country: that of the publicans, professional tax officers who on a private basis were allowed to enrich themselves by demanding surplus taxes from the people.

Such a situation of general well-being should result in stable political conditions. However, Judaism, with its nationalistic aspirations, became a threat to stability. This is not the place to write the early history of Judaism, although it was a decisive factor during the Maccabean revolt against the Greeks. Political Judaism developed in the time of Hasmonean rulership to become a dominating religious and political factor, split into many fiercely competing factions.

The tradition from the Maccabees and the Hasmoneans lived on as a nationalistic movement that ended in two revolts against the Romans. The first one has been extensively covered by Josephus, who participated in it, in his *Jewish War*. It lasted 66–73 CE. The reasons for the revolt and the course of events are immaterial here, but it led to extensive destruction of Jewish settlements in Palestine. Jerusalem and its temple were reduced to ashes.

Sixty years later, troubles began again in the suicidal Bar Kokhba rebellion, which ended with Jerusalem being rebuilt, but as a Hellenistic city named Aelia Capitolina, where Jews were not allowed to travel.

An Overview of the History of Palestine after the Jewish Rebellions

From the long perspective and in respect of the general conditions of this country, these rebellions were of little consequence—apart from those that directly involved Judaism. The country did not suffer from the Roman presence. On the contrary, it grew richer and richer. Peace reigned for centuries and was seriously interrupted only by the Arab conquest in 634 CE. The richest period of them all was the time when Palestine was governed from Constantinople as part of the Byzantine Empire. Thus the area of Beth-shan (Scythopolis) more than doubled in the Byzantine period. The elevation of Christianity to being the official religion of the empire in the fourth century CE also had positive consequences for the economy of Palestine, which now became the center of pilgrimage. Pilgrims traveled to Palestine in great numbers, and wealthy Christians sometimes chose to settle here, bringing with them their capital for investment in local affairs.

The Arab conquest had few consequences for the general economic and cultural situation. In the first period of Arab dominion, Palestine became one of the political centers, as the rulers of the Ummayad dynasty (661–749 CE) showed a definite interest in the country.

The time of the Crusades (1091–1291) remains an intermezzo in the history of Palestine, although from a historical point of view it follows a pattern also seen before, in which a central power, the kingdom of Jerusalem (1091–1187), was "assisted" by a series of local patrons who as masters of their castles controlled the Palestinian landscape. The political power play of these patrons is not unlike the one of, say, the local rulers of the Amarna Age.

Although the period following the expulsion of the crusaders resulted in a partial cultural and economic recession along the Mediterranean coast, the decline first became serious after the Turkish conquest in 1526 CE. The Sultans ruled their vast empire from the shores of the Bosporus. This was not very different from Roman emperors' residing in Rome and later Byzantium. However, unlike the Romans, they invested little energy in the welfare of their province. Local *publicani* chosen among the magnates of the country put such heavy burdens on local people that it resulted in a collapse of settled life. Between 1500 and about 1850 CE, the population of Syria, Jordan, and Palestine was reduced by up to 75 percent.

No climatic conditions contributed to this development, which from an archaeological point of view looks familiar. The climate in this period was not different from the one in the Arab period and only slightly worse than the one in Byzantine times. Neglect was the primary reason behind the decline. The Turks invested little interest in their provinces, and there was no Turkish control or Turkish military presence that could stop local *publicani* from destroying their country. The path toward the collapse can be tracked in documents preserved in Istanbul, the center of Turkish government.

This period saw a nomadization of the Near East. We have already met this phenomenon before. The sources are plentiful. Pressed by local magnates who disregarded the welfare of the general population, many people chose another economic strategy for survival and became nomads organized in family systems and tribes. Soon the nomads contributed their part to the general decline, when they began to extort taxes from the settled farmers, who in the end would have no option except to leave their settled way of life and become nomads themselves.

This development is extensively documented and had fatal consequences for all of the Near East. Thus when Bonaparte in 1799 moved from Egypt into Palestine, he was confronted not by any Turkish army but by local riffraff led by local magnates. Although his campaign broke down in front of Akko's walls, Napoleon showed in the battle of Nazareth that these local forces were not worthy opponents.

The subsequent history of the country, from the middle of the nineteenth century CE, is dominated by two and then later three factors. In 1866 CE, after it had lost its provinces in Europe in a series of liberation wars in the Balkans, the corrupt and incompetent Turkish government was overturned and replaced by the movement of the so-called Young Turks. The new government brought the Turks back to the Near East and introduced a series of economic and administrative reforms, including the stationing of Turkish troops in Palestine. When the First World War was fought fifty years later, a very different landscape met the allied forces, with a rapidly growing settled civilization and a reduction of the activity of the nomads.

The second phenomenon includes the immigrations of European Jews, who from the middle of the nineteenth century in ever greater numbers arrived in Palestine, where they created Jewish settlements in a number of places. Finally these immigrants in 1948 CE created their own state, modern Israel. The history of this state is still to be written.

The Long, Middle, and Short Perspective: The History of Palestine

The Israeli archaeologist Israel Finkelstein describes the history of Palestine as "cyclic." He is right. During the period reviewed here, which spans about 10,000 years, a constant shift of the occupational pattern took place, from a mainly settled civilization to an "empty" land, suggesting that settled life has been replaced by other ways of living.

From the long perspective, already characterized as depending on the natural conditions that change only very slowly, it seems as if the geography of Palestine was the decisive factor behind these constant changes. The gradual change, especially in the south and in the southeast, from arable land to desert conditions creates a continuum of life forms between urban settlers and nomads. Thus, what from the outside may look like dramatic changes, may for the people involved have been almost insignificant. It was never the case that the population in one region from one day to the next changed its way of living. In certain periods the population, including several different groups in the continuum between nomadism and urban life, drifted slowly in one direction or the other.

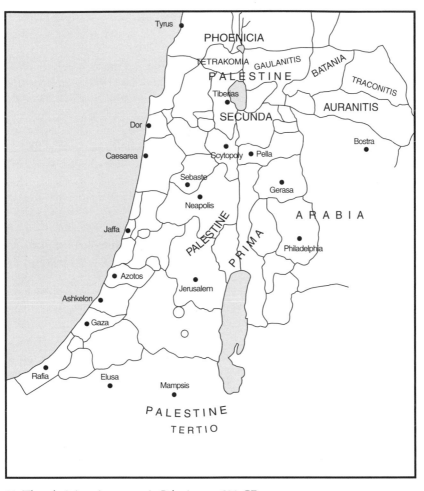

11. The administrative system in Palestine ca. 500 CE
(According to A. Giardani, M. Liverani, and B. Scarcia, *La Palestina* [Rome: Editori Riuniti, 1987], 96)

Another geographical condition has to do with the regional makeup of Palestine. Although it is very small, the historical picture shows a society that has almost always been highly fragmented. The map of the political system of the Amarna Age (see p. 431) is closer to this normal picture than the present situation, although the country is still divided into different regional units that are comparable to at least two previous episodes: the consequences of the arrival of the Sea People in the transition period between the Bronze and Iron ages, and after the crusaders' conquest of the country in 1091 CE.

In spite of many attempts to control this country, no foreign ruler, from the Egyptian Pharaohs in the Bronze Age to Arab emirs and Turkish sultans, has been able to change the regional arrangement of the country in any fundamental way. The system of the Amarna Age and the one at the middle of the first millennium CE are almost the same.

Climatic conditions—the second main factor behind the long perspective— have fluctuated through history between periods of drought and periods of relative high precipitation. Such changes have primarily been gradual and lasted for centuries. The Palestinian population subjected to such changes had no daily news informing them about the dangers of the greenhouse effect. The final result was, however, just as decisive as if the changes had occurred once and for all. Fertile land was given up because of drought and was put into use again if precipitation was sufficient for agriculture.

Both processes may have happened relatively quickly, but an archaeological analysis will show only the often dramatic end to a development that may have lasted for many years. The collapse of urban life toward the end of the Early Bronze Age may be an indication of this, when pressure on settled life increased until it became intolerable and could not be countered by the technology of the time. The process had lasted for about a thousand years, beginning before 3000 BCE. It would thus be possible to view the appearance of the cities of the Early Bronze Age as a consequence of the same factor that hundreds of years later brought about their destruction.

Traditional European historiography worked for generations with the concept of migrations involving huge numbers of people moving from one region to another as the underlying theory. European national literature includes many such examples, like the migration of the Cimbrians and the Teutons from cold and dark Scandinavia to Italy. The Germanic invasion of the Roman Empire in the fourth century CE was seen as a migratory wave, although it only completed what had been underway for perhaps 500 years.

It is said that it is the last straw that breaks the camel's back. This is correct, but this straw would be unimportant if it were not for the presence of all the other straws. The events attached to the last straw are dramatic. The back of the camel breaks. However, if the historian were interested only in the last straw, the process that led to the catastrophe would remain incomprehensible and invisible.

The theory that the many changes in Palestinian civilization in ancient times were caused by large-scale migration waves was popular for another reason. The European entertained the rather stereotyped idea of the "unchangeable Orient." From the perspective of modern times, including the explosive developments of western Europe and later North America, the Near East may seem almost totally static. However, static societies have never existed. A society is always on the move, although the tempo may change from place to place. The apparent monotony means that scholars have ignored slow developments within ancient societies, which were always changing.

When major changes occurred, as sometimes happened in the long history of Palestine, the European observer believed this to be the consequence of dramatic events caused by newcomers, immigrants. Thus the changes at the beginning of the Bronze Age were related to migrant Amorites, and the changing conditions at the end of the Late Bronze Age to roaming Aramaic nomads. Although people have always been on the move between Palestine and its surrounding countries, large-scale migration is an exception, at least as seen in the short perspective. The modern Jewish immigration to Palestine lasted a hundred years before the establishment of the Jewish state.

The middle perspective has to do with the development of economics. Changes here are considered less permanent than geographic and climatic conditions. This is not automatically a correct observation. Economic changes may last for as many years as climatic conditions, or even longer than that. A clear example is the Neolithic revolution that changed human existence from a hunter and gatherer culture to settled agricultural life. This revolution should be seen within the middle perspective but has now lasted for almost 10,000 years. It created a totally different demographic situation and paved the way for changes that belong within the short perspective.

The deforestation of the mountains around the Mediterranean is another economic development that had significant consequences, although they have not been discussed here. This process of deforestation changed the vegetation from woodland to *maki*, that is, a bush land. Scholars still discuss when the process began, whether in the last part of the Stone Age or in the Bronze Age or even later. The consequences were, however, obvious. The soil on the mountains eroded, and technology improved to allow for terracing of the mountain slopes to keep the soil still left. Deforestation may also lead to climatic changes creating changing conditions for the amount of rain received. Human activity is able to change even factors relating to the long perspective.

Economic life in Palestine was always relative to the country's geographical position and dependent on international stability, which allowed for the unimpeded transition of goods between two continents. Here it is not important if two great powers are in conflict. Even in case of an open war, this conflict will normally be only temporary. The great powers—when their differences have been settled—will still exist as well-organized states insisting on the maintenance of good trade relations.

The political problems become important if one of the great powers collapses, as happened at the end of the Late Bronze Age, when a system of three great powers broke down. Egypt and the Hittite Empire fought a series of wars for control of Syria, but the economic system survived in spite of this. When there was no Hittite Empire anymore, the system was not able to survive. A political power vacuum appeared, which resulted in economic regression, because the lack of political and military control over the trade routes made the life of a merchant precarious.

The period of turmoil that followed the Late Bronze Age also saw the large-scale domestication of the camel. Because of the remarkable ability of the camel to travel long distances, even under desertlike conditions, caravans making use of the camel could travel outside of areas not infested with all kinds of troubles, especially brigands. Now a new factor arose that in the course of the next two millennia steadily grew in importance: Arab tribes roaming the wastelands of the Syrian and Arabian deserts. The appearance of this nomadic culture based on the camel changed life in the Near East considerably, both politically and economically.

This picture of Near Eastern society did not change much in the Hellenistic-Roman period or during Arab rule. Although the Near East has often been a problematic place to live because of unstable political conditions, traders had more than one option.

The aforementioned relationships among the long, the middle, and the short perspectives are still valid. The long perspective is about the scene of action. It provides the physical boundaries. The scene does not decide what is played out here. Other rules prevail, such as the playwright's decisions, the director's choices. The playwrights and their instructors will have to think and act within the limits set by the scene, but they decide the course of action. It is a kind of play including several factors, but the human one will, in the end, be the decisive one. Then as in real life, a third factor is important, the actor on the stage. The good actor may change something mediocre into a remarkable piece of art; a bad actor may destroy an excellent arrangement. Whatever the limitations of the scene and the insufficiency of the manuscript, the good actor may make the spectators forget these limitations.

Palestine's history is characterized by this cyclic fluctuation between the center and the periphery. From the perspective of an outsider, the pattern seems repetitive. The same thing happens over and over again. This is true—but only as a consequence of an outsider's point of view. Most processes were different, and the factors that decided the course of events at one instance may not have had any influence the next time the same thing seems to have happened. The eyes of the outsider see only the consequences of the process, but have no idea of what really caused it. Here other perspectives will have to assist interpretation, both economic and human factors.

. . . and Israel

What happened to Israel? It almost disappeared. The history of the ancient state of Israel lasted for only about two hundred years. The political independence of this state was even shorter. The state of Israel gained regional importance in the southern part of the Levant in the Iron Age but had soon to submit to foreign powers. Two hundred years doesn't count for much from the perspective of 10,000 years. The only reason this state is interesting is because of its position within the biblical narrative. Otherwise, historical Israel represents a peripheral phenomenon of a very short duration.

This does not imply that the population of this state did not have a history much longer than that of the state itself. The history of the population living in the state of Israel may go back to very early times, and it did not end with the disappearance of this state. The obvious question then is, what caused the state to appear? A state like this derived in its days its name from the founder of the state, whether real or legendary. The state of Israel was perhaps founded by a general, Omri, and ruled by his dynasty. Omri's name may be Arabic, and Omri thus only one among plenty of foreigners who rose to power there. It would of course be a bit ironic if he really was an Arab by birth.

Ethnic identity and nationalism meant little to the people of those times. The important element in life was the small circle around individuals, their family and kinfolk, their village or town, and the authority that collected taxes. The king was only a "person" insofar as it was the duty of the king to protect the life of his subjects. In periods of crisis it was a good thing to be ruled by a king. Otherwise he was dispensable, although hard to get rid of.

The Old Testament has a different history to relate. It has little to do with what really happened in Palestine in ancient times—although at the same time it shows that history is not limited to the long perspective. In its case the decision to narrate a history that never happened became more important than anything that really happened even in the long perspective. It is the final proof that the decision made by a group of people to tell their story has more significance than all the other factors, such as geography, climate, and economy.

Index of Ancient Sources

OLD TESTAMENT

Genesis

1	9, 46, 319
1–2	9, 46, 47
1–11	9, 187, 209
1:28	187
2	46, 319
2:7	390
3	9, 46
4	9, 46
4:1.17–26	9
5	9
6–8	47, 55
6:5–8:21	48–52
7:7–10	47
7:22–23	47
8:7	244
9	9
9:1	187
9:18–19	9
10	9, 187
11	9
11:10–32	9
12–36	9
12	9, 10, 66, 69, 190
	207n11
12:2–3	188
12:10–20	67, 68, 69
12–25:11	9
13:1–3	190
14:13	136
15	46
15:6	189n2
15:13	189
15:13–14.18–21	188
16	9, 286
17:2–8	188
17:9	189
17:14	189, 207
18	190, 191
19	190, 323
19:29–38	10
20	10, 66, 68
20:1–18	67, 68
21	286
22	191
23	10
24	9
25:7–10	9
25:19–36:43	9
25:20–26	9
26	9, 10, 66, 69
26:1–11	67, 68
26:2–5	189
27	9
27–28	207n11
28:13–15	189
29	207n11
29:15–30:24	10
32:29	190
33	207n11
33–35	10
35:11–12	190
35:16–20	10
36	10
37	10, 207n11
37–50	9, 62, 189
38	10, 319
39:14, 18	136
40:15	136
41:12	136
42–45	10
43:32	136
46	10
46:3–4	190
49	10, 13, 90
49:3–4, 8, 27	11

Exodus

1–15	10
1:1–14	53, 54
1:15–19	136
2:6–7	136
2:11–13	136
2:16–22	46
3	46, 191, 290
3:6	374
3:7–8	191
3:18	136
6:1–8	191
13:21	11
14	11, 59
14–15	10, 11
15	59, 90
15:1–18	11

16:3	11, 207
16–18	10
18	46
18–19	10
19	12
19:5	82
19—Num 9	10
20—Num 10	244
20	59, 61, 346
20:1–17	12, 57
20:2	374
20:2–17	60, 61
20:3	247
20:4–5	249, 274
20:24–26	12
21–23	12, 244
21:1–22:18	244
21:2	136
21:18–19	57
21:28–32, 35–36	245
22:19–23:19	244
23	192
23:20–33	192
24	12
25–40	12
32	90, 203n9, 207
32–34	12
32:4	203n9
32:25–29	14
34:6–7	360
34:10–16	193
34:12–16	193
34:13–14	249

Leviticus

1–7	12
8–10	12
11–15	12
16	12
17–26	12
18:1–5	193
18:9	69
18:29	69
26	193
26:5	193
26:30–34	207
26:44–45	193

Numbers

1–4	12
4–9	12
6:24–26	179
10–33	10
13–14	12

13:30	90
14:6	90
21:21–31	89
22–24	59, 90
24:23–24	38
25	207
32	13
33:41–49	12
33:50–56	194
33:55	194

Deuteronomy

1–3	12
1–30	12
4:1–40	12
4:23–24	249
5	59, 61, 346
5:6–21	12, 60, 61
5:8–9	249
6:4–7	350
6:4–13	194
6:14–15	249
6:20–23	350
11:22	194
11:24	194
12–26	12, 86, 184
15:12	137
26	12
26:5–9	346
27:1–10	12
27:12–28:68	13
28:68	38
29:21–27	195
30	195
30:1–14	207
30:4	207
30:1–7	195
31	13
32	13, 90
33	13
33:6–7, 12	11
34	13, 37

Joshua

1–12	13
1:1–9	196
2	13
3	11
3–5	13
3:10	196
6	13
7	13
7:24–26	56
8	13

9	13
10	13
11	13
12	13
13–19	13
13	13
14–17	14
15:13–19	90
18–19	14
20	13, 14
21	13, 114
22	13
22:3	196
23	13, 14, 196
23:16	14, 197
24	13, 14, 82, 196, 197
24:19–22	197
24:29–33	13
24:29–30	208

Judges

1–12	14
1	140, 198
1:12–15	90
2	14
2:1–3	14, 197
2:8–9	208
2:11–15	198, 208
3:7–8	198
3:7–11	208
3:12	198
3:12–30	140, 208
4	75
4–5	14, 204
4:1–2	198
4:17–22	319
5	75, 90
6:1–2	198
8:13–17	208
8:18–21	210n14
8:20–21	208
8:22–23	208
8:33–35	198
9	142, 208
10:1–5	140
10:6–8	198
11	208
12	75
12:8–15	140
13:1	198
13–16	14, 15, 208
16:30	199

17–18	15	8	16	3:27	149
17–21	14, 199	8:7	208	8:16–19	204
17:6	199	8:16–18	181	9–17	17
18:1	199	8–20	16	10:15–16	85
19–20	141, 142	8–1 Kings 2	93, 144, 209	10:29–31	203
19–21	15	14–19	16	14:25	19
19:1	199	20	16	15:29–30	152
21:25	15, 141, 191	20:23–26	181	17	203, 204
		23:1–7	16	17:6	185
Ruth		23:8–39	16	17:7–23	17, 204, 205
4:18–22	10, 26	24	16	17:13–14	205
				17:24	147n45
1 Samuel		**1 Kings**		18:13–16	117, 118,
1–3	15	1–2	16		151, 161
1–8	15	1–2:11	17	18:13–19:37	117, 161
4–6	15	2–11	17	18:14–16	118
4:6–9	137	3	201	18:16	118
7	15	3:11, 14	201	18:17–35	151
8:5	15, 75	3:16–27	17	18–19	19
8:7	208	4:2–6	181	18–20	17, 19, 95n40
8:8	199	5–8	17	19:20–34	151
9:9	214	5:12	25	19:35	118
9–10	15	6–8	143	19:37	118
9–15	15	8	201	20:20	178
10:10–13	213	8:3–9	202	21	17
10:17–25	15	8:25	208	21:2	93
11	15	8:46–51	201	21:16	205
12	15	10	111	22:2	206
12:13–15	200	10:1–13	17	21:10–15	205
13–14	15	11	17, 202	21:16	205
13:1	76	11:9–13	202	22	160, 185
13:3, 7	137	11–22	17	22–23	95n40
13:19	137	12	17, 76, 146, 203	22:2	93, 206
13–2 Sam 6	200	12:1–19	203	22:14–20	206
14:11	137	12:28	203	22:16–20	196
14:21	137	14:22–24	203, 204	22:19–20	202
15–16	15	14:25–26	439	23	17
16–31	15	15:3	93	23:6–7	251
16–2 Sam 6	200	15:11	93	23:7	318
16–2 Samuel 7	62, 93	15:25–26	203	24–25	20, 155
23:19	24	15:26	93	24:2–4	206
25	25	15:33–34	203	24:10–17	116
26:1	24	16:23–28	92	24:14	155
29:3	137	16:25–26	94	24:14–16	154
31	15, 16, 76	16:27	93	25	17
		16:30	93	25:8–12	155
2 Samuel		17–2 Kings 9	17, 93, 210	25:18–21	160
1–6	16	18	216	25:26	155
6	143	22	216, 312	25:27–30	93
7	16	22:27	216		
7:5–17	200	22:41–44	204	**1 Chronicles**	
7:11–16	208			22	27
7:11–12, 16	16	**2 Kings**		28–29	95n41
7:24	200	3	149, 151		

2 Chronicles
29–31 — 27
29–32 — 95n40
35–35 — 95n40
36:17–21 — 155

Ezra
1:2–4 — 156, 157
1:64–65 — 156
2 — 27
3–6 — 159
4 — 159
7–10 — 27
7:1 — 27
7:1–5 — 160
10 — 27, 248

Nehemiah
1–6 — 159
2–6 — 27
2:11–15 — 27
4–5 — 157
7 — 27
7–13 — 27
7:66–67 — 156
8 — 27
10 — 27
11–12 — 27

Job
1 — 25
4–26 — 25
32–37 — 25
38–41 — 25
42 — 25

Psalms
1–2 — 23, 24, 237
1–15 — 236
1–41 — 24
1 — 24, 237, 337
2 — 24, 25
2:2 — 25, 391
3 — 391
6:3 — 361
10:1 — 361
15 — 238
22 — 377, 378
23 — 389
23:5 — 389
24 — 238
24:3–6 — 238
36:5–6 — 238
36:8 — 238
40:6 — 239

40:6–8 — 240
42–49 — 235
42–72 — 24
42:3 — 361
47 — 57
50 — 235, 240
50:7–15 — 239
54 — 24
72 — 235, 236, 240
73–89 — 24, 235
82 — 252n19, 386
84–88 — 235
87–88 — 235
89:3–4 — 16
90 — 235
90–106 — 24
93 — 57
97 — 57
99 — 57
104–106 — 236
107–150 — 24
110–118 — 236
120–134 — 236
127 — 235, 236
132:11–12 — 16
135–136 — 236
137 — 97
137:9 — 282
146–150 — 236
149–150 — 23, 24
150:6 — 390

Proverbs
1–9 — 25
10–22 — 25, 241
22:17–24:22 — 26, 241
22:17–21 — 242

Isaiah
1 — 227n20
1–12 — 18
1–39 — 96, 218, 277
1:1 — 18
1:11, 16–17 — 239
4 — 387
4:2–6 — 232
5:1–7 — 18
5:8–24 — 222, 223, 234
5:24 — 225n19, 229
6–9 — 377
6 — 18
6:8–10 — 222
6:11–13 — 222
6:13 — 224

7:1–20 — 357
7:3 — 18, 19
7:10–17 — 45
7:11–17 — 231n25
7:14 — 391
8:23–9:6 — 231n25
11 — 231n25
13–23 — 19
18–35 — 19
24–27 — 19, 97, 221n13, 277, 334
27:12–13 — 220, 221
36–37 — 117
36–39 — 19
40–55 — 19, 96, 277
42:1–9 — 20
45:6–7 — 330
49:1–13 — 20
50:4–11 — 20
52:13–53:12 — 20, 377
53:3 — 37
56–66 — 20, 96, 233, 277

Jeremiah
6:19 — 229
6:20 — 239
7:21–23 — 239n2
9 — 230
9:11–15 — 230
9:12–16 — 229
9:15 — 230
16:14–15 — 220, 231
30 — 229, 231
31 — 2, 20, 229, 231, 232
31:7–9 — 231, 232
31:29 — 230, 376
31:30 — 388
31:31–34 — 1, 163, 195, 231, 375, 377
31:33 — 323
34:8–14 — 137
35 — 85
36 — 218
39–43 — 155
39:3 — 148
42–43 — 221
46–51 — 20
52 — 20

Ezekiel
3:15 — 221
6:8–9 — 214
14:14 — 280
16 — 21

25–32	21, 35	7–12	21	**DOCUMENTS FROM**
25:13	251	14:21	243	**THE ANCIENT**
36	21			**NEAR EAST**
40–48	21, 155, 232	**Malachi**		
		4:5–6	272	**Amarna Letters**
Daniel				73:26–33	137
1–6	26	**NEW TESTAMENT**		144:24–30	138
2	26			148:41–45	138
2:4–7:28	27	**Matthew**		288:43–44	138
3	26	5:17	24	74	138
5	26	6:13	377	286	176
7–12	26	7:12	24	287	176
		11:13	24	276	430
Hosea		15:24	377	280	432
1:4	85	27:43	377		
4:4–6	226	27:46	377	**Egyptian Documents**	
4:6	21	27:47	272	Amenope's wisdom	242
4:12	227			Cheti's wisdom	243
6:6	239n2	**Mark**		Merneptah's victory	
8:1–2	226	4:13–20	265	("Israel") stele	131
8:9	227	9:12	377		
8:13	227	15:24	377	**Ugarit**	
11	227, 228	15:29	377	Baal epos	
11:3	227	15:34	377	*KTU* 1.5 ii	223n17
11:8–11	228	15:35	272		
11:10–11	228			**Mesopotamian Documents**	
11–14	227	**Luke**		Codex Hammurabi,	
		6:20–21	377	prologue	84
Joel		23:35	377	§250–252	245
1–2	21	24:44	24, 280	Cyrus cylinder	158
3–4	21			Esar-haddon's annals	153
		John		Eshnunna laws	
Amos		1:18	377	§§53–55	245
2:4	225, 229	14:6	391	Gilgamesh epos XI	322, 323
2:4–5	21	19:24	377	Mari Prophecy	216
2:5	225			Mesopotamian liver	
5:21–26	239n2	**Acts**		omens	215
5:27	225	13:33	24	Neo-Assyrian prophecy	217
6:7	225			Neo-Babylonian	
9:11–12	226	**1 Corinthians**		Chronicle	116, 153
9:11–15	21	11:25	377	Sennacherib's annals	117
				Tiglat-pileser III's	
Jonah		**2 Corinthians**		annals	152
1:9	137	3	377	Tukulti-Ninurta I	158
Micah		**Galatians**		**Palestinian Documents**	
5	21	3:13	224	Ketef Hinnom amulets	179
6:6–8	239n2			Kuntillet ᶜAjrud ostraca	250
		Hebrews		Siloam inscription	179
Habakkuk		2:12	377	Tel Dan inscription	113, 114
1–2	22	5:	377		
		8:8–12	377	**Transjordanian Documents**	
Zephaniah				Mesha stele	150
3:4	21	**Revelation**			
		11:15	377	**Greek Authors**	
Zechariah		21:9–27	232	Herodotus VII, 144	248
1–6	21, 159	21:22–27	232		

Index of Modern Authors

Abegg, Martin, 2n2, 168n1
Ackroyd, Peter R., 88n27
Ahlström, Gösta W., 73, 396n5
Aland, Kurt, 283
Albertz, Rainer, 82n19, 109, 127, 267, 268, 296, 305–2, 336, 337, 349, 356, 386n9
Albright, William Foxwell, 72, 90, 108, 122, 125n11, 133, 287, 301, 302, 315, 321, 354, 355, 384
Alt, Albrecht, 57, 71, 75n10, 79, 81, 128n19, 133n30, 302n4, 341, 381, 384
Andersen, Knud Tage, 77n12
Arndt, Moritz, 314

Barr, James, 121n7, 172, 267, 268, 275, 285, 291, 297, 298, 307, 352, 353n1, 358, 359, 363, 364n15, 369n8, 371, 384n6, 420
Barstad, Hans M., 96n42, 386n9
Barth, Fredrik, 104n1, 106n6, 247, 291, 314
Barth, Karl, 268, 333, 369, 370, 371, 374
Bauer, G. L., 366
Berger, P.-R., 158n56
Binger, Tilde, 350nn16–17, 318n9
Biran, Avraham, 113, 114n4
Blenkinsopp, Joseph, 156n53, 441n19
Bloch, Marcel, 399
Braudel, Fernand, 399
Briant, Pierre, 442n21
Bright, John, 41n17, 72, 125, 126, 133n30, 287, 355n6, 396n4
Brønsted, Johannes, 418n16
Brown, Alfred Radcliffe, 105n2
Brown, William P., 355n6
Brueggemann, Walter, 285, 304, 356, 358n8, 359–64, 375
Brunner, Emil, 369
Budge, E. Wallis, 174n4
Buhl, Frantz, 303, 352
Bultmann, Rudolf, 58n18, 268, 368, 370, 371, 373, 378, 380

Carroll, Robert P., 218, 230
Champollion, Jean-François, 39
Charlesworth, Jame H., 6n6, 131n27
Childs, Brevard S., 268, 280, 327, 328, 331–39, 364, 372, 379
Collins, John J., 317n4
Cook, Edward, 2n2
Cross, Frank Moore, 90n30
Cryer, Frederick H., 214n2, 323

Dalley, Stephanie, 243n5, 323n12
Daniels, Peter, 39n15
Davies, Philip R., xix, 162, 330, 337, 380, 381, 386n11
Dearman, Andrew, 150n48–9
Dever, William G., 123
Diebner, Bernd Jörg, 124n10, 290
Dietrich, Manfred, 42n18
Dietrich, Walter, 94n36
Dodd, Charles H., 376, 377
Donner, Herbert, 71, 150n48, 179n11
Dossin, George, 216n5
Doudna, Greg, 281
Driver, Samuel Rolles, 88n27
Droysen, Gustav, 35, 36n5, 126, 128
Dundes, Alan, 63n22

Edelman, Diana, 73n8, 159n58, 284n1
Einstein, Albert, 101
Eichrodt, Walter, 268, 291–93, 295–97, 301, 347
Eissfeldt, Otto, 47, 58nn8–9; 66, 88n27, 290
Engnell, Ivan, 85n25
Erslev, Kristian, 35
Exum, J. Cheryl, 403n13

Fales, F. Mario, 333n6
Feyerabend, Paul, 111n2
Finkelstein, Israel, 134, 145n42, 146n43, 448
Flint, Peter, 168n1

Frankfort, Henry, 84n22
Freedman, David Noel, 80n14, 109, 271n2, 294n25
Freud, Sigmund, 103
Fried, Morton H., 105n5
Friis, Heike, 107
Fronzarolli, Pelio, 333n6
Frye, Northrop, 304

Gabler, Johann Philip, 257–63, 267, 294, 297, 298, 300, 303, 306, 310, 319, 337, 338, 366, 379, 380
Garbini, Giovanni, 333n6
Gerstenberger, Erhard, 296, 310, 311
Gibbon, Edward, 260
Gibson, John C. L., 150n48
Gingrich, Andre, 106n6
Gnuse, Robert, 347n9
Goethe, Johann Wolfgang von, 260
Goshen-Gottstein, M. H., 3n4
Gottwald, Norman K., 106, 133n31
Grabbe, Lester L., 385n8, 386n9
Graf, Karl Heinrich, 37, 45
Greenspahn, Frederick, 276
Greenspoon, Leonard Jay, 276n10
Greenstein, Edwad L., 85n24
Grimm, Jakob, 55, 304
Grimm, Wilhelm, 55, 304
Grundtvig, N. F. S., 387n5
Guilleou, Jean, 265
Gunkel, Hermann, 55, 56, 57, 58n18, 343, 368
Gunneweg, Antonius H. J., 296, 305, 307
Gurney, O. R., 400n11

Hagelia, Harvard, 113n3
Hallbäck, Geert, 149n47
Hallo, William W., 26n12, 85n24
Harnack, Adolf von, 285, 286, 367
Hegel, Georg Wilhelm Friedrich, 261, 352
Herrmann, Siegfried, 71, 125
Hesse, Franz, 268, 340, 347
Hjelm, Ingrid, 443n22
Hoffmeier, James K., 131n24
Holm, Katrine Winkel, 368n6
Holloway, Steven W., 264n6
Hornung, Erik, 174n4
Hübner, Hans, 272n6
Hvidberg, Flemming Friis, 174n6

Ilgen, Karl David, 38, 39n9, 259, 286n5
Irving, David, 301n3
Iversen, Erik, 39n12

Jamieson-Drake, David, 441
Jensen, Hans Jørgen Lundager, 310, 311, 323
Jensen, Jørgen, 418n16
Jeppesen, Knud, 218, 219
Johnson, Aubrey R., 85n25

Kaiser, Otto, 88n27, 218, 268, 296, 298, 305, 307, 341, 362, 363
Kant, Immanuel, 32, 122, 259, 261, 352
Keel, Othmar, 88n28, 307, 369
Keller, Werner, 122n8
Kenyon, Kathleen M., 123

Kierkegaard, Søren, 191, 370, 371
Kitchen, Kenneth A., 130n22
Kittel, Rudolf, 71, 271
Knauf, Ernst, 284
Knight, Douglas A., 44n1, 63n21
Knudtzon, J. A., 131n25
Koch, Klaus, 56n12
Köhler, Ludwig, 288
Kofoed, Jens Bruun, xvii, 341
Kraus, F. R., 246n10
Kuenen, Abraham, 37, 45
Kuhn, Thomas, 31n1
Kuhrt, Amélie, 158n57

Lang, Berhard, 86, 222n14, 224, 233, 348
Lord, A. B., 63n23
Larsen, Mogens Trolle, 39n14, 40n16
Leach, Edmund, 304
LeBeau, Bryan F., 276n10
Lemaire, André, 180n13
Lemche, Niels Peter, 73n7, 149n47, 222n16, 246n11, 247n13, 304n8, 333n7, 385nn8, 11; 387n12
Lessing, Gotthold Ephraim, 128
Levenson, Jon D., 276n11, 287n6, 334, 365, 366
Lévi, Israel, 278n13
Levi-Strauss, Claude, 105
Lewis, C. S., 391
Lewis, Jack P., 279n4
Lichtheim, Miriam, 243n4
Lightstone, Jack N., 279n15
Lipschits, Oded, 156n53, 161, 441n19
Liverani, Mario, xix, 106, 130n22, 133, 300, 333n6, 382–84, 388n13, 398n7, 449
Long, Burke O., 125n11
Long, Victor Philips, xvii, 73n6
Longman, Tremper, 73n6
Lorton, David, 174n4
Loretz, Oswald, 42n8

McDonald, Lee Martin, 279n15
Macqueen, J. G., 400n11
Malinowski, Bronislaw Kasper, 195n2
Margueron, Jean-Claude, 215n3
Martínez, Florentino García, 2n2, 168n1, 277n12, 333n8
Marx, Karl, 399
Maxwell, James C.. 292
Mayes, Andrew D. H., 142n39
Mendenhall, George E., 106n8, 133n31, 294
Merlo, Paolo, 319n9
Meyer, Eduard, 125, 126
Mildenberger, Friedrich, 288
Moor, Johannes de, 174n6
Moran, William L., 131n25
Moscati, Sabatino, 333
Mowinckel, Sigmund, 57, 96n42, 108, 229, 230, 287
Müller, Mogens, 273, 279n15, 286

Naveh, Joseph, 113, 114n4
Nelson, Richard D., 94n37
Niehr, Herbert, 253n20
Nielsen, Eduard, 44, 45, 62n20, 222n15, 303

Nielsen, Flemming A. N., 206n10
Nissinen, Martti, 215n4, 217n7, 218, 219n11, 234
Noack, Bent, 44n1
Noth, Martin, 41n17, 71–73, 78n13, 90, 92, 94, 108, 126, 128, 133n30, 140, 301, 341, 342n2, 345, 354, 360, 381, 384

Oeming, Manfred, 161n60, 307, 308n12, 372, 373, 378
Oesterley, W. O. E., 72
Ollenburger, Ben C., 257n1
Olrik, Aksel, 63, 69
Oppenheim, A. Leo, 84n23

Pardee, Dennis, 42n18, 85n24, 174n5
Parker, Simon B., 85n24
Parkin, Robert, 106n6
Parry, Milman, 63n23
Pedersen, Johannes, 287, 303
Perdue, Leo G., xvii, 299, 300, 317n4, 320, 355, 356, 358, 363, 364
Perlitt, Lothar, 294
Pfeiffer, Robert H., 88n27
Pintore, Franco, 333n6
Popper, Karl, 111
Preuß, Horst Dietrich, 263, 293, 305, 307, 309, 341
Prior, Michael, 316n3
Pritchard, E. Evans, 105n2
Pritchard, James B., 26n12, 84n21, 156n52, 157n54
Provan, Iain, xvii, 73n6

Rad, Gerhard von, 64, 91n32, 94n36, 108, 141n38, 199n6, 263, 268, 291–297, 301, 305, 307, 308n12, 310, 328, 329, 335, 336, 338–49, 353, 354, 360, 367, 372, 381, 384
Ranke, Leopold von, 36
Rasmussen, Kaare L., 282n18
Reimarus, Herrmann Samuel, 128, 259
Rendtorff, Rolf, 268, 327, 331, 334–39, 341, 364
Renz, Johannes, 179n12, 250n17, 251n18
Ringgren, Helmar, 80
Robertson, R. G., 131n27
Robinson, Theodore H., 72
Rogerson, John W., 55n11
Röllig, W., 150n48, 179n11
Römer, Thomas, 94n38
Rosseau, Jean-Jacques, 259
Rost, Leonhard, 200n7, 209
Roth, Martha, 244n7, 245n8

Said, Edward, 393n2
Sanders, James A., 268, 279n15, 327–32, 334–39, 364, 372
Sanmartín, Joaquín, 42n18
Sasson, Jack M., 39n15, 130n22, 400n11
Schaudig, Hanspeter, 158n56

Schmid, Konrad, 307
Schmidt, Werner H., 80
Schroer, Silvia, 88n28, 307, 369
Schüle, Andreas, 307, 308
Schüssler Fiorenza, Elisabeth, 318, 332
Segert, Stanislav, 178n9
Seidel, Bodo, 39n9
Sellin, Ernst, 71
Service, Elman R., 105n5, 402n12
Shiffman, L., 282n18
Silberman, Neil Asher, 145n42, 146n43
Silverman, Sydel, 106n6
Ska, Jean-Louis, 52n7
Smend, Rudolf, 94n36
Smith, Morton, 86n26, 105n5, 221, 222, 224, 233, 234, 348
Smith, W. Robertson, 303, 352
Speiser, Ephraim, 47n6
Spiegelberg, W., 130n23
Spinoza, Baruch, 37
Strange, John, 304–6, 309, 356

Thompson, Thomas L., xvii, 109, 126, 187n1, 234, 302, 373, 380–84
Tigchelaar, Eibert, J. C, 277n12
Tolkien, John Ronald Reuel, 304
Tov, Emanuel, 168n1
Toynbee, Arnold, 354
Tronier, Henrik, 247n11

Ulrich, Eugene, 168n1

Valerio, Karolina de, 368
VanderKam, J., 282n18
Van Seters, John, 45n2, 66, 126, 127
Vaux, Roland de, 108, 125, 126
Vernes, Maurice, 303
Vriezen, Theodore C., 88n27, 289–91

Weidner, Ernst, 158n55
Wellhausen, Julius, 37, 39n10, 45, 71, 74, 91, 225n18, 286, 287n6, 302, 352
Westermann, Claus, 296, 305
Wette, Wilhelm Martin Leberecht de, 71, 126n16, 259
Whitelam, Keith W., 316n3, 383, 393
Wilson, John A., 57n17, 242n3
Wilson, R. A., 71n2
Wise, Michael, 2n2
Wiseman, D. J., 116n5
Wolff, Hans Walter, 94n36, 213n1
Woude, A. S. van der, 88n27
Wright, George Ernest, 353–55
Wyatt, N., 42n18, 85n24, 223n17

Yadin, Yigal, 277n12
Yon, Marguerite, 42n18

Zaccagnini, Carlo, 333n6
Zachariae, Gotthilf T., 258
Zimmerli, Walther, 296

Index of Subjects

Aaron, 12, 160, 180, 203n9, 207
Aaronite blessing, 179
Abdi-Ḥeba, 176
Abiathar, 144, 181
Abihu, 203n9
Abimelech
    king of Gerar, 69
    son of Gideon, 208, 210
Abraham, 9, 66–69, 71, 73, 74, 161, 162, 191,
    194, 200, 207, 244, 247–49, 323, 342,
    374, 388
    as Hebrew, 135, 136
    covenant, 196
    divine promise, 188–90
    election, 4, 9
    historical Abraham, 290, 309, 356
    narratives, 56, 65
Akko, 405, 427, 431, 448
Administration, administrators
    Egyptian administration, 175, 176, 430
    Hittite administration, 433
    Mari, 426
    Persian administration, 442
    royal administration in Jerusalem, 143,
    144, 182, 440
    Syrian administration, 439
Adonai, 46n4, 83, 272
Aegean Archipelago, 75, 434
Aelia Capitolina, 446
Aeneid, 171
Afghanistan, 388
Agriculture, 402–8, 412–14, 423, 450
Ahab, 17, 77, 78, 92, 93, 115, 147, 149, 150,
    203–5, 210, 216
Ahaz, 19, 45, 77, 89, 147, 266, 391
Ahijah
    king, 181, 203
    prophet, 205
Ai, 13

Akhetaten, 370, 429
Akitu festival, 174
Akkadian, 42, 102, 107, 175–77, 244, 253,
    425, 437
Akko, 427, 431, 448
    plain of, 405
Alexander the Great, 38, 310, 443, 444
Alexander Yannaeus, 445
Alexandria, 131n27, 443
Alexandria, school of, 36, 258
Allegory, allegorical reading, 36, 258, 264, 265,
    286, 322
Aleppo, 271, 419, 422, 425, 428
Aleppo Codex, 22n9, 26, 271, 272
Alphabet, 177, 178, 183, 242
    Greek and Latin alphabet, 177
    Paleo-Hebrew (Phoenician) alphabet, 178
    Ugaritic alphabet, 175, 177, 178
Amarna age, 139, 429–32, 439, 447, 449, 450
Amarna letters, 131, 135, 137, 139, 175, 176,
    388n13, 429, 430, 432
Amenhotep IV, 429
Amenope, 26, 241, 242
Amenophis, 83
America, North, 3, 105, 107, 108, 125, 126,
    287, 316, 324, 325, 341, 351–55, 367,
    384, 388, 389, 450
    North American biblical scholarship, 72,
    73, 80, 90, 94, 108, 133, 264, 274,
    301, 302, 307, 320, 321, 340, 344,
    351, 352, 357, 364n15, 381, 393
America, Latin and South, 105n2, 316, 320, 321
Amman, 411
Ammon, Ammonites, 10, 76, 83, 89, 144
Amonite language, 15
Amorite, Amorites, 89, 136, 188, 191, 192,
    196, 205, 423–26, 428, 437, 451
Amorite language, 176, 248, 413, 424, 425,
    436, 438

463

Amos, 4, 7, 8, 19, 21, 96, 225–27, 296, 348
Amphictyony, 73, 82, 83, 90, 126, 140–43, 222n15, 354
Amurru, 137, 138, 424, 431
ʿAnat, 84
Anatolia, 400, 401, 403
Ancient Israel, 17, 40, 43, 56, 58, 70, 73, 88, 94, 109, 110, 140, 143, 161, 169, 246, 252, 299, 328, 329, 335, 347, 348
   ancient Israel and Palestine, 382
   Bible and history, xix, 35, 38, 64, 65, 70, 73, 96, 161, 248, 251
   concept of time, 343
   covenant, 292, 294, 299
   definition, xix, 2n1, 162
   ideological concept, xvi
   a historical construct, 43, 71, 79, 98, 107, 109, 110, 124, 261, 262, 263, 300, 301, 341, 352, 354, 363, 381, 382, 384, 393
   literature, xix, 87, 88
   magic society, 324
   New Testament and ancient Israel, 286
   religion, xviii, 38, 39, 41, 57, 70, 80, 81, 85, 87, 89, 127, 252n19, 260, 262, 297, 311, 312, 344, 345, 348, 367, 381, 390
   tradition, 346
Anchor Bible Dictionary, 80, 109, 262
Ansariye Mountains, 421
Antioch, 443
Antiochene school, 36, 258
Antiochus I, 444
Antiochus IV, 97, 445
Anti-Jewish, 371
Anti-Semitism, 286, 314, 371
Apamea, 445
Apocryphal books, 6, 79, 267, 273, 274, 278, 376, 442
Apodictic law, 57–59
Aqaba, 404
Arab conquest, 437, 447
Arabic, 437
Arad, 421
Aram, Arameans, 78, 144, 149, 157, 346, 362, 436, 437, 451
Aramaic language, 4, 27, 107, 113, 248, 270, 271, 278, 436–39
Aramaic literature, 365
Archaeology, archaeological, archaeologist, xix, 36n6, 106, 118–20, 122–24, 133, 156, 178, 184, 185, 304, 344, 354, 355, 382, 402, 406, 410, 412, 413, 415, 416, 418, 419, 428, 433, 438, 440, 441, 442, 447, 450
   American archaeology, 72, 120, 122
   ancient Near Eastern archaeology, 40
   archaeology and the Bible, 122, 123, 133, 145, 146, 162, 340, 355
   biblical archaeology, 121, 122, 162, 353
   British archaeology, 120, 122
   cultural identification in archaeology, 415
   external evidence, 119
   French archaeology, 122, 426
   fundamentalism and archaeology, 121
   German archaeology, 71
   history and archaeology, 121
   inscriptions and archaeology, 41
   Israeli archaeology, 120, 160, 448
   nontextual sources, xv, 88
   Palestinian archaeology, 40, 41, 119, 120–22, 355
   religion and archaeology, 249, 312
   surface surveys, 135, 160, 435, 436
Armageddon, 389
Aryan race, 314
Aristotle, Aristotelian, 32, 34, 122, 261
Ark of Covenant, 17, 142
Artaxerxes (I, II, III), 27, 159, 160, 278
Arvad, 156
Asaph, 235
Ashdod, 411
Asherah, 84, 193, 196, 250, 251, 318, 332, 348
Ashkelon, 120, 131, 411, 425
Ashur, 175
Ashurbanipal, 152
Asia Minor, 78, 401, 433, 444
Assyria, Assyrians, 17, 19, 38, 40, 78, 149, 153, 157, 175, 433, 435, 441
   Assyrian texts and inscriptions, 115, 147, 148, 152, 219, 436, 438–40
   attack on Judah, 78, 96, 117–19, 121, 151, 185, 397
   conquest of Israel, 21, 78, 146, 154, 162, 184, 220, 348, 397, 439, 440
   deportations, 154, 205, 220, 221, 227
   empire, 22, 175, 185, 401, 440
   fall, 78, 221n12
   law tradition, 244
   prophecy, 215–17, 219
   religion, 175
   war against Ahab, 149
Astrologers, 214
Augustine, 268, 277
Augustus, 446
Avaris, 428

Baal, 76n11, 81, 84, 85, 174, 193, 198, 203, 204, 216, 223n17, 227, 229, 253
Babel-Bibel-Streit, 40
Babylon, Babylonians, 19, 20, 26, 40, 78, 84, 146, 147n45, 157, 158, 388, 394, 425, 426, 433, 438, 443, 444
   conquest of Jerusalem, xvi, 17, 79, 87, 115, 154, 155, 160, 180, 229, 233, 397, 441
   flood story, 47, 244
   inscriptions, 115–17, 148, 153, 154, 156
   law, 244
   Pan-Babylonism, 40
   Persian conquest, 79, 158
   religion, 174, 244, 253
Babylonian chronicle, 115–17, 153, 154, 441
Babylonian exile and return, 19, 27, 74, 79, 87, 92, 93, 95, 97, 107, 154, 156, 159–62, 195, 220, 221, 228, 230, 233, 277, 329, 387, 442

Babylonian law, 244
Bagoas, 157
Balkans, 434, 448
Barak, 208
Bar Kokhba, 390, 446
Barmen Declaration, 369n7
Baruch
    Book of Baruch, 5, 6, 8
    Baruch the scribe of Jeremiah, 5, 97, 218
Bathsheba, 16, 319
Battle Axe Culture, 418
Bedouins, 104, 394, 395
Beersheba, 120, 411, 435–37
Beirut, 427, 431
Benjamin, Benjaminites, 11, 15, 57, 75,
    140–42, 216, 426
Ben Sira, 278, 297
Beqaa Valley, 404, 405, 411
Bethel, 189, 203, 225, 407, 411
Bethlehem, 15, 76, 208, 374, 431, 443
Beth-Shan, 76, 120, 139, 411, 433, 446, 447
Bible, 144, 156, 244, 270, 272, 274, 276, 279,
    288, 305, 307, 315, 318, 320, 335,
    337, 363, 374, 375, 386, 395, 396,
    398
    archaeology, 121–23
    authority, 37, 275, 277, 317, 320, 371
    Bible and biblical theology, 316
    Bible and colonialism, 314–16
    Bible and feministic theology, 319, 320
    Bible and history, 162, 298, 300, 301, 304,
        311, 313, 340, 356, 357, 381–84
    Bible and law, 275
    Bible and theology, 259, 274, 330, 379
    Bible and the ancient Near East, 40
    Bible and the laity, 274
    Bible as an idol, 274, 275
    Bible interpretation, 36, 108, 171, 258,
        274, 276, 277, 317, 321, 324, 325,
        327, 356
    Bible traditions, 6, 18, 22, 37, 267
    canon and Bible, 334
    Christian Bible, xix, 2–6, 18, 22, 42, 175,
        265, 271, 273, 279, 280, 334, 353,
        364, 366, 370, 376, 385
    contextual reading, 265, 322
    critical study of the Bible, 257, 260, 290,
        395
    inerrancy, 121, 161, 172, 352
    Orthodox Bible, 334
    postmodern Bible, 391
    Protestant Bible, 6, 275
    reception, 103
    synchronic reading, 304
    unity, 265, 282, 286, 367, 372
Bible, rewritten, 295, 372, 381
Biblia Hebraica, 3, 58, 278, 279
    Biblia Hebraica (Kittel), 271
    Biblia Hebraica Quinta, 271, 283
    Biblia Hebraica Stuttgartensia, 271, 283
Biblical archaeology, 121, 122, 162, 353
Biblical theology, xviii, 172, 257–67, 270,
    272–74, 280, 281, 283, 292, 305, 307,
    326, 327, 334, 336–39, 344, 348, 350,
351, 356, 364, 372, 373, 378, 379,
    380, 390, 391
Biblical Theology Movement, 287, 340,
    351–56, 358, 359, 381, 384
Bit-Adana, 439
Bit-Gusi, 439
Blessing of Jacob, 10, 11, 13
Bomberg Bible, 271
Book of the covenant, 12, 244, 246
Book of the Dead, 174
Bronze, 416
Byblos, 137, 138, 388n13, 427, 431, 432
Byzantine Period, 394, 447
Byzantium, 447

Caesar, Julius, 446
Caesarea, 446
Caleb, 12, 90
Camel, 65, 67, 117, 450, 452
    domestication, 408, 413, 440, 451
Canaan, 10–12, 56, 76, 128, 131, 142, 188,
    191, 192, 196, 199, 207, 253, 259,
    315, 316, 319, 395, 423, 426
    Canaan and Israel, xv, 79, 81, 83, 90, 132,
        133, 135, 207, 247, 249, 321
    religion, xv, 42, 81–85, 193, 198, 208,
        213, 251, 292, 348
    the patriarchs and Canaan, 9, 10, 187,
        190, 244
    Israelite conquest, 13, 14, 74, 80, 139,
        140, 162, 189, 192, 195, 196, 208,
        296, 315, 345, 354
    ethnic cleansing, 75, 192, 194, 196, 198,
        199, 206, 207, 387
    war between Israel and Canaan, 75, 141,
        208
Canaanite enclaves, 144, 197
Canaanites and modern Palestinians, 315
Canon, canonical, 174, 266, 267, 273, 274,
    276, 277, 280, 281, 283, 327–31, 338,
    372, 377
    canonical history of Israel, 295
    canonical literature, xvi, 173, 175, 266,
        267, 273, 277
    canonical theology, 263, 268, 270, 280,
        282, 283, 298, 311, 329–31, 334–39,
        364
    canonization, 28, 70, 276, 277, 327–29,
        333, 336, 338
    canon of the New Testament, 331
    canon of the Old Testament, 169, 273,
        276, 329, 331, 367
    canon within the canon, 272, 377
    Christian canon, 43, 172, 279, 286–88,
        338
    collections, xvi, 6, 174, 175, 328, 334
    Hebrew canon, 179, 277, 331, 338
    Jewish canon, 5, 24, 267, 276, 330
Carchemish, 221n12
Carmel, 216, 405, 411, 427, 434, 435
Carthage, 444
Casuistic law, 57
Cattle breeding, 407, 408, 413, 414, 415n15,
    423, 424

Central Highlands, 397, 405, 419, 427, 434, 440, 441, 443, 444, 446
Chalcedon, confession, 274
Chalcolitic Period, 394, 416–21, 427
Chiefdom, chieftainship, 105, 402, 416
China, 177n7, 316
Christian Bible, 2–6, 18, 22, 42, 175, 271, 273, 334, 353, 364, 366, 370, 385
Christian dogmatics, 259, 288, 289, 370
Christian translations, 272
Christianity, xvi, xix, 18, 121, 141, 171, 224, 225, 232, 258, 264–67, 275, 279, 282, 285, 287, 304, 307, 308, 317, 325, 327, 328, 353, 354, 365, 367–71, 374, 375, 377, 390, 391, 447
    attitude to Judaism, 371
    early Christianity, xix, 218, 281, 365, 378
    the church as the new Israel, 2, 38, 286, 291
    concept of canon, 276
    conservative Christianity, 172, 340, 352
    context of the Old Testament, 2, 3, 42, 80, 272, 279, 285, 286, 306, 307, 345, 364, 366, 370
    dogmatics and doctrine, 259, 273, 276, 277, 282, 288, 289, 306, 333, 334, 351, 366, 395
    religion, 308
    theology, 43, 269, 289, 365, 366, 395
    tradition, 6, 8, 18, 22, 171, 271, 272, 368, 375, 376
Christological interpretation, 37, 171, 322
Chronicles, 4, 7, 8, 21, 22, 27, 76n11, 94, 95, 155, 184, 235, 272, 296
Chronicles of the Kings of Judah, 152
Chronistic literature, 95, 243
Church fathers, 268, 277, 333
Cimbrians, 450
City state, 182, 397, 410, 419–21, 423, 427, 446
Climate, 400, 401, 403, 405, 406, 408, 409, 422, 427, 447, 453
Credo, 346
Codex, 279
Codex Aleppo, 271
Codex Hammurabi, 158, 244
Codex Leningradiensis, 271, 272, 283
Colonianism, 314, 317, 325
Colonization, 314, 316
Collapse of history, xviii, 264, 267, 293, 299, 300, 302, 304, 310, 313, 316, 320, 355
Conquest, Israelite, 13, 13, 73, 74, 75, 76, 79, 90, 132, 133, 139, 140, 189, 191, 193–96, 197n3, 198, 207, 208, 221, 295, 315, 345, 354, 355, 385
Conquistadores, 316, 321
Constantine the Great, 317
Constantinople, 447
Copenhagen school, xvi, xix, 254, 303, 324, 349, 379, 380, 381, 384, 385, 390
Covenant, 1, 14, 83, 94, 190, 191, 193–95, 197, 204, 20608, 226, 227, 229, 234, 247, 249, 292–95, 297, 299, 335, 346, 347, 386, 387

Canaanites, 13, 192, 193, 196, 316
    covenant formula, 82, 347
    David and Solomon, 16, 201, 202
    Hittite treaties, 294
    new covenant, xviii, xix, 1, 2, 20, 162, 231, 232, 375, 376, 387, 390
    Noah, 9, 46, 48
    old covenant, 1, 2n1, 20, 162, 252, 375, 376, 390
    patriarchs, 188, 189, 196
    Shechem, 13, 14
    Sinai, 10, 12, 13, 82, 83, 207, 232, 294, 299, 387
    Zedekiah, 137
Creation, 4, 9, 46, 47, 59, 73, 84, 101, 174, 186, 187, 206, 269, 288, 290, 297, 307, 311, 319, 343, 360, 362, 368, 369, 374
Critical scholarship, 109n14, 167
Crusades, crusaders, 447, 449
Crusoe, Robinson, 371
Cultural evolutionism, 105, 106, 402
Cuneiform writing, 39, 40, 42, 127, 175, 177, 419
Cuthah, 147n45
Cyprus, 434
Cyrus, 19, 27, 79, 156, 158, 159
Cyrus cylinder, 157, 158

Damascus, 78, 225, 385n7, 397, 411, 431, 437, 439
Dan, tribe, 53
    city, 113
    inscription, 113–15, 144, 148, 439
Daniel, 4–8, 26, 27, 97, 278, 280, 281, 297, 333, 334, 366n3, 377
Danish Arabia Expedition, 39
Dante, 335
Darius (I, II), 5, 19, 21, 27, 97, 159, 160
Darwin, Charles, 395, 399
David, house of, 113–15, 144, 148, 201, 205, 226, 231, 266
Dead Sea, 405, 417
Dead Sea scrolls, 2, 24n10, 168, 253, 278, 299n16, 281, 282n18, 322, 333n8, 377, 385
Debir, 120
Deborah, 208
Deborah, Song, 75, 90
Decalogue, 57, 59–62, 244, 247, 346, 369
Decapolis, 446
Deforestation, 451, 454
Delphi, 141, 142
Denmark, 73, 418
Deportations, 154, 167, 221, 228, 443
Descartes, 352
Deutero-Isaiah, 18–20, 96, 270, 296, 377
Deuteronomism, 86, 184, 230, 329
Deuteronomist, Deuteronomistic literature, 45, 46, 63, 65, 86, 87, 92–97, 183, 184, 217, 218, 225, 230, 233, 243, 329, 346n7
Deuteronomistic history, 58, 92–95, 184, 186, 196, 198, 199n6, 206n10, 219, 228, 230n23, 296, 297, 342

Deuteronomy, 3, 4, 7, 12, 13, 20, 37, 46, 59, 61, 86, 92, 184, 191, 194, 199n6, 207
Dialectical theology, 263, 269, 288, 304, 307, 233, 234, 252, 315
Diaspora, Jewish, 87, 195, 207, 211, 221, 228, 230, 233, 234, 252, 315
Dielheimer Blätter zum Alten Testament, 108, 124n10
Differentiated society, 409, 410, 421
Diodorus Siculus, 132n28
Discoveries in the Judean Desert, 168n1
Divine Comedy, 335
Divination, 205
Documentary hypothesis, 37, 46n3.5, 47, 52, 91
Dogmatic theology, 257–59, 379
Domestication
    animals and cattle, 413
    camel, 440, 451
Drought, 190, 201, 401, 405, 406, 409, 413, 433, 435, 450

Early Bronze Age, 394, 418–24, 426, 450
Early Iron Age, 89, 123, 135
Eber Nahri, 442
Ebla, 419, 422
Ecclesiastes, 4, 5, 7, 8, 26, 97, 235, 278, 297
Eden, 244
Edom, Edomites, 10, 22, 76, 83, 226, 251, 439, 443
Egalitarian society, 409
Eglon, 140
Egypt, Egyptians, 1, 3, 11, 14, 21, 38, 60, 65, 66, 71, 75, 78, 82, 128–33, 137, 139, 144, 153, 155, 157, 162, 175, 182, 188–98, 200–5, 220, 221, 227, 228, 231, 243, 252, 253, 259, 261, 278, 346, 374, 375, 387, 395, 404, 411, 412, 417, 421, 423, 427, 428, 440, 442, 444, 445, 448, 451
    Abraham in Egypt, 9, 67
    archaeology, 40, 119, 121
    European interest in Egypt, 39
    history, 129
    Israel in Egypt, 47, 53, 59, 73, 82, 90, 135, 136, 207, 320, 350
    Jacob in Egypt, 10, 74
    Jeremiah in Egypt, 20, 218, 221
    Joseph in Egypt, 10
    kingship, 84, 85
    language, 107, 413
    plagues, 90, 261
    religious texts, 174
    rule of Palestine, 139, 175, 176, 422, 426, 429–33, 435
    texts and inscriptions, 115, 130, 412, 419
    wisdom literature, 26, 211, 242
Egyptology, 106, 129
Ehud, 140, 208
Ekron, 120, 148
El, 84
Elath, 405
Elephantine, 157, 442
Elijah, 17, 22, 85, 93, 153, 205, 210, 216, 272
Elisha, 17, 85, 93, 153, 205, 210

Elohim, 46, 48, 98
Elohist, 45, 46, 52, 63, 65, 66, 91, 342, 380
Emic, 394, 424, 430
Empire, Davidic, 184, 381
En-gedi, 405, 417
Enlightenment, 32, 34, 37–39, 91, 128, 259, 260, 300, 340, 352, 358, 359, 369, 393, 395, 398
Enoch, 6
Enthronement festival, Enthronement psalms, 57
Enuma Elish, 174, 370
Ephraim, 13–15, 228, 232
Epic laws, 63, 69
Erasmus, 283
Esar-haddon, 152, 153, 216, 217
Essenes, 389
Eshter, 4, 5, 7, 8, 22, 26, 235, 281, 385
Ethnicity, 247, 249, 291, 314, 371, 387
    ethnic groups and differentiation, 75, 79, 125, 139, 246, 247, 248, 249, 251, 291, 415, 417, 423, 453
    ethnic term, 2n1
    ethnic cleansing, 27, 75, 160, 248, 315
    ethnic exegesis, 307
    ethnic theology, 320, 325
    ethnic tag in archaeology, 415
Ethnology, 162
Etic, 394, 395, 424
Etiological narrative, 55, 56, 94
Etymology, 102, 224
Euphrates, 129, 188, 192, 194, 215, 220, 424, 426, 429, 442
Eurocentric, Eurocentrism, 264, 314, 322, 393
Europeanization, 316
Evangelical, evangelicals, xvii, 43, 73, 121, 172, 263, 266, 268, 302, 308, 340, 353, 356, 384
Execration texts, 425, 426, 427
Exodus
    book of, 3, 7, 10, 12, 47, 53, 59, 61, 65, 82, 131, 191, 387
    event, 10, 19, 73, 74, 82, 83, 90, 128–32, 195, 197, 221, 230, 259, 346, 355
    narrative, story, 128, 129, 131, 132, 189, 320, 321, 354
    myth, 387
Exegesis, 44, 257, 258, 260, 262, 265, 202, 321, 340, 370
    ancient and medieval, 36, 318, 322
    Christian, 371
    ethnic, 307
    European, 324, 325
    exegesis of faith, 370
    feministic, 319
    historical-critical, 229, 357
    Jewish, 366
    North American, 357
    Paul, 286
    postcolonial, 320
    postmodern, 351, 358
    reader-response, 103, 357
    reformatory, 36, 264, 322
    synchronic, 335
    third world, 324, 325

Exile, xvi, 2n1, 17, 20, 21, 73, 94, 154,
    193–96, 201, 206–8, 220–23, 225–28,
    230, 232, 233, 315
  Babylonian exile, 17, 20, 74, 79, 80, 92,
    93, 95, 97, 107, 154–57, 159–62, 195,
    196, 202, 206, 211, 220, 221, 224,
    225, 228, 230, 231, 233, 246, 277,
    296, 311, 315, 329, 330, 343, 354,
    383, 387, 388, 438, 443
  Deutero-Isaiah and exile, 96n42
  exile and biblical history, 201
  exile in Assyria, 205
  Jacob's exile in Haran, 189
  Jehoiachin's exile, 19
  Jeremiah's exile in Egypt, 20, 218
External evidence, 72, 111, 112, 115, 118,
    119, 122, 131, 133, 152, 159
Ezra, 4–8, 21, 22, 27, 73, 79, 94, 95, 157,
    160, 161, 169, 235, 248, 278, 281,
    315, 329
Ezekiel, 3n4, 4, 5, 7, 8, 17, 19–21, 154, 155,
    232, 296, 333
Ezekiel the tragedian, 131n27

Fauna, 406
Feministic theology, 264, 317–20, 332
Fertile Crescent, 403
Fertility religion, 81, 82, 315
Fertility of the land, 81, 193, 213, 405
Flood, story of, 9, 37, 47–52, 55, 121n7, 243,
    244, 322, 323
Flora, 406
Florilegia, 376
Folklore studies, 55, 103
Form Criticism, 45, 56–58, 61, 64, 69, 186
Foundation myth, xvi, 74, 83, 128, 131
France, 35n3, 326, 408
French Revolution, 34, 248, 260, 313
Frode the Peacemaker, 126
Fundamentalism, fundamentalists, 71, 121,
    122n8, 167, 172, 266, 340, 352, 353,
    358
Fundamentals, 121n5

Galilee, 152, 404, 406, 407, 411, 419, 427,
    434, 446
Gaza, 411, 430, 431
Gedaliah, 20, 155, 221
Genesis, 3, 4, 7, 9, 54, 66, 81, 127, 169, 171,
    186, 187, 195, 206, 207, 211, 243,
    302, 384
Gennesaret, 404, 405
Geography, 243, 257, 400, 403, 406, 448, 453
Gerar, 66, 67, 69
Germanic invasion, 450
Gezer, 120, 131, 175, 431, 432, 440
Gibeon, 13, 201
Gideon, 208, 210
Gihon, 178
Gilboa, 76, 144
Gilgamesh, 47, 243, 244, 322
Globalization, 321, 325
Godless, the, 20, 222, 224, 236–238, 240, 241,
    247, 252, 253, 337, 389, 390, 395

Golan Heights, 404, 416
Gospel, Gospels, 91, 218, 224, 273, 274, 280,
    281, 353, 368, 373, 374, 377, 388
Graff-Kuenen-Wellhausen documentary
    hypothesis, 37
Greece, 42, 434, 441, 444
Greek language, 6, 102, 107
Greek authors, 40
Greek Bible, 5, 18, 267, 270, 273, 279, 334, 375
Greek literature, 41, 266
Greek philosophy, 98, 266, 370
Greek New Testament, 283, 338
Greeks, 129, 148, 156, 173, 369, 427, 446

Ḥabiru, 135, 137–39, 432
Hagar, 9, 191, 286
Haggai, 4, 7, 8, 19, 21, 96, 159, 296
Hallelujah psalms, 236
Hama, 78, 147n45
Hamitic languages, 413
Hamlet, 171
Hammurabi, 84, 158, 244–46, 425, 426
Haran, 9, 19, 189, 244
Hasmonean, Hasmoneans, 446
Hatti, 116, 131, 433
Hattushash, 401
Hazael, 78, 147
Hazor, 75, 120, 238, 152, 411, 425, 427, 430,
    431, 434, 440
Hebrew, 22, 76
  alphabet, 178
  canon, 179, 331
  language, 4–6, 27, 41, 42, 102, 107, 177,
    183, 248, 267n7, 270–73, 277–82,
    285, 327, 329–31, 334, 338, 364–66,
    375, 385, 389, 390
  people, 135–39
  Bible, xix, 3, 5, 6, 8, 17, 22, 24–28, 70, 89,
    94, 160, 169, 270–73, 277–82, 285,
    327, 329–34, 338, 364–66, 375, 389,
    390
  kingdom, 75
Hebrews, letter, 377
Hebron, 10, 90, 251, 407, 411, 431, 443
Hecataeus, 132
Hellenistic period, xvi, 124, 173, 230, 246,
    252, 286, 297, 303, 309, 334, 380,
    386, 394, 396, 426, 442, 443, 445,
    446
Hellenistic-Roman Period, 174, 380, 396, 438
Hellenistic-Roman Judaism, 2, 333
Hellenism, 354, 446
Hellenization, 319, 444
Henotheism, 83, 349
Hermeneutic, 259, 264, 297, 313, 318, 335,
    352, 356, 368
  hermeneutic of faith, 368, 371, 373, 378,
    380
  hermeneutic of suspicion, 318, 319, 324,
    332
  hermeneutical circle, xviii, 110, 124, 167,
    210, 292, 371, 378
Hermon, 404, 405
Herod, 439, 443, 446

Herod's temple, 390
Herodotus, 206n10, 248, 249, 398, 442
Hexateuch, 64, 199n6, 296, 346
Hezekiah, 17, 19, 27, 77, 78, 95, 117, 118,
    151, 152, 154, 178, 184, 185, 203,
    439, 440
Hieroglyphs, 39, 40, 175, 177, 419
Hilkiah, 160
Historical-Critical scholarship, xvii, xviii, 28,
    36, 42–44, 73, 98, 103, 331, 337, 338,
    351, 352, 356, 358, 383
  amphictyony, 141
  ancient Israel, 70, 109, 162, 363
  archaeology, 123
  canon, 280, 282, 367
  development of historical-critical scholar-
    ship, 31, 32, 259, 260, 262, 265, 300,
    324, 366
  exegesis, 45, 357
  gap between the Old and New Testaments,
    265, 266, 368, 370, 380
  German tradition of scholarship, 73, 108
  hermeneutic circle, 110–12, 172, 210
  historical paradigm, 43, 107, 108, 124,
    222, 262, 344
  house of cards, 111, 172, 185, 301
  Israel's history, 74, 75, 77, 79, 80, 96, 132,
    139, 172, 313
  Israel's literature, 88, 95, 97, 183
  Israel's religion, 81–83, 87
  law, 225
  logics, 124, 264
  methodology, 52, 64, 109, 121, 142, 167,
    258, 294, 309, 318, 340, 356
  prophets, 212, 219, 283, 357
  rationalistic paraphrase, 341
  response from conservative scholarship,
    121, 123
Historiography, 161, 186, 199, 399
  biblical, xvi, 2n1, 122, 123, 149, 151, 152,
    154, 156, 161–63, 185–87, 209, 217
  ancient, 34, 151
  Deuteronomistic, 92
  historicity, 172
  modern, 313, 381, 398, 399, 402, 403, 450
History, concept of, 37, 142, 260, 286, 294,
    300, 304, 306, 313, 316, 379
History writing, xv, 34, 36, 206n10, 313, 398,
    402
History of Israel, xvi–xix, 17, 41, 70, 73, 74,
    80, 81, 88, 91, 92, 133n3, 146, 157,
    217, 257, 306, 309, 343, 344, 356,
    393, 396
  biblical history, 73, 94, 153, 154, 186,
    200, 207, 209, 219, 344, 348
  collapse of Israel's history, 303
  Deuteronomists, 184, 329
  exile and history, 201
  Gerhard von Rad, 292, 294, 295, 341, 345
  German histories, 125, 341
  inscriptions, 149, 152
  John Bright, 125, 287, 355, 396n4
  modern reconstructions, 71, 72, 88, 125,
    161

narrative, 40, 79, 247
prophets, 169, 226
tragic history, 342
William Foxwell Albright, 302, 354
Hitler, Adolf, 398
Hittite, 400, 401, 426, 428, 429, 432, 433
  Hittite Empire, 401, 433, 435, 451
  Hittite language, 426
  Hittites in the OT, 16, 188, 191, 192, 196
  Hittite treaties, 294
Hobab, 46n3
Holocaust, xvii, 291, 301n3, 315, 371, 398n8
Holy scriptures, 173, 289, 369n7
Holy war, 141
Homer, Homeric poems, 42, 45n2, 126, 143,
    173, 175
Horace, 171
Horeb, 191
Horites, 426
Hosea (prophet), 4, 7, 8, 19, 21, 96, 212, 218,
    219, 226–28, 230, 234, 296, 348
Hosea (king), 147, 152
House of Omri, 77, 146, 147, 149, 150, 152,
    161, 319, 396, 439
Huleh Valley, 404, 405, 407
Hulda, 206
Hurrian
  language, 426
  people, 426, 428, 429
Husbandry, 407, 413, 414
Hyksos, 129–32, 427, 428

Iceland, 141
Icelandic sagas, 143
Ideology
  of humanism, 33
  ancient, 138
  Assyrian, 151
  biblical historiography, 156, 248
  Judean, 185, 231
  prophets, 232
  Aryan-German, 314
  Joshua and violence, 320, 383
  critical scholars, 340, 341
  existentialism, 370
  empty land, 315
Idol, idols, 14, 92, 194, 220, 227, 249, 329,
    347
Idumea, Idumeans, 443, 445
Immanuel, 19, 45. 231n25, 357, 384, 391
Imperialism, 316, 317, 324
Inscriptions, 39, 40, 112, 115, 118, 119, 144,
    146, 149, 158, 177, 178, 183, 440
  Assyrian, 115, 147, 148, 154, 436
  Babylonian, 115, 148
  Egyptian, 130, 131, 139, 412, 429, 433,
    439
  Kuntillet ʿAjrud, 250, 251, 318
  Mesha, 149–51, 439
  Palestinian, 41, 115, 332, 425, 438
  Persian, 157, 158
  Rosetta stone, 39
  Siloam, 178, 179
  Tel Dan, 113–15, 144, 425, 439

Indo-European
    languages, 413, 426
    nomads, 418
Iron Age, xvi, 87, 115, 134, 177, 178, 180,
        182–85, 247–49, 262, 286, 318, 332,
        382, 394, 397, 413, 433, 434, 438–40,
        449, 452
    archaeology, xix
    early Iron Age, 89, 123, 135
    language, 380
    religion, 251, 252, 348, 349
Isaac, 9, 67, 69, 71, 74, 188, 189, 190, 191,
        194, 196, 207n11, 309, 356, 374
Isaiah
    book, 3n4, 4, 7, 8, 17–20, 95–97, 111,
        218, 220, 221, 223, 224, 233, 239,
        270, 277, 278, 281, 333, 336, 348,
        392
    prophet, 19, 20, 45, 96, 111, 118, 151,
        213, 219, 221, 226, 234, 266, 296,
        357, 370, 391
Ishbaal, 76
Ishboshet, 76n11
Islamist, 252, 325
Israel as a concept, xvi, 337
    ancient Israel, xix, 2n1, 35, 40, 43, 70, 71
    biblical Israel, xix, 4, 121, 162, 163, 209,
        211, 212, 234, 237, 300, 363, 384, 387
    historical Israel, xv, xvi, xix, 74, 162, 163,
        290, 348, 397, 452
    Israel of the new covenant, xviii, xix, 1, 2,
        162, 390
    new Israel, 2, 21, 25, 163, 286, 291, 315,
        390, 395
    old Israel, 2, 163, 232, 291, 316, 375, 376,
        387, 290
Israelite religion, xv, xvi, xviii, 38, 39, 41, 43,
        58, 65, 70, 80–83, 95, 87–89, 109,
        110, 121, 127, 169, 213, 217, 252n19,
        260, 263, 296, 297, 301, 305, 306,
        309, 310, 336, 342–44, 348, 349, 362
    polytheistic, xvi, 233
    Josiah's reform, 17
    Yahwistic religion, 82, 83, 141, 290
    patriarchal religion, 82, 127, 128, 290,
        302, 309
    syncretism, 84
    private religion, 127, 310, 312
    Moses's religion, 128, 290, 292
    prophetic religion, 213, 225
    religion of the Old Testament, 306,
        310–12
Israel stele, 396, 130, 131
ʿIzbet Ṣarṭah, 177

Jacob, 9, 10, 11, 13, 53, 71, 74, 90, 143,
        188–90, 194, 196, 207n11, 231, 238,
        309, 356, 374
Jael, 319
Jahwist, 46n5
Jamnia, 279
Jehoram, 149, 204
Jehoiachin, 19, 77, 116, 148, 154, 156
Jehoiakim, 77, 206

Jehoshaphat, 149, 181, 204
Jehovah, 46n4, 272
Jehovah's Witnesses, 389
Jehu, 77, 78, 85, 147, 203
Jephthah, 14, 75, 208
Jeremiah
    book, 3n4, 4, 5, 7, 8, 17, 20, 85, 96, 97,
        155, 195, 217, 218, 228–32, 281, 387
    prophet, xix, 19, 20, 26, 85, 96, 137, 218,
        221, 229, 230, 296, 376
Jeremiah, letter of, 5, 278
Jericho, 12, 13, 41, 56, 71, 120, 194, 405,
        412–14, 416
Jeroboam
    I, 77, 92, 203, 205, 207
    II, 19, 77
Jerome, 267n7, 272
Jerusalem, 18, 20, 26, 78, 86, 137, 138, 140,
        148, 156, 159, 160, 180, 184, 202,
        205, 206, 229, 231–33, 242, 242, 407,
        411, 425, 431, 439, 444–46
    Amarna Jerusalem, 176, 432
    archaeology, 40, 119, 120, 123, 145, 178,
        170
    Babylonian conquest, xvi, 17, 20, 21, 79,
        115, 116, 154, 155, 180, 206, 218,
        220, 221, 229, 348, 387, 397, 441
    capital of Judah, 76
    chosen by Yahweh, 86, 87
    cult of Yahweh, 162
    David and Jerusalem, 16, 76, 115, 142–44,
        200, 237, 305
    Deuteronomism and Jerusalem, 183, 184
    Ezra in Jerusalem, 27, 159, 160, 278
    Jerusalem and Samaria, 222n15
    Josiah's reform, 184
    Nehemiah in Jerusalem, 27, 159
    new Jerusalem, 155, 232, 333
    next year in Jerusalem, 233, 252
    Persian period, 161
    Sennacherib's attack, 17, 19, 117, 118,
        151, 185, 439
    Shoshenq and Jerusalem, 439
    Solomon and Jerusalem, 111
    temple, 4, 17, 21, 57, 73, 86, 87, 96, 97,
        155–57, 159, 201, 206, 208, 243, 251,
        318, 348, 446
Jesus, 218, 220, 265, 266, 268, 279, 281, 289,
        331, 353, 354, 369, 374, 378, 381,
        390, 391
Jew, Jews, 25–27, 97, 131, 156–58, 171, 221,
        233, 252, 262, 272, 279, 286, 308,
        315, 326, 325, 328, 366, 370, 383,
        385, 389, 442, 443, 446, 448
Jewish Bible, 2, 3, 4
Jewish exegesis, 4
Jewish monotheism, xv, xvi
Jewish rebellion, 443, 444, 447
Jewish tradition, 2, 3
Jewish War, 446
Jezebel, 17, 319
Jezreel Valley, 405, 411, 432
Job, 4, 5, 7, 22, 25, 97, 235, 241, 261, 280,
        297, 345, 368

Jonadab the son of Rechab, 85
Jonah, 4, 7, 8, 18, 19, 21, 22, 135, 137, 233, 296
Jonathan, 76, 137
Jordan, territory, 40, 71, 143, 149, 177, 397, 414, 415, 447
Jordan River, 11–13, 76, 78, 128, 137, 151, 196, 397, 404, 405, 406, 407, 411, 431, 438, 445, 446
Jordan Valley, 41, 120, 190, 405, 411, 412, 419
Joseph, story of Joseph, 9, 10, 14, 53, 62, 136, 189, 190, 207n11
Josephus, 2, 5, 79, 131, 132, 383, 396, 442, 446
Joshua
    book, 4, 5, 7–9, 11, 13–15, 17, 18, 21, 47, 75, 82, 92, 133n30, 139, 140, 183, 184, 192, 196–98, 199n6, 207, 280, 296, 315, 320, 342, 346n7, 347, 387
    person, 12–14, 56, 74, 196–98, 208, 354, 355
Joshua–2 Kings, 8, 9, 13, 17, 18, 21, 92, 183, 184, 280, 342, 347
Josiah, 17, 19, 27, 77, 78, 86, 87, 93, 95, 96, 160, 183, 184, 185, 202, 203, 206, 251
Josiah's reform, 17, 27, 86, 160, 184
Jubilees, 6, 278, 279
Judah
    state, xvi, 17, 20, 27, 74, 76–79, 86, 92, 93, 96, 113, 115, 118, 145–49, 151–57, 159, 161, 177, 178, 184, 185, 213, 217, 218, 225, 229, 234, 346, 375, 388, 397, 439, 440, 443
    tribe, 11, 13, 14, 56, 76, 205
    person, 10, 53
    landscape, 10, 53
Judeans, 20, 76, 79, 86, 118, 137, 156, 157, 18420, 76, 79, 86, 118, 137, 156, 157, 184, 185, 206, 221, 225, 231, 249, 440, 441
Judaism, xvi, xix, 2, 71, 160, 171, 211, 233, 246, 247, 252, 262, 278, 280, 298, 318, 325, 330, 345, 366, 367, 380, 383, 385, 386, 388–90, 443, 445–47
    Bible of Judaism, 3
    early Judaism, 76, 81, 87, 225, 232, 233, 240, 253, 349
    European attitude toward Judaism, 368
    Hellenistic Judaism, 2, 97, 354
    Judaism and Christianity, 224, 225, 289, 371, 380, 390, 391
    Judaism and religion, 83, 233, 253, 342, 391
    post-exilic, 70, 87, 91, 97, 344, 345
    rabbinic Judaism, 280
    writings of Judaism, 2
Judges
    book, 4, 7, 14, 15, 75, 140–42, 146, 192, 197–99, 208, 210, 318, 346, 387
    persons, 14, 15, 58, 74, 79, 140, 143, 146, 198, 199, 208, 293, 346, 383
Judges, period, 73–75, 79–81, 90, 126, 132, 139–43, 198, 199, 208, 345

Kadesh, battle, 130n22, 433, 434
Kemosh, 83, 150
Ketef Hinnom, 179, 182
Ketuvim, 8
Khirbet el-Kom, 251
King Arthur, 143
Kingdom, 15–17, 75, 142, 194, 206, 231, 313, 343, 401, 419, 420
    divided kingdom, 13, 76, 146
    divine kingship, 84
    Egypt, 129, 130, 132, 174
    Hasmonean kingdom, 445, 446
    Hittite kingdom, 433
    House of Omri, 146
    kingdom of Assyria, 221
    kingdom of David and Solomon, 21, 76, 95, 112, 143, 144, 146, 189, 200, 203, 388
    kingdom of God, 233, 253, 266, 343, 376, 388, 390
    kingdom of Israel, 17, 74, 77, 86, 95, 96, 147, 148, 161, 177, 184, 185, 220, 234, 243, 397
    Kingdom of Jerusalem (crusader), 447
    kingdom of Judah, 17, 74, 78, 96, 115, 118, 147, 148, 161, 177, 185, 203, 305, 213, 217, 218, 234, 397
    kingdom of Mari, 215
    messiah's kingdom, 238, 389
    Neo-Babylonian kingdom, 154
    Yahweh's kingdom, 240
King, kingship, 75, 76, 84, 85, 208
Kings, books of, 4, 7, 17–19, 27, 148, 152, 153, 168, 182, 183, 185, 205, 210, 218, 226, 230, 335
    1 Kings, 7, 17, 111, 201, 202, 208
    2 Kings, 4, 5, 7, 17, 22, 117, 118, 152, 155, 169, 171, 187, 195, 211, 251
King's Highway, 89, 411
Kings, period, 93, 168, 213, 219, 231, 233, 310, 332
Kir-hareshet, 149
Kirta, epic, 85
Korah, 235
Kumidi, 430, 431
Kuntillet ʿAjrud, 249–51

Labayu, 432
Lachish, 117–21, 135, 138, 227, 397, 440
Laenas, C. Porphilius, 445
Latakia, 42, 427
Late Bronze Age, 42, 123, 133–35, 176, 177, 182, 394, 401, 419, 421, 426, 428, 429, 433–35, 438–40, 444, 451
Latin America, 316
Law, 61, 141, 224, 241, 242, 275, 343, 344
    as Torah, 23, 71, 72, 91, 189, 193, 194, 196, 203, 204, 223, 224, 229, 246, 278, 286, 328, 342, 368, 369, 375, 388, 391
    biblical law, 2, 12, 57
        God's (Yahweh's) law, 1, 10, 12, 23, 85, 193, 196, 206, 224–26, 228, 229, 297, 298, 377, 388

Law (*continued*)
    Law, dead letter of, 342, 368, 371, 373,
        376, 380
    Law and the prophets, 273, 280, 281
    Law book, Josiah's, 184, 185
    Mesopotamian law, 244–46
    Moses's law, 3, 24, 27, 196, 225, 244, 258,
        290
    natural law, 32, 33, 87, 91, 170, 357
    Pentateuch as law, 2–4, 8, 9, 24, 224, 225,
        280, 375
Lebanon, 40, 41, 71, 115, 136, 177, 182, 248,
        325, 404, 405, 411, 422, 427, 430,
        432, 438
Legal tradition, Mesopotamian, 244
Legal tradition, Old Testament, 246
Les annals, school, 344
Levant, Levantine Coast, 41, 42, 75, 78, 112,
        135, 253n20, 403, 416, 422, 425, 427,
        434, 444, 445, 452
Liberal theology, 263, 370
Liberation theology, 264, 316, 317, 320, 321,
        325, 339, 351, 356, 357
Libyan Desert, 441
Linguistics, 101
Literacy, 180n13
Literal reading, 258, 265, 322
Literary criticism, 45–47, 52, 55, 64–66, 69,
        103, 111, 170, 186, 235
Livy, 398
LMK-stamps, 440
Long perspective, 447, 449–53
Lot, 14, 15
Luke, 280n17, 374
Luther, 6–8, 36–38, 258, 266–68, 271, 272,
        274, 276, 282, 322, 333, 342, 368,
        369
Lutheran Orthodoxy, 37, 275
Lydia, Lydians, 78, 156

Maccabean period, 97
Maccabean revolt, 444–46
Maccabees, 38, 337, 444
Maccabees, books, 5–8, 79, 267, 273, 442
Macedonia, Macedonians, 38, 401, 443, 444
Madeba, 149
Magnesia, battle, 445
Malachi, 4, 7, 8, 17–19, 21, 22, 97, 272, 296
Manetho, 131, 132, 428
Manasseh
    king, 12, 14, 142, 196
    tribe, 13, 14, 142, 196
Mandarins, 241
Marcion, Marcionism, 265, 285, 353, 374,
        378
Marduk, 158, 174, 253
Mari, 215, 216, 425, 426
Mark, 265
Matthew, 374
Matriarch, 66
Medes, 78
Mediterranean, 40, 182, 401, 411,
        413, 421, 423, 427, 433, 445,
        447, 451

Megiddo, 41, 71, 78, 120, 184n15, 411, 431,
        432, 440
Melanchton, 352
Merneptah, 130, 131, 396
Mesha, Mesha inscription, 149, 150
Mesolithic Period, 412, 415
Mesopotamia, xvi, 21, 40, 71, 139, 158, 175,
        182, 183, 189, 214, 221, 241, 242,
        401, 403, 411, 417, 419, 422, 424,
        425, 426, 437, 439, 442–44
    archaeology, 40, 119, 121
    deportation and exile in Mesopotamia, 20,
        78, 79, 154, 159, 211, 388, 440, 441,
        443
    divination, 214, 215
    inscriptions, 40
    Jewish diaspora, 195
    Judaism and Mesopotamia, 246, 252
    Law, 244, 246
    Mesopotamian influence on the Old Testa-
        ment, 40, 55, 244
    modern discovery, 39n14
    monotheism in Mesopotamia, 253
    patriarchs and Mesopotamia, 9, 187, 190,
        244
    return from Mesopotamia, 383
    texts, 174
    trade, 423
Messages, 89, 176, 177, 180, 182, 216
Messiah, 18, 25, 76, 236–38, 240, 266,
        289, 297, 368, 373–75, 381, 387,
        389–92
Micah, 4, 7, 8, 19, 21, 96, 212, 218, 219, 226,
        296
Micaiah son of Imla, 216, 362
Middle Bronze Age, 125, 394, 422, 425–29,
        433
Middle Kingdom in Egypt, 129
Middle perspective, 402, 406, 412, 451
Milkom, 83
Milton, John, 335
Miqra', 276
Mitanni, 426, 429
Moab, 10, 19, 76, 83, 140, 144, 147, 149,
        150, 194, 207, 208, 319, 439
Monarchy, Period, 80, 84
Monolatry, 83, 349
Monotheism, xv, xvi, 252, 253, 297, 315, 318,
        329, 330, 348, 349, 354, 361, 386,
        387
Moses, 11, 22, 24, 27, 37, 87, 90, 91, 160,
        225, 235, 244, 258
    books, 2–4, 7, 37, 45, 47, 86, 92, 184,
        224, 276, 296, 320, 375
    person, 10–13, 37, 46, 47, 80, 83, 92,
        128–30, 132, 133, 136, 180, 191, 193,
        194, 196, 207, 219, 278, 290, 293,
        294, 346, 354, 358, 369, 398
Mot, 174
Muslim tradition, 276

Nabi', 213, 214
Nadab, 77, 93, 203
Napoleon, 35n3, 39, 326, 395, 398, 448

Nathan, 16, 181, 200, 206, 208
Nationalism, 314, 453
National history, 36, 74, 206, 314
Natural laws, 32, 33, 170
Natural Science, 32–34, 98, 112, 170, 242, 357, 358
Natural theology, 259, 268, 290, 307, 370, 374
Nazareth, 390, 448
Nebuchadnezzar, 5, 17, 26, 27, 79, 93, 97, 115, 116, 148, 155, 206, 221, 233, 278, 348, 387, 388, 439, 441
Nebuzaradan, 155, 160
Neco, 184
Negev, 397, 404, 405, 411, 416, 419, 421, 427, 434
Nehemiah
    book, 3, 5, 7, 8, 21, 22, 27, 94, 95, 157, 160, 169, 235, 315
    person, 27, 73, 79, 157, 159–61
Neo-Assyrian prophecy, 215–17
Neo-Babylonian Chronicle, 148, 153, 331
Neo-Babylonian kingdom, 154
Neo-Babylonian empire, 221n12, 438
Neo-Babylonian Period, 244, 394, 438, 441
Neolithic, 415
    moist interval, 413, 419
    period, 394, 412, 413, 417
    revolution, 451
Nevi'im, 2, 8
New covenant, xviii, xix, 1, 2, 20, 162, 231, 232, 375, 390
New Revised Standard Version, xix, 283
New Testament, 2, 3, 5, 6, 22, 24, 36, 43, 58n18, 91, 121, 258–62, 264, 265, 266, 268, 269, 272–74, 276, 280–83, 285–87, 289–91, 295, 298, 306, 309, 316, 320, 327, 331, 333, 334, 338, 343, 353, 357, 358, 364–71, 373–78, 380, 389, 391, 392, 395, 443
New Israel, 2, 21, 25, 163, 286, 291, 315, 316, 390, 395
New Kingdom in Egypt, 129, 130, 132, 174
Newton, Isaac, 32, 101, 292, 357
Nibelungenlied, 143
Nicaea, confession, 274
Nile, Nile valley, 10, 130, 403, 411, 428, 434
Nippur, 221
Nineveh, 22, 117, 118, 148, 221n12
Noah, 46, 48–52, 187, 244, 280, 323
Nomads, nomadism, nomadization, 74, 81–83, 85, 89, 213, 215, 407, 408, 414, 418, 422–24, 426, 435, 436, 447, 448, 451, 452
Northern Africa, 426
Northwest Semitic, 248, 438
Nubia, 118

Odes of Solomon, 5, 273
Old Kingdom (Egypt), 129
Olives, 421
Omri, Kingdom of Omri, 76–78, 85, 92–94, 146, 147, 149, 150, 152, 161, 203, 319, 396, 439, 453

Oral literature and tradition, 55, 56, 63, 64, 89, 90, 173, 175, 176, 180–82
Orientalism, 264, 314, 393, 395
Orthodox Church, 267
Othniel, 208
Ottoman Empire, 414

Paleoanthropology, 412
Paleo-Hebrew alphabet, 177, 178
Paleolithic Period, 412, 415
Palestine, xv, xvi, 40, 66, 75, 76, 85, 90, 112, 113, 115, 118, 125, 127, 130, 139, 144, 145, 148, 152, 154, 157, 159, 177, 182, 221, 222, 233, 300, 349, 382, 394, 396, 397, 408, 414, 415, 417, 419, 420, 422–24, 427, 439, 441, 443, 448, 449, 451, 453
    agriculture and animal breeding, 408, 409, 414
    Amarna age and letters, 131, 135, 175, 176, 429, 430, 431
    Amorites, 424
    archaeology, 40, 41, 71, 72, 119–23, 172, 178n10, 344, 355
    Assyrian conquest, 440
    Babylonian conquest, 441
    climate and geography, 257, 397, 400, 409, 411, 423
    deportations, 221, 228
    diaspora and Palestine, 315
    Egyptian rule, 139, 422, 429, 433, 435
    hellenization, 441, 446
    history, xviii, xix, 41, 106, 115, 123, 302, 382, 383, 393, 395–98, 403, 412, 419, 425, 426, 447, 450, 452
    Hyksos, 428
    inscriptions, 115, 149, 177, 251, 318, 332
    Israelite conquest and settlement, 74, 82, 90, 130, 133
    Israelite origins, 81, 83, 133
    Israelite tribes in Palestine, 140, 143
    Judaism, 252
    kingdom of Israel, 146
    language, 248, 380, 413, 425, 436, 438
    Late Bronze Age–Early Iron Age transition, 134, 135, 435
    origins of the Old Testament, 41, 243, 246, 247
    Persian rule, 442
    Philistines, 434
    religion, 42, 87, 182, 249, 252, 332, 348
    right to Palestine, 156
    Roman rule, 445
    trade, 410, 411, 421
    traditional political organization, 409, 410
    writing, 175, 180, 182, 183, 242
    Yahweh, 83, 251
Palmyra, 144
Pan-Deuteronomism, 329
Paradise Lost, 335
Passover, 10, 13, 26
Patriarchs, 10, 66, 68, 90, 124–27, 187, 191, 207, 230, 290, 302, 335, 354, 369, 383, 396n4

Patriarchal age, 71, 73, 74, 124, 125, 190, 207, 302, 309, 355
Patriarchs, promise to, 81, 188, 190, 191
Patriarchal narratives, 9, 10, 58, 62, 74, 81, 125, 126, 127, 128, 132, 302
Patriarchal religion, 80–82, 127, 128n19, 290, 302
Patron, patronage, 34, 313, 386, 420, 421, 425, 428, 430, 432, 439, 446, 447
Paul, 224, 258, 282, 286, 289, 291, 320, 333, 342, 353, 365, 368, 374
Peasants, 83, 132, 133, 213, 407–10, 413, 414, 422, 424
Peasant fertility religion, 82
Peisistratos, 173n1
Pekah, 77, 147, 152
Pekaiah, 77
Pentateuch, 3, 8, 12, 37, 38, 45–47, 58, 63–65, 88, 90, 91, 103, 111, 128, 180, 183, 186, 194, 198, 199, 210, 225, 228, 262, 277, 296, 297, 342, 346, 354, 360, 380
People of God, 185, 195, 206, 208, 234, 240, 247, 248, 290, 291, 297, 329, 330, 337, 347, 352, 276, 386, 387
Peer Gynt, 341
Persia, Persians, 19, 21, 26, 27, 73, 78, 70, 87, 124, 129, 158, 195, 210, 211, 230, 246, 252, 278, 297, 386n9, 401, 438
Persian Gulf, 403
Persian Period, 74, 97, 109, 156–59, 160, 161, 380, 394, 441, 442
Perspective, long, middle, and short, 400
Pharisees, Pharisaical, 253, 365, 389
Philology, 34, 101, 106
Philistines, 10, 15, 16, 19, 67, 75, 76, 135, 137, 144, 192, 199, 208, 396, 434
Phoenicia, Phoenicians, 158, 182, 411, 440, 442
   alphabet, 177, 178
   language, 248, 425
   religion, 41, 42
Pilgrims, pilgrimage, 396, 417, 447
Pilgrimage psalms, 236
Plagues of Egypt, 10, 62, 90, 261
Plato, 124, 370
Poem of Roland, 143
Polytheism, 348, 349
Pompey, 444, 445
Positivism, 32, 102, 124
Postcolonial exegesis and theology, 263, 264, 317, 320, 339
Postmodern, postmodernism, xviii, 212, 268, 299, 317, 339, 351, 352, 356–59, 363, 371, 381, 384, 385, 391
Pottery, 135, 410, 415, 416, 434
Priests, priesthood, 12, 14, 15, 27, 46, 131, 143, 144, 180, 181, 226, 227, 417, 418
   Josiah's reform, 86
   high priest, 87, 160, 225, 389
   amphictyony, 140
   Egyptian, 175
   divinity and prophecy, 214

Priestly writer, document or source, 45–52, 55, 63, 65, 380
Primeval history, 9, 187, 206, 243, 244, 295, 333, 412
prophetism, 87, 205, 213, 225, 348
Prophets
   former prophets (Joshua–2 Kings), 8, 13, 21
   near eastern prophecy, 213–17, 219
   prophetic books and literature, 4, 5, 17, 18, 21, 22, 25, 86, 95, 97, 111, 168, 169, 195, 212, 213, 217–21, 223, 224, 226–29, 231–34, 237, 239, 240, 246, 251, 273, 277, 280, 281, 334, 357, 368, 375
   prophetic persons, 15, 17–22, 71, 85–87, 95–97, 111, 118, 135, 153–55, 196, 200, 208, 210, 212–14, 216–20, 224–30, 233, 234, 240, 277, 278, 286, 348, 349, 375, 388
   prophets and law, 71, 72, 91, 225, 273, 280, 281, 286
   prophets as part of the Old Testament, 2, 4–6, 8, 9, 24, 169, 273, 280, 297, 375
   prophets of doom, 86, 226, 229, 348
Protestantism, 275, 285, 369
Proto-Isaiah, 18, 96, 270
Proto-Masoretic, 281
Protourban Period, 419
Proverbs, 89, 241
   book, 4, 5, 7, 25, 26, 97, 235, 241, 278
Psalms of David, 4, 23, 24, 235, 390
Psalms of Solomon, 5, 6, 8, 273
Pseudepigraphs, 6, 273, 278, 281n18
Ptolemy I, 444
Publicans, 446, 447

Qatna, 425, 428
Qaus, 83
Queen of Sheba, 17, 111
Qumran, 24n10, 277, 278, 279n16, 281
Qur'an, 175, 276, 385n7

Rabbat Ammon, 411
Rabbis, 279, 281, 338
   Rabbis and the Hebrew Bible, 365
   Rabbinic commentaries, 276
   Rabbinic editors, 279n14
   Rabbinic commentaries, 276
   Rabbinic editors, 279n14
   Rabbinic manuscripts, 271
   Rabbinic Judaism, 280, 389
Ramesses, 83, 432
Ramesses II, 130, 139, 432
Ramesses III, 434
Ramesside Period, 432
Ras Shamra, 42
Rationalistic paraphrase, 79, 87, 126, 132, 261, 263, 300, 328, 341, 344, 381
Reader-Response exegesis, 103, 357, 381
Redaction history, 45, 52, 58, 64–69, 97, 103, 186
Reformation, 38, 258, 264, 267, 274, 277, 285, 338

Reformers, 36, 37, 86, 258, 267, 275, 322, 334
Regionalism, 440
Rehoboam, 76, 77, 146, 203
Retribalization, 424
Return from exile, 156
Reuben, 11, 13, 53, 196
Reuel, 46
Revisionism, revisionists, xvii, 107, 122, 301
Rib-Adda, 388n13
Risk spreading, 423
Road along the Sea, 411
Roman Empire, 171, 447, 450
Roman Period, 394, 442, 444, 445, 452
Romans, 38, 129, 389, 390, 444–47
Romantic Period, 34, 37, 360–62, 300, 304, 395
Rome, 444–47
Rosh Hanikra, 405
Rosseau, Jean-Jacques, 259
Ruth, 4, 7, 8, 10, 26, 319

Sabbath, 12, 20, 59, 62, 233, 263, 388
Sadducees, 389
Sahara, 406
Salvation history, 268, 293, 295, 297, 309,
      310, 329, 332, 340, 346–48, 381, 382
Samaria, 17, 21, 77, 78, 86, 92, 120, 146–48,
      154, 157, 159, 161, 184, 250, 251,
      396, 397, 439, 440, 442, 445, 446
Samaritans, 222n15, 443, 445
Samson, 14, 15, 199, 208
Samuel, 15, 196, 199, 200, 205, 208, 219, 278
      books, 4, 5, 7, 27, 76n11, 85, 145, 146,
            180, 182, 199, 205, 208, 226
      1 Sam, 15, 16, 135
      2 Sam, 16, 27
Sanballat, 157, 159, 442
Sarah, 4, 9, 66–68, 190, 191
Satan, 25, 252n19, 326
Satrap, satrapy, 442
Saul, 15, 16, 24, 73, 75–77, 137, 143, 144,
      200, 208
Saxo, 126, 398
Schools and education, 97, 98, 182, 241, 258
Scribes, 177, 187, 216, 141, 424
Scythopolis, 446
Sea People, 433–35, 449
Sebaste, 446
Sect, sectarianism, sectarian movement, 104,
      234, 253, 337, 386–88
Seleucia, 443
Seleucid Empire, 445
Seleucids, 444, 445
Seleucus I, 444
Semitic languages, 4, 183, 413, 424, 438
Sennacherib, 17, 19, 78, 117–19, 121, 148,
      151–54, 161, 185, 227, 233, 297, 439,
      440
Septuagint, xix, 5, 6, 7n7, 271–73, 279–81,
      283, 334, 338, 366, 375, 385, 390
Seraiah, 160, 181
Servant songs, 377, 392
Sethos I, 139, 433
Shakespeare, William, 171, 172, 275
Sharon Plain, 405, 407

Shechem, 12–14, 82, 90, 120, 146, 210,
      222n15, 407, 411, 425, 432, 445
Shema, 194
Sherden, 434
Shilo, 13–15, 142, 205, 407
Shishak, 439
Short perspective, 400, 401, 403, 412, 415,
      448, 451, 452
Shoshenq, 438
Shuppiluliumash I, 401, 429
Sidon, 138, 427
Siloam inscription, 178, 179
Siloam pool, 178
Sinai, 10, 82, 83, 128, 132, 192, 250, 411
      tradition, 10, 12, 64, 83
      revelation, 74, 83, 90, 347, 354, 355, 369
      covenant, 82, 207, 232, 294, 299, 387
Single grave people, 418
Sitz im Leben, 56, 286, 381
Social anthropology, xv, 72, 102, 104, 105,
      109, 123, 247, 291, 394, 402, 409, 415
Social sciences, 101
Sociology, xv, 72, 101, 102, 402
Socrates, 343
Sola Scriptura, 37, 268, 274
Solomon, 5, 6, 16, 17, 25–27, 73, 74, 76, 77,
      91, 95, 111–13, 116, 143–46, 181–83,
      185, 235, 236, 273, 278, 319, 382
Song of Songs, 4, 5, 7, 8, 26, 235, 278
South America, 105n2, 316, 317, 320, 321
Spinoza, Baruch, 37, 259
Stalin, Joseph, 398
State, centralized, 414, 423
Story of Joseph, 9, 10, 62, 189, 396
Structuralism, 105
Sub-Sahara Africa, 104, 105n2
Succession history, 93, 144, 200, 209
Surveys, archaeological, 135, 160, 402
Syncretism, 81, 85, 86, 348
Syrian-Arabian Desert, 423
Syria, 40–42, 71, 76, 78, 85, 115, 135, 144,
      145, 159, 174, 175, 177, 183, 195,
      242, 251, 253, 333, 401, 403, 404,
      411, 414, 415, 417, 419, 421–30, 432,
      435, 436, 438, 439, 443–47, 451
Syro-Ephraimite War, 78
Systematic theology, 258, 305, 337, 338, 360,
      379
Tadmor, 144
Taliban, 337, 388
Talmud, 276, 364
Tamar, 10, 26, 319
TaNaK, Tanakh, 2, 4–8, 17, 22, 26, 276, 375
Taxation, 76, 410, 412, 446
Tel-abib, 221
Tel Dan inscription, 113–15, 144, 148, 439
Tell Beit Mirsim, 120
Teleilat Ghassul, 416
Tell el-Amarna, 429
Tel Masos, 436
Teman, 250, 251
Temple scroll, 277
Temple of Jerusalem, 17, 21, 27, 73, 86, 87,
      97, 159, 208, 251, 318

Ten Commandments, 12, 59, 61, 62, 238
Territorialgeschichte, 79
Testamentum, 1, 376
Tetrateuch, 199n6
Teutons, 450
Text archaeology, 89, 91, 95, 169, 277, 342, 348
Textus receptus, 283
Thomas Aquinas, 261
Thucydides, 398, 442
Thutmosis, 83, 132
Thutmosis III, 429
Tiamat, 174
Time, concept of, 343
Tiglath-pileser I, 436, 437
Tiglath-pileser III, 78, 147, 152
Tobit, 5–7, 278
Torah, 2, 8, 18, 20–22, 25, 71, 82, 87, 222, 238, 273, 275, 276, 280, 297, 329
Tower of Babel, 9, 71, 187, 206, 325
Trade, 410–12, 416, 421–23, 426, 427, 433, 435, 438–40, 443, 444, 451
Traditional societies, 55, 63, 105
Tradition history, 45, 52, 58, 59, 61–64, 69, 127, 186, 294, 295, 327, 328, 331, 336, 341, 342, 344, 345, 349, 354, 372, 381
Transhumance, 408, 423
Tribal league, 73–75, 83, 91, 107, 128, 131, 132, 140–42, 310
Tribal society, 105
Trito-Isaiah, 18, 20, 96, 97, 233, 270, 278, 296
Turkey, 400
Turkish conquest, 447
Turks, 120, 414, 415, 447, 448
Twelve Prophets, 4, 21, 95
Tyre, 138, 156, 253, 427

Überlieferungsgeschichte, 63
Ugarit, Ugaritic literature, 42, 57, 85, 102, 107, 174, 175, 177, 178, 223n17, 427, 435

Ummayad dynasty, 447
Uppsala school, 44n1, 85n25, 287
Urban civilization, 134, 403, 409, 422, 423, 426, 428, 434, 435, 441
Ur in Chaldea, 244

Vaticinium ex eventu, 38, 225
Verbal inspiration, 121, 287
Village, village culture, 61, 134, 310, 394, 407–10, 412, 414, 415, 419, 434–36, 453
Virgil, 171
Virtual history, 403
Vulgate, 6–8, 267n7, 272, 279n16

Wine, 85, 407, 411, 421
Wisdom literature, 6, 25, 97, 98, 269, 235, 240–42, 297, 345, 363
Writings, the, 2,4, 5, 8, 9, 22, 26n13, 27, 169, 235, 236, 240, 273, 279, 280, 333, 375, 376

Xenophon, 442

Yahweh-alone-movement, 86, 195, 222, 224, 233, 247, 252, 253, 348, 349
Yahwism, 82, 83, 85, 141n37, 332, 345, 367
Yahwist, 45–52, 53n9, 55, 63, 65, 66, 82, 91, 111, 141, 183, 224, 315, 342, 348, 380
Yamḥad, 425, 426, 428
Yarim-Lim, 425

Zagros, 410
Zedekiah
    prophet, 19, 77, 79, 116, 137
    king, 77
Zechariah, 4, 7, 8, 19, 21, 96, 253, 296
Zealots, 389
Zephaniah, 4, 7, 8, 19, 21, 226
Zion, 18, 21, 22, 143, 225, 229, 233, 236, 297, 387